# WAGNER

CURT VON WESTERNHAGEN

# WAGNER

A BIOGRAPHY

TRANSLATED BY MARY WHITTALL

CAMBRIDGE UNIVERSITY PRESS

CAMBRIDGE
LONDON   NEW YORK   NEW ROCHELLE
MELBOURNE   SYDNEY

Published by the Press Syndicate of the University of Cambridge
The Pitt Building, Trumpington Street, Cambridge CB2 1RP
32 East 57th Street, New York, NY 10022, USA
296 Beaconsfield Parade, Middle Park, Melbourne 3206, Australia

First published in English translation 1978
First paperback edition, in one volume, 1981

Printed in the United States of America


*British Library Cataloguing in Publication Data*

Westernhagen, Curt von
Wagner.
1. Wagner, Richard
2. Composers – Germany – Biography
3. Opera – Germany – Biography
782.1′092′4   ML410.W1   78–2397

ISBN 0 521 28254 3 one-volume paperback
ISBN 0 521 21930 2 Volume I (hard covers)
ISBN 0 521 21932 9 Volume II (hard covers)

# CONTENTS

**VOLUME I**

| | | |
|---|---|---|
| *List of Illustrations* | *page* | vii |
| *Preface* | | ix |
| *Postscript to the Preface* | | xvii |
| *Acknowledgements* | | xxiii |
| *Summary Bibliography* | | xxv |

**Part I. The Early Years (1813–1840)**

| | | |
|---|---|---|
| 1 | The Wagner Family | 3 |
| 2 | Wagner's Mother | 11 |
| 3 | Boyhood | 17 |
| 4 | Beethoven | 22 |
| 5 | Studiosus Musicae | 27 |
| 6 | The First Three Operas | 35 |
| 7 | *Rienzi* | 45 |

**Part II. The First Creative Period (1841–1848)**

| | | |
|---|---|---|
| 8 | *Der Fliegende Holländer* | 59 |
| 9 | *Tannhäuser* | 69 |
| 10 | Hofkapellmeister in Dresden | 80 |
| 11 | Germanic Myth and Greek Tragedy | 93 |
| 12 | *Lohengrin* | 101 |
| 13 | Money Troubles | 113 |

**Part III. The Revolutionary (1848–1852)**

| | | |
|---|---|---|
| 14 | Revolutionary Ideas | 127 |
| 15 | *Wieland der Schmied* | 142 |
| 16 | From Heroic Opera to Mythic Drama | 151 |

# Contents

**Part IV. *Der Ring des Nibelungen* (I) (1853–1857)**
17 The Vision of La Spezia                                      169
18 The Myth Becomes Music                                       183
19 The London Inferno                                           197
20 The *Ring* Crisis                                            211

**Part V. *Tristan* and *Die Meistersinger* (1857–1868)**
21 In Asyl                                                      231
22 Venice and Lucerne                                           250
23 *Tannhäuser* in Paris                                        267
24 Odyssey                                                      294

*Notes to Volume I*                                             319

**VOLUME II**

25 Munich                                                       329
26 *Die Meistersinger*                                          365

**Part VI. *Der Ring des Nibelungen* (II) (1868–1877)**
27 From Tribschen to Bayreuth                                   401
28 The First Festival                                           449
29 Nietzsche in Bayreuth                                        499
30 The Nations Thanks                                           506

**Part VII. *Parsifal* (1877–1883)**
31 'My Farewell to the World'                                   527
32 La lugubre gondola                                           585

*Appendices I–IV*                                               595
*Chronological Summary of Wagner's Life and Work*               604
*List of works*                                                 611
*Correspondence of Richard and Cosima Wagner*                   615
*Notes to Volume II*                                            618
*Bibliography*                                                  629
*Index to Volumes I and II*                                     639

# ILLUSTRATIONS

between pages 36 and 37

1 View of Leipzig from the east, around 1850
2a Ludwig Geyer
2b Johanna Rosine Wagner, née Pätz
3a Adolf Wagner
3b Theodor Weinlig
4a Vincenzo Bellini
4b Giacomo Meyerbeer
5a Wagner around 1850: drawing by Ernst Benedikt Kietz
5b Wagner's house in Riga
6 The warrant for Wagner's arrest after the revolution of 1849, from Eberhardt's *Allgemeiner Polizei-Anzeiger* 1853
7a Minna Planer
7b Arthur Schopenhauer
8a Eduard Devrient
8b Anton Pusinelli
9a Dresden Opera House, designed by Gottfried Semper
9b Villa Wesendonk, near Zürich
10a Otto Wesendonk
10b Mathilde Wesendonk
11 The end of the Prelude to *Tristan und Isolde*: a piano arrangement dated 15 December 1859
12a Charles Baudelaire
12b Hans von Bülow
13 Letter from Wagner to King

Ludwig dated 3 May 1864: 'Theurer huldvoller König!'
14a King Ludwig II
14b Eduard Hanslick
15a Eliza Wille
15b Jessie Laussot-Taylor
16a Cosima von Bülow around 1860: drawing by Claire Charnacé
16b Wagner around 1864: painting by Friedrich Pecht, with a bust of King Ludwig in the background

**Sources**
Archiv für Kunst und Geschichte, Berlin: plates 1, 5b, 6, 9a, 9b, 11, 13, 16a
Bibliothèque Nationale, Paris: plate 12a
Historisches Museum der Stadt Wien, Vienna: plate 14b
Metropolitan Museum of Art (Gift of Frederick Loeser, 1889): plate 16b
Radio Times Hulton Picture Library: plates 4a, 7a, 7b
Richard Wagner Gedenkstätte, Bayreuth: plates 2a, 2b, 3a, 3b, 4b, 5a, 8a, 8b, 10a, 10b, 12b, 14a, 15a, 15b

between pages 356 and 357

**1** Wagner and his circle, Munich 1865
**2a** Heinrich Porges
**2b** Hans Richter
**3a** Friedrich Nietzsche
**3b** Elisabeth Förster-Nietzsche
**4a** Dionysus among the Muses of Apollo by Bonaventura Genelli
**4b** Wagner's house Tribschen
**5a** Mathilde Maier
**5b** Liszt with his daughter Cosima in 1867
**6** Autograph title-page of the Siegfried Idyll, 1870
**7** Wagner and Cosima, Vienna 1872
**8a** Wagner: sketch in red pencil by Franz von Lenbach, Munich 1880 (based on photographs of 1871)
**8b** Judith Gautier
**9a** Karl Tausig
**9b** Angelo Neumann
**10a** The Festspielhaus in Bayreuth: wood-engraving around 1880
**10b** The Festspielhaus: a modern photograph
**11a** Heinrich von Stein, Carl Friedrich Glasenapp and Hans von Wolzogen
**11b** Engelbert Humperdinck

**12** Family photograph on the steps of Wahnfried, 1881: Isolde and Daniela von Bülow, the dog Marke, Eva and Siegfried Wagner, Blandine von Bülow, Heinrich von Stein, Cosima, Wagner, Paul Zhukovsky
**13a** Wahnfried seen from the front
**13b** Tea at Wahnfried, 1881: Wagner, Cosima, Heinrich von Stein, Paul Zhukovsky, Daniela and Blandine von Bülow
**14a** Titian's Assumption of the Virgin (detail)
**14b** The Grail scene in Parsifal: Zhukovsky's sketch of 1882
**15a** Paul Zhukovsky
**15b** Hermann Levi
**16a** Arthur, Count Gobineau
**16b** Zhukovsky's pencil sketch of Wagner, Venice 1883: the inscription in Cosima's handwriting reads 'R. lesend 12. Febr. 1883'

**Sources**

Archiv für Kunst und Geschichte, Berlin: plates 4b, 6, 7, 10a, 10b, 13a
Richard Wagner Gedenkstätte, Bayreuth: plates 1, 2a, 2b, 3a, 3b, 5a, 5b, 8a, 8b, 9a, 9b, 11a, 11b, 12, 13b, 14b, 15a, 15b, 16a, 16b

# PREFACE TO THE ENGLISH EDITION

When Ernest Newman published the first volume of his *Life of Richard Wagner* in 1933 he justified the undertaking on the grounds that during the previous twenty years 'so much new and vital first-hand matter has come to light that one's old conception of the story has had to be modified at a hundred points' (p. vii). Since his final volume appeared in 1946 another thirty years have passed, during which a new perspective has opened on the Wagner phenomenon, and a wealth of new material has become available.

I must say at once that the importance of Newman's *Life* as the standard work has in no way been diminished. There are many delicate issues which can be presented with sufficient detail and thoroughness only in a work of so large a compass. Outstanding in this respect is his treatment of the 'Nietzsche affair': no one should forgo the pleasure and instruction of reading his chapters on that subject. I am equally sure that Newman himself would have welcomed my additions to the tale.

The bibliography of the present work gives some idea of the variety of publications that have appeared since 1946. I will confine myself here to mentioning those that contain documentary material of biographical importance. Foremost among them are the Burrell Collection, consisting almost entirely of letters, previously known only through the inadequate and misleading *Catalogue of the Burrell Collection* (London, 1929), and the second volume of Max Fehr's *Richard Wagners Schweizer Zeit*. Then there are Cosima's intimate letters to Judith Gautier, and two other collections which, though published before 1946, escaped Newman's net: her letters to Gobineau, published in the *Revue Hebdomaire* in 1938, and the second volume of her letters to Nietzsche (1871–7), which appeared in 1940. The edition of Wagner's complete correspondence in chronological order is planned to be in fifteen volumes in all; the three volumes published to date go up to 1851 and contain some new documents, but for the most part they republish, as far as possible in their original form, letters that have appeared in print before. As well as these collections, a number of isolated letters have been published which have helped to correct misconceptions (or worse) that had been current for decades: for instance the three letters from Nietzsche to Cosima discovered in 1964 by Joachim Bergfeld, and the letter from the philosopher's sister Elisabeth Förster-Nietzsche to Frau Overbeck, published by Erich F. Podach, in which Elisabeth admits that she did not dare call on Wagner when she was in Bayreuth for *Parsifal* in 1882, thereby giving the lie to her touching story of her 'farewell visit' and Wagner's heart-rending message for Nietzsche. (EFWN, p. 279) This more than confirms Newman's suspicions about 'Elisabeth's false witness', yet innocents still rely on her testimony even today.

Podach was the first Nietzsche scholar to take account of the findings of Wagnerian scholarship as well, among other things the documents from the Wagner Archives that I published in the appendix of my book *Richard Wagner. Sein Werk, sein Wesen, seine Welt* (1956), which included Wagner's correspondence with Nietzsche's doctor, Dr Otto Eiser of Frankfurt am Main, and the three short letters Nietzsche sent to Cosima–Ariadne at the onset of his madness (the one commonly circulated before that date was apocryphal and was based, according to Podach, on an oral communication of Elisabeth's). Podach's own publications have been of the greatest importance to the reassessment of the popular Nietzsche–Wagner legend, notably his *Friedrich Nietzsches Werke des Zusammenbruchs*, containing authentic texts of *Nietzsche contra Wagner* and *Ecce Homo* based on the original manuscripts in the Nietzsche Archives, and his *Ein Blick in Notizbücher Nietzsches*, which includes an analysis of Nietzsche's 'Ariadne' fantasies.

International interest was aroused in 1976 by the publication of a letter Wagner wrote to his American dentist Dr Jenkins, on 8 February 1880, discussing his idea of emigrating to the United States. It gave rise to my article 'Wagner's Emigration Utopia', in the Bayreuth Festival programme for *Götterdämmerung* in 1976.

Newman lamented in the mid–1930s: 'It is a thousand pities that his brother-in-law Brockhaus [actually Heinrich, the brother of his brothers-in-law] confiscated his library on his flight from Dresden: the mere titles of some of the books might have told us a good deal we should like to know about Wagner's reading and thinking.' (NLRW, II, p. 51) In 1966, through the kind cooperation of the publishing firm of F. A. Brockhaus of Wiesbaden, I not only had access to that library (which they have now presented to the Richard Wagner Foundation in Bayreuth) for my own use, but also published a catalogue of it, with commentary, for the use of others. I have also had the opportunity to consult the unpublished manuscript catalogue of the Wahnfried library, and so familiarize myself with the books Wagner read in his later years, from the Upanishads to the works of his 'great eccentric' contemporary, Thomas Carlyle.[1] As a result I have been able to incorporate in my biographical account of the events of Wagner's life a parallel history of his intellectual life.

Other interesting documents have been published in G. Leprince's *Présence de Wagner* and Martin Vogel's *Apollinisch und Dionysisch*, while the iconography has been enriched by Willi Schuh's *Renoir und Wagner* and Martin Geck's *Die Bildnisse Richard Wagners*, an anthology of portraits including the one painted for King Ludwig by Friedrich Pecht, which is now in the Metropolitan Museum of Art in New York.

New material in the field of Wagner's compositions ranges from exercises dating from his teens, done for his teacher Theodor Weinlig – including a four-part vocal fugue 'Dein ist das Reich' and a sonata in A major with a fugato in place of a scherzo (published by Otto Daube) – to the 1850 'Washington Sketch' for *Siegfrieds Tod* (published by Robert W. Bailey), the composition sketch of thirty bars that did not, in the end, go into *Tristan*, and my own study, with numerous musical examples, of the composition sketches for the *Ring*.

In the last year or two considerable attention has been focused for various reasons on Cosima's diaries. Carl Friedrich Glasenapp, the friend of my own youth in Riga, had the complete manuscript in front of him in 1907–9, when he was writing the sixth volume (838 pp., published 1911) of his *Das Leben Richard Wagners* and was preparing the fifth edition of Volume V (416 pp., published 1912), though he did not actually identify the diaries as his source. A copy he made of them at the time is no longer in existence. He wove his extracts from the diaries into his text in indirect speech, only very occasionally giving verbatim quotations between quotation marks, and confined his selection to the realm of ideas and art, but Richard Graf du Moulin Eckart also cited more personal events in the first volume of his life of Cosima (1929), such as her last interview with Hans von Bülow. In his preface Du Moulin writes: 'I cannot forget how she even made her diaries available to me for my work . . . Naturally I made the fullest use of them [pp. 422–999 of his book], although it will never be possible to exhaust their riches. But they afforded the basis of the depiction of her unique relationship to Richard Wagner and of the light in which his wife regarded his genius.' Du Moulin here pinpoints the value of his extracts: they are the 'basis', the primary source of any biography, and they already reflect the 'riches' that a complete edition of the diaries can only enhance.

Eva Chamberlain, Richard and Cosima's younger daughter, made a selection of 'entries from Mama's diaries for Maestro Toscanini' (15 April 1874 to 30 January 1883), amounting to 130 quarto pages of Wagner's observations about his own work and about literature, music and life in general. The same selection was published, with some unimportant differences, by Hans von Wolzogen in *Bayreuther Blätter* between 1936 and 1938.

My own quotations from the diaries are taken from these three sources. (In the case of the *Bayreuther Blätter* extracts I compared the printed text with Eva Chamberlain's original manuscript.) At the time of writing, the first volume of the complete edition of the diaries has appeared (CT, I, covering the years 1869–77 – and see the Postscript to the Preface, below), and in general it confirms the reliability of the earlier selections; they may contain occasional minor errors in interpretation or the decipherment of Cosima's handwriting, but CT itself is not faultless in that respect. Some of Wagner's remarks on his compositional procedures at the time when he was writing *Parsifal*, which are given in exactly the same form in BBL and CT, were obviously misunderstood and wrongly taken down by Cosima herself; where quoted here they have been corrected, without comment, after comparison with the score.

CT can make a valuable contribution to the dating of letters which have previously been uncertainly or mistakenly dated: one instance is the correspondence between Wagner and Catulle Mendès, immediately before and after the Siege of Paris, where the precise dating is of some importance.

It should be emphasized that Glasenapp and Du Moulin did not

overlook or deliberately suppress anything of biographical importance in their use of the diaries. Since Cosima wrote them expressly
and intentionally for her children there was never any question of
their containing any 'sensations'. On the other hand, if one com-
pares the accounts of certain episodes where the details are of the
essence (such as the Munich productions of *Rheingold* and *Walküre*)
in the diaries and in the biographies, the latter are unquestionably
superior in being able to draw on a wider range of documentation.

The diaries are fascinating precisely because of their subjective
limitations: the reader feels as though he or she were actually
present, from the night and its dreams, through the morning and its
work to the evenings spent reading and making music. There is,
however, no overlooking the fact that the underlying mood of the
diaries stems from Cosima and not Richard. Even actual facts are
given a surprising colouring for being seen through her eyes. For
instance, though she records a large number of the nonentities who
called at Wahnfried she does not even mention Anton Bruckner's
visit in September 1873; he is referred to only once, apropos of
Wagner's running through his Third Symphony on 8 February
1875, when she calls him the 'poor organist Bruckner from Vienna'.

If the diaries were our only source we should never have heard
about Wagner's extraordinary love affair with Judith Gautier and all
its fantasies. The only reference is in the entry for 24 December
1877, when Cosima notes that the purchase of Christmas presents
in Paris for herself had given rise to a lengthy correspondence
between Richard and Judith. The true character of the correspondence cannot have remained a secret from her, but she had the
good sense to say nothing whatever about it, in the certainty that it
was a passing fancy that would die down of its own accord.

On the other hand it is disappointing to find so little about
Nietzsche's visits to Tribschen and Bayreuth. By contrast, her
numerous letters to him are a mine of information. Nietzsche's
French biographer, Charles Andler, has a shrewd comment on
this: 'Cosima Wagner, entre les deux hommes, supérieurement
coquette, attisait à son insu leur rivalité.'

The earlier published extracts failed me in only one instance: they
do not refer to Wagner's acquaintance with Gustav Nottebohm's
edition of Beethoven's sketches for the Choral Symphony, and his
recognition of the parallels with his own way of working. 'Richard
says it's similar for him, it's almost never possible for him to use

something in the form in which he first wrote it down, it's like a mark to indicate that one has got something in one's head, but quite different, and so one finds it eventually.'(CT, I, p. 917) The comment confirms the thesis I advanced in *The Forging of the 'Ring'*.

The case of Wagner's Brown Book, published entire for the first time in 1975, is rather different. This diary-cum-notebook kept by Wagner from 1865 to 1882 was intended for Cosima's eyes only, and it was started at a moment when their relationship had reached its crisis. Its private nature is emphasized by the fact that Eva Chamberlain thought fit to paste over five sides (which have now been uncovered again) and to cut out and destroy seven further pages (fourteen sides). Since it was published by my own publishers, Atlantis Verlag of Zürich, I have been able to add some valuable material from it to the English and the second German editions of this biography, thanks to the cooperation of Atlantis Verlag and the editor, Joachim Bergfeld.

I would like at this point to avert one possible misunderstanding: if I have spoken hitherto exclusively of the biographical value of documentation, it does not mean that I am a champion of the current fashion for so-called 'documentary biographies' or 'studies'. Their alleged greater 'objectivity' is deceptive: the subjective answerability of the compilers begins with the selection of material, indeed with the selection of the sources, for the general reader is not in the position to judge the reliability or credibility of the witnesses.

In addition, there is something I like to call the 'counterpoint' of facts, which is particularly pertinent to an account of the life and work of Wagner. One need do no more than contemplate the events of a two-year period such as 1856–7: the completion of *Die Walküre*, the prose scenario of *Die Sieger*, the conception of a new ending for *Götterdämmerung*, the start of the composition of *Siegfried*, the first musical ideas for *Tristan*, the prose scenario of *Parsifal*, the text of *Tristan* and the composition sketch of the first act, the first Wesendonk songs – surely no one can believe that a reversion to a primitive chronicle method could begin to give an adequate idea of the strains and tensions, both personal and artistic, that are concealed behind those dates and facts!

Finally I must refer to an element in this book which Giulio Cogni, in his review of the Italian edition, called (perhaps a little grandiloquently) the 'valore artistico del volume'.[2] I would like to

think that the 'valore artistico' consists above all in the mastery of
the immense quantities of material. I have spotlighted elements in
the first half of Wagner's life, of which he left a perceptive and
reliable account in *Mein Leben*, in a series of essay-like chapters, and
then adopted a narrative sequence of epic scenes as the means of
giving an impression of the second half in its entirety, so far as the
limitations of space permitted.

The reader may be puzzled by the absence of one thing: the raised
eyebrows of the moralist. As Furtwängler once observed, a complaint about 'Wagner's bad character' is a normal part of the ritual.[3]
Nor was Wagner the first: 'They would all like to be shot of me,'
Goethe said to Eckermann two years before his death, 'and as
there's nothing they can touch in my talent, they have a go at my
character instead.' Schopenhauer's comment on that particular
school of Goethean biography was that because a great mind and
spirit had made the human race an incomparable gift they thought
they were justified in 'dragging his moral personality before their
judgement seat'.[4]

My own intention, by contrast, is to display the personality
complete with its inner contradictions, its *creative polarity*, and to
leave judgement to the reader. This is perhaps not unconnected
with the fact that, of the four academic disciplines Goethe's Faust
lists with such disgust (philosophy, medicine, law 'and, alas', theology), my own life has been spent in medicine, the one least likely to
predispose its practitioners to moralizing.

Curt von Westernhagen

Preetz/Holstein. May 1977

# POSTSCRIPT TO THE PREFACE

The second volume of Cosima Wagner's diaries was published in July 1977, shortly after the second German edition and the English edition of this biography had both gone to press. As the editors point out in their preface, it differs from the first volume in two important respects: in its greater depth and detail – the period from 1 January 1878 to 12 February 1883 occupies no fewer than 1081 pages (whereas the first volume covers nearly ten years) – and in the stronger light this greater length throws on the personality and attitudes of Cosima herself. From a detailed record of the activities of Richard Wagner, the diaries become the intimate chronicle of their married life; the change is reflected even in the style, especially of such epic passages as the months in Palermo. On the other hand, the account of the vicissitudes attending the rehearsals and the performances of *Parsifal* suffers from the lack of the broader, general lines a more detached narrator might have given.

Although these daily notes were inevitably written in haste, they are stamped with Cosima's own personal style, as we know it from her letters to Chamberlain and Nietzsche, even if they never aspire to the elegance of her correspondence in French with Gobineau and Judith Gautier. Her own sympathies and antipathies are more strongly in evidence than in her earlier volume, not only in the expression of her anti-Semitic and anti-French feelings – in the latter one recognizes the renegade – but also in her attitude towards individuals in Wagner's life. Even in the Munich period his friends had the sense that she was cutting him off from direct contact with others, which was perhaps the outcome not so much of a real dislike on her part as of a conscious lack of gregariousness.

This is particularly obvious in her treatment of the women

Wagner knew, especially Minna and Mathilde Wesendonk. The fact that Wagner had made Mathilde Maier a formal proposal of marriage (conditional on Minna's death) on 25 June 1864 inspired Cosima to commemorate religiously each anniversary of that 28 November 1863 in Berlin when she and Wagner had 'vowed to belong only to each other', in order to assert her own prior claim on him.

As for Wagner's last romance, with Judith Gautier, Cosima certainly knew of it by 27 January 1878, at the very latest. Writing to Judith on that day, after joking about the 'fâcheries' they were both experiencing in their attempts to translate *Parsifal*, she went on a little more seriously: 'Cependant vous savez bien, méchante, que toutes les questions ne sont pas vidées, mais motus, je compte sur vous pour prendre un bel élan de confiance, digne de vous et de notre amitié!'

I do not believe that the apostrophes to 'suffering – O my old companion' in her entries in the diary in 12 and 14 February 1878 have anything to do with that, however, but rather express the effect on her of three letters from Bülow (29 December 1877, 14 and 17 January 1878) which, after two years of silence, reopened her old wound, the trauma of her guilt towards him. (The letters are referred to in DMCW, I, pp. 816f., but for the full texts one must go to NBB, pp. 516–20.)

She had nothing to fear from Judith: 'Vous avez trouvé un ami digne de vous [Benedictus], "ce que l'on rêve et ne trouve pas", me disiez-vous ici.' (26 February 1878) The correspondence between the two women continued until 1893, conducted for the most part on terms of cordial friendship. Nevertheless, Cosima found it advisable to shield Richard from seeing too much of Judith during her visits to Bayreuth in 1881 and again, for *Parsifal*, in 1882 – and to say as little about them as possible in her diary. She mentions the presence of Mathilde Maier, and the delight with which Wagner greeted her, at the dinner for the artists and other friends on the day after the dress rehearsal (CT, II, p. 984), but it is left to an impeccable witness, Friedrich Eckstein, who made the pilgrimage from Vienna to Bayreuth on foot, to tell us in all innocence that Wagner's neighbour at table was a young woman in a linen sailor's blouse with a bright red neckerchief, who laughed a great deal and chattered to the Meister in melodious French.

Quite apart from such retouching, one must always bear in mind, when reading memoirs, that everyone involved in a conversation

hears – and records – something different. The classic case is the
different records of conversations with Goethe made by Eckermann and by Chancellor von Müller, on the frequent occasions
when both were present at the same time. There is a striking
example in Wagner's case, too. Ludwig Schemann's account of a
conversation on the afternoon of 31 May 1882, when Hans von
Wolzogen was also present, is cited in Chapter 31 of this book. It
made an indelible impression on Schemann, because he sensed that
what Wagner said was a testament. He ended his account: 'Wagner
had become increasingly sad, he prolonged our leavetaking, bade us
farewell over and over again and accompanied us right to the front
door. I may have seen him grander and more overpowering on
other occasions, but never nobler.' The reader should set that,
and the rest of the account on pp. 579–80, against what stuck in
Cosima's memory:

> 31 May 1882. A visit from Dr Schemann and Wolzogen
> rather upset Richard, he came back to Cherubini and
> said people ought to exercise much more criticism. 'You
> bury your noses in books, and all the time there's so
> much that needs doing. Military band music, for
> instance: am I to endure it that my son, or someone like
> Stein, will have to march to that music? Conservatories,
> concert organizations, they all need taking in hand, but
> instead of that we just nibble at I don't know what.'

There is material evidence, in the form of some of Cosima's
notebooks preserved in the Richard Wagner Museum in Bayreuth,
which makes it all the more appropriate to compare her practice
with that of Eckermann, who wrote up his records of Goethe's
conversations from notes taken on the spot. In April 1972 *Fränkischer Heimatbote*, the monthly supplement of Bayreuth's daily
newspaper *Nordbayerischer Kurier*, published an article about one of
these notebooks, describing it as the 'original manuscript of Cosima
Wagner's last diary'. Now that the texts of the diaries are available
in full, we can see that this document was not one of the actual
diaries but the 'second notebook' which Wagner gave Cosima on
26 October 1882 in the Piazza San Marco, after he had been on
an independent shopping expedition. (CT, II, p. 1033; the 'first'
notebook was presumably the one 'with a swallow on it' that he
gave her the day before.) He wrote an inscription on the first page:

> Gemeines Karnickel
> für Tages-Artikel!
> Mach mich nur schlecht,
> dann geschieht mir recht!
> > Adieu! – Oh!
> > 26. Oct. 1882.
> > R. W. Ges. Schr. T. II.

('A common "carnicle" for the daily article! Make me out to be bad, it'll only serve me right! Adieu! Oh! 26 October 1882. R. W. Collected Writings, Vol. II.')

The sense of this curious 'dedication' is that Wagner, possessing little Italian, had spoken French in order to make his purchase, referring to the notebook as 'un carnet'; perhaps by way of an Italian word of his own imagining ('carnuccio'?) he ended up with the German word 'Karnickel' (which means a 'rabbit' in the zoological sense but also a 'donkey' of the human variety). 'Article' has the same range of meaning in German as in English, so a 'daily article' is not only an article for daily use but suggests here that he knew perfectly well that Cosima would use the notebook for her daily 'piece' about him in her diary – which is probably also the point of the reference to his 'collected writings'. It's a typical piece of Wagner's punning light verse.

The next entry on the same page is in pencil and in Cosima's handwriting: '27ten Freitag. Gute Nacht trotz Kaffee. Gespräch kath. Kirche, Professoren über lieben.' ('27th, Friday. Good night in spite of coffee. Conversation Catholic church, professors on dear' [i.e. 'on the dear Lord'].) These are the topics that provide the substance of the entry in her diary for that date. (CT, II, p. 1033)

A second facsimile accompanying the *Fränkischer Heimatbote* article gives her notes for what became the entries for Wednesday and Thursday, 27 and 28 December 1882. A line has been drawn across the page from bottom left to top right, as if to signify that it is finished with. The article also includes facsimiles of the two drawings Paul Zhukovsky made of Wagner in the same notebook on 10 and 12 February 1883 (cf. Martin Geck, *Die Bildnisse Richard Wagners*, p. 157).

There can be no doubt that this notebook contains the original notes from which Cosima wrote up her diary from 27 October 1882 to 12 February 1883. That it was not the first such notebook is demonstrated by Cosima's reference to her 'little notebook' on 14 October 1882 (CT, II, p. 1024); the editors' note at this juncture is somewhat perfunctory (p. 1278). It would be interesting to compare the text of the notebooks with that of the diaries. It might well reveal a subjective bias on Cosima's part. As a 'well-informed Frenchwoman' remarked, 'elle n'est pas pour rien la fille de Madame d'Agoult'. (Ludwig Schemann, *Lebensfahrten eines Deutschen*, pp. 135f.)

That is not to deny the positive value of Cosima's use of preliminary notes in writing up her diaries; it is the guarantee of the accuracy of her dating of events, which, as we shall see, is of crucial importance on some occasions.

The editorial annotation and comment in this second volume of Cosima's diaries are lavish and, in the main, exemplary. It includes an appendix of errata from the first volume.

C.v.W.

January 1978

# ACKNOWLEDGEMENTS

The author wishes to thank all those whose assistance and cooperation have helped him in his work: Frau Winifred Wagner for permission to publish material from the Wagner Archives in Bayreuth, and for the run of the library in Wahnfried; Frau Gertrud Strobel for looking out the archival material; Verlag F. A. Brockhaus of Wiesbaden for access to Wagner's Dresden library and Frau Susanne Brockhaus for her catalogue of it; Dr Joachim Bergfeld and Dr Manfred Eger, Bayreuth, for the use of documents from the Richard-Wagner-Gedenkstätte; Dr Dietrich Mack, Bayreuth, for information about Cosima's diaries; Herr Erich Neumann, East Berlin, for the emendation of some points arising in the first edition; Dr Arnold Whittall, London, for making English-language additions to the bibliography; and last but not least Mrs Mary Whittall for the skill and care she has again shown in translating one of my books.

C. v. W.

The translator wishes to acknowledge the kind permission of Thames & Hudson Ltd to re-use her versions of a number of documents that appeared previously in *Wagner: A Documentary Study*, compiled and edited by Herbert Barth et al. (London, 1975).

M. W.

# SUMMARY BIBLIOGRAPHY

With a key to the abbreviations employed in the text

A comprehensive bibliography appears at the end of Vol. II.

BB   Bülow, Hans von, *Briefe*. 7 vols. Leipzig, 1899–1908

BBL   *Bayreuther Blätter*. Monthly, later quarterly periodical, ed. by Hans von Wolzogen. Chemnitz, later Bayreuth, 1878–1938

CT   Wagner, Cosima, *Die Tagebücher*, ed. by M. Gregor-Dellin and D. Mack. 2 vols. Munich, 1976–7. (See the Preface and its postscript, above)

CWFN   *Die Briefe Cosima Wagners an Friedrich Nietzsche*, ed. by E. Thierbach. 2 vols. Weimar, 1938–40

DMCW   Du Moulin Eckart, Richard Graf, *Cosima Wagner. Ein Lebens- und Charakterbild*. 2 vols. Munich, 1929–31

EFWN   Förster-Nietzsche, Elisabeth, *Wagner und Nietzsche zur Zeit ihrer Freundschaft*. Munich, 1915

FHKF   Herzfeld, Friedrich, *Königsfreundschaft. Ludwig II. und Richard Wagner*. Leipzig, 1939

FWSZ   Fehr, Max, *Richard Wagners Schweizer Zeit*. 2 vols. Aarau, 1934–53

GLRW   Glasenapp, Carl Friedrich, *Das Leben Richard Wagners*. Definitive edn, 6 vols. Leipzig, 1905–12. (Modern reprint, Wiesbaden and Liechtenstein) (First edn, 2 vols, 1876–7)

JKWF   Kapp, Julius, *Wagner und die Frauen*. Final edn, Berlin–Wunsiedel, 1951. (First edn, 1912; numerous subsequent edns)

KLRW   König Ludwig II. und Richard Wagner, *Briefwechsel*, ed. by Otto Strobel. 5 vols. Karlsruhe, 1936–9

LJG   Wagner, Richard and Cosima, *Lettres à Judith Gautier*. ed. by Léon Guichard. Paris, 1964

LWVR   Lippert, Woldemar, *Richard Wagners Verbannung und Rückkehr 1849–62*. Dresden, 1927

ML   Wagner, Richard, *Mein Leben*. 1st authentic edn. Munich, 1963. (First edn, 1911)

MMCW   Millenkovich-Morold, Max, *Cosima Wagner. Ein Lebensbild*. Leipzig, 1937

MWKS    Morold, Max, *Wagners Kampf und Sieg, dargestellt in seinen
        Beziehungen zu Wien*. 2 vols. Zürich, Leipzig, Vienna, 1950 (First edn,
        1930)

NBB     Bülow, Hans von, *Neue Briefe*, ed. by R. du Moulin Eckart. Munich,
        1927

NLRW    Newman, Ernest, *The life of Richard Wagner*. 4 vols. New York,
        1933–46. (There are some discrepancies between the pagination of the
        New York printing and the London edn of 1933–47. The author's
        references are to the New York edn, which is also that reprinted,
        London and Cambridge, 1976)

RWAP    *The letters of Richard Wagner to Anton Pusinelli*, ed. by E. Lenrow.
        New York, 1932

RWBC    Wagner, Richard, *Briefe. Die Sammlung Burrell*, ed. by J. N. Burk.
        Frankfurt am Main, 1953. (*Letters of Richard Wagner: The Burrell
        Collection*, ed. with notes by John N. Burk, was first publ. in New
        York, 1950, with the documents in translation. The German edn has
        the documents in the original and the editorial matter in translation.
        Page references in the present work are to the German edn, and
        quotations from the documents are newly translated for the sake of
        stylistic consistency)

RWGB    *Richard Wagners Gesammelte Briefe*, ed. by J. Kapp and E. Kastner.
        2 vols. Leipzig, 1914

RWGS    Wagner, Richard, *Gesammelte Schriften und Dichtungen*, vols 1–10.
        4th edn. Leipzig, 1907 (Reprint, Hildesheim, 1976)
        – *Sämtliche Schriften und Dichtungen*. Vols 11–16. 6th edn. Leipzig,
        n. d.

RWSB    Wagner, Richard, *Sämtliche Briefe*, ed. by G. Strobel and W. Wolf.
        Leipzig, 1967– (See below, Vol. II, p. 617)

SERD    Richard Wagner, *Skizzen und Entwürfe zur 'Ring'-Dichtung*, ed. by
        Otto Strobel. Munich, 1930

SRLW    Röckl, Sebastian, *Ludwig II. und Richard Wagner*, 2 vols. Munich,
        1913–19

TWLF    Tiersot, Julien, ed. *Lettres françaises de Richard Wagner*. Paris, 1935

Part I: The Early Years (1813–1840)

# 1

## The Wagner Family[1]

Germany was only beginning to recover from the horrors of the Thirty Years' War in 1651 when Martin Wagner, a schoolmaster and son of a silver-miner, Moritz Wagner, left Freiberg in Saxony, where he had been born in 1603. His destination was the village of Hohburg, seventeen miles east of Leipzig, and his journey took him past Wurzen, which the Swedes had razed to the ground in spite of its defences. Hohburg, too, had been devastated, the inhabitants had fled and the benefice had been vacant for years. Now, as the villagers gradually returned, their first move was to appoint a schoolmaster to make good their children's neglected education, to work diligently and in the fear of God at instructing them in the true Christian religion and in all Christian doctrines and virtues. It was another four years before a pastor arrived, and then Martin had additionally to assume the duties of sexton, hearing catechisms, singing in the church and playing the organ.

The Wagners remained in the district of the Hohburg hills for the next hundred years, working as village schoolmasters and cantors. In 1666 Martin's son Samuel 'satisfied the examiners' in Thammenhain. In those years there was little enough cause for satisfaction in life or work in those poverty-stricken villages. The plague stalked the land; warning placards were erected on the roads. An appeal was made to the monastery of Meissen to help the 'poor schoolmaster' of Thammenhain. In 1703 his son Emanuel was appointed schoolmaster and organist in Kühren, after having been 'heard by several in singing and in reading and well liked'. 'May God prosper and bless his appointment,' the scribe continues, 'because he has played the clavier for several years too.'

Emanuel's eldest son, Samuel, Richard Wagner's great-grandfather, was the last of the composer's ancestors to follow this career. After contact with a loftier educational sphere as servant–pupil to the Evangelical Superintendent in Borna, he went to Müglenz, at first as deputy to the old teacher there – who had to pay him from his own meagre salary – and eventually, after qualifying, as schoolmaster, cantor and organist 'with singing, reading and organ-playing, likewise bellringing and winding the church clock'.

When Samuel died in 1750, the same year as Bach, his eldest son Gottlob Friedrich was fourteen. He is next heard of in Leipzig in 1755 as a Thomaner, a pupil at the Thomasschule. 'The *subjectum* is not bad *in litteris*,' a friendly cleric wrote in a letter of recommendation to the pastor of Müglenz, 'and since he is young you ought to be able to mould him yet. I think the best thing he could do would be to leave Leipzig, because otherwise the all too great licence of the other Thomaner may lead his as yet innocent nature astray!' This advice was not followed, however, and in 1759 Gottlob Friedrich enrolled at Leipzig University to read theology.

Saxony was doing badly in the war with Prussia at that time and Frederick the Great made his winter quarters in what was then known as the Königshaus (later the Thomäsches Haus) in the market square in Leipzig. Napoleon stayed in the same house before the Battle of the Nations in 1813 and later, as a child, Richard Wagner spent the night there when he visited his father's sister, his aunt Friederike. The portraits of fine ladies in hooped skirts, with youthful faces and powdered hair, that still hung on the walls of its abandoned state apartments, filled his imagination with terrifying visions of ghosts.

His friend's fears about the harm that might be done to Gottlob Friedrich's innocent nature were not unfounded: in the thirteenth semester of his university studies he appears in the register of the Thomaskirche, on 23 March 1765, as the father of a child born to Johanna Sophie Eichelin, spinster, the daughter of the respected schoolmaster Gottlob Friedrich Eichel. That was the end of his career as a theologian, and he was lucky to get the job of excise officer at the Ranstadt gate of the city. When young Goethe arrived from Frankfurt to study in Leipzig that October, he must have paid his gate dues to Richard Wagner's grandfather. Unlike Goethe, who assiduously suppressed the information that his grandfather was a tailor, Wagner was not the least ashamed of his forebear. When a caller at Wahnfried mentioned that his father had been

musical director (a municipal appointment) in his home town,
Wagner interrupted him with '*Stadtmusikus*, you say? You do us an
honour then. My grandfather was a tollgate-keeper in Leipzig.'

It was four years before Gottlob Friedrich was able to marry
Johanna Sophie. He wanted their two sons (the first child had died)
to succeed where he had failed. The elder, Karl Friedrich (born 18
June 1770) – Richard's father – studied law, the younger theology.
Friedrich Wagner became registrar at the police headquarters in
Leipzig. In 1798 he married Johanna Rosine Pätz, the twenty-
three-year-old daughter of a master baker from Weissenfels. They
had nine children in fourteen years of marriage, the youngest,
Richard, born only six months before his father's death, so that he
had no memory of him at all; and as though Friedrich Wagner was
destined to remain completely unknown to posterity, no portrait of
him survives.

Among what is known of him, the outstanding characteristic was
a passion for the theatre, not unmixed with a gallant enthusiasm for
some of the actresses, as Richard gathered from his mother's recollections. As well as other lawyers and tradesmen and their families,
the regular visitors to their home included the members of the
Seconda troupe. The plays of Lessing and Schiller were in the
company's repertory and the first performance ever of *Die Jungfrau
von Orleans* was a red-letter day for the Wagner family; as the crowd
pressed around the theatre exit, all heads were bared as Schiller's tall
figure appeared, and mothers lifted their children up to see: 'Look,
here he comes, that's him!'

Friedrich Wagner himself acted, in Goethe's *Die Mitschuldigen* for
instance, in amateur performances in a room in the Thomäsches
Haus. When E. T. A. Hoffmann came to Leipzig in 1813, as musical
director of the Seconda company, the first thing he did was visit the
inn the actors always patronized. 'Evening in the Grüne Linde', he
wrote in his diary. 'Registrar Wagner, an exotic character who
imitates Opitz, Iffland etc., really rather well – he seems to be an
adherent of the better school, *un poco exaltato* after imbibing a lot of
rum.'

They were stirring times when Richard Wagner first glimpsed
the light of day on 22 May 1813, between the allied defeat at
Bautzen and the Battle of the Nations outside Leipzig. He was born
in the house of the Red and White Lion in a street called Der Brühl,
and the majestic lion crouching over the porch of the house sends

one's thoughts forward over seven decades to that other house, on the Grand Canal, adorned with a frieze of eagles, where his life ended. The birth of a genius is enveloped in a kind of mystery. And in Wagner's case there are in addition two genealogical mysteries.

The truce agreed on 4 June gave his parents the chance to take a holiday with their new baby in the pretty village of Stötteritz just outside the city, where Friedrich celebrated his forty-third birthday. He was recalled to Leipzig in July, when Napoleon arrived to review his troops, and he was appointed interpreter and acting chief of police by Marshal Davoust. Then at last, on 16 August, the child's christening, delayed by the events of the war, was able to take place in the Thomaskirche, where he received the names Wilhelm Richard.

The truce expired and on 16 October the thunder of cannon announced the start of the battle of Leipzig. The fighting reached the suburbs of the city by 19 October. The tocsin was rung in Der Brühl and when Johanna Wagner leant out of the window she saw the emperor galloping past bareheaded, having lost his hat in his haste. The following days and weeks demanded every ounce of strength Friedrich Wagner possessed, as he worked to restore order. The bodies of men and horses littered the streets in the suburbs, the dead and wounded lay together in the great hall of the Gewandhaus, and an epidemic of typhus broke out, eventually claiming Friedrich himself as one of its victims. His wife published an announcement in the local newspaper:

> A victim of his duties, my husband Carl Friedrich
> Wilhelm Wagner, chief registrar at the Royal Police
> Headquarters, died on 23 November, in his
> fourty-fourth year, far too early for me and my eight
> growing children. His worth as man and as friend has
> been proved to me especially by the exceptionally
> delicate concern his friends have shown for the
> well-being of me and my children at this time, but
> this has also made me all the more sensible of the
> magnitude of my loss.

There was one friend in particular who at once took the family into his care: Ludwig Geyer. Ludwig Heinrich Christian Geyer was born on 21 January 1779 in Eisleben, in the district of Halle, the son of the clerk to the justices, Christian Gottlieb Geyer. He enrolled at

Leipzig University in 1798 to study law, but had to give up his studies when his father died. Portrait-painting had been a hobby of his, and he now started to attend classes at Oeser's (later Tischbein's) 'Academy of Drawing, Painting and Architecture', where he painted 'old men and young girls'. He became friendly with Friedrich Wagner in 1800, and it was Friedrich who discovered his acting talent, invited him to take part in amateur performances and so set him on the professional career that led Geyer eventually to the Saxon court theatre.

In the summer of 1813 he was playing in Teplitz (now Teplice) in Bohemia with the Seconda company. 'I would have loved to come to Leipzig,' he wrote to Friedrich in Stötteritz on 6 June; 'Teplitz arouses my indifference, not to say dislike.' He invited his friends to visit him in Teplitz, and as her husband was recalled to Leipzig in July Johanna went without him, and was inscribed in the register of visitors on 21 July 1813. Ernest Newman's argument (NLRW, II, pp. 608ff.) that the only explanation for this journey of Johanna's in wartime was that she was anxious to show her two-month-old son to his alleged natural father – so indirectly supporting the hypothesis of Geyer's paternity – does not stand up to close scrutiny. Johanna used to take the warm baths at Teplitz every year, and the spa was more secure against war and war's alarums at that particular time than Leipzig, the centre of military activity. Goethe was in Teplitz at the same time, and his diary confirms that the town was quiet, with its descriptions of the comings and goings of other visitors, of his own mineralogical expeditions, of parties and visits to the theatre. A performance of Schiller's *Don Carlos* that he mentions will have given him the opportunity to see Geyer as King Philip, one of his best parts. There is only one reference to the war, a 'gloomy military–political conversation' on 25 July. The idyllic calm ended with the expiry of the truce on 10 August. All visitors had to leave Teplitz, and Johanna too returned to Leipzig.

Geyer hurried to Leipzig to offer help and comfort immediately after Friedrich's death, but had to return to Dresden, where the Seconda company was playing. When his daughter Cäcilie, in 1870, sent her half-brother Richard the letters Geyer had written to their mother at that period, he told her that he had been not just touched, but profoundly moved by them. 'It is seldom in civil life that we see so plain an example of complete self-sacrifice for a noble purpose as we find in this case . . . I think I now understand this relationship completely, although I find it extremely difficult to express my view of it. It seems to me as if our father Geyer believed he was expiating some guilt in sacrificing himself for the whole family.' (14 January 1870)

And yet the whole tone and content of the letters contradict the suspicion Wagner was voicing. 'Over the bier of 1813 you allow the ties of friendship to be fastened yet more tightly,' Geyer wrote to Johanna at the end of the year; 'the invitation to do so is great and noble.' It is only very gradually that the note of love and longing enters what he writes. 'Heaven is very well disposed towards us, it has given me the gratifying vocation of being your friend,' he wrote on 28 January 1814. 'I have a great deal to talk to you about, and I can barely wait until the time when I shall be able to have a heart-to-heart talk with you on the dear old sofa.' Johanna was of one mind with him, and they were married on 28 August 1814.

If Wagner's suspicion was well founded, why should Geyer have expressed himself with such restraint in these letters? (He even uses the formal 'Sie' in addressing her.) Indeed, Wagner himself later changed his mind. The entry in Cosima's diary for 26 November 1878 includes the following: 'I ask Richard: "I suppose Father Geyer was your father?" Richard replies: "I don't think so – my mother loved him – 'elective affinities'." '

But in 1870, still under the impression Geyer's letters had first made on him, he must have said something to Friedrich Nietzsche about his initial suspicion, for in 1888 the latter inserted a footnote in *The Wagner Case*: 'Was Wagner German at all? There is some reason to ask . . . His father was an actor called Geyer. A vulture [Geyer] is almost the same as an eagle [Adler].' Readers at once seized upon what he was hinting – that Wagner was a Jew. They assumed that his one-time friend, who had read the first proofs of Wagner's autobiography, which was still not generally available, must have more, and more reliable, information about the matter. But the inference was Nietzsche's own invention. Geyer is an old German surname, the most famous bearer of it being Florian Geyer, a nobleman who sided with the peasants in the Peasants' War in the early sixteenth century, and there is no onomastic justification for linking it with Adler, which is almost exclusively Jewish. Otto Bournot's research into the family background of Wagner's step-father, published in 1913, revealed that Geyer's ancestors had been organists and cantors at the Evangelical church in Eisleben (where

Luther was born and died) since the seventeenth century. The earliest known, Benjamin Geyer (died 1720), was the municipal director of music; the fact that he lived in the so-called 'church house' in Watzdorf from 1686 to 1693 shows that he held a post at the Andreaskirche there.

The other genealogical 'mystery' concerns Johanna Wagner. In *Mein Leben* Wagner says that she never gave any of her children a full account, or many details, of her own origins. 'She came from Weissenfels and acknowledged that her parents had been bakers there . . . A remarkable circumstance was that she was sent to a select educational establishment in Leipzig and enjoyed there the care of one she called a "high-ranking fatherly friend", whom she later identified as a prince of Weimar, to whom her family in Weissenfels was greatly obliged. Her education at the establishment seems to have ended abruptly on the sudden death of that fatherly friend.'

It was to this that Houston Stewart Chamberlain, Wagner's son-in-law, was alluding when he wrote to a teacher, one Hellmundt, on 12 December 1913: 'There is not a single missing link in his mother's descent, and the little secret it contains is no secret to initiates, and allows her family tree to be traced back to the twelfth century.'[2] In other words, it was assumed that Wagner's mother was the natural daughter of Prince Friedrich Ferdinand Constantin of Weimar (1758–93), the younger brother of Goethe's patron, Grand Duke Karl August. Prince Constantin is known to have been musical and a libertine. His military tutor, Karl von Knebel, wrote: 'The prince passed his time in reading, writing and, above all, music. This was his favourite occupation, and he possessed no small talent in it. He found nearly every instrument easy; indeed, he cured himself of an indisposition by prolonged music-making.' His youthful amours did not always lack consequences: he once returned to Weimar from Paris with a Madame Darsaincourt, who bore him a son who was raised in a forester's family.[3]

The Prince Constantin hypothesis was accepted not only in the inner circle at Wahnfried but – more important – even by so dispassionate an enquirer as Newman. Why, he argued, would a prince of Weimar have sent the daughter of a Weissenfels baker to receive an education above the average for her class in Leipzig, 'unless for very good reasons of his own'? He met the objection that Constantin was only sixteen when Johanna was born by referring to his, and his brother's, known precocity. (NLRW, II, pp. 613ff.)

The one curious thing is that Mrs Burrell, the founder of the famous collection of Wagner documents now in the Curtis Institute of Music in Philadelphia, never heard of the hypothesis. She began her researches in the 1890s, when there must still have been memories in a small town like Weissenfels of the mother of so famous a person as Wagner. And what did she learn there? She heard 'from more than one source', 'with variations', that Johanna Rosine Pätz was selected by Karl August and Goethe for the theatre in Weimar, and that Friedrich Wagner had made her acquaintance through Goethe. (NLRW, II, pp. 617ff.)

After the accretions of legend have been removed, the most likely facts are these: after the death of her mother in 1789 and her father's remarriage, Johanna was selected for a career as an actress, not by Karl August but by Constantin; her education for the stage was then ended four years later when the prince died.

But it is almost symptomatic of the extraordinary impression Wagner made, especially on his contemporaries, that even his parentage was a matter to be surrounded by mystery and legend.

No less remarkable is the prophecy made over his cradle. Jean Paul wrote in his preface to E. T. A. Hoffmann's *Fantasiestücke*: 'Until now Apollo has always cast the gift of poetry with his right hand and the gift of music with his left to two people so far apart from each other that to this day we still await the man who will write both the text and the music of a true opera.' That preface, dated 24 November 1813, was written in Jean Paul's home town, Bayreuth.

# 2

## Wagner's Mother

In the autumn of 1814 the family moved to Dresden, where Geyer was well known as a portrait-painter, actor at the court theatre and playwright. His play *Der Bethlehemitische Kindermord* – in spite of its title, 'The Massacre of the Innocents', it is a comedy about the ups and downs of an artist's life – even earned him a certain posthumous reputation when it was published many years later in the cheap and comprehensive series of popular classics, Reclams Universalbibliothek.

Johanna reigned in the hospitable house in the Moritzstrasse, amidst her flock of children, which was increased in the following year by a black-haired daughter, Cäcilie. Geyer's portrait of his wife shows her as still youthful, apparently on the point of going out in her bonnet and shawl, then suddenly turning back, perhaps in response to a call from the artist, and catching at her shawl, as it slides from her shoulder, with her left hand; her full oval face is turned towards the spectator, smiling and with some surprise in her large eyes.

Wagner described her as 'a woman remarkable in the eyes of all who knew her'. Certainly in his own case the memory of her is a thread running through his whole life and work. Only a few days before his death he dreamed of her, 'young and graceful, a radiant vision'.

Her chief attributes were a good temper and a sense of humour, according to *Mein Leben*, but the strain of caring for her large family stifled the expression of maternal tenderness. Wagner could hardly remember ever having been caressed by her, and so was the more strongly affected by one occasion when, as he was being borne sleepily off to bed and raised tearful eyes to her,

11

she smiled warmly and made an affectionate remark about him to a visitor.

'What made the strongest impression upon me was the unusual, almost histrionic fervour with which she spoke of the great and beautiful in art. But she always told me that she did not include theatrical art in her enthusiasm, but only poetry, music and painting; indeed she frequently came close to threatening to curse me, if I, too, should ever want to go into the theatre.' (ML, pp. 18f.)

She had good reason to fear that he might, for four of her other children did. Her eldest son, Albert, who was very like Richard in appearance, gave up his medical studies, to Geyer's displeasure, and became an opera singer; Rosalie and Luise were trained as actresses, at the wish of their father, and made their debuts at an early age in little plays Geyer wrote specially for them – Rosalie with such success that she was engaged for the court theatre; and a younger sister, Klara, possessing a pretty voice, could not resist the lure of opera.

In spite of Johanna's pleas and threats, Richard, too, embarked on a theatrical career at the age of nineteen. Two letters she wrote him, the only ones by her to survive, assail the wretchedness of the life he had chosen, which she feared would estrange him from her and from his own better self.

The first was written apropos of his falling out with the husband of his sister Luise, the wealthy publisher and bookseller Friedrich Brockhaus, who had remonstrated with the young director of music at the Magdeburg theatre when he arrived home in 1835 with nothing to his name but debts and 'a very intelligent poodle'. 'This humiliation in front of Fritz is buried in the very depths of my heart,' Richard had complained to her, 'and I am tormented by the bitterest self-reproach for having handed him the right to humiliate me.' (25 July 1835) He must have expressed his feelings even more strongly in a later letter announcing the forthcoming première of *Das Liebesverbot*, to which she replied on 9 March 1836. (Her attitude to German orthographic conventions was even more wilful than that of Goethe's mother; her spelling, notably, was coloured by the Saxon tendency, in speech, to lengthen vowels and voice all consonants.)

My dear boy, pray tell me how this false, ever bitterer trait got into your once guileless heart? it will be 3, 4

years before you realize that you were certainly wrong;
the letter got into Rosalie's hands . . .: your heartlessness
upset her the whole day . . .

I am greatly relieved that you have now decided to
present your opera in Magdeburg and conduct it
yourself, but good Richard what did you want to let
that great advantage slip out of your hands for? . . .
Now may God bless you and your plan; oh only believe
that I really yearn for you! I am always afraid time, and
things, will snatch your heart from me! God preserve
this one reward for me on earth! . . .

And another thing dear Richard, you have made me
very worried about your circumstances in Magdeburg, I
can . . . very well imagine that you often have great
money trouble now, but my dear good son! if you are
victorious it will gain you a lot of respect and so you
will show what the resolution of a noble youth can do,
what a comfort! what a hope for your mother! my good
heart's boy!

Yes yes I rejoice over you greatly in private! for I know
your purpose is good and noble.

The second letter was written in the following year, after he had
moved to Riga. It had been a painful year for her: Richard had
married the actress Minna Planer against his family's wishes, only
to have her run off with another man soon afterwards, and Rosalie,
who was married to Dr Oswald Marbach, had died in childbirth on
12 October 1837.

My heart's dear son! That's what you were before you
tore yourself out of my heart; but a mother's heart
remains the same, only the circumstances are changed!
Yes! dear Dear God!! It was you three, you, my sainted
angel Rosalie, poor Cecilie, who I had at my side
longest. The final loss of your heart and filial love cost
me many sleep less nights . . .

I heard the description of your Domestic
Circumstances in Königsberg with true distress, I cannot
understand how *a Female Creature can Hurt and Use so
young a man in this way!* . . . A well-brought-up
gentlewoman is certainly incapable of behaving so after

the worst treatment if she ever loved a man, and he so young!

My angel Rosalie was too pure to go into a better world unreconciled with you; before I left she had a long talk with me about you on a walk, she said that Louise Brockhaus had too little faith in you, and your talent! but, she had great hopes for the future, if only! you are surrounded by people with enough understanding intelligence and a measure of nobility! for only that, and it can still all go well with him! that's what she said! and I said Amen![1]

The apparent estrangement was only an expression of youthful defiance. 'I hope you did not believe that I had ever for a moment forgotten you,' Wagner wrote from Meudon on 12 September 1841, after hearing of the reception of *Rienzi* in Dresden,

even when you heard nothing from me! Oh, I'm sure I've already told you that there were times when I really went out of my way not to stir up your sympathy for my affairs again. But I was praying to God to preserve your life and health, for I hoped that in time my own efforts would win me a prize which would add to the pleasure of showing my face at home once more . . . Everyone who wants to attain true inward and outward independence must uncompromisingly . . . follow the path that his earnest inclination and a certain inner, irresistible prompting tell him to follow . . .

I would look foolish if I put into words what I think of – what I hope for – for what are thoughts and hopes! But things *must* turn out right eventually, and the person who most deserves his good fortune is one who has come through the tempest safely and has known bad fortune!

Even later, the memory of the years during which, for the sake of his career in the theatre, he had kept himself aloof from his mother, who was 'good but ignorant in this respect', was painful to him. Nevertheless he encouraged the young Hans von Bülow, whose wish to be a professional musician was opposed by his parents, to muster the same energy as he had himself when he had not allowed even the most noble of natural ties to hinder him in his right to self-determination. (To Franziska von Bülow, 19 September 1850)

Johanna lived to witness the beginning of her son's success. She tried to be reconciled with Minna, whose behaviour in Königsberg she was unable to forgive; even so they seem to have quarrelled again over the old grievance, when they were both taking the waters in Teplitz in July 1842. Wagner passionately took his wife's part in a letter headed 'for you alone', in which he commiserated with her over his mother's 'nagging', which he felt to be beneath his own notice. 'But it is quite different for you. Everybody ought to treat you, my dear wife, with special consideration, firstly because you deserve it in every way, and secondly because rough treatment hurts you more deeply than anybody else, for reasons that are very easily understood.' (Undated, RWBC, pp. 612f.)

In the end Minna's domestic virtues prevailed on her mother-in-law to forgive and forget. In a letter that can probably be dated just before the first performance of *Tannhäuser* in 1845, she thanked Minna most warmly for the love and attention she had been shown while she was staying with the couple. 'A mother's greeting and a kiss to my good old Richard! It makes me happy to see him prosper in everything he undertakes.' (RWBC, p. 621)

After spending her last years in a state of near childishness, she died in February 1848, shortly before the revolution broke out, and so was spared Richard's exile. It was a bitterly cold morning, Wagner wrote, when they laid her coffin in the grave. Instead of scattering earth in the grave in light handfuls, they had to drop it in frozen clods, which startled him by their rumble. 'On my short journey back to Dresden, the clear sense of my complete isolation came over me for the first time.'

His mother meant security to him, and this is the role assigned to motherhood in his works. It is not particularly overt in his auto-biographical and anecdotal writing or dicta, but operates at a deeper level of his subconscious. Once, in later life, recalling how he had taken a risky climb on to the school roof as a boy, he added that he had had a fit of vertigo and thought he was done for. In his terror he had thought of his mother, and that thought, like invoking the protection of a higher power, had given him the courage to reach the safety of the skylight again. In just the same way Siegfried calls on his mother in the moment when he learns fear.

There is even a letter Wagner wrote to his mother, dated 19

September 1846, which anticipates Siegfried's state of mind in the scene under the linden tree: 'My good little mother, however many strange things have come between us, how quickly they all vanish! When I leave the smoke of the town for a beautiful leafy valley, lie down on the moss, look at the slender trees, listen to a bird singing, until in my sense of ease a tear forms that I am happy to leave undried – it's as though I were stretching out my hand to you from the whole chaos of strange events.' And later he once, in conversation, referred to the Woodbird in *Siegfried* as the voice of 'Sieglinde's maternal soul'.

Cosima noted in her diary on 4 January 1878 that Wagner told her that 'when he had argued with his mother as a child he had shown a compulsion to confess'. This is like Parsifal, who has run away from his mother and is stricken with a passionate metaphysical sense of guilt in the second act, as the reality of her death comes home to him.

Such elements rose out of Wagner's subconscious and appeared in his work involuntarily. The connection is even more mysterious when the theme of Parsifal's self-reproach in the second act – 'Die Mutter, die Mutter konnt' ich vergessen!' – is recalled in a majestic fortissimo by the woodwind and horns in the third-act transformation music, as if, on the point of assuming his royal office, Parsifal remembers the security his mother gave him.

It is characteristic of Wagner and his work that a few pages about his mother should open perspectives of this breadth and depth. His life and his work are a fabric closely woven together from threads that run continuously from the earliest experiences of his childhood to the work that was his 'farewell to the world'.

# 3

Boyhood

It was a small thin boy that grew up in the charge of his sisters, pale, with a high forehead and bright blue eyes – 'blue as the sea', Judith Gautier wrote when she first met Wagner at Tribschen. His health was poor and caused his mother great and constant anxiety; once, when he was particularly ill with a childhood disease, she almost gave him up altogether. He suffered from a very early age from an allergic sensitivity of the skin, which continued to trouble him throughout his life and was the reason for the famous silk underwear. But just as the grown man, forever suffering and complaining about it, had an incredible capacity for hard work, so the child, for all his delicacy, possessed a prodigious fund of vitality and was always ready for mischief and hair-raising adventures – Geyer called him 'the cossack'. On a visit to Geyer's brother, a goldsmith, in Eisleben, he never stopped fighting the local boys, and when a troupe of rope-walkers set up their act in the marketplace, he at once tried to imitate them; to the end of his days he used to horrify Cosima by climbing every tree in the garden.

He himself denied that he was an infant prodigy. It would have been hard, indeed, to discover one particular outstanding talent in the abundance of his gifts. But there were signs that he was different from other children: he was observant far beyond his years, and he possessed an imagination which brought even inanimate objects so vividly to life that he was sometimes terrified by them. Mime's vision of Fafner in Act I of *Siegfried* is an objectification of his own earliest fears put to comic use.

His stepfather had plans for him, though they did not include the theatre. It would have pleased him best if Richard had shown a talent for painting, but after a number of fruitless attempts to

17

capture the boy's interest, he had to admit defeat on that particular front.

In his autobiography Wagner describes how he was summoned home from Possendorf, where he had started school with the pastor, because his stepfather was dying. He was taken to the bedside and experienced the sensation that it was all happening in a dream. 'In the next room my mother invited me to play what I had learned on the piano, her intention being to distract father with the sound: I played "Üb' immer Treu und Redlichkeit"; then father asked my mother, "Do you think he might have a talent for music?"'

'At first light the next morning mother entered the large room where we children slept, came to each bed in turn and told us, sobbing, that our father was dead, saying something to each of us like a blessing; to me she said, "He hoped to make something out of you." '

'I recollect', Wagner confessed, 'that for a long time I imagined that I would come to something.'

Geyer died too soon (on 30 September 1821) to have been able to influence the boy's development. His most lasting effect on him was perhaps through his friendship with Carl Maria von Weber. 'He inspired me with enthusiasm for music. I wish somebody could have seen me at the performance of *Der Freischütz*, in the little old theatre, conducted by Weber. It is a blessing to experience the impact of an elect being in childhood.' When Weber passed the house after rehearsals, Richard called his little sister Cäcilie to the window: 'Look, there's the greatest man alive! You can't have any idea how great he is!' 'Not to be emperor, not to be king, but to stand there like that and conduct like that': that was his sole desire when he saw and heard Weber conducting *Freischütz* once again. And the composer of *Parsifal* could still remember the 'tonic–harmonic thrill', the sense of the 'daemonic' that came over him on hearing the first bars of the overture, 'something peculiar to me, too'. 'Formal beauty, on its own, was a matter of indifference to me . . . Nobody else had much of a chance after I had heard that adagio introduction.'

His stepfather and his brothers and sisters introduced the child to the world of the theatre. Artists were frequent visitors in the Geyer household; they made trips into the country together, picnicking in the open air, and once Weber acted as cook. While Dresden, the capital of Saxony, was described at that date as a 'colony of court officials', with an appropriate decorum prevailing in social behaviour, manners in this charming, lively-minded circle were friendly and relaxed.

What attracted him to the theatre was, by Wagner's own account, not so much the search for entertainment as the pleasurable excitement of a purely imaginary world, a fascination often close to horror, 'something mysteriously ghostly about the beards, wigs and costumes, which the addition of music only intensified'. Through his sisters he was able to go behind the scenes and explore backstage and the wardrobe rooms, and a single piece of scenery or a costume was enough to transport him at a stroke to 'that fascinating daemonium'. He used to watch his sisters sewing the more delicate costumes at home, and just touching them was enough to set his heart racing.

The discovery of a puppet theatre that had belonged to his stepfather, with lovely sets Geyer had painted himself, at once inspired the boy to write a play of derring-do, which made his sisters laugh uncontrollably when they found it and must have been his first essay in dramatic form. Seeing a puppet theatre half a century later, after he had written *Götterdämmerung*, moved him, as we shall see, to comment on the essence of mimic art, present even in this primordial form of theatre.

The whole of the boy's small world was filled with marvellous happenings; it is characteristic that E. T. A. Hoffmann's fairy tale *Der Goldene Topf*, which was set in Dresden (and which was written in the year of Richard's birth), remained a favourite of his all his life, with its mixture of the realistic and the fantastic, reminding him of his first childhood.

Wagner's first experience of the wider world took the shape of a journey to Prague, on foot, and his account of it – including his falling passionately in love with two pretty sisters and even encountering a blind harpist – reads like a chapter out of *Wilhelm Meister*. The volcanic soil of Bohemia was to stir his imagination mysteriously again on a later occasion.

The five years he spent as a pupil at the Kreuzschule in Dresden (1822–7) provided an important classical counterbalance to the romanticism on which his imagination fed. It is rare for an artist of genius to praise his school as highly as Wagner did in his autobiography. Greek history and mythology aroused so great an enthusiasm in him that, while his neglect of Latin incurred punish-

ment, he plunged into the study of Greek, so as to be able to hear his heroes speaking in their own language. His teacher, Magister Sillig, confidently predicted a career as a classical scholar for him. Newman's doubts as to the accuracy of these claims are refuted by the record of extra work done by the third-form pupils on their own initiative in the Michaelmas term of 1826: the thirteen-year-old Wagner was the only one in the class to submit a translation of the first three books of the *Odyssey*. (GLRW, I, p. 103)

His early classical studies ranged widely. Professor Friedrich Creuzer of Heidelberg published a book entitled *Symbolism and Mythology of Ancient Peoples, with Special Reference to the Greeks*, which stirred up quite a controversy. Johann Heinrich Voss, whose translation of Homer is still the standard German version, wrote an *Antisymbolism* in reply. It is astonishing to read Wagner reminding an old school friend, in a letter from Riga in November 1838, of how they had sworn 'death to Creuzer's *Symbolism*' – when still in the third form! He later formed a less harsh opinion of Creuzer's thesis and had the book in his library in Wahnfried.

When the family moved back to Leipzig in 1827 his interest in classics was encouraged by his father's younger brother, Adolf Wagner. 'God, when I remember Uncle Adolf!' he said to Cosima. 'I would have been proud to introduce you to him, and to tell you I was descended from the same stock. His conversation was refined and mild, his mind was cultivated, noble and free. He was a true disciple of Goethe.'

Adolf Wagner had just published his magnum opus, *Parnasso italiano*, an anthology including texts by Dante, Petrarch, Ariosto and Tasso. He dedicated it 'al principe de' poeti, Goethe', who sent him a silver goblet in thanks. 'I have used it for many years in joy and sorrow, and it has witnessed manifold events. Use it yourself as often and refresh your memory of me in the enjoyment of wine, which belongs, like poetry, to those products of spirit and intelligence with which humanity has come close to rivalling nature itself.' (29 October 1827)

Richard used to accompany his uncle on afternoon walks outside the city gates and the sight of them deep in talk may well have raised a smile in passers-by. He liked to spend his evenings in his uncle's house, too: when Adolf read a Sophoclean tragedy aloud, it revealed a new, previously unknown side of the Greek spirit to him, one which was to be of decisive importance for his own work.

He had in the meantime discovered Shakespeare by his own initiative, and his enthusiasm grew to an obsession. 'I can remember dreaming in my early adolescence that Shakespeare was *alive*, and I saw him and spoke to him, face to face.'

For all his passion for music, the bent for poetry seemed to be winning the upper hand. While still at the Kreuzschule he had won the prize for a poem on the death of a fellow-pupil. It had even been printed and his mother folded her hands in prayerful gratitude at this first proof of her youngest son's gifts.

'It was now beyond doubt that I was going to be a poet.' The outcome of this conviction was a five-act tragedy, *Leubald*, at which he worked in secret for two years (1826–8). (RWGS, XVI, pp. 179ff.) The only person in the secret was his sister Ottilie. Once when he was reading her one of the most blood-curdling scenes, a violent thunderstorm broke out. 'As the lightning flashed and the thunder rolled right overhead, my sister tried to persuade me to abandon the reading, but she soon realized it was impossible to stop me, and sat it out with a touching devotion.'

He laughed at it later in life: it was compounded of *Hamlet* and *Lear*, forty-two people died in it and most of them had to reappear as ghosts in the last act, since he had run out of characters. But he took it very seriously at the time, and the monstrous progeny of his imagination sprang up from his bedroom floor with such vitality that they frightened even their creator.

At fourteen he believed he had found his vocation, chosen his future path.

# 4

Beethoven

'Then came Beethoven.' The look and tone of voice with which
Wagner once spoke these words, in the course of a conversation
tracing the development of German music, amounted to an experience in themselves, according to Hans von Wolzogen: as if the name
of Beethoven heralded the dawn of a new world.

Beethoven did open a new world to Wagner himself. The start of
the overture to *Fidelio*, with its use of horns and woodwind, had an
effect on him similar to that of the *Freischütz* overture. He asked his
sisters about Beethoven and was told that he had just died. His
deafness, his lonely life, a lithographed portrait and now his
untimely death conjured up the impression of the 'most sublime,
transcendental originality'. And when he heard the incidental music
to *Egmont* he knew he had to write music like that for his own
tragedy.

Beethoven, too, was admitted to the world of his imagination,
and in his dreams Beethoven's image was mingled now with
Shakespeare's. This conjunction of the poet and the composer was a
first, confused intimation of his own future creative activity. It was
while he was in this state of mind that he had two great Beethovenian experiences: he saw Schröder-Devrient in the part of Fidelio
and he immersed himself in the score of the Ninth Symphony.

The Leipzig theatre reopened in August 1829, after a closure of
over a year, now under the supervision of the intendant of the court
theatre in Dresden. Its priorities included not only high production
standards but also a varied and worthwhile repertory. Since his
sister Rosalie was a member of the company, Wagner had no
difficulty in getting into performances whenever he wanted to. If it
had been the mysterious and fantastic elements in the theatre that

had attracted him as a child, now, at sixteen, under the spell of Shakespeare, Schiller and Goethe, he was seized for the first time by a more 'aware' passion for the stage.

It was then that a kind of miracle occurred, turning his artistic sensibility in a new direction, determining the course of his whole life: Wilhelmine Schröder-Devrient, then twenty-four and at the height of her fame, came from Dresden for a short season as guest artist, and sang the title role in *Fidelio*.

In the opera's second act, as the music transfigures the drama, and as Leonora frees her husband from the darkness of his cell, it was to the boy, listening with bated breath, as if she was leading him, too, into the broad daylight of his hitherto dimly perceived artistic ideal. He scribbled a hasty note, handed it in at the singer's hotel and ran off into the night like a madman. From that day forward, he wrote, his life would have a new meaning, and if she should ever hear his name acclaimed in the world of art, then she might care to remember that it was she who had made him that evening what he thereupon swore to become. 'When I look back at the whole of my life,' he affirmed years later, 'I can discover no other experience that I could compare with this for the effect it had on me.'

He would have written a work worthy of that great woman there and then, if he had been able. The fact that he could not filled him with despair over his literary and musical experiments and cast him for a while into a frenzy of youthful excesses. He dedicated his essay *On Actors and Singers* (1872) to her memory, and the figure of Tragedy in the sgraffito over the front door of Wahnfried bears the face of Schröder-Devrient, a mysterious yet overt memorial to that seminal experience of his teens.

No such ideal interpreter guided him in his other Beethovenian experience. He had to find the meaning and the soul in the dumb notation of the score for himself. Some of the earliest of his childhood impressions were revived. As a small boy he had never been able to go past the palace of Prince Anton in Dresden without trembling at the mysterious sound of fifths that seemed to come from the violin held by one of the stone figures decorating the baroque façade. The haunting impression was the stronger because of a picture he knew well in which Death played the violin to a dying man. Later, when he attended afternoon concerts in the Grosser Garten park, on the outskirts of Dresden, the sound of the orchestra tuning struck him like the summoning of a spirit world in which he first set foot with the opening bars of the *Freischütz* overture.

Music was a 'daemonium' to him, a 'mystically sublime immensity', and tonic, third and fifth appeared to him in half-waking dreams as tangible, physical entities. Reading his favourite author, E. T. A. Hoffmann, fed his susceptibilities, and he even believed he had found the original of one of Hoffmann's characters, Kapellmeister Kreisler, in a half-crazy musical fanatic in Leipzig. This mysticism was only a youthful manifestation of the completely individual sensitivity to music that gives his works their special character: the sounds perceptible to sense are only the surface layer of the impulses contracting and relaxing in the depth of the soul: the music is more than music.

Opening the score to the Choral Symphony, he was struck by the fifths, the ghostly echo from his childhood, the 'Fundamental' of his own life. This symphony must contain the secret of all secrets! He set to, to copy the score laboriously by hand, until late into the night. Once the first light of day surprised him at his task and with a shriek he buried his face in the pillows as if he had seen a ghost. Since there was no piano reduction for two hands at that time, this seventeen-year-old undertook the task. The specimens of it published by Otto Daube show that his mysticism was allied to a genuine musical understanding: not only does it offer a clear, playable piano version, but there are places in the Adagio where its rendering of the melodic line is superior to Otto Singer's later version.[1]

After he had finished the first movement he wrote to Franz Schott, the publisher, in Mainz, on 6 October 1830 – the letter is the earliest by him that survives:

> Beethoven's last glorious symphony has long been the
> subject of my study, and the closer my acquaintance
> with its high quality, the more saddened I have been
> that it is still so much misunderstood, so much
> disregarded by the majority of the musical public . . .
> My enthusiasm was great enough to embolden me to
> undertake a two-hand piano version of it myself, and so
> it is that I have so far arranged the first, and perhaps the
> most difficult, movement as clearly and as fully as
> possible. I am now therefore approaching your respected

publishing house, to enquire whether you would be interested in taking an arrangement of this kind (for naturally I am unwilling to proceed further with such a laborious task without that assurance) . . . I therefore ask you most respectfully for a speedy reply.

Schott's reply was noncommittal, but he met Wagner at the next Easter Fair in Leipzig and took the complete piano score away with him to study it. He was obviously amazed to find his would-be collaborator so young. After waiting several months for Schott's decision, Wagner wrote to him again on 6 August 1831:

Since I have been waiting vainly for an offer from you for over three months, I have come to the conclusion that you have been expecting me to state my terms, which I herewith hasten to do. I am sure, Sir, that you will not think it exorbitant if I ask for 1 louisdor per fascicle for this protracted, difficult and important task, which no one else has as yet attempted in view of its unusual demands, that is a total of 8 louisdor, which will certainly be recouped tenfold by the sales of this important work.

Even this tempting commercial prospect could not persuade Schott to undertake publication. After he had returned the manuscript at the end of 1831, Wagner sent it back to him in June 1832:

I do not ask for any honorarium for it, but if you would care to make me a gift in return you would make me your grateful debtor. Might I perhaps request you to send me, through Herr Härtel: Beethoven 1) Missa Solemnis (D major), full score and piano reduction; 2) Beethoven Symphony no, 9, full score; 3) idem 2 quartets, score, and 4) Hummel's arrangements of Beethoven's symphonies? The sooner, the more gratifying.

Schott complied with this request but did not publish the arrangement of the Choral Symphony. Forty years later Wagner asked him for it again, as a present for Cosima: 'My dear wife is in a perpetual state of excitement, as much at the thought of the gift you are sending her . . . as at the continuing delay in its arrival. You would have to be as truly obsessed with my poor manuscript as this dear woman is, to be able to understand her state.' (3 January 1872) In return he dedicated a piano piece, *Albumblatt* in E♭ major, to Frau Betty Schott.

This earliest publishing venture not only gives a glimpse of his study of Beethoven, but it also reveals Wagner in toto, his enthusiasm, his persistence and not least his not unjustified self-confidence.

In the short story he wrote in Paris in 1840, *A Pilgrimage to Beethoven*, Wagner recounts the impact of Beethoven on him in fictional terms, when he has a German musician say, 'I don't really know what career had been planned for me, I only remember that one evening I heard a Beethoven symphony for the first time, that I thereupon fell ill with a fever, and when I recovered, I had become a musician.' (*Eine Pilgerfahrt zu Beethoven*, RWGS, I, pp. 90ff.) The extraordinary and unique thing about his further development was that he had been separately inspired by two Beethovens, first the dramatist and then the symphonist. Each of the experiences addressed itself to a different side of his own talent – hence the initial 'fever'. The ambition to combine these two strands in a single work of art sprang from his own genius. The whole story of his artistic endeavours, as theorist and practitioner, is the struggle to synthesize music as drama with music as symphony, in symphonic drama. That is what distinguishes him not only from other musicians, but also from his master Beethoven.

# 5

## Studiosus Musicae

The address Wagner gave on his early letters to Schott was 'Leipzig, in the Pichhof by the Halle Gate'. His mother and three of his sisters lived in a comfortable apartment on the first floor, with a fine view of the Promenade, a broad leafy avenue following the line of the old city walls, and the scene of Richard's secret poetic and musical experiments was a 'wonderfully small bedroom'.

Outside that room he ran wild. His self-esteem suffered a blow when he was put into a class in the Nikolaischule in Leipzig lower than the one he had been in in Dresden, and his enjoyment of his lessons was completely spoiled. He abandoned everything else and studied only music. By the time his family found out about it, he had not attended school for six months.

The family in conclave decided that there was no further way of preventing him from devoting himself to music, and his brother-in-law Friedrich Brockhaus proposed sending him to Weimar to study the piano with Hummel.

How was he to explain that music to him did not mean playing an instrument, but composing? He felt that the only course open to him was to make a complete break with his surroundings. It was the first of many times in his life when he was to feel the same. Whenever external circumstances threatened to overwhelm him, he was always able to find an escape route. On this occasion he gained admission to the Thomasschule in order to continue studying, but, as he said, he left that, too, without having made the least effort to reap any advantage from it. On 23 February 1831 he matriculated at the university in Leipzig as a music student.

Not the least of the university's attractions was the glamour attached to the status of student, which had impressed him even as a schoolboy. He joined the 'Saxonia' fraternity and even before the session began he already had fights pending with several experienced duellists. That he escaped with a whole skin from these challenges was due to a series of remarkable accidents of the kind that continued to help him in tight corners throughout his life. His account of this wild, dissipated period is written with such disarming frankness that Mrs Burrell, his admirer and biographer, who secretly got hold of a copy of the private printing of *Mein Leben*, could not bring herself to believe it but took it to be a fabrication of Cosima, whom she detested.

His inner life can be gauged from the fact that he still found the time for music and the self-possession to compose a number of pieces which, as he later remarked, bore much the same relationship to Beethoven as *Leubald* to Shakespeare. All the same, at the age of seventeen and still a schoolboy, he had an Overture in B♭ major performed in the theatre in Leipzig, on 24 December 1830. With gleeful self-mockery he tells in *Mein Leben* of how the drumbeat that recurred in every fifth bar put the audience into fits of laughter. The conductor, Heinrich Dorn, found the work unusual but recognized something in it that commanded attention.

Ever since Eduard Hanslick called Wagner a 'dilettante' and Nietzsche repeated it with rhetorical insistence, it has been bandied about, not only by laymen but by musical scholars who ought to have known that his 'miraculous scores', in Richard Strauss's phrase,[1] could not possibly have been written by an amateur.

The more detailed account found in *Mein Leben* already demonstrated that Wagner's remark in the *Autobiographical Sketch* of 1842 – that his study with Weinlig came to a halt within less than six months – cannot be taken literally. But the full extent of his formal studies has only been known since Otto Daube published his survey of Wagner's 'apprenticeship'.

At fifteen he borrowed Johann Bernhard Logier's newly published *Methode des Generalbasses* from the lending library run by Friedrich Wieck, Clara Schumann's father, so as to be able to paint the apparitions in his great tragedy in the proper musical colours. He found it tougher going than he had expected, and the accumulating library dues were, he asserted, the first and root cause of the financial difficulties that troubled him throughout the rest of his life.

Seeing that he would make no progress on his own, without

telling his family he began lessons in harmony with Christian Gottlieb Müller, a violinist in the theatre orchestra. He soon found the rules Müller expounded and the work he set too arid, and he went back to the 'artistic hauntings' of Hoffmann's *Fantasiestücke*, which were far more to his taste as a source of instruction. Even when he resumed lessons with Müller, after he had had to confess to his family the amounts he owed him in fees, harmonic theory could not hold his interest for long, and by summer he was neglecting his studies entirely. His move to the university brought no improvement – on the contrary, that was when his career in taverns and gaming houses really got under way.

At this point his mother plucked up her courage and went to ask Christian Theodor Weinlig, the cantor of the Thomaskirche, to give her son lessons. Weinlig, born in 1780, had studied in Bologna and was an adherent of Padre Martini's conservative Italian school. He had a formidable reputation as a contrapuntalist and had been appointed to J. S. Bach's old post in 1823. His health was poor and at first he would not yield to Johanna's fervent pleas to teach her son, but a fugue Richard had brought with him and shyly proffered changed his mind: he saw at once that the prospective pupil had talent and only lacked instruction. He agreed to teach him but made one condition: for six months he was to compose nothing at all but only to follow his master's precepts.

At first it seemed that the course was doomed to end like all the others; things reached the point at which Weinlig told him he wanted nothing more to do with him. But this coincided with another harrowing event: Richard had collected his mother's pension and in the course of a single evening's card playing had lost it and won it back again in one desperate play; thereupon he had sworn never to touch a card again. It was, he later confessed, the turning point of his life. But it also signified the turning point of his career as a musician. He begged his teacher's forgiveness and Weinlig agreed to persist with him. From then on the lessons were a joy to Wagner; the most difficult technical problems seemed to solve themselves like a game, so that he sometimes wondered if he was really learning anything.

When his English friend Edward Dannreuther asked him in 1877 for the secret of Weinlig's method, which had effected such results, Wagner replied:

Weinlig had no special method, but he was clear headed and practical. Indeed, you cannot teach composition . . . All you can do is, to point to some working example, some particular piece, set a task in that direction, and correct the pupil's work. This is what Weinlig did with me. He chose a piece, generally something of Mozart's, drew attention to its construction, relative length and balance of sections, principal modulations, number and quality of themes, and general character of the movement. Then he set the task: you shall write about so many bars, divide into so many sections with modulations to correspond so and so, the themes shall be so many, and of such and such a character. Similarly he would set contrapuntal exercises, canons, fugues – he analysed an example minutely and then gave simple directions how I was to go to work . . . With infinite kindness he would put his finger on some defective bit and explain the why and wherefore of the alterations he thought desirable. I readily saw what he was aiming at and soon managed to please him . . . Music should be taught all round on such a simple plan.[2]

This understanding between teacher and pupil, as Daube observes, lives on in Hans Sachs's workshop, as he explains the rules of mastersong to Walther.

Wagner regretted, in later life, the loss of an exercise book containing the fugues of the Leipzig period. But some of the counterpoint exercises, with Weinlig's corrections, are preserved in the Wagner Archives and very attractively illustrate Wagner's account of his lessons, above all a four-part vocal fugue on the text 'Dein ist das Reich von Ewigkeit zu Ewigkeit, Amen' (published by Daube).

Wagner's mother had the shock of her life one day when Weinlig paid her a formal call. Accustomed to hearing nothing but complaints from Richard's teachers, she was prepared for the worst, but instead the cantor explained that he had considered it his duty to call on her to render account of his pupil's progress. It was quite remarkable, but the young man already knew for himself everything he could have taught him. And when she enquired about the fees due after six months of lessons Weinlig replied that it would be wrong of him to expect payment in addition to the pleasure it had been to teach her son. His pupil's diligence and the hopes he himself nurtured for him were payment enough.

To give his student the chance to show that he had got rid of all his bombast, Weinlig set him the task of writing a sonata after the pattern of one of a childlike simplicity by Pleyel. Although Wagner constructed his B♭ major Sonata from the simplest harmonic and thematic relationships, it breathes the spirit, not of Pleyel, but of Mozart, whom he was then just coming fully to know and love. In recognition of his self-restraint Weinlig got Breitkopf & Härtel to publish it, and his acceptance of the dedication on the title page shows he saw no reason to be ashamed of this piece qualifying the apprentice as journeyman.

As a reward Wagner was then allowed to compose his Fantasia in F♯ minor for piano in as free a form as he liked. Its interest lies in the fact that for the first time we encounter here anticipations of the kind of uniquely Wagnerian thematic shapes that were later to characterize *Die Walküre* and *Tristan*.

Finally, one day when he presented his teacher with a particularly elaborate double fugue, Weinlig told him he might as well frame it and hang it on the wall, he had nothing more to teach him. 'You will probably never write canons or fugues; but what you have acquired is independence. You can stand on your own feet now, and you know that you are capable of the utmost expertise, if you ever need it.' Although this marked the end of a good six months of strict apprenticeship, Weinlig remained his 'friendly adviser'.

Wagner now proceeded to study on his own. What he still had to learn could only be learned from the masters, Mozart, Beethoven and Bach, whose *Well-tempered Clavier* he tried to unlock on his own. Newman devotes several pages of inimitable irony to Wagner's 'academic enemies', who could not conceive how anybody could even dare to compose without having been through their school; what conservatory of any age could ever have taught him what he found out for himself? The truth is that he went on learning all his life, but he could do it only in his own way, aiming straight at a target that his contemporaries could not even see.

That his study of Beethoven had profited from Weinlig's instruction is illustrated by the A major Piano Sonata and the C major Symphony, both of 1832. The sonata, which Daube publishes, is decidedly the most important of Wagner's juvenilia. The main

theme of the first movement, stated at the outset, is a true symphonic theme in the Beethovenian sense, driven forward by an
inner dynamic and providing the material for a lively development
section. Its pulsating rhythm persists in the quieter final bars, as if
preparing for the impassioned, sombre Adagio molto e assai espres-
sivo (F♯ minor). It was a bold stroke to follow this with a free
three-part fugue instead of a scherzo, finishing with a cadenza
which already prefigures the succeeding theme and leads without a
break into the finale (A major), which is also in first-movement
form.

Wagner's next composition, in the early summer of 1832, was the
C major Symphony. He had been completely cut off from external
life, he wrote to his friend Theodor Apel, and his interior life was all
the stronger for it. 'I was forsaken by God and the world. So my
godlike music had to come, and you must believe me when I say
that in this state I worked on my most powerful work to date,
my symphony, and finished it within six weeks.' (16 December
1832)

This early work still gave him pleasure at the end of his life; he
thought it a not uninteresting example of the effect Beethoven's
works, then still not well known, had on a young man like him. 'I
also enjoyed putting my study of counterpoint to the test: there are
some stretto passages in it I can only call devilish.' When the
symphony was performed again in 1882 he wrote of it, in Fritzsch's
*Musikalisches Wochenblatt*, that if it contained any recognizable trait
of Richard Wagner it was probably the boundless confidence that
he already possessed, caring for nothing even then, and remaining
immune to the hypocrisy that since then had infected the Germans
totally. (RWGS, X, pp. 309ff.) He then goes on to say that 'the
theme – no! let's call it the melody of the second movement
(Andante)' shows the capacity he already had for writing in an
elegiac vein, 'although it would probably never have seen the light
of day without the Andante of [Beethoven's] C minor Symphony
and the Allegretto of the A major', but, as Paul Bekker very rightly
comments, his dependence on Beethoven is no greater than that of
Brahms in his most mature works.

After finishing his symphony Wagner went to Bohemia again,
on the track of his early love, in particular of the elder of the two
young sisters. 'Picture Jenny as an Ideal of beauty, and add my
ardent fantasy, and you have it in a nutshell,' he told Apel. But a

bitter disappointment was in store for him. He found the young ladies surrounded by a gang of witless, horsy admirers, whom they permitted to pay clumsy court to them in the most unfeeling fashion. 'Oh, and – you can imagine all the things that can wound an ardent love; – but what is capable of killing it is more dreadful by far! – learn it from me and send me your sympathy: – she was not worthy of my love!' He had some consolation in an artistic triumph, however, when Dionys Weber, the director of the Prague Conservatory, conducted his students in the first performance of the C major Symphony. The occasion induced a friend to write what was probably the first of those satiric verse apostrophes, not always so good-natured, that rained on Wagner throughout his later career, likening his approach to Weber to the assault on Dionysius the tyrant in Schiller's *Die Bürgschaft*.

The symphony was played before the Euterpe Society in Leipzig in the December, followed by a performance in the Gewandhaus on 10 January 1833. Demoiselle Clara Wieck played a concerto by Pixis in the same concert. 'Now, listen to this,' she had already written to Robert Schumann after the Euterpe concert; 'Herr Wagner has soared above you. They performed a symphony by him that is said to be as like Beethoven's A major Symphony as two peas.'

Wagner managed to get three other orchestral works performed during the course of 1832: a Concert Overture in D minor in the Gewandhaus, an overture to Raupach's play *König Enzio* in the theatre, and a Concert Overture in C major, again in the Gewandhaus. His teacher Weinlig had used all his influence to help him, Wagner explained, in the belief that public performance was an experience of cardinal importance, 'and I am happy to say that it never did me any harm, but on the contrary, I had two great advantages from it: in addition to finding out increasingly clearly, by listening to the things myself, what was needed to achieve my ends, I also had the pleasure of having the eyes of the public directed towards me with interest.'

Half a century later he spoke of what had motivated him in his early works. The conversation had turned to the spread of his fame. 'Oh, yes,' he said, 'one has in abundance in age what one wished for in youth, but I can't say I ever wished for fame – no, for something that was distinctly mine, a real melody that was my own, something that wasn't Beethoven or Weber. That was all I aimed at when

I started to compose; I never went in for sophisticated ponderings like Schumann.' (2 March 1882)

In the meantime, during his visit to Bohemia, his manner of working had taken a new turn that was to prove of decisive importance.

# 6

## The First Three Operas

Wagner brought home with him from Prague his first text for an opera, *Die Hochzeit* ('The Wedding'). The letter in which he poured out his heartache to Apel ended, 'Enough, enough, all too much already. For in spite of the endless void in my bosom I still discover in myself a longing for love; – and what makes me really angry is that I look thoroughly well and in the best of health!' It was hardly surprising, for he had applied the time-honoured remedy of all unhappy lovers and worked off his anguish in writing: 'Such were the circumstances in which I drew up the text of my opera, and it was finished by the time I got back to Leipzig about a fortnight ago.' (16 December 1832)

He later called it a night-piece of the blackest hue, devoid of any gleam of light, any of the usual operatic adornments. *Werther* was much on his mind at the time: not only did he give his characters Ossianic names but a passage in another letter to Apel, describing Jenny at the piano, was stolen from Goethe's novel, as he confessed in the margin. (14 March 1833)

The subject was one he had found years before in J. G. Büsching's history of medieval chivalry, *Ritterzeit und Ritterwesen*. Two kings wish to set the seal on a peace made after years of enmity, so the son of one is invited to attend the wedding of the other's daughter. The young man falls passionately in love with the bride. As she comes out of the church their eyes meet. She tries to collect herself: 'Mein Gatte, sprich, wer ist der fremde Mann?' ('Husband, tell me, who is that stranger?'; cf. Senta's 'Mein Vater, sprich, wer ist der Fremde?'). That night the disturbing guest climbs up to the window of the room where she is waiting for her bridegroom. After a moment of hesitation she struggles with the intruder and succeeds in hurling him down to the courtyard below. The cause of his death remains a mystery, but as the court observes the proper ceremonies the princess collapses lifeless on his bier.

It is an early variant on the *Tristan* theme: 'Er sah mir in die Augen'. Wagner wrote the music for the first scene, and a septet won Weinlig's approval for its clarity and singability. There is even an authentic Wagnerian motive repeated several times in the accompaniment to a recitative. But his sister Rosalie, whose opinion meant more to him than anyone else's, felt nothing but revulsion for the grisly story, so he 'annulled and tore up' his text. The score of the first scene is all that survives, and it was performed in Rostock in February 1933, exactly one hundred years after its composition.

It was not offended vanity that made him abandon it. Rosalie, 'little sprite' as her stepfather called her, was his 'maternal' sister. There is a picture of her at the piano: while her fingers seem to be gliding over the keys, she looks out at us, clear-eyed. She believed in Richard from the first and suffered immeasurably at his teenage dissipation. Now that her faith in him was restored he wanted to prove by this summary act how much he valued her judgement. It was she who, by her playing of Gretchen in 1830, had inspired him to write his Seven Compositions for Goethe's *Faust*; he revised the sketches in 1832 and proudly inscribed them 'opus 5'. The melodrama 'Ach neige, du Schmerzensreiche' already foreshadows the future composer of music dramas.

There is reason to regret that he did not complete his first opera: it would have been much more personal, much less 'operatic', in short much more Wagnerian than the next three. But he may have been guided by a sure instinct that he was not yet musically ready for this tragedy of love and death.

He now made another important discovery. Heinrich Laube, the young editor of the *Zeitung für die Elegante Welt*, who had recognized the promise in the C major Symphony when he reviewed it, offered him a libretto which he had originally thought of sending to Meyerbeer. It gave Wagner a shock. He had renounced his boyish ambitions to be a poet and his only aim now was to be a composer, but only he could know what sort of text would serve for an opera of his own composing.

He had already started another text of his own. He took the plot of *Die Feen* ('The Fairies') from Gozzi's fairy tale *La donna serpente*,

1. View of Leipzig from the east, around 1850

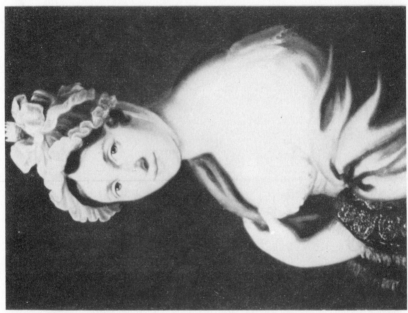

2b. Johanna Rosine Wagner, née Pätz

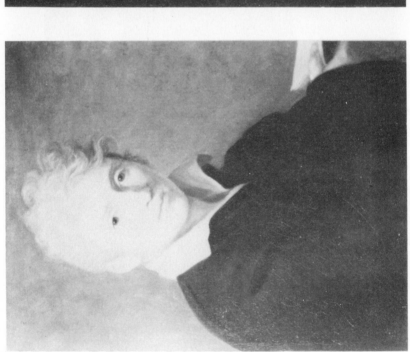

2a. Ludwig Geyer

3b. Theodor Weinlig

3a. Adolf Wagner

5b. Wagner's house in Riga

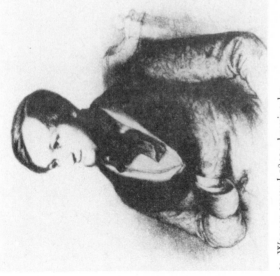

5a. Wagner around 1850: drawing by
Ernest Benedikt Kietz

6. The warrant for Wagner's arrest after the revolution of 1849, from Eberhardt's *Allgemeiner Polizei-Anzeiger* 1853

7b. Arthur Schopenhauer

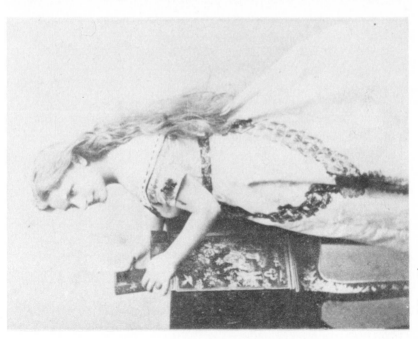

7a. Minna Planer

8a. Eduard Devrient

8b. Anton Pusinelli

9a. Dresden Opera House, designed by Gottfried Semper

9b. Villa Wesendonk, near Zürich

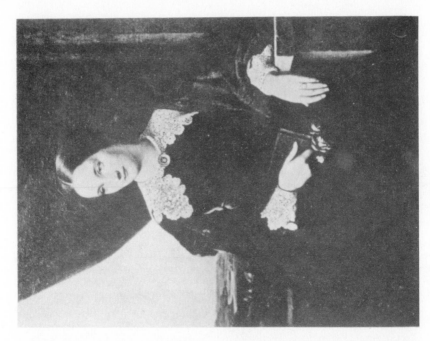

10b. Mathilde Wesendonk

10a. Otto Wesendonk

11. The end of the Prelude to *Tristan und Isolde*: a piano arrangement dated 15 December 1859

12b. Hans von Bülow

12a. Charles Baudelaire

13. Letter from Wagner to King Ludwig dated 3 May 1864: 'Theurer huldvoller König!'

14b. Eduard Hanslick

14a. King Ludwig II

15b. Jessie Laussot-Taylor

15a. Eliza Wille

16b. Wagner around 1864: painting by Friedrich Pecht, with a bust of King Ludwig in the background

16a. Cosima von Bülow around 1860: drawing by Claire Charnacé

but made some characteristic changes to it. The fairy Ada is cursed by her human husband Arindal, who fails the tests he has to undergo; she turns to stone until he releases her through the power of music and both enter the realm of fairyland together as immortals. This simple tale, which again is set in an Ossianic ambience, bears some typical Wagnerian trademarks: the forbidden question, the hunter's pity for the animal he has wounded, the idea of redemption. But these features are planted in an operatic hothouse of transformation scenes, choruses and ballets, and the ideal couple are flanked by a more down-to-earth pair as well as a burlesque pair.

In order to devote himself to the composition of his opera Richard turned down the offer of a post in Zürich, though with a bad conscience as he was being supported by Rosalie. At the end of January 1833 he accepted an offer from his brother Albert, who was working in the theatre in Würzburg, directing opera. By chance there was a vacancy there for a lowly post as chorus master, constituting Wagner's first practical engagement in a theatre.

'Yes, Theodor, now my future is bearing down hard on me,' he wrote to Apel, 'life is beginning to take a serious shape externally as well. I shall have to find myself a sanctuary for the summer, so that I can finish my opera by the winter.' (14 March 1833) His months in Würzburg were not so oppressive and serious that he failed to find inclination and opportunity for amatory escapades, but he nevertheless pursued his work with characteristic obsession. He had finished the finale of the last act the day before yesterday, he wrote to Rosalie on 11 December. 'It was exactly twelve noon, and the bells were ringing from all the towers as I wrote Finis at the bottom.' All that remained for him to do was orchestrate the last act, and here another characteristic reveals itself: his 'somewhat pedantic manner' of writing out even the first draft of the score as cleanly and tidily as possible would probably hold him up for another three weeks. It was dreadful, he complained nearly half a century later when he made a mistake in scoring *Parsifal*, to have been given 'pedantry and genius' in one bag – veritable torture! But the compensation for posterity is that his own fair copies of his scores are masterpieces of calligraphy.

He was unshakably convinced that his opera would be a success. 'It all flowed from my inmost soul – and they say that's how to reach into the souls of others.' His sisters had already put in a word for him at the Leipzig theatre. He was allowed to submit his score, and his only concern was that the forces there might not be adequate to its demands. 'It's a pity about the female principals in your company – I really need a first-rate voice and compelling acting ability – someone like Devrient would be no bad thing,' he wrote to Rosalie. (11 December 1833)

However, the bass singer and producer Franz Hauser, on whose sole judgement acceptance of *Die Feen* depended, was the last person in the world to like it. He was a knowledgeable and competent musician, but he thought Mozart over-elaborate, approved only of Gluck and regretted that Bach had written no operas. The twenty-year-old composer wrote him not so much a letter as a dissertation, which began with an expression of appreciation of Hauser's profound discernment and warm-hearted frankness, but then erupted in total youthful self-confidence: 'You dislike my opera; even more, you dislike the whole direction that I follow.' (March 1834)

*Die Feen* was not refused but postponed until Wagner had lost interest in it: 'If they don't stop fouling things up soon, I'll take the score back from under their noses.' It was eventually performed for the first time in Munich in 1888, but by then its only interest was historical. It is in fact very informative about the stage in Wagner's development at which it was written. The overture, for a start, is not just a medley of the opera's tunes, but a dramatically motivated symphonic movement after the models of Beethoven and Weber. The two themes of the Allegro are well shaped, only the energetic cantilena which ends the whole is no more than perfunctory: it was not until the coda to Elisabeth's greeting of the Hall of Song that he managed to write one with his own authentic stamp. All the operatic accessories are conventional, but the dramatic high spots – Arindal's 'echo' aria, Ada's scene and aria 'Weh mir, so nah der fürchterlichen Stunde', Arindal's mad scene – are uncannily competent for so young and inexperienced a composer. One particularly impressive feature is the use, probably quite unthinking, of a kind of leitmotiv: the opening bars of the romance of the wicked witch Dilnovaz are quoted several times, in various rhythmic and harmonic transformations, as a 'witchery' motive.[1]

Even while a production of *Die Feen* was still being discussed, Wagner had an artistic experience that seemed to cast doubt on all his ideals. Once again Schröder-Devrient came to Leipzig, but this time to sing Romeo in Bellini's *Montecchi e Capuletti*, a work with a ridiculously facile libretto and music of a vapidness that left Wagner under no illusions. How was it possible, he wondered, that it nevertheless made an impression far stronger than all those contemporary German operas that were so much better made? The search for the answer to this unsettling question drew his first piece of critical writing from him, on German opera (*Die deutsche Oper*, RWGS, XII, pp. 1ff.), which was published in the *Zeitung für die Elegante Welt* in June 1834. In it he renounced the 'academic' music of Spohr and Marschner, not sparing even his idol Weber's *Euryanthe*, and paid homage to the vocal beauty of Italian opera, in which the singing is as natural as speech and fills the characters with warm life. With youthful extremism he wrote off all the achievements of German opera: he would never forget, he wrote, the impression that the recent performance of Bellini's opera had made on him, blessing his ears – heartily weary of eternal allegorizing orchestral tumult – with simple, noble song again. When he wrote about Bellini again, five years later, he still voiced the wish that German composers would think of a way of treating singing in such a fashion: 'Song, song, and again I say, song, you Germans!' (*Bellini*, 1839; RWGS, XII, pp. 19ff.)

The time had not yet come when he would realize that the sure way to produce an incomparable work of art would be to combine this elemental song with texts and music of a high quality. From this point of view his enthusiasm for Bellini was not wasted and he always retained a sense of gratitude to the Italian. Once, when he was playing over melodies from *Romeo*, *La Straniera* and *Norma* at Wahnfried, he said: 'For all its *pauvreté*, there's true passion and emotion there, it only needs the right soprano to stand up and sing it and it can sweep you off your feet. I learned something from this that Messrs Brahms and Co. never learned, and put it into my melody.'

Intoxicated with Bellini, Heinse's *Ardinghello* and Heinrich Laube's *Das Junge Europa*, he and Theodor Apel set off for Bohemia, the land of his youthful romances, in June 1834. He tells in his autobiography of the easy life they led in Teplitz and how, driving back to their inn in the dusk of a summer night, stretched out comfortably in their elegant carriage, they felt they had passed the day like young gods.

On some fine mornings he stole away from Apel to climb the hill to the Schlackenburg castle. Here, with a rolling view of sunny hills and valleys spread before him, he wrote the first outline of a new opera, *Das Liebesverbot* ('The Ban on Love'), which was to be the artistic expression of his new 'young European' outlook on life. This time his source was *Measure for Measure*, treated rather freely. He transposed the scene from Shakespeare's never-never Vienna to sixteenth-century Palermo – perhaps in homage to the Sicilian Bellini – and transformed the basically serious theme of the operation of justice into a condemnation of hypocrisy and moral bigotry and a glorification of free love.

But he was overcome with forebodings in the midst of this heady mood. 'Will the happy days I am enjoying at the moment perhaps soon take revenge on me?' he wondered in a letter to Rosalie. 'I am often overcome . . . by a distressing sense of unrest which urges me to return home the sooner the better, I feel as though something is waiting for me there, which I will need all my resources to encounter.' (3 July 1834) His instinct was correct. When he did return to Leipzig he found a letter waiting, offering him the post of musical director to the Magdeburg theatre company, which was spending the summer playing in Bad Lauchstädt, between Leipzig and Halle. It marked the end of his youth, he declared in *Mein Leben*. While he had not remained altogether a stranger to excitements and errors, it was not until this moment that care entered his life.

Wagner's account of what he found in Lauchstädt is a classic description of a provincial theatrical company: the schnapps-drinking manager Bethmann, whom a subvention from the king of Prussia could not keep from chronic bankruptcy; Frau Bethmann reclining on a couch, whiling away the hours with an ageing bass; the producer Schmale discussing with the stage manager, a toothless bag of bones, just how they were to put on *Don Giovanni* the following Sunday now that the Merseburg municipal band were unable to come to rehearsals.

Wagner saw at once that it was no place for him. Intent solely on escaping as politely as possible, he asked for assistance in finding somewhere to stay. A young actor promised to find him lodgings in the same house as the prettiest and most adorable girl in Lauchstädt, the company's leading lady, Minna Planer.

Chance brought him face to face with her at the door of the house. The sight of her was in striking contrast to the bad impressions he had hitherto received on that fateful morning. 'Very graceful and fresh as a daisy in appearance, the young actress was decorous and gravely assured in her movement and demeanour, which lent an agreeably enchanting dignity to the kind expression on her face . . . After I had been presented to her in the front entrance hall as the new musical director, and she, surprised to see one so young bearing this title, had formed a first impression of me, she kindly introduced me to the landlady, asking her to be sure and make me comfortable, and then went off down the street, with a calm, self-confident gait, to attend the rehearsal.'

He took the room on the spot and agreed to conduct *Don Giovanni* on the Sunday.

The description of Minna and his wooing of her that he dictated to Cosima in 1866 has every appearance of being scrupulously fair. When the love letters he wrote to her at that time were published in 1950 along with the rest of the Burrell Collection, the editor, John N. Burk, expressed the view that comparing them with the account in *Mein Leben* revealed the astonishing accuracy of Wagner's later recollection, and agreement in every essential between the letters and the autobiography.

Minna had embarked on a theatrical career not out of inclination but in order to support herself and her parents. At fifteen she had been seduced by an army officer, Ernst Rudolf von Einsiedel, and had a daughter, Natalie, who passed as her younger sister all her life. Natalie often spent long periods in the Wagner home and achieved fame later, as Minna's heir, as the owner of important Wagner papers which she sold to Mrs Burrell in the 1890s.

Without any particular gift for the expression of deeper emotions, Minna's success on the stage was due to the beauty and distinction of her appearance. She was much in demand as an actress and much courted as a woman. While she maintained a polite reserve in the face of the often all too blunt offers she received, she believed it was in the interests of her career not to refuse small favours to theatre directors and well-to-do patrons. When Wagner remonstrated with her she replied that people like that were less importunate than certain young conductors. She fended off his passionate advances for a long time, and even when they were acknowledged lovers she tried time and again to withdraw from the relationship.

One evening she told him that she wanted to leave Magdeburg and take up an engagement at the Königstadt theatre in Berlin. She left early the next morning, to cut short all his objections. 'The morning mist in which I saw you rolling away shivered in my tears. Minna, Minna, I suddenly became horribly certain that the coach was tearing you away from me for ever and ever.' A year earlier he had outlined his plans for his artistic future to Apel: after seeing *Das Liebesverbot* performed, he was going to go to Italy to write an Italian opera: in short, lead the itinerant life of a freelance composer. By his attachment to Minna he had condemned himself to abandon that plan and stay in the small-theatre milieu he detested; now he reminded her of it: 'I have sacrificed every condition of my life to you and you cannot sacrifice two good parts for me!' (4 November 1835)

'What a state I'm in now,' he wrote to Apel the next day. 'My God! My God! – If I wanted to be up-to-date, now would surely be the right moment for separation – but it's no good. My heart is broken – broken like any bourgeois.'

What it was that attracted Wagner so irresistibly to Minna is a perennial question. She lacked the intelligence to understand him and the heart to have faith in him. Did she ever love him? She was incapable of a great passion. His mother and sisters all tried to dissuade him from the liaison, he could see the truth of all this for himself – and walked on to his fate and hers with his eyes wide open.

The first meeting in Lauchstädt, which left so indelible an impression on him, gives the answer: it was the maternal quality in her that drew and held him. Eros and the dependence on a mother-figure conjoined, deep down in his nature, to exercise a power stronger than all reason.

The passion of his love letters overflowed into the music of *Das Liebesverbot*. 'At seven o'clock in the morning I sit down and write to you,' he told his 'ferne Geliebte' in a letter of 8 November. 'Then I work steadily until one at my opera, which has grown back to its full strength in me again and has become one within me with the possession of you.'

When he once played the *Liebesverbot* overture to Cosima, she said she preferred that of *Die Feen*, to which he replied that the later one had more genius in it. The element of personal experience gave his third opera, for all its weaknesses, a spark of real life, which time has not extinguished. The British première at University College, London in 1965 surprised the critics with its melodiousness: its Italianisms look back to Rossini and forward to the young Verdi.

One composer rarely encountered in it is the mature Wagner.

The adagio ensemble 'Sie schweiget in stummem Schmerz' already has something in its structure, though not in its melodic writing, of the great ensemble in the second act of *Tannhäuser*, 'Seht mich, die Jungfrau . . . ', just as Isabella is in general terms a precursor of Elisabeth. The relentless theme of the decree forbidding love, which runs through the whole opera, has the function of a genuine leitmotiv, while the melody and harmonization of the 'Salve regina coeli' already contains, note for note, the Grace theme from *Tannhäuser*.

In *A Communication to my Friends*, the review of his artistic development to date that Wagner made in 1851, as much (or more) for his own benefit as for his friends, he wrote that a comparison of *Das Liebesverbot* with *Die Feen* would show that he had it in him to develop in either of two totally contrary directions: the earlier work showed the sacred earnest with which his instincts had originally responded to stimulus, but his experiences had nurtured an unabashed inclination to unbridled sensuality, which ran directly counter. Then he makes an admission that allows a glimpse of his struggle to improve and refine his work: 'Striking the right balance between the two was the task of my subsequent artistic development.'

His later opinion of his 'wild' early work was not very high; with a few exceptions everything about it was 'horrifying, atrocious, revolting'; only the orchestration was good, it was something he had been able to do from his mother's womb. He dedicated the score to King Ludwig in 1866 with a quatrain at once penitential and rueful:

> Ich irrte einst und möcht' es nun verbüßen,
> wie mach' ich mich der Jugendsünde frei?
> Ihr Werk leg' ich demütig Dir zu Füßen,
> daß Deine Gnade ihm Erlösung sei.

(Once I erred and now I would do penance; how can I be rid of my youthful sin? I humbly lay its work at your feet, so that your grace may redeem it.)

The first performance of *Das Liebesverbot* took place in Magdeburg on 29 March 1836, conducted by the composer. As the police objected to the title it was changed to 'The Novice of Palermo'. The company was on the point of breaking up altogether, and none of the singers had troubled to learn their parts properly, so that what happened on the stage was more like a 'musical shadow-play'. Wagner had placed great hopes on the second performance, as it was to be his benefit, but the auditorium was almost empty. The stage stayed empty, too. Certain of the principals chose that evening to allow their amorous wrangles to come to a head, a knife was pulled and blood was shed behind the scenes. The producer had to step before the curtain and inform the tiny audience that unforeseen circumstances prevented the performance from taking place.

That was the end of Wagner's career in Magdeburg. He arrived in Berlin on 18 May to enter into fruitless negotiations to get his opera staged at the Königstadt theatre and on 7 July he went to Königsberg in pursuit of Minna, who had been engaged at the theatre there.

They were married in the church at Tragheim near Königsberg on 24 November. As the pastor held out the closed prayerbook for the couple to place on it the rings they were to exchange, the bridegroom seemed not to be paying attention. It had struck him at that moment, with the clarity of a vision, that his whole being was caught in two separate currents at different depths: 'The upper, open to the sunlight, swept me away as if in a dream, while the lower held me fast in the grip of a profound, incomprehensible terror.'

# 7

*Rienzi*

Wagner's premonition that his ill-considered marriage would prove doubly culpable was confirmed all too soon. The debts he had already amassed before the wedding, and Minna's belief that she owed it to herself to improve her financial position by 'making the most of her personal popularity' gave rise to violent scenes. He was at last appointed musical director of the Königsberg theatre on 1 April 1837. He returned home from rehearsals one evening to make the dreadful discovery that Minna had run off with a rich merchant called Dietrich, whose familiarity with her had aroused his resentment from the first. 'Death in his heart', he hurried after her and at last caught up with her in Dresden, at her parents' house, where she had taken refuge after Dietrich had left her. Her reproachful avowals that she had only wanted to escape from a hopeless situation that was all his fault turned his indignation into pity and self-recrimination. After he had succeeded in obtaining the musical directorship in Riga she was ready to go with him to Blasewitz, just outside Dresden, to spend the time before he was due in Riga. Her mood really seemed much improved. But when she failed to return from a short trip she had told him she was making with a family of friends, he learned that she had stayed in a hotel in Dresden with Dietrich for several days and that both had since disappeared.[1]

'With that I knew enough to ask my fate why, when I was still so young, I was doomed to undergo so frightful an experience, one, it seemed, that would poison the whole of my life.' As he relates in *Mein Leben*, he poured out his anguish to his sister Ottilie, who had now been married for several years to the Indianologist Hermann Brockhaus, and lived in a lovely villa in the Grosser Garten in

Dresden. Walking there from Blasewitz every day, he felt as though he was leaving a desert for a paradise. Brother and sister understood each other without the need for explanations, and he found in his brother-in-law a man of scholarship and intelligence, who re-awoke his dormant desire for a better education and was the first to introduce him to the literature of India.

At this time of great emotional suffering, his peculiar strength asserted itself, instinctively countering the pain with increased artistic activity. He had read Bulwer Lytton's novel *Rienzi, the Last of the Roman Tribunes*, and conceived an admiration for the hero, while Minna was still with him at Blasewitz. Now he sat down and drafted the scenario of a five-act opera based on it, deliberately making it on such a scale that getting it performed must of necessity take him out of the sphere of small theatres.

He was due to sail from Lübeck to Riga early in August, but the sailing was delayed by contrary winds, so he was forced to spend a week in a squalid sailors' tavern in Travemünde. He spent the time reading *Till Eulenspiegel*, which first gave him the idea of writing an 'authentically German comic opera'. When he drafted the text of *Der Junge Siegfried* fourteen years later, the memory of it came back to him, he claimed. It was another of the secrets of his creative processes that a seed, once planted in his mind, never died but germinated sooner or later. The maturing was a process of continual enrichment.

Karl von Holtei, the director of the Riga theatre, had been under the impression that he was engaging an advocate of the light Italian and French repertory expected by his audiences. He had no suspicion that Wagner's recent experiences, culminating in the shock of the death of his sister Rosalie, had set in train an inner transformation, leading him back to the 'sacred earnest' of his original artistic ideas. From this initial misunderstanding relations between the two men grew steadily worse, till Wagner reached the point of regarding Holtei as his worst enemy. Despite that, Holtei never had any reason to complain of a lack of zeal on the part of his young musical director, whose rehearsals, he averred, would be the death of his singers.

A new prima donna expected at the theatre failed to arrive, so Holtei welcomed Wagner's suggestion that Minna's younger sister Amalie be engaged in her place. Amalie wrote to accept and reported that Minna was ill and unhappy and living with her parents. Wagner, aware that his wife had been staying in a hotel in Hamburg with Dietrich for a substantial period, asked Amalie to spare him any news of her and instructed a friend in Königsberg to start divorce proceedings.

'Hereupon, Minna herself appealed to me with a truly affecting letter, in which she frankly admitted her infidelity . . . I had never heard such words from Minna, and I was never to hear their like from her again, except on one moving occasion many years later, when the same mode of expression had an equally upsetting effect on me and completely won me over.'

He replied that he himself had been most to blame in what had occurred and that they should never mention the matter again. 'Come to me, my wife,' he pleaded in a second letter, 'let me heal your wounds, it shall be the office of my love.' (Riga, undated; RWBC, pp. 115ff.) The two sisters arrived in Riga on 19 October.

It has been objected that the only evidence of Minna's infidelity is Wagner's own account of the episode in his autobiography. Newman shrewdly pointed out that the *absence* from the Burrell Collection of the first letter asking him to forgive her is the conclusive proof of her guilt. She forgot that Wagner had referred to it at some length in a letter of 18 May 1859,[2] thus irrefutably proving its existence. 'Poor Minna little foresaw', Newman concludes, 'that by thus covering her tracks, as she imagined, she was delivering herself up to the hunters!' (NLRW, I, p. 234)

Wagner's Riga repertory included operas by Mozart, Weber, Cherubini, Bellini, Rossini, Boieldieu, Auber and Meyerbeer. Forty years later he recalled the elevated, ennobled sentiments Méhul's magnificent *Joseph* had inspired in him. However, his theatrical activities were not enough to satisfy him, and he planned a series of six symphony concerts for the winter season of 1838–9. To win the support of the twenty-four members of his little orchestra he composed the first of his proposals for orchestral and theatrical reform, distinguished, like all its successors, by its blend of idealism and grasp of the practical.

> I think I am safe in saying that I am doing no more than meeting the wishes of my respected colleagues in the orchestra when I hereby propose to them a cycle of orchestral concerts, to take place during this coming

winter, which shall be regarded expressly as an
enterprise of the orchestra and undertaken for its own
benefit.

He goes on to suggest subscription and admission prices, the basis
on which profits should be calculated and shared, the fees for
soloists and so on.

Our audiences as a whole will probably never have been
accustomed to the more serious musical pleasures of the
kind we shall offer them in due course, and it will
therefore be necessary to attract them with more
obvious enjoyments as well; in this respect I have in
mind the Leipzig subscription concerts . . . Following
that precedent, not only must the knowledgeable be
offered the prospect of elevating musical pleasures, but
the other sectors of the audience must also be given the
opportunity to see and converse with one another,
which could take place easily in the long interval.

He does not omit to advocate a buffet, in the charge of a Swiss
baker. The pecuniary gains might be but small in the first season, he
warned, but it was to be hoped that the success of the undertaking
would grow from one year to the next. Apart from that, every artist
was bound to value the idea behind the concerts. For his part, he
declared in advance, he renounced all financial gain and refused a
fee. (11 September 1838; RWBC, pp. 455ff.)

His popularity with the orchestra may be judged from the fact
that all twenty-four signed the document. Contrary to the note
made by the editor of the Burrell Collection, the first series of
concerts did in fact take place. For the first time since his teens
Wagner again had first-hand contact with Beethoven, conducting
six of the symphonies (nos. 3–8) and the Leonora Overture no. 3
(RWSB, I, p. 350). He also encountered the other great inspirational
genius of his youth, Shakespeare, when a production of *King Lear*
gave him the chance to attend rehearsals as well as the performance.

In a mood of enthusiasm that could not but strike him as a
mockery of his actual situation, he also completed the text of *Rienzi*
and composed the first two acts during the autumn of 1838. Hans
von Bülow's *bon mot*, that *Rienzi* was Meyerbeer's best opera, has
more than a grain of truth in it, but it is even more Spontini than

Meyerbeer. During his short stay in Berlin in June 1836 Wagner had heard *Fernand Cortez*, conducted by the composer. Although the soloists left him cold, he had been surprised by the precision and vigour of the chorus and corps de ballet: his eyes were opened to the 'peculiar impressiveness of theatrical presentation on the large scale'. The impression remained with him while he was thinking out *Rienzi*.

Compared with the character in the novel, Wagner's hero is nobler, a tragic spirit in the mould of Lohengrin. Although he was aiming at strong dramatic effects Wagner avoided everything in his source that would have seemed merely theatrical on the stage. He played through each scene to his friends in the evenings, as he finished them. Heinrich Dorn, who had conducted the first performance of the 'drumbeat' overture and had now also been washed ashore in Riga, described the occasions: Amalie sang the female roles, the men sang whatever they could make out from the sketches, and Minna wiped the sweat from Wagner's brow as he accompanied them on the elderly borrowed grand piano, while the clatter of the broken strings mingled with the rousing strains of Freedom.

Two of the occasional compositions of the Riga period should be mentioned. One is the setting of a poem, *Der Tannenbaum*, by Georg Scheurlin, in E♭ minor, a key Wagner called 'Livonian'. It is interesting to see how he develops an eloquent accompaniment out of a flowing, animated motive, rather in the style of the string figurations accompanying Brünnhilde's defence of her actions in the third act of *Die Walküre*: 'Weil für dich im Auge das Eine ich hielt . . .' The other is the orchestration of a duet from Rossini's *I Marinari*: adding low horn notes to the low strings and using the bassoon to link string phrases in order to depict the gentle stir of the sea at dusk are truly Wagnerian effects, in the view of Alfred Einstein. When it comes to the storm he uses all the available registers of the orchestra, from the piccolo to the drumroll, but the most inspired feature is the sparing, and therefore all the more effective, use of trombones. In that respect it looks beyond *Rienzi* and might be a study for the *Holländer*.

Ever since Wagner had begun to set his sights on Paris, he had been trying to establish connections there. In the autumn of 1836 he sent the scenario of an opera, *Die Hohe Braut* ('The High-Born Bride'), to Eugène Scribe, suggesting to the librettist that he might make a French libretto from it and then get the Opéra Comique to commission Wagner to compose it. Receiving no reply he wrote again in the spring of 1837 and included the score of *Das Liebesverbot* as his credentials. At the same time he wrote to 'Monsieur Meyer-beer, compositeur et chevalier de légion d'honneur à Paris', telling him that he had sent *Das Liebesverbot* to Scribe with the request that he would show it to Meyerbeer. 'It would be . . . quite out of order for me to give vent to clumsy praises of your genius, but I will this much: I see in you the complete fulfilment of the German composer who has mastered the superior elements of the Italian and French school, in order to make the creations of his genius *universal*.' He made so bold, he went on, as to cherish the hope that it would be from Meyerbeer himself that he would learn his fate, 'which I place herewith wholly in your hands, appealing to your heart'.[3] It was also in this period that he wrote an essay, not published at the time, on Meyerbeer's *Les Huguenots*, which also praises the cosmopolitan, universal qualities of his style. This was once given the date of 1840 but Richard Sternfeld, the editor of the later volumes of RWGS, pointed out that Wagner's attitude towards Meyerbeer had already cooled considerably by then. (XII, pp. 22ff., 422) Newman, too, demonstrates that his admiration of Meyerbeer's 'successful eclec-ticism' yielded, after he had left Riga, to a consciousness of his own German mission. (NLRW, I, p. 224)

This time Scribe replied, politely but noncommittally, in June 1837 and Wagner consoled himself with the thought that he had at least established a Parisian connection. 'There is no quashing me now, with my hopes and plans.' (To August Lewald, November 1838) In fact his Paris sortie became a matter of urgency rather sooner than he wished. Holtei, who had to leave Riga suddenly in January 1839 to escape embarrassing disclosures, had already sec-retly engaged Wagner's friend Dorn as conductor for the coming season. Since the new director was bound by his contract, Wagner asked him at least to pay him an advance that had been agreed on: in return he declared himself available for any work the management might wish to offload on to him, unless it were polishing boots or drawing water, which would be the last straw. Though he and Minna made every effort to supplement their income with concerts and benefit performances, he could not scrape enough to pay off all his debts, so they were forced to leave secretly and without pass-ports.

The story of their flight over the Russian frontier and their rough sea passage from Pillau (now Baltiysk) to London is one of the most exciting episodes of *Mein Leben*. We will return to it when we reach the composition of *Der Fliegende Holländer*, which owed its 'individual poetico-musical colouring' to the voyage. It was characteristic of Wagner's later works, too, that while he was still working on one piece the characters and melodies of another, often diametrically different, work were already taking shape and maturing in a half-conscious region of his mind.

They landed in Boulogne on 20 August and stayed four weeks there, during which time Wagner completed the orchestration of the second act of *Rienzi* and seized the opportunity to call on Meyerbeer, who was also staying in the town and whose proverbial amiability made the most favourable impression on Wagner. He patiently listened as Wagner read him the text of the first three acts and agreed to read the score of the first two, which Wagner left with him. On a subsequent visit he assured Wagner of his interest in the work and promised to recommend him to the manager and chef d'orchestre of the Opéra, so that Wagner was ready to thank his stars for having brought him to Boulogne just at that time.

Only a very short time elapsed after his arrival in Paris on 17 September before he found that all the recommendations from others and all his own efforts were of no consequence. The manager of the Grand Opéra took impassive note of Meyerbeer's letter of recommendation but Wagner heard no more from him: evidently he had read large numbers of such letters in his time. At an orchestral rehearsal Habeneck, the chef d'orchestre, played through an overture that Wagner had written in Magdeburg for Theodor Apel's play *Columbus* and decided that he had no further obligation for the time being. In order to make himself known Wagner composed French romances for famous singers, who were kind enough to sing them to him but confessed for the rest that they did not know what else they should do about them.

Of these vocal pieces, *Dors mon enfant* is a charming trial run for the Spinning chorus in the *Holländer*. *Les deux grenadiers* was a setting of a French translation of Heine's poem. 'I hear that you have composed Heine's "Grenadiers",' Wagner wrote to Schumann on 29 December 1840, 'and that the *Marseillaise* turns up in it at the end. I set it, too, last winter, and I used the *Marseillaise* at the end, too. Highly significant!' It is typical that the lyric composer gave the tune to the voice, while the dramatist put it in the accompaniment.

At last a possibility of success seemed to beckon. Meyerbeer had referred Wagner and *Das Liebesverbot* to Anténor Joly, the director of the Théâtre de la Renaissance. Since Joly demurred, Wagner turned to his 'dear master' with another cry for help: if he still remembered him, perhaps he would care to compel the wicked Anténor to produce the opera by issuing a kind of ukase or bull. 'Terrorization is the only way and you, revered Autocrat of all the Notes, are the only one who can apply it. I have no other hope of salvation in this world but through you.' (18 January 1840)

It worked. Joly agreed to put the opera on, subject only to an audition of some of its numbers by the committee. With typical optimism Wagner believed he was home and dry. He at once signed the lease for a comfortable apartment in the Rue du Helder, instead of the *hôtel garni* where they had been living. On 15 April 1840, the day they moved in with their few worldly goods, he heard that the Théâtre de la Renaissance was bankrupt and had closed. This bolt from the blue revealed the vanity of the prospects that had opened before him. Cynics, Newman remarks, hinted to him later that Meyerbeer must have known of the impending bankruptcy and had his own reasons for detaching Wagner from the Opéra and directing him towards this moribund institution. This is another case, he goes on resignedly, in which there does not seem the least likelihood of our ever knowing the whole truth. (NLRW, I, p. 280)

Wagner's only friends in Paris were a few Germans as poor and lacking in influence as himself: a musical historian, who kept his real name a secret and called himself Anders (a German surname, but the word also means 'other' or 'otherwise'), and who in spite of his extensive learning had risen no higher than a post in the music department of the Bibliothèque Royale; Samuel Lehrs, a classical scholar from Königsberg, whose abilities were ruthlessly exploited by the publisher Ambroise-Firmin Didot in his famous editions of the Greek classics; Ernst Benedikt Kietz, a portrait-painter who, according to Wagner, worked so slowly that his models died of old age before he finished. They were all drawn to Wagner by his enthusiasm, some of which he imparted to them.

The painter Friedrich Pecht became another friend. He was an acquaintance of Heinrich Laube, who was newly arrived from Germany, and was taking him on a tour of the Louvre galleries one day when Laube announced that he was about to meet another fellow-countryman. A few minutes later they were greeted by a handsome young couple and the notably elegant, even distinguished-looking young man was introduced to him as Richard Wagner. 'Evidently distrait and with his mind on other things than Rubens and Paul Veronese,' Pecht recalled, 'Wagner seemed to me very agreeable, but he did not strike me as a particularly impressive personality: I found him decidedly too good-looking and too dainty. There was a certain delicate sheen to him, but there was certainly something unapproachable about him too, which might have roused the attention of a more careful observer.'

On one occasion, when Laube introduced them to Heinrich Heine, the reserve Wagner had hitherto maintained thawed and he demonstrated his peculiar resilience, his rare ability to preserve his freedom, his loftiest aspirations, intact in the midst of the greatest need and distress. He was a superb raconteur and possessed the most discerning eye for the comic, the sharpest ear for the sound of nature and the surest taste for all kinds of beauty, including the visual arts. He held listeners spellbound with the story of his recent adventures at sea, one event following another like a 'flurry of snow'. Heine, whom normally nothing could move, raised his hands in supplication at such confidence in a German.

Pecht remarks in his memoirs that Wagner's friends had noticed how this one year in Paris had matured him, made him another person altogether. It made another artist of him, too. On a murky evening in November 1839, at a rehearsal by Habeneck and the Conservatoire orchestra of the first three movements of the Choral Symphony, the return to the ideals of his boyhood, which had already started in Riga, was shatteringly and immediately accomplished. His adolescent enthusiasm for the symphony had known no bounds, as long as he had known it only from the score, but a performance he heard in the Gewandhaus at seventeen had shaken his faith in Beethoven and himself. Now, in his own words, the scales fell from his eyes: he realized the crucial importance of a good performance. Habeneck had rehearsed the Ninth for years, bar by bar, until he and the orchestra had gradually come to a clear view of its musical substance. The French instrumentalists, trained in the lyric Italian school, understood that the melody, the song, was the essence of all music – that was their secret. 'That magnificent orchestra simply *sang* the symphony.'

This powerful experience, and the reaction against the misery of his circumstances, inspired him with the wish to write something that would give him inward satisfaction. 'So I wrote an overture to *Faust*.' Finished on 12 January 1840, it was intended to be the first movement of a *Faust* symphony, the second movement of which, 'Gretchen', he already had in his head. The overture is his first wholly underivative work of substantial size. The key, D minor, looks both backward to the Ninth and forward to the *Holländer*.

The experience also had a literary outcome in the short story *A Pilgrimage to Beethoven*, which appeared in the *Gazette Musicale*, 19 November–3 December 1840. He put into Beethoven's mouth his own interpretation of the final chorus of the Choral Symphony: 'Think of the wild, primitive feelings, soaring out and away into the infinite, presented by the orchestra, as being brought up against the clear, defined emotion of the human heart, presented by the chorus.' The encounter would have a beneficial, soothing effect on the turmoil of the primitive feelings, while the human heart, opening to admit those feelings, would be infinitely strengthened and enlarged. This was the first time Wagner put into words what he conceived to be his own life's work, the synthesis of symphony and song.

He was even drawn to the idea of a monumental biography of Beethoven in the following year. His friend Anders, who owned a comprehensive collection of data and documents, but possessed no literary talent, offered him the use of his material. Looking first for a publisher, Wagner wrote that the book would be no mere pedantic parade of learning and undigested quotations. It would be more like a novel about an artist's life than a chronological enumeration of dates and anecdotes. For all that, however, it would contain nothing that would not stand up to the most rigorous critical scrutiny. Woven into the historical narrative would be a comprehensive account of the musical epoch which, created by Beethoven's genius, cast its mantle over all music written since. (To Heinrich Laube, 13 March 1841)

For all his winning words, he failed to interest a single German publisher in the project. It would undoubtedly have been a very idiosyncratic but also a very stimulating book.

In the meantime Wagner had resumed the composition of *Rienzi*, starting the orchestral sketch of the third act on 15 February 1840, but with the composition of the *Faust* Overture a few weeks before he had already advanced far beyond the opera.

He undoubtedly cast the material of *Rienzi* in a dramatic mould but, as he later said himself, viewed through the glass of an operatic composer, as a 'grand opera' with brilliant finales to each of the five acts, hymns, processions and the musical clash of arms. It possesses some wonderful things which are already completely and authentically Wagner: the swelling A on the trumpets which, like the A major chord of the *Lohengrin* prelude or the E♭ major of the *Rheingold* introduction, raised the curtain on the magic realm of the soul where the drama is to be enacted; or the way a melodic line is filled with an inner dynamic by harmonic impulses, as for example in isolated bars of the Prayer; but above all the audacious, exhilarating development of the melody of 'Santo Spirito, cavaliere' at the end of the overture and of the whole opera, which already attains the height of similar motivic intensification in the later works. But in the midst of these, without warning, it plummets down to banal melodies à la Spontini and Meyerbeer.

There is no way to disguise this dichotomy, which is rooted in the basic conception of the work. The most unfortunate kind of retouching, however well meant, is when directors try to turn the opera into a music drama, which only succeeds in underlining its musical inadequacies. If *Rienzi* is produced in the style of grand opera, which is what it is, then the hearer accepts its weaknesses as those of the genre and is all the more delighted by the elements of inspiration which go beyond the limitations. The most important thing is to preserve the youthful exuberance, for better or for worse, as the one thing that lends a particular charm to the ineptitude of any artist's early works.

Even so, Wagner's own liking for his 'bawler *Rienzi*' soon cooled. 'I am very sorry to learn that you have made the acquaintance of my *Rienzi*,' he wrote to his Berlin admirer Alwine Frommann on 27 October 1845; 'I do not like the monster.' If the composer of *Tristan* defended the work in a letter, virtually a dissertation, that he wrote to the tenor Albert Niemann, long after he had lost all interest or sympathy with it, it was only because he desperately needed the money that a revival would bring. (25 January 1859) But he politely declined the invitation to its Paris première in 1869: he had always regarded it as one of the many ironies of his career that *Rienzi*, specifically written with Paris in mind, had never been performed there 'when this work of my young manhood still retained the whole of its youthful freshness for me'. (To Judith Gautier, early March 1869)

Part II: The First Creative Period (1841–1848)

# 8

*Der Fliegende Holländer*

The notes Wagner made in his Red Book during the voyage from Pillau to London include the following:

> 27 [July 1839] in storm on the Skager-Rack [sic].
> 28 Storm.
> 29 Stormy west wind forced us to run into a Norwegian small harbour in the region of Arendal. Ashore with Minna in the evening. Marvellous blocks of rock in the sea. Place Sand-Wigke.

It was one of the most wonderful impressions of his life, he later confirmed in his autobiography, when the ship slipped into the gigantic rocky chasm of a Norwegian fjord. 'An inexpressible happiness seized hold of me when the echo of the immense granite walls threw back the shout of the crew as they dropped anchor and hoisted sail [sic: a landlubber, Wagner evidently thought this expression meant its opposite]. The short rhythmic cries settled in me like a mightily comforting portent and soon formed into the theme of the sailors' song in my *Fliegender Holländer*, the idea of which I already carried within me.' He learned that the fishing village where they were was called Sandwike and was a few miles from Arendal. On the hundredth anniversary of the landfall, in 1939, the Norwegian Wagnerian singer Gunnar Graarud proved that, of the six places with the same name in the vicinity of Arendal, it must have been Sandviken on Boröya. It was with some excitement that he himself set the echo flying which had once resounded to the 'Hallojos' of the crew of the *Thetis*.[1]

This account of the genesis of the *Holländer* is complemented by a tale, recalled by Pecht, that Wagner told his friends in Paris when the experience was still fresh in his mind: the whistling of the wind in the rigging had seemed such an extraordinarily demonic sound that when another ship suddenly came into sight and as suddenly disappeared again in the darkness he had thought it must be the Flying Dutchman, and ever since then he had been composing music to the legend in his head.

The legend was well known and there were versions in several different languages. Wagner had come across it in Riga, and his creative imagination had at once been stirred by the version in Heine's *Memoiren des Herrn von Schnabelewopski*, according to which the damned sea-captain could be redeemed only by the love of a woman. This is apparently Heine's own invention, and it is obvious that he introduced it for a purely satirical purpose: 'The moral of the tale for women is that they take care not to marry a Flying Dutchman; and we men can learn from it how women are our destruction at the best of times.'

Wagner ignored Heine's moral but took up the idea of redemption with passionate sincerity and stored it away in his memory, where the dramatic and musical seeds ripened for another two years while he went on working on *Rienzi*.

To gain a conception of Paris in the 1830s and 1840s, the reader needs only to turn to Flaubert's *Education sentimentale*. There is a very close link between the milieu of the novel and that in which Wagner found himself. Flaubert's heroine, the sensitive, noble wife of the art-dealer, is based on the wife of the music publisher Maurice Schlesinger, Wagner's strange patron and employer. Perhaps we may even go so far as to glimpse in the poor devil of a painter, who scrapes a living with badly paid occasional work for the owner of the art gallery, the shadowy outline of the unknown German musician who was grateful when Schlesinger commissioned him to make arrangements for piano and cornet of operatic numbers by Donizetti and Halévy.

'Dearest Monsieur Schlesinger,' Wagner wrote in December 1840, 'I have been sitting here over the proofs of the score [of Donizetti's *La favorita*] since eight o'clock on Saturday morning until this moment, with a few hours' sleep. There were times, I can assure you, when I was on the verge of going out of my mind, and closer to tears than laughter . . . I am a poor devil and must be satisfied with whatever I can earn; but I am often driven to the despairing question: What is Monsieur Schlesinger paying me for this work!. . . A most cordial greeting from your obedient servant, R. Wagner. Tuesday morning, nine o'clock.'

A few pages of a diary from this period have survived. 'Tears came unbidden to my eyes again just now; is it cowardly or a sign of unhappiness to surrender gladly to tears? – a sick German apprentice was here – I told him to come to breakfast again; Minna reminded me that she would have to spend the last of our money just to buy bread. You poor, poor creature! I suppose you're right – things are bad with us.' And a week later: 'Explained to my wife, on our walk, what our financial position is; I am sorry for the poor woman from the bottom of my soul! It's a sad business! I want to work!' (RWGS, XVI, pp. 4ff.)

His work was not enough to save him from the debtors' prison. He does not mention it in *Mein Leben*, but a letter Minna wrote to Theodor Apel on 28 October 1840 gives him away. 'Richard had to leave me this morning and go into the debtors' prison,' she wrote. The Burrell Collection includes four tiny numbered scraps of paper in Richard's hand – evidently all he could get hold of in prison – which are a draft of that letter. The first of the scraps, with the admission of being in prison, is missing, presumably suppressed by Minna or Natalie, which demonstrates once again that the destruction of a document can conclusively prove its content.[2]

Many years later, a reference by Malwida von Meysenbug to his Paris days was still enough to bring the tears to Wagner's eyes: it had been a pit of baseness, he said, and added, turning to Cosima, she could not begin to imagine the atmosphere in which he had lived.

He admits in his autobiography that his short story *An End in Paris* was written in revenge for all the shame he had endured. It was published in the *Gazette Musicale*, 31 January – 11 February 1841, under the title *Un musicien étranger à Paris*. 'Hoffmann could never have written anything like this!' Heine exclaimed in admiration. The underlying note of authentic experience is what makes it so much more impressive than any mere 'tales of the imagination'. Wagner never wrote simpler prose than this. 'We buried him. It was a cold, grey day and there were but a few of us . . . The first chill air of winter made us breathless; none of us could speak and there was no funeral oration. Nevertheless, let it be known to you that he whom we buried was a good man and a fine German musician.' The whole story ends with the famous credo: 'I believe in God, Mozart and Beethoven.' (*Ein Ende in Paris*, RWGS, I, pp. 114ff.) It was Wagner's way of telling the small group of friends who used to meet at his lodgings of an evening that the young man who had come to Paris with such high hopes two years earlier really was dead now.

His intellectual horizons had changed, too. After the recall to his own destiny that hearing the Ninth Symphony again had meant, a new world had been opened for him by the music of Berlioz. 'The bad taste in the externals' of the *Romeo and Juliet* Symphony, Wagner wrote to Ferdinand Heine, a producer at the Dresden theatre, had made him recoil violently from a composer whom he nonetheless regarded as a musician of genius. Berlioz was so isolated among the French that the proper development of his immense powers was made exceptionally hard for him. 'His is a highly poetic nature, and this is all the more amazing since he is a thorough Frenchman in every other respect and can express himself only in extremes. It is not long since I made up my mind about Berlioz, really only since I heard his *Symphonie fantastique* about three months ago.' (27 March 1841)

'Anybody here in Paris who hears this symphony', Wagner wrote in one of his articles for the *Dresdner Abendzeitung* (5 May 1841),

> must truly believe that he is listening to a wonder, the
> like of which he has never heard before. An immense
> inner wealth, a heroic imagination, force out a flood of
> passions as if from a crater; what we behold are clouds
> of smoke of colossal proportions, broken and shaped
> into fleeting forms only by flashes of lightning and jets
> of flame. It is all immense, bold but infinitely agonizing.
> Nowhere is there any formal beauty, nowhere the
> majestically serene flow to whose assured motion we
> might entrust ourselves in hope. After the *Symphonie
> fantastique*, the first movement of Beethoven's C minor
> Symphony would have been a welcome relief. (RWGS,
> XII, pp. 87ff.)

His third musical experience was another to recall him to himself: a performance of *Der Freischütz*. In spite of the vow he had once made to his friend Apel – 'Now and for all time, I shall never again pay homage to our Germanity, and all the glories of your Leipzig classicism are not enough to lead me back to that course' – it was precisely the German qualities in the music of the opera that fell on his ear like the far-off but never forgotten voice of home and childhood. Berlioz had forced the simple words of the huntsmen and peasants into the straitjacket of recitative, the director of the Opéra saw fit to cast it with singers of the second rank, and the performers were unaware of the difference between *Romantik* and *romantisme*. But as the lads of the village clasped their girls by the hand and led them into the inn, as night started to fall in the shadow of the tall pine trees and the sound of the dance music died away in the evening stillness, it was like a stab in the heart to the unhappy German musician: 'I felt a burning hot wound . . . O dreaming, dear to every German heart! O romance of forest, of evening, of stars, of the village clock striking seven! How happy is *he* who can believe, feel, dream with you! How glad am *I* to be German!' (RWGS, I, pp. 220ff.)

But at the same time something was set in train in him that was to have revolutionary consequences: a reaction against the ideal of 'modern civilization'. Paris was the 'point of culmination' of the direction in which the world was now running, he wrote to King Ludwig on 18 July 1867. All other cities were only 'stations' on the same road. Paris

> is the heart of modern civilization, whither its blood flows and whence it circulates to the members again. Once when it was my ambition to be a famous opera composer my good genius took me straight to that heart; there I was at the fountainhead, and there I was able to recognize in full and at once what I might have spent half a lifetime learning in any of the 'stations'. For this sure recognition of the true and proper face of things, it is Paris that I must thank.

The personal and artistic experiences outlined here combined to rid Wagner of the chimera of being a 'famous opera composer'. He had first had to lose himself in order to find himself again with the conception of *Der Fliegende Holländer*. The letter of 3 May 1840 in which he told Meyerbeer about the first prose sketch of the work reveals not only the desperation of his position but also a far more disquieting sense that his whole personality was in dissolution.

> I have reached a point where I have no choice but to sell
> myself to somebody in return for help in the most
> material sense. But my head and my heart are already no
> longer mine – they belong to you, my master; – all I
> have left are at most my hands – do you want to make
> use of them? – I can see that I must become your slave
> in mind and body in order to obtain the food and the
> strength to carry out the work which will express my
> gratitude to you one day. (RWSB, I, pp. 384ff.)

But he had hardly taken the letter to the post before he regretted
it. 'You will understand', he wrote on 4 June,

> the shame and bitter self-reproach that I now feel for
> having permitted myself, in an hour when all the painful
> and worrying experiences of the most recent period of
> my life were thronging through my head, to reach a
> degree of exaltation where I failed to see that I totally
> overstepped the boundary of modesty and delicate
> feeling.

He enclosed the prose sketch of the *Holländer* with this letter, asking
Meyerbeer to bring it to the attention of the new director of the
Opéra, Léon Pillet. (RWSB, I, pp. 392ff.)

Hearing nothing, he wrote to Meyerbeer again on 26 July. 'I
venture only this one request: if, with your superior insight and the
degree of interest which you perhaps still have in me, you think it
proper and it is convenient for you, then I beseech you in all
humility to put in a good word for me and my "winged Dutchman" (one act), of which I have a few numbers ready for audition.'
(RWSB, I, pp. 400ff.) He heard at last that Pillet liked the subject and
wanted to buy it so that he could have it set by one of the composers
he had under contract. Pleas and representations were of no avail:
Wagner was told it would be at least seven years before it could be
his turn to be offered even the smallest commission. He had the wit
to accept the 500 francs he was offered and use the money to finance
his own composition of *Der Fliegende Holländer*, abandoning *Le
Vaisseau Fantôme* to its fate. (2 July 1841)

Pillet commissioned a libretto from two writers who 'botched'
the tale, to Heine's distress, and the music was written by the
director of the Opéra chorus, Pierre-Louis Dietsch. The opera was
first performed in 1842 and was given ten further performances.

When the prose sketch for the *Holländer* was published in 1933 it was revealed that the action still took place on the coast of Scotland, as in Heine. Daland was called 'the father', Mary 'the nurse', Erik 'Georg'. The daughter was called 'Anna', which apparently contradicted Julius Kapp's claim that her name was originally 'Minna'. But in Dietsch's opera the girl actually is called Minna, a name that can only have originated in Wagner's very first draft, in homage to his wife, who may well have appeared to him on occasion like a comforter 'im nächtigen Gewühl'.[3] He obviously changed the names later to put a distance between his own text and the sketch he had sold. The name 'Senta' presents something of a mystery: there is no trace whatever of its existence before he used it, even in Scandinavia. Hans von Wolzogen thought that the girl who waited on Wagner in the house of a Norwegian captain in Sandviken may have been introduced to him as 'tjenta' ('servant'), which he took to be her name and later remembered inexactly as Senta.

The fact that Wagner had written the texts and music of three numbers – the Norwegian sailors' chorus, the song of the Dutchman's ghostly crew and Senta's Ballad – for an audition that never took place, proved in the end to be the most significant outcome of his struggle for recognition in Paris, affecting not only the composition of the *Holländer* itself but the whole development of his creative technique. In writing the Ballad he unknowingly planted the 'thematic seed' of the whole work. When he moved from Paris to Meudon in the summer of 1841 and wrote the composition sketch, he found that the existing thematic idea involuntarily permeated the entire work, showing him how to shape the legend in which the surge of the sea is ever present. He later said that the *Holländer* marked the beginning of his career as a poet – as opposed to a mere manufacturer of librettos – but it would be even more true to say that it was also the start of his career as a musician, for this was the first demonstration of his peculiar ability to develop the themes of a whole work from the motivic germs of a single original melody. The only thing lacking at this stage was the technique for pursuing this principle to its fullest extent: the *Holländer* still contains operatic passages which do not cohere organically with the thematic fabric.

He tried later to alleviate the discrepancy between his artistic intention and his musical ability at the time of composition. In 1852 he purged the writing for the brass of some crudities. The reasons he gave for altering the chord accompanying Senta's scream in the second act were typical of the process as a whole: the original instrumentation was too coarse, too literal; the sudden appearance of the Dutchman is what should startle the audience, not the sound of the brass and kettledrum. On 19 January 1860, after writing *Tristan*, he added the final theme of redemption to the end of the overture. He wrote to Mathilde Wesendonk that he had not been able to find the right ending before. 'We shall become omnipotent, if we just go on playing with the world.' (10 April 1860) A letter Cosima wrote to King Ludwig reveals that in 1865, between the completion of *Meistersinger* and the resumption of the *Ring*, Wagner considered revising the *Holländer* to make it worthy to stand beside *Tannhäuser* and *Lohengrin*. (DMCW, I, pp. 319f.) One might suppose that he meant only the eradication of the more conventional elements, but his intentions went much further. 'He is thinking of revising *Der Fliegende Holländer*,' Cosima wrote in 1878. 'Senta's Ballad is in a folk style, he thinks, but it is not truly characteristic of the *Holländer*.' (DMCW, I, p. 846) And in 1881 he told her about the new version he had written of the Ballad but had unfortunately lost. (BBL 1938, p. 3)

However, the new, Wagnerian characteristics of this early work are so overwhelming that they made him forget his reservations on each occasion. 'On the whole I found the work very interesting, going back to it,' he confessed to Theodor Uhlig in 1852; 'it has an uncommonly penetrating colouring, of the utmost sureness.' (Letter of 25 March) Later he once said that it was without precedent in operatic history: what distinguished the *Holländer* from similar romantic operas by Marschner or Weber was that the supernatural, the miraculous or demonic elements, were not external forces but proceeded directly out of the characters of the protagonists and were therefore artistically credible.

When Wagner heard the opera again in Munich in 1880, despite the deficiencies of the performance he was moved to tears. What he went through while writing the work is revealed by three annotations to the orchestral sketch. At the end of the second act: '13 August. Money troubles start again tomorrow!!' At the end of the third: 'Finis. Richard Wagner. Meudon, 22 August 1841, in need and tribulation.' But at the end of the overture, written last, we find: 'Paris, 5 November 1841. Per asp[e]ra ad astra. God grant it! Richard Wagner.'

For his fortunes had taken a turn for the better in the interval, encouraging him to have faith in his star. After all his efforts to get *Rienzi* performed in Paris had proved vain, he set his hopes on Dresden: not only would the ideal tenor, Tichatschek, be available for the name part, but he would also be able to make something of his personal connections. He had finished the score on 19 November 1840. On 1 December he addressed a petition to the King of Saxony, Friedrich August, not forgetting to remind him of his stepfather's years at the Saxon court theatre, and expressing the wish that his first large-scale work might see the light on the soil of his homeland, with the favour of the patronage of his all-gracious lord and king. On 4 December he sent the score to the intendant, Freiherr von Lüttichau, and in the covering letter pointed out how the visual splendours the work demanded for its production would demonstrate the magnificent appurtenances of the new opera house.

At the same time he wrote to a whole string of the leading figures in the theatre in Dresden: Schröder-Devrient, who still remembered the favourable impression he had made on her in Magdeburg; Hofrat Winkler, the theatre secretary and an old friend of his family, who had published Wagner's articles from Paris in his newspaper, the *Abendzeitung*; the musical director, Kapellmeister Reissiger, with whom Wagner remembered enjoying a drinking spree and who had to be approached with particular tact as an opera composer himself. The most valuable friends and helpers proved to be the producer Ferdinand Heine, who had been one of Geyer's colleagues, and the chorus master Wilhelm Fischer.

In the end Meyerbeer too lent his support with a letter to Lüttichau, dated 18 March 1841: 'Herr Richard Wagner of Leipzig is a young composer who possesses not only a thorough musical grounding but also a great deal of imagination, and whose situation as a whole seems to deserve active sympathy in his homeland in every respect.'

An impatient second letter from Wagner crossed with Lüttichau's reply, dated 29 June 1841: after giving the libretto and the score his careful consideration, he was happy to assure him that his opera had been accepted 'and will be presented at the Court Theatre as soon as possible, I hope during the course of next winter'.

Hoping to steal a march on the Parisian *Vaisseau Fantôme*, Wagner sent the text of the *Holländer*, which had been rejected by the intendant of the Munich opera, Küstner, as 'unsuitable for Germany', to the intendant of the Berlin Court Opera, Count von Redern, with a covering letter dated 27 June 1841 asking for the honour of a first performance: 'This. . . is quite a short opera, at least not intended to fill an evening, but rather to share a programme with a short ballet or play.'

Although he had received no answer he sent Redern the score as well on 20 November, venturing to hope that the opera might be performed before the current season was out. At the same time he appealed to Meyerbeer again: having a stupid libretto and a sizeable chunk of score on his hands he had been able to think of nothing better to do with them than to pack them both up and send them off to Berlin, where he knew they would be left to rot. 'Then the gospel was revealed to me, for it is written by your own venerated hand: "I will try to find favour in the eyes of Count von Redern!" . . . God grant that every day of your blessed life be a joy to you and may He never darken your vision with sorrow: that is the sincere prayer of your most sincere pupil and servant Richard Wagner.' (Early December 1841)

Meyerbeer's diary has the following entry for 7 December 1841: 'Call on Redern, to recommend the score of *Der Fliegende Holländer* by Richard Wagner to him.' He took the score away with him to read and sent it back to Redern on 9 December. 'I have already had the privilege, the day before yesterday, of talking to Your Honour about this promising composer who doubly deserves, both for his talent and for his extremely straitened circumstances, that the major court theatres, as the official guardians of German art, should not bar their stages to him.' A few days later, on 14 December, Wagner at last received the news that the text and the score had been approved and had been particularly warmly recommended by Meyerbeer.

'Think of me and accept in advance my warmest thanks for the inestimable services your friendship has rendered me', Wagner hastened to write to his champion. 'If I thought that you could be much happier than you are I would wish you the attainment of the highest happiness; as it is I must be merely an egoist and ask you to let me share a small part of your good fortune and your fame.' (Mid-December 1841)

It very soon transpired, however, that Redern's approval, gratifying though it was, was not at all the same thing as a binding commitment to stage the work.

# 9

*Tannhäuser*

Yet another experience of Wagner's time in Paris that set his thinking along a new path was reading Friedrich Raumer's history of the Hohenstaufens, of which Goethe said that it brought the 'faded ghosts' of the past back to life. The one thing that most fascinated Wagner in the book was Raumer's depiction of the character of Frederick II, a masterpiece of historico-psychological reconstruction. He struggled in vain to find the proper artistic channel for portraying Frederick until it occurred to him that his son Manfred offered a more tractable related subject. During the winter of 1841–2 he wrote the text of a five-act historical opera, *Die Sarazenin* ('The Saracen Woman'). It is prophesied that the heroine Fatima, the love-child of Frederick and a Saracen princess, will perform miracles in advancing Manfred's renown, as long as she does not surrender to him in love. She appears to him with inspired prophecies at decisive moments in battle and leads him on from one victory to another. When Manfred falls passionately in love with her, she is stabbed to death by the young Saracen who has loved her since childhood, and Manfred realizes that he will never know happiness again. (RWGS, XI, pp. 230ff.)

Though it seemed reasonably effective to him, Wagner was unable to feel any great enthusiasm for the text. He later showed it to Schröder-Devrient, when she complained that she was 'pining' for his music, if only he would write the right part for her, but she rejected it: she had known too many lovers herself to have any sympathy for the idea that a prophetess, like Schiller's Joan of Arc, might not with impunity be a woman too.

Steeping himself in the atmosphere of the German Middle Ages to which Raumer had introduced him, Wagner had also encountered the old folk ballad of Tannhäuser and Venus. He had already known the story from Ludwig Tieck's *Phantasus*, but that modern retelling, with its 'mystical titillation, its Catholic frivolity', had not inspired him to put it in dramatic form. The tale of the Singers' War at the Wartburg, which has no connection with Tannhäuser at all, had also been known to him since boyhood from E. T. A. Hoffmann's version.

But then one day one of the companions of his Parisian misfortune, Samuel Lehrs, lent him a volume of the historical and literary proceedings of the Royal German Society of Königsberg, with a paper on the Wartburg 'war' by C. T. L. Lucas, which acquainted Wagner with the legend's original form. The most important thing he culled from it was the hypothesis, advanced by Lucas with some caution, that the Heinrich von Ofterdingen of the poem may have been identical with the minnesinger Tannhäuser. This was the spark that led to the fusion of the two subjects in Wagner's imagination: all at once he had a drama that threw the *Sarazenin* into the shade.

Now that *Rienzi* and the *Holländer* had been accepted for performance, he was impatient to get back to Germany. He and Minna took a tearful leave from Lehrs, Kietz and Anders on 7 April 1842. They sensed that they would not see Lehrs again, for he suffered from a severe pulmonary disease. The *diligence* carried them along the boulevards on a smiling spring morning. On the far side of the Rhine the weather was cold and grey, and Wagner took it as a good omen that the first rays of sunshine they saw again were falling on the Wartburg. As they drove through the valley towards it he sketched the scenery which he later described to the Parisian stage designer who painted the sets for the first production of *Tannhäuser* in Dresden.

He spent his first days in Leipzig and Dresden in a dream, meeting his mother and sisters again. He had to pull himself together sharply to attend to his affairs. In Berlin he learned that Redern had resigned and his successor was to be Küstner – the same Küstner who had turned down the *Holländer* for Munich as 'unsuitable for Germany'. Although not now able to refuse a work which met 'every requirement of the critical standards of the Royal Prussian Court Opera', he delayed production long enough for the première finally to take place in Dresden on 2 January 1843, while the first performance in Berlin was not until 7 January 1844.

This setback in Berlin was not the only disappointment of the high hopes Wagner had had of Germany. The Dresden opera, too, failed to conceal from him that it found him all too tempestuous. Only Ferdinand Heine and Wilhelm Fischer greeted his arrival with sincere pleasure. In every other respect the Dresden he had known had vanished: the hundred friends he had once had no longer existed. The city itself no longer meant anything to him, and if he was going to be a failure he felt he would rather be one in Paris than in Dresden. 'I have no geographical preferences and my homeland, apart from its beautiful ranges of hills, its valleys and its woodlands, is actually repellent to me. These Saxons are an accursed race – mean, dozy, cloddish, idle and coarse – what have I to do with them?' (To Lehrs, 12 June 1842)

Above all he was still the same 'penniless Johnny', as he complained to his half-sister Cäcilie, 'with glorious prospects and a meaningless present'. His sisters and their husbands had joined forces to ensure him a modest monthly income until the profits he hoped for from *Rienzi* materialized. He would have been well off if it had not been for his old creditors . . . and for his Parisian debts! He was obliged to make some operatic arrangements to pay off an advance from Maurice Schlesinger. He sent him one such piece of forced labour from Teplitz, where he had gone for a cure, on 25 June 1842: '*La Reine de Chypre* – Airs arrangés en quatuor pour 2 violons, alto et basse en 3 suites par Richard Wagner. Musique de F. Halévy.' 'My damned Parisian obligations still weigh abominably upon me, just when I would be gloriously ready to get on with a new work, I have got to force it all back inside myself – in order to write arrangements.' (To Ernst Benedikt Kietz, 1 July 1842)

He managed to get away, though, for a walking holiday as in the old days, going to the Schreckenstein in the Erzgebirge near Aussig (now Ústí) on the Elbe to think out the plot of the 'Venusberg', as the new work was still called. He slept on straw in the small guest room, and the solitude so fired his imagination that in a recrudescence of his teenage japes he spent an entire night clambering about among the castle ruins wearing nothing but a sheet, a living apparition. One day he climbed the Wostrai, the highest mountain in the district, and suddenly came upon a shepherd, lying on a slope and playing a lively dance tune. 'At once I was in the chorus of pilgrims, passing the shepherd as they wend their way through the valley.' He saw Carlo Dolci's *Madonna* in the parish church in Aussig, and told Kietz that he had found the painting extraordinarily delightful, and that if Tannhäuser had seen it, it would have explained fully how he came to transfer his devotion from Venus to the Virgin without any great access of piety. 'Anyway, now I have a clear idea of the saintly Elisabeth.' (6 September; RWBC, p. 188)

Saint Elisabeth of Hungary was the daughter-in-law of Landgrave Hermann of Thuringia and does not appear in Wagner's sources. In the medieval version of the Singers' War it is the landgrave's wife, Sophia, who spreads out her cloak to shield Ofterdingen as the knights advance upon him. Hoffmann turns this figure into a beautiful widow, Mathilde von Falkenstein, who is wooed by Wolfram and Ofterdingen. It was a stroke of genius on Wagner's part to substitute Saint Elisabeth, and make her the landgrave's virginal niece, so gaining a worthy counterpart to Venus.

Some of the pages of the notebook in which Wagner wrote the prose sketch have survived in the Burrell Collection: '2–8 June 1842. Schreckenstein bei Aussig. Spacious grotto with side galleries hidden from view . . . Luxuriant circle of the half-naked forms of beautiful virgins, scattered amorous groups. Singing. *Celebration of love.*'

Glasenapp also published a page of music sketches of the same date, comprising the first version of the principal themes: 'Venusberg', 'Pilgrims', 'Act II finale', 'Act III opening' and so on. The shepherd boy's shawm solo is sketched on another page, in a form totally different from the eventual version. (GLRW, I, pp. 445f.)

The prospect of seeing *Rienzi* take the stage in full panoply in the very near future brought Wagner hurrying back from Teplitz on 18 July, to keep an eye on the 'idlers in Dresden'. He had sent a list of enquiries while he was still in Paris: 'How have the parts been cast? Are my suggestions useful and good, and are they being adopted? . . . The management must spare no expense or trouble – because with operas like mine there's no middle way – you know what I mean! – Just listen to me! An emperor is nothing to me: "Do this! Do that!" as if I had only to command!' (To Ferdinand Heine, undated; RWBC, p. 145)

He had no reason to complain of any lack of zeal on the part of the performers. The work and his own presence at rehearsals increased their enthusiasm daily. The first time they rehearsed the scene with the messengers of peace at the beginning of Act II, Schröder-Devrient was unable to restrain her tears, while Tichatschek, who was singing Rienzi, declared that the B minor ensemble in the Act III finale was so fine that they ought to pay for the privilege of singing it, whereupon he produced a silver groschen and the others followed his example. This charade was repeated at every rehearsal – 'Here comes the new groschen passage' – until Schröder-Devrient wailed that it would make a pauper of her. 'And none of them suspected', Wagner confessed, 'that this honorarium they paid as a joke was only too welcome to my wife and me, to pay for our dinner.'

He wooed the easygoing musical director Reissiger, who attributed his own failures as a composer to bad librettos, with a verse text of *Die Hohe Braut*, the scenario of which he had sent to Scribe in 1836. Reissiger's initial interest was cooled by his wife's suspicion that it was some kind of trap, so he turned it down and had an actor write him another libretto on the wreck of the *Medusa*. Wagner later adopted the title as an appropriate expression for the failure of operatic hopes: if Liszt had not championed him, he said, he too might have sunk without trace like Reissiger's *Medusa*.

Lüttichau was the only person of whom he complained, in a letter to Kietz: the countless misunderstandings that arose daily from the intendant's 'uncommon obtuseness and stupidity' placed continual obstacles in his way, and removing them was like forever mucking out a stable. (To E. B. Kietz, 6 September 1842, RWBC, p. 146)

Nothing in his previous or ensuing experience resembled the state of mind in which he looked forward to the first performance on 20 October. The success went far beyond his wildest expectations. People recognized that, *Euryanthe* and *Les Huguenots* notwithstanding, here was something audacious and new. Financially, too, it was unusually successful: the management could put it on again and again and always fill the house, initially at increased prices. The composer was not so lucky: except for Berlin, no German opera house paid royalties, but only made a single payment, which varied with the size of the house. Lüttichau believed he was being extremely generous when he offered Wagner 300 talers.

At the same time he was preparing the first performance of *Der Fliegende Holländer*. Schröder-Devrient, who had had to be content with a supporting role in *Rienzi*, was singing Senta. She did not find it easy to learn a new part and her moods sometimes made Wagner despair. His patience gave out: Devrient was a sow and a bitch, he wrote to Minna, no one knew the trouble she was giving him. But he was soon reconciled with her again: 'I dare say it will be a long time before our Creator produces anyone like her again,' he wrote to Kietz; 'the wealth, the power of her passion, the turbulence and force of the inner daemon, combined with such genuine femininity, lovableness and kindness of heart . . . our artistic collaboration was quite remarkable: a whole book could be written about us working on the part of Senta!' (8 April 1843; RWBC, pp. 246f.) When he came to create his Brünnhilde, he wrote later, it was her example that showed him how: 'the example that she, the mime, set the dramatist and that I alone, of all those to whom she gave it, have followed'. It was certainly her inspired performance as Senta, seemingly completely isolated on the stage, that made the first performance of the *Holländer* a success. Wagner could not disguise from himself the fact that his stark, sombre dramatic ballad was not greatly to the public taste: for the first time he had cause to consider that his inner promptings might be at odds with outward success.

While he was still pondering this new problem he received an offer from Lüttichau of an assistant conductor's post, which had become vacant through a death. 'I hasten to inform Your Excellency', he replied on 5 January 1843, 'that after mature reflection on my part I believe it necessary to explain, with regard to the proposals kindly made to me by Your Excellency this morning, why I find it impossible, in the given circumstances, to accept a probationary appointment as a conductor to the royal orchestra.' The example of the leading Parisian orchestras had shown him the extent of the organizational measures that would be necessary to raise the standards of artistic discipline in Dresden. 'To have any success in this latter, highly important matter, I would need authority in the full sense of the word.'

Instinct warned him against accepting a post which would certainly conflict with his vocation, and he thought his stipulations would avert the impending disaster. 'I am still in a very great dilemma,' he wrote to his brother Albert; 'of course I would like to keep my freedom for the next few years. I am in my prime now, when my productive powers are at their most vigorous.' (3 December 1842)

But everything seemed to conspire against him: Lüttichau offered him the post on a permanent basis at an annual salary of 1500 talers and without a probationary year; it was Minna's dearest wish to relinquish the 'vagabond life' for middle-class security and respectability; Weber's widow implored him not to abandon her husband's life work.

'More than anything else,' he confessed, 'I was moved by my own enthusiastic faith, never completely extinguished at any time in my life, that the place to which fate had led me – Dresden, as it then chanced – was where the first step might be taken in transforming the familiar, where the unknown might be born.' (ML, p. 293)

The appointment of Richard Wagner as kapellmeister to the court of the King of Saxony was announced on 2 February 1843. 'I often have stupid expenses,' he wrote to Lehrs; 'now I've got to have a court uniform made, which is going to cost me about 100 talers! Isn't it nonsense?' Eliza Wille tells of an evening ten years later in Zürich, when he disappeared for a moment during dinner, to return wearing his court dress. Stooping slightly, rubbing his hands, and with a sarcastic smile on his lips, he turned to his wife: 'Oh yes, Minna, I dare say it was very nice, and you were pleased with me in those days. My poor wife, what a shame the uniform got too tight for me!'

At last he found time, after this eventful winter, to devote himself to *Tannhäuser* again. He finished the text early in April. He meant to start composing during a summer holiday in Teplitz, but a feverish excitement prevented him from getting anywhere with it. The beginning of the composition sketch, which is in the Burrell Collection, is dated as late as November 1843. Like all the composition sketches of the later works, this first continuous draft on two or three staves was written down in sequence and with hardly any alterations. Here and there details of characteristic instrumentation are given. Even a chord as completely without precedent as the sustained dissonance at 'Naht euch dem *Stran*–de' in the chorus of Sirens is found there, exactly as if such an effect was common currency.

He spent six happy weeks in the autumn of 1844 at Fischer's vineyard outside Loschwitz, where he completed the sketch of the second act on 15 October. He sketched the third act after his return to Dresden, keeping himself in form with frequent, solitary walks. He finished the full score on 13 April 1845. 'My whole being had been so consumed in the work that the closer I got to the end, the more convinced I grew that sudden death would prevent me from reaching it, so that as I wrote the last note I rejoiced as if I had just escaped some mortal danger.'

The reason for this degree of involvement lies in the fact that this work expresses the essence of his own nature as no other does. The two opposing tendencies in himself which he described, apropos of *Die Feen* and *Das Liebesverbot*, as the 'sacred earnest' of his instinctive responses and the 'inclination to unbridled sensuality' are also the two dominating characteristics of his protagonist. Wagner went on to say, in that context, that the object of his further development as an artist would be to achieve a balance between the two: the conflict between them is the actual subject of *Tannhäuser* and it is triumphantly resolved. As Wagner pointed out in his note on the overture, the distinguishing feature of *Tannhäuser* is that it ends with the reconciliation of the two elements: 'Spirit and senses, God and Nature embrace in the holy, uniting kiss of love.' (RWGS, V, pp. 177ff.)

It is one of the ironies of Wagner's career that this very conciliatory resolution dragged him into an interconfessional wrangle, with the charge of having been got at by the Catholics. Then and later nothing was further from him than any kind of sectarian commitment. When the Berlin music critic Karl Gaillard took exception to the wording of the concluding couplet:

> Hoch über aller Welt ist Gott,
> und sein Erbarmen ist kein Spott!

he replied that he had left the lines like that 'because in my view "Spott" ['mockery'] is not a forced rhyme, but the most apt poetic word to express the perversion of divine mercy by a hard-hearted priesthood. God be my help!' (5 June 1845)

Gaillard had in fact criticized several passages in the text, and it shows how seriously Wagner now took the words, that he reconsidered and changed the lines in Wolfram's song to the Evening Star:

> Wie Todesahnung, Dämm'rung sinkt hernieder,
> umhüllt das Tal mit schwärzlichem Gefieder

to:

> Wie Todesahnung, Dämm'rung deckt die Lande,
> umhüllt das Tal mit schwärzlichem Gewande

substituting the image of dusk covering the valley with a dark cloak instead of the rather precious plumage of the first version. After finishing the prose scenario, he had written to Kietz that he would try to make the verse text 'as good as possible'.

But Wagner's poetry consists not only in his words but also in his visual imagery. Wilhelm Furtwängler cites the transformation of the Venusberg into the valley below the Wartburg as a particularly remarkable example:

> We think that we have never experienced a May morning quite like it, God's world has never seemed so beautiful as now. The reason is psychological: we are seeing the scene with Tannhäuser's eyes, and his cry 'Allmächtiger, dir sei Dank! [sic] Groß sind die Wunder deiner Gnade!' is thus one of the most sublime moments in world literature. And what else can you call the person who was capable of creating such a moment but a poet?[1]

It is very hard for us today to realize how daring and strange the music first sounded to Wagner's contemporaries. 'Wagner has finished another opera,' Schumann wrote to Mendelssohn, 'the fellow is certainly inventive and bold beyond belief. . . but truly he isn't capable of thinking out and writing four bars in succession of beautiful, or hardly even competent, music.' After hearing a performance, however, he admitted: 'I must take back some of what I said. . . it's all quite different on the stage. I was quite carried away.' Later still, it is true, this enthusiasm abated somewhat. He wrote to a friend that when he heard the operas in the theatre, he could not help but be deeply moved at many passages; though it was not bright sunlight that Wagner's genius radiated, it was often a mysterious magic that mastered the senses. But he found the music slight divorced from the stage, often downright dilettante, insubstantial and distasteful. 'The future will be its judge.' (To Karl Debrois von Bruyck, 8 May 1853)

Mendelssohn conducted the overture in the Gewandhaus in 1846, but adopted so fast a tempo that no sense could be made of it. The young Hans von Bülow described it as an 'execution' in every sense of the word. Hans Pfitzner tells how his father, who was an orchestral violinist, caught a supercilious smile on Mendelssohn's face as the last note died away, as much as to say 'we classicists know what to think of music like this'. Newman comments on the harm the performance did Wagner.

But he had been prepared for hostility. He had written to Kietz that he expected this opera to be a 'great revolution; I feel that I have made giant strides towards my ideal in it. Strictly between ourselves!' (18 December 1844; RWBC, pp. 188f.)

When the curtain fell on the première in Dresden in 19 October 1845, in spite of the friendly reception from the audience Wagner had the distinct impression that the dramatic climaxes had misfired. Tichatschek, vocally overwhelming as Rienzi, had been unable to project the contrition of 'Zum Heil den Sündigen zu führen' in the Act II finale, or to lend conviction to the dramatic motivation of the Rome narration. Wagner's niece Johanna, too, whose youth gave general delight in the second act, was not up to the demands of the Prayer in the third – a passage Wagner always valued particularly highly for its simplicity – which had to be partly cut in the following performances.

There was, additionally, a weakness in the work which Wagner attributed to his lack of dramaturgical experience. In its original version the opera ended without the appearance of Venus or of the cortège with Elisabeth's body, but only with a glow from the mountain and the distant sound of a bell tolling, so that it was not at all clear to the audience what was happening. Wagner rewrote the close twice before arriving at the eventual version.

Wagner was conscious even then of another weakness, the 'sketchy and awkward' writing of the part of Venus, but he was unable to do anything about it until he revised the work for Paris in 1861.

In the last years of his life he used to say he wanted to produce Tannhäuser at Bayreuth: as a drama it was now perfected – and yet not quite, after all, because there were things in the music that had not been sufficiently worked out. On 22 January 1883, only a few days before his death, Cosima noted in her diary: 'Conversation this evening, which Richard brought to a close with the Shepherd's Song and Pilgrims' Chorus. He said he still owed the world a Tannhäuser.' Whether he meant another version of the work or just a production is not altogether clear. Another remark of a few weeks earlier, whose meaning is quite clear, has hitherto been overlooked. Speaking of his dispute with the Berlin publisher Fürstner, who had withheld his opera from him, he added: 'If I want to revise Tannhäuser now, I haven't got a score.' (GLRW, VI, p. 716)

The work was a turning point in his career in one more, very particular sense: in it he attained at last to full awareness of his creative processes. Immediately after finishing the composition sketch of the first act he wrote to Gaillard on 30 January 1844:

> Before I begin to write a single line of verse, or even to outline a scene, I am already intoxicated by the musical aroma of my creation, I have all the notes, all the characteristic motives in my head, so that when the verses have been written and the scenes satisfactorily constructed, then so far as I am concerned the opera itself is already finished.

Some eighteen months later a court official, Hofrat Gustav Klemm, sent him a libretto by a lady, asking him to set it. Wagner replied that, with the greatest respect for the librettist, he hoped, in the name of Heaven, that she would not be offended by his refusal. It was not that he had a low opinion of her work, but he had arrived at the conclusion that if anything more of significance was to be accomplished in opera, it could only come about by the union of poet and composer in one person. He went on with an admission that tells much about his creative psychology: the whole of his productive power, and especially his musical power, was founded on the fact that he shaped and developed his material in such a way that even he himself could not distinguish between 'what is done by the poet and what by the musician'. (20 June 1845)

# 10

Hofkapellmeister in Dresden

'I have been told quite frankly that I am expected to reorganize musical affairs here on genuinely artistic lines', Wagner wrote to Lehrs on 7 April 1843, a few weeks after his appointment to the musical directorship in Dresden. The expectations seemed justified by the success of the first opera entrusted to his direction, Gluck's *Armide* – a sign of especial confidence in him, as it had never been performed in Dresden before. He had taken pains to render the score less stiff by careful modification of the incessant crotchet movement of the instrumental accompaniment. 'Everyone was beside themselves with the nuances that I got the orchestra and the singers to observe: the king . . . sent me a message of thanks and the most extravagant praise while the performance was still going on.'

One aspect of the performance that everybody commented on was the accompaniment, restrained, soft, yet always perfectly clear; and later in life Wagner himself liked to recall the expressive style of the singing. He used to sing the second-act chorus, 'Beklagt sei er, der nie genossen, wo ihm Nektarströme flossen' ('Ah, quelle erreur, quelle folie, de ne pas jouir de la vie!') as an example, first in the style he had once heard in Berlin and then as he had performed it in Dresden. His parody of the stiff, dry delivery of the Berlin singers was extremely funny; the serious, wonderfully subtle nuances of the second version seemed to demonstrate the abundance of his dramatic skill almost as fully as if it were a live stage performance.

It is not surprising that at the time this success earned him the reputation of a particular love for Gluck. When he conducted *Don Giovanni* three weeks later he had to take over a production originally conducted by someone else and by then hallowed by tradition. He had only one rehearsal in which to loosen the stranglehold of familiarity, and he wrestled in vain with the resistance of the orchestra and its ambitious leader Lipinski, whom Wagner indeed respected as an artist. The press complained of Wagner's 'Parisian tempos'. At the next meeting of the general board of management, Lipinski launched a violent attack to which Wagner replied, aroused, as he confessed, 'to a state where I forgot the propriety due to the occasion'.

He attempted to justify himself the following day in a letter to the intendant. He repeated his promise not to try to alter the accepted tempos of familiar operas without consultation, but pointed out that 'traditions' of that kind were not always so sacrosanct as they appeared. Before he conducted a rehearsal of *Euryanthe*, Weber's widow had implored him to do away at last with the errors of tempo that had taken root. 'Your Excellency will see from this how performance of an opera originally rehearsed and conducted by the composer, with the same performers and in the same theatre, can diverge from the original and authentic conception in the course of twenty years; and my question now is, who will vouch for the authenticity of the tradition in the case of an opera that was first given here fifty or more years ago and was never performed here under the direction of the composer?' (2 May 1843)

It is significant that the anti-Wagner faction took his attitude to Mozart as the grounds for an attack on him. There was nothing that could so discredit a musician in public opinion as the assertion that he despised Mozart. Wagner retorted: 'A stupid remark that I feel almost ashamed even to protest about.' (RWGS, XII, p. 210)

It had been no empty rhetoric when the German musician in his Parisian tale died professing his faith in Beethoven and Mozart. A biography of Mozart, read to him when he was only six, had made an undying impression on him. The only musical biography he bought during this period in Dresden was the German translation of Alexander Ulibishev's life of Mozart (1847); and in spite of the persistent hostility shown toward himself by Otto Jahn (hostility that did not always leave him untouched, as Jahn had the ear of his publisher Härtel), he had a copy of Jahn's *Mozart* in the library at Wahnfried.

He was possessed by a sense of the tragedy of Mozart's life, spent 'as if under the vivisector's knife'. His finest works had been written between present exultancy and anxiety about what the next hour might bring. When Wagner saw an *Adoration of the Kings* in a church in Siena he exclaimed: 'All these signs of honour in childhood, the shepherds and the kings and the angels – where were they later? Mozart suffered the same fate!'

The overture to *Die Zauberflöte* was his earliest musical love: it captured so exactly the note of a fairy tale. He conducted it in Mannheim in 1871 at the concert celebrating the founding of the German Richard Wagner Society. He often reminisced about his childhood impressions when Mozart was played at Wahnfried. He had discovered the C minor Fantasy at his Uncle Adolf's house and had dreamt about it for ages afterwards. The Requiem had aroused wild enthusiasm in him: it was beautiful, he said at Wahnfried, the work of a pious spirit, one who went to church and was moved by religion, and yet totally unecclesiastical. Going through the maskers' quartet from *Don Giovanni*, he said that it was what he had always hoped to emulate when he was young. One evening they sang the trio from Act II of *Zauberflöte*, 'Die Stunde schlägt, nun müßt ihr scheiden'; as a boy he had thought it the most sublime of all music, melancholy and consoling at the same time.

During his studies with Weinlig he had tried to discover the secret of Mozart's fluency and lightness in solving difficult technical problems. In particular he tried to emulate the fugal finale of the great C major Symphony, 'magnificent, never surpassed', as he called it years later, and at eighteen he wrote a fugato as the finale of his C major Concert Overture, 'the very best that I could do, as I thought at the time, in honour of my new exemplar'. In the last years of his life he liked to call himself the 'last Mozartian'. He played Brünnhilde's E major passage from the last act of *Die Walküre*, 'Der diese Liebe mir ins Herz gelegt', and lamented the general failure to appreciate his sense of beauty which, he believed, made him 'Mozart's successor'.

He worked hard to introduce Mozart to his friends. Wolzogen records that, reared as he had been in unquestioning veneration of Mozart, it was through Wagner that he had first been made fully aware of the genius of *Figaro*. Humperdinck says that the most interesting evenings at Wahnfried were those when Wagner performed scenes from Mozart's operas, *Die Entführung* for example, giving them a freshness that was wholly delightful.

He believed the key to Mozartian performance lay in singing. He explained to Luise Dustmann how to take breath in Donna Anna's great aria so as to be able to sing the bar leading into the return of the main theme and the theme itself in one breath. He wrote in the album of a young soprano, who had just sung Susanna's aria for him, 'Long breath – beautiful soul'. Mozart, he said, had breathed the same expressive beauty into his orchestral writing: 'The whole of the Andante of the C major Symphony is a vocal aria; I would like to write words to it and then hear it sung by a Catalani.' He gave Hans von Bülow advice on how the famous 'Swan' Andante of the Eb major Symphony should be played: the difficulty here, he wrote, lay in finding an overall tempo that did not drag, and yet still allowing the main theme its due. If it was played without any nuance in the tempo the whole magic of it was lost. (18 March 1868)

What aroused the Dresden public in the 1840s to protest at what they called 'Parisian tempos' was Wagner's effort to breathe the life back into Mozart's cantilenas, which they were accustomed to hear played 'smoothly and neatly', very much as a matter of course.

When the Dresden critic Carl Banck accused him, after a performance of *Figaro* in 1846, three years after that first *Don Giovanni*, of the wrong tempos and of ignorance of Mozart, Wagner was provoked to reply:

> C. B. is wrong in supposing he needs to tell me to enquire among older musicians about the authentic tradition of tempos in Mozart's operas. In the case of *Figaro*, in particular, I have assembled a large number of very reliable testimonies, notably from the late director of the Prague Conservatory, Dionys Weber; as an eye-and-ear-witness of the first performance of *Figaro* and of the rehearsals that preceded it, under Mozart's own direction, he told me that, for instance, the master could never get the tempo of the overture fast enough and, in order to maintain the momentum, continually whipped up the pace wherever the nature of the theme allowed it.

Wagner gave a number of other examples and finally, in full consciousness of his own quality, took a stand above the level of theoretical discussion: when the development of creative powers of his own had given a conductor a finer instinct for the performance of the work of another genius, he communicated that instinct to the musicians, too, and the resulting performance could justly be regarded as perfect in itself, even though there might be differences of opinion over details; 'above all we may assume that the creator of the work would prefer this kind of performance to every other, because every creative artist knows from experience that, for his own work as for every other, the letter kills and the spirit gives life'. (RWGS, XII, pp. 208ff.)

Wagner's court appointment and his conductorship of the Dresden Liedertafel choral society meant that he sometimes had to write music for special occasions. At the unveiling of a memorial to King Friedrich August I in the Zwinger in Dresden, he conducted a performance of a 'simple song for men's voices of a restrained character', and when Friedrich August II returned from a journey to England on 12 August 1844, Wagner greeted him at the royal country palace at Pillnitz with a choral and orchestral work, 'His loyal subjects' greeting to Friedrich August the beloved', in which the march from *Tannhäuser* was already to be heard.

He broke new ground when asked to write a large-scale work for a festival. Instead of an oratorio, in order to alleviate the monotony of male-voice choral singing, he wrote a 'biblical scene', *Das Liebesmahl der Apostel* ('The Love-Feast of the Apostles'), dedicated to the widow of his teacher, Theodor Weinlig.

A choir of twelve hundred singers, on a platform that almost entirely filled the nave of the Frauenkirche, was divided into separate choruses of disciples and apostles, greeting and answering each other, lamenting and comforting and finally uniting in a mighty crescendo: 'Send' uns deinen heiligen Geist' ('Send us Thy Holy Spirit'). In reply a choir of forty of the best voices was heard from high up in the dome: 'Seid getrost, ich bin euch nah' ('Take comfort, I am near you'). Then the one-hundred-strong orchestra, placed out of sight of the audience, began to play. The disciples asked each other, wonderingly, 'Welch Brausen erfüllt die Luft?' ('What rushing fills the air?') The work ended with the affirmation: 'Wir sind bereit, in alle Welt zu ziehen, kräftig zu trotzen jeder Schmach und Not!' ('We are ready to go out into all lands, doughtily defying every disgrace and hardship') – words that almost anticipate the chorus of the Grail knights: 'Treu bis zum Tod, fest jedem Müh'n, zu wirken des Heilands Werke.' The ethereal quality of the voices high in the roof, the powerful sound of the 'rushing mighty wind' as the orchestra entered at the outpouring of the Holy Spirit, made an unforgettable impression, the critic Richard Pohl recalled. Wagner himself was not altogether satisfied with this occasional piece: it was over thirty years before he was able to realize the scenic and musical potential of his vision, when he came to write the Grail scenes in *Parsifal*.

There was another ceremony very close to his heart. For years efforts had been made to get the mortal remains of Carl Maria von Weber brought to Dresden from London, but they had always met with obstacles. Now Wagner was elected to the committee, in the hope that his energy would overcome the difficulties. The most stubborn opposition came from the intendant, and a strong light is thrown on Lüttichau's capacities by his asking why so much fuss should be made about Weber. What if the widows of all the hofkapellmeisters who happened to die abroad claimed the right to have their husbands' bodies brought home with pomp and circumstance?

But at last all the obstacles were overcome. On 14 December 1844, on an icy winter evening, thousands of people lined the streets as the procession with the coffin, followed by a sea of blazing torches, made its way from the bank of the Elbe to the chapel of the Catholic cemetery. Wagner had written a funeral march, using motives from *Euryanthe*, for eighty wind instruments, carefully employing them in their softer registers and replacing viola tremolos with muffled drums. He gave a moving address at the graveside the following day: 'Rest here, then. Let this unadorned spot watch over the remains that are so dear to us . . . (RWGS, II, pp. 46ff.) Hearing his own voice, he seemed to see himself as a separate person, standing in front of him and speaking. He stopped for a moment, till he remembered that he was there to speak, not to listen. It was one of those moments of self-forgetting that he experienced sometimes when he was inwardly tense. The ceremony ended with a chorus he had composed for the occasion, 'Hebt an den Sang, ihr Zeugen dieser Stunde'. (RWGS, II, p. 49)

The generous imagination Wagner brought to his post at the opera is illustrated by an episode that immediately preceded Weber's burial. A new production of *La Vestale* was scheduled and he had pressed for Spontini to be invited to conduct his opera. Spontini, by now an old man, accepted, but his orchestral requirements – 'six ou sept excellentes contrebasses' were a minimum (RWBC, pp. 295f.) – appalled all concerned. Wagner's description of this episode, a mixture of respect and amusement, is one of the funniest passages in *Mein Leben*. 'He has character,' he said later.

'You see before you a proud devil who doesn't understand a joke, who wears all his orders. But what a difference belief in oneself makes, how decidedly drastic it is, when compared with Brahms, for instance.' He acknowledged a large debt to Spontini: the first-act finale of *Lohengrin*, 'this continuity of singing', really derived from him more than Weber. One evening he played from *La Vestale* to Cosima, Julia's plea to the High Priestess and her monologue, and then said, 'a man who wrote something like that is sacred to me'.

The greatest moment of Wagner's career in Dresden was the performance of the Choral Symphony on 5 April 1846. For the third time the 'Fundamental of his own life' was sounded at a critical moment in his development. The first time had been in his teens, he wrote, as a mystical sign of his vocation; the second in Paris, recalling him to his true path and lighting his way. Much that he had experienced since then had driven him to despair and doubt, as yet unexpressed. But the despair he had tried to hide from his friends was now transformed into enthusiastic optimism by the Ninth Symphony. Anyone who had come upon him unawares with the score open in front of him would have asked if this was the behaviour to be expected of a conductor by appointment to His Majesty the King of Saxony. Fortunately, he concluded, he was spared visits from the respectable musicians, well versed in the classical masters, who were his colleagues.

Reissiger had conducted the symphony in Dresden eight years earlier, on which occasion it had been a dismal failure – a judgement which the conductor fully endorsed. Now when Wagner proposed it for the annual Palm Sunday concert in aid of the orchestral pension fund he roused general dismay. The orchestral management wanted to take the matter to the king himself, and a newspaper asked if this 'carnival music' could be considered appropriate to the solemnity of the day.

By a masterpiece of diplomacy, in spite of all the opposition, Wagner had his way. The performance was to be given in what was known as the Old Opera House, where, in the days when the Electors of Saxony were also Kings of Poland, spectacular operatic productions had been mounted with processions of horsemen and wild animals, and which was now used for court balls and concerts. On those occasions the orchestra was seated in a wide semicircle only two desks deep, an arrangement which, Wagner remarked, broke every rule and was probably without parallel anywhere in the world. His diplomacy scored a further success in that he won from Lüttichau not only the permission to have the platform rebuilt but also the 200 talers to do it. In his request he wrote that he and the theatre machinist had calculated the design for the fairly complicated structure with mathematical accuracy. 'May it please Your Excellency to observe, in studying the plan, that the areas coloured red designate the position of the choir, rising in amphitheatrical tiers at the sides to above the level of the orchestra, and presenting an imposing spectacle, while it will face the conductor from every side and, not being buried in itself, will be heard very strongly and clearly from every seat in the audience.' (4 March 1846)

When Wagner stepped on to the podium at the first rehearsal he slammed shut the score that had been placed there for him and began to conduct the gigantic work by heart, something that was unheard of in those days. He met the full force of the players' resistance in these rehearsals. Time and again, as he rapped his baton to stop them, they shouted, 'But we haven't got D♭, we've got D♮!' Whereupon Wagner replied, calmly but firmly, 'Well, alter it, it must be D♭.' He paid particular attention to the woodwind. The famous oboist Kummer later confessed that at every emendation he had whispered furiously to his neighbour, 'if only the beggar knew what he was up to!'

Wagner's method of conducting rehearsals was quite different from that of Habeneck, the director of the Paris Conservatoire orchestra, who, according to Berlioz, conducted Beethoven's symphonies from the first violin part. While Habeneck gradually picked his way from the part to the whole, from technical accuracy to interpretative understanding, Wagner already had an overall conception of the work when he arrived at the first rehearsal. Within this framework he then sought to bring out the 'melos' – for him the quintessence of all music – from the broad, sweeping melodic lines down to the tiniest fragments to which the composer had reduced his themes. He made fun of German conductors who could not sing a melody rightly or even wrongly and for whom music was 'a curiously abstract thing floating somewhere between grammar, arithmetic and gymnastics'. At his rehearsals of the Ninth Symphony in London, many years later, he did not hesitate, for his part, to sing the recitative of the cellos and basses, which the players at first took as a joke until the meaning of the unusual phrase suddenly dawned on them.

In Dresden, too, he devoted twelve special rehearsals to the string recitative passages, until they really sounded like human voices singing. Niels Gade, who had come over from Leipzig, said he would gladly have paid twice as much for his ticket if he could only have heard that recitative again. It was only in the rendering of some of the more delicate passages that Wagner found he could not match, then or later, the quality of the Paris orchestra: neither in Dresden nor in London could he prevent the strings, at the rising semiquaver figurations in bars 116–23 of the first movement, from falling straight into the usual crescendo instead of observing the even pianissimo expressly required, which he had heard from the French players who had been trained in the lyrical Italian school. It was true that the passage expressed dissatisfaction, unrest, yearning, whatever the dynamics; but the precise nature of those feelings could only be expressed when it was performed as Beethoven directed: when the delicately 'sung' G♭ was answered by an equally delicately 'sung' G, then the hearer was initiated, as if by magic, into the mysteries of the spirit that was speaking there. (RWGS, VIII, pp. 271ff.)

As well as technical problems of that kind, Wagner believed that a further cause of lack of clarity in the projection of Beethoven's melodies lay in certain weaknesses in the scoring. The instrumental grouping was always superb, but the composer was sometimes mistaken about the relative strengths of individual instruments, and anyone who could help to remedy that was doing him a service. On this occasion in Dresden he went no further himself than doubling the woodwind in the second theme of the Scherzo, so that they could be heard against the string accompaniment in octaves. As a result, he felt, the theme was heard properly for the first time in the symphony's existence.

It was of the highest significance, Wagner said, that Beethoven had marked the tempestuous, anguished first movement 'Maestoso'. Wagner always regarded 'Allegro maestoso', in any music, as possessing a wider range of meaning than any other tempo; no other had such a need of modification when maintained over a long period and particularly when the treatment of the thematic material was markedly episodic. By selecting not too fast a main tempo and keeping to it, with modifications, throughout the movement, Wagner imbued it with an inner tension, so that even in the brief moments of wistful happiness the listener did not forget that he was on the edge of the abyss. 'That's the demonic cauldron,' he once commented, 'which has always been there, bubbling, but nobody heard it.'

He was convinced from the first that the success of the performance would stand or fall by the effectiveness of the singing. He made Mitterwurzer – who, as Wolfram, had been the only member of the cast to understand the stylistic requirements of *Tannhäuser* – sing 'O Freunde, nicht diese Töne' over and over again and then exclaimed impatiently, 'That won't do, if you can't sing it better than that, you'd better not sing it at all.' Mitterwurzer said nothing but looked at him intently; then he started again and sang the line thrillingly.

Recognizing that only a massive array of enthusiastic singers would be able to meet the demands of the choral writing, Wagner enrolled a choir of three hundred, whom he roused to a pitch of genuine ecstasy in rehearsals. He showed them that 'Seid umschlungen, Millionen!' and above all the line 'Brüder, überm Sternenzelt' cannot be sung in an ordinary manner but must be proclaimed exaltedly. Untiringly he sang these lines with them with the enthusiasm he knew how to impart, and did not stop until his own voice, which penetrated the sound of the chorus in every bar to begin with, could no longer be heard. The result, according to someone who attended the rehearsals, was something no one who heard it would ever forget.[1]

In performance Wagner stood very still: his head raised, the upper part of his body hardly moving, his left hand at his side, his right hand holding the baton, conducting with the wrist, not the whole arm. His passion was now outwardly restrained, expressing itself in his face, above all in his eyes, which he called the most important means of communicating his wishes. As he conducted without a score – which the Dresden press decried as an affectation – he looked at his players all the time and each felt that his eye was on him. Now and again he stopped beating time in order to let a melodic line, such as the low strings' recitative, 'speak'. At other times he showed the power he wielded over the players with his baton, coaxing from them the most delicate pianissimo, outbursts of despair, ecstasies of enthusiasm. He said once that the spell he seemed to cast on an orchestra was admired, but no one realized what his magic cost him.

His programme note for the Dresden Ninth consisted of quotations from Goethe's *Faust*; it was taken by some as proof of a purely literary and imagistic approach to Beethoven's music, though the performance itself should have proved otherwise. As he said himself later: what was expressed in that first movement could not be put into words, though he had tried. Instead, he had sought to induce in the audience, by reference to one of the greatest works of poetry, that 'elevation of sensibility' without which Beethoven could neither be performed nor appreciated.

About a month before the performance, Wagner sent the intendant a memorandum on the court orchestra. It was published for the first time by Julius Kapp in 1910, and Richard Sternfeld included it in the twelfth volume of the complete writings in 1912. It runs to more than fifty pages of print and is one of the most important documents of Wagner's life.

> I have spent the last three months, taking the greatest pains, in subjecting everything I thought necessary to the strictest and most exact scrutiny, carefully weighing every point, leading to the revision and rewriting of some paragraphs two, three and even four times, and have now at last completed the enclosed work, in respect of which I beg to assure Your Excellency that I have not been motivated by any ulterior consideration. I trust that Your Excellency will accept the outcome of my labours with your accustomed kindness and above all will remain favourably inclined towards me, who have so much reason to be obliged to you.

The document is a detailed plan for improving the court orchestra and bringing it up to strength. Nothing is overlooked : the manning of the individual sections with 'Kammermusiker' and 'Akzessisten' (full-timers and part-timers), in which section we learn that at that time one of the double basses also had to play the bass tuba, prompting Wagner to urge a rise of at least 50 talers a year for the overworked man, 'because he has to play two instruments and needs the best nourishment possible to give him the strength'; the purchase of new instruments such as a double-pedal harp; a roster for the string-players, dividing their duties fairly between operas with their widely varying requirements, farces, ballets and divertissements, and summer performances; above all, a concentrated seating plan for the orchestra: for good ensemble, the width should never be more than twice the depth. The paper culminates in two proposals: the institution of orchestral concerts, and the erection of a new concert-hall complex facing the Zwinger, with elegant apartments at the front of the building that could be let at very advantageous rents, and two concert halls, a large and a small, at the back. Finally there are tables with exact reckonings of the current expenditure on the orchestra and of the additional sums needed if the plan were put into operation: the difference would be no more than 1750 talers a year.

There is not a sentence in the memorandum, Newman remarks, that does not carry its own justification. It is the work of an idealist, but not a fantasist. Above all, it is the work of a man who places the interests of art above his own personal interest. Why else should Wagner care about the future of the King of Saxony's orchestra? His sacrifice of three months of his scanty leisure to this work is an example of selflessness almost without parallel in the history of musical institutions. The people who accused him of egoism simply did not know him. He may well have shown egoism in daily life, like most of us. 'But as an artist he was from first to last beyond fear and above reproach.' (NLRW, I, pp. 463ff.)

He had to wait a year for an answer and when it came, early in 1847, his plan was rejected. The experience played a decisive part in driving him into the arms of political discontent and revolution. Another factor was the appointment of a new dramaturg to the court theatre in the person of Karl Gutzkow, who did not restrict the exercise of his dictatorial power to plays but extended it to operas. 'My pain at being condemned, under these conditions, to suffer ever greater dissatisfaction and consequent lack of activity . . . is so great and sincere that, were external circumstances more favourable, I would undoubtedly already have sought to leave His Majesty's service altogether,' Wagner wrote to Lüttichau on 9 July 1847. 'Notwithstanding, however, I cannot remain in thrall to these circumstances, and should Your Excellency not see your way, officially, at the very least to removing Dr Gutzkow from any involvement in operatic matters . . . I am fully determined to leave it to the wisdom of His Majesty the King to decide to what extent and in what manner my proven abilities as dramatic composer and conductor of good music in His Majesty's service could be employed so that an honorarium could be paid me, sufficient at the least to insure the obligations I have already incurred towards the pension fund, but without laying on me any official connections or duties in relation to operatic matters.'

He could not regard it as other than a curse that the whole of his creative prompting was towards dramatic form, he wrote to Ferdinand Heine on 6 August, because he was forced to see the complete mockery of all his aspirations in the miserable constitution of the Dresden theatre. 'Perhaps you've already heard something of my break with Lüttichau about three weeks ago; it was so completely decisive that there can be no thought of reconciliation, especially from my side: the occasion of it was Gutzkow. But in fact the particular circumstances are quite unimportant: it's the old fight of knowledge and conviction against the brute despotism of ignorance.'

# 11

## Germanic Myth and Greek Tragedy

Two intellectual experiences while Wagner was in Dresden, though apparently remote from his musical activities, proved to be of decisive importance in his further development: his encounters with Germanic myth and with Greek tragedy.

Ever since Lehrs, whose interests embraced German antiquities as well as the classics, had introduced him in Paris to the legends of the Wartburg War, Tannhäuser and Lohengrin, he had not rested in his efforts to learn more. Now in Dresden a major book on the subject had fallen into his hands, and when he went to Teplitz on holiday in July 1843 people noticed that on his solitary walks he always took with him a bottle of mineral water and the one book. It was Jacob Grimm's *German Mythology*.[1]

The first impression was extraordinarily exciting. He could discern only a 'rough, fissured terrain, overgrown with tangled scrub', and looked in vain for any structural outlines or defined forms. And yet the book exerted a magical fascination over him. This was the feverish excitement that prevented him from composing *Tannhäuser* during that summer.

Slowly the tangle of gods and heroes, heaven and earth, time and eternity, fate and salvation – assembled by Grimm with a true 'devotion to the insignificant' – began to clear, and he began to make out a world of living figures, 'three-dimensional and primevally akin': he saw them before him, understood their speech and could not fathom how it was that he already knew their ways so well. 'I can describe the effect of this on my spirit in no other way but by calling it a complete rebirth,' he wrote a quarter of a century later in *Mein Leben*, 'and just as we are moved and amazed at the intoxicating joy of children when they experience their first, new, instantaneous perceptions, so too my own looks radiated delight at a similar miraculous perception of a world in which, until then, I had been like a child in the womb, apprehending but blind.'

Wagner improved on this initial experience, which bears all the signs of an intuition of genius, with further study. In October 1843 he moved into a pleasant, spacious flat on the Ostra-Allee, with a view of the Zwinger. There were three things that made it particularly dear to him: a concert grand by Breitkopf & Härtel; Cornelius's title-page to the *Nibelungenlied* (it still exists, in its original frame, in the Wagner Archives in Bayreuth); but above all the library that he built up in accordance with the programme of reading he set himself, in the classics, medieval German and history. After his flight the library was retained by Heinrich Brockhaus, the brother of his brothers-in-law Friedrich and Hermann, as security for 500 talers he had lent Wagner in 1846. To begin with Wagner hoped he would soon be able to redeem his books. 'One other request, my dear Hermann,' he wrote on 2 February 1851, 'please ask Heinrich from me to keep the library together, as he acquired it. He will probably be relieved of it before long, when he has had his money back, so I would be obliged to him if he would look on the books only as security, not as payment.' But Wagner's constantly fluctuating fortunes and his perennial financial troubles meant that he had to give up the hope of redeeming the library. In the end he lost interest in it altogether, when he began to form a new collection in Tribschen and Bayreuth.[2]

What he could not buy he borrowed from the State Library, with the help and advice of the librarian, Hofrat Dr Grässe, himself an authority on Germanic myth and legend and a literary historian – and, incidentally, the founding father of 'Wagnerology'. Stimulated by the Grimm brothers, he went back to the Nordic sources: the Eddas, the Vilkina and Niflunga sagas, the Heimskringla and the Volsunga saga. Paul Hermann, whose German translation of Icelandic sagas was published in 1923, came to the conclusion that Wagner must have acquired a good enough command of Old Norse to be able to understand the original texts, using F. H. von der Hagen's translation as a crib: that, at least, is the inference to be drawn from his characteristic use of certain words, such as 'fahren', 'fällen' and 'taugen', in their archaic senses. In *Mein Leben* Wagner claimed to have made himself as familiar with Old Norse literature as was possible without a 'fluent' knowledge of the language –

which does not exclude the possibility of his having a rudimentary knowledge of it. This hypothesis was confirmed by the discovery of a copy of Ludwig Ettmüller's edition of the Vaulu-Spá (Völuspa, 'Sayings of the Prophetess'), comprising the original Old Norse text, a German translation, a commentary and a vocabulary, in Wagner's Dresden library. This is an important key to the language of his texts, especially the *Ring*.

Goethe confessed that though he had known the tales from the Eddas from an early age and enjoyed retelling them, he had never been able to draw them into the orbit of his poetry because, unlike the figures of Greek mythology, they completely eluded his power of visualization.[3] What was it then that gave Wagner the power to breathe life into the nebulous Nordic figures of Germanic myth so effectively that they gained a validity that held good beyond the frontiers of the German nations? It was that perception of them as 'primevally akin', 'primevally indigenous'. He was helped to this by the example of Jacob Grimm, who had made a thorough exploration of the Norse myths in order to rediscover the lost German myths. It was supremely fascinating, Grimm wrote to F. C. Dahlmann, to learn to distinguish between what was typical and what was individual. He took from the Nordic sources whatever the German folk tradition confirmed as being common Germanic material, and added some traits from German legend, folk tales, popular superstition and custom, which – though often handed down in a pallid and distorted form – nevertheless betrayed mythic origins. In this way he succeeded against all odds in restoring to view the *German* mythology, the outlines of which had been obliterated and obscured by the accretions of a thousand years.

Wagner was to adapt Grimm's methods to the composition of his poetic text: he 'translated' the Germanic myths from Scandinavian into German, or rather, so far as the heroic sagas are concerned, he translated them back into German, for long before Icelandic skalds had told of the exploits of Sigurd, German singers at the courts of Frankish kings in the sixth century had sung of Siegfried. The difference between the old German and the old Scandinavian poems should not be under-estimated. Andreas Heusler, one of the great authorities on ancient Germanic literature, said that the difference between the character and the environment of the two societies meant that a gentler spirit pervaded the German epics, while the

Germanic heroic ideal was pushed to its extreme in the Nordic cycles.

The long and half-unconscious process of assimilation and Germanization of the Germanic myths was spread out over the years from the seminal experience in Teplitz in the summer of 1843 to the first version he wrote down in 1848, *The Nibelung Myth as the Scenario for a Drama (Der Nibelungenmythos als Entwurf zu einem Drama*, RWGS, II, pp. 156ff.).[4] One obvious outward sign of it is the use of German forms of the names, and Oswald Spengler's use of the Norse form 'Fafnir' in his critique of the *Ring* in *The Decline of the West* indicates that at the time of writing he knew it only at second-hand.[5] The scene of the action is transferred from chill, foggy cliffs and coastlines to an Alpine landscape, to German forests and the autumnal Rhine valley. The Nordic savagery of the characters is tempered by generosity and warmth of heart, gruesomeness is transformed into grandeur. Characteristics from German folk tales are introduced as well, in the spirit of Jacob Grimm: Wagner even discerns the prototype of Till Eulenspiegel in Siegfried, the boy who sets out to learn fear, just as Grimm, too, sees something of 'Eulenspiegel's temper' in Siegfried in the smithy. Mime's exclamation

> Nun ward ich so alt
> wie Höhl und Wald
> und hab' nicht sowas gesehn!

comes almost word for word out of the Grimm brothers' version of the Hessian tale of the goblin changeling (who, when tricked into revealing himself, cries out: 'Nun bin ich so alt wie der Westerwald und hab' nicht gesehn, daß man in Schalen kocht').

Finally, Wagner's setting of the tales to music can be regarded as another act of Germanization, for whereas the Norwegian and Icelandic poets recited their lays, the Germans – at least as represented by the Goths, Franks, Friesians and Angles – sang them to the accompaniment of the harp.[6]

In his later phase Nietzsche borrowed a term from Paul Bourget's writing on French *romantisme*, and spoke of a kind of *'exotisme'* in Wagner's 'Edda personages', comparable to that in Victor Hugo's *Les Orientales*, a yearning of the modern soul for the piquant attractions of what was remote and foreign: but it is abundantly plain that the comparison is completely without foundation. Even if Wagner had wanted to, he would have been incapable of creating a work of art out of nothing more than an impulsive yearning for the exotic.

On the other hand, the champions of a Nordic ideal have accused him of precisely the opposite: that he failed to preserve the spirit of the Old Norse poems. They are quite right, though not in the sense they meant: Wagner simply never intended to preserve that spirit. His aim was more specifically German: he was confident that even the text on its own was something the nation would treasure in years to come as well as in the present. His purpose was simultaneously more than merely German. He made fun of his imitators, who stuffed their works with unpronounceable gods and heroes and for whom the exotic, the curious, was precisely the attraction. For him the transposition of the Germanic myths to a more local, German setting was the means whereby he could develop the universally human elements of the myths: 'My heart, my spirit were inhabited by an ultimate, supreme world glory; the old German World-Ash, the Norns' tree, through me was to spread its mighty crown of foliage over every feeling human heart.' (KLRW, II, p. 215)

But before he was ready for that, another, seemingly unrelated precondition had to be fulfilled. His boyhood reading of Greek literature under the tutelage of his Uncle Adolf and his schoolmaster Sillig had ended prematurely when he stopped going to school. But the desire for the 'eternals of humanist culture' stayed with him even during the distractions of his wanderjahre, and in the midst of his Parisian misery he used to say to Lehrs that he wished he could read the Greek Classical authors in the original. With the wisdom of experience Lehrs advised him against the attempt: Greek could be read with true enjoyment only if it were studied seriously. He added, as a well-meaning consolation, that with the music he had in him Wagner would probably manage to learn as much as he pleased without the help of lexicons or grammars. In saying so he expressed an awareness of an inner association, though he could hardly have realized its full significance at the time.

As Wagner took up the Greeks again now in Dresden, he did it 'in order to approach the studies I had undertaken in Old and Middle High German in the proper frame of mind'. He made it easier for himself this time by reading them in translation.

In April 1847 his debts had driven him to move into a less expensive flat in the Marcolini Palais some distance from the city

centre. The mansion had a quiet, spacious garden at the rear, laid out
in the French style. After spending his mornings working on the
orchestral sketch of *Lohengrin*, he used to take refuge from the
summer heat in the shade of the old trees and there steep himself in
the world of Greek civilization.

The 'intoxicating picture of a day in the Attic theatre' arose
before him out of the pages of Droysen's translation of Aeschylus
and the accompanying description of performances of the tragedies.
He imagined the sight of twenty thousand Greeks filling the wide
semicircle of the theatre of Dionysus at the foot of the Acropolis,
and himself sitting among them as the action unfolded, watching
the chorus of Argive elders, decked in wreaths, enter the *orchestra*
and, to the accompaniment of the Apollonian cithara and the
Dionysian aulos, begin to intone the mighty *parodos* of the *Oresteia*,
in which, as Walter Kranz says, we first hear the soft, deep, heavy
notes which form the mysterious primeval source of the trilogy,
'just as the prelude of Wagner's Nibelung trilogy is a sea of sound
out of which the giant work rises up'.[7]

Ancient destiny is fulfilled on the *skene* in front of the palace of the
Atrides. Between the exchanges of dialogue the action is ever
present in the songs of the chorus, dipping down into the primeval
origins of music. Narratives and commentaries give the background to the tragic action in words, music and dance. 'One can
only marvel . . . at the weave of the primeval tapestry,' Goethe
wrote to Wilhelm von Humboldt after reading the *Agamemnon*.
'The intermingling of past, present and future is so felicitous that
one becomes oneself a seer, that is, like a god.'

After the crushing weight of the first play comes *The Libation-
Bearers* with its persistent, ever renewed wail of lamentation. Many
years later, after reading the *commos* of the *Choephori* aloud, Wagner
said it reminded him of his own *Tristan*.

The third play, *The Eumenides*, strikes yet another note. The
elders tell of the horror that seized all the onlookers at the Furies'
sudden appearance. Beginning with the earliest sounds of childish
babbling, they sing the invocation, accompanied only by the deepest notes of the aulos, and, wearing the black, snake-haired masks of
the Furies themselves, they tread the measured dance 'to chain and
ensnare the guilty one's mind'.

Athena appears at the door of her temple, lifts the curse and
grants redemption through mercy and kindness where the stricter

evaluations of justice have failed. Night has fallen on the festival crowd. Women and girls in white robes, with flowers in their hair and torches in their hands, come out of the stage temple to accompany the chorus, transformed from Furies to Kindly Ones, to their new shrine.

Wagner experienced as vividly as if he were there how the tragedy was transformed, as it ran its course, into a celebration in which the goddess, the Eumenides, and the whole audience all had a part to play. He confessed that as he read he was in a transport, from which he never recovered to the extent of being fully reconciled to modern literature again. 'My ideas about the significance of drama, and of the theatre in particular, took their definitive shape under the impact of those impressions.'(ML, pp. 402f.)

Greek drama had for far too long been regarded as a purely literary creation, in which music played at most an ancillary, decorative role. 'It was different in Athens,' Herder has a Greek say; 'our pronunciation, our declamation, our gestures and music are all lost to you, yet your room feels too small, your house is filled with ringing spirits of the air, when you but read our Greek dramas. Imagine this determinedly advancing, ever-changing melos; hear it in your mind and fall silent over your silent theatre.'

Wagner's reliving of the Greek experience through the spirit of music was not just a consequence of antiquarian studies, but was a response of his creative disposition and practice. With the music he had in him, as Lehrs had prophesied, he was able to experience the work of Aeschylus across more than two millennia, with an immediacy that had been granted to no other person in modern times. Nietzsche writes: 'There are such affinities between Aeschylus and Wagner as to be an almost tangible reminder of the relative nature of all concepts of time; it is very nearly as though some things belong next to each other and time is only a mist that makes it hard for our eyes to see that they do.'

That this was more than a rhetorical conceit has been confirmed by more recent research showing that the example of Aeschylus was the essential factor that enabled Wagner to create his drama out of the ruins of Germanic myth. It is a successor to Greek art of a very different order from the classicism of the Renaissance or the eighteenth century, lying not in the adoption of material or the imitation of forms but in an inner affinity.

In the course of this Greek summer of 1847 he pressed on through the other tragedians to Aristophanes, whose *Birds* exhilarated and delighted him, and to Plato, whose *Symposium* afforded him such a view of the beauty of life in Athens that he felt more at home there than in the modern world. The musicians, artists and writers among whom he moved were puzzled to hear him talking about Greek literature and history and not about music. A young Austrian poet, Johannes Nordmann, who was introduced to him by Wilhelmine Schröder-Devrient, was impressed above all by the profundity of Wagner's general culture: 'He talked about the Greek dramatists with a sympathy and understanding that one would seek in vain among some university professors; but even at that date I noticed that his favourite topic was German myth. The hour that I spent under the spell of his conversation became, in recollection, like attendance at a sacrament of the mind.' (GLRW, II, p. 203)

In the midst of his financial worries, professional frustrations and efforts to gain public recognition for his operas, it was his Greek studies that enabled Wagner to escape time and the world and filled him with a happiness more durable than he ever experienced before.

# 12

*Lohengrin*

At the same time as he had read the poem of the Singers' War in Paris, Wagner had read a long-winded Middle High German version of the legend of Lohengrin, the son of Parsifal the Grail King, placed by its author in the mouth of Wolfram von Eschenbach, who in fact wrote a very brief outline of the tale at the end of his *Parzival*. Far from stimulating his creative imagination, if anything this version put Wagner off: he found it bathed the figure of Lohengrin in a mystic gloom that inspired the same distaste that he felt for crudely carved and painted images of saints. 'The old German poem which records this most poetic of legends is the paltriest and most pedestrian thing of its kind that has come down to us.' (To Albert Wagner, 4 August 1845)

But as the first impression faded, the essence of the legend grew clearer in his mind. Significantly he came to recognize a prototype in Greek mythology, in the story of the fateful love of the god Zeus for a human woman, Semele. For the time being, however, he was unable to discover the right form in which to cast the legend, which was left to mature, half-forgotten, at the back of his mind until it was ready for realization.

In June 1845, immediately after finishing *Tannhäuser*, Wagner vowed solemnly to do nothing for a year but 'live off the fat' of his library, for if a dramatic work was to have any significance and originality he felt that it must be the product of a distinct period in the creator's life that was a recognizable advance on previous stages. 'An advance, a period of that importance is not going to be made every six months; only several years will suffice to produce the stage of full maturity.' (To Karl Gaillard, 5 June 1845) He did not realize that he had already made the advance and embarked on the next period.

A few weeks later he went to Marienbad to take the cure. On the way he made a brief stop in Leipzig; Heinrich Brockhaus, who took him on the town, noted in his diary that he was in a state of extreme nervous debility, and that music was a torment to him for the present. But Marienbad was enjoying magnificent weather and this soon restored his spirits. Every morning he went walking in the woods on the outskirts of the town, carrying a fat volume that contained Wolfram's *Titurel* and *Parzival* and the epic poem of Lohengrin. Lying beside a stream in the shade of the trees, he communed with the strange and yet familiar figures of the cycle of Grail legends. Once again, as with *Das Liebesverbot* and *Tannhäuser*, the volcanic soil of Bohemia stimulated his imagination: suddenly the Grail knight stood before him fully armed in a finished dramatic form. Mindful of his doctor's warning to avoid any work of an agitating or exciting character, he sought diversion in drafting a comedy on the mastersingers' guild of Nuremberg, to be an appendage, like a satyr play, to the more serious minstrels' conflict of *Tannhäuser*.

But in vain. One day, while sitting in a bath of medicinal waters, the longing to get on with *Lohengrin* overcame him with such force that he cut short the prescribed time for soaking, pulled on his clothes, rushed home like a madman and began to write the prose scenario. He even sketched one of the principal musical themes of the third act, 'Fühl' ich zu dir so süß mein Herz entbrennen', in the margin.[1]

He had spent nearly all the time in the woods and on the hills, he wrote to his brother Albert, but his thoughts had been unable to rest, 'and consequently yesterday I finished writing out a very detailed plan for *Lohengrin*, which I am greatly pleased with, indeed I freely confess that it fills me with joy and pride . . . My inventive and creative powers are fully engaged in this work.' (4 August 1845)

Once back in Dresden he took only a few weeks to write the verse text. The structure of the text of *Tannhäuser* had demonstrated Wagner's skill in its blending of the two legends of the Wartburg and the Venusberg; now he united countless threads from legendary and historical sources in a simple, easily comprehensible action. The sources are a particularly rewarding field of research in the case of *Lohengrin* but, without going into detail, suffice it to mention here the works by C. T. Lucas, Joseph Görres, the Grimms, Karl Lachmann, San Marte and Karl Simrock that Wagner owned in Dresden. One work, which he himself acknowledged as a source, was missing from his library, but that may have been due to its size: Jacob Grimm's *Weistümer*, about early German legal precedents, three of the seven volumes of which had been published by 1842. Several elements in the plot show that he must also have known Grimm's *Deutsche Rechtsaltertümer* ('Antiquities of German Law') of 1828: the conduct of the trial in the first act, Telramund's defiance of sentence (the offence of 'Urteilsschelte') in the second, and Lohengrin's bringing of a 'charge against the dead' in the third.[2] After the failure of *Konradin*, Ferdinand Hiller's opera about the last of the Hohenstaufens, Wagner admitted that perhaps he was partly to blame, for not having advised Hiller to read the *Weistümer*.

Many years later he told Cosima he was about to say something that would sound very like self-praise: he thought that in *Lohengrin* he had painted a 'perfect picture of the Middle Ages'.

Specifically, *Lohengrin* portrays the early, Romanesque Middle Ages, as opposed to the High Gothic era of *Tannhäuser*. 'There is much too much ceremonial for the noble, naïve simplicity of that time,' he wrote to Ferdinand Heine in 1853, apropos of the Weimar production:

> What gives my *Lohengrin* its individual colouring is precisely the fact that what we see is an old *German* kingdom in its loveliest, most ideal form. Nobody here does anything for reasons merely of the custom or etiquette of the court, but on the contrary everyone present takes a personal interest in every move; there is no despotic splendour here, with 'bodyguards' (oh! oh!) pressing back the crowd to 'make way' for the lords and ladies, but small boys in attendance on a young woman, for whom everyone gladly moves aside voluntarily . . . Look at my herald, how he sings as if everything affected him personally! (RWBC, p. 444)

This historical setting is necessary if the arrival of Lohengrin is to have the effect of a supernatural world invading the real world, and there is nothing worse than enveloping the work in a generalized fairy-tale atmosphere and so blurring the contrast between the two worlds which are destined from the outset to conflict tragically. The accurate representation of the historical setting fulfils another important dramaturgical function: the relationship of Lohengrin and Elsa is not another tragedy of the passions, like *Tannhäuser*. Their tragedy is grounded in a very sensitive area of male and female psychology and the sphere of action is a purely mental one. This inner action needs the powerful contrast and counterweight on the stage of an external action, provided here by the historical conflicts of immediate national interests and the larger concepts of empire, and of paganism and Christianity.

One consequence of the interiority of the conflict between Lohengrin and Elsa was that Wagner himself hesitated for a time over the necessity of a tragic outcome. One of the people in Dresden to whom he read the text was a literary amateur, Dr Hermann Franck, by whose opinion, delivered with cool discrimination and restraint, he set particular store. Franck considered that the punishment of Elsa by the departure of Lohengrin was repugnant. He recognized that it was in accord with the elevated poetic ambience of the legend, but doubted whether it would satisfy an audience's tragic sense in the theatre. Infected by this doubt, Wagner considered alternative endings, with Lohengrin forgoing his higher nature in order to remain with Elsa, or with both undertaking a penance and withdrawing from the world together. But when he discussed the question with Frau von Lüttichau, the intendant's wife, a woman of discernment, she retorted that Franck must be completely devoid of poetry if he could not see that *Lohengrin* could only end tragically.

Four years after he had finished it Wagner was again stricken with doubts about the ending, when the writer Adolf Stahr raised the same objections as Franck. The identical nature of his criticism made Wagner – who by then had moved some way away from the frame of mind in which he had written the work – hesitate again, and he wrote a hasty letter to Stahr conceding that he was right. This upset Liszt, who had defended Lohengrin's behaviour against Stahr, but Wagner soon changed his mind again. At the time he was writing the autobiographical essay *A Communication to my Friends*, which recalled to him the spirit in which he had written *Lohengrin*, and he now recognized the work as the tragedy of the artist, who puts his faith in the power of love to understand, when the world about him has lost the ability to love or understand – an archetype, even, of the tragedy of life in the modern world. (*Eine Mitteilung an meine Freunde*, RWGS, IV, p. 297)

On the day that he took the manuscript of the *Communication* to the post in Zürich he wrote to Liszt: 'Just two words – *you* were *right* about *Lohengrin* – not Stahr. I retract my endorsement of his opinion – it was too hasty!' (23 August 1851)

That was not the last occasion on which Wagner was to consider the implications of the tragedy of *Lohengrin*. When he was writing a preface for a French prose translation of the texts of his operas, in 1860, he was obliged to subject them all to close scrutiny. In doing so he was greatly moved by *Lohengrin*, he told Mathilde Wesendonk, and he could not help regarding it as the most tragic, because reconcilement was to be found only if a fearfully wide view of the world was taken. But he no longer dreamt of denying the necessity of the tragedy: he had read Schopenhauer and the Indian philosophers and now he sought reconcilement, at least notionally, beyond the bounds of time and space, in the idea of the myth of rebirth. (Early August 1860)

In spite of his complete absorption by his subject Wagner did not immediately throw himself into the composition of the music after completing the text in November 1845. The work lay fallow throughout the winter while he immersed himself ever deeper in its underlying mood: the sense of his isolation as a creative artist had overpowered him, he said. It is reflected in the short notices he published in the press around that time, in anticipation of his performance of the Choral Symphony: the world with which Beethoven had grown familiar was, alas, the world of loneliness. He had been seized by an immense longing to turn to the real world and to share its joys and happiness. 'Receive him, take him to your hearts, listen in amazement to the wonders of his language, in whose new-found wealth you will soon experience wonders and sublimities such as you have never heard before.' (RWGS, XII, pp. 205ff.)

In May 1846 Wagner and Minna, with a dog called Peps and a parrot called Papo, retired for three months to the peace of the village of Gross-Graupa, near the royal summer palace of Pillnitz. 'God be praised, I am in the country! . . . I am living in a completely unspoiled village – I am the first townie who has ever rented rooms here.' (To Gaillard, 21 May) The sculptor Gustav Adolf Kietz, the younger brother of Ernst Benedikt, who visited them there, recorded how Wagner, returning home from a walk, greeted him in the highest of spirits. After dining Kietz had seen over the accommodation, which consisted of two whitewashed rooms with the most primitive furnishings. And in a place like that, he added, Richard Wagner, whose love of luxury was already a byword, felt completely happy![3]

But before he started composing he had, as always, to get his theories clear in his head, which he did this time in a letter to Franck: 'Of course I've argued with you a great deal: we are still not of one mind over *Lohengrin*; but I've settled down to it again feeling completely fresh, and I'm now quite clear about it in *my own* mind.' The music would leave nobody in any doubt as to how Lohengrin himself felt: the one great advantage of uniting a text with music seemed to him to be that it enabled characters to be presented in a certain 'three-dimensional concentration and entirety', which would only be weakened by too much 'subsidiary motivation'. 'If your conscience lets you, do give me your blessing for my work, for I am buckling down to it now with inexpressible pleasure and great hopes: – you will like my music this time – I think that I have again learned a great deal.' (30 May 1846) He finished the composition sketch of the whole opera on 30 July, just two and a half months after starting it.[4]

On 29 July he received a visit from the sixteen-year-old Hans von Bülow, already an ardent admirer of his works. Wagner wrote in his album: 'If there glows in you a true, pure warmth for art, then the fair flame will surely kindle one day; but knowledge is what will feed and fan the glow until it becomes a strong flame.'

He began the orchestral sketch in September, after returning to Dresden, and for the first and only time he started with the third act of the work. Clearly he wanted to establish the controversial tragic ending as soon as possible.

He interrupted the composition in December, in order to prepare Gluck's *Iphigenia in Aulis* for performance. Discovering the customary Spontinian retouchings in the Berlin score, he sent for the Paris edition, the text and music of which he then revised as sparingly as possible, so that his own hand should be imperceptible. The only part he had to alter completely was the customary happy ending, which Goethe's *Iphigenie* had rendered quite unacceptable; in place of the marriage of Iphigenia, he had Artemis appear *ex machina* and wrote for her an arioso recitative in which she claims

Iphigenia as her priestess, to serve her on a distant shore, and exhorts the quarrelling Greeks to make up their differences:

> Nicht dürste ich nach Iphigenias Blut,
> es ist ihr hoher Geist, den ich erkor!
> Mein Opfer führ ich in ein fernes Land,
> als Priesterin dort meine Huld zu lehren . . .
> Nun seid versöhnt, versöhnet bin auch ich!
> Die Winde wehn, ruhmvoll sei eure Fahrt!

A marginal note in his own copy refers to his reading of Euripides.

Most important of all, he corrected a long-standing error about Gluck's intentions as to the tempos of the overture. When in 1854 Wagner wrote a concert ending for the overture to replace Mozart's, he defended his views in an article published in the *Neue Zeitschrift für Musik*. (RWGS, V, pp. 111ff.) Newman commented that no one today would think of disputing Wagner's reading of the overture.

This revival of *Iphigenia in Aulis*, which was decried at that time as Gluck's most dated work, was an act of the same order as the performance of the Choral Symphony. It is interesting to note that Wagner's edition of the opera still met with Hanslick's approval at the time of his feud with Wagner: he said that it combined a conservative sense of the characteristic features of the past with a clear-eyed recognition of the needs of the present day. The additions in the last act increased the dramatic effect without forcing themselves into the foreground of the attention.[5]

We can perceive an inner association between Wagner's interest in Greek society and literature, his editing of *Iphigenia* in the spirit of Euripidean tragedy and the composition of *Lohengrin*: just as Artemis's recitative recalls the style of *Lohengrin*, so *Lohengrin* breathes something of the Apollonian spirit of Greek drama. The good spirits nurtured by his Greek studies enabled Wagner to finish the orchestral sketch of the first and second acts and the prelude by 28 August 1847, and he wrote the full score in an incredibly short time, between 1 January and 28 April 1848.

'I took pains this time to place the music in so sure and plastic a relationship to the text and action that I can feel completely confident in the result. Trust me, and don't just put it down to infatuation with my own work,' he wrote to Liszt. (2 July 1850)

The plasticity to which he refers is well prepared by the text itself, in its avoidance of any secondary elements to distract from the central plot. The first act is a model of exposition. The events prior to the stage action are recounted in the charges made by Telramund and in Elsa's narration of her dream in such a form that they become active elements, anticipating the intervention of a higher power. The fact that Lohengrin's arrival with the swan has become the butt of endless facetious comment is due to the shortcomings of naturalistic representation when it comes to miraculous events, not to the poetry of the event itself: Pfitzner calls it 'one of the most marvellous moments, for both the eye and the heart, in all Wagner's work, and thus in all drama'.[6] After the trial by combat has revealed the 'judgement of Heaven', the feelings of everyone present, which have been poised tensely between hope and fear, find release in the joyful outpouring of the final chorus. As a result the musical line is at liberty to develop without restraint. Richard Strauss wrote to his librettist Hugo von Hofmannsthal that when he was asked to name a model operatic first act he always came back to the first act of *Lohengrin*.[7]

The spirit of the music governs even details of the text. While they were working on *Der Rosenkavalier* Strauss wrote to Hofmannsthal that he would like to have a 'contemplative ensemble' in the second act: after the bursting of some dramatic bombshell the action ought to stand suspended while everyone was lost in thought. As an example he cited the ensemble 'In wildem Brüten darf ich sie gewahren' from the second act of *Lohengrin*,[8] and in fact Wagner already anticipated this ensemble in his prose sketch, to play precisely the role of a general reflective pause after a dramatic explosion, the sudden appearance of Telramund. In the margin he noted 'Adagio', the only tempo marking in the whole of the scenario (in the score the passage is marked 'moderately slow' after a 'fast', which amounts to the same, relatively speaking). Strauss and Wagner both recognized the same deep-seated musical need.

There is one instance, too, where the process of melodic invention can be observed in action. One day in 1850, when Wagner was leafing through the vocal score, he noticed how, at Elsa's appearance at her window before dawn in the second act, the clarinet plays a motive in B♭ major which is then heard again, 'fully developed, broad and resounding', as she goes to the church in her bridal array in broad daylight. This brought it home to him, he told Uhlig, just how his themes came into existence 'always in the context and in accord with the character of a plastic phenomenon'. 'Might it not interest you to speak your mind about how the thematic formal structure is bound to lead on to ever new formations along the lines I have started to explore?' He was by then alive to the principle of motivic development that he had used unconsciously in the *Holländer* and would bring to the peak of perfection in the *Ring*.

It is even possible to discern in *Lohengrin* the outlines of those extended musical forms which Alfred Lorenz traced in the later works. The first act, for instance, falls into three main sections: the first, concluding with Elsa's narration of her dream, ends with Lohengrin's motive in A♭ major; the second, of equal length, reaches to Lohengrin's entrance and ends with the same motive in A major; the third, twice as long and more excited in mood, culminates in the motive in B♭ major. Each time, therefore, the motive is raised a semitone: an indication that Wagner was conscious of these three large-scale periods as such. The resulting schema could be called a Bar-form on a very large scale, with the first Stollen of 270 bars, the second of 297 bars and the Abgesang of 562 bars.[9]

The musical framework of the entire opera is equally well constructed: the A major prelude to the first act is paralleled by its reprise in the third act in Lohengrin's Grail narration in the same key. Wagner cut the second part of this narration just before the first performance, from 'Nun höret noch, wie ich zu euch gekommen' to 'wo ihr in Gott mich alle landen saht'.[10] 'I have sung it to myself over and over again and am convinced that this second section would only lower the temperature,' he wrote to Liszt. (2 July 1850) Though he only referred here to the dramatic effect of the cut, it can also be justified in terms of the musical form: it meant that the narration as revised corresponds to the Act I prelude in length, too.

The harmonic technique is more sophisticated than in *Tannhäuser*. Wagner cited as an example the three polyphonic woodwind phrases accompanying Elsa's entrance in Act I, 'Sie naht, die hart Beklagte'. Uhlig, who was going to do the vocal score, was amazed when he saw how far the music modulated in so few bars, and even more amazed when he played them through and discovered how natural the modulation sounded. (RWGS, X, pp. 191f.) Heinrich Porges wrote an introduction to *Lohengrin* for King Ludwig,[11] and when he read it to Wagner the latter drew his attention to the significance of modulations of that kind: when Elsa's theme is played after her line 'Dir geb' ich alles, was ich bin!', the modulation to A♭ major represents the expression in her eyes, which strikes to Lohengrin's innermost soul and kindles love in his heart. Whereas up to that moment his words have sounded rather studied, he now speaks from the bottom of his heart. 'He got out the vocal score', Porges goes on, 'and sang the passage with truly thrilling expression. He is inimitable in his ability to strike home to the unique point of a psychological motive.'

The use of the chorus, going far beyond its conventional operatic role, illustrates the influence of Wagner's reading of Aeschylus. Porges draws attention to some of the particular felicities. At Lohengrin's entrance the male half of the chorus is divided into two four-part ensembles, who toss brief exclamations to and fro between small groups, until they all come together in a resounding fortissimo cry of 'Ein Wunder! Ein Wunder!', and only then do the women, falling on their knees, join in with 'Dank, du Herr und Gott . . . '. Then, while Lohengrin gazes sadly after the swan, in the sempre pianissimo 'Wie faßt uns selig süßes Grauen', Wagner uses the new technique of having the altos and tenors (the first tenors falsetto) sing in unison, which results in a unique veiled timbre.

*Lohengrin* marks the end of Wagner's first creative period, but it already belongs to the second in one respect: the instrumentation. Before the pupil advances to the polyphonic writing of *Tristan* and *Meistersinger*, Richard Strauss advises in his edition of Berlioz's treatise on instrumentation, he ought to study the 'model compendium' of the score of *Lohengrin*: the treatment of the wind instruments, in particular, is on an unprecedented level of perfection. Wagner assigns specific timbres to individual characters and situations, which had never previously been done with complete consistency. In order to enrich his palette for this purpose he extended the romantic principle of 'tonal blending', devising new instrumental combinations, and he also adapted the preclassical principle of employing the various timbral groups like the different stops of an organ. Supplementing the woodwind with the so-called 'third group' – cor anglais and bass clarinet – meant that he could now paint any triad in any homogeneous primary colour he chose.

Wagner used his new orchestral sound most perfectly in two utterly different passages: in the prelude to the opera and in the scene between Ortrud and Telramund at the beginning of the second act. In the latter he succeeded in expressing the threatening and seductive power of evil in pure sound, above all by the use of the bass clarinet and of the flute in its very lowest register. The 'blue–silver beauty' of the prelude, as Thomas Mann called it, is achieved by the following means: the four strophic variations on the Grail theme, played in changing registers in a slow crescendo by the violins, woodwind, horns and other brass in turn, are framed by the violins in eight parts – four solo instruments and the rest divided – during which the accompanimental figures gradually develop into individual melodic lines, to which the players can lend individual expression.

Wagner himself, Liszt, Baudelaire, all tried to interpret the prelude in words. At the climactic unfurling of the Grail theme in full, Porges astonished Wagner by quoting the lines of the Pater ecstaticus from the last scene of *Faust*:

> Arrows, pierce through me, and
> Lances, subdue me, and
> Clubs, leave no form in me,
> Thunderstorms, storm in me![12]

But at a performance of *Lohengrin* the prelude has a dramatic function in addition to its musical effect. It has been asked how Lohengrin convincingly established his higher nature and mission, in view of the tragic conflict that results from them. It is a pertinent question if based on the text on its own: but the prelude entirely satisfies our instincts on that score in its evocation of the realm of the Grail whence he comes, and which is recalled at every decisive moment in the action. This is one of those instances that prove that no proper assessment can be made of Wagner's skill in characterization and motivation without taking the music into account.

Although he had whole-heartedly adopted Lohengrin's cause from the first, he demonstrated, as in his other works, the genuine dramatist's ability to penetrate the other characters objectively. This power of empathy enabled him to enter so fully into Elsa's femininity that he felt a real, deep distress on her behalf that often moved him to tears. Porges found particularly interesting a comment he made about Ortrud and Telramund which showed the profound sympathy he brought even to them: they epitomized the 'misery of the outcast'.

On the title-page *Lohengrin* is designated a 'romantic opera', and it was customarily represented as such, although Wagner himself was energetically rebutting the term as early as 1851. 'Anyone who does not see anything in *Lohengrin* that goes beyond the "Christian–romantic" category, sees only a fortuitous exteriority, but has failed to grasp its essence.' (*A Communication to my Friends*, RWGS, IV, p. 298) In the final analysis romantics are reactionary beings: with their medieval subjects they are liable to medieval ideals. For himself, Wagner affirms, 'all our wishes and burning desires are in fact carrying us on into the future, and we search among the images of the past for the forms in which to give them an existence discernible to the senses, because the present day cannot furnish the forms they need.' (RWGS, IV, p. 311)

Thomas Mann concluded his memorial address on the occasion of the fiftieth anniversary of Wagner's death with a consideration of his relationship to the past and the future. It was possible, he said, to interpret Wagner's love of myth and the past as reactionary, and yet every grain of understanding of the true character of his artistry, instinct as it was with the drive towards innovation and liberation, categorically forbade taking his language and mode of expression literally instead of seeing them for what they were: an artistic idiom of a peculiarly uncharacteristic kind, conveying at every turn something quite different, something completely revolutionary. 'Every will that is directed towards the future can invoke him in its cause.'[13]

Wagner's origins lay in romanticism, but the disciple of the Greeks, the herald of Beethoven, the poet of mythology was on the point of leaving romanticism behind him.

# 13

## Money Troubles

'Do you know what money troubles are?' Wagner asked Gaillard at the time of his retreat to Gross-Graupa in May 1846 to write *Lohengrin*. 'Lucky man, if you don't!' Newman remarks that we have been told in great detail about 'the women in Wagner's life', but the story of 'the talers in Wagner's life' is much more important. So a chapter devoted to the subject, in addition to passing references, hardly needs an apology.

In spite of his full-time appointment at the Dresden opera this perennial problem was once more on the point of developing from a crisis to a catastrophe. He had been 'penniless Johnny' when he returned to Dresden in 1842, but no sooner had he scored a success with *Rienzi* and been appointed hofkapellmeister than his old creditors, going back even to his schooldays, presented themselves again, so that he exclaimed that he fully expected a bill for services rendered from his wet-nurse.

As a consequence he never enjoyed his monthly salary of 125 talers to the full, while on the other hand he was never remotely near paying off all his debts. On a generous impulse Schröder-Devrient lent him 1000 talers at 5 per cent – a loan that was to prove fateful. Half of it was immediately despatched to Paris, to Kietz who was as poor as a church mouse, to his patient tailor Monsieur Loizeau, to the shoemaker, and to the pawnbroker with whom he had left his watch and silver cutlery. The other half had to go to pacify his Magdeburg creditors, who were threatening to sue. After meeting the most pressing demands in this way he was still left with commitments of a not immediately 'hostile' character, the sum total of which he was not precisely sure of himself. Chief among them was the new, large debt with which he had paid off some of the old ones.

This method of dealing with his debts is typical of Wagner's financial management. It could be described as an improvident gamble, staking everything on a single card. But from his point of view it all looked quite different. At no time did he ever experience a moment's doubt that he would triumph in the end, and even in a situation as desperate as he found himself in in London in 1855 – exiled from his homeland, hounded by the press, without any prospect of ever seeing his new works performed – he amused Berlioz with his assurance that in fifty years' time he would be supreme in the world of music: a prophecy that proved literally true.

Wagner was convinced that he possessed incomparably greater assets with which to balance out his ludicrous liabilities, only that he had not yet had the chance to realize them. The error in this calculation was simply that he was the only person who saw things that way, except perhaps for a loyal friend here and there who shared his faith. 'The one thing on which it all depends for me is: *winning time*, which is *winning life*,' he wrote to Ferdinand Heine in 1849. Those who loved him, who regarded the survival of his art as a matter of prime importance, would have to help him. 'They must not look on me as someone who needs help on his own account, but as an artist and a movement in art which they want to preserve for the future and not allow to founder. They shall own the works that I am eager to create, until such a time as they are able to present them to the *people*, as a property preserved for them.' (19 November; RWBC, pp. 352ff.)

Once *Rienzi* and the *Holländer* had been performed, his first priority was to find a publisher, so that he could supply scores as well as the performing rights which he confidently expected would very soon be in demand. The success *Der Fliegende Holländer* had enjoyed in three theatres, he wrote to Raymund Härtel on 11 July 1843, meant that he could no longer postpone the steps necessary to publication. 'If I do myself the honour to offer you herewith the publication . . . I am confident of making you a not unadvantageous proposition.' At first Breitkopf & Härtel expressed delight, especially as he had not mentioned the matter of an honorarium, and asked him for more details. But when he asked for a fee, and one of the order of 2000 talers, they found themselves regretfully obliged to decline his proposal.

Their letter revealed, Wagner replied, that they regarded his opera as worth the substantial costs of publication, but not worth a fee for him. 'Great as is my amazement, because I cannot grasp how anyone can risk a considerable capital outlay on something of which one is not sure whether it is worth the purchase price, yet at the same time it confirms the sorrowful opinion I have hitherto held that an original *German* opera, however fortunate the auspices under which it made its appearance, does not seem as safe a business proposition to a *German* publisher as a *French* opera, even though . . . it saw the light under the most inauspicious signs.' As Newman says, he was simply telling them, politely enough, what he thought of this attempt 'to rook a poor German composer'. (NLRW, I, p. 410)

Relations between the parties remained amicable, however, Breitkopf & Härtel undertook the publication of *Das Liebesmahl der Apostel*, and early in January 1844 Wagner even made them two further proposals with regard to the *Holländer*, suggesting that his fee should be made entirely dependent on its success. When, after renewed hesitation, they replied that they could not see their way to pay any royalties until sales had reached one hundred copies of the vocal score, Wagner realized that it was useless to pursue the matter any further.

We have no way of knowing whether it was his own idea or put to him by someone else; at all events Wagner now made one of the most fateful decisions of his whole life: to publish his scores himself. At first everything went smoothly. Schröder-Devrient approved his estimates and was ready to lend him the necessary capital at an appropriate rate of interest, and the court music publisher C. F. Meser was willing to publish on a 10 per cent commission. But after the contract had been signed, and substantial orders had already been placed with suppliers, an engraver and a printer, Devrient announced out of the blue that she had entrusted the management of her finances to her latest lover and husband-to-be. Wagner could not withdraw from his commitments and so had to try to raise the capital elsewhere.

Three of his friends in Dresden had the confidence in him to advance the money: the oboist Hiebendahl, the actor Hans Kriete and Anton Pusinelli. Pusinelli, a medical practitioner and amateur singer, had first approached Wagner to express his admiration of *Rienzi* when the Liedertafel male-voice choir serenaded their conductor on his thirtieth birthday. 'I have few friends,' Wagner wrote to him in August 1843, 'because I lack entirely the talent for going out to seek them. I am able to win very few by my own deserts, I have to rely on my good star to grant me them. But there is a certain look by which one at once recognizes another person – we only need to exchange names and we have gained a friend. And this brings happiness – so how could anyone doubt your faith? Let us both hold to it and be friends for life!'

His wish was granted, in spite of the occasional strains placed on the friendship by Wagner's financial demands. Pusinelli attended the Bayreuth Festival in 1876 and was able to offer his congratulations and share in the triumph for which he too had made sacrifices. He died two years later. On his deathbed he whispered 'My Richard, O my Richard, how you have had to fight, how misunderstood you have been! Only future centuries will know how to appreciate you! And you have been my friend.' 'He had a great heart, an unshakably great heart, which enabled him to understand everything,' Wagner mourned when he had the news of his death. 'It is hard to think of anyone who stood by me with the same heartfelt, unwavering loyalty.'

In 1844, when Pusinelli became the principal creditor in the young conductor's publishing venture, it was certainly a gesture of great confidence in his future. A contract was concluded on 25 June 1844 between Wagner on the one hand and Pusinelli, Hiebendahl and Kriete on the other, whereby the latter were to receive the proceeds from the publishing rights as collateral and interest. The success of the undertaking rested on two factors: the growth in demand and Meser's business efficiency. It emerged that Wagner had been mistaken about both.

He had twenty-five copies each of *Rienzi* and the *Holländer* printed by lithography. He wrote *Tannhäuser* straight out on to a paper suitable for reproducing by the same method and had a hundred copies of it printed. Every one of the copies of the full score that he sent out to theatres was sent back, Munich not even having troubled to open the package. 'I am learning by experience that here in Germany the more stir my works have created and the more they have made my name, the slower they are to spread,' he complained in a letter to Kietz in December 1844; 'why that should be, God alone knows!' In the final resort it was because his successes in Dresden remained of local importance, and only success in Berlin would have counted for anything more. And those in Dresden who envied or disagreed with him, unable to shake his popularity with the Dresden public, saw to it that in Berlin, as had been the case with the *Holländer*, he was received by a press that was already predisposed against him.

The other important factor in Wagner's calculations, the court music publisher, soon proved completely useless. Even when demand for the music did pick up, from 1850 onwards, Meser was incapable of exploiting the opportunities. 'Of all the music publishers in the world he is the least fit for such a business,' Wagner raged in 1851, 'and if you distil the quintessence of the most shit-scared, unreliable and cowardly philistine, what you get is Meser.' (RWBC, p. 777)

By the end of 1845 at the latest, Wagner must have abandoned the hopes he had placed in the publishing venture. 'I couldn't any longer put off taking steps I found most repugnant to ward off the impending catastrophe in my financial status.' A ridiculous accident struck him as an omen. Meser had arranged to meet him in a wine-parlour to discuss the idea of doing business at the next Easter trade fair. Wanting to encourage him, Wagner ordered a bottle of the best Sauternes so that they could drink to success at the fair. Suddenly they both shrieked and tried to spew out the tarragon vinegar which had been served them by mistake. 'Good Lord!' Meser gasped, 'that couldn't have been worse timed.' 'You're right,' Wagner agreed, 'I think it bodes that a lot of things will turn sour on us.' His sense of humour showed him in a flash that he would have to save himself by some other means than dabbling in trade fairs.

He had already had recourse to his usual method of raising money by incurring new debts, with only partial success. He tried in vain to borrow 2000 talers for two years from Ferdinand Hiller. His luck was better with Pusinelli: 'God willing, this is the last time that I shall bother you with a request like this.' He also borrowed 500 talers on this occasion from Heinrich Brockhaus, the brother of his two brothers-in-law – this was the debt for which Heinrich took his library as collateral in 1849. It is not known whether Heinrich Schletter, a Leipzig patron of the arts who was a friend of his sister Luise, lent him the 1000 or 1200 talers he asked for or not. He even took it into his head to borrow the same sum from Meyerbeer, who noted in his diary on 26 November 1846: 'wrote to Richard Wagner (turned down his request for a loan of 1200 talers).'[1] He was, in short, like a drowning man clutching at every straw to keep his head above water.

His economic circumstances could not be kept a secret any longer, and the rumours that spread in the city were fanned to the utmost by his opponents. 'You exhort me to do something about the gossip in the city, which is taking such an unprecedented and assiduous interest in me at the present time': the only answer he had for these fictions and exaggerations was contempt. Pusinelli published this letter in the *Dresdener Anzeiger*, giving it as his belief that to do so was in the best interests of his greatly maligned friend.

What finally caused the catastrophe to break over him came from a quarter where he had least looked for it. The arrival in Dresden of Wagner's niece Johanna, the stepdaughter of his brother Albert, unleashed first the jealousy and then the hatred of Schröder-Devrient, who sensed that she had passed her peak. She announced in public that Wagner had helped to oust her from her position, called in the 1000 talers she had lent him, together with the accumulated interest, and started legal proceedings.

Wagner had no alternative but to render Lüttichau an account of his debts. It says much for the intendant's esteem for him, in spite of everything, that on 16 August 1846 he was awarded an advance from the court orchestra pension fund of 5000 talers at 5 per cent to be repaid in instalments of at least 500 talers per annum from 1851. Since it was a condition of the loan that Wagner had to take out life insurance at an annual premium of 3 per cent of the borrowed capital, Lüttichau could hardly be accused of rash irresponsibility in the light of reasonable expectations, for no one could have foreseen Wagner's flight and exile. The payment of what amounted in effect to interest at 8 per cent – without taking the later amortization into account – took up almost two months' salary in a year, so Wagner succumbed to the temptation of not declaring some of his commitments, which he considered less urgent, and this in turn was a source of new embarrassments.

But his efforts to get the better of his desperate situation were not confined to making new debts. In spite of the experience he had had with the *Holländer* in Berlin, in spite of the failure of his attempt to dedicate the score of *Tannhäuser* to the King of Prussia – which had elicited the suggestion that he should set numbers from it for military band and get them performed at a colour-trooping – his hopes nonetheless rose again when the king commanded a performance of *Rienzi* in 1847. He travelled to Berlin in September to direct the rehearsals and conduct the first three performances. His letters to Minna show that he was doing his best to interpret all the signs favourably and that he even dreamt of a post in Berlin: '*Here* is more the place for my works, there's no denying it! – Well, – let us leave these fantasies!'

It is no wonder that the rumour became current that he was trying for an appointment as conductor and even that he had good prospects of getting one, garnished with special powers. Of course it spread at once to Dresden. 'You foolish friend, do you still allow yourself to be misled by gossip?' he reassured Ferdinand Hiller. 'As long as I am unable to exist without kapellmeistering, I much prefer to do it in Dresden, for a thousand reasons, all of which I will swear to on oath. You know how much I would like an adequate pension, enough to allow me to read all the books I already own and those I have yet to add to my collection.' (6 October 1847)

Secretly his wishes were more ambitious: apart from scoring a success with *Rienzi* he hoped for an audience with the king, word of whose interest in his operas had reached him. He wanted to obtain leave to read the text of *Lohengrin* aloud to him, in the hope of getting a first performance for it in Berlin. But all these hopes were dashed. *Rienzi*, handicapped by the shortcomings of the singer in the title role, nevertheless pleased the audiences, but the critics were the more ruthless for that very reason in demolishing it. Furthermore, a hunting party prevented the king from attending the first performance. Wagner set himself a date up to which he would leave the door open for the sudden summons to Potsdam that might seal his fate, but when the date was past he was forced to admit the failure of all his hopes of Berlin.

Just how deeply these hopes and disappointments had stirred him, more profoundly perhaps than he admitted to himself, is shown by the fact that in later years he had the same dream over and over again: Friedrich Wilhelm IV showed him boundless love and heaped consideration and favours upon him, so that when he stood before Ludwig II for the first time it was as though his dream was at last coming true. (DMCW, I, p. 554)

Since Count von Redern, who would have been the intermediary in arranging an audience, was a friend of Meyerbeer, it used to be surmised that the latter in some way influenced Wagner's lack of success. But his letters and diaries for the period in question offer no evidence whatever to support the suspicion. 'Today I am dining with Meyerbeer,' Wagner wrote to Minna on 3 October. 'He is leaving Berlin soon – so much the better' – presumably because he feared that a success with *Rienzi* might arouse Meyerbeer's jealousy. On the same day Meyerbeer wrote in his diary: 'Took Kapellmeister Richard Wagner to dine at mother's.' 23 October: 'In the evening to the dress rehearsal of Richard Wagner's opera *Rienzi*.' 26 October: 'First performance of the opera *Rienzi* by Wagner under the composer's direction. Wagner took two curtain calls.' The reason for his not writing anything about the work itself is that he had already heard it in Dresden. He had noted on 20 September 1844: 'In the evening I went to *Rienzi*, grand opera in five acts by Richard Wagner. Although dulled by a senseless over-abundance in the orchestration, there really are some truly beautiful, excellent things in it.' For the rest Meyerbeer proves to mention Wagner far less often than was generally expected. He was interested in the Wagner phenomenon, but he had as little inner sympathy for his work as Mendelssohn and Schumann, witness an entry in his diary for 23 October 1862: 'Because of the mental fatigue that listening to Wagner's *Lohengrin* caused me, I had never listened properly to the third act, never even stayed until the end. In order to accomplish it I went to the third act alone today.'

The last straw was when Küstner, the intendant, revealed to Wagner that he could not claim any fee for the two months he had spent rehearsing the work, since the management had only expressed a 'wish', but had not issued an 'invitation'. The only money he received was royalties for the three performances he had conducted 'as an advance'.

It was in a bad mood, Wagner wrote in his autobiography, that he finally took his leave from Berlin and his Berlin hopes. Seldom had he suffered so much from the eternal grey skies and the cold, damp weather. Moreover everything his friend Hermann Franck had told him about political and social circumstances in Prussia contributed to discouraging him completely. 'As I travelled with my wife along the homeward road through the bleak landscape of the Mark, I felt that the deep despair I was experiencing was a mood that I could be plunged into only once in a lifetime.'

Lüttichau was amazed when his second conductor came to him, straight from his guest appearance in Berlin, with the request for more money and for an increase in salary and parity with the principal conductor, Reissiger.[2] Even so he promised to pass on the request with his own recommendation that it should be granted. Wagner was astonished and ashamed when the intendant sent for him one day and showed him his letter of recommendation together with the king's consent. Wagner's version of it in *Mein Leben* could be taken for an overstatement, if it were not surpassed by the original, published by Glasenapp (II, pp. 262f).

'I beg most humbly to offer in the following my unqualified approval of Kapellmeister Wagner's deferential petition.' After the preamble, Lüttichau began by expressing the view that Wagner's stay in Paris had unfortunately given him so light-hearted a view of life that experiences as serious as the difficulties he was now undergoing were probably the only means of curing him. He had not known how to appreciate properly his good fortune in obtaining his post as kapellmeister with a salary of 1500 talers. Inflated praise of his talent had strengthened him in his extravagant ideas, so that he had envisaged making as much money with his operas as Meyerbeer had earned in Paris. The illusory notion of channelling the profit from his compositions to himself instead of leaving it to his publisher had led him to undertake their publication at his own risk and expense. After the disappointment of the hopes he had entertained of the Berlin production of *Rienzi*, he found himself in such straits that he was emboldened to approach the king directly with a petition for an increase in salary of 500 talers.

The intendant's letter concluded,

> As to the question of whether his retention here would
> be of sufficient value to justify granting him so
> exceptional an increment, I must indeed confess that it
> does not really appear proportionate to his overall
> achievement so far; nevertheless it is beyond dispute that
> in particular cases, where it matters, as for instance in
> the production of the opera *Iphigenia in Aulis* last year,
> or in the current series of subscription concerts, he does
> exert all his powers and displays a zeal that can only
> redound to his credit and would make his loss a matter
> for regret.

Wagner handed the sheet of paper back to his advocate without a word. Sensing the hostile reaction, Lüttichau hastened to emphasize that his request had in fact been granted. In fact the consent depended, at the intendant's suggestion, on two conditions: that the sum in question was to be regarded not as an increase in salary, which would have put Wagner on the same footing as the principal conductor, but as an *ex gratia* payment; and that if he got into new financial difficulties he would be instantly dismissed.

Still Wagner was to know no respite from his troubles. Perturbed by a speech he made to the Dresden Vaterlandsverein on 15 June 1848, some of the creditors of his publishing concern terminated his credit. His first move, as five years previously, was to approach Breitkopf & Härtel. He had been ill-advised enough to publish three of his operas on his own account, he wrote on 17 June; even now he would not regret it, if the money had been his own. But now some of the principal had been called in and he sought a speedy settlement of the matter in order to recover the peace to devote himself to artistic creation. 'I therefore offer you the opportunity to purchase this business: namely, the three operas *Rienzi, Der Fliegende Holländer* and *Tannhäuser* . . . Since my previous dealings with you give me reason to suppose that, had I asked for no fee, you would have been willing to undertake the publication of my operas on your own account, I am reasonably confident that you will not have any substantial objections to such an arrangement.'

But Breitkopf & Härtel were no longer disposed to agree even to those terms. They feared that the uncertainty of the times threatened the theatre. They declined the offer and at the same time asked Wagner not even to inform them further about his new opera *Lohengrin*, which he had already mentioned to them. (20 June 1848)

Without losing any time he next turned to Liszt, on 23 June: 'For a number of contributory reasons the matter is becoming very perilous for me: and privately I wonder what will become of me. The sum involved is 5000 talers: after deducting what has already been gained from the investment, and forgoing any fee for myself, this is the money spent on publishing my operas. Can you raise the money? Wouldn't it interest you to be my publisher? . . . I should become a human being again, a human being for whom existence had become possible . . . Dear Liszt, with that money you buy me out of slavery!' And a week later: 'I am fighting for my life here, and do not know how it will end.' But Liszt, who had given up his career in the concert hall, could not help him.

By the end of July the situation had grown unendurable and only Pusinelli remained as the last hope. Wagner proposed that he should buy the publishing concern, but he replied to Wagner's lawyer: 'I cannot permit my friendship for Wagner, my respect for his talent or my admiration of his art to lead me to take any further rash steps. I have shown my readiness to make sacrifices, great sacrifices, but my conscience forbids me to do any more and I am fully resolved not to consider his proposal of a sale in any circumstances whatever. I may lose much, very much indeed, by acting in this way, but I must console myself with the conviction that I was fired with enthusiasm for an ideal, and that I have paid a heavy price for that enthusiasm.' (1 August)

To Wagner himself he wrote begging him not to make any personal approach about the transaction: he feared that he might then weaken after all. Wagner replied that this request aroused many bitter thoughts: while it showed no change in Pusinelli's feelings for him personally, it confirmed his views on the devastating effect money could have on the human soul. The full significance of the comment can be seen only if one remembers that by that time he was fully absorbed in the thoughts he was eventually to formulate in his essay on the Nibelung myths. A coolness was created between the two friends, which thawed only slowly.

Wagner's flight from Dresden did not entirely put an end to the publishing venture. The after-effects caught up with him nearly thirty years later, when the publisher Fürstner, one of Meser's business assignees, laid claim to the performing rights of *Tannhäuser*, but on 2 January 1877 Wagner at last emerged victorious from the case.

It is interesting to read the interpretation that Newman, with his no-nonsense grasp of affairs, places on the whole episode. Time was to prove that, in begging his friends one by one to pay his debts in return for the rights to his scores, Wagner was making them a perfectly sound proposition.

> In 1848, anyone could have become the out-and-out proprietor of *Rienzi*, the *Flying Dutchman*, and *Tannhäuser* for about £750 in all – an investment that would have one day brought him in some hundreds per cent. The commonsense of the thing seemed so self-evident to Wagner that he frankly could not understand why it was not equally and immediately self-evident to others. (NLRW, I, pp. 419f.)

# Part III: The Revolutionary (1848–1852)

# 14

## Revolutionary Ideas

It is as well to remind ourselves at this stage, immediately prior to the great turning point in Wagner's life and work, that the various threads we have traced in his Dresden years were all unwinding simultaneously. At the same time that he was writing *Tannhäuser* and *Lohengrin* he was delving into Greek and German antiquities, conducting operas and concerts, devising theatrical reforms, publishing his own music and fighting for his financial life, but he was also already bringing an artistic ideal into being that led him far beyond the confines of his own century.

The first products of his classical and German studies were the scenarios of two historical plays on Alexander the Great and Frederick Barbarossa. The former is known only from what Wagner told Cosima about it: 'I had written a sketch for a play, "Alexander"; the first act was the murder of Cleitus, the second the decision to withdraw from Asia, the third his death. Nowadays they usually go for the burning of Persepolis, Thais with a torch, something lyric. I also sketched a three-act "Achilles" and a "Barbarossa".' (1 April 1878; BBL 1937, p. 5)

Wagner read the life of Alexander in Droysen's *Geschichte Alexanders des Großen und des Hellenismus*, and from that one can imagine quite vividly his three scenes in the royal tent at Marakanda, the encampment on the bank of the Hyphasis and the palace in Babylon. It was the incommensurable, as Jacob Burckhardt calls it, that attracted him to the figure of Alexander throughout his life.

His 'Barbarossa' survives as a brief sketch entitled *Friedrich I.*, written on 31 October 1846 – that is, during the composition of *Lohengrin* – with some additions made in 1848. (RWGS, XI, pp. 270ff.) In it, the concept of kingship is invested with the most

127

powerful and immense significance possible; the emperor's dignified yielding to the impossibility of putting his great ideals into
practice would have gained sympathy for the hero and, at the same
time, demonstrated the proper recognition of the 'self-activating
multiformity of the things of this world'. Wagner was thinking, as
with 'Alexander', of a play without music, to be written in 'popular
rhyming form', in the style of the twelfth-century *Alexanderlied* by
Pfaffe Lamprecht. The scenario is only a few pages long, but it must
have been preceded by a long process of cogitation, just as it
stimulated further thought and writing that eventually crystallized
in the text of the *Ring*.

But before that final step could be taken one more powerful
stimulus was needed: the experience of revolution.

'What is the use of all our preaching at the public?' he wrote on 23
November 1847, after the collapse of his Berlin hopes, to the writer
Ernst Kossak, who had told him about *Rienzi*'s fortunes. 'I am so
sorry that you are giving yourself all this trouble over it and, in the
last analysis, doing it for my sake! What we have here is a dam that
we must force our way through, and the means to that end is:
Revolution!'

There for the first time he uttered the fateful word that was to
direct his thinking from then on. It is significant that it was not the
February revolution in Paris that first gave him the idea; indeed it
was not inspired by politics at all. The heights and depths the
thought opened to him are suggested in a letter he wrote on 4
January 1848 to his old friend Johann Kittl, by then the director of
the Prague Conservatory, who had helped him in his publishing
difficulties and whom he had thanked by giving him the text of *Die
Hohe Braut*, which Reissiger had rejected. Kittl had suggested some
changes, and Wagner replied that the excitement and lightning
speed of the ending were quite intentional and the frightful catastrophe was not to be softened in any way. 'The one dreadful,
exalting element is the inexorable advance of a great world destiny,
personified here by the French revolutionary army, marching in
terrible glory over the ruins of the old order.' The great reconciling
factor lay in the fact that 'we see literally before our own eyes the
entrance of a new world order, whose birth-pangs were the sufferings in the events of the drama up till then'.[1]

All he meant here, of course, was an operatic revolution – he did
not believe that there would be a real revolution, even in France: he

had seen the construction of the circle of *forts détachés* around Paris while he was living there. When August Röckel interrupted a rehearsal of *Martha* with the triumphant announcement of the flight of Louis Philippe and the proclamation of the republic, he was extremely surprised, even though he expressed his doubts as to the significance of these events with a slight smile.

As long as he was preoccupied with the composition of *Lohengrin* (finished 28 April 1848), he was shielded by the aura of the Grail kingdom and could not be touched inwardly by events in Paris, Vienna or Berlin. He welcomed Friedrich August's appointment of a liberal government in Saxony in March, but feared that changes to the constitution in the democratic interest could mean cuts in the Civil List and thus, as the first economy, in the subsidy of the court theatre. To forestall this possibility he worked out a plan for the 'organization of a German national theatre for the kingdom of Saxony', which, taught by his experience with his plan for reforming the orchestra, he sent direct to the ministry rather than to the intendant.

The gist of this very detailed document, filling forty pages in print, was that the theatre should be taken out of the competence of the court bureaucracy and placed directly under the control of the elected representatives of the people. 'The king . . . could not but enhance the standing of this institution, if he appointed the authorities through whom he imparts his wishes to it from the members of the Ministry of State and not any longer from the officials of the court.' (11 May)

The manuscript ended up in the royal archives in Dresden, and later study revealed that, when Wagner published the text in his collected writings in 1871, he left out a passage about the competence of the intendant, to the effect that the position might be filled by one of the two principal conductors; but since a divided rule was always less efficient the reorganization should be entrusted to only one of them, together with the responsible minister, while the other might be put in charge of church music.

One of the people to whom the document was referred, obviously Reissiger, wrote in the margin against this 'That's the poodle's heart!' – in other words, here the author betrayed his true purpose. In another marginal note replying to the 'honoured reader' who had written the first comment, Wagner explained that no material benefit, at any event, would come to himself if he were to be given such a position; on the other hand, since the choice would have to fall on the most industrious and energetic, he had indeed meant it for himself, as the previous annotator had correctly guessed. He assumed that no one who read his document would believe that he had gone to so much trouble for purely egotistical reasons. 'So I am deeply grieved that the honoured reader regards the whole of this plan merely as a poodle, and its heart my own self-seeking.' (RWBC, pp. 297ff.)

After the referees had come out against the document the ministry put it aside, and the revolution that broke out shortly afterwards made it out of date in any case. In 1850, in exile, Wagner toyed with the idea of publishing it with a preface, solely in order to demonstrate that the infamous revolutionary had busied himself with plans for practical reforms until the last moment. (To Uhlig, 18 September 1850)

If his ideas on theatrical reform already had political implications, it was not long before he moved on to overtly political acts. In May he hailed the Austrian revolutionaries' recognition of the 'true nature of freedom' in a poem which appeared, with his name, in the *Allgemeine Österreichische Zeitung*.

> Ihr habt der Freiheit Art erkannt,
> nicht halb wird sie gewonnen . . . (RWGS, XII, pp. 358ff.)

He joined the revolutionary Vaterlandsverein, which was particularly absorbed at the time in discussion of the question: monarchy or republic? Recoiling from the narrow either–or, Wagner put forward a compromise view in a speech which was published in the *Dresdener Anzeiger* under the title 'What relation do republican aims bear to the monarchy?' and which he delivered on 15 June before thousands of people at a meeting of the Verein in a public park.

After proposing the abolition of the Upper Chamber and the formation of a People's Army, he put forward his economic ideals which, by emancipating mankind from the devilish concept of money, would put into practice the unadulterated teachings of Christ.

> Or do you scent the theories of communism in this?
> Are you foolish or malevolent enough to equate the
> necessary release of the human race from the clumsiest
> and most demoralizing form of enslavement to base

matter with the realization of communism, the silliest and most meaningless of theories? . . . Recognize the rights bestowed on mankind by God, or you might well see the day when nature, forcibly denied, will gird itself for a bitter battle, and the wild shriek of victory might really be the communism you fear, and even though the impossibility of its principles enduring is the inherent assurance that its rule would be of the shortest, nevertheless that short rule would have been sufficient to eradicate all the achievements of two thousand years of civilization. Do you think this is a threat? No, it is a warning!

He appealed to the king to place himself at the head of the new movement, for his mystical conception of kingship among the Germanic tribes was combined with a quite personal respect for Friedrich August II.

That is the man of Providence! . . . This prince, the noblest, the worthiest of kings, let him say it: 'I proclaim Saxony a free state.' And let the first law of this free state, giving him the most perfect assurance of his possession, be; 'The supreme executive power resides in the royal house of Wettin and continues in it from generation to generation according to the law of primogeniture.' (RWGS, XII, pp. 220ff.)

Wagner spoke with all his considerable powers of persuasion, and the applause was tumultuous. But his hearers had understood nothing more than that the hofkapellmeister had made a speech attacking the court toadies. The town talked of nothing else for days. Newspapers published anonymous articles and verses denigrating and lampooning Wagner, to which he replied with an 'Open Declaration' in the *Anzeiger*: 'The rogues and scoundrels are hereby informed that I make no answer to their anonymous attacks.' He tried to explain himself in a long letter to Lüttichau: he had attempted to present a poetic image of kingship, as he saw it, to a predominantly prosaic crowd. That it might not have pleased the demagogues gave him no concern; but it was a different matter if he had reason to fear that he had been completely misunderstood by the other side as well. (18 June)

He asked, and was readily given, leave of absence, and went to Vienna to find out whether conditions there would be more favourable to his plans for theatrical reform. He found the city in the grip of nationalist and revolutionary fervour: the National Guard wearing black, red and gold sashes, students in Old German tunics, sporting plumed hats and bayonets, the women with tricolour ribbons in their hats, and a German flag waving on nearly every house. Vienna had five theatres, which dragged themselves laboriously along. With the sense of the practicable that never deserted Wagner when he was on his own ground, he worked out a plan for a federative constitution for them, which he read to a number of leading figures in the musical and theatrical world. But politics took first place for the time being, and when the entry of Prince Windischgrätz's troops in October put power back in the hands of the reactionaries, it was an end of any plans for theatrical reform as well.

By the time Wagner got back to Dresden the unwelcome attention aroused by his speech to the Vaterlandsverein had so far abated that he was able to resume his conducting duties. The celebration of the orchestra's third centenary on 24 September, when Wagner proposed the toast, had the effect of a feast of reconciliation. (RWGS, II, pp. 229ff.)

Foremost among those who had introduced Wagner to politics was August Röckel, whose father occupies a place in musical history as the Florestan in the 1806 revival of *Fidelio* in Vienna. Röckel had been an enthusiastic socialist ever since witnessing the July revolution in Paris at the age of fifteen. He was appointed assistant conductor in Dresden in 1843, and when he got to know *Rienzi* and the *Holländer* he voluntarily withdrew an opera of his own which he had submitted for performance. He was the young musician whose sympathy went to such lengths, as Wagner wrote in *A Communication to my Friends*, that he surrendered his natural preference for his own works. It was not long before he came to view his badly paid post as forced labour and devoted himself to reading books on economics, which he discussed on walks with Wagner. In 1848 he at once took the side of the radical Socialists and announced that he had at last found his true vocation, as an 'agitator'. All at once, to the general amazement of his acquaintances, he stood revealed as the 'voice crying in the wilderness'. After losing his job for addressing an appeal to the army, he published weekly newssheets, the *Volksblätter*: three articles published anonymously in them were obviously by Wagner – 'Germany and her princes' (15 October 1848), 'Man and society as it is' (10 February 1849) and 'The Revolution' (8 April 1849). (RWGS, XII, pp. 414ff., 240ff., 245ff.) The increasingly strident tone betrays the general heightening of political excitement in the face of the threat of reaction.

The apocalyptic language of the last article is thought to be a sign of the influence of the Russian revolutionary Mikhail Bakunin. Wagner had met him through Röckel and had been fascinated by the 'colossus', the flowing mane that gave his Slav features a leonine air, the combination of ruthlessly challenging energy with refined delicacy of feeling. Without halting the flow of his terrible doctrines, Bakunin once held up his hand for a full hour to shield a bright light which he saw was dazzling Wagner. Neither succeeded in making a convert of the other: to Bakunin, Wagner's hopes for a future human society shaped by artists were the purest castles in the air, while Wagner could not help but see that Bakunin's insistence on the need to destroy all cultural institutions rested on premises of vertiginous implications. When Wagner conducted the Choral Symphony for the third and last time on Palm Sunday 1849 Bakunin secretly attended the performance. 'All, all will perish,' he exclaimed, 'not only music, the other arts too, even your Cornelius' – he had seen the *Nibelungenlied* print over Wagner's desk – 'only one thing will not perish but last for ever: the Ninth Symphony.'

In view of the profound differences between their outlooks, it is ludicrous to call Wagner a Bakuninist and to see a portrait of Bakunin in his Siegfried, as Bernard Shaw did. But it only needs one intelligent mind to propose an amusing paradox for ten less intelligent ones to spring up and adopt it in all seriousness. Bakunin for his part had nothing but contempt mingled with pity for Wagner's politics. According to the minutes of the hearing at Königstein on 19 September 1849 he said: 'Wagner I at once recognized as a dreamer, and although I discussed politics with him I never undertook any joint action with him.' (LWVR, p. 214)

Newman regretted that no catalogue of Wagner's Dresden library existed, which would have shown whether he had read Marx and Engels; now that the library has come to light and been catalogued we can see that it contained no political texts whatever. It is another piece of evidence that, in spite of his activities in the field, politics as such hardly impinged at all on his inner life.

It was during this period that he told Gustav Adolf Kietz, on one of their walks, that he was contemplating a work drawn from German mythology. His only fear was that he was already too old to be able to master the immense subject: he should have undertaken it earlier in his life.

When he had taken up his Barbarossa sketch again to make some additions to it, it occurred to him that the subject had a 'generic similarity' – one that only the eye of faith will perceive – to the Nibelung myths. The train of thought set off by this led to an extraordinary essay written in the late summer of 1848, 'The Wibelungs: World History from Saga', in which he attempted to show that the history of the Hohenstaufen dynasty derived from the Nibelung sagas, by associating 'Waiblingen' (the name of the Hohenstaufen stronghold Italianized as 'Ghibelline') with 'Wibelung' and thence 'Nibelung'. It was all fantasy, of course, but interesting insofar as it shows how the historical subject was being transformed in his mind into the mythological one.

The Nibelung myth had developed for him into a form which 'contained much and yet [was] compressed down to its principal elements', and the time was ripe for him to work out a dramatic text from it. What he said to Kietz gives some notion of his struggle with the immensity of the subject which, as he guessed, would be his fate. The first prose outline of all, *The Nibelung Myth as the Scenario for a Drama*, finished on 4 October 1848, already contains in narrative form the whole of the eventual plot of the *Ring* apart from a few, admittedly significant, factors. The fragmentary nature of the literary tradition vanishes from sight and the sketch reads like a new-minted original text from the authors of the Edda and the Volsunga saga. It owed its homogeneity to the Greeks: the close interrelation of the divine and the heroic myths, in particular, was quite unknown to the early Germans and was inconceivable without the example of the *Iliad*.

Even in this first version, Wagner's text broke spontaneously into dialogue at the point where Brünnhilde recognizes the ring on Siegfried's hand, and Wagner realized that the final stages of the fable would serve as the material for a 'drama executed in music'. In view of the contemporary state of the lyric theatre he was slow to muster any great enthusiasm for the prospect: only when he had nothing left to lose did he find the courage for the task.

Precisely there, in the creative courage born of despair, lay the deeper significance of the revolution for the conception of the *Ring*.

Even if Wagner himself had not stressed the matter, it would be clear enough that social factors also played a part, but such factors have no bearing on the value or non-value of a work of art. If the artist does not succeed in sublimating those factors, whatever they may be, into the substance of pure art then there remains a sediment that draws the work down to the level of its time and allows it to perish with its time. To translate the *Ring* back, nowadays, into a piece 'about' those factors and to pride oneself on doing so amounts to a failure to recognize the timeless substance behind the temporal, and indeed renders it unrecognizable.

The last straw for Wagner came when the production of *Lohengrin*, for which the sets had already been commissioned, was abruptly postponed by Lüttichau without a word of explanation. 'Silently abandoning my last hope of reconciling myself to the theatre by means of a fine production of my *Lohengrin*, from that moment, absolutely and fundamentally, I turned my back on the theatre and on every attempt to come to terms with it. . . Now I set to work to carry out the plan that I had long nurtured in seclusion, of *Siegfrieds Tod*.' (ML, pp. 445f.)

He completed the first full prose sketch, in dialogue form, on 20 October 1848. (SERD, pp. 38ff.) When he read it to Eduard Devrient, the dramaturg of the Dresden theatre, the latter pointed out that in order to enter into the quarrel between Siegfried and Brünnhilde it was essential for the listener to have known them in their earlier, unclouded relationship. Wagner at once sketched the introductory scene in which they take leave of each other and, while he was at it, the Norns' scene, an addition of much greater consequence, referring the 'great heroic opera' to its mythological background for the first time.[2]

Rewriting the text in verse took him from 11 to 28 November. For the first time, he used not iambics but the 'free rhythmic verse' that he developed out of the requirements of musical declamation. Early in December Gustav Kietz had a note from Wagner inviting him to a reading of the new text, 'if you have nothing better to do'.

> I arrived punctually [Kietz wrote in his memoirs], and found Professor Semper, Fischer the chorus master, Heine the costume-designer and his son already there. The last arrivals were the musicians Hans von Bülow and Karl Ritter, who made their entrance in full evening

dress, tails and white tie, balancing top hats on their
arms. Laughing, Wagner met them with the words, 'Ah,
gentlemen, you do me too much honour.' . . . Now he
began to read the text in a clear voice and with the
enthralling expressiveness which lay uniquely at his
command . . . His listeners were spellbound, the general
excitement grew from act to act! The reading was
followed by a discussion about the musical realization of
it with old Fischer, who kept on shaking his head.
Excited by his demurrings, Wagner explained the
important part the orchestra would play in the dramatic
expression, and how the 'word' projected from the stage
would have to carry more weight than hitherto.

It was, Kietz concluded, an unforgettable evening for everyone
present – and, we may add, a red-letter day in the history of the
writing of the *Ring*, not least because it shows how clearly Wagner
already envisaged the new kind of musical realization.

But the immediate effect of writing the text was to bring home to
him even more painfully his isolation as a creative artist. He had
been immersing himself in the Gospels, and the copy of the New
Testament that he owned at that time bears more underlinings than
any other book in the whole of his Dresden library. His reading
made him very aware of the man Jesus as opposed to the symbolic
Christ, and drove him to sketch a drama 'for the ideal theatre of the
future', presenting the self-sacrifice of Jesus as the revolt of a spirit
that loved, and needed love, against a loveless world. The sketch of
*Jesus von Nazareth* runs to more than fifty pages in print. (RWGS,
XII, pp. 273ff.) The first act, outside the house of Levi the publican,
expounds the contrast between Judas and Barabbas, who are planning an insurrection, and Jesus, who develops his teaching of love
(the tribute money and the woman taken in adultery). The second
act takes place on the Sea of Gennesaret and ends with the sermon
on the lake. The third depicts the entry into Jerusalem, the fourth
the last supper and the agony in the garden. In the fifth, the trial
takes place outside Pilate's palace, and the two Marys and John,
returning from Calvary, recount the end and look forward hope-
fully to the founding of the communion of followers. Arthur
Drews believed that it was probably no exaggeration to describe
Wagner's version of the life of Christ as one of the most successful.

It is significant of the relationship between Wagner and Bakunin that the latter was no more interested in the *Jesus von Nazareth* project than he was in the Nibelung plans: he begged Wagner to spare him, but in any case to present Jesus as a weak character. He recommended musical variations on a single text: the tenor singing 'Behead him!', the soprano 'Hang him!' and the bass 'Fire, fire!'

Wagner passed the spring of 1849 in a state of numb expectation. The political situation seemed to be heading straight for a catastrophe, and it gave him a certain satisfaction to picture his personal fate as bound in with the general position. Indignation with the reactionary party reached a peak when the king, contrary to the constitution, dissolved both chambers of the Landtag on 30 April, and sent a government commissioner to order the deputies home. In the face of deputations from every sector of his kingdom appealing to him to reverse his decision, the king, normally the most malleable of men, preserved a firmness of purpose worthy of a better cause. He understood very well that his refusal was bound to lead to civil war, but he relied on his troops and the military aid promised by Prussia. The government's moral position was as poor as could be in the eyes of the country: the dissolution of the Landtag was seen as a breach of the constitution and the threatened Prussian aid as an invasion, and the expression 'revolution from above' was heard.

The dissolution of the Landtag deprived Röckel of his immunity as a member of it, and he fled to Prague. Wagner wrote to him on 2 May: 'It is very unsettled here . . . People are preparing themselves for a decisive confrontation, if not with the king, then at any rate with the Prussian army; the only fear is that a revolution may break out too early.' That sentence turned out to be fateful for Wagner, when the letter was later found on Röckel. Item 5 in the Saxon Ministry of Justice document of 1862, collating all the charges against him, reads: 'The letter written on that account by Wagner to Röckel compromises the former to the utmost.' (LWVR, p. 18) In this the court was over-estimating Wagner's political status, for if a date had really been set for the revolution, the last person to whom the secret would have been confided was the musician shrugged off by Bakunin as a 'dreamer'.

The chapter about the revolution is one of the most exciting in *Mein Leben*. It is very possible that he represented his own part in it as less active than it really was. The reader must not forget that when he began to dictate the autobiography his exile, after lasting thirteen years, had been lifted only two years previously, on 28 March 1862. Apart from that, there is the consideration that he had perhaps already admitted almost too much for a reader like King Ludwig, at whose behest he was writing the book.

There are some undisputed facts. He had handbills printed saying 'Are you with us against foreign troops?', which he distributed in person during a cease-fire to the Saxon soldiers stationed on the square outside the palace and on the Elbe bridge. It was a miracle, according to an eyewitness, that he was not arrested or even shot while he was doing it. He spent the night of 6–7 May on the tower of the Kreuzkirche and watched the approach of bands of insurgents from the Erz mountains in the early morning. He did not go to the barricades and join in the hand-to-hand fighting; nor was it he, contrary to what was claimed, who set fire to the Old Opera House. A curious incident made that particular event unforgettable for him. As he went past the Annenkirche on his way home on the morning of 7 May, he heard a shout: 'Herr Kapellmeister!' and when he turned round he saw a fine figure of a man on the barricade who called to him 'Joy's beautiful divine spark has *kindled!*' ('Der Freude schöner Götterfunken hat *gezündet!*'). When Wagner told this 'peculiar story' in 1873 he also made the movement of the arm with which the man had visibly underlined the word 'gezündet'. 'It was very strange', he added in a voice that betrayed emotion.

Some things remain obscure, for instance whether Wagner – as alleged by the brassfounder Oehme, one of the 'most severely incriminated persons' – really did order a substantial number of hand grenades for Prague from him. The protocols give a general impression that the revolutionaries who were arrested – not excepting Wagner's friend Röckel – did not scruple to lay as much as they could at the door of one who had managed to escape.

But our concern here is less with the legal side of the affair than with the psychological. While the elemental force of an event of such a nature seems to draw Wagner wholly in its wake, his better conscious judgement remains untouched by it, like an uninvolved spectator. When the tocsin suddenly started to ring as he was crossing the Postplatz he experienced a phenomenon which, he realized, was exactly the same as Goethe had experienced during the cannonade of Valmy: 'The whole of the square before me seemed to be lit with a dark yellow, almost brownish light' (Goethe: 'as if the world had a certain brownish tint'). There were others on the tower of the Kreuzkirche with him. While they were trying to keep out of the line of fire of the Prussian snipers on the tower of the Frauen-kirche, he started a philosophical discussion with a schoolteacher called Berthold, which led them to the remotest areas of religion. A Professor Thum, who was also on the tower that night, recalled that he had a long and lively conversation with Wagner about the classical and Christian views of the world. 'In this way,' Wagner wrote, 'in the immediate proximity of the terrible clamour of the bell and under the constant hail of Prussian bullets against the tower wall, I spent one of the most remarkable nights of my life.' Slowly making his long way home past the numerous abatis during the short cease-fire on the morning of 7 May, he worked out in his head the plot of a play about Achilles. Thetis would appear to her son as he was mourning for Patroclus and offer him immortality if he would forgo vengeance for his friend. But Achilles would disdain-fully reject divine immortality at the cost of the loss of human striving. Then the goddess would bow before him, recognizing that he was greater than the gods. 'Man is god perfected. The eternal gods are only the elements which create man. Creation finds its ultimate conclusion in man. Achilles is higher and more perfect than the elemental Thetis.' (RWGS, XII, p. 283)

Wagner kept the project in mind for years. In 1865, after complet-ing the prose sketch of *Parsifal*, he wrote to King Ludwig that he still hoped his *Achilleus* would see the light of day eventually. (16 September 1865) In the meantime one of its important features had been transferred to the figure of Brünnhilde in the third act of *Siegfried*, renouncing divinity and accepting her humanity.

Wagner avoided arrest after the failure of the revolution solely because of one of those remarkable chances that always played a large part at the turning points of his life: travelling on from Freiberg he lost contact with the members of the provisional gov-ernment with whom he had fled from Dresden and with whom he would otherwise have been arrested in Chemnitz. 'My soul was transfixed as if by lightning, remembering the extraordinary way that once before, when I was a student, I had been saved from certain defeat in the duel I was to have fought with the experienced bully-boy.' Fate had some other strokes of luck in store for him: the fact that his brother-in-law Heinrich Wolfram lived in Chemnitz and was able to hide him and drive him secretly to Altenburg; that

Liszt was able to give him advice and practical assistance in Weimar; that a Professor Widmann in Jena was ready to give him his passport, so that he could cross the Saxon border under a false name. If any one of the links in this chain had been missing, his flight would have failed.

The account in *Mein Leben* is supplemented by what Wagner wrote at the time in letters to Minna and his brother-in-law from Weimar and Eisenach. (RWBC, pp. 303ff.) What these principally reveal is his concern for his wife: he had been so happy to have a letter from her on his arrival in Weimar: 'the evidence of your pure, warm love which you assure me of this time without torturing me with reproaches'. He went on that he would not leave Germany without having seen her again.

'The ways of human fate are incomprehensible! The dreadful catastrophe I have just experienced and the day I spent yesterday in Weimar have made a different person of me and have shown me a new path.' In his extreme dissatisfaction with his position and almost with his art, he had been at odds with the world and ceased to be an artist. While he had spent the journey to Weimar thinking about finding a quiet place in the country, Liszt had turned his thoughts to the whole wide world, to London and Paris. 'That gave me fresh heart, and at a stroke I am once again all artist, *love* my art again and *hope*, too, that it will be the means whereby I will make my poor, sorely tried wife happy again.'

He was in a state of 'dreamy detachment' which made it hard for him to judge how far he had compromised himself. To comfort Minna he wrote: 'To be sure, if the reactionaries wanted revenge on everyone who took any kind of part in the rising – they would have to prosecute half Saxony!' With all the insouciance of Goethe's Egmont he went off to Eisenach, intending to explore the Thuringian countryside on foot and visit the Wartburg. By chance the Grand Duchess Maria Pavlovna was on his train and she invited him to call on her in Eisenach that evening. He presented himself at the castle in his travelling clothes, and she received him among all her noble guests with uncommon kindness, talked to him for a long time and made him promise to visit her later in Weimar.

On his return he used his first free hour to write a long letter to Eduard Devrient, giving him a full account of his part in the rising and clearly intended for the eyes of Lüttichau. 'I shall hold out the olive branch, so as not to make the breach with Dresden irreconcilable,' he told Minna.[3]

While he was lulling himself in such illusions, the warrant for his arrest had already been drawn up. He heard from Minna on 19 May that its issue was imminent. At Liszt's urging he went into hiding in the nearby ducal domain of Magdala under the name of 'Professor Werder from Berlin', and there Minna paid him a birthday visit on 22 May. Their initial conciliatory mood quickly dispersed under the pressure of events and she could see in him only an 'ill-advised and thoughtless man', who had plunged them both into the most dreadful situation. When they took leave of each other in Jena on 24 May the breach, which was never again to be completely mended, had already taken place within them.

On 27 May Wagner travelled by express coach via Rudolstadt, Saalfeld, Coburg, Lichtenfels and Nuremberg to Lindau on Lake Constance. Stepping on to the steamer for Rorschach the next day, on a beautiful spring morning, with the Swiss mountains shimmering on the other shore of the lake, he was quite unaware that he had escaped a sentence of death.

But he had incurred one lifelong enemy. Among the Prussian troops who fought in Dresden in May 1849 was a lieutenant in the Grenadiers called Botho von Hülsen, who was appointed general intendant of the Berlin court opera two years later. The reluctance with which he allowed Wagner to be performed in the theatre is already well known, the motive less so. When Wagner wanted to call on him in 1863, after his amnesty, Hülsen wrote to Hans von Bülow on 14 February: 'I cannot deny my personal feelings, and after our encounter in Dresden in May 1849 it is repugnant to me to enter into any kind of personal relationship with the aforesaid.'[4] And when it was expected, after Wagner's death, that the Berlin opera would commemorate a great German composer in some fitting way, Hülsen refused the Wagner Society permission to hold such a ceremony in the house, on the grounds that the theatre could not be made available for private functions.

# 15

*Wieland der Schmied*

On the night of 29 May 1849 the doorbell began to ring loudly in the house of the musician Alexander Müller in the Rennweg in Zürich. Müller put his head out of the window. 'Who's that at this hour?' 'Hurry up and open the door,' came a voice from below, 'it's me, Richard Wagner!' Müller's daughter said later that she would never forget Wagner's arrival at their house. 'He stormed up the stairs, threw his arms round my father and cried: "Alexander, you must let me stay with you, I'm safe here!" '

He and Müller had become friends in Würzburg in 1833, and it was another of the strokes of luck that helped him on his flight that Müller now lived in Zürich and could take him in, introduce him to two cantonal officials, Jakob Sulzer and Franz Hagenbuch, and help him to get a Swiss passport for his journey on to Paris. 'To my complete astonishment I have found that I am famous here,' Wagner wrote to Theodor Uhlig, his friend in the Dresden orchestra, 'thanks to the vocal scores of all my operas, whole acts of which have been frequently performed at concerts and by choral societies.' (9 August)

He arrived with no luggage but a lightweight brown coat and what he could carry in a single bag slung over his shoulder. At the moment when he caught his first glimpse of the Lake of Zürich framed by the Glarner Alps as he approached Zürich from Oberstrass, he made a subconscious decision that he wanted to stay there. All at once he felt a surge of new strength to create the most important work of his life but, to please Liszt and Minna, he tried to persuade himself that he had to do it in Paris. Planning to leave Switzerland again after only two days, he felt like closing his eyes to the land he was travelling through, like Tannhäuser: 'Verschloßnen

Aug's, ihr Wunder nicht zu schauen'. (29 May, RWBC, pp. 319ff.)

Renewing his acquaintance with Paris was worse than he had anticipated. 'What is going on inside me is indescribable,' he complained to Minna. 'Memories, the present and the future, are all pressing in on me . . . Alas, my Swiss courage has already nearly gone.' While he still held fast to the necessity of Paris for his future, he confessed to Liszt that he would not be able to create works with which to storm the French capital if he stayed there. 'I cannot work in Paris and without hearth and home – by which I mean peace of mind: I must find a new spot where I can feel at home and resolve to stay at home. I think that Zürich is that spot.' (18 June) Meanwhile he passed the time by reading Proudhon's *De la propriété*, which afforded him in those circumstances, as he said, strangely lavish consolations.

He returned to Zürich early in July, with the idea for an essay on art and revolution as his sole gain. He submitted it to one of the larger French periodicals, which returned it with the remark that it would be of no interest to their readers. He promptly sent it to the Leipzig publisher Otto Wigand, who paid him 5 louisdor, in view of the stir it was likely to cause.

*Art and Revolution* was the first of the Zürich essays which were, in a sense, the means of sublimating his revolutionary ideas. In the one-sidedness of their point of view, in their simplification of the problems they discuss, they cannot be described as contributions to an objective philosophy of art. But those same qualities make them all the more valuable as the documents of Wagner's struggle to create a new artistic ideal, which can be seen taking an ever surer form from one essay to the next: *Art and Revolution, The Artwork of the Future, Opera and Drama* and *A Communication to my Friends*.

Even in the first of these essays we can see him 'hewing out' this ideal for himself from the Greek experience: re-creating a day at a festival in the Attic theatre, the references to *Prometheus* – the profoundest of all the tragedies – and to Apollo in *The Eumenides* – evoked by the tragedian under the inspiration of Bacchus – these are the products of his reading of Droysen and Karl Otfried Müller in Dresden. (*Die Kunst und die Revolution*, RWGS, III, pp. 8ff.)

Forced though his exile was, it was freedom to Wagner; he enjoyed the understanding and sympathy of his new friends, especially Jakob Sulzer, and when he read the text of *Siegfrieds Tod* to a small group he declared that he had never had a more attentive male audience. The one cloud in his happiness was Minna's obstinate silence to his imploring letters: 'I must always feel that I have a home – and only you, my dear wife, are my home.' (29 May; RWBC, pp. 319ff.) At last on 18 July she announced her readiness to join him in Zürich. 'I hope you will appreciate, my dear Richard, that in coming to you I am making *no small sacrifice*. What kind of future lies in store for me, what can you offer me?' (RWBC, pp. 337ff.)

She finally arrived at the beginning of September, with the dog, the parrot and Natalie. Her immediate threat that she would go straight back to Dresden if her husband did not behave himself cast a slight chill on the joy of their reunion, so he had to fall back on the affection of Peps and Papo. The odd little family moved into a modest apartment in the Hintere Escherhäuser, where Minna made them quite comfortable, thanks to her domestic talents and the generosity of Sulzer – whose office of 'Staatsschreiber' (secretary in the employ of the cantonal government) she initially understood to be the loftier position of 'Stadtschreiber' (town clerk).

Wagner, who had had to promise her to make an effort to have an operatic success in Paris, devoted himself to theorizing about art the while. Sitting in the Café Littéraire one afternoon, surrounded by card-players and tobacco fumes, he was dreamily surveying the cheap wallpaper covered with scenes from classical mythology, when his thoughts turned from the recent upheavals in the world at large to his own inner life. And suddenly a picture he had seen as a boy flashed upon his mind: Bonaventura Genelli's *Dionysus among the Muses of Apollo*. 'There and then I conceived the ideas of my *Artwork of the Future*.'

It must have been at about the time when he first saw Schröder-Devrient as Fidelio, while he was still a pupil at the Nikolaischule, that he first saw Genelli's watercolour in the house of his brother-in-law Brockhaus. He often stood gazing at it in enchantment, and confessed that it was one of the first things to give him an idea of the Greek spirit of beauty. When he visited Genelli's patron, Count Schack, in Munich thirty years later, he spent a long time looking at the works he owned by this neglected artist, especially at his *Bacchus among the Muses*, another version of the Leipzig painting. He told the count that he had known the artist in his youth, and his compositions had exercised an important influence on his own work. What attracted him to Genelli was the intimation of a new conception of

Greek culture that went beyond Winckelmann's classical ideal of 'noble simplicity and reposeful grandeur' and that was here epitomized in the encounter of the Dionysian and the Apollonian. It is significant that *The Artwork of the Future* was conceived under this sign. (*Das Kunstwerk der Zukunft*, RWGS, III, pp. 42ff.)

Keeping up a running battle with the cold in their sunless apartment and the worry as to where their next meal was coming from, Wagner finished the essay on 4 November. He later dedicated it to the philosopher Ludwig Feuerbach: 'To none but you, honoured sir, can I dedicate this work, for with it I have given back to you what is your own.' (RWGS, XII, pp. 284f.) Feuerbach's reply gave him great joy: he did not understand how opinion could be divided over the book; he had read it with enthusiasm, even delight, and he had to assure him of his fullest sympathy, his warmest thanks. (Quoted by Wagner to Uhlig, 20 September 1850)

Wagner confessed that it had always been his ambition to immerse himself in philosophy in much the same way as he had plunged into the depths of music under the mystical influence of the Choral Symphony. After wrestling in vain with Schelling's *System of Transcendental Idealism* in his youth, he had later tried again with Hegel's *Lectures on the Philosophy of History*, which was in his Dresden library: much of it had impressed him deeply and the greater the difficulty he had in understanding some things the harder he had tried to get to the bottom of the 'absolute'. During the retreat from Dresden a German Catholic preacher, a serious young man in an enormous sombrero, had recommended Feuerbach to him as the 'right and only philosopher of modern times'. In Zürich Wagner lost no time in acquiring a copy of his *Thoughts on Death and Immortality*, which was banned in Germany; it had struck him as bold and rewarding to find that true immortality was conferred solely on sublime deeds or inspired works of art.

Feuerbach's influence can already be seen in *Art and the Revolution*, but the claims to have traced it in *Jesus von Nazareth* or even in the articles published in Röckel's *Volksblätter* are refuted in the first place by Wagner's own account of his reading of Feuerbach and above all by the total absence of any of his works from the Dresden library.

It is because it was conceived as a vision that *The Artwork of the Future* is so difficult a text to understand: it is as a vision that it must be read. 'I have no desire to make any alterations,' Wagner wrote when he sent the manuscript to Uhlig; 'once something like this has been written it has to be allowed to stand as it is: the strengths and weaknesses are quite accurately related to each other for the most part.' In the event it was fundamentally misunderstood and only gave rise to two indestructible new catch-phrases. Professor Bischoff, the editor of the Cologne *Niederrheinische Musikzeitung*, achieved immortality of a kind by coining the howler 'music of the future', but Wagner's friends on Brendel's *Neue Zeitschrift für Musik* hung a worse millstone round his neck with their theorizing about the 'total artwork'. Anyone who goes to the original sixteen volumes of Wagner's *Schriften und Dichtungen*, in search of further information about this apparently central concept, will encounter an initial difficulty: the term is not to be found in the 132-page index. Wagner does in fact use it once, in *The Artwork of the Future*, at a point where he is contemplating the supplementation of the 'three purely human arts' – music, poetry and the dance – with what, in an unpublished note, he called the 'ancillary aids of drama': architecture, sculpture and painting. The Utopian character of a work of art that would absorb all the separate arts into itself in such a way is further emphasized by the proviso that it would be the creation not of a single genius but of the 'genius of community', of a free association of artists, led by the performer, who is both the writer and the composer. That is the context in which Wagner used the expression 'total artwork', or to be more precise 'total artwork of the future'. It is obvious that he meant two complementary things by it: a totality of the arts and a totality of artists.

But disciples are usually the same: with unerring skill they single out the exceptional and extravagant among their teacher's dicta. Not content with rallying to the 'artwork of the future', they plucked 'total artwork' out of its context in the book, so that Wagner was to write to Liszt in complete despair that they weren't even capable of understanding his writings when they read them. (16 August 1853) 'There is no other reason why the fruit of all my efforts should be this wretched "special art" and "total art". Honestly: it makes me sick to talk to people without intelligence about things they do not and never will understand, because they simply have no trace of artistic and true human essence in them. If I were ever to write another polemic it would be far more likely to be against these "enlightened" wretches . . . But first and foremost, no mention of that wretched "total art" in the title!!!' It is as though he foresaw that the 'wretched' total artwork would still be a topic of discussion a hundred years later.

Wagner concludes his vision of the 'artwork of the future' with a vigorous coda in which he interprets the legend of Wayland Smith as a parable of the artist driven to forge wings for himself out of his own distress. When he finally had to give way to Liszt's and Minna's urgings to produce an operatic project for Paris, that was the subject he wrote up in a prose sketch, with dialogue, for a three-act drama, with the idea that the librettist Gustave Vaez should put it into French verse.

Then what seemed to be a last-minute chance of escaping the Parisian doom presented itself. Frau Julie Ritter, the widow of a merchant from Narva, now resident in Dresden and the mother of the young Karl Ritter, had heard of his straits and sent him 500 talers, as the first instance of the help she was to give him in the future. Furthermore, a young friend of hers, Jessie Taylor, who had visited Wagner with Karl Ritter the previous year in order to express her admiration of his work, and who was now married to a Bordeaux wine merchant, Eugène Laussot, wrote in terms of heartfelt sympathy. But when he put it to Minna that they would be able to manage on what they could get in Zürich after all, she completely lost her temper: if he did not make a serious effort to succeed in Paris then she would have to wash her hands of him; she was not going to sit and watch him go to the dogs in Zürich as a penniless writer and conductor of hole-and-corner concerts.

Wagner returned to Paris on 1 February 1850 and found, as he had expected, that the city where Meyerbeer was just celebrating the triumph of *Le Prophète* was no place for him. 'I am ill and my illness is called Paris,' he wrote to Sulzer. 'The struggle between my inner unwillingness and the urging of some of my friends and my good wife in particular has perhaps been sowing the seeds of my present illness for a long time . . . How can people fail to understand that no activity satisfies us and makes us happy, no activity is useful, in fact, except one that is in sympathy with our whole true nature!' (22 February 1850, FWSZ, I, p. 355)

Then something happened that threatened to bring about another fateful change in his destiny. It remained a secret for many years, until the publication of *Mein Leben* in 1911. The tale Wagner told there was confirmed and amplified by the publication of his correspondence with Frau Ritter in 1920 and of documents from the Burrell Collection in 1950.

In a letter to Liszt dated 6 February 1850 – not included in the official edition of their correspondence – he had mentioned that a third person – obviously Frau Ritter – had told him that a Madame Laussot of Bordeaux had put aside a not inconsiderable sum of money for him, with the intention that it should assure him a modest living. 'You know, my dear Liszt, I have few friends . . . Acknowledge that woman as your sister and one of like mind with you.' We now know, in fact, that the Ritters and the Laussots planned jointly to provide him with an annual income of 3000 francs. (RWBC, pp. 368ff.)

Now, in Paris, at the beginning of March, he received an invitation from the Laussots to visit them in Bordeaux. His meeting with Jessie in Dresden had been very brief, and it was only now that he got to know her well: she was young, beautiful and gifted and, since hearing *Tannhäuser* in Dresden, an ardent admirer of him and his work. She listened enthralled as he read the texts of *Siegfrieds Tod* and *Wieland der Schmied*, preferring the latter, as she found it easier to identify with the part of Wieland's bride Schwanhilde than with the unhappy Gutrune. For her part, she demonstrated her musical talent by playing him Beethoven's Hammerklavier Sonata with great understanding. Her intellectual and artistic calibre is further confirmed by the life she led, after divorcing Laussot, with her second husband the historian Karl Hillebrand, in Florence, where she took up a position at the centre of musical life, founding and directing the Società Cherubini, for which Liszt wrote her twelve anthems. She also wrote scholarly treatises and translated Schopenhauer's *Fourfold Root of Sufficient Reason* into English.

Bordeaux was like a new world for Wagner. The belief in his mission that he encountered there restored his self-confidence. He was now determined not to allow himself to be forced back into the operatic rat-race in Paris. When he confided to Jessie that all he really wanted to do was seek oblivion in Greece and the Orient, far from European civilization, she was surprised and overjoyed, and told him she was ready to share his lot.

Returning to Paris his first task was to inform Minna of his decision to leave her. He may have thought that, having made the same threat herself, she would agree to it with not too heavy a heart. But since she had just received a letter from Jessie, telling her of

Wagner's visit to Bordeaux and expressing the wish that he might now live and work entirely according to the promptings of his heart and advance towards his great goal unhindered by any exterior considerations, her female instinct recognized a rival to whom she could not afford to concede a single inch of ground. 'O false, treacherous creature!' she scribbled at the foot of the letter. (RWBC, pp. 376f.) She rallied their friends in Zürich to write an imploring letter to her husband, and herself set out for Paris, where she missed him, as he had gone to Geneva to avoid her.

He had already planned his flight, via Marseilles and Malta to Greece, and from there to the Near East. Jessie declared her determination to accompany him without hesitation. But on the point of departure he had a letter from her confessing that she had let her mother into the secret, that her husband had forthwith threatened to shoot Wagner, and that she herself had made up her mind not to follow him. Thunderstruck, Wagner wrote to tell Laussot that he was coming to Bordeaux to see him. But the house was empty: the outraged husband had preferred to take his household to the country and leave it to the police to send his rival packing.

Wagner retreated to Villeneuve on Lake Geneva, where he met Karl Ritter, whose mother also came hurrying when she received a despairing letter from him. They spent his thirty-seventh birthday together. The most bitter disappointment was yet to come, when Karl had a letter from Jessie letting it be known that in future she would throw any letters in Wagner's hand into the fire unread. It is easy enough to guess what induced her to make the break. The Burrell Collection contains a letter from her mother accompanying 'important papers' returned to Minna. Obviously some of Wagner's letters to Minna were used to turn Jessie against him. (RWBC, pp. 412f.)

One of the few people who knew of the episode, Hans von Bülow, a friend of Jessie's in her youth and again in age, later wrote to Karl Klindworth that this very attractive, intelligent and musical woman had some years earlier experienced an uncommon passion for Wagner, 'a passion that was, moreover, mutual and was brought to a sudden rift solely by the crossgrained counterpoint of unfavourable circumstances'. If she should visit Klindworth in London in the immediate future, Bülow went on, he could give her immense pleasure by playing her some of the music from the *Ring*:

'she deserves, as few others do, to be initiated in it'. (10 October 1858, NBB, p. 2)

In Villeneuve Frau Ritter's maternal solicitude restored Wagner's spirits. The way she stood by him even then and did not withdraw her hand from him was the best reassurance he could have had. Karl was despatched to Zürich to intercede with Minna, and gave so favourable a report of her reaction that Wagner himself wrote her a long letter recapitulating everything that had happened. (RWBC, pp. 403ff.) At the bottom of it she wrote: 'Not this letter, which contains many accusations that are untrue as well as hurtful, only my all too great love, which lets me forgive and forget what happened, do I thank for our reunion.'

'I arrived in Zürich with Karl Ritter four days ago', he wrote on 7 July to Ernst Benedikt Kietz, whom he had told of his plan for flight in Paris, 'without my horsetail and turban' – the oriental insignia of manhood. (RWBC, pp. 413f.)

On the face of it, the Jessie Laussot episode was an ordinary love affair, but at bottom it was yet another of the often violent attempts that Wagner the artist made to free himself. As the revolution had torn him from his position as kapellmeister, so the Bordeaux adventure released him from the phantom of making an operatic career in Paris. That subject was no longer mentioned.

In May, while he was still in Villeneuve, he had written a preface for *Siegfrieds Tod*, which he was thinking of publishing, believing that he would have to abandon the idea of ever setting it to music. 'So receive this work of literature that I offer you as what an honourable artist, after mature deliberation, can now offer only to his friends.' (RWGS, XVI, pp. 84f.) But in Zürich he wrote a composition sketch of the first two scenes, and with that we move into a new phase in the history of the creation of the *Ring*.

# 16

## From Heroic Opera to Mythic Drama

Minna had set up house in a modest apartment in Enge, the first suburb of Zürich along the left-hand shore of the lake. There was nowhere else in the whole wide world he wanted to live but here, Wagner wrote to Uhlig after his return. 'I go down in my house coat and bathe in the lake. There's a boat, which we row ourselves. And an excellent race of people, sympathy, kindness, the most touching readiness to be of service at every turn . . . Let me . . . say nothing of the very recent past and tell you briefly only this much, that I have got a new wife.'

Things were looking much better outside the home, too. 'Perform my *Lohengrin!*' he had appealed to Liszt from Paris. Now the first performance was due to take place in Weimar on 28 August, on Goethe's birthday and the occasion of the unveiling of a memorial to Herder. The theatre management had spared no expense and Liszt had spared himself no pains. He even touched on the possibility of performing *Siegfrieds Tod* and hoped to be able to procure Wagner an advance payment so that he could work without worries. 'I need the actors to play heroes such as our theatre has never yet seen,' Wagner replied; 'where are they to be found?' But in the first flush of enthusiasm he was ready to put such doubts on one side: 'I believe you are going about things in the best way to get them growing out of the ground for me.' (20 July 1850)

In this optimistic frame of mind, on 12 August he drafted a composition sketch for the Norns' scene and the opening of the Leavetaking scene between Siegfried and Brünnhilde.[1] The very first bars reveal an astonishing coincidence. The Norns' scene of *Siegfrieds Tod* differs somewhat in the text, but the music begins – as in *Götterdämmerung*, composed twenty years later – in E♭ minor (and in 6/4 time): a proof of how involuntarily and compellingly in Wagner the key proceeds from the situation. In both versions the rondo-like refrain of the question-and-answer framework returns, after temporary modulations, to the mysterious atmosphere of E♭ minor in the end. There are motivic reminiscences, too: the words the Norns repeat like a formula, 'In osten wob ich . . . ', anticipate the theme of the Ride of the Valkyries, though without the final modulation into the major; according to Jacob Grimm the Norns and the Valkyries were related. The setting of the Leavetaking scene is particularly interesting, since the words are the same as in *Götterdämmerung*: a piece of luck which will allow us to make a stylistic comparison in due course.

The composition sketch breaks off at Siegfried's words 'Brünnhildes zu gedenken!' and although Wagner assured Liszt on 16 August that the music for his 'Siegfried' (as he then called it) was haunting him in his very bones, he did not resume it. There were three reasons for this. His courage failed at the thought of finding, within a year, a singer capable of giving life to his Brünnhilde; there seemed to be too much bald narrative of events that had preceded curtain-rise; but the principal reason was the third, though as yet he was only dimly aware of it: the composition sketch is written in an astringent saga style, completely *sui generis*, but does not reveal the extensive background of the myth. His writing and thinking during the next six months were devoted to the problem of how to open up those perspectives.

Meanwhile he plunged once more into polemics, which he had believed himself to have done with. There was an association from his past that had long been irking him. As we have seen he had tried to accommodate his liking for Meyerbeer the man with his distaste for the composer. Then, in 1847, on the occasion of the Berlin *Rienzi*, he lost confidence in the man as well, suspecting some intrigue, although, as we now know, there is not the slightest shred of evidence for it even in Meyerbeer's diaries. When Meyerbeer tried to avoid him on a chance encounter in Paris in 1850, Wagner interpreted it as the sign of a bad conscience, though it is much more probable that Meyerbeer feared that a meeting with a man wanted for insurrection and high treason would compromise him, in his position as General Musical Director to the King of Prussia.

At all events, Wagner now believed that he was no longer under an obligation. His dislike of Meyerbeer's work had recently been revived by a performance of *Le Prophète* in Paris, and when he came upon the term 'Hebraic taste in art' in a review in the *Neue Zeitschrift für Musik* it became the watchword of his *Jewry in Music*.

He frankly admitted to Liszt in a letter of 18 April 1851 that the article was aimed solely at Meyerbeer: his relationship to Meyerbeer was odd and quite unique; he reminded him of what might almost be called the most vicious period of his life. 'It was the period of old-pal networks and backstairs arrangements, when we are made fools of by patrons to whom inwardly we are most decidedly not devoted. It is a relationship of the utmost dishonour: neither is sincere in his dealings with the other.' Meyerbeer's favours made it impossible for Wagner to make him the least reproach, so that he was actually glad not to be so much in his debt as, for instance, Berlioz. 'But it was time to free myself completely from the dishonest relationship to him: outwardly I did not have the least cause to do so . . . But inward reasons eventually forced me to abandon every regard for normal circumspection where he was concerned: I cannot exist as an artist in my own sight or that of my friends . . . without roundly declaring that in Meyerbeer I find in every respect my opposite . . . This is an act necessary for the complete birth of my mature being.'

Anticipating Liszt's disapproval, he added: 'These are secular matters, on which we can from time to time disagree, without ever being divided on sacred matters. – Whatever you don't care for here, just shut your eyes to!'

Wagner had never objected to Jewish origins among his friends and acquaintances before this time: he has often been accused of ingratitude, and yet he wrote in *Mein Leben* of Samuel Lehrs, for instance, by then long dead, with affection and gratitude. That he now singled out Meyerbeer's race for attack was the outcome of his efforts to give his criticism a completely personal edge. In the last resort that edge was directed against himself, against 'the most vicious period of his life'.

He returned to the subject of Meyerbeer in *Opera and Drama*, when he criticized contemporary grand opera. After sending the manuscript to Uhlig he began to have second thoughts: 'It would be dreadful if it proved possible to take the book as just an attack on Meyerbeer. I wish I could take back some of the things in that vein: when I am reading it, the mockery never sounds venomous – but perhaps when others read it it often sounds passionately embittered to them, which is not how I would wish to appear even to my enemies.' (10 March 1851)

The criticism in *Opera and Drama*, which refrained from any attack on his ancestry, wounded Meyerbeer more deeply than the earlier pamphlet. He felt so debilitated by an illness, he wrote in his diary on 24 November 1851, that he could not carry out his intention of getting on with the composition of his new opera. 'Moreover I am greatly demoralized by hearing from Burguy [his mother's secretary] that Richard Wagner has attacked me violently in his book on the future of opera.' He goes on to refer to his turning up again a manuscript essay by Wagner 'on the standpoint of Meyerbeer's music', in which Wagner praised him extravagantly and which he had sent him for publication ten years ago; this can only be the essay mentioned in Chapter 7, on *Les Huguenots*, to which Richard Sternfeld gave a date of 1837, since its wording corresponds to a letter Wagner wrote to Meyerbeer in that year. (*Über Meyerbeers Huguenotten*, RWGS, XII, pp. 22, 422; RWGB, I, p. 101)[2]

In the meantime *Lohengrin* had been performed for the first time, on 28 August 1850 in Weimar. Wagner and Minna celebrated in advance by making an excursion up the Rigi, and took it as a good omen when they saw the rare phenomenon of the Rigi spectre, when Richard, who had advanced to the very edge of the precipice, was reflected giant-size in the sky in the evening sunlight. They spent the evening of the performance itself in the inn Zum Schwanen in Lucerne. Stirred by a multitude of emotions, Wagner kept his watch in his hand to time the start and the probable ending, but he always felt a little strained, ill at ease and irritable, he later confessed, when he tried to share what should have been agreeable and exciting occasions with Minna.

The whole opera was a single, indivisible miracle, Liszt reported, and like the pious priest who had gone through the *Imitation of Christ* underlining the text word by word, he could underline *Lohengrin* note by note, though if he did he would go first to the duet in the third act, which to him was the acme of beauty and truth in art. (2 September)

'As far as I can now . . . judge the overall character of the Weimar production of my *Lohengrin*,' Wagner replied, 'the first most certain and incontestable thing that emerges from all the accounts is your incomparable exertion and dedication for the sake of my work, your touching love and the manifestation of your genius for doing the impossible as well as it possibly can be done.' (8 September) When he dedicated the score to Liszt two years later he wrote: 'You it was who awoke the dumb notation of this score to the bright life of sound: but for your rare love to me my work would still lie silent – perhaps forgotten by myself – in a box with my domestic effects: no ear would have been reached by what moved my heart and delighted my imagination when I wrote it, nearly five years ago now, performance always vivid in my mind.' (May 1852)

Though the theatre at Weimar was not one of the great houses of Germany, this première marked a new epoch in Wagner's career. The world was accustomed to look on the first performances of his works as local, Dresden occasions and waited to read about them in the spiteful columns of the local critics, Carl Banck and Julius Schladebach. But *Lohengrin* had been presented to a new forum, an audience of strangers, and its success could neither be denied nor concealed. The mere fact of the presence at the première of leading figures from the musical world both in Germany and abroad proved the standing of the exiled composer. For the first time, too, voices were heard expressing good will, even enthusiasm: Franz Müller, a senior civil servant in Weimar, who wrote for the *Konversationsblatt* of Frankfurt, Adolf Stahr in the Berlin *Nationalzeitung*, J. C. Lobe in the Leipzig *Signale*, Uhlig in the *Neue Zeitschrift für Musik*, and Gérard de Nerval in *La Presse* of Paris. If Nerval showed more good will than actual understanding, he nevertheless deserves to be hailed as the precursor of the French *wagnéristes*. Wagner was now a phenomenon so widely discussed that even adverse criticism could no longer put him down but, as Newman points out, only added to his publicity. Moreover the Weimar production broke a taboo, the idea that only theatres with performers of the calibre of Tichatschek and Schröder-Devrient at their disposal could dare to stage Wagner's works. From now on there began a steadily increasing demand for them at the smaller houses – or at those where the musical director had no operatic aspirations of his own – the most sought after, to begin with, being *Tannhäuser*. If Wagner had earned any royalties from the performances he would soon have been in the position to support himself without being a burden on his friends.

The Weimar *Lohengrin* had no less profound consequences for his new work. According to Karl Ritter, his emissary at the first performance, the musical execution was good, but the dramatic side was all wrong. This had a decisive effect on the fate of *Siegfrieds Tod*. The first person to whom he mentioned it was his old Parisian friend Ernst Benedikt Kietz. He was still thinking of setting his 'Siegfried', he wrote on 14 September, but he was not prepared to let it be performed in just any theatre that happened to make an offer for it. On the contrary, he was laying the most audacious of plans, the realization of which could not cost less than 10,000 talers. With that sum he would build a wooden theatre right there where he was and employ the most suitable singers. He would invite all those who were interested in his works and give – gratis, of course – three consecutive performances in one week, after which the theatre would be pulled down and that would be the end of the whole affair. Something on those lines was all that appealed to him now. now. 'If Karl Ritter's uncle dies I shall get the money!' (RWBC, p. 415)

A week later he wrote to Uhlig that whether he would let Weimar give the first performance of 'Siegfried' was a question he would probably be able to answer only with an unconditional No. Although the intendant had assured him that *Lohengrin* was and would remain a success at the box office, nevertheless he probably didn't need to emphasize that he hoped 'Siegfried's' launching on the world would be different from what the good people there were capable of giving it. Then he again unfolded the plan he had revealed to Kietz which, he admitted, looked a real chimera on the face of it. 'Now do I seem downright mad to you? It may be so, but I assure you that achieving it is the hope of my life!' (20 September)

For the time being these were dreams of the future which he confided to no one else. 'I have had a great deal to think about again,' he told Liszt, 'alas, to think about *again*! But now once and for all I've come to a point where I cannot go back: I *must* think things through to their conclusion, before I can become an instinctive, completely confident artist again.' (2 October) And even more urgently after quite a long silence: 'I regard the eventual adoption of my artistic plans, to which I am now applying myself, as one of the most important factors in my life. . . I had to make a clean sweep of a whole life, bring all that was dawning in me to full consciousness, master by its own agency the reflection that inexorably rose upon me.' (25 November)

He was referring to an article he was writing on the 'nature of opera', which grew during the course of the winter to a whole book, *Opera and Drama*. 'It is a very remarkable work,' he told Cosima in 1879, 'and I was very excited when I wrote it, for it is without a predecessor in the history of art, and I was really aiming at a target no one could see.' (BBL 1937, p. 106)

The excitement that pursued him on his lonely way vented itself in some strange, exalted ideas. With true fanaticism he prescribed a 'water cure' for himself and his friends, on the grounds that 'radical water' is the only release any of us have from an unnatural physical state. At the same time he proposed a 'fire cure' for mankind in the form of a new revolution which was to start with the firing of Paris as a beacon. 'You'll see how much better we shall be after this fire cure!' he exclaimed to the horrified Uhlig.[3] The following year he survived two months of a hydropathic cure in Albisbrunn, though he was in a terrible nervous state and lost a great deal of weight, which goes to show the fundamental soundness of his constitution in spite of all his complaints and suffering.

*Opera and Drama* was nothing less than the theoretical expression of an 'artistic–productive process' – the outward manifestation of his great drama on the Nibelung's ring, which was developing deep within him while he was writing the book. The third part of it, 'Poetry and Music in the Drama of the Future', as he told Uhlig, penetrates to the fundamentals. It is illuminating that artistic practice had already preceded the theory. 'I had to wait until now to realize that I would not have discovered the most important factors in the shaping of the drama of the future, if I had not already stumbled upon them completely unawares as an artist in my "Siegfried".' The great significance of the 1850 composition sketch lies in its illustration of how the preliminary practice was not confined to the text alone, but also affected the musical setting as well.

'Here is my testament,' he told Uhlig when he sent him the manuscript. 'I wrote the last pages . . . in a mood that I could not describe lucidly to anyone.' He had withdrawn so far from the present that it had grown completely still about him and he had sometimes seemed to himself to be dead.

Shortly before completing the book, he had suffered the loss of his familiar spirit and domestic genius: the little parrot, which had always had a cheerful whistle to greet him with, had died. 'Oh – if I could tell you all that has died for me with that little creature!!! I don't care in the least if people laugh at me: what I feel, I feel . . . It happened three days ago – and still nothing can soothe me: – and it's just the same with my wife: – the bird was something unforced between us and for us.' (To Uhlig, mid–February; to Liszt, 18 February 1851)

It had not been long before it emerged that they had little left in common; and the pets, the dog and the bird, had had to take the place of the children and interests that might have linked them. For all Minna's excellent qualities she unfortunately did not have the least understanding of his essential being, he complained to Liszt: 'I am inwardly a stranger to her.' (9 March)

At the same time that he was working on the book, he had not been able to rid himself all winter of an idea for a comic opera based on the Grimms' fairy tale about 'the boy who left home to learn fear', which threatened to distract his attention from Siegfried altogether. 'Imagine the shock I had', he wrote to Uhlig on 10 May, 'when I suddenly recognized that that boy is none other than – young Siegfried, who wins the treasure and wakes Brünnhilde.' *Der Junge Siegfried* would have the immense advantage of presenting the myth to the audience playfully, as a fairy tale does to a child, and it would moreover prepare the performers for the daunting task of *Siegfrieds Tod*.

He had just drafted the first prose sketch before he wrote that letter, and the confidence of the scenario reveals how much the plan had already matured in his head. He wrote the full-scale prose draft between 24 May and 1 June and completed the verse text in the following three weeks, 3–24 June. *Der Junge Siegfried* had entered the world, entire and well rhymed, that very morning, he wrote hastily on 24 June to Uhlig, who was on the point of leaving Dresden to come and visit him in Switzerland.

Liszt, too, was made privy to the new plan, partly because it occurred to Wagner that perhaps it would after all be possible to entrust the two 'Siegfrieds' to the Weimar theatre. But he hesitated to send him the text: 'What I have written is – I'm afraid – not good enough for my purpose, but if I can read it aloud to you – giving some idea of how I think it ought to be – then that would completely reassure me as to the impression I want my text to make on you.' (29 June)

But although he had thought that this text would absolve him once and for all from ever writing prose again, he had, once more, crowed too soon. Breitkopf & Härtel were going to publish an edition of the texts of *Der Fliegende Holländer, Tannhäuser* and *Lohengrin*, and for this he wrote a long autobiographical preface, the *Communication to my Friends. (Eine Mitteilung an meine Freunde,* RWGS, IV, pp. 230ff.)* As he put it in a letter to Liszt, the *Communication* is an admission of how far he too had wandered trying to find the right artistic path, and he was not one of those elect of God into whose mouths the one true, solid food of art drops as manna from heaven. Only the *completed Tannhäuser*, the *completed Lohengrin* made him conscious of the direction in which an unconscious instinct had steered him. What he wanted to explain to his friends was the turn he was now making away from romantic opera to mythic drama. (22 May)

As chance would have it, the printing was held up because Breitkopf & Härtel took the preface for a delayed revolutionary tract: as businessmen, they indicated, they held aloof from political involvement of any kind; but as Wagner lived outside the frontiers of the German Federation, they would be held accountable. By the time the offending passages had been altered and the book had gone to press the situation had fundamentally changed.

Wagner had embarked on his drastic hydropathic cure at Albisbrunn on 15 September: the idea of being in perfect health when he went back to his 'Siegfried' appealed to him as both pleasing and seemly. After only a fortnight he reported to Uhlig that Albisbrunn was doing him the world of good: whereas to begin with he had still been plagued by theory, it was now gradually dispersing from his brain like a grey mist. Two weeks later still, on 12 October, came the first announcement of the tetralogy: 'More big ideas for "Siegfried"': three dramas with a three-act prologue – if all the theatres in Germany collapse, I will put up a new one on the Rhine, issue my summons and perform the whole work in the course of one week.' In November he made the first drafts of the prose sketches of *Das Rheingold* and *Die Walküre* and returned to Zürich on 23 November, where he had in the meantime moved to rooms on Zeltweg.

It was clear to him that his plan entailed a break not only with Weimar but with the contemporary theatre as a whole. 'With this conception of mine I *totally* abandon all connection with the theatre and audiences of today: I break decisively and forever with the formulas of the present time,' he told Uhlig. And then followed an admission that was omitted from the edition of their correspondence and first published in *Bayreuther Blätter* in 1892: 'I cannot think of a *performance* until *after the revolution*, only the revolution can give me the artists and the audiences . . . Then I will summon what I need out of the ruins: I will find *then* what I must have.' (12 November; RWBC, p. 783)

He had hoped that *A Communication to my Friends* would appear before his new plans became known, so that Liszt would have been assured of his original good intentions, at least, in respect of Weimar. As a result of the delay he was obliged to alter the conclusion so as to announce the project of three dramas and a prologue, of which it was as yet still quite uncertain when and how they would eventually reach the public. At the same time, on 20 November, he wrote Liszt a letter, running to ten pages in print, rendering him a full account of the development of his idea from the first draft of 1848 to the tetralogy: the expansion was not the product of wilful calculation of extraneous factors, he explained but had forced itself upon him as the necessary consequence of the nature and content of the material.

'You just get on with it,' Liszt replied, 'and don't concern yourself with anything but your work, for which we might as well now give you the same commission as the cathedral chapter in Seville gave their architect: "Build us a temple such that future generations will surely say that the chapter was mad to undertake something so extraordinary." And yet the cathedral stands!' (1 December)

It was another of the eleventh-hour strokes of luck in Wagner's life that a sudden legacy enabled Frau Ritter to ensure him an annuity of 800 talers. That it should have come precisely at that moment could not but seem almost providential. 'Thanks to this security I am . . . as one newborn,' he wrote to the friend who had become like a mother to him; 'my head is full of the most provocative and exhilarating artistic plans.' (9 December)

All the time his plan was growing, he was alive to the natural beauties of Switzerland. In a letter to Otto Wesendonk in 1859 he wrote with nostalgia of 'glorious Switzerland', where he had conceived his works 'with the sublime, gold-crowned mountains before my eyes'. Before going to Albisbrunn, inspired by the quincentennial celebrations in Zürich, he had spent a week with Uhlig following the paths traced in Schiller's *Wilhelm Tell*, which led them from Brunnen on the east shore of the Lake of Lucerne through 'the fearful mountains of the Surennes' to the Maderaner valley, where the 'sublime Alpine world' of the Tödi came into view. He made no further progress with his work during the winter, but he wrote the full prose draft of *Das Rheingold* in March 1852, and both the prose sketch and the verse text of *Die Walküre* in May and June, while staying in the Pension Rinderknecht on the slopes of the Zürichberg, 'in the open air, with unimpeded views of the lake and the distant Alps'. It was here that he first thought of the episode of the May night bursting its way into Hunding's hut, which is absent from the earlier sketches: in the full prose sketch, 'Siegmund points to the beauty of the spring night, no one has gone out: Spring has opened the door and entered; the fresh, intoxicating scents of the forest reach us; the nightingale tells her sad tale . . .'

On 2 July he told Uhlig that he had finished *Die Walküre* the day before after a month's work, 'I am rather worn out once again: I am simply putting too much passion into my work!' So the next thing he did was set off on another tour, mostly on foot, from Interlaken via the Gries glacier to Domodossola, climbing en route the Faulhorn and the Siedelhorn, which gave him amazing views of Mont Blanc and Monte Rosa.

After that, he found the courage in the autumn to write the verse text of *Das Rheingold* and make a final revision of *Der Junge Siegfried* and *Siegfrieds Tod*. 'My only major concern now is the Nibelung poem,' he confessed in the middle of his work, 'that is the only thing, it uplifts me, high and powerfully, whenever I turn to it. I am averse to the thought of posterity, and yet this vanity of vanities creeps up on me now and then, when my poem issues out of my soul into the world. It is and it contains everything I can do and everything I have.' (To Uhlig, 14 October)

The fundamental structure of the fable of the *Ring* was already present in the 1848 essay, *The Nibelung Myth as the Scenario for a Drama*, but it acquired certain new characters and new situations during the next four years. The *Scenario* lacked Loge, Freia and Erda: the last is unknown to German mythology and was Wagner's own invention, a Greco-German mother–prophetess, uniting Aeschylus's Gaea (*The Eumenides*, V, 2) and the Eddic Völva (from whom Jacob Grimm deduced an Old High German Wala).

Two important elements were not incorporated until quite a late stage. Alberich's curse on love took from the ring its purely magical power and made it an ethical symbol of universal significance: as the material shaped itself in Wagner's hands, the renunciation – or the denial – of love became the governing dramatic motive up to the moment of Siegfried's death. And the World-Ash, slowly withering away from the wound incurred when Wotan tore off a branch to make his spear, now provided the mythic background to the revised version of the Norns' scene, Waltraute's narration and the finale.

But the most significant departure from the 1848 sketch is the turn the work takes into tragedy. Originally *Siegfrieds Tod* ended with Brünnhilde proclaiming the restoration of Wotan's reign:

> Nur einer herrsche:
> Allvater! Herrlicher du!

('Let one alone rule: Allfather, Lord, you!');

while *Götterdämmerung* ends with his freely chosen eclipse:

> Ruhe! Ruhe, du Gott!

Two interpretations have been put on this, one philosophical, the other political, and both mistaken. The former, attributing the change to the influence of Schopenhauer, is easily answered: the Annals record Wagner's first reading of *The World as Will and Idea* in September 1854, eighteen months after the private first edition of the text of the *Ring* in February 1853.

According to the other interpretation, Wagner the revolutionary, disillusioned by Louis Napoleon's *coup d'état* of 2 December 1851, inwardly admitted defeat, gave up the struggle against the nineteenth century and gave the *Ring* a pessimistic, nihilistic construction. The reasoning is attractive, but it is false for all that. Apart from the version of *Siegfrieds Tod* published in the complete edition of Wagner's writings, there is a later manuscript copy that can be dated early in 1849, owned by the Sulzer family of Zürich. In that, Brünnhilde's final words are crossed out and replaced initially by a few lines in which she speaks to the guilt of the gods and promises them 'blessed expiation'. But this change still did not satisfy Wagner: following a sudden inspiration, he scribbled a third version sideways up the margin:

> erbleichet in Wonne vor des Menschen Tat,
> vor dem Helden, den ihr gezeugt!
> Aus eurer bangen Furcht
> verkünd ich euch selige Todeserlösung!

('Grow pale in bliss before the deed of the man, before the hero you begot! Out of your dread I proclaim to you blessed absolution in death!')

This is no less than the complete reversal of Wotan's destiny into a tragic one. The note in the margin can moreover be dated fairly precisely: since it is in the old German script it must have been written before Wagner changed to using Latin script, which he did in 1850. Nothing tangible came of it for some time, but when Wagner started to draft the first sketches for *Der Junge Siegfried* in May 1851, the following immediately meets the eye:

> Wodan and the Wala: the gods' end. Wodan's decision: the Wala sinks away.

The tragic theme crystallizes here, in the scene between the Wanderer and Erda in the third act, the 'heart of the great cosmic tragedy', and from here it reaches out to inform every section of the tetralogy. The sketches for *Rheingold* and *Walküre* followed in November, with the greatest space allotted to the tragic catastrophe in the second act of the latter, and by the time the news of the coup in Paris on 2 December 1851 broke on the world, the tragic turn to the *Ring*, which had started to take shape two years before, had already been accomplished.

But while the political event was too late to exercise any influence on his text, it inflamed rather than dampened his thoughts. Together with the poet Georg Herwegh, he wrote to Uhlig on 18 December, he had decided on something which could prove to be a turning point in history. He was going to devote his literary activity to nothing else from that time forth, his goal being a positive, practical purpose of immeasurable consequence and moreover one that no reactionary power in the world would be able to hinder. (RWBC, p. 784) Whatever these cryptic hints may have meant, the last thing they suggest is inward defeat.

He expressed himself in even more radical terms to Ernst Benedikt Kietz: 'The whole of my political creed is nothing other than the bloodiest hatred of our whole civilization, contempt for everything that springs from it, and longing for nature . . . Everything in our country is riddled with servility: there is nobody in all France who knows that we are nonetheless human beings, except perhaps Proudhon – and even he is none too clear about it! – In all Europe I prefer the dogs to these doglike people. And yet I do not despair of a *future*; but only the most fearful and destructive of revolutions can make our civilized beasts "human" again.' And then he voices for the first time an idea that stirred him again a quarter of a century later: 'I am thinking about America a great deal now! Not that I would find right there, but because it would be easier to implant there.' (30 December; RWBC, p. 257)

But violent outbursts like this do not disguise the fact that his belief in revolution was by now only a habit of thought essential to his creative work. As the hope of a revolution in 1848 had given him the desperate courage necessary to embark on the Nibelung plan, so now he had to sustain the illusion so as not to lose his courage in the face of the dissatisfactions of his present circumstances. Once he had established the dimensions of his plan, laid down the width, height and depth of it, the idea of revolution lost its creative importance and nothing more was heard of it all the time that he was at work on the music.

It was neither philosophy nor politics that dictated the tragic turn taken by Wotan's fate in the *Ring*: his tragedy revealed itself to Wagner in exactly the degree that the mythological figure took on the attributes of individuality, of *humanity*.

The many stages in the composition of the text, from the first notes and sketches to the first and then the final drafts of the poem, amounting to more than 750 pages in all, can be traced more completely in the case of the *Ring* than any other of the major works. It emerges all the more surely that research into the sources, or historico-biographical interpretations, will not plumb the mystery of its genesis. The final form of the work was not the product of wilful calculation, Wagner had told Liszt: it forced itself on him as the necessary consequence of the material. As Thomas Mann remarks, we have to relive the 'ecstatic amazement' Wagner himself experienced in the course of writing the text, if we are to realize how little the artist originally knew about his work. 'The ambition is not the artist's, it is the work's: the work's own will to be far greater than the artist believed he might hope, or dare, imposes itself upon him.'

'The work imposes its will upon the artist' – and how relentlessly! His whole day was a strict regimen, he told Frau Ritter, in order to gain two beneficial hours in the morning to work in. 'As the result of a gestation like this I have now brought the complete poem of my *Ring* into the world: this birth gives me great joy; like an enfeebled mother I have diverted my best fluids to it and with luck no one will notice how it came about.' (29 December 1852) As usual he was impatient to unveil the new work to his friends. On 18 December he set off with Georg Herwegh to read it to their friends François and Eliza Wille in Mariafeld on two consecutive days. He spent a fee that he had had for *Tannhäuser* on printing fifty copies of it for private circulation. He derived especial pleasure from the thought of sending it to his friend Uhlig already in print, but it was too late: Uhlig died on 3 January 1853. In the middle of February Wagner arranged a reading of the tetralogy on four evenings in the Hotel Baur au Lac, and was astonished to find the room was fuller on each successive evening.

Part IV: *Der Ring des Nibelungen* (I) (1853–1857)

# 17

The Vision of La Spezia

'I am greatly occupied with the musical setting now', Wagner wrote to Frau Ritter on 29 December 1852, a fortnight after he had finished his text. But the preoccupation had started much earlier. Even before the composition sketch of August 1850 he wrote down some preliminary sketches for *Siegfrieds Tod* on a folio sheet which has survived:[1] fragments of the Norns' scene and the Leavetaking scene, and the Valkyries' chorus from the first act ('Nach süden wir ziehen, siege zu zeugen . . . '), sung to a melody that later became the orchestral form of the Valkyries' motive. This theme, so very characteristic of the style inaugurated in the *Ring*, is thus the earliest surviving leitmotiv of the entire work. (The theme turns up again in an *Albumblatt* of 23 July 1851 and in an inscription in an autograph album dated 12 November 1852.)

It is less easy to know precisely what other musical developments came out of these years of preparation, apart from notes of individual motives and remarks Wagner made during the period about singing the free, rhythmic Nibelung line. Certainly the most important thing was that, although against his will, Wagner engaged once again in the performance of music. On his recommendation Karl Ritter had been appointed conductor at the Zürich municipal theatre for the 1850–1 season. However, when it became all too apparent at Ritter's first rehearsals that he was almost completely unequipped for the post, Wagner recognized that he had an obligation to the management to take his place. The fact that Hans von Bülow also wanted to come to Zürich to study conducting with him was, in his eyes, yet another burden.

Bülow, though consumed by a passion for music, was being forced by his parents to study law. 'Pray allow . . . a man who, now

169

in his maturity, has become accustomed to think and to act not by halves but always whole-heartedly – so far as it lies in his power – to tell you his opinion on this matter,' Wagner implored Frau von Bülow. He had observed, he wrote, that her son's love of music was founded on great, indeed exceptional, ability. 'Give your consent, freely, gladly and soon, to your son's not living an instant longer under a yoke that is incompatible with his well-founded and tested inclination.' His plea was in vain. Bülow asked him once more for advice, to which Wagner replied: '*You alone* must know the strength of your love for art and your dislike for the law; I have no doubts about your ability.' (5 October 1850) That message was conveyed to him by Karl Ritter at his father's house, Schloss Ötlishausen in the Thurgau. After walking through foul weather for two days the two young men arrived on Wagner's doorstep in Zürich on 7 October. 'I had to act,' Bülow wrote to his mother, 'act wholly, leave no bridge behind for return, for possible repentance. There is no going back on this decision now. I am going to be a musician.'

By contrast with Ritter, he at once demonstrated an innate ability to govern an orchestra. But he had the misfortune to earn the displeasure of the all-powerful prima donna, and had to resign after only two months. The post was filled by Franz Abt, while Wagner, carefully avoiding any permanent appointment, continued to conduct certain works until the end of the season.

The choice he made from the limited Zürich repertory, with the *Ring* stirring inside him, is illuminating. He began with *Der Frei-schütz* and finished with *Fidelio*. *Norma* was a voice from the past, recalling his enthusiasm for Bellini when he was twenty-four. As he said in a letter to Liszt, he regarded the works of the older French school as the most suitable for developing a dramatic performance style, because they embodied a natural dramatic intention in the most easily assimilable form. How was a company that could not put on competent and effective performances of works by Cheru-bini, Méhul or Boieldieu to cope in the fullness of time with the enormous demands of his operas? (22 May 1851) In fact he only had the opportunity to conduct *La Dame Blanche* during that season, and the deficiencies of the Zürich theatre are illustrated by the fact that, in the absence of a harp, the music for that instrument which accompanies the appearance of the White Lady had to be played by Bülow on the piano; he did it 'with a wonderfully beautiful effect'.

Of the two works by Mozart that he conducted, *Die Zauberflöte* and *Don Giovanni*, the latter has a certain significance in that he did not limit himself to preparing the musical performance, but undertook also a cautious editing of the text and the recitatives. He told Uhlig that he had put in some careful shading in the orchestral part, made a new translation of the dialogue and run some of the scenes together, to reduce the need for changing the set. As an instance of this he cited the combination of the scene in the cemetery with Donna Anna's aria. 'After Don Juan and Leporello have gone off over the wall, the orchestra softly holds the F major chord: the two mourners [Donna Anna and Ottavio] enter (accompanied by servants with torches) to lay a wreath on the Commendatore's tomb; a short dialogue takes place (to music), leading directly into the aria, which gains a very beautiful, elegiac colouring from being sung in the graveyard.' (26 February 1852)

Wagner and his two apprentices spent several days and nights correcting the deficient orchestral parts, and making up for the lack of some instruments by rewriting the parts for others – low trumpets in place of trombones, for instance. Bülow wrote of how angry it made him to recall that Wagner had been accused in Dresden of deliberately conducting Mozart's operas badly because he detested them out of sheer conceit: the warm sense of piety that Wagner expressed in his selfless action would never be displayed by any of those pseudo-admirers.

Unfortunately the edition has been lost. It was probably destroyed when the theatre caught fire on the night of New Year's day 1890. Throughout his life Wagner opposed the fashionable idea of making a serious opera of *Don Giovanni*. Of course the work was divine, incomparable, but that was precisely due to the fact that its perspectives opened out from a popular basis: to take those wider perspectives as the starting point was to destroy them, to make nonsense of the frivolous and light-hearted elements, to render the work as a whole stiff and dull. In short, it was *opera giocosa*. (BBL 1937, p. 53)

The stimulus he received from this renewed contact with the theatre is shown in the pamphlet he wrote in April 1851, *A Theatre in Zürich*, which approached the question of theatrical reform, which he had already tackled in Dresden and Vienna, from a completely different angle. Instead of entrusting the fortunes of the institution to the arbitrament of chance, he suggested the evolution of an 'original theatre' out of a root-stock of local, indigenous forces. 'Let us take a look . . . at Zürich! Are there no artistically creative forces to be found here? Unrecognized they may be, but they surely exist.' (*Ein Theater in Zürich*, RWGS, V, pp. 20ff.)

The Zürich writer Gottfried Keller, then in Berlin, at once sent for a copy of Wagner's pamphlet and read it rejoicing, as he told Wilhelm Baumgartner, a Zürich musician who knew them both. In his opinion, it would unfortunately have little effect in the immediate future, but it strengthened his hope of finding somewhere where he could work in the air of his own home.

Wagner also conducted concerts in Zürich, and this activity had a direct bearing on his principal concern, the composition of the *Ring*. The Music Society in Zürich, in competition with the theatre, maintained its own orchestra, consisting of twenty-four professional players assisted by some dozen amateurs. After Wagner had accepted their invitation to conduct Beethoven's A major Symphony 'with an augmented orchestra' in January 1850, the society were bold enough to engage him as a guest conductor for future concerts. During the winter seasons of 1850–1 and 1851–2, in addition to the overtures to *Euryanthe, La Vestale* (to mark the death of Spontini), *Coriolan* and *Tannhäuser*, Wagner conducted the *Egmont* music and Beethoven's Third, Fifth, Sixth, Seventh and Eighth Symphonies, some of them on two occasions.

Even the rehearsals, with musicians who in some cases had travelled long distances to play, were in a sense solemn occasions. And since Wagner was able to concentrate on one overture and one symphony at a time, he had the leisure to refine his interpretation and performing style as never before. He rehearsed the oboist in his part like a singer, with such success that the little adagio passage in the first movement of the C minor Symphony was played more movingly than he ever heard it again. He put a gifted horn-player in charge of the brass section, under whose leadership they played the loud sustained chords in the last movement with an intensity that reminded him of the Paris Conservatoire orchestra.

When rehearsing the *Coriolan* Overture, the first thing he did was give the players a programmatic exposition as a foundation, in terms of a dramatic scenario which he explained to them step by step as they went through the work. (RWGS, V, pp. 173ff.) The result was striking: he made ordinary dance-band musicians capable of achievements that they themselves had never dreamed of. And later, when he was rehearsing the *Tannhäuser* overture with them, they asked him on their own initiative for a similar exposition, as it would help them to 'play better'.

'A miracle!' Bülow exclaimed after the 'Eroica', 'beyond belief!' What particularly pleased Wagner, however, was the effect his performance had even on such as his friend Jacob Sulzer, who had had no interest in music until then.

The effect that performing Beethoven had on Wagner himself was to stimulate him to reflect on the other composer's procedures of melodic formation and development: how he burst the narrow mould, broke up the melody into its separate motivic elements, mixed these elements together in all kinds of different associations, in order to link them all together again during the course of the piece in a new organic whole – that is, his presentation, not of a completed melody, but of the act of its creation. (*Opera and Drama*, RWGS, III, p. 315)

The only person with whom Wagner could discuss matters like this was another musician given to thinking about music, like Uhlig. He read his articles in the *Neue Zeitschrift für Musik* and wrote to tell him what immense pleasure they gave him and, more important, how much they frequently taught him as well. 'I am very grateful to you. You are a master in your field, there is nothing more that I can say.' When the two of them went on their walking tour of the four Forest Cantons in July 1851, Uhlig had the misfortune to fall into a mountain stream. Making the best of it, he spread his clothes out in the sun and walked up and down stark naked waiting for them to dry, while continuing his conversation with Wagner about the weightier problems of Beethovenian thematic processes, until at last Wagner shook his aplomb by declaring that he had just caught sight of a respected Hofrat from Dresden and his family coming along the path towards them.

The outcome of these exchanges was an essay by Uhlig on the 'choice of motives and the manner of their deployment in larger instrumental compositions'. After his death Wagner offered it, together with other essays by his friend, to Breitkopf & Härtel for publication: he believed it to be no exaggeration, he wrote, to regard it as the most significant work of its kind. (5 April 1856) 'But, however,' went their reply, declining, 'collected essays in the field of music are very hazardous projects for the publisher.' When Uhlig's writings were eventually published, nearly sixty years later, the manuscript of his most important work had vanished without trace.[2]

Motivic development was the musical problem that exercised Wagner most with the *Ring*. In the case of the *Holländer* he had been unaware of what he was doing when he set the motivic germs in Senta's Ballad, whence they had grown to spread a complete network over the entire drama; but since then he had become aware of the process, and it must have been a wonderful moment for him when he recognized that the principle of motivic development, with its wealth of emotional associations and its capacity for recalling the past and foreshadowing the future, was ideally suited to the task of creating the omnipresent mythic background to his drama.

It can be said that it was the poet who refined the process of musical motivic development for the sake of his drama. But it could be asserted with equal truth that it was the musician who made his text go back to the very beginning of things for the sake of these new musical possibilities. It is probable that Wagner's musical instinct, always the stronger force, had the last word here, as elsewhere. At all events the first and perhaps the most difficult step on the road to understanding the Wagnerian work of art is the realization that the text and the music are only two different facets of one and the same thing.

It is significant that this stage in the development of his compositional technique took place under the aegis of Beethoven: 'I would not have been able to compose as I have, had it not been for Beethoven.' (GLRW, VI, p. 408)

Wagner's appearances on the podium in Zürich were the occasion of his at once stepping, as he was fated to do wherever he went, into the centre of controversy, This time, however, there was a comical exchange of roles: while the conservative *Eidgenössische Zeitung* espoused the cause of the revolutionary musician, the *Neue Züricher Zeitung*, then a radical, liberal paper, took the side of his opponents, on account of the various choral societies and their director, Franz Abt, who were among its readers. On the occasion of a performance of the *Holländer* overture in 1852, the *Tagblatt* published a poem by 'an Aargauer', accusing the opera of immorality, to which Wagner replied with an antistrophe:

Daran erken ich schnell, mit leichtem Rat,
du Ärmster seist ein – ganzer Literat . . .

('Therein I see at once, as well I can,
poor wretch, thou art – a literary man.')

His conducting had a more serious consequence, however, in that it drew him to the attention of the police of the German Federation. A young violinist from Lemberg (Lwow) called Haimberger, whom Wagner had known at the time of the Dresden rising and who had also fled to Switzerland, appeared at one of his concerts. An enquiry went from Prague to Dresden as to whether the Wagner who was one of the ringleaders of the Swiss Revolutionary Party in Zürich, associated with the Galician fugitive Haimberger, and had Austrian connections, was identical with the 'known Richard Wagner'. The Dresden police enquired of the Zürich police about the 'said individual', and received the following reply: 'The refugee Richard Wagner from Dresden composes and occasionally obliges by conducting the orchestra in concerts and in the theatre here; he holds no specific appointment. The Jewish embezzler Lehmann Samuel, *vulgo* Braunschweig, was handed over to the district magistrates in Hall on 1 February. The notorious confidence trickster and counterfeiter Mitalis Georg, alleged Prince of Smyrna' – and so on. (LWVR, p. 28) Wagner knew nothing of the illustrious company in which he had been included. But we can see the effect that the Saxon police's interest in him was to have on his future.

To begin with Wagner refused even to think of appealing for pardon. As late as 13 April 1852 he asked Liszt to deny as firmly as possible the rumour that he had made any such application. By accepted standards he could count himself satisfied with his lot: a refugee without means, he had found friends here who helped him, and was the centre of a circle who admired him as an artist.

Of all his Swiss friends, it was Sulzer whom he singled out in his autobiography for the highest praise: if he was asked if he had ever encountered in his life what could be called true moral character, then, after very careful thought, he had to name Jakob Sulzer. Another intimate in Zürich was Wilhelm Baumgartner, 'Boom' to his friends, whose settings of poems by Gottfried Keller Wagner actually reviewed in the *Eidgenössiche Zeitung*: 'May . . . true song, no more separable from the poem than from the melody, blossom from the common creative power of these two.' (RWGS, XII, pp.

286ff.) The attempt to introduce him to the senior members of the university was less successful: 'Recently I was invited to take tea with some of the German professors here – horror seized me and drove me, pining, back into the arms of my Swiss friends.'

After her initial reluctance, Minna, too, had settled down in Zürich. 'My wife is radiantly happy,' Wagner wrote to Frau Ritter in April 1852, 'she has lovely clothes and a lot of lady friends; she has never, anywhere we have been, enjoyed a winter so much as this last.'

But all of a sudden, in the following autumn, he began to complain: 'The desert in which I now find myself is becoming intolerable,' he wrote to Liszt on 3 October 1852. Then, even more passionately, 'I shall very shortly be ruined here and everything – everything will come *too late*!!' He weighed up all the possibilities open to him: should he appeal for pardon to the King of Saxony, or rather to his scoundrels of ministers? Who would ever expect that of him? But there were princes – and here he was hinting at Liszt's employer, the Grand Duke of Weimar – who loved his works and could bring about his return without his needing to humiliate himself. 'You, my only friend, the dearest that I have, you who are prince and world – everything in one to me, have pity on me!' (9 November)

What had happened? Wagner suffered from depression throughout the whole of this winter of 1852–3. 'I wanted to work,' he told Uhlig, 'but felt so bad that I had to spend the whole morning on the couch, half sleeping, half waking.' He had no doubts as to the inner cause of his malaise. 'Something has got to happen, to wrest me out of this eternal existing only in my thoughts. This occupying myself with art *à distance* is killing me!' 'I am suffering from "mind",' he wrote to Kietz, 'and the mind is an incurable disease.' (7 September; RWBC, p. 263)

Early in 1853, immediately following his readings of the text of the *Ring*, he felt so ill that he feared he was on the verge of following poor Uhlig. Again, it was the constriction on his material circumstances that sapped his strength for living and creating. 'Give my new poem the greatest attention,' he exclaimed to Liszt, 'it includes the beginning and the end of the world!' The prospect of setting it all to music stimulated him greatly: 'in its form' it was completely finished in his mind, and he had never been so certain about a composition as now. All he needed was some pleasure in his life to induce the cheerful temper where motives would pour out freely and gladly. 'I *must* hear *Lohengrin* once: until I have, I neither want, nor am able, to make music again!!' He outlined a new scheme: the Grand Duke should arrange a safe conduct to Weimar for him for four weeks, and then he would punctiliously return to Switzerland. (11 February 1853) 'I am afraid that I can hold out only very timorous hopes,' Liszt replied.

So Wagner had to help himself. On 22 February 1853 he wrote to the committee of the Zürich Music Society, proposing to give a special concert *hors saison* in the civic theatre in May, with a programme of excerpts from his operas, which he would repeat twice. 'I would . . . look for my sole reward in the artistic execution, in the joy of success itself, and I expressly decline any part of any kind of pecuniary profit.'

It was in fact the first Wagner Festival. An orchestra of seventy was assembled from far and wide – only Munich refused its players leave. Zürich provided a choir of 110 singers, of both sexes. The programme consisted of items from *Rienzi, Holländer, Tannhäuser* and, most important of all, from *Lohengrin*: for the first time Wagner heard the sound of the eight-part string writing in the prelude, the woodwind chords enriched by the 'third group'. The third of the concerts took place on his fortieth birthday. At the end a singer stepped forward and read a poem in his honour. As the whole house applauded Wagner was presented with a silver cup and a laurel wreath. 'It made an uncommonly moving impression on me,' he told Liszt; 'I had to take a good grip on myself not to break down.' Artistically it was an immense success: there was a demand for more repeat performances, but Wagner wanted to preserve the special character of the occasion. 'There is *one* beautiful woman . . . at whose feet I laid the entire festival,' he confessed to Liszt. It was Mathilde Wesendonk.

Not only did these concerts permit him to hear how his *Lohengrin* orchestra sounded; they also revived his hopes of performing the *Ring* in Zürich and he actually selected a beautiful meadow at Hottingen as a site for his timber festival theatre. 'My music festival was wonderful,' he wrote to his old friend Ferdinand Heine in Dresden on 10 June, 'and has given me great hopes of accomplishing unheard-of things here in the future. Certainly I shall perform . . . the "Nibelungs" here too.'

It even seemed now as though his pardon was likely to come

through. There was to be a wedding in the Saxon royal family, and Wagner's friends counted on his being included in the amnesty usual on such occasions. They took it as a good omen that the theatre in Dresden, obviously acting on instructions from above, had recently revived *Tannhäuser*.

Then a mere week before the wedding ceremony, there appeared in the Dresden police bulletin, under the rubric 'politically dangerous individuals', the old warrant, adorned with the old portrait by Kietz printed on its side, such was the official haste: Wagner, who was believed to be intending to leave Zürich for Munich, was to be detained if he should cross the border, and handed over to the jurisdiction of the Dresden magistrates. The whole procedure smacks of a desire on the part of the reactionary court bureaucracy to forestall the chance of a royal pardon. Not only did it put paid to any hopes of a safe conduct to Weimar; it also diverted Wagner on to a course that took him further and further away from Germany.

But in the mood that he was now in Wagner was not to be discouraged by the news. In May, at a banquet given by the patrician music-lover Konrad Ott-Imhof, he had outlined the plan for a larger orchestra to be available both to the theatre and to concert-promoters. On one of his mountain rambles he now spent a rainy day drawing up a nine-point programme – first published in the Burrell Collection – which neglected none of the organizational and financial aspects involved. (RWBC, pp. 459ff.) It was, after Riga and Dresden, his third plan for orchestral reform and, like the Dresden plan, it was not put into practice.

At last on 2 July his passionate wish to see Liszt again was granted. They came close to smothering each other in their embraces, Liszt reported to Princess Wittgenstein. 'At times Wagner has something of the cry of a young eagle in his voice.' Their friendship was of a rare kind, not one to be measured by the usual standards. Wagner often said that a large piece of him remained alien and incomprehensible to Liszt. But in spite of all reservations and some estrangements there was one thing that bound them together for life: the secret affinity between the souls of two men of genius.

Wagner had just moved from no. 11 Zeltweg to a larger apartment in no. 13, marked today with a plaque. 'You will find I've got things very nicely,' he had written to Liszt, 'the demon of luxury has got into me' – as was usually the case when he was turning from writing words to writing music. 'When one can't get what is exactly right, one does the best one can!' Liszt was amazed by the 'petite élégance', though he found it 'fort modérée'. (The furnishing of the new flat contributed in no small measure to Wagner's pecuniary difficulties over the next few years.)

'A veritable tempest of news and views raged between us,' Wagner told Otto Wesendonk. He read to Liszt from the *Ring*, and Liszt played some of his own compositions.[3] They went up the Rütli with Herwegh, and drank brotherhood in the three springs on the mountain. Liszt recalled years later how he and Wagner had chanted the Eddic lay of Helgi the slayer of Hunding: 'In days of old, when eagles sang and sacred waters flowed from the mountains . . .' 'Eagles – that's what we are,' he wrote to his daughter Cosima in 1877, 'and the sacred waters are flowing.'

They also discussed the possibility of performing the *Ring* in Zürich, and Wagner was amazed by Liszt's enthusiasm for the plan: he was ready to ask for contributions from every source under the sun and was confident of being able to raise enough money. When François Wille asked Liszt whether he did not have the influence in Weimar to arrange for Wagner to return to Germany, Liszt replied that he knew of no theatre suitable for Wagner: the theatre, the singers, the orchestra – in short, everything, would have to be exactly as he wanted them to be. 'That could cost a million,' Wille said, to which Liszt, speaking French as usual when he was excited, exclaimed: 'Il l'aura! Le million se trouvera!'

There was more ceremony to come, to conclude the exhilarating events of that spring, when the choral societies of Zürich united to bring Wagner a torchlight serenade on 13 July. Zeltweg was packed and there was loud applause when a spokesman voiced the wish that the man who had been driven from his homeland would continue to live, to the country's honour, in free, beautiful Switzerland.

There seemed to be no obstacle now to his making a start on the composition. But still Wagner shrank back from this 'gigantic task'. 'He had before him a task', Newman writes, 'such as had faced no other composer in the whole history of music, the task not merely of "setting the text to music" but of giving organic musical unity to the enormous dramatic mass.' His themes had not only to be musical in themselves but also to sustain the most varied, subtle musical and psychological relationships to one another. In addition they had to possess an inexhaustible capacity for variation and furthermore lend themselves to contrapuntal treatment. 'At every point in the score he would have to look both before and after, seeing the whole in each part, and each part as contributing to the whole.' (NLRW, II, p. 389)

The importance for him of the study of motivic formation and development in Beethoven is understandable, even if the technical difficulties of the process in a four-part drama went far beyond what they are in a symphonic movement.

At the same time he was assailed again by the dangerous longing to break with the past that had recurred repeatedly since the revolution, to rid himself of all compromises and seek out new, virgin territory for his life. He had to close the door behind him on a whole section of his life, in order to begin a new one, he wrote to Otto Wesendonk. For that he needed new impressions: Italy, perhaps Paris too, in order to find creative peace. And Wesendonk was generous enough to finance his journey to Italy, in the form of a loan for which royalties for *Tannhäuser* expected from Berlin stood as security.

But first Wagner wanted to recover his health completely. He persuaded Herwegh to go to St Moritz with him to take a cure. Forced to spend time in Chur he read *Der West–Östliche Diwan*. The only accommodation they could find in St Moritz was primitive, and Wagner complained about 'food fit only for dogs'. Once again he discovered that he was not a fit subject for this kind of 'cure': the mineral waters and baths agitated him more than they soothed. To aid recovery he read *Die Wahlverwandschaften*, swallowing down every word, disagreed with Herwegh about the character of Charlotte, and in the end would gladly have been rid of his companion in order to have peace and quiet.

But he received two indelible impressions from the mountains. When he saw the Julier on the way from Chur to St Moritz, he was able to imagine Wotan and Fricka on its heights: 'there, where all is silent, one pictures the beings who reign there, no longer touched by growth and becoming'. On an excursion to the Roseg glacier he received once more, more strongly than the first time, 'the sublime impression of the holiness of the empty waste'. Both impressions became music: the 'open space on a mountain summit' depicted at the beginning of the second scene of *Das Rheingold*, and the 'blessed emptiness on blissful height' where Siegfried finds the sleeping

Brünnhilde. But it was not only the artist in Wagner who was susceptible to the majesty of the mountains; the man, too, felt the challenge to prove himself through danger. Wagner once told Heinrich von Stein that he had climbed the Alps in his younger days with the feeling that he must be able to overcome even them.

At last he set out for Italy on 24 August. In Turin he enjoyed a performance of *Il Barbiere di Siviglia*. In Genoa he encountered for the first time a genuine Italian city, beside which London and Paris seemed to him to be mere agglomerations of houses. On the very first evening he had his courier Signor Raffaele take him on a tour of the streets around the old mansions of the nobility and enjoyed a night fit for the gods beneath flowering oleander trees as high as houses in the garden of one of the Palazzi Brignole-Sale, where a café had installed itself on the ground floor. But the noise from the harbour, right outside his hotel, drove him along the coast to La Spezia. And there, suddenly, there came the moment that released everything that had been building up in his musical imagination for five years – 'unasked-for, unsought', as Egmont says, and 'unimpeded flows the circle of inner harmonies'.

Wagner recounted in his autobiography how, after a night spent in sleepless fever, he forced himself to go for a walk and in the afternoon, exhausted, lay down on a hard couch in his inn in the hope of sleeping at last. But sleep did not come: 'Instead I sank into a kind of somnambulist state, in which I suddenly got the feeling that I was sinking into a strong current of water. Its rushing soon developed into a musical sound as the chord of Eb major, surging incessantly in broken chords; these presented themselves as melodic figurations of increasing motion, but the pure chord of Eb major never altered, seeming by its persistence to give the element into which I was sinking an infinite significance. With the sensation that the waves were now flowing high above me I woke with a violent start from my half-sleep. I recognized immediately that the orchestral prelude to *Das Rheingold* had come to me, as I had borne it in me but had been unable to find exactly; and quickly, too, I understood the essence of my own nature: it was not from without but only from within that the current of life was to flow to me.'

'Whether it be a demon or a good genius that often takes control of us in decisive hours,' he wrote to Arrigo Boito in 1871, 'enough:

the impetus for the music of *Das Rheingold* came to me as I lay sleepless in an inn in La Spezia; and without delay I returned to my dismal home to set about writing the immense work, whose fate, more than anything else, binds me to Germany.'

# 18

---

The Myth Becomes Music

On the same day that Wagner experienced his 'vision' in La Spezia, 5 September 1853, he wrote to Minna, complaining of his loneliness and the state of his health: 'I have only one thought in my head: how to get back home to you quickly.' This was published for the first time with the Burrell Collection, but the editor is wrong in assuming that Wagner deliberately concealed from Minna the true reason for his wish to go home, because she would not have understood it: he overlooks the fact that the letter was written in the morning, while the vision did not occur until the afternoon. As Wagner travelled back towards Genoa by stagecoach, his pleasure in the Italian scenery revived, and in the midst of the musical sensation that now filled him, it was the colours that made a particularly strong, even impressionistic, appeal to him: the blue of the sea, the red of the cliffs, the green of the pine trees, the white of a herd of cattle. But the mere thought of postponing his departure was enough to cloud his spirits again.

Since he had arranged to meet Liszt in Basel at the beginning of October he had to possess his soul in patience for a while, in any case. Princess Wittgenstein also put in an appearance, with her fifteen-year-old daughter Marie, whose youthful grace earned her the title of 'the Child' from Wagner. 'I have come to venerate the Child,' he confessed to Bülow, 'now, as I compose, I live under her blessing.' (25 November) It is not too fanciful to see a reflection of this feeling in Freia's delightful D major melody. His letters to Princess Marie during the next few years contain a number of revealing comments on his work, but this did not prevent her from joining the camp of his enemies in Vienna, after her marriage to Prince Konstantin Hohenlohe. He told Cosima that he regretted every confidential and enthusiastic remark he had ever made to such a deceitful being.

From Basel the party set out together for Paris, where two events occurred of great significance for Wagner. Liszt took him to visit his children, who were being brought up there under the strict tutelage of Madame Patersi. Wagner read them the third act of *Siegfrieds Tod* and was particularly struck by the exceptional shyness of the sixteen-year-old Cosima.

The other event was a performance of Beethoven's Eb major and C# minor Quartets, by the Maurin–Chevillard quartet, whom Wagner used to cite as exemplifying the blend of thoroughness, imagination and intelligence typical of the best French musicians. Even as a boy he had been drawn to the late quartets, and at sixteen a copy of the Eb major had been his most treasured possession. But just as it had been a performance by the Paris Conservatoire orchestra that had first enabled him to recognize the full stature of the Choral Symphony, so it was only now that the C# minor Quartet was fully revealed to him. 'If I remembered nothing else of that visit to Paris, it would rank as unforgettable for that alone.' This is a significant admission, above all because the 'differentiated texture' of these quartets became the model for the polyphonic writing of the works of his second creative period: in them, as in the quartets, linearity is wrested out of the predominantly homophonic textures.

At last, on 1 November, he was back in his study on the Zeltweg and wrote down the chord of Eb major that had sounded for him in La Spezia, with the famous sustained pedal point on the low Eb. But any expectation that the visionary nature of its inspiration would have led to a free fantasy is disproved by the first version, with its regular sequence of four, precisely compartmented, sixteen-bar variations, with a note already anticipating the 'poco dim.' in the last bar of the fourth of them. 'Friend, I stand amazed!' he wrote to Liszt after finishing the first scene. 'A new world is revealed to me. The great scene in *Das Rheingold* is finished: I see an abundance before me greater than I ever dared to hope. Now I believe my capabilities are limitless: the making of music floods through every fibre of my being.'

As always he began with a continuous composition sketch, written in pencil and later inked in for the most part, usually combining the vocal and instrumental parts on two staves, occasionally three.

He used a kind of shorthand, decipherable for us only by reference to the score, which made it possible to write out the whole of *Das Rheingold*, words and music, on thirty-nine half-sheets of manuscript paper, with fourteen staves on each side.

The first remarkable thing is the shortness of the time in which he wrote it, and the second is how complete the sketch is. It is dated at the end '14 January 1854', followed by the cryptic question: 'And nothing more?? Nothing more??' That means that, not counting a period when he was laid up with a feverish cold, Wagner took only nine weeks to set down on paper this composition which not only was completely new in style but also laid the thematic and compositional foundations of the whole tetralogy. This could only have been possible if he had it all fixed and ready in his mind when he started, which in turn presupposes that its essential elements must already have been present in his mind when he was writing the text. And so the claim he had made to Liszt at the beginning of 1853, that the form of the music was already finished in his mind, was no exaggeration.

But this means, furthermore, that the verse itself must owe its form to the music that already existed within the composer, in a way such as had never been known before. The well-meaning literary critics of Wagner's texts concede readily enough that they ought to be judged only in association with the music, but they then invariably proceed to judge them from a purely literary point of view. It is only in perusing the documents of his creative processes, pre-eminently the composition sketches, that we can appreciate how close, how mutually dependent, how organic the relationships are between the words and the music.

From the very first words – 'Weia! Waga!', the undying target of so many pawky jokes at Wagner's expense – it is quite obvious that the melody is the primary consideration, and the words, developed from the Middle High German 'heilawâc' ('holy wave'), which Wagner had found in Jacob Grimm and elaborated after the model of the 'Eiapopeia' refrain of German nursery rhymes, are secondary. But coming after the impersonal natural phenomenon of the orchestral prelude, how effectively words and music combine to create the first impression of conscious life and sensation!

This close alliance of words and music is not confined to the emotional content, it extends to the linguistic expression as well. From a few examples in the second scene of *Das Rheingold*, August

Halm illustrated how Wagner even composed the syntax: an antecedent clause ends with the triad not in its root position, but in the second inversion that indicates the statement is incomplete; a parenthesis is declaimed as such in the musical line; an unsingable pluperfect tense, for which an imperfect verb does service in the text, is yet discernibly present through the medium of the accompanimental motive. These are isolated fingerposts for a future assessment of Wagner's texts.[1]

No less astonishing than the speed with which the composition sketch was written down is its correspondence to the completed score: everything is already there. It is as if it was written at one sitting, taken down in great haste from uninterrupted dictation. There can be no question of its having been composed at the piano. Wagner never created anything at the keyboard, though he found that improvising stimulated his 'creative memory' to recall ideas that had occurred to him 'God knows how or when'. Moreover, playing things at the piano after he had thought of them prevented him from writing down something that was permissible according to the rules but did not sound right.

The concision of the composition sketches allowed him to take a general, bird's-eye view of lengthy passages and large-scale forms: it kept him from getting bogged down in too much detail. Since the frequent changes of key signature sometimes obscure the overall, *real* key of a period, he often used to write that key down in letters and words for his own reference as he worked: 'F major', 'A major', 'B minor'. Against Alberich's 'Holder Sang singt zu mir her' he wrote expressively 'flat keys'. This bears out Alfred Lorenz's analyses of Wagnerian form, which mark off the periods according to their underlying, though not always obvious, tonalities. It also demonstrates that Wagner was always conscious of what he was about in his construction of musical forms.

Some occasional alterations were made later to the vocal line without affecting its essence, but all the themes are already in their final form in the composition sketch. The harmonization is also already fully realized, not only within the themes but in their development as well. When Donner vanishes into the gathering stormcloud, for instance, already in the sketch the tonality, too, darkens threateningly at the impending catastrophe, sinking into low B♭ harmonies, like the development section of the first movement of Beethoven's 'Appassionata' (cf. Ernst Kurth).

There are already notes indicating the characteristic instrumentation: even such specks of colour as the pianissimo strokes on triangle and cymbal after Fricka's 'Gewänne mein Gatte sich wohl das Gold?' are already marked – evidence that Wagner's instrumentation was not a gloss that he worked out separately later. Only the statement of the Valhalla theme at the beginning of the second scene differs in being assigned to trombones, although it is already distinguished by the metallic demisemiquaver triplets on the trumpets – the idea of devising his own tubas specially for this work (a development of the horn from the romantic into the mythological) had not yet occurred to him.

Emendations and later alterations are few and far between, and are confined to relatively unimportant matters, with two exceptions. The first concerns the Rhinemaidens' final song: the original two bars setting 'Um dich, du klares, wir nun klagen' are replaced already in the sketch by the version found in the score, with the characterful sharpening effect of the chord of the dominant seventh. The result is what Ernst Kurth calls 'one of the most marvellous refractions of colour': as he says, shading like this is too subtle to be expressed in words.

Yet there is nothing in the least rarefied about this subtlety. Furtwängler once noted: 'Some composer, any composer in the world, should just try to cap Richard Wagner in the Rhinemaidens' final song in *Das Rheingold*, if nothing else! This power to speak from the very depths of popular feeling, and yet in a completely direct and original voice, was something only he possessed.'[2]

The other change affected the introduction to the first scene – the last place, in view of its inspiration, where one would expect to find any alterations. It is an astonishing discovery which gives completely new insights into the origination of one of the most important musical symbols in the *Ring*. In the sketch the introduction is admittedly in E♭ major and in 6/8 time, it comprises variations that roll on, steadily crescendoing, over the pedal point of the low E♭. The melodic line of the very first horn motive is already indicated, developing out of the E♭ major triad. But the profound difference between the version in the sketch and the eventual version in the score is the total absence from the former of the two variants of that motive which now set their stamp indelibly on the introduction. In its place there are figurations for the strings, running up and down as in the transition to the second scene.

It is as Wagner had heard it, but it is as yet nothing more than pure nature-painting. How it was to be informed with a symbolic content worthy of the cosmic drama it begins was still hidden from Wagner. The solution to that problem – indeed, the problem itself – occurred to him only at a later stage in the work, at a moment that had nothing to do with the Rhine or its waters: at the apparition of Erda in the fourth scene. We do not know how the idea came to him, but we do know how he felt his powers increasing, in the conviction that his work would succeed and that he himself would win through in the end. To others he appeared taciturn and introspective: but what visions he beheld within! 'Believe me,' he wrote to Liszt, 'nothing has ever been composed like this before; it seems to me my music . . . is a morass of horrors and sublimities!'

It was one of the great moments in the process of composition when the idea came to him of projecting the two themes associated with Erda back to the prelude and blending them into the music of his vision. The two images, the flowing water and the goddess rising up out of the earth, are now merged in a single image of inconceivable simplicity and symbolic potency, and each of the two passages, the prelude and Erda's appearance, gains a deeper significance thereby. It is true that when we first hear the prelude we do not know the themes' associations, but we sense that the music is more than a depiction of natural phenomena. What is truly remarkable is that the symbolism was not premeditated: the writer of the text knew nothing about it: it was born to the composer out of the spirit of the music.

Finally, has enough credit yet been paid to Wagner's accommodation here of the demands of poetry and the idea with those of music and form? In the terms of the latter, Erda's apparition is no longer an isolated episode: unbidden, one hears it as a varied reprise of the prelude, and one's sense of musical form approves it.

He had achieved, after all, what he had despaired of when he started the composition sketch of *Siegfrieds Tod*, when it was no more than an idea: beyond the foreground action played out on the stage there lay the broad background of the myth, revealed by the orchestra. Completing the composition of *Das Rheingold*, so difficult and so important a work, had restored a great confidence to him, he wrote to August Röckel on 25 January 1854. He was now again able to recognize how much of the intention of his text was disclosed only with the music: as a result he could no longer bear to

look at the words without the music. 'In due course,' he went on, 'I
expect to be able to let you see the music too. For the moment I will
say just this much, that it has turned out to be a firmly entwined
unity: there is scarcely a bar in the orchestral writing that does not
develop out of preceding motives.' He was now fully alive to
the technique of motivic development that he had first used
unconsciously in *Der Fliegende Holländer* and had then studied in
Beethoven, but significantly the creative process itself still remained a mystery to him: 'it is something that will not be spoken
of.'

This is still not the end of the story of the *Rheingold* prelude. The
newness of its conception obliged Wagner to abandon what was
usually the second stage in composition, the writing of an orchestral
sketch on three staves. 'I am now writing *Das Rheingold* straight out
in full score, with the instrumentation: I couldn't think of any way
of writing out the prelude . . . comprehensibly as [an orchestral]
sketch.' (To Liszt, 7 February 1854)

This first draft of the full score of *Das Rheingold* had an eventful
history, typical of many of Wagner's manuscripts. From the estate
of Karl Klindworth, who had made the vocal score, it made its way
to New York, where it was sold at auction in 1927 for $15,400. In
1928 it became the property of Mr John H. Scheide of Titusville,
Pennsylvania, and it is now in the Scheide Library at Princetown
University (as Dr Daniel Bodmer of Zürich tells me). But this copy
was not complete: it lacked the first two fascicles, which had been
given by Liszt to the pianist Louis Köhler of Königsberg, who
returned them to Cosima on 17 September 1878.[3] These eight pages
of thirty staves each, now in the Wagner archives in Bayreuth,
contain the opening of the prelude, up to six bars after the entry of
the trumpets. At the head the first page is dated 'Zürich, 1 Febr.
54', that is, a fortnight after the completion of the composition
sketch.

And from this manuscript, the very first draft of the score, we see
that the synthesis of the La Spezia vision and the apparition of Erda
had already taken place: the draft corresponds to the final version.
Only the first horn theme is still as follows:

while it was, of course, eventually to take the following form:

It is an apparently insignificant alteration. But its effect is twofold: the larger interval, a fifth, coming right at the start, gives the motive a stronger lift, and the mediant (G) to which it now rises imbues the final note, too, with a latent tension. It demonstrates the simplicity that was as much part of Wagner's genius as his complexity: at one stroke an ordinary sequence of notes has become a living tonal shape.

Up to the last few bars, the dynamic swelling in the prelude is due entirely to the successive entrances of new groups of instruments, and not to any crescendo marking: as Wagner stressed at the 1876 rehearsals, it should make the impression throughout of a natural phenomenon unfolding of its own volition. It is therefore interesting to observe that the first draft of the score is marked with small expressive crescendos and decrescendos, subsequently crossed out in pencil, however, never to appear in any later version.

In the letter Wagner wrote on 15 January to tell Liszt of the completion of the sketch, he was already complaining: 'Ah, how the want of gold encompasses me, too!' By the summer his situation was menacing. 'I am sending you . . . a shipment of "Rhine gold",' he wrote to Bülow, who was originally to have made the vocal score; 'how I wish it was minted.'

Apart from the 3000 francs he received yearly from Frau Ritter, he had no regular income. The Dresden publishing company could not even meet the pressing demands of its creditors. The fourteen concerts of the Zürich Music Society that he took part in between 1850 and 1854 earned him 1400 francs altogether. There were also occasional fees for articles and pamphlets. Breitkopf & Härtel took on *Lohengrin* in 1851, after all, but since his payment for that consisted of the cancellation of an old debt of 200 talers for a concert grand, he could not help but feel that their decision to publish the score was an act of charity, of which he could almost be ashamed.

Then suddenly in 1852 applications to perform *Tannhäuser* began to flood in: requests from twenty-two theatres within a period of eighteen months, and they made single payments of between 10 and

25 louisdor – Hamburg, exceptionally, paid 50. This brought him in 7500 francs. Since there were still a number of theatres where he had hopes that *Tannhäuser* would be staged – apart from Berlin and Vienna, where he met with particular difficulties – and since *Lohengrin* had as yet been performed in only four houses, he believed he could afford to furnish his new lodgings in 1853 with the 'petite élégance' Liszt admired; Liszt was also pleased to find that his larder and his cellar were well stocked to provide for the friends who were always welcome at the Wagners' supper table.

But Wagner's expectations were severely disappointed, when the hoped-for applications to do *Tannhäuser* failed to arrive by the autumn of 1853. 'If opera money doesn't come from Germany soon, and in massive amounts, then I shall be in truly the most disagreeable position I have yet to know.' (To E. B. Kietz; RWBC, p. 269)

The German theatres had good reason for their caution: the recent re-issue of the warrant for Wagner's arrest inhibited them from having anything to do with a man who would be thrown into gaol if he set foot on German soil.

In his predicament Wagner hit on the idea of selling to Breitkopf & Härtel the performing rights for *Lohengrin* as well. On the basis of his earnings from *Tannhäuser* he decided to ask them for 15,000 francs. 'If you think, my dear Franz,' he wrote to Liszt on 16 November 1853, 'that what I'm offering for sale is not rubbish . . . then you will probably agree that my price is not, after all, unreasonable, and – here it comes!!! – *recommend it to Härtel's.*' Liszt passed on this proposition in person, when he went to Leipzig for the première there of *Lohengrin* on 7 January 1854, but he met with a point-blank refusal. It was hardly surprising, for Dr Härtel was a close friend of Otto Jahn, the future biographer of Mozart, who had recently published in the *Grenzboten* an article on *Tannhäuser* which was, as Newman observes, 'of a quite monumental stupidity, even for a "classicist" of that epoch'. (NLRW, II, p. 399)

In the event, the production of *Lohengrin* in Wagner's birthplace, under the direction of Julius Rietz, who was simply not up to its demands, gave so false an impression of the work that the agent Michaelson, who was supposed to negotiate the purchase of the performance rights for the Berlin firm of Bote & Bock, decided that it was not a commercial proposition.

Some bills of exchange were due for payment in April. 'God

knows what I am to pay them with! If I could only manage to hang on till the autumn, then I shall be getting something from the theatres again,' he told Liszt. 'Well, that's how it is, when one acquires a taste for luxury, but is in reality condemned to sackcloth and ashes.' But no theatres applied to perform anything during the summer or autumn of 1854. It was no secret to his friends in Zürich that his situation was now desperate. 'Whether and how to render any assistance can only be decided when all the circumstances are known,' Wesendonk wrote to Sulzer on 26 July. 'This much is clear: no money must be given to him directly . . . From the very first I thought of giving funds to Madame Wagner, but it seemed too humiliating.'

Wagner finally opened his heart to Sulzer in a long letter on 14 September: he had nothing with which to meet the reproaches, silent or open, which he had brought upon himself on account of his domestic expenditure, except by pleading that certain processes were going on inside himself which no one could understand, unless they could imagine themselves in his position and with his nature, and faced with a task of that kind and that scale. 'So I say nothing of that, and willingly admit that anyone who accuses me of folly is right. And I am also completely ready to atone for my folly.' He had earlier expressed himself more explicitly to Liszt: his senses were uncommonly delicate, sensitive, strongly responsive to any stimulus, and needed to feel pampered in some way or other if he was to succeed in the 'desperately difficult task of bringing a non-existent world into being'. (15 January 1854)

He asked Sulzer to be his intermediary with Wesendonk in launching a rescue action. His debts amounted to 10,000 francs, and he estimated that *Tannhäuser* and *Lohengrin* would still bring in a minimum of 21,000 francs. If Wesendonk would let him have the means to settle the debts and also allow him 500 francs a quarter for the next three years, then all his income from theatres should go to Sulzer and be administered by him. (FWSZ, I, pp. 309ff.)

Wesendonk agreed to this proposal, but he authorized Sulzer to say on his behalf that he was not prepared to listen to any further requests of the same nature. Sulzer acquitted himself in the delicate task of managing Wagner's income for him with tact and efficiency, and was rewarded by the affectionate title of 'my dear guardian'.

During the summer, while the financial crisis was at its height, Wagner put the final draft of the score of *Das Rheingold* on one side, in the hope that starting a new work would rescue him from the despair that threatened to crush him: he began the composition sketch of *Die Walküre* on 28 June. 'You know, now it really *is* getting started!' he exclaimed to Liszt. 'Extraordinary, these contrasts between the first love scene in *Die Walküre* and the scene in *Das Rheingold*!' He was now leaving the world of elemental beings for the human world, and the 'plastic nature motives' of the first part of his tetralogy were now re-forming as the 'vehicles for the promptings of the passions' roused by the action and experienced by the characters. Or, as he was to express it later to Brahms, when he sent him a copy of the score of *Das Rheingold* in 1875, ironically alluding to Hanslick: his music had been accused of being 'painted scenery' and the same would certainly be said of this work. All the same, he thought Brahms would be interested to see the variety of thematic material he had been able to construct in the later scores of the *Ring* from the 'scenery' set up in the first part.

*Das Rheingold* ends and *Die Walküre* begins with a thunderstorm. But what a contrast! The first is seen through the eyes of the gods, the second is part of the experience of human distress: 'Gewitterbrunst brach meinen Leib', Siegmund says. But as well as the skilful, stretto-like treatment of the string figures, stormily overrunning each other, the prelude to the first act of *Die Walküre* also features the call with which Donner summoned the thunder, now played on the tubas and trombones, and so this orchestral passage, like the *Rheingold* prelude, is more than a mere depiction of nature: we sense the god's authority. 'Play it with more awareness!' Wagner exhorted his brass-players in 1876.

Divine authority has a very special role to play in the first act itself. In the earliest prose sketch Wotan actually puts in an appearance; he does not reveal his identity and is received warily by Hunding, while Sieglinde and Siegmund dimly sense who he might be. He drives the sword into the trunk of the tree and spends the night behind a partition at the back of the stage, the unseen witness of his children's love. The intention was to rid the theme of love between siblings, an essential and basic element of the Volsunga saga in Wilhelm Grimm's view, of any taint of moral aberration and present it as Wotan's will. But Wagner soon abandoned the idea and trusted in the power of his music's 'associative magic', as Thomas Mann called it, to express Wotan's presence *in spirit*.

In the margin of the sketch, against Sieglinde's 'Gast, wer du bist, wüßt' ich gern', there is the note 'Answer, when I get back from Sitten, 13–14 July'. Wagner had agreed to conduct Beethoven's A major Symphony and the *Tannhäuser* overture at the Confederation Music Festival at Sitten, on condition that he first approved the arrangements for himself. He found them so unsatisfactory that he left without conducting a note, fuming at the 'village fair'. Sheer vexation prevented him from resuming his work at once, as the next entry in the manuscript shows: '3 August!!' It is followed by a further note, 'W. d. n. w., G.!!!', decipherable as 'Wenn du nicht wärst, Geliebte' ('Were it not for you, beloved'), which relates to the adjacent stage direction and Siegmund's words: 'Siegmund looks up, gazes into her eyes and begins: "Friedmund darf ich nicht heißen".' There are sixteen similar notes in the first act of *Die Walküre*, all of them undoubtedly to be interpreted in the light of his growing love for Mathilde Wesendonk.

He confided in only a few: Liszt, Bülow, Julie Ritter. To her sympathetic, motherly ear he confessed that he was living a life completely divorced from reality; in the mornings he sat down in his 'luxury' and *worked*; in the afternoons, solitary walks in the mist; on some evenings he called on the Wesendonks, where he could still find the one thing that roused his spirits: 'the graceful woman remains loyal and devoted to me, even though much else in this association is necessarily a torment to me'. (20 January 1854)

Having resumed the composition sketch of the first act on 3 August with Siegmund's narration, Wagner finished it on 1 September, thus composing the major part of the act in thirty days. The music had been present in his mind for a long time, as we know by chance. He had made a note of the characteristic rocking rhythm of the Spring Song in the margin of the manuscript when he wrote the verse text in 1852. While he was writing it he used to go for morning walks with the writer Hermann Rollett, to whom he read each new part of the text as he finished it. When Rollett said he hoped he would write a 'really full-blown melody' to this 'in every sense poetic passage', Wagner tore a page out of his notebook, drew a five-line stave in pencil, wrote out the text and its melody and then sang it, more or less as he intended it to be. This first version of the melody, later published in facsimile, cries out for the rocking to go on longer, to arch across a wider span; that in turn demanded an expansion of the text, such as Wagner wrote out one day in his pocketbook. But he still had to make further alterations to the words and the melody and even to the metre – replacing the 3/4 time with its triplets by 9/8 – before the song reached the score in the form we know today.[4]

At the rehearsals in 1876 Wagner explained that he did not want it performed like a kind of concert number, but so as to make the effect of an episode which momentarily halts the dramatic progress without interrupting it. Porges, in his record of these rehearsals, defines the overriding characteristic of the style of *Die Walküre* as the way in which essentially reflective sensations are expressed in a completely spontaneous fashion.[5] Some of the questions and answers ought to sound exactly as if they were spoken; the temptation to draw out emotionally charged, extended melodic phrases was to be resisted, until at the end the primitive force of elemental passion sweeps all before it in a whirlwind.

This unleashing of passion is mirrored in the manuscript of the composition sketch; to begin with the handwriting is a model of calligraphic beauty, but it becomes increasingly hurried, and by the end of the act the pen can hardly keep up with the pace of the invention.

'I have finished the first act of *Die Walküre*,' Wagner wrote to Bülow a day or two after doing so; 'when I shall get on to the second, God knows – I am in a very bad mood now!' In fact he started it within three days of ending the first, on 4 September. In an undated letter to Liszt he poured out all his rage at the world: 'It is bad, *bad, fundamentally bad*, and only the heart of a friend, only the tears of a woman can redeem it from its curse.' Then he went on: 'I have started the second act of *Die Walküre*: Wotan and Fricka: as you can see, I'm bound to succeed with it.'

In the middle of this crisis in his economic, intellectual and emotional affairs, Wagner began the composition of the second scene, in which Wotan's despairing renunciation of the will to power marks the turning point of the entire drama:

> Auf geb ich mein Werk;
> nur eines will ich noch:
> das Ende.

And then, after a long pause, in which he seems to be communing with himself in the very depths of his spirit, once more, accompanied by the disturbing pianissimo of the chord of C minor:

das Ende!

Then one day Georg Herwegh entered his lonely study with a copy of Schopenhauer's *The World as Will and Idea*.

# 19

The London Inferno

The history of Schopenhauer's major work aroused Wagner's fellow-feeling: it was completely ignored by an entire generation of academic philosophers, until attention was focused on it in 1853 by a brilliant article in an English journal, published soon afterwards in translation in Germany.[1] The 'great clarity and manly precision' of the language at once captured Wagner's interest. The importance Schopenhauer attached to music in his aesthetics surprised him, but when, as one passionately aroused by the business of being alive, he turned to the philosopher's handling of the ultimate questions of ethics, he was appalled to read of denial of the will as the only means of release from the trammels of the world. It was Herwegh who pointed out to him that recognition of the worthlessness of the world of appearances was the only *tragic* world view: intuitively, it must dwell in the heart of every great creative artist, and of every great human being.

Then Wagner looked again at the text of the *Ring* and suddenly realized that the idea that perturbed him when he read Schopenhauer's theory had long been familiar to him in his own poetry. Had not a poetic impulse inspired him to refashion his drama so that tragic resignation became a principal theme? 'So at last I myself understood my Wotan and, shaken, I began to study Schopenhauer's book more closely.' The fundamental idea was dreadfully serious, he told Liszt, and no one could begin to understand it unless it was already alive in him. (16 December 1854)

*The World as Will and Idea* affected him as the Choral Symphony once had, as the 'Fundamental of his own life'; more than the thoughts expressed, Schopenhauer's metaphysics and Wagner's music share something that is outside the province of reason. It was

197

more than a book, it was a friend who entered his loneliness like a gift from heaven. Wagner wanted everyone to share in his experience. He undertook personally the initiation of Karl Ritter and Robert von Hornstein, and hoped that they would be his emissaries on a pilgrimage to Frankfurt. He exhorted Hans von Bülow to get a copy as quickly as possible: he would be amazed when he made the acquaintance of Schopenhauer's intellect. (Late 1854) He even sent a copy to his comrade of the revolution, August Röckel, now languishing in Waldheim prison, expressing the hope that he would find in it the consolation more necessary to the strongest spirit than to all others. (5 February 1855)

Only with Liszt, who was so close to him in friendship and in art, and often so distant in things of the mind and spirit, did he abstain from any attempt at proselytization. But he had to affirm his belief in their essential unanimity in a matter that had become so important to him. 'It is queer that I have often . . . recognized your thoughts as my own,' he wrote, 'even if you express them differently because you are religious, yet I know you mean exactly the same thing.' (16 December 1854)

On fine Sundays he and Herwegh walked out to visit the Willes, who owned the patriarchal country house of Mariafeld overlooking the Lake of Zürich. François Wille, who had represented Schleswig–Holstein in the Bundestag for a time, had returned to the land of his fathers to get away from the forces of reaction in Germany. He too was made a convert, and the conversation often turned to questions of Schopenhauerian philosophy. His wife Eliza, who sewed while the men talked, was amazed by the speed with which Wagner had absorbed the philosopher's ideas. He later compared their effect on him with the benefit he had had from his rigorous study of counterpoint with Weinlig: he meant that what he had assimilated from Schopenhauer consisted not in preformed conclusions but in a mode of thought. Even here his intellectual freedom was important to him; once, fearing that Princess Wittgenstein would 'scent Schopenhauer again' in what he said, he complained that people would not credit him with any independence in crucial matters: 'It only remains for someone to prove that Reissiger wrote my operas.' (FWSZ, II, pp. 376f.)

The small community's greatest wish was to receive the Sage of Frankfurt in their midst. 'A whole coterie of fine minds . . . ', Schopenhauer growled, 'invited me in all seriousness to travel to

Zürich in December, to satisfy their curiosity! Replied in a polite and friendly tone but briefly that I could not embark in a controversy in writing and that I no longer travel anywhere. This brought me a book from Richard Wagner, printed only for his friends, not for the trade, on superb, thick paper and in a decent binding: it is called *Der Ring des Nibelungen*, a series of four operas which he intends to compose one day – the artwork of the future itself, I suppose: seems very fantastic: have only read the prologue: I'll read the rest before making up my mind. No letter with it, just an inscription: "in respect and gratitude". ' (To Julius Frauenstädt, 30 December 1854) Wagner had thought that if Schopenhauer could not tell what manner of person he was from the poem, then no letter, however long, would make any difference.

As is well known, Schopenhauer wrote disapproving notes all over the margins of the book, complaining especially of the, in his view, 'hair-raising morality' of some passages.[2] Nevertheless, comments he made in conversation with Wagner's friends show that his overall impression of the work was more favourable than would appear from the notes. 'Thank your friend Wagner on my behalf for sending me his "Nibelungs",' he said to Dr Wille, 'but he ought to forget about the music, he has more genius as a poet! I, Schopenhauer, remain true to Rossini and Mozart!' To Robert von Hornstein he said, 'the man's a poet, not a musician', and Karl Ritter reported that while Schopenhauer thought highly of Wagner as a poet, he could not agree on the 'joint stockholding' of words and music. He praised the *Ring* as a work of poetry: the language was in every way worthy of the subject, which he meant as high praise.[3]

But Wagner was never quite able to get over the fact that Schopenhauer never wrote him a line in acknowledgement of the book. 'I cannot think of any other poem which depicts the will – and what a will! one that has created a world for its own pleasure – broken without the intervention of grace, solely through the strength of its possessor's own proud nature, as Wotan's is . . . I am convinced that Schopenhauer must have been annoyed that I created this before I knew his philosophy: I, a political refugee, whose theories were shown to be untenable in the light of his own philosophy by his disciple Kossak, on the grounds that I have 'no melody'! But it doesn't look well. It's exactly how Goethe treated Kleist, whom he ought to have hailed as joyfully as Schumann did

Brahms. But that', he added cheerfully without a shred of bitterness, '– that seems to happen only among donkeys!' (GLRW, VI, pp. 62f.)

It did not prevent him from trying to do something for Schopenhauer, who wrote to his apostle Julius Frauenstädt on 28 March 1856: 'Jam de re nova magnaque: arrigite aures! Four days ago Ritter came to see me from Zürich . . . He disclosed to me that they are thinking of founding a chair of my, and exclusively my, philosophy at Zürich University, and they think the best occupant for it would be you.' Going on to say that the scheme was being promoted by a Regierungsrat Sulzer, he evidently had no idea that Sulzer was acting solely in response to Wagner's urging. What Schopenhauer thought of this plan – which came to nothing in the end – can be judged from the glowing colours in which he painted the prospect to Frauenstädt: life in that 'Swiss Athens' would be very different from what it was in 'horrible, pinched Berlin . . . I should be greatly honoured by it.'

Besides occupying himself with Schopenhauer – he read *The World as Will and Idea* from cover to cover four times in the course of a year – Wagner continued to work on the composition sketch of *Die Walküre*. By now, as he admitted, he was having to hold a new creative idea forcibly at bay. 'Conceived *Tristan*', he wrote in the Annals. The entry is undated but clearly relates to October 1854. He gave Liszt a fuller explanation in the letter of 16 December: since he had never enjoyed the true happiness of love in his life, he wanted at least to set up a monument to that most beautiful of all dreams, in which his yearning should for once be completely satisfied. He was less extravagant in *Mein Leben*: the earnest frame of mind engendered in him by Schopenhauer had induced the urgent need to give ecstatic expression to its fundamentals. Finally, in conversation with Cosima in 1878, he commented on people's ignorance of how remote the creative processes are from all experience, all reality. 'I felt the need to let myself rage in music, just as if I had to write a symphony.'[4] These are three very different admissions over a period of twenty-five years, and the full truth emerges only from placing all three together. Even if the third was tempered by consideration for Cosima, we can see today that it delves deepest into his creativity: the composer, conscious of the mastery he now possessed, had to express himself without restraint, 'let himself rage'. Mathilde Wesendonk and Arthur Schopenhauer were the two par-

ticular experiences that his genius needed and that destiny generously granted him.

In November he wrote to Princess Wittgenstein that he had been
able to continue working away on *Die Walküre* but it was going
much more slowly than he had expected. What he finally sketched
was always the best he could do, but the mood to work visited him
less and less often in his dreary life. And then, he found the subject
of *Die Walküre* too painful by far: there was really not one of the
world's sorrows that it did not express, and in the most painful way.
Playing artistic games with that pain was taking its revenge on him:
several times it had already made him so ill that he had had to stop
altogether. 'I am now on the second act, in the scene where Brünnhilde appears to Siegmund to foretell his death: something like that
can hardly be called composing any more!'

The beginning of the Annunciation of Death scene is one of the
few passages in the composition sketch which Wagner had to cross
out twice before eventually getting it right the third time. The
trouble was caused by the second motive, which is subsequently
taken up by the voice at the words 'Wer bist du, sag', and which, so
far as it is possible to decipher the first deleted version, originally
lacked the rising interrogative cadence at the end. The sketch of this
scene offers a particularly large number of instances of Wagner's use
of letters and words to keep the overall key of longer musical
periods in mind when he was working. The indivisibility of expression and form in his work is well illustrated by the fact that precisely
this most moving of scenes was, as shown by the formal analysis of
Alfred Lorenz, one that required the highest degree of artistic
contrivance.[5]

It was while he was working on the second act that Wagner wrote
a letter to Bülow discussing the latter's compositions very
thoroughly and tactfully – a rebuttal of the charge that he had no
time for his friends' works. He knew from his own experience, he
wrote, that there were some things that could not be expressed
musically in any other way than by the use of harmonies that were
bound to affront the ear of the musical philistine. When he recognized this in his own work he always made an effort to disguise the
difficult nature of the harmony as much as possible. The art consisted in 'communicating precisely the strangest, least familiar sensations to the listener in such a way that he is not distracted by the
material substance of what he hears but surrenders to my blandish-

ments unresisting, so to speak, and willingly accepts even the most unaccustomed of sounds'. (26 October 1854)[6]

He was writing there of something he had just been putting into practice, setting Wotan's despairing outbreaks in the great second scene of Act II. The notes he made in the margins of the composition sketch show he was already thinking out the instrumental blends that would distract attention from the difficult harmonies. The readiness with which his imagination was able to give him what he wanted is well illustrated by the note against the line 'Ich berührte Alberichs Ring': the cor anglais, three clarinets, horns, bassoons and tubas listed in the sketch all appear in the scoring of the following passage.

The composition sketch of the second act was finished on 18 November 1854, having taken two and a half months. Below the date Wagner wrote 'that was a bad time!!!'

He began the third act directly, on 20 November, and, relieved now of his financial worries, finished it in the incredibly short time of five weeks, on 27 December. It was written down in great haste, some of it no more than the bare indication of his intentions: the elaborate ensemble for the eight Valkyries at 'Unsern Schutz flehte sie an' appears here in the form of a single unison line, and at the close of the act he wrote out only the sustaining melody of the wind, without the Magic Fire figuration.[7]

But the sketch of this act has one most unusual feature, of which the prelude to *Das Rheingold* is probably the only other example: it lacks an important musical motive. Sieglinde's thanks to Brünnhilde, 'O hehrstes Wunder! Herrlichste Maid!', is set merely to a declamatory phrase, not to the melody of Redemption through Love. It has been asked why Wagner should have destined this motive, which occurs only at this one place, for its transfiguring role in the finale of *Götterdämmerung*, but it would appear from the sketch that Wagner originally conceived the motive for that role, and only subsequently decided to anticipate it in *Die Walküre*, so as to allow a ray of that transfiguration to fall upon Sieglinde in her grief.

As he now came to start scoring, Wagner was glad of the opportunity to work with an orchestra again. He replied to another invitation from the Zürich Music Society with a letter, dated 23 November, that, as Max Fehr says, is a masterpiece in both substance and form. While reminding them of the lack of results from his efforts of the last five years, he affirmed his readiness to conduct for them again, if the society and the theatre would come to an 'arrangement' over their two separate orchestras. This was accomplished, and he undertook a performance of the 'Eroica' on 9 January 1855. For the next concert, as he told the orchestral manager, Salomon Pestalozzi, he had something special in mind which would require extra players. 'I recognize, to my sorrow, that this will cause you a great deal of trouble and that I am driving the Music Society into certain bankruptcy.' (FWSZ, I, p. 411)

The 'something special' was the first performance of the *Faust* Overture he had originally composed in Paris and had just re-written in a single week. 'I cannot be vexed with this composition,' he had told Liszt back in 1852, 'even though it has things in it that would not flow from my pen now.' Now he wrote a completely new score, expanding the middle section with cadential phrases, toning down the brass throughout, and adding a 'dying fall' coda. He felt that revision of that nature showed more clearly than anything else what sort of person the composer had become and what crudenesses he had sloughed off. According to Mathilde Wesendonk he originally intended to dedicate the overture to her, but had suddenly decided that it was 'impossible for me to burden you with the dreadful motto [from *Faust*]:

The God who dwells within my bosom
Can make my inmost soul react;
The God who sways my every power
Is powerless with external fact.
And so existence weighs upon my breast,
I long for death, and life – life I detest.'

So he contented himself with presenting her with the score and inscribing it on the last page: 'R. W. Zürich 17. Jan. 55, to his dear friend, in remembrance.'

When he performed the work on 23 January he discovered that it was difficult to put across. He soon regretted having published the score: it had been more than rash, it had been foolish and irresponsible to place a composition like that in the hands of the time-beaters without any assurance of an even tolerable degree of understanding. (To H. Gottwald, 30 December 1855; FWSZ, II, pp. 353f.)

As well as his own works, the four concerts he conducted in January and February 1855 included the overtures to *Die Zauber-*

*flöte*, *Iphigenia in Aulis* and *Der Freischütz*, and Beethoven's Septet and Fifth and Seventh Symphonies. He also took a great deal of trouble rehearsing some members of the orchestra in Beethoven's C♯ minor Quartet, observing the while that simply teaching dynamic nuances by rote could never achieve the kind of results that were only to be obtained through the individual cultivation of a higher artistic taste.

When Wagner mentioned his loneliness during these months it was no more than the literal truth, for Minna had left Zürich at the beginning of September, ostensibly to visit relatives in Germany, but in reality on a special mission. As long ago as the summer of 1852, an enquiry about the terms for performing *Tannhäuser* had come from Botho von Hülsen, the intendant of the court opera in Berlin, transmitted through Wagner's brother Albert, whose daughter Johanna was now one of the stars of the Berlin company. In order to avoid repeating the experience he had had with *Rienzi* and the *Holländer*, of the performances being cancelled after he had done a lot of work for nothing, Wagner's terms included a payment of 1000 talers in advance, as well as the supervision of rehearsals by his 'other self', Liszt. The negotiations had come to grief on the latter condition, and when they were resumed in May 1854 between Hülsen and Liszt personally, there was again no agreement, in the face of Liszt's insistence on a completely free hand. In his financial predicament, Wagner was embarrassed by his friend's lack of diplomatic compliance, but could not bring himself to let him down. The easiest way for Liszt to retreat honourably would be if Wagner himself could assume control of the rehearsals.

So when Minna arrived in Dresden in October she presented a personal petition to the king: 'May Your Majesty accord grace and pardon to my husband, Richard Wagner, who was led astray, and grant him leave to attend the performances of his works in person.' The answer from the Ministry of Justice did not reach her until she was back in Zürich: the petition was refused. (LWVR, pp. 48ff.)

Before that, Hülsen had condescended to see Minna in Berlin on 9 October, when he gave her a number of empty assurances, so that she was encouraged to write to him from Zürich on 4 November, probably at Wagner's dictation, asking him to lend support to her petition. Quite apart from Hülsen's total lack of any desire to intercede for the amnesty of someone found guilty of high treason, it was not long before the refusal arrived from Dresden, so shelving the whole rescue operation.

Unless Wagner was prepared to renounce the royalties from Berlin, he had no remaining recourse but to capitulate. He could not afford to defer the Berlin *Tannhäuser* business any longer, he told Liszt in mid-March 1855; his financial situation was too grave. A friend in Zürich (i.e. Wesendonk) had rescued him from catastrophe the previous year, paying his debts in return for supervisory rights over all his future income. The person in question was a businessman, and a sincere friend, but, being a businessman, was unable to grasp why they did not give way, since it had become clear that there was no hope of Liszt being employed. 'Let us allow the matter to take what now seems to be the only course it can take. I regret bitterly that you have expended so much trouble in fulfilling my condition, and have had to endure so much tiresomeness.'

To Hülsen he wrote on 23 March: 'I hereby authorize you to perform this work, without attaching any further conditions.' His only request was for an advance payment of 100 friedrichsdor. *Tannhäuser* was at last performed in Berlin on 7 January 1856. By the fiftieth anniversary of Wagner's death, 13 February 1933, it had been given 711 times.[8]

Meanwhile Zürich had stolen a march on Berlin, and *Tannhäuser* was performed there in February 1855. He complained to Bülow that he had been squeezed dry. 'To please Frau Wesendonk I even consented to conduct one performance in their divine theatre. What stupid things one does!' The modest scale of the production can be judged from the scene-painter's bills, quoted by Fehr: 'Background to Venus Grotto with transparency, fr.55.–; repainting the horizon, fr.15.–; image of the Virgin, fr.8.–; two tiger skins, fr.3.–.' In addition, the soubrette cast as Elisabeth sang her role in white kid gloves with a fan dangling from her wrist. But modest as the singers' abilities were, Wagner wrote to Frau Ritter, they showed such willingness that he was moved to play a larger part in the production than he had originally intended, 'and to my sincere astonishment my – admittedly appalling! – exertions resulted in a success far beyond what I had expected. I did not conduct [the first two performances] myself. . . and so, as a listener for the first time, I had a truly thrilling impression of my work.' After conducting the third performance himself he addressed a few guarded words to his audience: if they now had only a feeble conception of his work, he was ready to do everything he could, if Zürich would also do its part.

He left Zürich on 26 February 1855 to travel to London by way of Paris. A Mr Anderson had turned up at the beginning of January, introducing himself as treasurer of the Old Philharmonic Society and offering him a fee of £200 for eight concerts. 'The prospect filled me with gloom,' Wagner wrote to Liszt, 'going to London to conduct philharmonic concerts is not my line of country.' But he had seen very clearly that if he did not accept the proffered hand it was tantamount to turning his back once and for all on the idea of making an impression in the artistic world as it was. (19 January)

It was soon plain that his forebodings had been justified. He had already learned before leaving Zürich that the London press was howling for the blood of the Old Philharmonic management committee over his engagement. As soon as he arrived he was advised to call on the most powerful critics, such as Chorley and Davison: they were of course rogues and fools, but they had influence, and it would be a pity if he allowed his talent to be wasted in London to no purpose. 'I don't know what *you* think of it,' he told Otto Wesendonk, 'but I have felt all along that there is nothing here for me with my talents, and I can really do without the praises of scoundrels.' (21 March)

He had to conduct those interminable programmes beloved of mid-nineteenth-century England in which one item followed another without rhyme or reason and was applauded with an equal lack of discrimination. He could not even console himself with the thought of his fee, for life in London was more expensive for a foreigner than he had anticipated. One cause for satisfaction was that the orchestra took a liking to him very quickly, although he brought them almost to despair at rehearsals with his 'Once more, please!' (in English). It was hard to wean them from the uniformly fast tempos and lack of dynamic variation instilled in them by Mendelssohn and persuade them to play in his own more richly shaded style. The 'faults' with which Henry Smart of *The Sunday Times* charged him give an approximate idea of his conducting: he took quick tempos faster than usual and slow tempos slower; he prefaced important entries or returns of themes with exaggerated ritardandos; he reduced the speed of Allegro movements by a third on the entry of cantabile phrases. This corresponds, broadly speaking, to his recommendations in his later essay *On Conducting*, which have been followed by all the great conductors since, especially in Beethoven.

He caused sufficient stir to bring Queen Victoria and Prince Albert to the seventh concert of the series, on 11 June. They asked for an encore of the *Tannhäuser* overture and received him, outlaw from Germany though he was, in their box during the interval. The queen's diary indicates that it was no empty act of courtesy: 'His own overture to *Tannhäuser* is a wonderful composition, quite overpowering, so grand, & in parts wild, striking and descriptive. We spoke to him afterwards.'[9]

But no amount of success could prevent him from comparing his lot in London to that of 'one of the damned in Hell'. He tried to spend the mornings scoring the second act of *Die Walküre* but felt so disorientated that he often sat staring at his pencilled sketches as if they were written in utterly foreign characters. Nevertheless, he managed to write the first draft of the score of the first and second scenes while he was there, including Wotan's great narration, of which Richard Strauss wrote in his edition of Berlioz's treatise on instrumentation: 'For all its simplicity, this passage is to me the rarest miracle of a genius more richly endowed than any other with the gift of transforming every nuance of feeling, every tremor of passion, into orchestral timbres, with an exactness that invincibly captivates and convinces every listener.'

In the afternoons Wagner threw himself despairingly into reading Dante, whose *Inferno*, he said, gained an unforgettable realism from the atmosphere of London. When Liszt told him he was going to write a *Dante* Symphony, he was aroused to write the long letter of 7 June which amounts to a complete treatise on the subject. He had followed Dante with sympathy through Hell and Purgatory, only to learn in Paradise that God had created the hell of existence to his own greater glory. He pointed out the contrast offered by Brahmanism and Buddhism: a sublime doctrine, the only satisfying one. For with Schopenhauer, another culture had dawned upon his spiritual horizon beside ancient Germany and Greece: India. He had brought Adolf Holtzmann's *Indische Sagen* to London with him: reading the legends had been his only pleasure there. They were all beautiful, but Savitri was divine. 'How hangdog our culture looks beside these pure revelations of noble humanity in the ancient East!' (To Mathilde Wesendonk, 30 April)

The external events of the four months in London were few: he struck up an acquaintance with the orchestra's leader Sainton, a Frenchman from Toulouse, and his friend Lüders, who were responsible for Wagner's engagement without knowing him: they had supposed that there must be some virtue in an artist who was so violently attacked. He met a young pupil of Liszt's, Karl Klindworth, who was supporting himself in London by giving lessons and in whom Wagner found only one fault, namely that he did not possess the voice for Siegfried. He met Malwida von Meysenbug, who had left Germany on account of her political ideals and was then living in London, and was later to become an intimate of the Wahnfried circle. He met Meyerbeer in the house of an English music-lover, who was astonished that two great composers should greet each other so coldly. He spent a few stirring evenings with Berlioz, who was in London to conduct the 'New' Philharmonic orchestra: they would have become even closer in their shared antipathy for the contemporary musical scene, had not Madame Berlioz, jealous of Wagner's fame, come between them. 'I have one genuine gain from London,' Wagner wrote to their mutual friend Liszt on 5 July, 'a sincere and intimate friendship with Berlioz, to which we are both party.' Berlioz, too, wrote to Liszt, 'Wagner a quelque chose de singulièrement attractif pour moi, et si nous avons des aspérités tous les deux, au moins nos aspérités s'emboîtent.' (Liszt to Wagner, 10 July)

The London tragedy does not lack its satyr play. Ferdinand Praeger, a German who lived in London teaching music, was recommended to Wagner by August Röckel's brother, and proved helpful in numerous mundane matters – 'an uncommonly good-natured fellow, only too touchy about his educational qualifications', as he was described in *Mein Leben*. Wagner corresponded with Praeger in later years, and the latter occasionally visited him in Zürich, Paris, Munich, Tribschen and Bayreuth.

To general astonishment, in 1892, a year after Praeger's death, a book by him entitled *Wagner as I Knew Him* appeared in both German and English editions, containing 'sensational revelations' about Wagner. To his personal 'reminiscences' were appended thirty-four letters to him from Wagner, but the discrepancies between the English and the German versions of these were so glaring as to arouse the suspicion of forgery. The following year Houston Stewart Chamberlain discovered twenty of the original letters in the possession of Lord Dysart, which he copied out in full. The result surpassed all expectations: not a single sentence corresponded to Praeger's text! When Chamberlain published the originals in 1894, together with a critique demolishing Praeger's book, Breitkopf & Härtel withdrew it, admitting that professional integrity required them to do so.

But what had become of the fourteen letters still missing? Chamberlain drew up a table demonstrating that these on the one hand were the most sensational, and on the other had no dates in Praeger's text, unlike those he had found, and contrary to Wagner's habit. It is not unreasonable to conclude that they were out-and-out fabrications or else distorted beyond recognition, so that Praeger had not dared to give dates, which would have led to their flat contradiction by other reliable sources.

And someone who forges letters will certainly not shrink from forging unsubstantiated conversations: the sheer impossibility of some of the dates and facts in Praeger's 'recollections' proves it. With anyone else that would have been an end of the matter, but not with Wagner. Praeger's inventions continued to be touted as facts for long after. It is only as an example of a very large sub-species of 'Wagnerian literature' that the case merits as detailed an exposition as it has received here.[10]

It is not even possible to attribute the line taken by Praeger in his book to senile decay, as has been suggested. Karl Klindworth warned Wagner in 1859 that Praeger was abusing his confidence. Wagner's reply, in a letter of 18 May, shows how easily he could be deceived by those who purported to be his friends: Klindworth had no cause for alarm on his behalf, it was impossible for Praeger to abuse any 'confidence': 'he really is not on such terms with me'.

Unproductive as his stay in London was so far as his creative work was concerned, it nevertheless represented another step in his growing awareness of alienation from contemporary artistic activities. This is most clearly expressed in a long letter to Sulzer of 10–12 May 1855: that he had once again allowed himself to be tempted to have truck with the world with which he had really long ago severed his ties was due to the contradiction within himself that would probably endure his life long. The realization that he could only sully himself by contacts with the public world of art had already led him to wish that he could slough off his artistic nature altogether. What would then be left for him? Probably Schopenhauerian sainthood!

> But there is no need for me to rack my brains over that one, because as long as a spark of life remains within me, it is unlikely that my artistic illusions will release me: they are really the decoys the life-urge uses to ensnare my judgement to do it service again and again. I really cannot imagine anything clearly and plainly that does not at once get mixed up with visions of that kind, and in the end it is my own judgement that time and again makes me the artistic dreamer that I am.

It was a nice state of affairs, he concluded. He probably hurt a lot of people in this way, but he caused none such hellish torments as himself, and he could assign the blame almost entirely to his artistic nature. 'Therefore anyone who gains some pleasure from the products of it really has nothing to complain about if I cause him any distress, for I certainly suffer more from it than he.' Resignedly he added, 'I hardly believe that you will be able to understand me entirely.'[11]

Although he was sometimes on the point of throwing away the baton he finally stuck it out for all eight concerts. 'I shall be bringing 1000 francs back from London with me,' he wrote to his 'guardian' on 15 May; 'it is simply *not possible* to save any more than that, and I can only assure you that this is the *hardest* money I have ever earned in my life, compared to which the piecework I once did for a Parisian music publisher, humiliating as it was, now seems child's play. I may say that I have had to pay for every one of these 1000 francs with a sense of bitterness such as I hope never to have to experience again.'

# 20

## The *Ring* Crisis

'London' had prolonged itself throughout the rest of the year, Wagner wrote to Julie Ritter, looking back over 1855. 'On my return, my old dog received me and lived just one more week to show me he had been waiting for me; then he died . . . it was yet another heavy blow for me.' He will have remembered Homer's lines about the dog Argus, who 'had no sooner set eyes on Odysseus after those nineteen years than he succumbed to the black hand of death'.

In the middle of July he and Minna went to Seelisberg, a resort high above the Lake of Lucerne with views across to the mountains of Schwyz and Uri. 'A few days ago I arrived up here in Paradise,' he wrote to Praeger. But his stay was spoiled by the weather and the other people, and he went back to Zürich on 15 August to take up the scoring of *Die Walküre* again, from the third scene of the second act. He was so unsettled that all memory of the ideas he had in London seemed to have abandoned him.

Then during the winter he began to suffer attacks of an inflammation that was diagnosed as erysipelas, though it is more likely to have been an allergy of some kind. Hardly had he started to settle to his work again, he complained to Julie Ritter, than a 'face-rose' [to give a literal translation of the German name for erysipelas] had flowered on the briars of his existence. Like a conscientious gardener he had been tending it carefully for almost three months, 'and I still have not been able to get my big child, the Valkyrie, to go to sleep yet'. (29 December)

In such periods of illness, which made it impossible for him to compose, his mind was always particularly active in adopting and elaborating new ideas. The Indian studies sparked off by his reading of Schopenhauer had led him to Eugène Burnouf's *Introduction à l'histoire du Bouddhisme indien*, where he read the legend of Prakriti, the Jandala girl, and Ananda, the Buddha's 'beloved disciple'.

Once on his wanderings Ananda came to a well where a girl was drawing water. When he asked her for a drink she replied that she was of the Jandala caste and not permitted to approach a holy man. Ananda answered: 'My sister, I did not seek to know your caste, I asked you for a drink of water.' And as she handed him the cup she was suddenly overcome by passionate love. She hurried to her mother and bewailed her distress. Her mother told her to adorn herself and put on her finest clothes. Then she wove a powerful love-spell that would bring the youth to the spot. When Ananda felt the pangs of love he prayed to the Buddha, and the Enlightened One heard him and destroyed the spell. But the girl did not abandon her desire. She went outside the city gate, sat down beneath a tree and waited for the Buddha. When he came past, begging for alms, she threw herself at his feet and confessed her love. Then the Enlightened One asked whether she was willing to wear the same robe as Ananda and to follow him wherever he went, and whether her parents consented. The girl, thinking only of her love, answered 'Yes'. But then she realized the deeper significance of the question and she joined the Buddha's followers.

When the Brahmans heard that the Buddha had taken a Jandala girl as a disciple they murmured together and went out to the garden where he taught. And the Enlightened One, knowing their thoughts, told them the story of the girl in her previous incarnation: then she had been the daughter of a Brahman king, and her father had rejected the proposals of a Jandala king who had wanted her as a bride for his son.

For the time being Wagner stored this legend in his heart. But it never left him, and he only finally abandoned the idea of composing it in 1882.

At least the state of his health guarded him against the temptation to throw himself into another adventure like the London one. America was working on him now, he told Klindworth, trying to persuade him to go to New York for six months, but they had small hope of success. 'I am too stupid even to earn money.' (4 October) When the Zürich Music Society invited him to conduct another series of subscription concerts, he refused on health grounds. He told Mathilde Wesendonk that his London experiences had made him determined to withdraw from public music-making. 'I need all my inner repose now, in order to complete my great work, which could easily . . . become a grotesque chimera, ruined by this everlasting, injurious contact with the second-rate and the unsatisfactory.'

Even so, he very nearly succumbed to the temptation of conducting Mozart's *Requiem* in celebration of the centenary of his birth in 1856. The arrangements came to grief, however, over the matter of finding a hall for the performance that satisfied Wagner: the German-language press seized this as a welcome excuse to accuse him of hostility to Mozart. He lost patience and wrote an 'explanation' for the *Eidgenössische Zeitung*: since his refusal had been exploited by a number of 'journalistic idiots' in the style that had become standard practice for use against him, he thought he might as well explain himself. He would be ready to sacrifice his health if the music-lovers would make corresponding sacrifices and provide him with a proper concert hall.[1]

As Wagner saw his hopes for Zürich as the location of his future artistic activities receding, he increasingly withdrew from the public eye. He had formed a small circle of tried and trusted friends, to whose number Gottfried Semper and Gottfried Keller were added in 1855.

Semper had gone through the Dresden uprising with Wagner, who commended him to Sulzer in 1850, writing from Paris: 'It would give me extraordinary happiness if so excellent a man and artist were to join you all – and me – there.' (FWSZ, I, pp. 355f.) He had then met him again in London, where Semper was struggling to gain a foothold. Thanks to the combined efforts of Wagner and Sulzer, in the autmn of 1855 he was appointed to the staff of the newly established federal Polytechnic in Zürich, where he became a stimulating member of the circle of friends, always ready for a lively argument. While Wagner followed with interest the writing of Semper's book on style, his chief theoretical work, and had a copy of it in his library in Wahnfried, Semper thought that the dramatist in Wagner took his work too seriously: what he particularly liked about *Don Giovanni* was that the tragic types were encountered in it only as in a masquerade, in masks and dominoes.

Gottfried Keller had returned to Zürich from Berlin in December 1855, and as early as 13 January 1856 he was writing to Lina Duncker, his publisher's wife, about dainty suppers at the house of an elegant member of the cantonal executive council – Sulzer – where Richard Wagner, Semper and some native Zürichers used to meet. Wagner himself sometimes offered a decent midday meal and didn't stint the wine. On 21 February Keller wrote to the literary historian Hermann Hettner: he often saw Richard Wagner these days: come what may, he was a very gifted and likable person. 'And he is certainly a poet too, for the text of his Nibelung trilogy is a treasure house of original national poetry.' In a letter of 16 April he repeated, emphatically, 'I am seeing a great deal of Richard Wagner, who is a genius and a good man as well. If you find the opportunity . . . do read his Nibelung trilogy. You will find it is informed by an impressive poetry, quintessentially German, but clarified by the spirit of classical tragedy.' His intuition of the Germanic and Greek elements behind the inspiration of the *Ring* is amazing. And on 21 April he wrote to Ludmilla Assing (another of his female friends) that Wagner was a genius and the most entertaining of men, extremely cultivated and a really profound thinker. 'His new libretto, the Nibelung trilogy, read simply as a poem on its own account, is full of passion and felicities, and has made a far deeper impression on me than any other book of poetry.'[2]

In view of these letters there is something curiously brazen about the assertion of Marcel Herwegh, Georg's son, in his memoirs (*Au banquet des dieux*, 1932), that after Wagner's public reading of the *Ring* in February 1853 his father had walked home with Keller, who had disparaged the work – the more so as Keller was not even in Zürich at the time! Evidently some people would give a great deal to be able to call Keller as witness for the prosecution. In 1951, in a review of the newly published Burrell Collection, Thomas Mann launched a furioso attack on Wagner, taking Keller's description of him as 'hairdresser and charlatan' as his text: of course a realist like Keller could have had no time for the Wagnerian hotch-potch of worldly renunciation and worldly lust, the arch-romantic exploitation of the unwholesome contrast of sensuality and chastity, and so on. Mann does not give the source of his quotation, but, coming from a man of his integrity, one takes it for granted that it must have been said in a context where Keller was discussing fundamental principles of art and life. It is therefore all the more surprising to track it down in a letter to Ferdinand Freiligrath of 30 April 1857 where Keller for once really lets off steam. After slandering a string of 'notabilities' he writes: 'Then there's Richard Wagner, a very gifted man, but something of a hairdresser and a charlatan as well. He has a bric-à-brac table, with a silver hairbrush in a crystal dish etc. etc. on it . . . But that's enough tittle-tattle.' And then in a postscript he tries to take back what he has said: 'Once again I've written a lot of feeble jokes, which I already regret.'[3]

For his part, Wagner had lost no time in asking Sulzer for a copy of Keller's novel *Der grüne Heinrich*, but he had the greatest pleasure from *Die Leute von Seldwyla*, Keller's collection of tales about the inhabitants of a mythical but archetypal small Swiss town. To the end of his days *Die drei gerechten Kammacher* and *Spiegel das Kätzchen* were, together with Hoffmann's *Der goldene Topf*, the stories that he most loved to read aloud. The 'town warlock of Hottingen', as he dubbed Keller, was much gratified by Wagner's special appreciation of these two tales, of whose formal excellence he himself had a high opinion. 'I have just passed one of the pleasantest hours of my life,' Wagner declared after reading the much later *Züricher Novellen* in 1879, and praised Switzerland for being a country where a writer like Keller was still possible. 'If only I could hear something comparable in music from a contemporary.' Then he recalled his memories of Keller from his years in Zürich: when he said something truly fine and witty, it came blurting out in a rush, as if somebody had tipped over a sack of potatoes. When he and Cosima read *Das Sinngedicht* together, when they were in Sicily in 1882, he made up his mind to see his old friend once more after so long an interval. The reunion did not take place. On 19 February 1883 Keller wrote to Cosima, asking if she would permit an old neighbour and friend to express his deep sympathy, sorrow and distress at Wagner's death. Daniela replied on her mother's behalf, saying how much Wagner had continued to admire and enjoy Keller's works – 'your charming, touching characters, the sublimity of your observation and thought' – in the last years of his life.

Of all his other friendships in Zürich, Wagner was affected most deeply by his relationship with the Wesendonks, embarrassed as it was during that winter of 1855–6 by his growing love for Mathilde and his dependence on Otto. His not daring to be godfather to their son Guido gives some insight into the conflict of his feelings. In the Annals he noted for September 1855: 'Bad, capricious moods, particularly against the Wesendonk family. Refused to be godfather, because unlucky.'

Forever interrupted by attacks of erysipelas, work on the third act of *Die Walküre* proceeded only slowly, which obliged him to put off once again the visit from Liszt that he was longing for. 'I am pining for him,' he told Princess Wittgenstein in November. Moreover, a year after the first mention of the idea, a new project was again urging itself upon him. 'More defined conception of *Tristan*,' he noted in the Annals for December 1855, 'third act the source of the mood of the whole (interweaving Parzival searching for the Grail).' A few lines about this earliest conception were preserved in a notebook dating from 1854–5.

> *3rd Act.* Tristan on his sickbed in the castle garth.
> Battlements to one side.
> Waking from slumber he calls to his squire, if he can
> see anything, thinking him to be on the battlements. He
> is not. He comes at last in response to the calls.
> Reproaches. Apology. There has been a pilgrim to make
> welcome. Then and now. Tristan's impatience. The
> squire still sees nothing. Tristan reflects. Doubt. Song
> from below, receding. What is it? Squire tells him about
> the pilgrim. – Parzival. Deep impression. Love as
> torment.
>
> My mother died when she bore me;
> now I live, I die of having been born.
> Why? – 'Parzival's Refrain' – repeated by the shepherd.
> = The whole world nothing but unsatisfied yearning!
> How shall it ever be satisfied? –
>                     Parzival's Refrain. (BBL 1915, p. 145)

The words and melody of 'Parzival's Refrain', with the rising sixths of the Grail theme coming at the end, have also survived, in a note Wagner wrote to Mathilde Wesendonk:

> Wo find' ich dich, du heil'ger Gral
> dich sucht voll Sehnsucht mein Herze.
> ('Where shall I find thee, thou holy grail,
> full of longing my heart seeks thee.')
>
> You dear, errant child! Look, that's what I was on the point of writing down, when I found your beautiful, noble verses![4]

At last, in March 1856, he was in the position to tell his friends that he had finished *Die Walküre*, after suffering agonies. 'It is more beautiful than anything I have ever written – but it has exhausted me dreadfully.' (To Pusinelli, 28 April)

Throughout the whole period he was dogged by his everlasting money troubles. A large debt to Karl Ritter had been left unpaid in the reorganization of his affairs in 1854, and repaying it now in instalments perceptibly diminished his income. In November he had approached Wesendonk, through Sulzer, with a plea for his subvention to be increased from two to three thousand francs a year, but Wesendonk mantled himself in silence. When the Wesendonks then paid him a formal call to congratulate him on the completion of his score, he spoke in such bitter terms, as he admits in his autobiography, about this manner of expressing interest in his works, that the visitors abruptly left in confusion: it cost him a good many laborious explanations to repair his offence.

On 26 April he invited his friends to hear a run-through of the first act with piano accompaniment, in which he sang both Siegmund and Hunding. While the impression this performance made on him was still fresh, Wesendonk wrote to tell Wagner how much he had enjoyed the evening and that he wished heartily that Wagner might be able to bring the work he had begun so magnificently to an equally magnificent conclusion, untroubled by mundane worries. 'I will take charge of that and authorize our friend Sulzer to pay you 250 francs a month forthwith, on the understanding that you regularly transmit all the income from your operas to Sulzer, as hitherto.' (FWSZ, II, p. 38)

As his hopes of Zürich faded Wagner was again directing his thoughts towards Germany. After the failure of Minna's attempt to win him an amnesty, he appealed to Liszt to seek an audience with King Johann of Saxony on his behalf, with Grand Duke Carl Alexander of Weimar acting as intermediary: in requesting pardon for him, Liszt was to put all the emphasis on the fact of his being an artist. 'Could you perhaps take the opportunity to give the king a copy of my *Ring* text?'

Liszt, recognizing the uselessness of such a step, advised Wagner to present instead a plea for permission for nothing more than to hear his works in Weimar, on the grounds that to do so was essential for his future works. For his part, in the meantime, he persuaded the duke to write personally to King Johann in the hope of influencing him to receive Wagner's request favourably.

The king's reply, on 25 April, was that many benefits had been bestowed on Wagner in the past, his thanks for which had been to take part in the May uprising: 'had he not absconded, he would probably have been sentenced to death for high treason. It is as clear as day that even the greatest talent cannot weigh in the scale against such ingrate and shameful conduct.' Nor did he refrain from administering a reprimand to his 'dearest cousin': in propriety he had to leave it to his conscience as to whether, in the circumstances, he wished to allow a man like Wagner to appear at his court.

Evidently Carl Alexander was so wounded by this letter that he did not even tell Liszt about it. It is otherwise improbable that Wagner would have composed his lengthy plea for pardon on 16 May, admitting and attempting to justify his error. Since he had once more become capable of conceiving a great, purely artistic work, in which he had regained his moral poise, an inner conversion had led him to a deeper insight into the essence of things, thanks to which he had now come to recognize that his previous opinion in one particular matter, the 'relationship of the ideal to the reality of all human, earthly affairs', had been erroneous. (LWVR, pp. 62ff.)

'Here is the letter to the King of Saxony,' he wrote to Liszt, 'it has cost me much, very much – even so, I am afraid that it may not serve its purpose, and let that be the end of the matter. For even this letter is a profanation; just to mention my "inner conversion" to the King of Saxony and his ministers amounts to sacrilege. But I thought I might go so far in this extremity.' His fears proved justified: the reply that came from the Ministry of Justice at the beginning of August held out no hope of his petition being granted. He sent it on to Liszt: 'Read the splendid answer to my letter to the king.'

After finishing *Die Walküre*, Wagner composed no more of the *Ring* for six months, but his imagination was busy. On the same day that he wrote his letter to the King of Saxony, 16 May 1856, he wrote down in his notebook the prose sketch for a drama to be called *Die Sieger* ('The Victors'), based on the legend of Ananda and Prakriti. (RWGS, XI, p. 325) It was not alone the beauty and the profundity of the subject that appealed to him, but also its peculiar suitability to the compositional procedures that he had now developed: as the life of every being in earlier incarnations is appar-

ent to the eye of the Buddha, so the listener should be able to share in
the previous lives of the two principal characters through the musical reminiscences heard throughout the action. This is an example
of how, in Wagner's work, the poetic and dramatic ideas on the one
hand and the musical techniques on the other mutually condition
and support each other.

It was in the same period that he devised a new ending for
*Siegfrieds Tod*, with a large-scale choral finale. On 22 June he wrote
to Franz Müller in Weimar that he was going to make changes of
some substance to the last two dramas, including their titles, which
would probably become plain *Siegfried* and *Götterdämmerung*. The
principal change would be in the finale of the latter, for which he
was going to write a completely new text: 'the interpretation of the
character of Brünnhilde, now that she has become all-knowing,
will be different, broader and more decisive. The men and women,
too – for the first time in the whole work – will take a larger part and
express a wider interest at the very end.'

He was referring not to the two versions of the concluding words
which are to be found in the complete edition of the writings (the
first beginning 'Nicht Gut, nicht Gold, noch göttliche Pracht . . .'
and the second 'Führ' ich nun nicht mehr nach Walhalls Feste . . .'),
but to a third version he had sketched, which was first published by
Otto Strobel in 1933. The second and third versions both introduce
the idea of rebirth, which has been regarded as an uncalled-for
fusion of the Germanic and the Indian ; but Ettmüller's commentary on the Vaulu-Spá (Völuspa), which Wagner is now known to
have had in his library in Dresden, lists some examples of the belief
in rebirth of the 'old Northmen', so Wagner must have believed
that he was not proposing anything contrary to the spirit of Germanic myth.[5]

If, in the end, he used none of the three, it was because 'the
meaning they had to convey is already expressed with utmost
clarity in the musical rendering of the drama'.

Before beginning the composition of *Siegfried* Wagner wanted to
overcome his susceptibility to erysipelas. On 5 June he set out on
one of the 'unhappiest and most wretched' journeys he had ever
made, by train, mail coach and steamer, to seek a cure in a change of
air. He had been recommended to consult a Dr Vaillant, who ran a
hydropathic institution in the small village of Mornex, in the vicinity of Geneva, at the foot of the Petit Salève, where the regime was

more like the milder observances of Priessnitz than the killing measures of Albisbrunn.

When Wagner had described his symptoms, Vaillant smiled: 'Monsieur, vous n'êtes que nerveux.' He promised to cure him so effectively within two months that he would never suffer from erysipelas again, and it was in fact another twenty-four years before he did. The only unwelcome aspect of the cure was that he had to abstain from all serious work, so he devoted his time to reading the novels of Sir Walter Scott and designing a house for himself, doing his best to draw plans as accurate as an architect's.

This ambition was born of negotiations he was conducting at the time with Breitkopf & Härtel, with a view to their publishing the *Ring*. There was no longer any reference to the resignation of two years previously, when he had declared that he wanted to perform it for Liszt and himself alone.

He saw very plainly, he wrote to the Härtels,

> that only the future in a quite literal sense (and not in the sense of the label that a number of empty-headed scribblers have stuck on me) will be able to establish the genuine, unquestionable success of my dramatic works; and if I was previously without hope in that respect, you must admit that after the extraordinary, quite unprecedented fate that has befallen my most recent works, I now have good reason for hope . . . It is impossible that I shall ever again conceive, let alone write, anything resembling my 'Nibelungs': rich and abundant, it is the most important work of my life, and in the text alone I believe that I have already given the nation a work that I am proud to think can be commended to it for the future as well.

He suggested that, as there were no precedents for so extraordinary a publication, his fee should be calculated according to what he would need to live on while he finished the work: 'That sum, for all four parts, is . . . 2000 louisdor, or 10,000 talers in gold.' He would make over the two parts already completed to them at once and unconditionally, on payment of half that sum; the remainder to be paid in instalments of 500 louisdor each on delivery of the scores of *Siegfried* and *Siegfrieds Tod*. Whatever their decision, he felt compelled to tell them that if they could come to no agreement he would find it impossible to finish the great work. In that case he would start something else, which he would be able to finish in a year. (20 June)

The Härtel brothers' counter-proposal revealed, to his delight, that they were by no means unwilling to bargain. He therefore invited them to join him and Liszt when they met, as they were planning to do, in Zürich. 'You will have no better opportunity, *before* hearing a performance, of getting a really clear idea of what is in hand.' But they unexpectedly revoked their proposal: 'Circumstances leave us no choice: we beg to withdraw.' Once again, Newman remarks, 'a fortune was to be lost to people whose business instincts were a guide to nothing but the immediate future'.

Wagner suspected, not without reason, the influence of Otto Jahn; instead of getting to know the work at the fountainhead, as he had suggested, they had preferred to trust the advice and opinion of a third party. 'My negotiations with the Härtels have come to nothing again,' he wrote to Princess Wittgenstein, 'and the little house I have so long been yearning for, as a quiet place to work, is still only a castle in the air, probably next door to Valhalla.' (4 September)

The collapse of his hopes in Weimar and Leipzig was followed by the failure of his attempt, through the good offices of Mathilde Wesendonk, to rent a cottage in Seefeld; but then Otto Wesendonk came up with the suggestion of providing something for the Wagners in the property overlooking the Lake of Zürich where he was having a house built for himself. 'Entre nous, do you really want to take the place, as far as you are able, of princes and publishers?' Wagner wrote in reply. 'I scarcely thank you for this wonderful offer, for I am sure that the sensation of being able to make one like it must be a joy that is more rewarding in itself than any expression of thanks could hope to be.' (1 September)

The prospect gave him the courage, in spite of five pianos and a flute in his immediate neighbourhood on Zeltweg, to begin the composition sketch of *Siegfried* in the middle of September. He reverted to his earlier practice of making an orchestral sketch while he was still working on the composition sketch, having often experienced difficulty in deciphering his hectic scrawl when he came to score *Rheingold* and *Walküre*. He started with Mime's 'Zwangvolle Plage! Müh' ohne Zweck!' and did not write the short prelude until he was on the verso of the second sheet of paper. 'It was utterly new ground,' he wrote to Frau Ritter, 'and after the dreadful tragedy of *Die Walküre* I entered upon it with a sensation of freshness such as I have never felt before.' But he came close to despair when a tinsmith across the road added his percussion to the other musicians in the street. In an access of comic rage he threw himself at the piano to sing Siegfried's G minor Allegro: 'Da hast du die Stücken, schändlicher Stümper . . .'

Work was interrupted on 13 October by the arrival of Liszt, followed a few days later by Princess Wittgenstein and her daughter Princess Marie. Liszt played his *Faust* and *Dante* Symphonies from the score, making Wagner exclaim that it was a miracle to hear him. Liszt's forty-fifth birthday on 22 October was the high point of his visit. A brilliant company gathered in the Hotel Baur au Lac to hear Wagner and a young Zürich soprano, with Liszt at the piano, perform the first act and the Annunciation of Death scene from *Die Walküre*. At the end Liszt held out both hands to his friend in admiration. A well-wisher wrote in the *Neue Zürcher Zeitung* that Wagner's efforts towards reform were realized in this composition, which was one of music's most magnificent creations; his ideas 'mark an epoch and will move the whole world'.

'I . . . have now luxuriated – without getting intoxicated – in Liszt's company for three weeks,' Wagner told Karl Klindworth on 1 November, 'and hope to keep him here for some time yet.' His desire to unbosom himself to Liszt on artistic matters was accompanied by a need to pour out his heart on more confidential concerns. Liszt had just had a letter from Jessie Laussot, telling him that she was on the point of creating an independent existence for herself by founding an educational institution. This prompted Wagner to tell him the whole story of his unhappy adventure in Bordeaux. Liszt was so moved that he walked home with him all the way from the Hotel Baur au Lac to Zeltweg, and kissed him as they parted. 'Were it possible', Wagner wrote to their mutual confidante, Julie Ritter, 'that Jessie has gathered the strength to withdraw from an unworthy dependence . . . no one would owe her the heartiest interest more than I; indeed, I could call myself shamed by her . . . I ought to draw some comfort from being able to offer Jessie my hand in friendship, now that passion need no longer cloud our relationship.' Clearly the pain of that experience still lodged in his heart.

But Wagner's pleasure in Liszt's company was clouded by the

hubbub Princess Wittgenstein created around her: it was, he said, as though Zürich had become some kind of metropolis overnight; dinner parties, supper parties followed hard upon one another; suddenly one found oneself surrounded by a throng of interesting people, of whose existence in Zürich one had previously had no inkling. His only choice was to put a good face on it or take refuge in illness. 'By all that you and I hold holy,' he excused himself to Liszt, 'believe me and my assurance that I am ill and need complete rest and care today, in the hope of being able to enjoy you again tomorrow.' (2 November) He particularly detested the princess's 'appalling mania for professors', now keeping each one individually to herself, now serving them en masse to her friends. Gottfried Keller remarked that the 'Ferschtin' (as her title of 'Fürstin' was pronounced in Zürich) had made a friend of every person of prominence, and was a clever woman, for all the learned fire-eaters and Brutuses sang her praises – he alone had remained in the outer darkness and was quite out of countenance. (To Lina Duncker, 8 March 1857) He had almost despaired of Wagner, who, encouraged in his follies by the presence of Liszt, had again become cracked in the head and very selfish.

Wagner, too, was taken aside for a tête-à-tête one day, as she wanted to know all about the 'plot' of the downfall of the gods in the *Ring*. She showed a keen interest in the finest and most abstruse elements, he recalled, but in somewhat too arithmetical, mathematical a spirit, so that by the time he had finished he had the feeling that he had been explaining the intrigues of some French play to her.

Liszt was often unwell and irritable during the six weeks and did not always have the self-control to sustain his usual air of serenity. Wagner observed this on several occasions with alarm: he was put on his guard by it, and things never reached a pitch of intensity between them, 'only it gave me the obscure feeling, which has never since left me, that it might come to such a pitch, and it would then be frightful'. (ML, p. 629)

One outburst he witnessed was directed against Karl Ritter, who was mortally offended and was not to be pacified even by a personal visit by Liszt. For the first and only time Wagner was reproached by Frau Ritter, because he had allowed her son to suffer offence in his house. As a consequence he felt he could not continue to accept her money: 'Permit me to tell you candidly that I could accept such a sacrifice only so long as I was sure that the source from which it flowed was a completely unclouded sympathy, a sympathy strong enough to extend forbearance even to my weaknesses and errors.' (24 December) To Sulzer he wrote that it gave him no pleasure to have to remind him that he was now without means of subsistence. The recognition that his financial affairs would never regulate themselves was gradually eating down so deep into him that he was afraid of becoming totally apathetic. (FWSZ, II, p. 373)

But in spite of all its drawbacks, Liszt's visit gave him a lift that is reflected in his letters to Princess Marie. After Liszt had gone he had swallowed Goethe and Schiller's correspondence hungrily. It was the case with him that he seldom read what was actually in front of him, but what he put between the lines. 'And now I was reading into it everything that I could promote, initiate and disseminate with Liszt if we were closer to each other! I even read our rare friendship into it, printed in letters of gold.' (January 1857)

He had resumed the composition of *Siegfried* on 1 December with Mime's 'Einst lag wimmernd ein Weib'. But he was already telling Princess Marie on 19 December that he had imperceptibly found himself in *Tristan*: 'for the present music without words'. A sheet of musical sketches of the same date has survived, with the heading 'Love scene. *Tristan und Isolde*', which includes not only the proto-type of the theme 'Lausch, Geliebter!' from the second act, and some variants on it, but also the famous rising chromatic motive of yearning which was destined to revolutionize the history of music – and this before a single line of the text or even of the prose sketch had been written! 'For some things I will sooner write the music than the words.'[6]

Nor was that all that was occupying his thoughts: three weeks later he told the princess of a new idea for *Die Sieger*, inspired by Count Schack's *Stimmen des Ganges*: the girl, now called Savitri after his favourite character in Holtzmann's *Indische Sagen*, who, while waiting for Ananda in the second act, 'rolls in the flowers in ecstasy, luxuriantly drinking in the sun, the trees, birds, waters – everything – the whole natural creation, is told by the Shakya, after she has taken the fatal vow, to look about her and then asked "How does it all seem to you?" – "No longer beautiful", she replies gravely and sadly, for now she sees the other side of the world.' Characteristi-cally, in view of the counterpoint of his creative activity, Wagner went on: 'In the second act of *Tristan* – but you shall not learn anything about that yet. All that is only music at present.' (January 1857)

Finally, he felt compelled to take arms on behalf of Liszt, who was under fire as a composer, in an open 'Letter to M[arie] W[ittgenstein] on Franz Liszt's Symphonic Poems', published in the *Neue Zeitschrift für Musik*. (*Brief an M. W. Über Franz Liszts symphonische Dichtungen*, RWGS, V, pp. 182ff.) It in fact mirrors something of Wagner's feelings on the subject: by keeping to general aesthetic reflections, he avoided having to touch on details that were unsympathetic to him. Privately he did not conceal from his friends his reservations about some of the more theatrical effects, such as the pompous conclusion of the Dante symphony: 'No, no! Not that! Away with it! No majestic Lord God!' 'You are quite right,' Liszt wrote back, 'I said the same; the princess persuaded me to write it like that: but now it shall be done as you think it should be.' Wagner was all the more distressed, then, that not only was the finale retained after all, but the original ending of the *Faust* Symphony, which died away gently, was replaced by a grandiose chorus with tenor solo. Nevertheless the open letter is an unequivocal affirmation of his high opinion of Liszt the composer. Thanking him, the latter wrote: 'You said it as no one else would have known how.' (19 April 1857)

In the meantime Wagner had finished the composition sketch of the first act of *Siegfried* on 20 January and the orchestral sketch on 5 February. He finished the first draft of the score on 31 March during a visit from Mathilde Wesendonk. This first act had succeeded beyond all his expectations, he told Julie Ritter, and he was now convinced that *Siegfried* would be his most popular work. He had not only trodden completely new ground in it, but developed a completely new compositional technique as well. Whereas there are still alternating passages of arioso and recitative in *Rheingold* and *Walküre*, which had confused Liszt at first in the third act of the latter, here Wagner succeeded for the first time in sustaining the uninterrupted flow of melody: one is hardly aware that the structure rests on a sequence of songlike periods.

He had just got to Siegfried's 'Des Vaters Stahl fügt sich wohl mir', and was actually thinking about the motive that was to define the beginning of the forging, when Wesendonk's letter arrived confirming the purchase of the cottage next to his villa on the

Gabler hill. 'You dear, good people!' he exclaimed. 'What shall I say to you? Everything around me is suddenly different, as if by magic!' (To Otto Wesendonk, January 1857) 'Wagner's letter truly warmed our hearts and was the best possible reward, if an action which in itself gives the greatest happiness even needed one,' Mathilde wrote to Minna. 'I hope this house will be a true haven ['Asyl'] of peace and friendship, a sanctuary in a world of envy and hatred.' (11 January) The house, henceforth called 'Asyl', was ready for them to move into on 28 April. Minna occupied the ground floor, Wagner the first. From his writing-desk he had a wonderful view of the lake and the Alps. A chaise-longue, on which he used to rest, stood in the middle of the room. He stood at a lectern to compose, often taking a turn up and down the room, sometimes going into the next room to try out a chord or a phrase on the grand piano there.

It seemed a good omen when the first letter to arrive in his new home was from Frau Ritter, offering to renew her support. With what melancholy he had thought of her all that time must remain his secret, he wrote in reply, for she was really the closest to him of all her family: her age and her frank, open character enabled her to maintain her boundless indulgence in the face of the fierce idiosyncracies of his own nature, 'which is something people like me need if we are in our turn to remain patient and persevering in our contact with a world that is always hostile at bottom, alien and injurious towards us'. (6 May)

On the first warm, sunny morning of spring he had taken a walk out to the new house while it was still in the builders' hands. Green buds were opening in the little garden, the birds were singing and bells were ringing in the distance. He recalled that it was Good Friday and then remembered the significance of the same reminder for the hero in Wolfram's *Parzival*. All the intransigence of existence subsided, and an inner voice cried out: 'God is in us – the world is vanquished! Who created it? Idle question! Who vanquished it? God in our hearts!' It acted as a pointer to the fundamental idea of the poem. 'Starting with the Good Friday idea, I rapidly conceived a complete three-act drama, which I at once sketched in outline.'

'Good Friday, fantasy on the terrace. Conceived "Parcival"', he wrote in the Annals. (10 April 1857)

But before turning to one of the new projects – *Tristan, Die*

*Sieger, Parsifal*[7] – that were clamouring for his attention, he made one last attempt to create a material basis on which he could then have proceeded to complete the *Ring*. With Liszt acting as mediator, he again resumed negotiations with Breitkopf & Härtel in March. The most important thing, he wrote to them, was to set right their misconceptions about the nature of the work. He was expecting some leading singers and a pianist of the first rank – Klindworth – during the summer. If they could come and see him at the same time, then he would gladly let them know the precise date. 'In issuing this invitation I assure you at the same time that no pressure of any kind from me will be exerted on you to make a decision.' (19 May)

Their noncommittal reply to this was an end of the matter, as far as Wagner was concerned. 'I shall have no more trouble with the Härtels now,' he told Liszt, 'as I have now decided at last to abandon the stubborn enterprise of finishing my "Nibelungs".' He had conducted his young Siegfried as far as the solitude of the forest and bidden him farewell with heartfelt tears. And he added that if he was to take the work up again after all, then it would have to be made possible for him to *give* it to the world, in the fullest sense of the word. (28 June)

But inspired by the walks he used to take in the nearby Sihltal, where he listened attentively to the songs of the forest birds, he did complete the composition and orchestral sketches of the second act of *Siegfried* before laying the work aside. What he took home with him of their songs he imitated by his art, and the music reproduces distinctly the songs of the yellowhammer (oboe), oriole (flute), nightingale (clarinet), tree-pipit (flute) and blackbird (flute and clarinet).

Sitting on the veranda on the evening of 22 May, his forty-fourth birthday, he was surprised by the song of the Rhinemaidens, which he had rehearsed with some singers in the previous year, and which now reached him across the gardens as if from some little distance. Coming now in the composition sketch to the point where Siegfried emerges from the cave with the ring and the Tarnhelm – 'Was ihr mir nützt, weiß ich nicht' – he added the melody of the Rhinemaidens' lament in the accompaniment, writing it very lightly in pencil. Scoring the passage twelve years later, he wrote to King Ludwig in similar terms, telling him that the melody was now heard on six horns, as if coming from a distant dream-world of nature: 'As we take in the full significance of it, our emotion is overwhelming!'(23 February 1869)

With the music of the Woodbird leading Siegfried off, he laid his most important work on one side as a 'chimera' – at the time it seemed that it might be for ever.

Part V: *Tristan* and *Die Meistersinger* (1857–1868)

# 21

## In Asyl

The Härtels' refusal to come to Zürich would not in itself have influenced Wagner to abandon the 'stubborn enterprise' of the *Ring*, but it was just one more in a series of reasons. He felt the necessity of appearing before the public with another new work, after an interval of seven years: his friends feared, so he wrote later, that he might have strayed into the realms of 'the unstageable and the unsingable'; the leading critics treated him as no longer in the land of the living; and in his own eyes, as he laid one unperformed score aside after another, he resembled a sleepwalker with no real idea of what he was doing. (RWGS, VI, pp. 266f.) Perhaps, too, he sensed that he was not yet ready to tackle the composition of *Götterdämmerung*. We, at any rate, with the advantage of hindsight, can see that he would not have been able to write it without first having mastered the harmonies of *Tristan* and the counterpoint of *Die Meistersinger*.

There was a psychological factor, too. Having severed one link with the outside world after another during the last few years, his need to immerse himself in an inner world had grown ever more imperative. Hence his yearning for the friendship of Liszt, his longing for the understanding and love of a woman who would open her soul before him like a blank sheet of paper; hence, too, his receptivity to Schopenhauer and Buddhism, and his attraction to the subject of *Tristan*.

His acquaintances, in different ways, must have sensed his isolation in those years. Wagner was indescribably lonely there, Eliza Wille wrote to Princess Wittgenstein, but would he not be so everywhere? And Eduard Devrient, the first guest the Wagners received in Asyl, wrote to his wife, 'He is a totally disquieting character.'

With great self-control, he was on the point of leaving Siegfried alone in the forest for a year, in order to give himself some relief in writing a *Tristan und Isolde*, as he reported to Frau Ritter. He shrank from admitting to this good friend, whose generosity had inspired him with the courage to start the tetralogy, that he saw no prospect of ever finishing it: she died in 1869 and never saw its completion. 'The text [of *Tristan*] is still dormant within me,' he went on: 'I shall shortly start to rouse it.' (4 July 1857)

The way for his new enterprise seemed to smooth itself of its own volition. In March Wagner had received a letter from a Dr Ernesto Ferreira-França, who introduced himself as the Brazilian consul in Dresden: the emperor, Dom Pedro II, an admirer of his music, wished to invite him to Rio de Janeiro, so that he could perform his operas there in Italian. Strangely enough, Wagner observed, the idea had attracted him: he thought he would have no difficulty in writing a libretto full of passion which would turn out excellently in Italian. He wrote to Liszt that he was thinking of getting *Tristan und Isolde* translated into Italian, dedicating it to the Emperor of Brazil, and offering it to the theatre in Rio for its first performance. His correspondence with Ferreira went on for several months, but in the end nothing came of it: in *Mein Leben* he wrote that he never heard from the Emperor of Brazil again. But ten years after he had dictated that section of his autobiography, a foreigner arrived in Bayreuth, on the day of the very first performance of *Rheingold*, who entered his name in the hotel register as 'Pedro'; profession, 'emperor'. Late that same evening he called at Wahnfried, and talked enthusiastically about his impressions of the performance.

The proposal Devrient made during his visit to Asyl held out more concrete hopes. As intendant at the Grand Duke of Baden's theatre in Karlsruhe, he offered to interest the duke, whose liking for Wagner's music was well known, in holding the première there. Wagner also had plans for a performance, with the Karlsruhe orchestra, in Strassburg, the home town of Gottfried, the author of the German medieval epic poem of *Tristan*, 'and so I believe that, with God and in my own way, I shall once again produce something in which I shall achieve renewal and self-awareness'. At all events, *Tristan* was going to be a thoroughly practicable work which would soon bring him in good financial returns. (To Liszt, 28 June)

On 22 August the Wesendonks moved into their new house,

built in the style of a patrician Renaissance villa. Mathilde had christened it 'Wahlheim' ('chosen home'), quite possibly at Wagner's suggestion, in allusion to the idyllic hamlet of that name where Werther decides to live. Wagner had begun the prose sketch of *Tristan und Isolde* two days before. The sense of seclusion, the beauty of his surroundings, the neighbourly association with Mathilde combined to speed the work, so that he had completed the verse text by 18 September. As he recounts in *Mein Leben*, he made the best use of his reading in Dresden, and the catalogue of his Dresden library reveals just how extensive that must have been. It includes Gottfried's poem, not only in the modern German translation by Hermann Kurtz, but also in the Middle High German editions of H. F. Massmann and F. H. von der Hagen, the latter also including the surviving texts of the Middle English, medieval French, Welsh and Spanish poems on the same subject. His possession of Ziemann's 750-page dictionary of Middle High German with grammatical introduction shows that he really made the effort to read Gottfried's text.

Even then Hermann Kurtz's comment that the legend has the stuff of a tragic drama in it must have stirred his imagination to trace the outline of its original form – perhaps we might say its ideal form. As was so often the case with him, the material lay dormant for years in a half-conscious creative sphere of his brain, then suddenly came to the fore and was written down, prose sketch and verse text, in twenty-nine days. Bülow, who was visiting Asyl at the time with Cosima on their honeymoon, had the feeling that Wagner was in a state bordering on 'transfiguration'.

Although he always aimed at stripping his legendary subjects of specific historical conventions, he recognized that the knightly ethos of the Middle Ages had to be retained as the necessary setting for Tristan's conflict of love and honour. It was in consequence of this that the language of the text is more deliberately archaic than usual. The language has been much abused, but it is strongly influenced by Middle High German, not only in the choice and inflection of the vocabulary, but even more in the sentence structure.

To give just one example in each category: in Kurwenal's 'Nun bist du daheim . . . auf eig'ner Weid' und Wonne', the word 'Wonne' (which means 'bliss', 'great joy' in modern German) is imbued with the double meaning of MHG 'wünne': not only 'what is longed for' but also 'pasture' (a synonym of 'Weide', so a non-singing translation of the line could be 'Now you are at home . . . among your own meadows and longed-for pastures'); in Isolde's 'den hell ich haßte', 'hell' ('bright', 'light' in modern German) is used in the original sense of 'resonant', extended to mean 'violent', and showing that it is cognate with 'hallen' (which still means 'to ring' or 'resound'); a form like 'sehren', lacking the usual prefix ('versehren'), is much closer to the medieval 'sêren'; case inflections are used to make their point on their own, without prepositions, as in the use of the genitive in Brangäne's cry 'Des unsel'gen Tranks!' ('[Because of] the accursed drink'). Then the sentences often use constructions that are medieval in inspiration: in 'Das Schwert – das ließ ich fallen' ('the sword – I let it drop') the caesura after the noun and the subsequent pronoun duplicating the noun reproduce a characteristic of Gottfried's own style ('liep und leit, diu sind alleins'); the placing of adjectival and adverbial phrases in front of, and outside, the main body of the sentence: 'Siech und matt, in meiner Macht, warum ich dich da nicht schlug', where the first two phrases refer to 'dich'; the placing of a whole relative clause, or even a series of them, in front of the main clause, before the noun to which they relate has been spoken: 'Die im Busen mir die Glut entfacht, die mir das Herze brennen macht, die mir als Tag der Seele lacht, Frau Minne will, es werde Nacht' ('[She] who . . . Dame Minne wills that it be night').[1]

There is nothing amateur about this archaicization, nor is it so abstruse that only scholars can appreciate it. It might nevertheless be open to a charge of artificiality, were it not also determined by the spirit of the music. The concise forms of words, the avoidance of auxiliaries and expletives, the more flexible construction, the defiance of linguistic logic make the sentences akin to the melody, which also knows only the logic of emotion. Yet even so sympathetic a critic as Erich von Schrenck can criticize the 'favourite advance positioning of the relative clause', which wearies by its artificiality.[2] He fails to see that the practice, as in the last of the examples in the preceding paragraph, results in a peculiarly intimate fitting of the words to the climbing melodic line, as it mounts to a climax of monumental grandeur. The sequence of short relative clauses anticipated the musical sequence: or rather, since it is quite clear that the music formed the words rather than vice versa, the sequence of clauses was determined by the needs of musical sequence.

Finally, towards the end of the great duet in the second act, there are passages where the words read on their own seem empty, because their emotional content is provided by the music alone: it would have been a contradiction of Wagner's concept of the living work of art to create a poetic illusion on the page which would then be annulled by the writing for the two voices and obliterated by the flow of the orchestra. The words here are nothing more than the raw material for the vocal parts.

On the other hand, all the passages where the words are intrinsically important possess the highest degree of poetic strength and beauty: Isolde's 'Mir erkoren – mir verloren', Marke's 'Mir – dies? Dies – Tristan – mir?', Tristan's 'Muß ich dich so verstehn, du alte, ernste Weise', can stand comparison for expressive pregnancy with any of the greatest works in dramatic literature.

But the poetry, as in *Tannhäuser*, is not confined to the expression and content of the words. Wagner presents a symbol at the beginning of each act – the young sailor's song, Isolde holding the torch, the doleful tune of the shepherd – which is then transposed on to a psychological and metaphysical plane. Interpreting a simple theme in a series of poetic variations like this is also an act of creation out of the spirit of music. As a matter of interest, the poetic motive of the torch is absent from the prose sketch: Brangäne stands on the steps leading to the gate and Isolde calls to her to open the gate to Tristan. The extinguishing of the torch, which is far more striking both as a visual image and as an imaginative association, appears for the first time in the verse text itself. 'Even the ancients', Wagner told Eliza Wille as he was playing to her from the second act, 'placed a lowered torch in the hand of Eros as the genius of death.'

The *Hymns to the Night* of Novalis are frequently referred to as the model for the love scene, and there are indeed reminiscences.[3] But Novalis's works were not in Wagner's library either in Dresden or in Bayreuth, nor is there any other evidence that he ever took any interest in the poet. If, instead of being content with comparing a few lines in isolation, one reads both poems in conjunction, then it is the differences that make the far stronger impression. The *Ring* is as remote from the verses the romantic poets wrote about elves and goblins as *Tristan* is from their poetry of love and death, and the affinities of the subject matter make the contrast with the spirit in which it was conceived all the more striking. The major difference between *Tristan* and the *Hymnen an die Nacht* is the complete absence of Christianity from the former. There is only one divinity in *Tristan*: Frau Minne, 'des Weltenwerdens Walterin'. The imaginative world is closer to that of India, as is the idea of the 'Weltatem' ('world breath'), and – say what you will – Schopenhauer: even though the longing for the night, 'wo Liebeswonne uns lacht', has nothing to do with the denial of the will to live, yet Thomas Mann is right in this instance when he demonstrates that such denial is only a secondary intellectual element of Schopenhauer's philosophy: his system is a metaphysic of the will, fundamentally erotic in character, and to the extent that it is so, *Tristan* is filled, saturated with it.[4]

'On 18 September', Wagner wrote in the Venetian Diary intended for Mathilde, 'I finished the text and took the last act to you. You went with me to the chair beside the sofa, embraced me and said "Now I wish for nothing more."'

A few days later an encounter of truly portentous significance took place in Asyl. When Wagner read the text aloud to a small gathering, the audience included Minna Wagner, Mathilde Wesendonk and Cosima von Bülow. Minna, as she told a friend, saw nothing in Tristan and Isolde but a 'much too odious and slippery couple'.[5] Cosima was then nineteen. Wagner found her shy and reticent, and complained to Hans that she was too reserved. But her reserve already concealed an instinctive animosity towards Frau Wesendonk. When the last act provoked a particularly emotional response from Mathilde, Wagner comforted her by saying that such an outcome was really the best, in an affair of such seriousness – and was supported by Cosima.

Who was Mathilde? Her importance as Wagner's muse was beyond all question sublime. But it is the privilege – or the fate – of the poet to see his muse through the eyes of love. Who was Mathilde Wesendonk in sober reality, and of what order were her mind and spirit? Ernest Newman, who can certainly not be accused of favouring Cosima unduly, was very sceptical about Mathilde. Was she able to follow Wagner's thoughts? Did she ever love him as much as he loved her? Her avowals of love, apart from her poems, have come to us only through Wagner's pen; she destroyed her own letters, except for a few from later in her life, and she made her own selection and edition of his letters for posthumous publication, some of them reaching the editor Wolfgang Golther only in copies in her handwriting.

Perhaps we shall do her the greatest justice by referring to a comment Wagner made in a letter to her after he had been reading Goethe's *Tasso* a year after leaving Asyl: 'The only important confrontation for those who seek the essence of things is that between the Princess and Tasso. . . If we look . . . beyond the play, we are left with only the Princess and Tasso: how will their differences be reconciled?' It is obvious that this remark had a personal relevance: when Wagner's passionate nature had made it hard for him to obey the stern command of voluntary renunciation, Mathilde had admonished him as the Princess admonishes Tasso: 'There are many things that we should grasp eagerly: but there are others that can only become ours through restraint and self-denial. Such, they say, is virtue; such is love, her kinswoman. Consider it well!' (II, 1) 'Will Tasso be taught by her?' Wagner asks.[6]

On 1 October 1857, twelve days after finishing the text, he began the composition sketch of the first act, which he finished by 31 December. The dates shed light on the 'force' with which the conception 'erupted' from him, in Ernst Kurth's words: there are few instances in the history of music of the evolution of harmony being similarly pressed forward in one enormous jolt by the genius of a single individual. An epoch was closed, and the assembled ranks of his contemporaries were able to witness it like a natural phenomenon.[7]

Not that there was anything new about the famous *Tristan* chord, the first chord of the prelude: it is to be found in the Andante of Bach's A minor Violin Concerto, and in the Andante of Mozart's Eb major Quartet. The chromaticism is even less of a novelty. What was new was the elevation of these two features into the form-giving principle of a whole work on a large scale. The chord provides an inner dynamic which sweeps the music on from tension to relaxation to renewed tension. 'You know the Buddhist theory of the origin of the world,' Wagner wrote to Mathilde: 'a breath clouds the clarity of heaven' (and here he writes the four chromatically rising notes which he had written down as early as 1856 as the germ of this music):

'This swells, grows denser until finally the whole world stands before me in impenetrable vastness.' (3 March 1860) His words act as a description of the impulse which led on to the creation of the musical world of *Tristan*.

For all its dynamism, the music is informed by a stream of thought that is, as Richard Pohl wrote of the prelude as early as 1859, 'of eminent logic and consistency'. Eighty years later Paul Hindemith analysed the logic and the consistency:

> The prelude to *Tristan* is one of the finest examples of the elaboration of a two-voice [i.e. two-part] framework. The observer of the intervals formed by the outside lines of the harmony will be astonished to see how intervals of varying tension are juxtaposed. The procedure is illustrated beginning with the very first chord . . . the tensional development of the framework is calculated from beginning to end.[8]

The epoch-making significance of the music of *Tristan* was so little a conscious intention on Wagner's part that to begin with he did not even notice it. The effect it had on him, when it did suddenly strike him, is recounted in a letter to Mathilde Wesendonk, written in January 1860: nothing that had happened to him in Paris (where he was at the time) was of any significance beside a realization, a discovery he had made during the first rehearsal with the orchestra for his concert series, because it would determine the whole of the rest of his life. 'I played the prelude to *Tristan* for the first time; and – saw, as though scales had fallen from my eyes, the immeasurable distance that I had travelled from the world during the last eight years. This little prelude was so incomprehensibly *new* to the players that I had to lead them directly from note to note, as though hunting for jewels in a mine.'

One cannot avoid the impression that in writing *Tristan* Wagner was the unconscious agent of a higher power, and all the personal and intellectual experiences that contributed to it were merely release mechanisms. This is in direct opposition to the popular belief, shared by Frau Mathilde, as Newman ironically remarks, that she was the work's onlie begetter. (NLRW, II, p. 524)

The direct artistic outcome of their relationship was the group of *Wesendonk Lieder*, composed between 30 November 1857 and 1 May 1858. He had spent a little time dabbling in trifles, he told Liszt, and had set some nice little verses that had been sent him, 'which is something I have never done before!' (1 January 1858) The order of composition of these 'five poems for a woman's voice' is somewhat different from that in which they were published: *Der Engel, Träume, Schmerzen, Stehe still, Im Treibhaus*. As one can see from the dates, Wagner must have set the poems virtually 'by return of post'. Only in the case of *Schmerzen* did he revise the setting, changing the coda twice in the following two days. Sending Mathilde the second version, he wrote on the manuscript: 'After a good, refreshing night, my first thought on waking was this improvement to the coda: we shall see if Señora Calderón [an allusion to what they had been reading together] likes it if I play it today in the depths [at Wahlheim].' Below the third version he wrote: 'Another ending, it must be getting more and more beautiful.' He explicitly identified two of the songs as studies for *Tristan*: *Träume* for the second act, and *Im Treibhaus* for the third, while the Destiny motive heard in *Stehe still* is a quotation from the first act, which had already been composed by then.

The first song, *Der Engel*, contains a delicate tribute to Mathilde: the melody of the words 'da der Engel niederschwebt' is taken from the first violin melody after Loge's words in *Rheingold*: 'In Wasser, Erd' und Luft, lassen will nichts von Lieb' und Weib.'

It was a difficult, artificial situation, the stability of which could be maintained only by scrupulous consideration of all the people concerned and was under threat at every instant. While Wesendonk was away from home on business, following a crisis in the American money market, Wagner serenaded Mathilde on her birthday, 23 December, with an arrangement of *Träume* for solo violin and small orchestra, performed in the hall of the villa. On 31 December he presented her with a dedicatory poem:

> Hochbeglückt.
> schmerzentrückt,
> frei und rein,
> ewig Dein –
> was sie sich klagten
> und versagten,
> Tristan und Isolde,
> in keuscher Töne Golde,
> ihr Weinen und ihr Küssen
> leg' ich zu Deinen Füßen
> daß sie den Engel loben,
> der mich so hoch erhoben!

('Enraptured, freed from pain, free and pure, ever thine – what Tristan and Isolde lamented and forwent in the gold of chaste music, their weeping and kissing I lay at thy feet, that they may praise the angel who raised me so high!')

Whether the serenade or the poem was the cause of it, there must at all events have been an exceptionally violent quarrel between the Wesendonks when Otto returned in the new year. A passage in a letter Wagner sent Liszt refers to it: 'For a moment it seemed to me that I would have to steel myself, quickly and decisively, to offer my protection.' (18–20 [?] January 1858) In his first wave of despair he turned once again to his friend in Weimar. 'This time you must come without delay. I am at the end of a conflict involving everything sacred to man: I must decide, and the choice facing me is so cruel that when I decide I must have at my side the *one* friend Heaven has granted me . . . Since I hope to find the path on which I shall cause the least harm, I am thinking for the present of going to Paris where – plausibly – my interests take me – at least in the eyes of the world at large and of my good wife in particular.' (Early January) Astonished, Liszt asked: 'Is your wife staying in Zürich? Are you thinking of perhaps going back there later? Where is Mme W.?' On 14 January Wagner left for Paris, and from there he wrote to Liszt that things had all turned out quite peaceably after all: '*For* me – only tenderness, resignation, pining, concern solely for me; *against* me – honourable suffering amidst great magnanimity and irreproachable considerateness towards the delicate, passive element in the conflict.' A passage in the Venetian Diary shows that he corresponded with Mathilde during this period: 'Do you remember, how we wrote to each other when I was in Paris, and our joint sorrow burst forth from us both at the same time, after we had fervently told each other of our plans?' (31 October 1858) Unfortunately those illuminating letters have not been published.

Wagner did in fact have a genuine business reason for his journey. Dr Hermann Härtel had visited him in Zürich in the previous autumn and reminded him of the necessity of establishing his copyrights in Paris. In pursuit of this end he now made contact with the lawyer Emile Ollivier, later a member of the French government, and the husband of Liszt's daughter Blandine. Wagner gave him powers of attorney to represent his rights in France. It must have been a picturesque scene when Wagner expounded the plot of

*Tannhäuser* to the 'most famous advocates in the world', strolling up and down at Ollivier's side in the Salle des Pas Perdus in the Palais de Justice.

The most tangible profit of his visit to Paris came from a visit he paid in Passy to the widow of the piano manufacturer Erard; he improvised from his operas in her music room, and she promised to give him one of her famous grand pianos – the 'swan', as he called it, which had a soft tone that for him became inseparable from the love scene of the second act.

During his visit Härtel had also pronounced an interest in buying the rights to the less demanding new opera. The great warmth of the subject, the music's fortunate propensity for melodic flow, the two effective principal parts which would soon be numbered among the most grateful in the soprano and tenor repertories – so Wagner wrote to the publishers on 4 January – all this made him confident that he had played his hand well. The contract was drawn up after his return from Zürich at the beginning of February, though not without all manner of demurrings on the Härtels' part, and a beating down of Wagner's price of 600 louisdor to 200, with the proviso of another hundred if it should prove an exceptional success. 'It was really funny!' Wagner told Liszt. 'I can do what I like, it will always seem completely or at least half impossible to the philistine.'

On 6 February Wagner resumed work on the score of the first act, which he had barely started before leaving for Paris, and finished it on 3 April, in the incredibly short time of scarcely two months.

It may have been intended as something more than a public gesture of reconciliation when Mathilde gave a soirée on 31 March in somewhat belated celebration of Otto's birthday, at which Wagner conducted an orchestra of thirty in ten separate movements from symphonies by Beethoven in the hall of the villa. After the serenade for 'sa belle Mathilde', a nocturne for Otto was appropriate, Cosima von Bülow commented in a letter to Frau Herwegh.

The whole of Zürich's *beau monde* were present, Eliza Wille reported. Gottfried Keller regretted having been prevented by an accident from attending this elegant concert, which was completely unprecedented for 'a private do in Zürich'.

Wagner's conducting desk, almost completely hidden by flowers, was placed in the vestibule opposite the front door, while the guests were seated in the adjoining rooms. Before the concert began the Wesendonks' seven-year-old daughter presented him with a baton carved with a design by Semper. Frau Wesendonk had received her first decisive impression of Wagner when he conducted Beethoven's Eighth at a subscription concert six years before, and the Allegretto scherzando, which had been one of her favourite pieces ever since, was on the programme on this occasion. It was typical of Wagner's own taste that the concert ended with the 'profoundly consoling' Adagio of the Ninth. Afterwards he went over to the table where Minna was sitting with the wife of the leader of the orchestra, and delightedly showed her the carved baton. The party went on till after midnight and the guests were royally entertained

Even the Wesendonks were deeply moved by the occasion, which was intended primarily as a tribute to them, Wagner recorded in *Mein Leben*. It 'had a melancholy effect on me as a warning that possibly the climax of a relationship between lives had been reached, that the real substance of it had indeed already been overtaken, and the bowstring overdrawn'. Before reproaching him with having concealed the true nature of his relationship with Mathilde in his autobiography, one should remember that he wrote it for King Ludwig and dictated it to Cosima. For those in the know that sentence said all.

Frau Wesendonk had some time previously engaged Francesco de Sanctis, a lecturer at the Polytechnic in Zürich, to give her private lessons in Italian. Since she displayed more interest in excursions and conversation at the tea table than zeal to learn the language of Dante, he asked her to release him, to which she replied that she received him 'en ami, non pas en qualité de professeur'. Her two friends now regarded each other with undisguised dislike, and an attempt to bring them together had failed. On 5 April, a few days after the concert, Wagner had had to do without his evening visit, since De Sanctis remained to tea after the lesson. His chagrin kept him awake all night, and the next day bad weather prevented him from meeting her in the garden.

When he went to see her that evening he was irritable, and they had a difference of opinion. The next morning he sent her the pencil sketch of the *Tristan* prelude as a peace-offering, with a letter. Minna stopped the messenger, took the rolled sheet of manuscript paper, found the letter and opened it. Had she been capable of understanding it, it ought to have allayed all her fears, for, as

Wagner wrote to his sister Klara, its theme was his resignation. She believed, instead, that she now had tangible proof of his infidelity and furiously went to confront him with it. With difficulty he succeeded in so far calming her that she promised to forgo a foolish revenge and to avoid any kind of scene. But behind his back she went to Frau Wesendonk and threatened: 'If I were an ordinary woman I would go to your husband with this letter!' Mathilde, who had no secrets from her husband, had no choice but to tell him of this visit and its cause.

And what was in that fateful letter? Since Minna had appropriated it, it was not to be found among those that were later published. Its history is as strange as the role it played in Wagner's life. Minna left it to her daughter Natalie, who sold it to Mrs Burrell in the 1890s. On her death, shortly afterwards, it was held in trust, together with the many other Wagneriana she had collected. In 1930 two literary adventurers, Hurn and Root, succeeded in gaining access to the Burrell Collection and its secrets. They published what they allegedly found there, together with some of their own inventions and smears, in a disgraceful book to which they gave the title *The Truth about Wagner*. The letter to Mathilde was one of the few documents that they had actually seen, and it was supposed that what they published was the authentic text, especially as Julius Kapp published it in the same form in the next edition of his book *Richard Wagner und die Frauen*. In the meantime the Burrell Collection had been taken to America, having been bought by a patron of music, Mrs Mary Curtis, for the Curtis Institute of Music in Philadelphia which she had founded. When at last, in 1950, the principal items of the collection were published, including the letter which had failed to reach its addressee nearly a century before, it transpired that what Hurn and Root had published twenty years earlier was only its beginning ·and its ending, and the main substance, and the reason for the letter, was a dissertation on Goethe's *Faust*.

Their disagreement the evening before had been about *Faust*. Wagner had become heated and Mathilde had reproved him for it. Now he had woken with a bad conscience and wanted to make a 'morning confession' to her, excusing his irritability by his 'dreadful hatred for all the De Sanctises of this world'. 'Wretch that I am! I had to say that to you: I had no other choice. But it was very petty of me and I deserved to be suitably punished.'

'What was that stupid quarrel over Goethe about?' he went on. Mathilde had said that Faust was the most significant human type any writer had ever created, while Wagner, with all due respect for Goethe, saw him as an 'over-imaginative scholar' who, sent out to study the world at first hand, instead of learning from Gretchen where salvation and redemption were to be found, woke up one morning and had forgotten the entire incident. 'In the end even the grey-haired sinner is aware of it and makes a visible effort to repair his omission in a final tableau – outside things, after death, where it's no longer inconvenient to him.' To the words of the dying Faust:

> Towards the Beyond the view has been cut off;
> Fool – who directs that way his dazzled eye,
> Contrives himself a double in the sky!
> Let him look round him here, not stray beyond;
> To a sound man this world must needs respond –

Wagner's response was 'Fool, to hope to win the world and peace from out there! Salvation dwells only within, in the inner depths!'

'Be good to me,' he concluded, 'and forgive my childish behaviour of yesterday: you were quite right to call it that! – Today seems mild. I shall go into the garden; as soon as I see you I hope to catch an uninterrupted moment with you! Take my whole soul as a morning greeting!' (RWBC, pp. 489ff.)

Some relaxation of the tension was to be expected after Wagner had taken Minna to the Brestenberg sanatorium on 15 May for three months, to receive treatment for her heart ailment – which had only been aggravated by a 'fearful amount of opium' – and after the Wesendonks, too, had left at the beginning of May to spend a month in Italy. The Erard had arrived on 3 May: this wonderfully soft, sweetly melancholy instrument had fully coaxed him back to music again. The next day he began the composition sketch of the second act, which he finished on 1 July. 'Still in Asyl' he wrote on the first sheet, between hope and fear. The existence he led in his isolation was curiously dreamlike, interrupted by visits from his few friends, and its external events were set down in twenty-nine letters to Minna.

The garden was a picture – but he didn't want to distress her. The gardener was taking care of the lawn, the peas had sprouted, the first asparagus was ready for pulling and if there was plenty she should be sent some. 'I am living so much inside myself now, that I simply do not notice whether anything has happened in the world . . . In addition to that I am now really in the mood for my work and all kinds of the loveliest themes have occurred to me.' As she had broken her ring he had the stone reset: 'Today I am sending you a whole ring for your broken one, and let us hope that it will last better than the old one.'

One morning Liszt's favourite pupil, the sixteen-year-old Karl Tausig turned up. 'He is a terrible boy,' Wagner exclaimed, when he had got to know his young visitor better. 'Musically at any rate he is enormously gifted, and his insane piano-playing makes me tremble.' It was not long before he had found a place in Wagner's affections and had to accompany him on one of his visits to Brestenberg. His 'little Thousand-tara [Tausendsasa]' had taken her to his heart too, Wagner told Minna, and he added, since she had evidently mentioned his Jewish descent, 'his father is a very honourable native of Bohemia, a thorough Christian'. Later, he was to choose Tausig to be the organizer of the society of patrons of the Bayreuth festivals.

At the end of May Minna came home for twenty-four hours to see that everything was in order. Since she mentioned, with a frivolity Wagner found disagreeable, the 'little love affair' she had set to rights, he felt obliged to warn her of the dangers that could jeopardize their remaining at Asyl. It was the first and only time since the devastating letter she had once sent him in Riga that he heard her 'lament in a gentle and dignified manner'. And as on that previous occasion he was ready to believe in a change of heart. 'Your tears and regret during the last night at home moved me more than any other kind of declaration.' Minna's version of this exchange was: 'Richard poured out his venom against me until two o'clock in the morning.' (To Frau Herwegh, JKWF, p. 147) We might despair of ever knowing the truth of the matter, had she not also often told her friends that her husband had again written her a letter full of cruel, mean things, whereupon reference to the letter in question on each occasion shows that, on the contrary, he had expressed himself warmly and affectionately. 'But if she wished posterity to share her opinion of Wagner', Newman observes, 'she ought to have avoided the cardinal blunder of preserving his letters.' (NLRW, III, pp. 175f.)

These were the foreground events of the two months in which

the composition sketch of the second act of *Tristan* was being written. The introduction starts piano in the sketch, with the motive of Impatience in the bass clarinet. The harsh Day motive at the beginning, played fortissimo on horns and woodwind, was not added until he wrote the full score – so presenting the theme of the discussion of Night/Day, that great variation movement, in a form that could not be mistaken.

On the sheet of sketches written on 19 December 1856 (mentioned in the previous chapter), Wagner had set the words of 'O sink hernieder, Nacht der Liebe . . .' to an early form of the 'Lausch, Geliebter' melody.[9] But instead of using that in the composition sketch he began with a melody that proves to be an arpeggiated form of the *Tristan* chord: evidently in the interests of providing a motivic link between the two major elements – the prelude and the love scene.

This scene also contains the only instances of lines set in the composition sketch being subsequently omitted from the score: the eight lines from 'Selbst um der Treu' to 'Geheimnis vertraut' and the fourteen lines from 'Soll der Tod' to 'den Weg uns gewiesen'. While the first omission, of fifteen bars, is of no formal significance, the second, of thirty-six bars, perceptibly shortens the reprise of the period in question, compared to its exposition in the first half of the duet. The gathering velocity of the dramatic action is reflected in the growing speed with which the scene approaches its end musically.[10]

Perhaps the most amazing thing, in view of the intensity of personal experience that seems to be so much in evidence here, is the level of artistic objectivity: one need only think, for instance, of his setting of King Marke's reproach. How much sympathy he had for Marke is demonstrated by his remonstrating with Heinrich Porges over a point in the latter's analysis of *Tristan*: Porges's assumption of a 'quasi-guilt' on Marke's part was uncalled for, in fact wrong: he had failed to notice that the basis of the melodic construction of the coda of the second act was Marke's principal motive, representing his benevolence; 'consequently it contains the motive of self-reproach, which Tristan conspicuously rejects'. (15 March 1867)

The Wesendonks had returned on 1 June, and Otto called on Wagner the next day to invite him to tea. 'I thereupon wrote to him to explain, very delicately, that in future we want to maintain a friendly relationship, but without personal contact.' (To Minna, 3

June) But he was unable to endure more than a month of this voluntary banishment. 'I shall not visit you often,' he wrote to Mathilde on 6 July, 'for from now on you shall see me only when I am sure of showing you a calm, smiling face.'

On 15 July he went to Brestenberg to fetch Minna. During his absence the gardener, 'a wily Saxon', erected a triumphal porch, covered with flowers, which, Minna was delighted to see when she arrived home, was in full view of her neighbour. When the Bülows, invited by Wagner to stay at Asyl, went to call on the Wesendonks, they discovered that this welcome had had its effect on Mathilde, who still nursed a sense of grievance. Wagner wrote in his auto-biography of her 'passionate excesses', retailed to him by the Bülows, and he also wrote to Eliza Wille, telling her that after he had made his last farewells, Frau Wesendonk had taken it into her head to torment him again 'with childish and senseless reproaches', conveyed by one of his friends, because of the terms she supposed him to be on with his wife. It made him painfully aware that she was hardly capable of appreciating what he suffered on her account.

He was not going to revoke his decision now: his only regret was that he had not taken it earlier, at the first catastrophe, in the new year. If he had weakened again then, he hoped he might be forgiven by her who had left him uncertain as to her wishes. 'I can see my continuing to live here in no other light than as a hell from which I daily long to be released.' (To Eliza Wille, second half of July) Twenty years later he viewed these events more dispassionately – perhaps too dispassionately, when he told Cosima about 'Frau Minna's battle with Frau Mathilde', how they had each tried to rile the other, 'and I – I had no thought of either'. (DMCW, I, p. 860)

When he told Minna of his decision to leave Asyl he had to admit that *her* behaviour was not the sole cause of his desperation. In terms of their personal relationships, Mathilde's refusal ever to have anything to do with Minna again was the decisive factor. But from a higher standpoint, it was *Tristan*, it was his work, which, if it was to be finished, demanded that he find peace and solitude and review his experiences in a transfigured light.

Putting his decision into practice was fated to suffer delay, as one party of visitors after another, from far and near, descended on Asyl: apart from Tausig and the Bülows, no sooner had one famous tenor, Albert Niemann, and his bride left, than another, Tichatschek, came, followed by Klindworth, Karl Ritter, a young musician called Wendelin Weissheimer, and Cosima's mother, the Comtesse d'Agoult, who had come to Zürich 'pour faire ici la connaissance de grands hommes'. 'And so the house was full every day,' *Mein Leben* says, 'and anxious, worried and uneasy friends sat down at our table, their wants catered for by her who was about to give up this household for ever.' The one friend who did not come was the one person Wagner longed for in his emotional turmoil: Franz Liszt.

With only half his mind on his guests, Wagner entertained them with a performance of *Rheingold* and *Walküre*, singing all the parts himself, as Bülow reported, 'with a magnificent unself-consciousness and expending all his forces', while Klindworth provided a thrilling accompaniment at the piano from his difficult vocal scores. The Wesendonks were not present. Mathilde had returned to Wagner a 'precious trifle' which she had kept until then – and about which we know nothing more – 'certainly in order to hurt me very deeply', as he told Eliza Wille. 'You will keep it then, until such time as *she* wants to have it again. Won't you? You will do this for me?' (7[?] August)

By a curious chance we can judge what effect all this had on Cosima. Before her arrival she had written to Frau Herwegh, saying that she was sorry for Minna but could not think it wrong of Richard, driven by his longing for the ideal and for peace at the same time, exhausted by incessant everyday cares of life, if he asked for a little happiness from 'une nature pâle et chétive, aussi incapable de vivre fortement d'une existence simple et droite, que de rompre avec ses engagements antérieurs pour s'abandonner à l'amour et soutenir son amant'. Now she left Zürich for a few days to accompany her mother to Geneva and meet her sister there, and Karl Ritter undertook to escort the ladies. She returned from the journey in a greatly excited state, which alarmed Wagner, to whom she showed it in 'convulsive, violent endearments'. From a passage in a letter from him to Mathilde Wesendonk which was suppressed in the published edition, we learn that in Geneva Cosima and Karl had been close to suicide. She suddenly begged him to kill her and he had declared himself ready to die with her. They both went out on the lake, Cosima intending to drown herself, Karl determined to follow her, and it was because she could not shake his determination that she abandoned her plan. They parted with an agreement to let each other know how they felt in three weeks' time, and in fact Karl did then receive a letter from Cosima, in which she expressed regret for her vehemence and thanked him for his delicacy and consideration. (JKWF, pp. 151ff.)

It was not a tragic mutual passion that led the two to this pass, but the sudden overwhelming recognition of the affinity between their fates. Karl had just separated from his young wife and Cosima had become aware in Zürich of the unhappiness of her own marriage. She was disturbed to the roots of her being by Wagner's personality, his destiny and his art.

Gradually the guests departed. Wagner gave notice of his intention to leave Asyl in a personal call on Wesendonk. He took his leave of Mathilde in the presence of Bülow, and his last words to her were a blessing for her children. The day before he himself was to leave, Hans and Cosima left: he in tears, she stern and silent. Early on the morning of 17 August 1858, after a sleepless night, Wagner left Asyl. Minna was composed, but going to the station in the carriage to see him off, she was overcome by the emotion of the occasion.

'The sky was bright and cloudless, it was a glorious summer's day,' Wagner recalled in *Mein Leben*; 'I do not remember once looking back, or even shedding a single tear at my departure, which almost alarmed me. But as I journeyed in the train I could not conceal from myself a growing sense of well-being; it was obvious that the totally useless torment of the last few months could not have been endured any longer, and a complete separation . . . was what the governing force of my life and my destiny demanded.'

# 22

Venice and Lucerne

'This is my address,' Wagner wrote to Minna on 1 September 1858: 'Canal Grande, Palazzo Giustiniani, Campiello Squillini no. 3228.' It had not been easy for him to decide where to go after leaving Asyl. In the end Venice seemed to have everything in its favour, except the possibility that there he was not really beyond the reach of the Saxon police. It was not part of the German League, but it was under Austrian rule. Liszt had passed on a warning from the Grand Duke of Weimar, but the Austrian ambassador in Berne believed that with the visa he had given him Wagner had nothing to fear, at least for a while.

'Grandeur, beauty and decay in close proximity.' This first impression, received as he went down the Grand Canal to the Piazzetta, was in harmony with his own grave, melancholy mood. Since his lodgings were important to him as the 'casing of his working mechanism', he decided on the fifteenth-century Gothic palazzo next door to the Palazzo Foscari, where he rented some furnished rooms on the first floor from the Hungarian landlord.

'It has, like all such apartments in a large, old-fashioned palace, large halls and rooms. For my living room I have an imposing chamber overlooking the Grand Canal; in addition a very spacious bedroom with a little closet off it as a wardrobe. Beautiful old ceiling painting, marvellous floor inlaid with splendid mosaic; badly painted walls (no doubt richly tapestried in the past), old-fashioned and at first glance elegant furniture with red velveteen covers, very fragile, miserably upholstered; nothing working properly, doors not shutting completely, everything a bit broken.' (To Minna, 28 September)

To make his living room more habitable he had the grey walls

papered in dark red, and ordered red curtains to hide the shoddy
doors that had been hung in the ancient frames.

Here were peace and solitude in abundance! He was the only
tenant in the whole house. From his balcony he could enjoy the
colourful bustle of life on the canal without any of the street noises
he detested. He looked forward to hearing the Erard in his large
room – twice the size of the Wesendonks' drawing room. The only
drawback was the cold, especially in the winter, when crosswinds
seemed to choose this corner of the canal to intersect.

In a smaller town he would have been unable to avoid social
distractions and would probably not have wanted to. Here he was
surrounded by a world that constantly provided stimulation, but
was alien, remote and moribund – exactly suited to his desire for
solitude. 'Nothing makes the immediate impact of real life; everything makes an objective effect, like a work of art. I will stay here.'
(Venetian Diary, 3 September) Visitors were turned away uncere-
moniously. Apart from Karl Ritter, whom he met in the afternoons
in the San Marco restaurant on the Piazzetta, the only people who
penetrated his fastness were Liszt's pupil Winterberger, a piano
teacher called Tessarin who was a passionate lover of German
music, and the cultured Russian Prince Dolgoruki.

Here he recovered the composure he needed to work and which
had deserted him during the last weeks in Asyl. He could not rid his
thoughts altogether of the two women who had become his fate
even here, but the distance tempered everything, showed much in a
different light.

Minna was still in Zürich, disbanding the household rather noisily and writing heart-rending letters of goodbye as 'the unhappiest
woman under the sun', as she signed herself to Sulzer. Before
leaving for Zwickau and Dresden she wrote one more letter to
Mathilde: her heart bled to tell her that she had succeeded in
separating her husband from her after twenty-two years of marriage. 'May this noble deed bring you consolation and happiness.'
And one to Wagner: he would curse himself in time for having
thrown everything over and wantonly banished his faithful wife.
'That isn't at all what I wanted to write to you about, even that will
come to an end, but it just flows from my pen of its own accord and
only a feeling of vengeance mounts in me, unfortunately there is no
God!' (RWBC, pp. 496ff.)

Wagner's only feeling for her was a boundless pity: he wrote to commiserate with her on her fate, bound once and for all to that of a man who, however much he might wish for contentment, was committed to so extraordinary a development that he had finally had to forgo his wishes in order to fulfil his life's work. 'All I want now is to collect myself inwardly, so as to be able to complete my works.' (To Minna, 1 September) He begged his friends to look after her: 'Be her doctor, her adviser and her helper – if you can,' he wrote to Pusinelli in Dresden, 'her comforter if you cannot.' (1 November) Then he had another letter from her 'and all the old misery starts again'.

Bülow, who had witnessed and played a part in the tragedy in Asyl and knew all the people intimately, formed his own ideas on the matter. He thought that Wagner was 'longing for his wife(!!!)', who kept on bewailing her imminent end and therefore naturally – paltry though the device was – roused his pity anew. 'He wrote in his last letter "no one shall die on my account"! I am afraid – I am afraid – I am afraid! Please heaven I am wrong!' (To Karl Klindworth, 10 October 1858) He could not restrain himself from pleading with Wagner on the same day. 'I have an inexpressible fear that you may profane yourself again out of pity and the goodness of your heart! Don't do it!' (NBB, p. 416)

On the Green Hill in Zürich it had been decided to avoid any contact with Wagner for the time being. 'Do you not even want letters?' he complained in his Venetian Diary. 'I have written to you and have every hope that with *this* letter I shall not be repulsed.' It was returned to him unopened two days later. '*That* shouldn't have happened! Not that!' Only from Eliza Wille did he receive brief bulletins: Mathilde was collected, calm, and determined on complete renunciation – parents, children, duties. 'How strange that sounded to me in my lofty mood of serious cheerfulness!' he commented. 'When I thought of you, parents, children, duties never entered my head: I only knew that you loved me and that everything sublime in the world must be unhappy.'

In fact this disagreement had already come into the open at Asyl. In 1873 he told Cosima that in the dreadful period of Mathilde's jealousy of Minna he had suggested that they should both get divorces and marry each other. She had replied that it would be 'sacrilege'. 'Anyway,' he went on, smiling, 'that incomprehensible word was quite appropriate, because in my heart of hearts and quite unconsciously I was not serious.' (DMCW, I, p. 654)

While the separation only bound Mathilde more closely to her house and family, longing threatened to overwhelm the resignation he had achieved so laboriously. In October Wesendonk informed him that their little son Guido had died. 'Your news distressed me profoundly,' Wagner wrote – an inexplicable apprehension had once prevented him from becoming the child's godfather. 'How gladly I would fly to your side to comfort you both.' The wish was expressed there as something impossible of fulfilment, but his longing soon represented it to him as a possibility. 'Decide on winter visit to Mariafeld,' it says in the Annals. In two unpublished letters he asked Eliza Wille to arrange for him to meet Mathilde again at Mariafeld at Christmas. The reply came from François Wille instead of his wife: Frau Wesendonk had sworn in the most solemn terms that she could not understand how she had given Wagner the least cause to write those two letters: she was horrified at his proposal and begged him not to proceed with it. In his blunt fashion Wille called him 'the most magnificent of all sophists and self-deceivers', who allowed his artistic imagination free rein in everything that flattered his own desires. (6 November) Wagner replied that the motive that had inspired this wish in him so suddenly was too delicate to lend itself to explanation. (13 November; FWSZ, II, p. 402) In his Venetian Diary he wrote: 'The mendicant Buddhist presented himself before the wrong house and hunger became his prayer.' His mood at this time is reflected in a sketch for a song, 'Es ist bestimmt in Gottes Rat' ('It is determined in God's counsels') in A minor. The bass descending stepwise through one and a half octaves, the impassioned cry at 'what we hold most dear' with its augmented triad, give the setting something unrelenting. These were the tones of someone at the convent gate, he commented when he played it to Cosima two decades later, 'and even more, complete renunciation, extinction'. (BBL 1937, p. 109)

He sought refuge from the storms of his passion in *Tristan* – and in writing letters and the diary for Mathilde. His hopes and despair are present in them all, but a world of ideas and observations soon suppressed all personal factors. As always his days were governed by a routine. The morning was reserved for work on his score. At about five he went by gondola to the usual restaurant on the Piazza San Marco, then to the Giardino Pubblico or the Lido where he took his walk. When he got home in the evening a lamp was already burning to greet him in the dark palazzo. At that hour he would open a book, read and think: whatever he read at once stimulated his own ideas. He read history, biography, poetry, philosophy; Count Daru's *Histoire de la république de Venise*, which led him to view the Venetians as 'superb statesmen, quite heartless as human beings'; Wilhelm von Humboldt's letters, which made him laugh at the author's 'nonsense about providence – which certainly provided very well for *him*!'; Schiller, to whom Wagner felt particularly close in the one respect in which he outshone Goethe – the desire for cognition. 'You would think that the man never lived at all, never did anything but peer about him for the light and warmth of the mind.'

'Very solitary,' the Annals say for the November, during a bout of illness, 'dreamy. No work: *Histoire de Venise*. – Schopenhauer. Frequent *Parizival* moods. Shepherd's tune, F minor.'

His renewed preoccupation with his friend Schopenhauer brought him up against what seemed to him to be two gaps in the philosopher's system. Schopenhauer expresses surprise that a pair of lovers should commit suicide, since losing their lives means simultaneously losing their greatest happiness: this moved Wagner to try to demonstrate that sexual love is the saving way to self-knowledge and self-denial of the will. 'You alone give me the material of the concepts through which my views become communicable along philosophical lines,' he started to write to Schopenhauer (RWGS, XII, p. 291), but instead of finishing the letter he asked Breitkopf & Härtel to send the philosopher a copy of the text of *Tristan*. (26 November)

The other problem lay in Schopenhauer's metaphysics of music, in relation to the other arts, especially poetry: this touched on matters that only he, Wagner, could explain properly, 'because there has never been anyone else who has been both poet and musician in the way that I am, and who could therefore have had insights into inner processes such as could be expected from none but myself'. (Venetian Diary, 8 December) These ideas remained with him and formed the subject of his essays on Beethoven in 1870.

The long, slow maturing that was characteristic of his creative processes meant that different works and interests occupied him at different levels simultaneously – like Goethe. While in the middle of composing *Tristan* he could not prevent the mood of *Parsifal* from overtaking him: in particular he was visited by the increasingly vivid and compelling conception of a woman, strange and wonder-

ful, but possessed by cosmic demons: the messenger of the Grail. 'If
I ever succeed in writing this text, it is bound to be something very
original.' (To Mathilde, 2 March 1859) At the same time, reading
Köppen's history of Buddhism encouraged him to expand his
scenario for *Die Sieger*. The difficulty was the representation of the
Buddha, the man who had shed all passions, in terms suitable for
dramatic and, above all, musical realization. The solution he found
now was that the Buddha himself, deeply moved by Savitri's fate,
should attain to a yet higher level of perception. It was a transfer of
emphasis towards the inner action similar to the one he later gave
the second scenario for *Die Meistersinger*, away from the foreground
action concerning Ananda and Savitri, or Walther and Eva, towards
the change that takes place in the heart of the sympathetic observer
Buddha, or Sachs. This gave the drama a far greater depth which is
revealed in the music.

'My work has become dearer to me than ever,' he wrote to Liszt
on 19 October. 'I took it up again recently; it's flowing like a gentle
current from my spirit.' Everything in his life in Venice conspired
to keep him in the mood for this 'art of resonant silence'. When he
rode to the Lido in a gondola of an evening, a sound like the 'soft
sustained note of a violin' seemed to waft round him. As he wrote
he could hear music outside his window: a brightly lit gondola was
gliding past, carrying singers with beautiful voices and players with
passable instruments; long after it was out of sight he could still hear
the sounds which, while they had no attraction for him as art, were
yet native here. One night when he could not sleep he heard the
gondoliers' antiphonal singing that had once stirred Goethe so
deeply: the melody was older than the verses of Tasso that they sang
to it, as old as the canals and palaces of Venice itself. One night,
when he was going home along the Grand Canal, a sudden cry
broke from the breast of the gondolier standing high above him on
the stern, wielding his powerful oar, a mournful sound not unlike
the howl of an animal, swelling up from a low, long-drawn-out
'Oh!' to end in the simple, musical cry 'Venezia!' Such were the
impressions that surrounded him while he finished the second act
and gave him the idea for the melancholy 'alte Weise' of the third
act.

His work was the only thing in his life, he told Eliza Wille. But
what a work! He was going at it as if he did not want ever to finish it,
as though he hoped to force death to surprise him at it. He had never

worked so privately: every line had an eternity's significance for him. It was astonishing: when he looked it over as a whole, he was sure he had never written anything possessing such musical unity, such an inexhaustible flow. '*Tristan* will be beautiful! But it is devouring me.' (21 February 1859; FWSZ, II, p. 411)

It was another characteristic of his creative processes that routine in itself could not help him. After an interruption of some length he sat for three days over the passage beginning 'Wen du umfangen, wem du gelacht': he could not pick up the right thread and was at a standstill. 'Then the goblin knocked at my door' – referring to the fairy tales about the goblin's power of inspiration – 'and proved to be the fair muse herself. In an instant the passage was clear. I sat down at the piano and wrote it down as fast as if I had long known it by heart.' (Venetian Diary, 22 December 1858) These are the bars which lead into the melody of Isolde's final transfiguration.

There were more interruptions and distractions than one might suppose from the pages of the Diary, which is saturated with the mood of *Tristan*. To Bülow, who was preparing the vocal score, he wrote that when he had got to know the second act he would sense how rarely and with what difficulty Wagner was able to wrest from his present way of life the hours when it was possible to write such music. (23 January 1859) There was letter after letter to write, so that he groaned that he really ought to have a secretary: about the Berlin production of *Lohengrin* (23 January 1859), which forced Hülsen to admit at last that he had not expected such an 'outrageous success'; about his efforts to 'exploit' *Rienzi* to earn some money, which brought him from Munich the news that it had once again been withdrawn there 'for religious reasons' – as a result he lost a royalty of 50 louisdor which he had unfortunately already spent in anticipation. In December he was approached again by the agent Dr Hartenfels, who had tried three years previously to persuade him to undertake an American tour. Wagner was once more so deep in financial trouble that this time he gave the proposal serious consideration: five months in New York, a prestigious German opera, he thought he would be well paid. His conditions were that he would conduct only his own operas and that Klindworth must be engaged as his assistant. After three months of negotiations he was finally relieved when the plan came to nothing: it would have been a little too much like London! (To Klindworth, 28 April 1859)

In November 1858 Breitkopf & Härtel, who were in touch with

him over the engraving of *Tristan*, raised the subject of the 'Nibelung' project again of their own accord: they proposed publishing it without making a down payment, but offered him a share of the net profits. They did not want to let slip the opportunity of doing business, but still had doubts about the practicability of so huge a work. Wagner replied that he not only thought his work was practicable, he knew it, in spite of all appearances. He possessed a particularly acute sense of the practical, which never deserted him in any of his ventures, however daring. After a protracted correspondence he broke off the negotiations on 6 February 1859: 'I can see that the time is not yet ripe.'

He lost no time in turning to Liszt instead. On 23 February, referring to a conversation he had had with Grand Duke Carl Alexander in Lucerne in the summer of the previous year, he wrote to Liszt offering the duke the rights to the score of the *Ring*, for the same fee that Breitkopf & Härtel were paying him for *Tristan*. Liszt reported back: 'Our Serenissimus did not find the thick "soup", as you call it, much to his taste. Neither the palate nor the stomach is ready for it.' (6 April 1859)

At the same time he was still corresponding with Eduard Devrient, in the belief that Karlsruhe was going to give the first performance of *Tristan*. He was relying on the Grand Duke of Baden to snap his fingers at Saxony and invite him personally to Karlsruhe, and was unaware that Devrient had long been playing a double game, as we learn from the letters he wrote to his wife from Asyl the year before.

So many plans; so many illusions. The only thing to come to fruition, in fact, was something he had ceased to expect. 'The police served me with my expulsion order today,' he wrote to Bülow on 3 February. 'Saxony has just kept on at Vienna about it.'

The Saxon government was not alone to blame: he had a powerful enemy in Austria, too, the General Inspector of Police, Lieutenant-Field-Marshal Johann Freiherr Kempen von Fichtenstamm. No sooner had he heard of Wagner's arrival in Venice on 29 August 1858 than he sent off a telegram in code to the Venetian police authorities, on 3 September, making enquiries. After receiving confirmation, he at once approached the Austrian foreign minister, Karl Graf von Buol-Schauenstein, representing to him that the presence on Austrian territory of a man notorious as one of the leaders of the May revolution in Dresden was not only unwelcome to the police but also likely to offend the government of Saxony. For the time being Buol ordered only that Wagner should be kept under strict police surveillance and that the Saxon government should be informed of this. Kempen had to be satisfied with that, and there was nothing Dresden could do but file the information.

The official documents published by Lippert (LWVR, pp. 94f.) read like a chilling satire on reactionary administrations, while all the more honour is due to Angelo Crespi, the minor police official in Venice who wrote the regular police reports to Kempen and gave Wagner what protection he could in them: Wagner was devoting himself to his work, to the exclusion of all other activities; thanks to his genius he had broken new ground in composition; the doctors had years ago ordered him to live in the south to restore his health. Good Wagnerians, Newman comments, ought to drink Crespi's health after each performance of the second act of *Tristan*.

Wagner's position got worse early in 1859, when the likelihood that Austria would soon be at war with France and the Kingdom of Sardinia engaged so much of Buol's attention that Kempen got a free hand and ordered his expulsion on 1 February. In order to win a little time to finish the second act, on the advice of his friends in the police, Wagner addressed a petition to Archduke Maximilian in Milan, then Governor General of Lombardy and later the ill-fated Emperor of Mexico, who telegraphed his consent without delay.

But as his residence permit was in any case due to expire in the spring, the question of his amnesty again became urgent. He decided to write to 'old Lüttichau', asking him to recommend that he be allowed to return without incurring further penalty: if he were refused yet again then he would have no other choice but, with a heavy heart, to abandon Germany once and for all. 'But it would make me very satisfactory amends that I should not need to denounce my harsh treatment myself: my epitaph would proclaim it, silently but for all the world to hear.' (9 February 1859) Without taking any action himself at all, Lüttichau left it to him to approach the king and so, encouraged by his success with Archduke Maximilian, Wagner wrote to the Saxon minister of justice on 22 February, pleading that his health did not permit him to face the stresses that a trial and the loss of liberty entailed would cause him. The petition was laid before the king; Minna received the refusal on 10 March.

A misunderstanding with Liszt was added to the worries of that winter. 'Thanks to Liszt I had a sad New Year,' Wagner wrote to Bülow on 23 January. It was cleared up in no time, but it left a slight distance between them: he recognized more clearly than ever that he could not let himself go completely with Liszt. 'He doesn't understand my sense of humour at all.' Bülow replied that he had only heard of his awkward passage with Liszt after it was all over. 'Thank God that it's all been settled. You are right to exercise a little diplomacy towards him now and then. He has become distrustful in the highest degree. Hardly a day passes without his being betrayed and traduced.' (5 February)

Wagner finished the orchestral sketch of Act II on 9 March 1859 and the score on 18 March. He wrote to tell Mathilde that he had at last dealt with the big musical problem that had caused everybody so much concern, and knew that he had found a solution such as had never been found before. 'It is the summit of my art so far.' (10 March) Not the least reason for his success, as Alfred Lorenz has shown, was his decision to cast the immensely extended dialogue in symphonic form, in broad outline Allegro – Adagio – Allegro.[1] It was thanks to the complete translation of all the ideas and concepts into musical and visual terms that, as Pfitzner said, a miracle was realized: for all its philosophical profundities and visionary realms of light, even the listener who remains unaware of its poetic depths enjoys it as an opera.

In the meantime the political situation had further deteriorated; troops had been sent to the Riva, and Milan was reported to be in a state of emergency. Since Wagner wanted to spend the summer in Switzerland he made haste and left Venice on 24 March. Coming to Milan and the noise of its streets was like entering a new world, he wrote to Mathilde the following day, and Venice already seemed like a fairy-tale dream. 'One day you will hear a dream that I roused to sound there!' During his short stay he also went to see Leonardo's *Last Supper*. As he looked from the copy, showing the painting as it had originally been, to the original, which was almost completely obliterated, he received for the first time, as he admitted, a clearer idea of the purely artistic significance of a masterpiece of painting. It was probably no coincidence that this revelation first came to him as the composer of *Tristan*. Nietzsche must have had an intimation of this affinity when he said that all the mysteries of Leonardo da Vinci are unravelled in the music of *Tristan*.

While the fruit trees were already in flower in Italy, the St Gotthard was clothed in an abominable cloak of mist, lined with snowflakes. 'A fine business, this snowy passage through wind and weather, on an open sledge.'(To Minna, 30 March) In Lucerne he put up at the Hotel Schweizerhof, managing to get a room in the annexe, which he had to himself until the end of June, with a large balcony and a magnificent view of his 'favourite lake'. At the weekend he visited the Wesendonks in Zürich. 'I feel as though I didn't really see you clearly,' he told Mathilde, 'thick fog lay between us, and even the sound of our voices could hardly penetrate it.' Since Wesendonk thought it was time to resume the appearance of a normal social relationship, to give the lie to gossip, a number of visits were exchanged between Zürich and Lucerne. 'It was, or so we both hope, a salutary demonstration,' Wagner dutifully reported to Minna. 'And I hope that you too will draw from it the conclusions that have given Wesendonk such satisfaction.' (18 April) The immediate consequence was that she at once got in touch with Jacob Sulzer: if his friend Wesendonk knew only a fraction of what she knew, he would abandon this naive idea that it was harmless to receive such a *dangerous* guest in the house. (24 April; FWSZ, II, pp. 164ff.)

After the Erard, delayed by troop movements and snowdrifts, finally arrived, Wagner began the composition sketch of the third act on 9 April. He felt as though he would never invent anything new again: the one period of flowering had produced so many shoots that now all he had to do was help himself from his store. In fact the act prelude is based on the song *Im Treibhaus*, transposed from D minor to F minor, the key of the 'traurige Weise' he had written in Venice, and more oppressive by the change of metre from triple to quadruple. But then the weather took a turn for the worse; he sat gazing out of the windows at the fog and could not get on with his work. In such times of reluctant inactivity he picked up Goethe's *Tasso*, which made him realize that he should not be in any hurry to have the text of *Tristan* published: the difference between a poem intended to be set to music and one intended as a straight play was so great that, if the former was read with the same eyes as the latter, the greater part of its real significance remained hidden. The poet–playwright had to assimilate his subject to real life in innumerable small details, which the poet–composer could simply make good in the 'endless detail of the music'. (To Mathilde, 15 April)

Liszt sent him his *Dante* Symphony at Eastertime. 'As Virgil guided Dante, you have led me through the mysterious regions of worlds of music, drenched in life. From my heart of hearts I cry: "Tu se' lo mio maestro e il mio autore!" and dedicate this work to you in steadfast, faithful love, your Liszt.'

The dedication reached Wagner at a moment of deep discouragement such as only genius knows, when it seems it would be better to smash the statue and have done with it. In his reply to Liszt he wrote: 'With this last act I am on the very brink of "to be or not to be" – the least featherweight pressure from some mundane accident . . . could kill the child in the act of its birth.' He suggested that they keep the words of the dedication to themselves: they had made him blush for shame. 'I simply can't tell you strongly enough how wretched a musician I am in my own eyes; from the bottom of my heart I despise myself as a complete bungler.' (8 May)[2]

'Dear Richard, your letter – what a dreadful tempest!' Liszt wrote back. 'Hamlet's dilemma does not apply to you, because you are and cannot help but be. Even your crazy injustice towards yourself . . . is a sign of your greatness.' (14 May)

But Wagner's mood had already changed. He wrote to Mathilde on 9 May to tell her that only the day before his attempt to work had been a dismal failure. He had been in an awful state and had poured it all out in a long letter to Liszt. But after he had been stuck at an awkward passage for a week her biscuits had reached him today. 'Now I am quite happy: the transition has succeeded beyond expectation, with a quite marvellous blend of two themes. Dear God, the things biscuits can do, when they're the right ones!'

The transition in question was that from Tristan's passionate outcry 'Im Sterben mich zu sehnen, vor Sehnsucht nicht zu sterben!' to his recall of his first lonely voyage to Ireland to be healed by Isolde. What he describes as simply the blend of two themes is the start of a musical period in which, after the words 'den Segel[3] blähte der Wind hin zu Irlands Kind', the polyphonic writing for the woodwind, horns and strings above the pianissimo pedal point on the timpani expands into the simultaneous blend of four independent themes, but is so fluent and transparent that the accents of each part can be heard and appreciated individually.

Over and above its intrinsic accomplishment, the passage marks an epoch in musical history. Richard Strauss commented that the contrapuntal theory of the old school, according to which the invention of a new melody had to take into account another melody with which it was expected to fit, had never interested him much. On that principle one could spend the livelong day writing fugues. But the yoking together of themes that were intractably opposed and had to be forced to accommodate each other – that was something else entirely! This modern 'psychological' counterpoint originated, Strauss concluded, in the third act of *Tristan*.[4]

Wagner took his technical inspiration for the passage from Bach and the Beethoven of the late quartets. He had tried to rehearse four Zürich musicians in the C♯ minor Quartet while he was still at Asyl. 'The beggars fiddled and squeaked away again so abominably', he told Minna, 'that Tausig grieved for me.' And an allusion in one of his letters to Mathilde reveals that during this summer while he was working on the third act, he played Bach to her, perhaps from the *Well-Tempered Clavier*, which he held particularly high. 'He has never given even me so much pleasure before, and I have never felt so close to him.' (9 July) Bülow's intuitive understanding of Wagner enabled him to appreciate the unique quality of the style of *Tristan* at once: 'Your *Tristan* bears the same relationship to *Lohengrin* as Beethoven's last quartets to his first. The analogy struck me forcibly. You will have to reckon with the audience of late Beethoven.' (NBB, 24 August)

Wagner, too, was pleased with himself. He had just played through the first half of the third act to himself, he wrote to Mathilde one day, and he had nobody to praise him, just like God on the sixth day of creation – 'and so I said to myself, among other things: Richard, you're a devil of a fellow!' (5 June) This act was like an intermittent fever, he complained while he was working on it. But while someone else might suppose that the passion and suffering in it were as much as his soul could bear, they were putting him into the frame of mind for *Parsifal* again: it was Amfortas who now filled his mind, appearing before him like Tristan in the third act but 'intensified beyond all imagining'. 'And do I really intend to create something like that? and actually set it to music as well? No, thank you very much!' (To Mathilde, 30 May)

Not if he could help it. The nearer he got to the end of *Tristan* the lighter his spirits became. He took up riding – riding! 'My doctor insisted.' He hadn't been on a horse since Riga, but he was managing quite well, with an 'English' seat. But he would have to beware of conceiving a passion for horses: the Wandering Jew had better not have a horse to accompany him on his travels. He had even made up a folksong while he was out riding, to celebrate finishing *Tristan*:

> Im Schweizerhof zu Luzern
> von Heim und Haus weit und fern –
> da starben Tristan und Isolde:
> so traurig er und sie so holde.

('In the Schweizerhof in Lucerne, far from hearth and home, Tristan and Isolde died, he so sad and she so fair.')

It went very well to a folk tune: he had sung it the same evening to Vreneli – Verena Weidmann, his faithful housekeeper, who later looked after him and Cosima in Munich and at Tribschen.

One morning he was woken up by the sound of an alphorn on the Rigi, and the cheerful noise it made inspired the 'lustige Weise' in *Tristan*. While he was pulling it into shape he suddenly thought of a different version of it, far more exultant, almost heroically so, and yet as natural as folk music. He was on the point of crossing out all he had written down when he was struck by yet another thought, namely that the new tune did not belong to Tristan's shepherd but to none other than Siegfried: 'Sie ist mir ewig, ist mir immer Erb und Eigen, Ein und All . . . ' 'And so I found myself all at once deep in *Siegfried*. Am I not right, after all, to have faith in my life, in my – ability to survive?' (To Mathilde, 9 July) Just as the first themes of *Tristan* had intruded as he was writing the second act of *Siegfried*, so now themes for *Siegfried* occurred to him while he worked to finish *Tristan*. As well as this jubilant theme, he made a sketch of a mournful cor anglais tune, heading it 'third act or *Tristan*'. He eventually changed its metre from 3/4 to 4/4 and used it in Act III of *Siegfried* at 'Dort seh ich Grane, mein selig Roß'.

His longing to complete the *Ring* revived, in spite of the Härtels and the Grand Duke of Weimar. When Otto Wesendonk offered him help Wagner at first refused. 'I cannot honourably accept a loan, for I know my position and constitution, which will probably never alter.' (24 August) But a few days later he followed this with: 'Can we perhaps make a *deal*?' He outlined the same proposals as he had made to Carl Alexander: Wesendonk should pay 6000 francs for each part completed, Wagner would sign over to him all the receipts from publication and would keep for himself only the income from public performance. He added that the offer would prove a bargain, even if it took time, which was if anything too modest a claim: it would have been the most profitable investment Wesendonk ever made – if it had not been for an event five years later which no one could have foreseen at the time. The contract was agreed, though it is hardly necessary to say that Wesendonk looked on it not as a commercial venture but merely as a means of saving Wagner's face.

Apart from the occasional society of his friends in Zürich, he felt very lonely. 'Do send me Tausig!' he begged Liszt. But Tausig could not come, and Liszt himself was rushed off his feet with the preparations for the Leipzig musicians' congress that was to lead to the foundation of the Allgemeiner Deutscher Musikverein. 'Don't laugh too much at me for always concerning myself with things like this: they are not without influence on your royalties, and from that point of view I beseech your tolerance.' (14 May) Instead of Tausig he sent the twenty-four-year-old composer Felix Draeseke, who arrived in Lucerne at the end of July and to begin with upset Wagner gravely with his account of the congress in Leipzig, at which his name had not been mentioned once, so as not to incur royal displeasure. Wagner addressed his anger to Bülow: instead of timidly avoiding mention of his name the honourable assembly should have submitted a petition on his behalf to the government of Saxony. 'Truly, I was stupid enough to expect just that . . . And ought I to blame Brendel and his cronies for it? Of course not – but you and Liszt – you I blame.' (2 September) 'You are right,' Bülow replied; ' "We" behaved badly. It is not my fault particularly.' He went on to tell Wagner that he had been so disgusted by Brendel's 'tactless, lickspittle toast' to King Johann, 'the jolly state-coachman, patron of the arts and sciences' – Bülow's allusion here to a well-known satirical poem makes this a far more savage comment on the king than it appears to be – that he had thrown his full glass of wine under the table, to the consternation of the assembled company.[5]

Draeseke stayed for four weeks and bequeathed us one of the few accounts of Wagner at work written by someone who possessed not only the musical training but the grounding in general culture needed to do the subject justice.

Wagner worked throughout the day, while Draeseke read the sections of the score that were finished. In the late afternoon they emerged from their separate rooms to talk and go for walks. One day, 6 August, Wagner received him with: 'Wait just a moment and *Tristan* will be finished.' 'I don't want to miss that!' Draeseke exclaimed and he was allowed to watch as Wagner wrote the last bars, with the opening motive dying away in the final, transfiguring chord. Looking at the score he asked why the cor anglais did not play in the last chord.[6] Wagner replied brusquely: 'Why should that old scoundrel still be grunting away?' The instrument that plays the 'traurige Weise' is silent in what Richard Strauss called 'the most beautifully orchestrated B major chord in the history of music'.

On their walks they held long conversations about art, philosophy, religion and politics. Draeseke soon noticed that Wagner's thought processes were completely different from Bülow's and especially from Liszt's: he would call their minds quick, but Wagner's profound. At the end of his life he still maintained that Wagner's was the greatest intellect that he had ever known.

Several times there arose the subject of the 'New German School', whose wilful harmonies incurred the severe condemnation of the composer of *Tristan*. On one of these occasions he taught Draeseke a lesson about melody which shed a completely new light on the subject for the younger man and was of more use to him than everything he had learnt at the Leipzig Conservatory. 'Quite out of the blue, I don't know what gave rise to it, he began to sing the first movement of the "Eroica" one very hot afternoon in August, got dreadfully carried away, sang on and on, grew very hot, was beside himself but wouldn't stop until he had finished the first section. "What's that?" he shouted at me, and I of course replied "the 'Eroica' ". "Well, isn't the plain melody enough? Must you always have your insane harmonies with it?" To begin with I didn't understand what he meant, but when he calmed down and explained how the melodic current in Beethoven's symphonies flows onwards inexhaustibly and the melody alone is all you need to be able to call the entire symphony clearly to mind, it set me thinking in a way that had a great influence on my work.'[7]

What Wagner so dramatically demonstrated to Draeseke on that occasion was the underlying principle of his own creative process: that the melody ought not to be set moving artificially by harmonic indulgences, but must flow inexhaustibly by its own power. 'I've experienced it all at first hand,' he wrote to Liszt, while he was composing *Rheingold*, 'and now I'm in a phase of development where I've turned to a completely different method of construction.' (4 March 1854) He believed that *Tristan* was the closest that he had got to his ideal so far.

He had finished the score of *Tristan* yesterday (actually the day before), he told Princess Marie Wittgenstein. He had saved up this important part of it as a greeting for her. 'Do you remember the trip to Paris? It was a feast of loving friendship fit for the gods, and you presided.' After it he had sat down to compose for the first time in six years. Since then he had finished *Rheingold*, *Walküre*, the greater part of *Siegfried*, and now *Tristan und Isolde*. It was impossible for him to say what the verdict on these works would be. It would certainly be said that they were too unremittingly full of the whole abundance of the subject. A single glance would show that these scores were far richer, more finely woven, more extravagant than all his earlier scores put together. 'Certainly a wonderful blessing must have been laid upon me, to enable me, in these years of worry, want and all kinds of sorrow, to produce what someone who does not know me may well imagine to have flowered from the luxurious womb of a harmonious existence.' (8 August 1859)

# 23

## *Tannhäuser* in Paris

This time the compulsion to see his new work staged was stronger than ever before. As Germany and Austria were barred to him, perhaps for ever, with Karlsruhe the one uncertain exception and with the alternative of Strassburg hardly to be taken seriously, that left Paris. 'God knows, Paris was not my choice: my readiness to seize it was only that of someone who has no other alternative.' (To Otto Wesendonk, 27 October 1859) Although he at first tried to persuade himself that the sole purpose of his journey was to hear a good orchestra or string quartet, once he was there his true purpose, as strong as fate, swept him ever more irresistibly on to undertakings which brought him to the very brink of disaster.

In 1839 he had believed that he was going to take Paris by storm; in 1849 he went there only at the insistence of Minna and Liszt; this time, in 1859, he obeyed the prompting of his own daemon. 'Something is wanted of me that is more important than consideration of my own personality.' (To Mathilde Wesendonk, 23 September 1859)

Since 1850, however, changes concerning himself had taken place in Paris, of which he was as yet unaware. Little enough had happened on the surface. The *Tannhäuser* overture had been performed twice, in 1850 and 1858, without the press paying it much attention. In October 1850 the *Journal des Débats* had published an article by Liszt about *Lohengrin*: a spirit of flame had sprung to life, whose destiny was to wear a double crown of fire and gold. But public opinion had been more decisively moulded by F. J. Fétis, a formidable scholar of European renown, who wrote a series of seven articles in 1852 in the *Gazette Musicale*, reprinted as a pamphlet, demonstrating that Wagner composed according to a 'system' and that that system was wrong.

But there were also a few finer, more discriminating spirits who felt drawn to him, who studied his scores and honoured him as their liberator. 'The truth is, it was a complete "milieu" that received him,' Maxime Leroy wrote, 'a spiritual milieu that had waited for him and wanted to celebrate his art.'[1]

Bülow had commended him to Auguste de Gaspérini, a retired naval doctor, who now devoted himself entirely to his twin passions of writing and travelling. When Wagner arrived in Paris on 11 September the entire city was on holiday. His letter reached Gaspérini in Marseilles. 'Quick, quick!' the latter wrote to his friend Léon Leroy, 'great news! Leave everything and hurry to no. 4 Avenue Matignon. Ask the concierge if Richard Wagner is at home! He has written me a charming letter. He is in Paris for a time. I beg you to deputize for me with the great man.'

'Thank you very much for Gaspérini,' Wagner wrote to Bülow in October; 'he is agreeable and lively and seems to possess a very obliging nature.' Our greatest debt to Gaspérini is for one of the rare portraits of Wagner as man and artist.

> Wagner was forty-six years old but could have passed for thirty-six. What first struck me was his coldness, his reserve, the severity of his features. But as the conversation got going his expression became more vivacious and I at last recognized him as I had imagined him from his works. Every one of his features was imprinted with the iron will that was the foundation of his character; it was apparent in everything: in the powerfully protuberant forehead, the strongly shaped chin, the thin, tight-pressed lips, the hollow cheeks, which bore the marks of the protracted turmoil of a life full of suffering. Yes, that was the man, the fighter whose history I knew, the thinker who, unsatisfied with the past, pressed ever onwards to the future. In the extraordinary mobility of his features, which his dominant will seemed to struggle against in vain, I saw the born dramatist and the untiring investigator of the human soul, which he explored down into its finest recesses.

In the alterations of his expression, I thought at times to discover in its depths Tristan in despair, the disciple of Buddha and of Schopenhauer. But when conversation turned to a different subject, one close to his heart, concerning his future plans and new prospects – he made courageous efforts in speaking French, though he had only a poor command of it at that time – I suddenly beheld a different man: young, enthusiastic, full of life and confidence and, in spite of all his theories, very far removed from Buddha and his fruitless contemplation.[2]

Wagner expected to settle in Paris for some time, so he took a three-year lease on a small house in the Rue Newton, a quiet side street linking two of the avenues radiating out from the Place de l'Etoile, where he hoped to resume work on *Siegfried*, undisturbed by neighbours' pianos. 'Here I am', he wrote to Mathilde, 'settling in somewhere new again – without faith, without love or hope, resting on the unfathomable foundation of dreamlike indifference.' (23 October) Something astonishing happened while he was arranging for his belongings to be sent from Lucerne. He went to the Customs bureau to make an enquiry, and when he gave his name a young official leapt to his feet: 'Je connais bien M. Richard Wagner, puisque j'ai son médaillon suspendu sur mon piano et je suis son plus ardent admirateur.' His name was Edmond Roche, and he was a fervent amateur poet and musician. Wagner invited him to call on him and later entrusted him with the translation of *Tannhäuser*.

Wagner informed Bülow that he was sending for his unhappy wife again, since he was the only person who could give her the care she needed: 'Her dependence on me is life and death to her and that in turn determines my behaviour towards her.' (7 October) 'So come here, be cheerful, don't get excited and don't worry,' he wrote to her. 'You will find that there is still a lot to do here, but there is nothing waiting for you that will wear you out: we shall be able to look forward to a bright, cloudless sunset.' (7 November) Their reunion was under an unlucky star from the first. A short time before, Wagner had written to Pusinelli: it was a delicate matter that he could discuss only with a friend and a doctor: in consideration of the state of her health would he advise her against a resumption of conjugal relations, a prohibition that she should understand as being in his interests as well as her own. Pusinelli for his part gave Minna a letter to deliver to Wagner, in which he reiterated the importance of avoiding all excitements that could affect her health adversely. She opened this letter en route and he now refused to accept it from her. There can be no doubt that she made generous use of its contents in future arguments. (RWAP, pp. 106ff.)

The house in the Rue Newton had been in a dilapidated condition and Wagner had had it redecorated at considerable expense. According to Malwida von Meysenbug it looked charming and comfortable; his workroom and the adjacent music room, in particular, were works of art, though tiny. 'Only when I hope to conjure the muse and keep her at my side do I think . . . of furnishing my house with peace and comfort', he wrote apologetically to Wesendonk. 'If I relinquish the muse, then it all ceases to have any importance for me.'

In spite of being in Paris he lived in considerable isolation. His books were his preferred companions. The society of living people cost him more than he could muster, he felt; for the most part it just wore him out. But a book by a noble spirit was the most precious friend anyone could have; all outside excitements fell silent and the voice of a departed, perfected being could speak to one in peace. (To his sister, Cäcilie Avenarius, 31 July 1860)

Wednesday evenings were an exception, when a brilliant company of poets, artists, musicians, writers, politicians and scholars used to assemble in his drawing room: Gaspérini brought his friends, the music critic Léon Leroy and his brother Adolphe, a professor at the Conservatoire, whom Wagner nicknamed 'Monsieur Clarinette'; the poet Jules Champfleury, who had also tried painting and sculpture, and who later became artistic director of the porcelain manufactory at Sèvres: his essay on Wagner said as much that was true and profound in its fourteen pages as a whole library of Wagneriana, in the opinion of Houston Stewart Chamberlain; Frédéric Villot, curator of the art collections in the Louvre, whom Wagner met in a music shop, where he was enquiring about the newly published score of *Tristan*: Wagner esteemed his shrewd judgement, including his opinion of the character of his own nation; the future husband of Judith Gautier, the writer Catulle Mendès, whose admiration for Wagner's music survived the events of 1870; the illustrator Gustave Doré, who wanted to portray Wagner as the conductor of an orchestra of spirits in an Alpine landscape;

there were the musicians Ernest Royer and Charles Gounod, the politicians Jules Ferry and Emile Ollivier, the critics Jules Janin and Emile Perrin; a Monsieur de Chabrol, who wrote for the papers under the name of Lorbac, and proposed the foundation of a 'Théâtre Wagner'; Challemel-Lacour, who translated four of Wagner's operatic texts (*Holländer, Tannhäuser, Lohengrin* and *Tristan*) into French prose, to Wagner's satisfaction; last but not least, the barrister Charles Truinet, who used the nom de plume of Nuitter: he was the second translator of *Tannhäuser*, and his tactful, reliable friendship was to be of lasting value to Wagner.

The host dominated the company so completely, according to Malwida von Meysenbug, that really she saw and heard only him. On one occasion he was talking to a number of people about the rarity of what is called happiness and quoted the Princess in *Tasso*: 'Who then is happy?' She could see in the others' faces that they did not understand him. 'Why does he throw these pearls away on people who can't appreciate them?' she asked herself.

When Klindworth came over from London the social evenings moved upstairs to the music room, and there was always a performance of something from *Lohengrin, Rheingold, Walküre* or *Tristan*; Wagner took all the various singing parts while Klindworth accompanied him. Malwida comments that this might seem very unlikely to create a good impression, 'and yet it did'. Nobody could communicate his intentions as clearly as he did.

Minna felt at a loss and very forlorn in these surroundings. 'I am just the housekeeper here,' she told a friend in Dresden, 'with nothing to do but give orders to three servants and lose my temper with them, but am also allowed into the drawing room to show off my silk dress.' All her hatred for the moment was directed against Blandine Ollivier, Liszt's daughter. 'Blandine is a very commonplace, not to say common, female.' But Madam had noticed that Minna did not want her company, and so she had given up the regular visits she had been in the habit of paying Wagner. (JKWF, p. 186) 'I hardly ever see Blandine now,' he confirmed in a letter to Bülow; 'her husband is always ill and my wife eyes her with implacable suspicion.' (21 May 1860) But it was left to the fecund imagination of Julius Kapp to construct an 'erotic relationship' out of this material and – 'quite comically', as Richard Sternfeld said in his review of Kapp's book[3] – make it the basis of the conception of the new Venusberg music.

Wagner's growing doubts about the Karlsruhe project were confirmed by a letter he received from Devrient on 23 October 1859, saying that in the given circumstances *Tristan* was impossible, indeed that it would be impossible to perform in any circumstances. 'The dramatic idyll in Karlsruhe is completely over and done with,' he wrote to Mathilde. She would accuse him of exaggeration if he tried to tell her how hostile and unscrupulous Devrient's treatment of him had been. He was only interested in an everyday theatrical institution, without any excursions into the exceptional: 'In this sense he was always instinctively opposed to my works.' (23 and 29 October 1859) That he did Devrient no injustice is confirmed by letters, already mentioned, that Devrient sent his wife during his visit to Asyl: while protesting his sincerity to Wagner's face, behind his back his comments on him personally and his works were hostile.[4]

With the abandonment of the Karlsruhe plan, the importance of Paris for Wagner's hopes was greater than ever. He eventually drew up a scheme for conquering the city with three concerts of excerpts from his works, which he thought would earn him the facilities for producing *Tannhäuser*, *Lohengrin* and, as the crowning glory, *Tristan*. So for the time being he put aside his intention of resuming work on *Siegfried* and plunged into an ocean of trouble and vexation.

To avoid having to pay the prohibitively high cost of hiring a hall, on Gaspérini's advice he approached Napoleon III's private secretary for permission to use the auditorium of the Opéra, as an act of imperial favour. Permission was duly granted but came too late: by then Wagner had already arranged to hire the Théâtre Italien for three nights in January and February 1860 at 4000 francs a night. It might have been taken as an ill omen that this was the theatre previously known as the Théâtre de la Renaissance, where *Das Liebesverbot* had *not* been performed twenty years before!

He had a foretaste of what he could expect from the French press from a joke in *Le Figaro* which called him the 'Marat of music', though he could derive some consolation from the designation of Berlioz as its Robespierre.[5] Wagner was provoked to reply in *L'Europe Artiste*: 'I am a foreigner and an exile, and I hoped to be received hospitably by France . . . I have been called the Marat of music. My compositions have no such revolutionary propensities

. . . The French press should wait just a little while; perhaps it will revise its opinion of me.' (RWGS, XVI, p. 28)

All the seats, more than 1500, were taken in the Théâtre Italien on the evening of 25 January 1860. Only the Tower of Babel or a session of the National Convention could give so much as a faint impression of the feverish excitement reigning in the whole auditorium, *Le Ménestrel* reported. Everyone of position and name was present. The court was represented by Marshal Magnan, the Académie by Auber. Meyerbeer, Berlioz, Gounod, Reyer, the Belgian composer Gevaert were all to be seen in the front few rows. The press also appeared en masse, though they had no official invitation. Wagner bowed, with an impassive face, in acknowledgement of the applause that greeted him, then turned to face the orchestra. 'What goes on in the mind of an artist', Champfleury speculated, 'when he turns his back on the audience in the knowledge that in five minutes' time he will hear the judgement of Parisians, that is, of beings who expect first and foremost to be entertained, and whose immediate representatives, the theatre managers, have from the very first protested against all innovations?'

The programme included excerpts from *Tannhäuser* and *Lohengrin*, the *Holländer* overture with the new ending with the Redemption theme, and the prelude to *Tristan* with the concert ending anticipating Isolde's transfiguration. The fact that Wagner conducted without a score created a sensation in those days. Apart from the *Tristan* prelude, which the orchestra too had disliked at the first rehearsal, every item was applauded enthusiastically. Wagner was later to refer to the storm of applause that broke out after sixteen bars of the first cantabile of the march from *Tannhäuser* as a sign of the devout attention with which the audience had followed the development of the melodic idea. (RWGS, X, pp. 73f.)

'A complete success, an immense impression', Gaspérini wrote in the *Courier du Dimanche*. But his was a lone voice. The rest of the press, of all shades, fired off the wildest invective after each of the three concerts: unable to deny the fact of Wagner's success, they did their best to devalue it. But neither applause nor criticism affected Wagner as deeply as his friends thought. 'Evenings like that remain somewhat outside me', he told Mathilde. Only three things made a more distinct impression on him: an article by Berlioz, a pamphlet by Champfleury and a letter from Charles Baudelaire.

He had dedicated the score of *Tristan* to Berlioz on 21 January 1860: 'Au grand et cher auteur de *Roméo et Juliette* l'auteur reconnaissant de *Tristan et Isolde*.' The copy, now in the Bibliothèque Nationale, bears Berlioz's marginal marks against all the musical liberties he took exception to. His applause under the immediate impact of the first concert had been noticed. Reviewing it in the *Journal des Débats* on 9 February, he expressed a not unfavourable opinion of the separate items, except the *Tristan* prelude, of which he admitted that he understood nothing, but at the end of the article he attributed to Wagner theories about an alleged 'music of the future', from which he solemnly dissociated himself: 'I raise my hand and aver: "Non credo".' Wagner's Swiss–French biographer Guy de Pourtalès is honest enough to call the review an 'article perfide'.

Wagner felt the same about it. All the more credit is due, therefore, to the friendly tone of his reply, published in the *Débats* of 22 February, in which he thanked Berlioz for his complimentary remarks and then corrected the distorted picture he had drawn of the 'music of the future' by reference to his ideal of Aeschylean tragedy.[6] Nor was that all: when he read Berlioz's article about *Fidelio* in May he could not restrain himself from writing to him, in his 'horrible French', to thank him for bearing witness to the fact that 'une chaîne ininterrompue d'intime parenté rallie entre eux les grands esprits'. 'God knows what he will make of my gibberish,' he wrote to Liszt, but was astonished to realize from Berlioz's answer that his words must have made a great impression on him: 'Vous êtes . . . plein d'ardeur, prêt à la lutte,' the Frenchman wrote, 'je ne suis prêt moi qu'à dormir et à mourir.'[7]

Champfleury's pamphlet was dated 'the night of 27 January', two days after the first concert. What moved Wagner was the author's understanding, greater than any he had ever encountered, of his suffering as an artist. The signs of exhaustion on Wagner's features, Champfleury wrote, were the result of fifteen years of worry and disappointment, but there was no trace in his works of the martyrdom of this artist, condemned not to hear or see his own creations. Wagner himself had remarked on the same thing in the letter he sent Princess Marie after finishing *Tristan*. He might express bitterness sometimes – in conversation, in letters, in his writings, in his autobiography – but his art lay under the arch of a heaven unclouded by earthly vapours.

Baudelaire had gone to hear the first concert without knowing that he was inwardly already prepared for Wagner's music: 'La musique souvent me prend comme une mer!' And that was how the music had taken him. He wrote to Wagner on 17 February, above all to thank him for the greatest musical experience he had ever known. He said that he would have hesitated to assure him of his admiration, were it not that every day his eye fell on unworthy, ludicrous articles that made every possible effort to denigrate his genius. What he had experienced in the Théâtre Italien had been indescribable, but if Wagner would be so kind as not to smile at him, he would try to put it into words. His next statement is a subtle psychological observation: it had at once seemed to him that he already knew the music – a sensation that others, too, have described on first hearing Wagner's music: completely new and yet completely familiar.

'Ever since the day when I heard your music, I say to myself repeatedly, above all when things look bleak: If only I were at least going to be able to hear some Wagner this evening!. . . Once again, Sir, I thank you; you have shown me the way back to myself.' (TWLF, pp. 198ff.)

Through diffidence he did not give his address, but Wagner managed to track him down and invited him to call on him. 'If you see him before me,' Baudelaire wrote to Champfleury, 'tell him that it will give me great happiness to shake the hand of a man who is reviled by the empty-headed common herd.' (TWLF, pp. 220ff.)

This is the place to mention yet another unexpected amicable encounter. A malicious joke at the expense of Wagner's music, currently going the rounds, was attributed to Rossini, who publicly repudiated it. Wagner thereupon paid him a call and thus made the acquaintance of an honourable, upright man and a cheerful sceptic. Rossini disavowed any ambition to be numbered with the heroes, but on the other hand he could not remain indifferent if he was held so low as to be included among the shabby spirits who derided serious endeavours. When he died in 1868 Wagner recalled their meeting in *A Souvenir of Rossini*, published in the Augsburg *Allgemeine Zeitung*, thereby atoning for the many attacks he had launched on him in his earlier writings. (*Eine Erinnerung an Rossini*, RWGS, VIII, pp. 220ff.)

Of more immediate importance to Wagner than reviews, criticism, applause or fame was the deficit of 11,000 francs remaining after the concerts, and the failure of a financier whom Gaspérini had introduced to him as a future guarantor of his operatic plans for Paris. That was the end of the plan that should have culminated in the performance of *Tristan*, and he counted himself lucky not to end up in gaol, which he accomplished by means of a tangled web of financial transactions of which Newman gives the best account.[8] His only remaining chance was to set all on getting *Tannhäuser* produced at the Opéra, he told Otto Wesendonk. 'Think of me caught up in my efforts, weigh my character and what it is that alone means anything to me: the shifts I shall be put to, the paths I must tread! – and you will know what frame of mind I am in!' (12 February 1860)

The most successful and momentous piece of business he did at this time was with Franz Schott, the proprietor of the Mainz firm of music publishers B. Schott's Söhne, to whom he had offered his transcription of the Choral Symphony thirty years before. Schott wanted to have an opera by the controversial composer on his list, and approached Wagner with this purpose in mind in November 1859 through the agency of his musical adviser Heinrich Esser, the kapellmeister to the imperial court in Vienna. Wagner replied that he had enough material to enter into immediate negotiations with Schott. Esser reported back to Schott, advising him that a certain degree of toughness towards Wagner would not be inappropriate; but apart from that an opera by him would redound to the credit of any publisher; he hoped very much that a satisfactory result would come of his mediation. 'I shall then claim the usual fee of a successful matchmaker.'

Having no new score to dispose of, Wagner quickly made up his mind and offered Schott *Das Rheingold* for 10,000 francs, cash down. To his astonishment Schott sent the money by return. Wagner had intended to repay the 6000 francs that Wesendonk had paid him for *Rheingold* out of the proceeds of his concerts, but the deficit frustrated that plan. In this desperate situation he hit on the extraordinary solution of asking his friend to regard the sum he owed him as an advance payment for the as yet unwritten last part of the tetralogy. Wesendonk agreed to this but, as Newman remarks dryly, as a businessman he must have smiled at this ingenious plan for 'feeding the dog its own tail'.

As usual in such crises Wagner also tried to help himself by his own efforts. He trustingly accepted an invitation to Brussels, to repeat his three Paris concerts in the Théâtre de la Monnaie, on the basis that he would receive half the net profits. Only after making the undertaking did he realize that he had overlooked a clause in the small print making him solely responsible for the musical expenses. After the second concert he decided to forgo the benefits of a third, since the outcome of the management's calculations was that, while he would not actually have to pay anything towards the concerts himself, he would have had to cover his lodging and travelling expenses out of his losses from the Paris concerts. (To Hans Richter, 19 October 1869)

His only gain from the journey to Brussels was making the acquaintance of the elderly diplomat Georg Heinrich Klindworth, a relative of the pianist, and his daughter Agnes Street, a former pupil and friend of Liszt. The meeting needs to be mentioned, because the two were to make one more brief but momentous appearance in Wagner's life, when he was in Munich. The only other consequence of the acquaintance was that Kapp once again leapt to the wrong conclusion, misinterpreting a remark in the catalogue of the Burrell Collection (the contents of the collection itself were of course not available to him) to mean that 'the lovely Agnes . . . seems to have harnessed Wagner also to her love-chariot', with the astonishing result that, as the editor of the Burrell Collection says, 'one more is added to the *Women in Wagner's Life*'.[9] A brief visit to Antwerp, to pay his respects to 'Madame Lohengrin, née Elsa', was disappointing. Wagner had imagined the citadel as being on a hill, but found instead a bleak, bare plain with defences dug into the ground. Thereafter he never saw a performance of *Lohengrin* without smiling to himself at the designer's imagination.

Help came in the end, unsolicited and unexpected, from a woman who had been present at the first performance of *Tannhäuser* in 1845, had made Wagner's acquaintance fleetingly in Paris in 1853, and now learned of his losses on her return from an extended journey: Marie Kalergis, born Countess Nesselrode, later to be Frau von Muchanoff, German on her father's side, Polish on her mother's, Russian by upbringing, Greek through her first husband, an internationally renowned beauty, pupil of Chopin and Liszt, dedicatee of Théophile Gautier's *Symphonie en blanc majeur*. An admirer of all progressive movements, she was also ready to support them out of her considerable means. She sent for Wagner and explained that her regret at having missed his concerts was the greater for her absence having caused her to miss the chance of being able to help him at the right time. She therefore asked him now to accept 10,000 francs from her to go to meet his losses. She was the first person, Wagner wrote to Mathilde, who amazed him quite spontaneously by a truly generous assessment of his position.

To thank her he mounted an impromptu private festival for her, with the first performance of the second act of *Tristan*. He summoned Karl Klindworth from London to play the piano and sang the part of Tristan himself, with Pauline Viardot-Garcia, in whose rooms the event took place, as Isolde. The audience consisted of Berlioz and Madame Kalergis. Her rescue action had been effected so quietly that only those closest to him knew about it. It thus came about that Glasenapp failed to mention it in the first edition of his biography in 1876, which Wagner represented to him as one of its most serious gaps. (GLRW, III, p. 265)

Liszt, too, was delighted at this intervention by his own old patroness: 'Beauty and nobility such as these are, alas, encountered all too rarely!' For the most part he was noticeably reticent during these months. 'Your friendship is indispensable to me; I cling to it with my last ounce of strength,' Wagner had written to him on 20 October 1859, for his birthday. 'When am I at last going to see you again?? Have you any idea of the position I am in? Of the miracles of loyalty and love I need, if I am to recover courage and patience over and over again?' And a month later: 'Believe me, my dear Franz, I find it very difficult to give you my news. Our lives do not coincide enough, and we are bound to grow further apart in an important aspect of friendship.' (23 November 1859) He complained to Bülow that Liszt would always remain sublime, deeply sympathetic, greatly admired and loved in his eyes, but – he would no longer be able to expect very much in the way of nurturing their friendship. 'I simply cannot *find* any words to say to him any more: my warmth has been answered with phrases too often. But phrases – are what I do not care to write to him: he is too dear to me for that.' (7 October)

Light is shed on the change in Liszt's attitude by his correspondence with his daughter Blandine. Writing about Wagner in Paris, Blandine said that there was no more dreadful sight than a genius combating the mundane obstructions of life. 'It's the old story, which never fails to move us, of Gulliver entangled in the thousand and one threads of the Lilliputians.' (29 December)

Of course it was regrettable, Liszt replied. But why could a great spirit not muster a little common sense to deal with the practical matters of life? He had himself advised Wagner more than once to settle in Paris, but he had also tried to make him understand that there would be no likelihood of his operas being performed there. 'In my opinion the best thing he could do would be to preserve a quiet, dignified and proud reserve . . . I shall abstain completely from interfering in his affairs, and confine myself to enduring his resentment against me in silence, as long as he is pleased to maintain it.'[10]

Liszt was right in his view that Wagner's activities in Paris were at odds with his true nature. But he failed to understand that there was no other course open to him but to write his works – and to have them performed; that he no longer had the time to wait in aristocratic reserve – until it was too late for him. Wagner knew that he was misunderstood, even though it was more painful for him on the part of his greatest friend. 'A life . . . like mine is bound to deceive the onlooker: he sees me involved in actions and enterprises which he supposes to be mine, whereas they are fundamentally alien to me; how often does anyone realize the reluctance that fills me when I am about these things? It will all be understood only when the sum and the final total are known.' (To Mathilde Wesendonk, 10 August 1860)

At times like these he took refuge in his inner world, as we can see from his correspondence with Mathilde, which underwent a last, late flowering. It is like a great self-communing: 'Mit mir nur rat' ich, red' ich mit dir'. He tells her what he has been reading: after Plutarch's *Lives of Great Men*, he thanks God not to be one of them; Schiller's *Maid of Orleans* inspires him with the desire to fill her glorious, wonderful silence with music. He writes about his 'art of transition' and its masterpiece, the great scene in the second act of *Tristan*. The Wesendonks went to Rome, which gave him occasion to compare Goethe's experience of Italy with his own: unlike Goethe, the great visual observer, he was not satisfied with the perception of the eye alone: there had to be an ineffable inner sense which was wide awake and active, when the external senses were only dreaming. *Parsifal* was occupying his imagination again: 'Have I already told you that the fabulous savage who is the messenger of the Grail is to be one and the same creature as the seductress in the second act?' And again and again he returned to the subject of nature. 'Clear understanding eases suffering; creases are smoothed and sleep regains its restorative power. And how good it is that the old man knows nothing at all of what he is to me, of what I am through him.'

While he was outwardly engaged in incessant and various activity, his spirit withdrew into a dream life. 'I dream much and often . . . But what poor assistance dreams give! If one is much aware of one's dreams it only indicates the emptiness of our waking existence. I always think of Keller's Green Heinrich, who in the end did nothing but dream.' (To Mathilde Wesendonk, 10 April 1860)

The necessity of limiting his plans to *Tannhäuser* suited the mood of the French public, which now associated his name exclusively with that work. His hopes of the Opéra, as his last chance, seemed threatened by the opposition of the minister of the household, Achille Fould, a friend of Meyerbeer. Then unexpectedly, in the middle of March 1860, Napoleon III commanded the performance of *Tannhäuser*. While his friends rejoiced, Wagner himself remained sceptical: he had no faith in it, and for good reasons, he told Liszt. He would greatly prefer to see *Tristan* performed in Germany and he was thinking seriously of settling his old score with Dresden, if only he could win some decent concessions. (29 March 1860) The course of events proved him right.

The imperial decree was the outcome of the interplay of personal and political factors, in which Bülow had played an enthusiastic part. Hans's diplomatic skill had procured him all manner of Parisian glories, which hovered teasingly before him now like a *fata morgana*. He had hurried to Paris with a letter of introduction from Princess Augusta of Prussia to the Prussian ambassador, Count Pourtalès. In particular, he had been successful in winning the good offices of the attaché at the embassy, Count Hatzfeld, on Wagner's behalf. Hatzfeld, a favourite of the Empress Eugénie, was approached at a masked ball in the Tuileries by a masked woman, in whom he recognized the empress. When they withdrew, at her suggestion, to one of the quieter rooms, he took the opportunity of recommending *Tannhäuser* to her. She promised to see what she could do and asked him to give her details of the matter in writing. This, according to Hatzfeld, was the beginning of a friendlier attitude at the court.[11]

But the decisive factor was the intervention of Princess Pauline Metternich-Sándor, the wife of the Austrian ambassador, who had got to know Wagner through Councillor Klindworth of Brussels. 'She is an imp of a woman,' he wrote to Bülow, 'a distinct oddity, but certainly useful.' Horace de Viel Castel, the chronicler of the Second Empire, describes her in the most repellent terms: this favourite of the empress drank, smoked and swore, was as ugly as sin and a scandal-monger. But we must make allowances for patriotic prejudice: it was generally believed that she had a political mission to improve relations between France and Austria, which made her detested in certain circles in Paris. One day, when Wagner was the subject of conversation at the court, the emperor asked the princess for her opinion. She spoke of *Tannhäuser* with such enthusiasm that he promised her to have it produced in Paris. Thereafter both good manners and policy obliged him, as a man of honour, to keep his word.

The question of the French translation had been a headache from the start. Finally Wagner remembered the customs official Edmond Roche, but as Roche understood no German he had to have a German-speaking collaborator, Rudolf Lindau. 'Travaillez, travaillez comme le diable,' Wagner exhorted his 'chère compagnie de traduction' as early as the beginning of February. And on 12 March: 'The devil's away! The emperor has ordered *Tannhäuser* to be performed . . . If Meyerbeer isn't paying you to lead me up the garden path, let me know if *Tannhäuser* is going to be put on before the end of the world. . . Au nom de l'empéreur, donnez-moi de vos nouvelles!'[12]

With a certain amount of fictional licence, Victorien Sardou describes how Wagner worked with Roche on Sundays, from first thing in the morning till late at night, striding up and down with flashing eyes and wild gestures, hammering something out on the piano, singing, shrieking 'Allez! Allez!' In the evening, when the lamp cast his perambulating shadow on to the wall like something out of Hoffmann, he was still as fresh as when they had started.

The translation was ready at last, but an unrhymed libretto was unheard of at the Opéra, and the manager, Royer, recommended that Truinet, the barrister, should re-do it in verse. Truinet duly produced a satisfactory version, but the matter did not end there. At an advanced stage of the rehearsals Rudolf Lindau brought an action against Wagner, because he wanted his name on the posters as the translator. Thanks to the advocacy of Emile Ollivier, who even offered to sing 'O du mein holder Abendstern' to the court, Wagner won the case easily.

The news from Paris had repercussions in Germany. In view of the facts that *Tannhäuser* was to be performed by order of the emperor, that both the Prussian and the Austrian embassies had intervened on Wagner's behalf and even the Saxon ambassador, Baron Seebach, had taken his part, and finally that Princess Augusta of Prussia put in a good word for him with King Johann in Baden-Baden in June 1860, the king had no choice but to bow to the inevitable. But instead of doing so with fitting dignity he remained true to his nature: he still did not want to see this undesirable person in his own country, and if other German rulers wanted him, then it must be only after consulting Dresden. The draft written by Minister Beust still exists: the clause requiring Wagner himself to apply for permission each time is changed in the king's own handwriting to the effect that the request must come from the *government* in question: he would have nothing to do with Wagner directly. (LWVR, pp. 139ff.)

On 22 July 1860 Baron Seebach notified Wagner of his partial amnesty. On 12 August Wagner set foot on German soil for the first time in eleven years, without, he confessed, feeling any particularly strong emotion. He was received in Baden-Baden on 17 August by the Regent of Prussia, Princess Augusta. He found her the intelligent, clever and vivacious woman that he had imagined her to be, who gladly accepted his thanks for her liking for his works but was skilfully evasive when he raised the subject of the Berlin Opera.

All in all the return to his homeland that he had so long looked forward to was a disappointment. He shuddered when he thought of Germany and of what he meant to undertake there in the future, he told Liszt, writing from Paris again on 13 September: 'Believe me, we have no fatherland! And if I am "German" then I surely carry my Germany within me.'

His French friends tried to counter his lack of faith in the Paris *Tannhäuser* by emphasizing the unprecedented importance of the impression that they expected it to make: how it was received was a matter of life and death for the cultural salvation of Parisian audiences. 'They say to me: "You see *how* things are, and *what* we expect and demand from you! . . . What you are offering is not remotely like anything that has ever been seen here before, for you offer the perfect and with the greatest expressive power." '(To Mathilde Wesendonk, 10 April 1860) It resounds like a foretelling of the unique '*wagnériste*' movement which grew up after Wagner's death and completely dominated French cultural and intellectual life for twenty years. 'He was the liberator!' exclaimed Maxime Leroy. André Suarès compared him with Prometheus the fire-bringer. Stéphane Mallarmé called him a god: 'Le dieu Richard Wagner irradiant un sacre.'[13]

To promote deeper understanding of his work, Wagner asked Challemel-Lacour to make French prose translations of the *Holländer*, *Tannhäuser*, *Lohengrin* and *Tristan*, which were published with a preface by himself in the form of a *Lettre sur la musique* addressed to Frédéric Villot. This letter, published in his collected writings with the title *Zukunftsmusik* (RWGS, VII, pp. 87ff.), moves away from his earlier theoretical works in placing the emphasis on the musical element – on his innovatory 'infinite melody', which is intended to make an impression on the hearer like that received by a solitary walker in a beautiful forest on a summer evening: however many parts and separate tunes he hears, the swelling notes will yet seem to be just 'the one great forest melody'.

'Meanwhile I must put myself into the right mood to write – a large-scale ballet,' he told Mathilde. 'What do you think of that? Do you find it hard to believe?' He had been asked to provide a ballet for the second act, since the holders of subscriptions to the Opéra, the aristocratic members of the Jockey Club, always arrived at the theatre rather late. 'I explained to them that I could not take any instructions from the Jockey Club and would rather withdraw my work. But I will help them out of their difficulty after all: the opera does not need to start before eight, and so I will rewrite the accursed Venusberg properly once and for all . . . So far I haven't written anything at all: I will try to jot something down here for the first time. Don't be surprised that this should happen in a letter to Elisabeth.'

The scenario he drafted in this letter gives a good idea of Wagner's eagerness to give rein to his poetic imagination again after a long pause. His primary concern was with the dramatic structure of *Tannhäuser*: the court of Venus was the weak part of the work, failing to fill in properly the important background to the tragedy that was to follow. Rectifying it required skills that he had only recently acquired.

It may well be, too, that now that he had expressed in artistic form something of his experience of the Germanic heritage, the desire revived in him to express his experience of ancient Greece, and in particular his conception of Greek culture as the struggle between the Dionysian and Apollonian principles. The Classical Witches' Sabbath (Walpurgisnacht) from the second part of *Faust*, which he admired as an inspired reconstruction of the Greek world, will have been in his mind as a remote model. Goethe introduced a Nordic element with Faust, Mephistopheles and Homunculus, and in this first draft Wagner did the same with the figure of the water sprite, the Strömkarl, who rises out of the whirlpool amid the rejoicing of the Bacchanalian throng and strikes up a dance on his big magic fiddle. 'You can imagine how I'm going to have to exercise my invention to give this dance the proper character.'

Wagner found the Strömkarl in Grimm's *German Mythology*: he plays a tune with eleven variations, of which men may dance to only ten. The eleventh belongs to the Spirit of Night and his horde; if it were to be played, then everything, animate and inanimate, would start to dance. 'I'm very pleased that I thought of using my Strömkarl and his eleventh variation. It also explains why Venus and her court have come to the north: it was only there that they could find the fiddler fit to play for the old gods.' (To Mathilde Wesendonk, 10 April 1860)

In the more detailed second sketch, too, where 'mythological beasts' driven forward from the background are added to the 'mythological rabble', the Strömkarl appears on a rock in the middle of a waterfall, 'an elderly figure of a gentle, jovial appearance, with a misshapen stringed instrument rather like a violin'. Drawing his bow across the strings, he rouses the young men, nymphs, griffins and sphinxes to a wild dance, in which they are joined by a band of centaurs, until a signal from Venus bestirs the slumbering Cupids, who fly up and let loose a hail of arrows on the dancers. Finally the Dionysian riot gives way to Apollonian visions, the Rape of Europa, Leda and the Swan: 'Leda reclining beside a pool: the swan swims towards her, arches his neck, which Leda caresses and draws to her.' This closely parallels the scene on the Lower Peneios in the Classical Walpurgisnacht:

> Now new marvels! Swans are coming,
> From their hidden waters swimming . . .

> But one most of all seems vaunting
> His audacity and flaunting
> Sails through all with eager pace . . .

The Apollonian visions are retained in the final version of the Bacchanal, on which Wagner based his composition. 'Sensuality is transformed into beauty.' But the inspired stroke of the Strömkarl was omitted, and it is an eternal shame that Wagner had to sacrifice it to the limitations of the Paris opera ballet of the time. The company was in any case completely at a loss with what had been written for them. When Wagner pointed out to Petipa that the dancers' little skipping steps were glaringly inappropriate to the music, and explained that he had wanted something 'bold and savage but sublime' in the style of the Bacchanalia depicted on classical reliefs, the ballet master whistled through his fingers: 'Oh, I understand very well!' But if he had said so much as a word of it to his dancers they would at once have found themselves with a cancan and all would be lost.

Yet another trial had been imposed on him to mock his position, Wagner wrote to Otto Wesendonk on 5 June 1860. He had heard from St Petersburg that the director of the Imperial Russian theatre was coming to Paris with the intention of engaging him on advantageous terms. The director duly arrived at the end of May, in the imposing person of a General Saburoff, prepared to conclude a formal contract, but issuing the following ultimatum: either Wagner would go to St Petersburg that summer, spend the winter there, produce *Tannhäuser* and conduct large orchestral concerts, all for a guaranteed sum of 50,000 francs, half to be paid immediately – or nothing at all. The general had been adamant in refusing any of the compromises Wagner suggested to fit in with his Parisian commitment. He couldn't simply sell himself just for the money like that, Wagner confessed to Wesendonk. 'I kept faith with Paris, loaded the apparently unending misery of my Parisian existence . . . on to my shoulders and trudged back to Newton Street.'

Another Parisian catastrophe was already impending. When Wagner had taken the house in the Rue Newton, he had had to pay the whole three years' rent, at 4000 francs a year, in advance. The landlord already knew that the street was due to be relaid at a lower level according to Prefect Haussmann's plans, and that the house would be pulled down. The first the unsuspecting composer knew of it was when the Rue Newton was 'lowered four metres under his very feet'. Litigation to recover the amount paid in rent for the remaining two years of his lease was unsuccessful, and he had to pay the costs of the action as well. When Malwida von Meysenbug visited him in his new lodgings in the dark, noisy Rue d'Aumale, she found him on the second floor of a large tenement house, full of other residents. 'It cut me to the heart to see it. I felt how dreadful it must be for Wagner to live in so uncongenial a house.'

She had heard the sound of music from outside. Wagner was in the act of coaching a young soprano (not a boy) in the shepherd boy's song. 'What a good thing you've come!' he exclaimed. 'You will never hear a better perfomance than this: it is going to be excellent.' This prospect was the only consolation he had. For the first time he had at his command all he needed: everything was going smoothly that would contribute to the success of the production. Whenever, from sheer force of habit, Minister Fould opposed the engagement of anyone Wagner needed to have, he had only to say a word to Princess Metternich and an order from the emperor settled the matter. (To Otto Wesendonk, 5 June)

While Wagner was content to accept the French or Italian singers suggested by Royer for most of the parts, for the title role he insisted on engaging the young tenor Albert Niemann from Hanover. He was admittedly somewhat taken aback when Niemann appeared on his doorstep and asked, without further ceremony, 'Well, do you want me or not?' After an audition, where his giant stature made as great an impression as his powerful voice, he was engaged for nine months from 1 September 1860 at 6000 francs a month, with no other commitments but to rehearse and perform the role of Tannhäuser. The conclusion of this extraordinary contract, Wagner admitted in *Mein Leben*, filled him with a sense of power such as he had never known before. And it was Niemann, of all his singers, who most disappointed him, not only professionally but personally.

In the early stages the rehearsals were encouraging: the artists began to understand him, he wrote, raised no objections to anything and looked forward eagerly to what was to come. In the meantime he was still working on the revision of the text and music of the great scene between Tannhäuser and Venus. He was satisfied with everything to do with Tannhäuser's longing for life and the freshness of nature, everything that breathed the air of the legend.

But he was amazed at his total failure, in the earlier version, to encompass everything to do with passion, specifically, the feminine ecstasy of Venus. 'Truly I am appalled at my greasepaint Venus of those days!' What he had to do was write a free verse sketch, get it translated and then set the French rhymed version. The German singing text that we now have is a somewhat contrived translation back from the French, which differs quite a lot from the text published in Wagner's complete writings. For instance, the original German lines:

> Da liegt er vor der Schwelle,
> wo einst ihm Freude floß:
> um Mitleid, nicht um Liebe,
> fleht bettelnd der Genoß!

appear in the score as:

> Auf der Schwelle, sieh' da!
> ausgestreckt liegt er nun,
> dort wo Freude einst ihm geflossen!
> Um Mitleid fleht er bettelnd,
> nicht um Liebe.

One Saturday towards the end of October Wagner sent his excuses to the chorus master: he was so exhausted, or rather over-wrought, that he urgently needed a few days of complete rest. His condition worsened rapidly and Gaspérini diagnosed a typhoid fever with the possibility of its developing into cerebral meningitis. The patient became delirious and later had no recollection whatever of the first week of his illness. But his tough constitution brought him through the crisis, and by 20 November he was again able to drag himself the short distance to the Opéra.

They had probably not been expecting him: the rehearsals had fallen off and then ceased altogether. His opponents had used his absence to shake the confidence of the artists. Niemann, in particular, had been susceptible to the insinuations of critics, who had prophesied the certain failure of the opera. He proved himself a wretch, both as man and as artist, Bülow wrote, although he had nothing but profit from the whole venture. (To Alexander Ritter, 10 April 1860)

In this very different atmosphere Wagner had to resume the

rehearsals and at the same time finish the Bacchanal and the scene with Venus. 'Do not entertain the least doubt . . . that I am making superhuman exertions at present', he told Wesendonk in a letter at the end of January 1861. 'Not until yesterday at half past two in the morning – after being up all night – did I finish my new music for *Tannhäuser*.' He had at least the compensation that the new material had turned out to be very significant and at last gave him some interest in the performance.

'One can become omnipotent, just by playing with the world,' he told Mathilde, and that characterizes the essentially new quality of this music. After surmounting the peak of art as experience, as represented by *Tristan*, a new element entered his work: art as play. This is the importance of the new Venusberg music in his artistic evolution. It was born not only from his improved technical mastery but also from the change in his attitude to the world: his desire now to rise above it and look down at it as a 'plaything'.

The 'abundance' of the music gave him lasting pleasure. It was far from easy to write so extensive an Allegro, he remarked in 1881, and he would not attempt it today. (GLRW, VI, p. 446) At the time he wrote it he had had no experience to inspire something like that. 'It is all a *cry*; it's the same in *Tristan* as in the Venusberg, in the latter it dissolves in grace, in the former in death – it is a cry, a lament, throughout. And those accents come from ever so slightly different a source than Berlioz's Sabbath.' (14 July 1880; BBL 1937, p. 159)

The stylistic difference from the Dresden version is obvious. It is revealed in the mere alteration of the Sirens' call from a 4/4 time to the passionate 3/4. The *Tristan* chord is also to be heard in the Paris version, in a different register, fortissimo, as the orgy reaches its climax: Eros here shows his other face – in *Tristan* the spirit of death with lowered torch, here Dionysus surrounded by Bacchantes. But in spite of that kind of harmonic reminiscence the Venusberg music is quite distinct from *Tristan*: nothing like Venus's lament, for instance, 'Wie hätt' ich das erworben, wie träf' mich solch Verschulden', with the painfully sweet, chromatically descending sixths at 'lächelnd unter Tränen', is to be found anywhere else in Wagner, not even in *Tristan* or the second act of *Parsifal*.

Nonetheless, the Dresden version is still often preferred because of the stylistic inconsistency of the Paris version. Even Wagner himself appears to have entertained similar doubts later in life. But when, in Richard Strauss's phrase, 'the opera *Tannhäuser* rose again as drama', in Cosima's Bayreuth production of the Paris version in 1891, it found another champion besides Strauss in Engelbert Humperdinck. He took the line that the important thing was to examine the stylistic discrepancy from the higher viewpoint of dramatic effectiveness as a whole. The simpler musical language in which the full spiritual depth of the Christian medieval world was so convincingly recreated seemed an authentic and appropriate means of expression to oppose to the heightened aural excitements of the pagan Venusberg music.[14]

It was a struggle for Wagner to keep his interest alive in coaching the singers in their parts day in and day out, but at rehearsals in the theatre 'the immediacy of art' exercised its old power over him again. But the two worst disappointments were yet to come. Niemann, who for some time had been given to voicing gloomy prognostications, finally announced that he could not sing the lines 'Zum Heil den Sündigen zu führen, die Gottgesandte nahte mir' in the second-act finale, a passage which is crucial to the character of Tannhäuser. With the first night imminent, Wagner sat down on 21 February 1861 and wrote him a letter about the part, running to eleven pages in print, which has been a bible to every interpreter of the role ever since. 'This is the last request that I shall address to you as author.'

There is a postscript: '11.30. I had got thus far when your letter reached me.' Niemann's brief letter, which is in the Burrell Collection, is an ultimatum: if Wagner did not cut the phrase 'venant en aide au misérable' he would have to look for another Tannhäuser. Wagner goes on: 'I see where you have now got to: you employ towards me a manner of speech which I find myself able to understand only by casting my mind back to the very first period of my painful career.'[15] But with Niemann's gun to his head he had no alternative but to sacrifice the dramatic climax of the second act and the turning point of the whole action.

The other and yet more painful blow came with his renewing his acquaintance with Pierre-Louis Dietsch, the former chorus master and composer of the ill-fated *Vaisseau Fantôme*. He was now the principal conductor at the Opéra and, according to the regulations of the Académie Impériale de Musique, had to conduct the performances of *Tannhäuser*. His inadequacy was obvious to Wagner at the rehearsals. A letter to Royer on 25 February, imploring him to allow Wagner himself to conduct at least the final dress rehearsal and the first three performances, was of no avail. He tried to help matters by sitting at the edge of the stage at rehearsals and conducting with both hands and feet, giving the beat to both singers on one side of him and the conductor on the other. But at the final dress rehearsal it was out of his hands. 'There is nothing more to be done now,' Bülow wrote to Alexander Ritter, 'Wagner is not conducting. Usus tyrannus. One of the shabbiest brutes . . . a dotard with no intelligence, no memory, totally incapable of benefiting from any instruction . . . with no ear – will wield the baton.'

As the prospect of a good rendering disappeared, so Wagner's interest died, so that the three performances had on him the effect 'only of purely physical blows'. There is no need to repeat here the tale of how the outcome of 164 rehearsals was engulfed in one of the biggest scandals in theatrical history. But what cannot be said too often is that it was not the audience as a whole, exercising their critical faculties, who howled *Tannhäuser* from the stage, but a small clique, who had vowed to wreck it in advance. In his report on the production, Wagner wrote that he continued to credit the Parisian public with the very agreeable attributes of a most lively receptivity and a truly magnanimous sense of justice – a verdict that does honour to his own sense of justice. (*Bericht über die Aufführung von Tannhäuser in Paris*, RWGS, VII, p. 144)

It is still astonishing to contemplate the mindless means whereby an entire theatre audience was terrorized throughout those three evenings. At the first performance the clique had agreed to bellow with laughter each time certain words were pronounced, but this failed in its effect as the laughter was drowned by clapping. For the second performance they purchased hunting whistles at a gunsmith's on the way to the theatre, which enabled them to create a far more effective din. The third performance was on a Sunday and outside the subscription series, which, it was hoped, would keep the Jockey Club away. But they were not to be so easily deterred and came in even greater numbers. Malwida recounts that they distributed silver whistles engraved 'pour Tannhaeuser', which they put to their lips each time their leader signalled with his white kid glove, and thereby interrupted the performance for up to a quarter of an hour at a time.

He had blushed for this barbarity enacted before his own eyes, Baudelaire wrote in 'Richard Wagner et le *Tannhaeuser* à Paris'. 'What will Europe think of us, and what will they say of Paris in

Germany? This handful of hooligans brings disgrace upon us all.'

Wagner thanked Baudelaire with the cordiality that this rare instance of tact and courage deserved. 'I can see that the young people, when they do not belong to the Jockey Club, possess a good helping of decent common sense. They understand me. And you, who have devoted so many handsome words to my work, you stand in the front rank of these sincere and likable young people. Et c'est pourquoi je crois que les vieux ont sifflé.'[16]

Jules Janin, the 'king of the Parisian feuilletonists', was another champion, writing one of his most elegant articles in the *Journal des Débats* on 'Princess Metternich's fan', which she broke on the ledge of her box in anger, and advising the gentlemen of the Jockey Club to get themselves a new coat of arms, 'un sifflet sur champ de gueules hurlantes, et pour exergue "Asinus ad Lyram" '.

The unanimity with which the Meyerbeerites in the press fell upon *Tannhäuser* used to be cited as evidence that he was behind the plot. Kapp even asserted that he was present in person.[17] But in fact he was in Berlin and wrote in his diary on 15 March 1861:

> News came today of the first performance of *Tannhäuser* in Paris, which is said to have been a complete fiasco. The audience is reported to have laughed, and at times whistled, many passages (music as well as text) out of court. Princess Metternich and Countess Seebach, whose patronage is held responsible for the production, met with such derision from the audience that they left the theatre after the second act. So extraordinarily unfavourable a reception of a by any standards very remarkable and talented work strikes me as the doing of a cabal and not of genuine public opinion, and in my view will actually benefit the work in subsequent performances.[18]

The rumour, widespread at the time, that Princess Metternich had fled the theatre, was not true: she did not desert in adversity the enterprise to which she had subscribed. When a Marshal of France accosted her with a *bon mot* as she did leave the theatre, 'Madame, you have exacted a cruel revenge today for the defeat at Solferino,' she replied: 'You have laughed Wagner to scorn this time; but in twenty-five years' time Paris will cheer him.'

After the third performance, which Wagner did not attend, Malwida and some other friends called to report events at two o'clock in the morning. They found him alone with Minna, in a cheerful mood. He drank his tea, smoked his pipe and teased Malwida's foster-daughter, Olga von Herzen (the daughter of Alexander): he heard, he said, that she had whistled him off. But when Malwida took her leave she noticed how his hand shook.

A note has survived, asking a friend to take part the following day in a conference 'pur discuter froidement des mesures nécessaires à prendre de ma part'. The outcome was a letter to the minister, Count Walewski, asking leave to withdraw his score as the only means of protecting his work and the artists who had placed their talents at his disposal from demonstrations that had overstepped the limits of criticism and had degenerated into a scandal from which the administration had shown itself incapable of shielding the public. (TWLF, pp. 245f.)

It was generous of the minister to agree to the withdrawal: the production had cost 250,000 francs to mount. The three performances had already brought in a tenth of that; the third alone had raised 10,790 francs, the highest sum since the first Universal Exhibition. The theatre could have reckoned on the opera continuing to be a draw and a box-office success. The only person to profit was Niemann with his 54,000 francs. No payment was due to Wagner for the rehearsals; a fee of 500 francs was due to him for each performance, but it had been settled that the translators should have half the fee for the first twenty performances. Wagner and Truinet agreed to hand over the entire sum from the *droits d'auteur* to poor Roche, all of whose hopes had been dashed by the fiasco. He did not long survive the disaster: he died of consumption before the year was out.[19]

In his friends' eyes Wagner's defeat meant nothing. Quite the contrary! 'Que dieu me donne une pareille chute!' exclaimed Gounod. The performances had acquired a complete 'nimbus', Wagner wrote to Bülow on 4 April. 'Sects are already forming that positively worship me: even among the ordinary people.' The only thing he regretted was what his friends had had to go through. And yet he himself had made a real gain from the whole affair, in that he had found these friends: however poor and inadequate the performance had been, it had nevertheless brought him into close contact with the most estimable and attractive element of the French spirit.

The circle of Wagner's Parisian friends was only a small one, as Houston Stewart Chamberlain remarked, but it included the best names of the day and it gave Wagner what he had not yet received in Germany, except from Liszt and Bülow: respect.

# 24

## Odyssey

'Your Richard Wagner, ὅς μάλα πολλὰ πλάγχθη' ('who roamed the wide world'): the quotation of the opening words of the *Odyssey* with which Wagner signed a letter from Paris to Hans von Bülow (7 January 1862) could serve as motto for the years 1861 to 1864. The letter was about his new work and his need to find somewhere to settle while he got on with it. The tragedy of his wanderings and his conception of the comedy of *Die Meistersinger* make up the tale of this, the most confused and tangled period of his life, in which he was forever on the move, between Paris and St Petersburg, Mainz and Vienna, Zürich and Stuttgart, in which old associations were dissolved and new ones formed, punctuated by incomparable artistic triumphs and an ignominious secret flight, and ending with a reversal of fortune from the darkness of complete despair to a miraculous salvation.

The worst aspect of the *Tannhäuser* débâcle for Wagner was that he not only had earned nothing for his eighteen months' work, but also had accumulated more debts. His friends did their best to help him, but many obligations remained unmet: in a letter of 29 March 1869 he told Ernst Benedikt Kietz that if *Rienzi* were now to catch on in Paris the profits from it, for a *long* time to come, would go to the banker Erlanger, whose loans had kept his head above water at the beginning of the decade. In the end, in 1895, twelve years after Wagner's death, it fell to Adolf von Gross, Cosima's business adviser, to clear things up in person in Paris, in a manner, as Cosima recorded, that was not without its funny side and scored a considerable success for Wahnfried. (DMCW, II, p. 390)

At first it had looked as though something might now come from Germany to make up for the buffeting the composer had suffered in

Paris. On a visit to Karlsruhe in April 1861 he found that the Grand Duke of Baden was again interested in securing the first performance of *Tristan* for his theatre. It was only a question of engaging the best soloists. With this end in view Wagner set off for Vienna, where he received an ovation from the singers and orchestra when he attended a rehearsal of *Lohengrin* under Heinrich Esser.

It was the first time that he had ever heard the work. The soloists wore their everyday clothes – Lohengrin in frock coat and top hat, Telramund with a walking stick, Elsa in an ordinary day-dress – but the chorus was in costume, the sets were in position and every aspect of the stage action was punctiliously observed. Wagner sat on the stage and did not stir throughout. He told Minna that the rehearsal had surpassed all his expectations, giving him a complete enjoyment that for the first time made all the pain and trouble he had endured in his career worthwhile. 'I went on sitting there without moving. The dear people came up and silently embraced me.' (13 May)

The critic Eduard Hanslick secured an introduction during one of the intervals. They had first met in 1845, in Marienbad, when Hanslick was a law student with hair curling to his shoulders and a passion for music. He had accosted Wagner as an enthusiastic admirer and the following year published a long essay on *Tannhäuser*, spread through eleven issues of the *Allgemeine Wiener Musik-Zeitung* and culminating in the sentence: 'I am convinced that Richard Wagner is the greatest dramatic talent among living composers.' (MWKS, I, p. 230) After 1850 he went back on that opinion – he later described it as showing 'all the immaturity of a cocky young member of the League of David' –and with his essay *On the Beautiful in Music* (1854) and his reviews in the *Neue Freie Presse* he became the spokesman of the anti-Wagner faction. It may perhaps have been embarrassment that made him hesitate to approach Wagner on this occasion without the friendly mediation of the Lohengrin, Alois Ander. Wagner greeted him laconically, as if he had never met him before, and when Ander insisted that they must know each other already, he simply replied that he remembered Herr Hanslick very well – and turned his attention back to the stage. He commented later that his friends in Vienna, as in London, seemed to have wasted their time in trying to persuade him to honour the dreaded critics with his regard.

After the emotions he experienced at the rehearsal Wagner was not unduly concerned that the actual performance was delayed. Its reception by the Viennese audience was more enthusiastic than anything he had seen in his life: 'A shout of joy, sounding like a thousand trombones.' (To Minna, 16 May) It weighed on him almost like a burden, he said in a speech afterwards. 'Allow me to carry this burden in humility, allow me to strive towards the goals of my art.' Only Hanslick saw himself obliged to perform the un-grateful task of 'pouring cold water on such a bacchanal'. He hoped that the city of Gluck, Mozart and Beethoven would not purchase a good reputation for Wagner's music at the cost of its own.

Wagner believed he had found the singers he was looking for in Ander and the Elsa, Luise Meyer-Dustmann. 'With these two – we must do *Tristan und Isolde!*' But when he asked the intendant, Count Lanckoronski, to give them leave to sing in Karlsruhe, his request was firmly refused, and instead he was offered the Vienna Hofoper itself for the première. The proposal suddenly threw a very differ-ent light on Wagner's plan for Karlsruhe, where he would have had to get everything together himself from scratch, to produce the work properly. 'I think I shall have to seize the opportunity here, where *everything, everything* I need is already to hand.' (To Minna, 13 May)[1]

As he was walking down the steps of the Hofburg, preoccupied with this new turn in his affairs, he was accosted by an imposing, congenial-looking man who offered to drive him to his hotel in his carriage. It was Josef Standhartner, chief medical officer at the General Hospital and physician to Empress Elisabeth, a passionate music-lover who had taken the composer Peter Cornelius under his wing. Together with Karl Tausig and his one-time 'discoverer' Heinrich Laube, who was now the director of the Burgtheater, Wagner won new devoted friends in Standhartner, his stepson Gustav Schönaich, Peter Cornelius, and Heinrich Porges, a young musician from Prague.

He set off back to Paris on 20 May, to wind up his household there, in a mood compounded of resignation and hope. Picking up *Wilhelm Meisters Wanderjahre* in a hotel room en route, he was particularly struck by the aptness to his own situation of the 'almost barbaric song' with which the band of journeymen set off on their travels: 'Can I say, can I know, what chances lie in wait for me as I now depart, as I now roam . . . betake myself far away from here?'

The events and the people he saw during his last weeks in Paris flit across the pages of his autobiography like a shadow-play, in which he himself plays the role of ironic spectator. The only thing to make a deeper impression on him was the loss of his dog: the pets had come to mean a great deal in his and Minna's childless household; their life together had long been an impossible burden and the sudden death of so cheery and lovable a companion seemed to denote the final rift.

After Minna's departure to take a cure in Bad Soden, Wagner moved temporarily into the Prussian embassy in Paris, and here he was overcome by a 'profound sense of well-being in the enjoyment of a complete lack of any possessions and freedom from everything that is usually understood by a stable way of life'. His window overlooked the garden; there was a pool where two black swans swam, and he felt a kind of dreamlike attraction towards them. It was there that he wrote his first music since the revisions for *Tannhäuser*, two small pieces for piano. The first, *Albumblatt* in A♭ major, 'Coming to the Black Swans', dedicated to his hostess Countess Pourtalès, is a reminiscence of Elisabeth's 'Sei mir gegrüßt' from *Tannhäuser*, but drenched in the atmosphere of the prelude to the third act of *Tristan*. The other, *Albumblatt* in C major, dedicated to Princess Metternich and well known in the transcription for violin by Wilhelmj, employs a charming motive that had been in his mind for some time and that seems to anticipate the melodic writing of *Die Meistersinger*.[2]

He spent one of his last evenings in Paris with his friends Gaspérini, Champfleury and Truinet in a café in the Rue Láfitte, and as he walked home in the company of Champfleury very late at night he was delighted by the extraordinary atmosphere of the deserted streets.

On his way to Vienna, to please Liszt, he put in an unexpected appearance at the musicians' congress in Weimar, where he was given an uproarious welcome. There was no question of relaxing and enjoying himself, he told Mathilde Wesendonk; he had had to recount the story of his life to yet another person every half-hour, so that in desperation he had surrendered to his old wild humour. 'I could not permit myself to turn serious, because it is now impossible for me to be so at all without going almost completely to pieces. This is a basic weakness of my temperament, which is increasingly gaining an upper hand nowadays: I fight it as best I can, because I feel as though I should weep uncontrollably if I once gave way to it.' (19 August)

His hectic high spirits continued as he resumed his journey, now in the company of the Olliviers. They had to spend a night in Nuremberg and enjoyed a morning's sightseeing: 'There are a lot of delightful things to be seen here,' he told Mathilde.

On 14 August, as he had informed the theatre management, Wagner arrived in Vienna to begin coaching the musicians in *Tristan*. To begin with he stayed at the Standhartners' house. The family was away on holiday, and he was looked after by the doctor's niece Seraphine Mauro, whom he nicknamed 'the doll' on account of her trim figure and hair curled 'à l'enfant'.

The people at the opera house were astonished that he had been so literal in observing the agreed starting date; they also told him that Ander was indisposed and had to rest his voice for several weeks. Wagner had already realized that the part of Tristan would not lie so well for him as that of Lohengrin, and had commissioned Cornelius to transpose certain individual low notes up by a third, a fifth or an octave. The weeks of Ander's vocal indisposition became months, and as neither Tichatschek nor Niemann was available Wagner was forced to make more and more concessions, including a cut in the third act of as much as 142 bars. Cornelius soon came to the conclusion that Tristan was too low for Ander's voice and too high for his intelligence.

Wagner had no idea that he would not get from Esser the support that the whole undertaking demanded. Esser belonged to the school of conscientious conductors who will not rest until every semi-quaver is correct. But as Cornelius recognized even then, 'The passion which alone brings a work like this to life, which makes its to-be-or-not-to-be a matter of his own life and death – that he lacks.' Nowadays we know more than Cornelius did: while Esser impressed Wagner in their walks together as an 'honest' and an 'upright and serious' man, what he said about Wagner in his letters to Schott was far from complimentary.

The tenor's illness was a misfortune that would be of no further consequence, Wagner wrote to Schott on 30 October, if it were not being used by his opponents as yet another piece of evidence that the opera was unperformable. But the real purpose of this letter was to tell the publisher about a new project that would afford the composer a more agreeable and entertaining occupation, the realization of one of his earlier ideas for a popular comic opera. 'The title is *Die Meistersinger von Nürnberg*, and the principal hero is the jovial poet Hans Sachs.' The subject was extraordinarily rich in pleasant humour, and he believed he could boast of having achieved something completely original in the plot, which was entirely his own invention. He proposed to send the text to Schott as soon as he had finished it. 'I sincerely wish, my dear Sir, that just as I lighten my own heart – in a sad hour – with this sudden inspiration, so the news of it will delight you too.'

The Standhartners had returned to Vienna, and Wagner had moved into a cheerless room in the Kaiserin Elisabeth hotel, where he had time to reflect on his position. 'So this is the outcome, for the time being, of my Viennese expedition which promised so much,' he wrote to Bülow. 'Remarkably, I have nothing to do. I am not expected anywhere, I have not been invited to go anywhere, I am not needed anywhere; I feel as though I'm in a state of the most absolute freedom, you could say the freedom of an outlaw – or a bird: "wie der Fink frei sich davon schwingt".'

It was in this bitter mood that he received a letter at the beginning of November from Otto Wesendonk, inviting him to meet them in Venice. 'God knows what I was thinking of, when I really set off at a venture in that grey November . . . for Venice,' he wrote in his autobiography. But a letter he wrote to Mathilde in the December betrays that one of his motives had been the hope of regaining his 'haven' in Zürich. An hour in her company in Venice had been enough to destroy that illusion, he wrote. He had quickly realized that his proximity robbed her of the freedom she needed. 'I cannot endure it if being near to you means seeing you confined and constricted, overwhelmed, subjected . . . That and that alone was what lay on my soul like lead, in Venice. Not my situation, my other misfortunes; that is, and has always been ever since I knew you, essentially indifferent to me.'

They also discussed his *Meistersinger* plan. Mathilde had kept the scenario he had written in Marienbad in 1845. He seemed so despondent in Venice that, as she later confessed to him, she had hardly dared to hope that he would take it up again. But one day, when he was in the Accademia di Belle Arti, standing in front of Titian's *Assumption of the Virgin* (which had not at that date been restored to its place in the Frari church), he was suddenly overcome by the most sublime sensation which brought all his old strength flooding back to revive him. During the long grey train journey back to Vienna, which lasted a night, a day and yet another night, 'pinned helplessly between Once and Now', the idea of the principal C major section of the prelude presented itself to him with the utmost clarity.

In Vienna Cornelius, who was 'out of his mind' with joy at the prospect, was despatched to borrow Wagenseil's *Nürnberger Chronik* from the Imperial Library. It is barely credible that Wagner then set to and wrote a first prose scenario, which differs considerably from the Marienbad sketch, in only five days and started a second on 18 November. The inner action was now developed for the first time, and its lyrical, contemplative climax, the third-act quintet, is already indicated, though at this stage Wagner anticipated a trio: 'All three sing together gracefully of their gratitude and tenderly of their hope.'

He sent a copy of the scenario to Schott with a letter that Ludwig Strecker, a more recent head of Schott's, has described as a 'magnificent document from Wagner's creative world'. In it he said that he had long been saving this blithe work for when he was older, because he had not expected to summon up the right frame of mind for it among the stresses of his life. But it was precisely the troubles his career was undergoing now that had suddenly recalled this pet project to his mind, because carrying it out was the only thing that would help him over his present difficulties. 'The subject permits me to write lucid, transparent and yet pithy music of the cheerfulest colouring; and yet merely in reading this sketch you will have found that my characteristic note will be struck just as fully and richly here, most persuasively in the blend of fervour and good humour. In sum, precisely at the present time I calculate that I have hit the essential nerve of German life, and in the guise that other countries, too, recognize and love as authentic.'

With his usual optimism he forecast that the opera would be ready for despatch to all the German theatres on 1 October 1862 and ought to have its première in Munich in mid-November. However, that would all depend on Schott's placing complete confidence in him and relieving him of all material worries for the next twelve months. (20 November 1861)

At last he found a haven where he could work. Princess Metternich was in Vienna just then, and he arranged an orchestral rehearsal of *Tristan* in her honour. She offered him the use of a pleasant apartment with access to a quiet garden in the Austrian embassy in Paris. Before he left Vienna a curious interlude took place. Luise Dustmann, foreseeing that he would have no success in the Austrian capital as long as Hanslick was his enemy, invited both of them to a party, at which Hanslick took Wagner aside and confessed with tears in his eyes that it was not malice that lay at the root of his criticism but the 'limitations of personality'. Wagner was so touched that he had no alternative but to comfort Hanslick and assure him of his understanding. Shortly afterwards Hanslick was said to be singing the praises of Wagner's kindness so loudly that the opera management decided the time was ripe to honour their obligation and announce the performance of *Tristan*.

On his way to Paris Wagner made a short stop in Mainz, where he read the *Meistersinger* sketch to Franz Schott and his wife Betty, a woman with a fine appreciation of the arts, and managed to obtain an advance of 10,000 francs after 'uncommonly difficult' bargaining. But in Paris a new disappointment awaited him that affected all his plans: Princess Metternich informed him with the greatest regret that she was unable to keep her promise as the unexpected death of her mother meant she had to take her half-crazy father into her house.

Wagner made do with a modest room in the Hôtel Voltaire on the eponymous Quai, where he settled down to write his text. Gradually his desperation gave way to a cheerful serenity, and he was later to describe these weeks to Malwida as the happiest of his life. He could hardly have failed to be struck with the humour of it, being met, each time he raised his eyes from the paper in order to reflect on the quaint verses and dicta of his Nurembergers, with the view from his third-floor window of the dense traffic on the *quais* and bridges, and the panorama of the Rive Droite from the Tuileries and the Louvre as far as the Hôtel de Ville.

The whim of fate that had tossed him there strengthened his inclination not to take the world seriously any more. Sometimes, he confessed to Mathilde, he had been unable to go on working, either from laughter or from tears. 'Steel your heart against Sachs: you will fall in love with him!' He used little or nothing from the old sketch. 'Ah, you have to have been in Paradise to find out what lies hidden in something like this!'

He lived very quietly, and his only evening entertainment was to visit one of the small theatres where he enjoyed in their original form the farces of which inferior copies were fed, year in, year out, to German audiences. Almost the only person he saw regularly was Truinet, whom he met at midday in the cheap Taverne Anglaise. On his way there one day, passing through the galleries of the Palais Royal, the melody of the 'Wach auf!' chorus suddenly burst upon him. Finding Truinet already at the restaurant, he asked him for pencil and paper so that he could write it down at once, while he softly sang it to him. 'Mais quelle gaieté d'esprit, cher maître!' Truinet exclaimed. Interestingly, none of the three prose scenarios has the least hint of the chorus, which is now the climax of the third act. Such elements in Wagner's work are always spontaneous inspirations, never the outcome of long forethought.[3]

Having finished the text in exactly thirty days, on 25 January 1862, he had to find somewhere quiet, another 'haven', to write the music. 'All the music is already in my head,' he had told Schott on 17 January, 'and God grant only that I fetch up as soon as possible within four suitable walls where . . . I can set my dear Erard sounding again!'

Since the response of the friends and relations of whom he made tentative enquiries was a uniform, undisguised alarm, he even thought of setting up house with Peter Cornelius: '*Friend, you must move in with me, once and for all!*' Since this would be quite impracticable without a woman to keep house for them, he thought of Seraphine Mauro: 'God, how I would like to have the poor doll there! In something like this I am of an indestructibly naïve morality. I could find nothing whatever wrong with it, if the girl came to me and was to me exactly what her nice little nature enables her to be. – But what should we say to society? Oh, heavens! – It makes me smile, but I am still sorry for it!'

But besides his fears for his own artistic identity, Peter was helplessly in love with Seraphine, in whom he saw, not a 'nice little nature' but 'a grim sphinx with the most beautiful bosom in the world and indescribably lovely eyes, but always with that ultimate riddle, threatening to cast me into the abyss if I cannot guess it'.

Finally Wagner decided to take somewhere near Mainz temporarily. 'What pleasure and encouragement it will give me', he told Schott, 'when I start bringing you something every week in the near future, and to a certain extent we complete the work together!' He arrived in Mainz on 4 February and read the text of *Die Meistersinger* aloud to quite a large gathering the following day. The room in the publishing house where this took place, later known as the Wagner-Saal, survived the destruction of old Mainz in the Second World War and is now preserved as a monument.

The young conductor and composer Wendelin Weissheimer was among those present, and his memoirs of Wagner, *Erlebnisse mit Richard Wagner*, contain some graphic scenes, in spite of their self-congratulatory tone. Of the *Meistersinger* reading he recounts that after the audience had all taken their seats Wagner continued to pace up and down restlessly, looking alternatively at the door and at his watch: 'We must wait a little longer, Cornelius is not here yet!' Just then there was a knock and Cornelius came in. Wagner had sent him the fare, and in the middle of winter, defying frost and flood, he had hastened from Vienna to Mainz. 'That's what I call loyalty!' Wagner exclaimed and flung his arms round him. The reading was a virtuoso performance. Wagner's ability to modulate his voice was so great that he soon no longer needed to name the characters. Even when all the mastersingers are talking at once each stood out individually and the audience really had the impression of listening to an ensemble. By the finish they all realized that they had been present at the baptism of an epoch-making work. Wagner's happiness was spoiled only because Cornelius insisted on leaving again the next day. He refused to be dissuaded, in order to preserve the extraordinary character of his expedition.

In the middle of February Wagner at last found a small house in Biebrich, midway between Mainz and Wiesbaden, with a big garden and a view of the Rhine. He had incautiously asked Minna, in a letter of 9 February, whether she would like to join him. Instead of replying she arrived in person on 21 February, as she said, to help him move in. He was moved to tears, and they immediately began to consider settling in Wiesbaden together. But as luck would have it, on the second day of her stay a letter arrived from Mathilde Wesendonk, announcing the belated despatch of a Christmas present, and the parcel itself came the following day. Minna had it opened at the customs office in the belief that it contained music but, as she wrote to Natalie, 'it was from that filthy woman again, an embroidered cushion, tea, Eau de Câlange [sic], pressed violets'. (RWBC, p. 540) Incapable of regarding his relationship with Mathilde in any but a cheapening light, she refused to accept any of his explanations, 'and the whole madhouse is back again, not a brick changed . . . we have been through ten days of hell, and those appalling ten days have at least had the beneficial effect of administering a final warning.' (To Cornelius, 4 March)

Minna went back to Dresden, and as Wagner was not in the mood to settle back to work immediately, he left for Karlsruhe on 8 March to read the text of *Die Meistersinger* to the grand duke and duchess, which he did, by a happy coincidence, sitting under a painting by his old friend Friedrich Pecht, depicting Goethe reading *Faust* to the duke's ancestors.

It was at an evening party given by the Schotts in Mainz that Wagner made the acquaintance of Mathilde Maier. He was at once greatly taken by her intelligent, candid expression. Her blue eyes and curling fair hair were reminiscent of the young Duke of York in Delaroche's painting. For her part, she admitted: 'When I saw you for the first time the mark left on you by deep suffering made an indelible impression on me. I wanted so much to gather together all the joys of the world in order to blot out your pain, if only for a moment.' He promised to visit her at her home in Mainz, and there he found an idyllic household such as he had hardly come across before. Mathilde, then twenty-eight years old, lived in modest circumstances with her mother, sister and two aunts, and enjoyed a wide circle of friends, including an old friend of Schopenhauer, Gerichtsrat Becker. When Wagner had business in Mainz, usually once a week, he called on her, and she sometimes visited him in Biebrich, accompanied by her sister or a friend.

'Not a love affair, that it was not,' Ulrike von Levetzow said of her relationship with Goethe, and Mathilde Maier could have said the same of her friendship with Wagner. His letters to her breathe the air of *Meistersinger*, and if we did not know that he had already finished the text when they met, we might well take her for the model for Eva. But she was constantly in his thoughts while he was composing the music, and in the turmoil of his existence she gave him peace and reminded him of his true nature and vocation. 'Had I not your dear, resolved, lucid nature, and the lovely person that goes with it, to encourage me, "Teufel möchte Schuster sein!" '

The first rays of spring sunshine revived his zest for work. 'As I sat on my balcony enjoying the magnificent view afforded by a beautiful sunset which shed a transfiguring light on golden Mainz and the majestic Rhine flowing between, suddenly the prelude to *Die Meistersinger* presented itself to me, close and clear, exactly as it had come once before, remote and insubstantial, out of a mood of dejection. I set to and wrote it out exactly as it stands today in the score, with all the principal motives of the whole work clearly delineated in it.'

In the composition sketch, started at the end of March, the majority of the prelude is written out on two staves, increasing to three at the end, where the three themes are welded together contrapuntally. The orchestral sketch, started immediately afterwards, took a week, 13–20 April. The first sketch of the chorale, 'Da zu dir der Heiland kam', survives on a separate sheet, with the chorus parts written in ink and the instrumental interludes very lightly in pencil, and may perhaps antedate the prelude.

While the composition sketch of *Die Meistersinger* has not quite survived complete, there are a large number of separate preliminary sketches still in existence: themes and melodies, some in various different versions, contrapuntal studies of ensembles, and some personal annotations. 'Something for my friend Standhartner's birthday' appears at the bottom of a sketch of Sachs's shoemaking song.

On 22 May Wagner wrote to Mathilde Wesendonk: it was his birthday and somebody had brought him some flowers. 'And there I sat alone. Suddenly I had an idea for the orchestral introduction to the third act.' He went on to describe how he had the bass instruments begin with a profoundly melancholy passage, with the character of complete resignation, and then the horns enter with the bright, joyful melody of 'Wach auf!', like the sound of a gospel. 'I now realize that this will be my most accomplished masterwork and – I shall accomplish it.'

This was one of the sketches that survive, headed 'Introduct. Act III / 22 May 62 morning'. In it the prelude is already in a 'perfect' arch form, that is, a palindromic a–b–c–b–a. It demonstrates that Wagner carved his music from a complete block and did not piece it together from fragments. The chorale melody appears already in its eventual form, whereas the melancholy passage based on the 'Wahn' motive is still very different from what it was to become.[4]

He was not left on his own for the whole of this birthday. Mathilde Maier came later, with a few other friends, and did the honours at the table, skilfully making the most of his deficient stock of china.

Wagner's progress with the first act was not as fast as he had hoped, partly because he was plagued by all kinds of worries and anxiety, and partly because of his attitude to the work: he was only pleased with what he had written down if it was all, to the smallest detail, the result of a happy inspiration. (To Otto Wesendonk, 26 July) Finally he had an accident. His landlord owned a dog and neglected it; when Wagner decided to give it a bath one day it bit him in the right thumb, which prevented him from writing legibly for quite a long time.

He got so behind with the instalments of his manuscript that Schott, who had been very generous to start with, refused to give him another advance. 'You are wrong, my very good Herr Schott!' Wagner wrote to him on 20 October. 'You are very wrong as to the way to treat a person like me. Starvation will compel people to do a great deal, but it will not produce works of a higher kind. Or do you suppose that if my worries will not let me sleep at night, I shall have the serene temper and good ideas that my work needs in the daytime? . . . This letter is the product of a sleepless night, and I thought I was merely following the immutable dictates of justice in not keeping it from you.'

'I had better refrain from comment on the product you have sent me of one of your sleepless nights, my very good Herr Wagner,' Schott replied the next day, 'for although I know what behaviour to adopt towards artists, I prefer not to say to you what I expect from artists . . . I cannot give you the rather large sum you ask for [Wagner had mentioned first 3000 gulden, then 1000]. No mere music publisher could satisfy your needs: it would take an enormously rich banker or a reigning prince with millions at his disposal.'

In their later dealings neither Wagner nor Schott bore the other a grudge over this exchange of letters, but it put an end to the period of happy cooperation and Wagner's life now took a turn which this time led inevitably to disaster. 'If you had supported me that time in Biebrich for another nine or ten months,' he wrote to Schott on 6 November 1867, 'our *Meistersinger* would have been playing in the theatres for the last three years. God knows! It was unfortunate that you made a mistake.'

His correspondence with Minna added to his troubles. While he persisted, with a patience that is hard for us to comprehend, in telling her about his day-to-day existence, she would not stop picking at old wounds until in the end she gave him a real fright with a letter that made him think she must have lost her reason (cf.

his letter to Klara Wolfram, 2 June 1862). He turned to her doctor, Pusinelli, in this predicament: would it not be better for Minna's health if they were to agree to live apart and write to each other as little as possible? He asked him to consult Luise Brockhaus on the matter. (RWAP, 14 June 1862) Wagner did not mention divorce in this letter, but Pusinelli evidently thought that that was what he had in mind and wrote to Minna along those lines. She replied that she would never even consider such a dreadful thing and Wagner had to write to conciliate her. 'In his sympathetic eagerness Pusinelli went further than I meant him to . . . I am sorry such a painful thought occurred to you, which never entered my head. I beg you to calm yourself about it!' (27 June, RWBC)

On the other hand he rejected as foolish and futile the idea that they might resume living together, perhaps in Dresden, which would have been possible by then, since he had been granted a complete amnesty on 18 March. Minna could keep a room ready for him and he would try and see her there, he told his sister Klara; and as long as he had a quiet refuge somewhere else to work in, she could conceal the breach from the world. 'The idea of divorce did not originate with me, although there is much to be said in its favour and although I think I would certainly be forgiven for harbouring the wish to spend my remaining years with a sympathetic being at my side to the greater benefit of my works.' (11 July)

After the rupture with Schott, Wagner had no alternative but to earn his living by giving concerts. The following two years could be regarded as a complete blank in the history of his creative life were it not for the opportunities they gave for audiences, and above all for himself, to hear excerpts from the *Ring, Tristan* and *Meistersinger*.

It was at a concert of his compositions that Weissheimer organized in the Gewandhaus in Leipzig on 1 November 1862 that Wagner conducted the very first performance of the *Meistersinger* prelude, in the city of his birth – in an almost empty hall. 'I have never experienced such a void on a comparable occasion,' he averred. The whole thing seemed to him and Bülow, who was also taking part, like something out of *Don Quixote* and infected them both with an uncomfortable hilarity, until the joyful solemnity of the prelude itself lifted them out of the poverty of the circumstances. It was applauded so vigorously that it had to be repeated, and at the end the orchestra honoured him with a ceremonial *Tusch*.[5]

From Leipzig he went to Dresden, where Minna met him and took him to her new home. Since his sister Klara was also staying with her, this, the couple's last meeting, was not spoiled by quarrels. 'I am alive and shall return in one day's time!' he wrote to Mathilde Maier. A new calamity awaited him in Biebrich: his landlord gave him notice. After a brief farewell from Mathilde he set off for Vienna on 13 November, to conduct a series of concerts in the Theater an der Wien. He travelled in the company of the actress Friederike Meyer, whom he knew from Frankfurt, which cost him the good will of his Isolde, her sister, Luise Meyer-Dustmann. He was staying in his old hotel again, he reported, where they did their best to anticipate his every unspoken wish; he was basking in his popularity and enjoying the sound of his music being played on barrel organs.

A week after his arrival in Vienna Standhartner organized a reading of *Meistersinger*, to which Hanslick was also invited. According to Wagner's account, the critic left at the end in an unmistakable rage, while Hanslick denied it – though not until years later, after Wagner's death. His version was that 'after the smoky heat of the *Ring*' *Die Meistersinger* had delighted him like a smiling landscape. (MWKS, I, pp. 323f.) The fact remains that he was from now on irreconcilably hostile to Wagner, after the short truce. It may be that he had heard that Beckmesser, the Marker, had been called Veit Hanslich in the scenario, and he suspected what kind of immortality might be bestowed on him. Indeed, as Newman says, he was preserved for posterity in Wagner's work like a fly in amber.

Wagner had done a lot of preparatory work for the concerts while he was still in Biebrich, extracting the items from their contexts in his scores, writing concert endings for them, transcribing some for orchestra alone, as in the case of the Ride of the Valkyries, or, as with the assembling of the mastersingers in the first act, quickly orchestrating them for the first time. The instrumental parts remained to be copied in Vienna, with the assistance of Cornelius, Tausig, Porges, Weissheimer and – perhaps surprisingly – Brahms. Brahms had been introduced by Tausig as 'a very good chap' and was entrusted with copying an excerpt from *Meistersinger*. 'I suppose I shall be called a Wagnerian,' he remarked to Joachim, 'principally, of course, because any reasonable person is bound to speak up against the silly tone which musicians here use against him.'

The Wagner tuba did not exist at that date, so Wagner had to supplement the opera orchestra with tuba-players from a military band for the pieces from the *Ring*. 'The trouble this concert is causing is out of all proportion,' he moaned to Mathilde Maier the evening before the first one took place; 'everything I do is just about as difficult as if the world had never known such an event before.' And then he added very seriously: 'I feel as if this may be the last time that I shall ask Fate what change I can expect in my position in the world: it's possible that from now on I shall turn my back on it completely and for ever.'

The first concert was given on 26 December in the presence of the empress and before a full house. With the exception of the *Meistersinger* prelude, every item was a first performance:

> *Meistersinger* prelude
> Assembly of the mastersingers (orchestral arrangement)
> Pogner's address
>
> Ride of the Valkyries (orchestral arrangement)
> Siegmund's Spring Song
> Wotan's Farewell and Magic Fire music
>
> Theft of the Rhine gold (second half of Scene 1)
> Donner's conjuration of the storm, *leading into*
> Entry of the gods into Valhalla

'I have never heard anything like the tumult that broke out when Wagner appeared,' Weissheimer recalled. 'Everyone clapped and shouted, the empress leaned out of her box applauding – it went on certainly for five or six minutes, and kept reviving, so that Wagner did not know how to go on acknowledging it and just stood there resignedly, with his arms extended, until the noise died down.' Each piece was applauded more enthusiastically than the one before, and the Ride of the Valkyries drove the excitable Viennese nearly mad.

'Dear child – it's over – but not done with!' he reported the next day. 'There's still an awful lot for me to do! Rebuilding the orchestra: sound not good enough!' He had a sound-board put up, which unfortunately cost 230 gulden. The second and third concerts took place on 1 and 11 January, with slight variations of programme. In the third, Wagner conducted the *Faust* Overture, which Weissheimer thought the most perfect orchestral composition he had ever heard. The applause was beyond belief, but 'Johannes Brahms sat next to me in the box . . . He remained cool and reserved throughout the whole concert. When I rallied him to join in the applause after the thrilling performance of the *Faust* Overture he said "Ah, Herr Weissheimer, you will tear your white kid gloves."'

The reception was the same as almost always: tumultuous applause, bad reviews – notably that of the playwright and non-musician Friedrich Hebbel, who had also tried his hand at dramatizing the Nibelungs – and a deficit. 'Tausig is running round, trying to raise the money to pay off part of my latest concert debts!' (To Bülow, 3 January)

Two significant events took place during the concert series. His various enterprises were proving a nerve-racking gamble, he told Mathilde Maier; a rehearsal with the piano had convinced him that an invalid like Ander, who had ruined his voice, would not possibly be able to sing Tristan. And so he had come to yet another dead end. In this sombre mood he put a question to her which he asked her to consider in a purely hypothetical light, in the first place, like a moral problem.

He needed, he said, a home, not so much a place as a person. He could not marry as long as his wife was alive, and he could not divorce her, because it would kill her. This was the sorry pass that was destroying him. 'I need a female being who, in spite of everything and everyone, will have the resolution to be to me what a wife can be in these miserable circumstances – must be, I say, if I am to thrive. Perhaps I am being blinded by excessive self-esteem when I go so far as to suppose that a woman with the resolution to devote herself to me in such inauspicious circumstances would abandon all human relationships that have no useful place in the life and work of a person like me . . . I want a loving woman at my side, and let her be a daughter at the same time!'

'What will you make of this?' he asked at the end. 'Well, after all, it was only a theoretical problem.' (4 January 1863) He was fairly sure that she would not want to give up her middle-class milieu.

The other event was the writing of a preface to the first edition of the text of the *Ring* to go on sale to the general public. He wrote that he no longer dared to hope that he would live to see it performed, or even that he would find the leisure and the inclination to complete the music. Thus it was really just a dramatic poem, a literary work, that he offered to the reading public. So much in a postscript. The preface itself ended with a pessimistic question. One of the German princes would be in a better position than any other person or group of people to promote the performance of the *Ring*: 'Is such a prince to be found?' (RWGS, VI, pp. 272ff.)

A concert he gave in Prague on 8 February, at which he was presented with a laurel wreath with streamers in the German national colours while the Czechs cheered him with their 'Sláva! sláva!', actually made a net profit of 1100 gulden. Ander surprised him agreeably by his performance at another piano run-through of *Tristan*, so it was in a generally more optimistic frame of mind that he accepted an invitation to go to St Petersburg. Before leaving he commissioned Mathilde to look out for a piece of land on the Rhine where he could build himself a house. 'There, you see, I'm after my quarry: St Peter with his net! And oh, let me catch peace and a home at last!'

'It was downright frightening,' he wrote after the first concert in St Petersburg. 'I've never known it so hot as here in Russia!!! The audience – three or four thousand people – nearly gobbled me up. I've thrown all other concerts into the shade, and my triumph is unheard of.' And he went on to describe what he later called his Jeanne d'Arc vision: 'When I was obliged to repeat the *Lohengrin* prelude my nerves began to sway, and it was as though the whole orchestra – 130 of them – had turned into angels and were greeting me with this strangely ecstatic music on my arrival in Heaven . . . Now may Heaven bless my settling down!' he went on. 'There ought not to be any shortage of money. Do your best! Goodbye – and stay fond of me!' (4 March)

There were another two concerts in St Petersburg, followed by three in Moscow. 'So now I'm in Asia, really in Asia, my girl! . . . It's all gaily coloured, bright, golden, domed – wondrous, wonderful – in my amazement I had to laugh aloud.' The tour finished with two more concerts in St Petersburg.

In spite of his triumph he felt it to be nothing but an interruption of his normal activity. The vision of a little house beside the Rhine was the reward he looked forward to. When Mathilde reported the find of a 'Rose Cottage' near Bingen he immediately sent a telegram telling her to take it whatever the rent; he was so accustomed to seeing every agreeable prospect dissolve again that anything good filled him with anxiety.

What now gave him hope for the future was the interest that the Grand Duchess Helene Pavlovna showed in him. Born Princess Charlotte of Württemberg, and the widow of Grand Duke Michael, she occupied a leading position at the court of St Petersburg, where she brought together all the men of intellectual distinction and also played a part in politics under Alexander II.

Wagner tells in *Mein Leben* of his introduction to her lady-in-waiting and confidante, Editha von Rhaden, after the success of his first concert. He found her a lady of the greatest culture, and she arranged for him to be invited to the Grand Duchess's evening tea circle. This gave him the opportunity to read the *Ring* and *Meistersinger* to the company. Before leaving Russia he told Fräulein von Rhaden of his plans for building a house and of the financial problems·they posed. 'Build and hope!' she exclaimed ardently. But a telegram reached him as he crossed the frontier: 'Not too bold!'

This account was supplemented by the publication of eleven important letters from Wagner to Editha von Rhaden, in the periodical *Die Musik* in 1924. 'What marvellous evenings they were!' he wrote from Vienna. 'As you know, the Greeks thought of the realm of Apollo as being in the far, Hyperborean north; there eternal sunshine reigned, there Apollo held his court! Ought I not to think of that Hyperborean court when I remember the quiet liberation from all mundane pressures that I enjoyed on those evenings, in those rooms? . . . And now on to a new life, to the old life, the only one dear to me! "Gib Vergessen, daß ich lebe!" my Tristan cries to the night of love – I cry it to my art.' (9 May)

After paying his own debts and sending Minna the allowance due to her – an obligation he always observed conscientiously, however hard pressed he was – he still had 4000 talers left. In spite of Mathilde's efforts 'Rose Cottage' came to nothing: 'Oh you did everything you could, my dear treasure!' In the meantime his friends in Vienna had been looking for a house in the vicinity with a garden and some trees, and a few days later he wrote to Mathilde again: 'I have some important news; what will you think of it, you dear?' An old Hungarian, Baron Rackowitz, deemed it an honour to place the upper storey of his house at Penzing, half an hour from Vienna, at Wagner's disposal. There was a large garden and some magnificent trees, and the rent was comparatively low, 1200 gulden a year. (10 May)

The next day he wrote to her again. Although he was aware of all the good reasons in favour of settling in Vienna and against a house on the Rhine, he could not rid himself of a sense of regret. He tried to console Mathilde and himself with hopes for the future. 'God knows how far you and your family's bourgeois bigotry will stretch – but suppose the whole family, aunts and all, moved here? – Oh yes! one more Russian campaign and I shall be able to offer you the equally beautiful ground-floor flat of my house. You shall all keep house for me. What about that? What do the aunties say to that?' (11 May)

The expense of decorating and furnishing his flat – which he described to Mathilde in great detail, including a plan he drew himself – gave him an uneasy conscience, though he tried to justify it: 'Good gracious! for how much must not the trivia of an agreeably decorated house be a substitute!'

He felt very lonely on his 'half-hundredth' birthday; only the Standhartners looked in for a moment in the evening. A torchlight procession of choral societies and students' associations made amends on 3 June. As the procession made its way towards him across the Hietzing bridge, the most splendid, glowing full moon suddenly rose above the tall trees in the garden of Schönbrunn. 'And so a dear, old, trusted friend rose to greet me and told me that I was not alone in the midst of all this crowd! (To Mathilde Maier, 5 June)

He was working on *Die Meistersinger* again. He told Editha von Rhaden how curiously attractive he found the work; in it, for the first time, a genial element was developing, an enjoyment of delicate, light-hearted detail such as had never manifested itself in his earlier, passionate dramas. 'I believe that completing this work in peace is the only thing that may heal me and make a new, light-hearted man of me.' (14 September) But his progress was very slow. Having orchestrated the prelude a year earlier, by the middle of June 1863 he had only just finished scoring the first scene of the first act (i.e., up to Eva and Magdalene's exit).

He was constantly being interrupted by conducting engagements: three concerts in Budapest in July, two in Prague and two in Karlsruhe in November, a concert with the private orchestra of the Prince of Hohenzollern-Hechingen at Löwenberg in December,

Breslau on 9 December, Vienna on 27 December. As a conductor he was a 'virtuoso': in that role he could offer the general public the 'personal' accomplishments which were all it knew how to appreciate, while his 'works' really existed for only a few. As a virtuoso he would be at home in St Petersburg, too, he told Editha von Rhaden, only he would not want to take up concert-giving as a career, but rather engage himself for a number of large-scale concerts: he would then build up the Petersburg orchestra into the best in the world. The terms would have to be such as to relieve him of the need to supplement his income in other ways. By his reckoning he would need an annual income of between five and six thousand roubles.

The grand duchess appeared not averse to lending this plan her support. Revolution in Poland, however, barred his way to St Petersburg. An enquiry addressed to Moscow, which he enclosed with a letter to Fräulein von Rhaden for her to forward, was posted in Vienna on 2 February 1864 yet did not reach its destination until 23 March. His friend in Moscow much regretted the delay, as a series of concerts could probably have been arranged had the letter arrived when it should have done. He thought of travelling to Kiev, too, via Odessa, taking Cornelius with him, but again was advised against it because of the political situation.

There remained one last glimmer of hope. At Löwenberg and in Breslau he renewed his acquaintance with Frau Harriet von Bissing, whom he had known in Zürich, a daughter of the wealthy Hamburg shipowner Sloman, and sister of Eliza Wille. She was moved by his exhausted appearance, would not hear of his undertaking another Russian tour and proposed giving him a large sum of money to make up for it. The promise was slow in taking effect, ostensibly because of the objections of her family. In the end Wagner was forced to ask her for an unequivocal declaration: not whether she *could* help him at once, but whether she *wanted* to help him at all. 'You want to know after all if I *want* to? Well then, in God's name: No!' This answer completely bewildered Wagner until Frau Wille gave him the astonishing explanation: in great agitation she told him that her sister had said to herself, 'And if I do rescue Wagner, he still loves the Wesendonk woman!'[6] 'In the end Frau von Bissing's jealousy (I had no idea!) was so powerful', Wagner wrote to Cornelius at the end of March, 'that her behaviour towards me only now – through this discovery – becomes comprehensible.' In 1887, four years after Wagner's death, she called on Mathilde Wesendonk in her home in Berlin, and her agitation on seeing Wagner's bust was such that she began to tremble.[7]

Wagner's fate in Vienna was now sealed. Since he had believed that he only needed to gain time while the help he was sure of getting from Frau von Bissing was delayed, he had been forced to meet the interest due on his debts by issuing bills of exchange. (To Mathilde Maier, 29 March) In the first flush of his hopes he had celebrated Christmas by giving each of his friends Cornelius, Porges, Tausig and Schönaich 'an appropriate little something'. 'That idiot Wagner put up a great big tree and piled a king's ransom in presents under it for me!' Cornelius wrote to his sister. 'Just imagine: a wonderful heavy overcoat – an elegant grey dressing gown – red scarf, blue cigarette case and lighter – beautiful silk handkerchiefs, magnificent gold buttons – *Struwwelpeter* – elegant penwiper embossed in gold, lovely ties – meerschaum cigar-holder with his initials on it – in short, everything an Oriental imagination can dream up – it made me heavy at heart.'

Cornelius's gratitude took the form of a poem wishing Wagner good fortune and immortality, which he recited on New Year's Eve at the Standhartners'.

Wagner must have realized the impossibility of maintaining his establishment in Penzing any longer by the beginning of February at the latest. He asked Mathilde whether she and her family would consider taking a house outside Mainz, 'where I would have a quiet, pretty sitting room and a bedroom; and would you be able to manage if I paid you 100 florins a month for my keep?' But events were moving too fast. 'What I am caught up in is not a catastrophe, it is my approaching end,' he told Editha von Rhaden on 14 March. He implored her to ask the grand duchess to provide a pension of 1000 talers for his wife to be paid in quarterly instalments to 'Frau Minna Wagner, at Walpurgisstrasse 16, in Dresden', the first to be paid on the coming 1 April, and to be discontinued at her death.

Finally Eduard Liszt, an uncle of Franz though younger than his nephew, and an official of the district court in Vienna, advised him to lose no time in leaving for Switzerland to avoid arrest for debt, as one of the larger bills of exchange was about to fall due.[8] On the same day that he wrote to St Petersburg, Wagner also approached Eliza Wille with the request to discuss with Mathilde Wesendonk the possibility of the latter giving him a home for the summer. He asked only for his keep and would not be any kind of a nuisance. By the time Eliza Wille's 'total refusal' reached him he had left Vienna. He had decided on flight. Schönaich and Cornelius went to the station with him. Peter was gripped by a kind of black humour, a mood of 'flippant excitement', but in his next letter to his sister he wrote: 'But Susanne, he is Wagner, after all – by far the most important poet of our time – and I tell you, in spite of everything he is a German through and through – in sorrow and joy, in his virtues and his sins – human, a child, a genius!'

On 23 March Wagner arrived in Munich. In a shop window on Good Friday he saw a portrait of the new king, the eighteen-year-old Ludwig II, who had just succeeded to the throne on the sudden death of Maximilian II. The picture 'gripped me with the special emotion that beauty and youth arouse in us in what one supposes must be an uncommonly difficult position'. 'While I was there I wrote a humorous epitaph for myself.' This is now in the Wagner Archives.

> Hier liegt Wagner, der nichts geworden,
> nicht einmal Ritter vom lumpigsten Orden;
> nicht einen Hund hinterm Ofen entlockt' er,
> Universitäten nicht mal 'nen Dokter.

> ('Here lies Wagner, who never throve,
> tempted no dog from behind the stove,
> earned not the shabbiest star or garter,
> honoured by no Alma Marter.')
> Munich, 25 March 1864

As on his flight fifteen years before, he crossed Lake Constance and made for Zürich. He sent a few lines announcing his imminent arrival to François Wille, who was away from home on a trip to the East. Eliza Wille barely had time to prepare the guest room. 'He arrived in a pathetic condition, resembling in every respect someone in need of asylum,' she wrote to her husband. In her memoirs she added: 'He was in a state of mind in which a son seeks out his mother.'

She had forwarded Wagner's notice of his arrival to Otto Wesendonk. 'I hope . . . that you will be able to give Wagner a refuge,' he replied on Easter Sunday. 'I can *not* do it; you can fully appreciate that.' So she took him in. 'That woman is beyond praise,' he wrote to Cornelius, 'beyond compare, absolutely unique.' And to Mathilde Maier: 'Frau Dr Wille is quite unique; she knows *everything* straight away. Also capable, busy and boundlessly kind-hearted. You will like her very much, in spite of her great ugliness.'

She provided him with books: Jean Paul's *Siebenkäs*, the diaries of Frederick the Great, the fourteenth-century monk Johannes Tauler. 'I'm reading the German mystics: today Tauler. The coming of "grace" is particularly enthralling. All the same, everything is more spacious, peaceful and serene on the Ganges than in the cells of these Christian monasteries. One can tell how much bad, grey weather we always have.' (To Mathilde Maier, 5 April) In his diary he noted: Buddha – Luther; India – North Germany . . . On the Ganges mild, pure renunciation; in Germany monastic impossibility . . . Our life here is such a torment that without "wine, women and song" we cannot endure it nor even serve God. Mariafeld, April 1864.' (RWGS, XII, p. 282)

One evening, just after sunset, he was sitting by the window and looking at the floor while Frau Wille talked about the magnificent future that surely lay in front of him. He listened impatiently then jumped up. 'What's the use of your talking about the future, when my manuscripts are gathering dust? Who is going to stage the work that I, only *I*, with the aid of *benevolent* spirits, can give substance to, so that the whole world can know that this is how it is, *this* is how the master envisaged his work?' He was pacing excitedly up and down the room and then suddenly stopped in front of her. 'I am a different kind of organism, my nerves are hypersensitive – I must have beauty, splendour and light! The world owes me what I need! I cannot live the miserable life of a town organist like your master Bach! Is it so shocking, if I think I deserve the little bit of luxury I like? I, who have so much enjoyment to give the world and thousands of people?' He raised his head defiantly and then sat down by the window again.

He slept badly, disturbed by dreams. One night he was King Lear on the heath, in the storm. The Fool sang mocking rhymes at him. With his royal soul Lear hurled his curse in the teeth of the darkness and the storm and felt great and wretched, but not degraded. 'What have you to say of such an experience, where the dreamer feels himself identical with what his dream conjures up?' He dreamed feverishly that Frederick the Great invited him to join Voltaire at his court. 'That's what my secret ambitions do for me!'

'My condition is very disquieting,' he wrote to Cornelius, 'it's balanced on a knife edge: a single push and that will be the end, and there will be nothing more to come from me, nothing, nothing more!' Conjuring fate with daemonic force, he added: '*A light* must shine: *a man* must come, who will help me whole-heartedly, now – while I still have the strength to use his help: or else it will be too late, I feel it!' (8 April)

When Wille returned in the second half of April, Wagner sensed that his presence worried him. He decided to go to Stuttgart and try to resume work on *Die Meistersinger* somewhere in the country. Before leaving Mariafeld he gave Frau Wille a letter for Mathilde Wesendonk, who, however, returned it to her unopened with an accompanying note. 'I am sending that childish little letter back to you,' Wagner wrote to Eliza; 'there is nobody else, dear lady, who can explain to her, as occasion offers, that the most shameful troubles that have befallen me have made me neither wicked nor *bad*, and that therefore the childish exhortation to be *good* is meaningless.'[9]

Wagner left Mariafeld on 29 April. He wrote to Frau Wille from Basel, telling her he would be back and asking her to keep the room and her friendship for him. Her reply, to the Stuttgart address he had given her, caused her some pain: she would not fall in with his plans, one future lay ahead for her, another for him. He replied from Stuttgart on 2 May: 'Your desire not to see me at Mariafeld again is in accordance with my own feelings on the matter. Let the tempestuous, fevered night that not even the loveliest sunshine had the power to lighten from outside be a thing of the past, and let us draw a veil over the changing phantasms that it produced. – My fate, even for the immediate future, is still uncertain.'

# NOTES TO VOLUME I

### Preface

1 Conversely, Wagner's *Religion und Kunst* was the last thing Carlyle read before his death on 5 February 1881. (Cosima to her daughter Daniela, 3 April 1881)
2 *L'Opera*, 4, nos. 12/13.
3 Furtwängler, *Ton und Wort*, p. 108.
4 Schopenhauer, *Parerga und Paralipomena*, II, §59.

### Chapter 1. The Wagner Family

1 W. Lange, *Richard Wagners Sippe*; Lange, *Richard Wagner und seine Vaterstadt*; O. Bournot, *Ludwig Heinrich Christian Geyer, der Stiefvater Richard Wagners*; W. K. von Arnswaldt, *Ahnentafel des Komponisten Richard Wagner*.
2 H. S. Chamberlain, *Briefe* (Munich, 1928), I, pp. 226ff.
3 Wilhelm Bode, *Der Musenhof der Herzogin Amalie* (Berlin, 1908), pp. 13ff.

### Chapter 2. Wagner's Mother

1 Both letters were published in the *Bayreuther Festspielführer*, 1933, p. 15.

### Chapter 4. Beethoven

1 Otto Daube, *'Ich schreibe keine Symphonien mehr'*, pp. 94ff.

### Chapter 5. Studiosus Musicae

1 In a letter to Dr Martin Hürlimann, 5 June 1946; published in Westernhagen, *Wagner* (1956), pp. 532f.
2 Dannreuther included the full text of what Wagner said in his article on Wagner in the first edition of *Grove's dictionary of music and musicians* (1879–89). On another occasion Wagner mentioned that Weinlig had purposely not recommended Bach as a model because of his tendency to break the rules. (Cosima's diary, 20 December 1878; BBL 1937, p. 61.)

### Chapter 6. The First Three Operas

1 Richard Sternfeld, 'Zur Entstehung des Leitmotivs bei Richard Wagner', *Richard-Wagner-Jahrbuch* 1907, pp. 106ff.

### Chapter 7. *Rienzi*

1 An entry in the autobiographical notebook known as the Red Book betrays that Wagner tried to challenge Dietrich on this occasion: 'Became master of myself and a man. Whip, pistols. Failed to find D.' (RWSB, I, p. 83)
2 In *Richard Wagner an Minna Wagner*, II (*Briefe in Originalausgaben*, vol. 2), pp. 90f.
3 The letter is much abbreviated in RWGB, I, p. 101; it is complete in RWSB, I, p. 323.

### Chapter 8. *Der Fliegende Holländer*

1 *Bayreuther Festspielführer*, 1939, pp. 61ff.
2 A note in RWSB, I, pp. 414ff., lists a number of points which might be interpreted as evidence that he did not go to prison, but these do not diminish the suspicion occasioned by the disappearance of the first, incriminating piece of paper.
3 G. Leprince, *Présence de Wagner*, pp. 320ff.: '*Le Vaisseau Fantôme* de P. Foucher'.

### Chapter 9. *Tannhäuser*

1 Furtwängler, *Ton und Wort*, pp. 163f.

### Chapter 10. Hofkapellmeister in Dresden

1 Gustav Adolf Kietz, *Richard Wagner . . . Erinnerungen*, pp. 45ff.

### Chapter 11. Germanic Myth and Greek Tragedy

1 J. Grimm, *Deutsche Mythologie*. It must have been a copy of the first edition. The second, which he had in his Dresden library, was published in 1844.
2 Westernhagen, *Richard Wagners Dresdener Bibliothek*. The collection of Wagner's books, stored in a deep bunker, was one of the few things that survived the destrucion of the publishers' quarter of Leipzig on 4 December 1943. After the war the firm of Brockhaus were able to transport it to their new base in Wiesbaden. Their publication of the catalogue in 1966 met a long-standing need among Wagnerian scholars.
3 *Dichtung und Wahrheit*, Book 12. It is interesting to note that when Goethe was writing the scenario for an opera, *Der Löwenstuhl*, in 1814, he thought of casting the narration of the tale of the 'Lions' Seat' in 'Eddic rhythms'.
4 The original title was *Die Nibelungensage* (*Mythus*). (SERD, pp. 26ff.)
5 Spengler, *Der Untergang des Abendlandes*, I: 'Fafnir's hoard' twice, pp.

480 and 482. Spengler heard the *Ring* at Bayreuth in 1931. There is no sign that he changed his views. Frau Gertrud Strobel, the wife of the Wahnfried archivist, sat next to him at dinner after one of the performances, and has told me that 'he didn't speak a single word the whole time'.

6 Andreas Heusler, *Die altgermanische Dichtung* (new edn, Darmstadt, 1957), p. 39.

7 Kranz, *Stasimon* (Berlin, 1933).

### Chapter 12. *Lohengrin*

1 The scenario was published in the *Bayreuther Festspielführer*, 1936, pp. 141 ff.

2 Günther Schulz, *Das Recht in den Bühnendichtungen Richard Wagners* (Cologne, 1962). Apart from the works mentioned in the text, Wagner also owned Leopold August Warnkönig's *Flandrische Staats- und Rechtsgeschichte bis zum Jahr 1305*, in three volumes.

3 The 'Lohengrin house' still stands in the 'Wagnerort Graupa', as it is now designated (in the district of Pirna), and the museum set up there is still maintained and, so the curator assures me, is popular with visitors.

4 Cf. Erich Rappl, 'Vom Werden der *Lohengrin*-Partitur', in Bayreuth Festival programme, *Lohengrin*, 1954, pp. 21 ff.

5 Hanslick, 'Gluck'sche Oper', in *Die moderne Oper*, I.

6 Pfitzner, *Werk und Wiedergabe*, p. 312.

7 Strauss, *Briefwechsel mit Hugo von Hofmannsthal*, p. 628.

8 Ibid., p. 62. Strauss gave the *Meistersinger* quintet as another example.

9 Lorenz, 'Der musikalische Aufbau des *Lohengrin*', in *Bayreuther Festspielführer*, 1936, pp. 189ff. On Bar-form, see note 11 to Chapter 26, in Vol. II of the present work.

10 The uncut version is to be found in Wagner, *Sämtliche Lieder*, ed. by Emil Liepe (Breitkopf & Härtel).

11 BBL 1909, 1910.

12 All quotations from Goethe's *Faust* are in the translation by Louis MacNeice (London, 1951).

13 Mann, *Wagner und unsere Zeit*, pp. 120f.

### Chapter 13. Money Troubles

1 Meyerbeer's diaries and correspondence are in the process of publication, under the editorship of Dr Heinz Becker; to date (early 1978) three volumes have been published, to 1845. I am much obliged to Dr Becker for placing material from the diaries at my disposal before publication.

2 Some comparative salaries: Eduard Devrient, dramaturg, 3000 talers; Reissiger, principal conductor, 2000 talers; Wagner, second conductor, 1500 talers; Schröder-Devrient, principal singer, 4000 talers, in addition to a pension claim of 1000 talers, wardrobe allowance of 200 talers, and a payment of 20 talers for each

performance she gave – and frequent leave of absence to make guest
appearances elsewhere. (GLRW, II, p. 261, note.)

## Chapter 14. Revolutionary Ideas

1 Kittl's setting, under the title *Die Franzosen vor Nizza* ('The French
  before Nice'), was a success when it was produced in Prague – the
  one occasion when Wagner appeared in the role of librettist!
2 The first prose sketch of the Norns' scene was published in *Die
  Musik*, February 1933, pp. 336ff.; the first verse text is in RWGS, II,
  pp. 167ff.
3 The letter of 17 May 1849 to Eduard Devrient is to be found in
  RWSB, II, pp. 660–9.
4 Julius Kapp, *Richard Wagner und die Berliner Oper* (Berlin 1933), p. 27.

## Chapter 16. From Heroic Opera to Mythic Drama

1 The manuscript found its way into the Bibliothèque Nationale in
  Paris as part of the Collection Louis Barthou and was published for
  the first time in 1933 in facsimile in *L'Illustration*. When I enquired
  about it in 1962, in connection with my 'new Wagner studies', *Vom
  Holländer zum Parsifal*, it transpired that this invaluable document had
  been sold to a private buyer in 1936 for 11,500 francs. I was therefore
  glad of the opportunity to reproduce the sketch from the facsimile in
  *L'Illustration* in the Wagner number of the *Neue Zeitschrift für Musik*,
  May 1963, with a transcription, to prevent it from being lost
  entirely.
2 Heinz Becker, 'Giacomo Meyerbeer', in the *Year Book of the Leo
  Baeck Institute*, IX (London, 1964). It is of no importance if
  Meyerbeer gives the essay a different title: he appears unsure of the
  title of *Opera and drama*, too.
3 The long section about the 'fire cure' was suppressed in the edition of
  Wagner's letters to Uhlig (*Briefe in Originalausgaben*, vol 4: letter 18,
  22 October 1850) and was published for the first time in RWBC,
  pp. 774f.

## Chapter 17. The Vision of La Spezia

1 It was shown at the Wagner Memorial Exhibition in Leipzig in 1913,
  when it was part of the Gustav Herrmann manuscript collection. It is
  now in the Library of Congress in Washington, D.C. Robert W.
  Bailey has demonstrated convincingly that it dates from on or after
  27 July 1850. Cf. Westernhagen, *The forging of the 'Ring'*, p. 13.
2 Uhlig, *Musikalische Schriften*, ed. Ludwig Frankenstein, Regensburg,
  n.d. [1913].
3 Wagner says in *Mein Leben* that Liszt played to him from his *Faust
  Symphony*, but he must have confused this occasion with their
  meeting in 1856.

### Chapter 18. The Myth becomes Music

1 Halm, *Von Grenzen und Ländern der Musik*, chapter 4, 'Musik und Sprache'.
2 Furtwängler, *Vermächtnis*, p. 31.
3 Otto Strobel, 'Die Originalpartitur von Richard Wagners *Rheingold*', and 'Die Kompositionsskizzen zum *Ring des Nibelungen*', in *Bayreuther Festspielführer*, 1928 and 1930 respectively.
4 Cf. SERD, p. 257. Strobel was mistaken in supposing that this first sketch was in C major: it has to be read in the tenor clef, which makes the key B♭ major. It would otherwise be a unique instance of Wagner conceiving a tune in quite the wrong key.
5 Porges actually used Schiller's terms 'sentimental' and 'naive'.

### Chapter 19. The London Inferno

1 John Oxenford, 'Iconoclasm in German philosophy', *Westminster and Foreign Quarterly Review*, LIX, no. 111 (1 April 1853), pp. 388–407.
2 These notes are given in full in W. A. Ellis, *Life of Richard Wagner*, IV, pp. 440–6.
3 Felix Gotthelf, 'Schopenhauer und Richard Wagner', in *Jahrbuch der Schopenhauergesellschaft*, IV (Kiel, 1915), pp. 24–42.
4 28 September; BBL 1937, pp. 55f. '. . . wie wenn ich eine Symphonie zu schreiben hätte'. The entry in Cosima's diary from which this comes (28 September) actually reads: '. . . as if I had written a symphony' ('Wie wenn ich eine Symphonie geschrieben hätte'), but she was clearly mistaken.
5 Lorenz, *Das Geheimnis der Form bei Richard Wagner*, I: *Der musikalische Aufbau des Bühnenfestspiels 'Der Ring des Nibelungen'*, pp. 179ff.
6 On the dating of this letter, see Wilhelm Altmann, *Richard Wagners Briefe nach Zeitfolge und Inhalt* (Leipzig, 1905), p. 180.
7 For a more detailed description of the sketch, cf. Westernhagen, *The forging of the 'Ring'*, pp. 101–27.
8 Julius Kapp, *Richard Wagner und die Berliner Oper* (Berlin, 1933).
9 Bert Coules, 'An extract from Queen Victoria's journal', in *Wagner 1976*, p. 212; ill. no. 16.
10 *Richard Wagner and Ferdinand Praeger*, ed. by H. S. Chamberlain (2nd edn, Leipzig, 1908); *Cosima Wagner und H. S. Chamberlain im Briefwechsel*, pp. 354ff.
11 FWSZ, II, pp. 343ff. Wagner praised Sulzer in *Mein Leben*, but that he was nevertheless justified in the reservation he expressed here is confirmed by a recently published letter Sulzer wrote to Mathilde Wesendonk, undated but replying to hers of 17 August 1887 (*Neue Zürcher Zeitung*, 20/21 March 1976; on her letter see FWSZ, II, p. 501). Sulzer's own reservations about Wagner's personality were based on his awareness of something irrational in him that remained a closed book to himself. It was what Goethe called the 'daemonic' and is found in music in the highest degree; because music is on a

plane inaccessible to reasoning or intellectual processes, musicians have more of the daemonic in them than all other artists. Cf. the chapter 'Das Dämonische' in Westernhagen, *Wagner* (1956), pp. 427ff.

### Chapter 20. The *Ring* Crisis

1  The version in RWGS, XVI, pp. 23f., is abridged; it is to be found in full in FWSZ, II, p. 28.

2  J. Baechtold and E. Ermatinger, *Gottfried Kellers Leben, Briefe und Tagebücher* (Stuttgart and Berlin, 1924), II.

3  This somewhat lengthy excursus is made necessary by the fact that Mann's review, published in the *Neue Schweizer Rundschau* in 1951, has acquired a form of eternal life through having been reprinted in book form in *Altes und Neues* (1953), *Gesammelte Werke*, X (1960) and *Wagner und unsere Zeit* (1963). It is in any case a classic example of Wagnerian legends of that kind. Keller's letter is in Baechtold and Ermatinger, op. cit., II, pp. 439ff.

4  From W. Golther's edition of the *Briefe an Mathilde Wesendonk* (*Briefe in Originalausgaben*, vol. 5), p. 26. The note is undated. Ashton Ellis suggests that Mathilde's poem may have been *Im Treibhaus*, which would give a date of April 1858.

5  Cf. Otto Strobel, 'Zur Entstehungsgeschichte der *Götterdämmerung*'; Westernhagen, *Vom Holländer zum Parsifal*, p. 86; Westernhagen, *Richard Wagners Dresdener Bibliothek*, pp. 37f. Newman published an English translation of the sketch of the third version (NLRW, II, pp. 354ff.).

6  Strobel, ' "Geschenke des Himmels" ', pp. 157ff.

7  There are about as many alternative spellings of the hero's name as there are medieval versions of the legend. Wagner himself did not settle for 'Parsifal' until 1877.

### Chapter 21. In Asyl

1  For a detailed appraisal see Johann Cerny, 'Die Sprache in Richard Wagners *Tristan und Isolde*', BBL 1934, pp. 14–30.

2  Schrenck, *Richard Wagner als Dichter*.

3  A. Prüfer, 'Novalis *Hymnen an die Nacht*', in the *Richard-Wagner-Jahrbuch* 1906, pp. 290ff.

4  Mann, *Leiden und Größe Richard Wagners*.

5  Friedrich Herzfeld, *Minna Planer*, p. 330.

6  The theme of the play, in a nutshell, is as follows: the art-lovers at the court of Tasso's patron acknowledge that, in an ideal world of the spirit, the poet's genius would make him the equal of any monarch; but in the real world the Princess is immeasurably his superior and the Prince, her brother, expels Tasso from the court for daring to love her. (Like Mathilde, the Princess is happy to play the Muse, but not to accept the full consequences of the artist's love.)

7  Kurth, *Romatische Harmonik und ihre Krise in Wagners 'Tristan'*, pp. 40ff.

8 Hindemith, *The craft of musical composition (Unterweisung im Tonsatz)*, transl. A. Mendel, rev. edn (New York, 1945), I, p. 214.

9 Early in 1857 Wagner sent Mathilde Wesendonk a 'musical letter', with the annotation 'sleepless', consisting of an elaboration of the earlier sketch. (Reproduced in facsimile in *Bayreuther Festspielführer* 1938.)

10 Part of the cut passage is reproduced in facsimile and transcription in Westernhagen, *Vom Holländer zum Parsifal*.

### Chapter 22. Venice and Lucerne

1 Lorenz, *Das Geheimnis der Form bei Richard Wagner*, II: *Der musikalische Aufbau von Richard Wagners 'Tristan und Isolde'*, pp. 88–124.

2 Earlier in the same letter he wrote: 'I, poor devil, have . . . absolutely no routine at all, and if it won't come naturally there's nothing I can do about it.' Arnold Schoenberg commented that Wagner, having something new to say, was able to say it: 'That's not routine, but that quasi-animal sureness that a physical organ always shows at the critical juncture. Wagner could not do anything *mechanical*!' (H. H. Stuckenschmidt, *Schönberg*, p. 208).

3 'Segel' is a word of neuter gender in modern German, but the masculine (accusative case) here is one of Wagner's medievalisms. Cf. Wolfram's *Parzival*, I, line 1715 (58⁵). 

4 Wille Schuh, '*Tristan und Isolde* im Leben und Wirken Richard Strauss' ', *Bayreuther Festspielbuch 1952*.

5 This reply is dated 24 August in NBB – evidently incorrectly, in the absence of any evidence of a previous letter to Bülow from Wagner or Draeseke.

6 'Bass tuba' in Roeder, which is presumably a mistake.

7 Erich Roeder, *Felix Draeseke*, pp. 102–12.

### Chapter 23. *Tannhäuser* in Paris

1 Leroy, *Les premiers amis français de Wagner*, preface.

2 Ibid., pp. 57ff.

3 In the *Richard-Wagner-Jahrbuch* (Berlin, 1913), pp. 339ff., Sternfeld also called Kapp 'hasty' ('schnellfertig') in his review, but, as he later told me, he had meant to write 'irresponsible' ('leichtfertig').

4 The edition planned by the Wagner Archives of Wagner's correspondence with the Grand Duke of Baden and with Devrient about the production of *Tristan* in Karlsruhe in 1859 was abandoned on the outbreak of the Second World War. (RWSB, I, p. 10)

5 Wagner was referring to this when he told Mathilde Wesendonk that a portrait photograph of himself taken in Paris, in a dramatic pose with his eyes turned to the side, made him look like a 'sentimental Marat'. (23 May 1860)

6 *Ein Brief an Hector Berlioz*, RWGS, VII, pp. 82ff.

7 Quoted by Wagner in his letter of 5 June 1860 to Otto Wesendonk.

8 NLRW III, passim. There is also an account of Wagner's relations with the publisher Flaxland and the banker Erlanger.

9 Three letters from Wagner to Agnes Street are published in RWBC, pp 696ff., though the editor wrongly describes her as the daughter of Karl Klindworth.

10 Daniel Ollivier, 'Lettres d'un père [Liszt] à sa fille [Blandine]', in *Revue des Deux Mondes*, 15 December 1935 and 1 January 1936.

11 *Briefwechsel zwischen Cosima Wagner und Fürst Ernst zu Hohenlohe–Langenburg*, pp. 88f.

12 TWLF, p. 214. Rudolf Lindau was the brother of the journalist Paul Lindau, who wrote the notorious *Nüchterne Briefe aus Bayreuth* ('Sober letters from Bayreuth') in 1876.

13 Cf. Westernhagen, *Wagner* (1956), pp. 265ff.

14 '*Tannhäuser*-Nachklänge', in BBL 1892: see Humperdinck, pp. 57ff., and Strauss, pp. 126ff.

15 RWBC, pp. 512f., and Wilhelm Altmann and Gottfried Niemann, *Richard Wagner und Albert Niemann* (Berlin, 1924), pp. 117ff.)

16 This letter is not to be found in TWLF, but is in Leroy, *Les premiers amis français de Wagner*, pp. 177ff. and is abridged in Westernhagen, *Wagner* (1956), pp. 267f.

17 *Die Musik*, 1923, p. 42.

18 Heinz Becker, 'Giacomo Meyerbeer', *Year Book of the Leo Baeck Institute*, 1964, pp. 191f.

19 Details in Nuitter (C. Truinet), 'Les 164 répétitions et les 3 représentations du *Tannhaeuser* à Paris', *Bayreuther Festblätter in Wort und Bild* (Munich, 1884).

**Chapter 24. Odyssey**

1 In any case, Eduard Devrient had again queered Wagner's pitch in Karlsruhe. Bülow wrote to Wagner on 1 May that he trusted the grand duke's good faith. 'But I have noticed *one* curious item: *shortly* before your arrival in Karlsruhe [in the previous month], something appeared in the *Didaskalie* [the house journal of the opera management], not merely inspired by Uncle Devrient, I'll swear to it, but probably written by his own fair hand, explaining yet again that *Tristan und Isolde* is impossible to perform. Perfidious scum!' (NBB, p. 452)

2 Cf. Anthony Lewis, 'A "pretty theme" and the Prize Song', *Musical Times*, September 1976, pp. 732f., and CT, I, p. 442: 'he had always thought it was by someone else . . .'

3 Wagner's Dresden library included Friedrich Furchau's *Hans Sachs* (Leipzig, 1820), a two-volume biography based entirely on the internal evidence of Sachs's works. The second volume contains a particularly vivid episode where the poet writes *Die Wittenbergisch Nachtigall* on a Sunday morning in his workshop.

4 The sketch is reproduced in Westernhagen, *Vom Holländer zum Parsifal*, p. 136.

5 Vividly described by Berlioz in the sixth of his first set of letters from Germany: 'An appalling hubbub . . . trombones, horns and trumpets blaring out fanfares in a selection of keys, energetically accompanied by the clatter of bows on the wood of the stringed instruments and the din of percussion.' (*Memoirs*, translated by David Cairns (London, 1969).)

6 This episode was omitted from the first published edition of *Mein Leben*; it is in the 1963 edition, p. 848.

7 Mariafeld Archives; FWSZ, II, p. 208.

8 In the *Meistersinger* programme of the 1975 Bayreuth Festival, Manfred Eger published a letter to Eduard Liszt of 25 March 1864, in which Wagner gave an account of his debts. The kind of usury to which he had fallen victim is particularly interesting: taking into consideration the amounts quoted and the shortness of the term, he was being asked to pay interest at rates up to 200 per cent per annum!

9 On his letter and its subsequent fate see Otto Strobel, 'Über einen unbekannten Brief Wagners an Mathilde Wesendonk und seine Geschichte', p. 152. Mathilde later offered the house 'Asyl' to Brahms and also invited him to set her poems – he declined both! See: Erich H. Müller von Asow, *Johannes Brahms und Mathilde Wesendonk, ein Briefwechsel* (Vienna, 1943).

# 25

Munich

'I am at the end of the road – I can go no further – I must disappear from the world somewhere.' With these words Wagner greeted Wendelin Weissheimer on Saturday 30 April 1864 in his Stuttgart hotel, whither he had summoned him by telegram, to discuss what steps he should next take. They decided to look for somewhere as remote as possible in the Rauhe Alb, the hill country of southern Württemberg, where Wagner would be able to finish the first act of *Die Meistersinger* in peace. Since he wanted to see a performance of *Don Giovanni* on the Sunday he decided to leave on Tuesday. On Monday evening he went to visit a friend, Kapellmeister Eckert, and there, at already quite a late hour, the visiting card of a gentleman calling himself the 'secrétaire aulique de S. M. le roi de Bavière' was brought to him. Surprised and annoyed that his presence in Stuttgart was known even to people passing through the city, he told the servant to say he was not there. On his return to his hotel he was again told that a gentleman from Munich wished to speak to him urgently. Wagner left a message for him to call again the next morning and passed a restless night, preparing for the worst.

The next morning the Secretary of the Cabinet to the King of Bavaria, Franz Seraph von Pfistermeister, was shown up to his room. He had already been to Penzing and Mariafeld in search of him and, had it not been for Wagner's delay in order to see *Don Giovanni*, he would have missed him in Stuttgart too. Pfistermeister brought him a photograph of Ludwig II, a valuable ring and the message that as the stone in the ring glowed, so the King was on fire to see the author and composer of *Lohengrin*. [1]

'This life, all the poetry and music of which it is yet capable, now belongs to you, my gracious young king,' Wagner replied, 'dispose

329

of it as of your own!' (3 May) One of the not infrequent symbolic chances of his life brought a telegram, as he lunched at the Eckerts the same day, with the news that Meyerbeer had died in Paris the day before. Wagner castigated Weissheimer in his autobiography for breaking into a 'yokelish laugh'.

By 4 May Wagner stood before King Ludwig in the Residenz palace in Munich. 'I should be the most ungrateful of men if I did not tell you at once of my immeasurable good fortune,' he wrote to Eliza Wille the very same day. 'You already know that the young King of Bavaria had sent to look for me. Today I was taken to him.' He went on, prophetically: 'He is so handsome, so great in spirit and in soul, so glorious that, alas, I fear that his life will evanesce in this mean world like a fleeting dream of godhood.' 'My heart is bursting,' he exclaimed to Mathilde Maier, 'I must share my news with someone dear to me. Look at this picture of a marvellous youth, whom Fate has chosen to be my saviour. This is he whom we expected, whom we knew existed, but to find him so handsome fills me with profound amazement . . . He offers me everything I need to live, to create, to have my works performed. All I need to be is his friend: no official appointment, no duties . . . And this now – now – in the darkest, deathlike night of my life!! I am crushed by it!' (5 May)

'If only you could have witnessed how his thanks shamed me', the king told his cousin and future fiancée, Duchess Sophie in Bavaria, 'when I gave him my hand with the assurance that his great Nibelung work would be not only completed but performed as he wished it to be, that I would faithfully see to it. At that he bowed deep over my hand and seemed moved by what was after all so natural, for he stayed in that position for a long time, without saying a word. I had the sensation that we had exchanged roles. I bent over him and drew him to my heart with a feeling as though I were silently taking the oath of fealty: to remain true to him for ever.' (KLRW, I, p. xxxv)

No wonder that the friendship soon passed into legend, for better and, even more, for worse. The publication of the complete correspondence between Ludwig and Wagner, in five volumes between 1936 and 1939, was of all the greater biographical value.

What is immediately apparent from the letters is that the popular conception of a favourite composer and a royal musical amateur does not apply here. A love of music was not the most important motive at work in Ludwig. Was he musical at all? It has been denied and Wagner himself sometimes expressed doubt about it. But he may have meant only that the king had not been properly educated in music; why else should he have encouraged him to let Bülow play Beethoven to him, to improve his knowledge of that master? There was also, from the first, no question of a princely patron condescending to a favourite commoner. Each regarded the other as an equal in his different way. The tone of courtly deference in Wagner's letters does not conceal the fact that he addresses the king as an equal. The king in his turn places himself on the same footing as the artist, in the belief that in realizing the composer's ideas he is only bodying forth his own dreams: he writes of 'our' ideals, 'our' efforts, 'our' work. 'When we have both long since ceased to be, our work will still serve posterity as a shining exemplar, to delight future centuries, and hearts will glow in enthusiasm for art, divinely begotten, immortal art!' (4 August 1865)

In view of the homosexual inclinations that the king was later to reveal, the suspicion was expressed at one time that his friendship with Wagner also rested on that, or a related basis. So far as Wagner is concerned it is of course absurd to suppose that he would have enjoyed an unnatural relationship with the king at the time of his consuming passion for Cosima. He stated his own views on the subject quite unambiguously. 'It is not for me to be to you what the world, your family, your high calling in life, a friend – and one day the woman of your choice can be to you,' he wrote to him on 24 March 1865. And he wrote in his diary in 1873, evidently after reading Plato: 'What we cannot understand in the Greek character, whatever the language we use, is what separates us completely from them: e.g. their love – pederasty.' The king, for his part, as Strobel emphasizes, had far too idealized a conception of his relationship to Wagner to have permitted the intrusion of any such feelings. Newman draws attention to Ludwig's diary, which testifies to his constant but hopeless struggle against his homosexuality, and in which he quotes lines from Wagner's works to strengthen and comfort himself. For instance, he once quotes some lines from Lohengrin's Grail narrative:

> Wer nun dem Gral zu dienen ist erkoren,
> den rüstet er mit überird'scher Macht;
> an ihm ist jedes Bösen Trug verloren,
> wenn ihn er sieht, weicht dem des Todes Nacht,

but alters the last phrase from 'the night of death yields to him' to 'the might of sin yields to him': '. . . weicht dem der *Sünde Macht.* Amen! Amen! Amen!'[2]

It was his idealization of art that drew Ludwig to Wagner, as to Schiller. Growing up in the castle of Hohenschwangau, whose walls his father, Maximilian II, had had decorated with pictures of emperors and dukes, including four of the Swan Knight, the decisive experience of the boy's life had been a performance of *Lohengrin* seen when he was fifteen. Even before then he had already read *The Artwork of the Future* and *Music of the Future*, the word 'future' ('Zukunft') exercising a mysterious fascination on him. He went on to immerse himself in *Opera and Drama* too, and when he came upon the question at the end of the preface of the text of the *Ring* – 'Is such a prince to be found? "In the beginning was the Deed"' – he felt it was addressed to him personally, although he had no idea at the time how soon he would be in a position to respond.

'Rest assured that I will do everything in my power to compensate you for your past suffering,' he wrote to Wagner after their first meeting. 'I want to lift the menial burdens of everyday life from your shoulders for ever, I want to enable you to enjoy the peace for which you long, so that you will be able to unfurl the mighty pinions of your genius unhindered in the pure ether of your rapturous art!

'Unknowingly you were the *sole source of my joys* from my earliest boyhood, my friend who spoke to my heart as *no other* could, my best mentor and teacher.' (5 May)

His first act to relieve Wagner of the burdens of everyday life was a provisional gift of 4000 gulden to meet his obligations in Vienna, followed by another 16,000 gulden in June. He lent him a house on the Starnberg Lake for the summer months, Haus Pellet, just outside Kempfenhausen, from which Wagner could drive over to see him at Schloss Berg in a quarter of an hour. There was not a blot, not the smallest cloud, Wagner wrote to Bülow, but the pure, deep, complete devotion of the disciple to the master. 'I have no other pupil so perfectly dedicated to me as this one.' And he referred to the king for the first time by the name of 'Parzival', as he was to be known to Wagner and his close friends. (18 May)

His experiences in Dresden had taught him that he could expect to meet with envy and rancour in Munich too. His good fortune and his power were now so great, he told Bülow, that his sole care was to avoid attracting the accusation of abusing them. (12 May) But the king had no such suspicions. 'Do you really believe that the composer of *Lohengrin* still has enemies?' he asked once. 'I think it is impossible!'

After the first heady delight had worn off, Wagner became conscious of his isolation in the 'bewitched castle', and it was all the more acute because he was not yet able to collect himself sufficiently to get down to work again. 'Shall I be able to renounce the "feminine" entirely?' he wondered in a letter to Eliza Wille. He plucked up enough courage to appeal yet again to Mathilde Maier: 'Will you come to me and keep house for me? . . . Must I still fear to put you in a fluster if I ask you to come to me? . . . God! God! These eternal petty bourgeois scruples; – and where there is so much love!' He went on, imploringly: 'I'm afraid you will lose me one day, if you do not give me your help entirely.' (22 June) Three days later he followed this: 'I have not yet set eyes on anyone who could take your place. It was not a threat, only the fear that I should be forced to *seek* someone else.'

With this letter he also enclosed a long one for her mother: 'Have you perhaps the courage in the sight of the world and enough confidence in me to entrust Mathilde to me? I know how disturbing, even destructive, a thing this is to ask of you. But I must ask you . . . Do I need to assure you that Mathilde's position in my house will be good and noble and that she will be protected in the most emphatic and energetic manner against every suspicion, every stain? Or may I even go so far, without nurturing an impious wish, as to take the possibility of my wife's death into account and to sue for your daughter's hand in that eventuality?'

Mathilde's answer is missing, but it is clear from Wagner's response that she had not given her mother the letter, for fear that it would indeed destroy her. 'Oh, my dear child! I do not want that at any price!' he exclaimed in horror, 'I can and will endure anything in the world from now onwards, save only new onslaughts of disturbance and strife, such as I now see would inevitably ensue if you were to give the letter to your good mother!' (29 June)

He added incidentally that he was expecting visitors: by a strange coincidence, on the very day that he received and replied to Mathilde's refusal, Cosima von Bülow and her daughters Daniela and Blandine arrived at Haus Pellet. On 30 June he told Eliza Wille that Frau von Bülow had arrived the day before, with two children and their nurse, and Bülow would be following. 'It makes things a little more lively, but I am in so peculiar a state that nothing seems to make any real impression on me any more.' So, instead of the middle-class girl from Mainz, his house received the daughter of the Comtesse d'Agoult, and the eight days that passed before Bülow's arrival sealed the fate of all three of them.

The letter that Bülow wrote to Liszt on 20 April 1856, asking for Cosima's hand, ended with the remarkable statement: 'I swear to you that, however much I feel myself bound to her by my love, I would never hesitate to sacrifice myself to her happiness and release her if she should come to realize that she had been deceived in me. Her will, her very whim, shall be sacred to me.' This almost morbid sense of his own 'insignificance', as he calls it here, contains the seeds of the eventual tragedy of his marriage. In the letter he wrote to congratulate his sister on her engagement in 1862 he confessed that as a rule it was the office of the husband to play the part of the protector, but he was painfully aware that in his own case the relationship was reversed: 'Mine is a nature that verges on the feminine; my wife has a strong character and has, alas, so little need of my protection that if anything she gives me hers.' (MMCW, p. 188)

When the Bülows visited the Wagners in Zürich during their honeymoon, Wagner was taken aback by Cosima's reserve towards him. Her reticence distressed him. 'If she found my manner too strange, if occasionally a brusque remark, a word of mockery . . . offended her, then I should truly have to regret having allowed myself to go a little too far in my familiarity.' (To Bülow, 18 January 1858) On her second visit to Asyl he again complained that she seemed more drawn to the Herweghs: 'I dare say she finds me rather unprepossessing; but we are excellent friends!' (To Liszt, 2 July 1858) It must have startled him all the more, therefore, when, as she said goodbye, she fell at his feet and covered his hands with tears and kisses. (JKWF, p. 152) What can she have said in the 'recent mad letter' for which she asked Hans to make her apologies to Wagner? (NBB, 5 February 1859) Wagner replied that he wished she would always send him letters that she regretted. Such regrettable letters were the only things he had to refresh him. 'Thanks to these outpourings I suddenly see myself clearly all at once; then a wonderful calm and a deep sense of inner peace take possession of me. Tell her so! And give her my warmest regards!' (6 February 1859)

When he heard that Hans was worried about her health he ventured the opinion that her temperament was the worst threat to her health: 'Her origins are simply too extraordinary and for that reason it is hard to shield her.' (4 April 1861) 'She's a wild child, is all I can say! But her aristocratic breeding shows.' (19 September 1861)

All this epistolary evidence points to the character of their relationship before her visit to Starnberg. Her tongue-tied and sometimes strange behaviour in Wagner's presence shows what he meant to her. His concern on her behalf was mixed with perplexity and admiration, but no word of love or passion had been spoken between them.

There is, however, a passage in *Mein Leben*, suppressed in the 1911 edition, according to which they had exchanged a vow 'to belong only to each other' on 28 November 1863, on a drive around Berlin during his brief visit to the city. (ML, p. 844) One of Cosima's biographers remarks that this statement was probably composed in the light of later feelings. (MMCW, p. 139) It is understandable that Wagner should have felt a need to give Cosima a place in his memoirs, which finish at the point of his summons to Munich, by thus advancing the date when they confessed their love.

The first direct evidence of the change in their relationship is in a letter she sent from Starnberg to her friend Marie von Buch, later Freifrau von Schleinitz. 'I'm writing to you . . . far from home, far from all disturbance, separated by the lake even from the little village of Starnberg, I feel far away from everything, as if everything has forgotten [me] and as if I have forgotten everything. When I have told you about it all, then you will not misunderstand my words. I have been here three days and it seems to me that it has already been a century and that it will last, how long, I don't know.' (DMCW, I, p. 233)

That was on 2 July 1864. Bülow himself arrived at Haus Pellet on 7 July. The entry for these weeks in Wagner's Annals reads: 'End of July: every day with Hans to the king in Munich. 29 July: Hans's appointment . . . Hans falls ill. 19 August: Cosima to Karlsruhe. Hans to Munich: to the hotel, ill and furious.'

The festival of the Allgemeiner Deutscher Musikverein was due to take place in Karlsruhe from 22 to 26 August. Since Bülow was ill and Wagner unable to get away because of the king's birthday (25 August), Liszt was obliged, against his will, to leave his refuge in Rome and undertake the direction of the festival. He told Princess

Caroline that he had refrained from inviting Cosima, so as not to influence her in any way. But on 19 August, on the same day that Bülow, ill, moved to the Bayerischer Hof hotel in Munich, Cosima went to Karlsruhe. Was it simply to keep her father company? In the light of what was known of the 'Wagner–Cosima–Bülow triangle', Newman felt it permissible to assume that she wanted to tell her father about the crisis that had recently come about and ask for his counsel and help. (NLRW, III, pp. 266ff.) This assumption has since been confirmed by the publication, in 1975, of the full text of Wagner's Brown Book.[3] The entry for 11 September 1865, while Cosima was away with Liszt and Bülow for a time, reads: 'God knows what you'll be like when you return. I know how you were a year ago, when your father brought you back here! It was dreadful: you sleepless, restless, weak, frail, miserable, ravaged!' This leaves no doubt that she went straight to Karlsruhe from Starnberg in order to pour out her heart to her father.

She arrived back in Munich on 28 August 1864, accompanied by Liszt, who visited not only Hans, still on his sickbed, but also Wagner. '*Liszt*', the latter wrote in the Annals, underlining the name significantly. '(Grey man.) Comes to Starnberg with me for one day and night. Praises my good sense. – Munich again: Bayerischer Hof . . . (Hans!). 3 September, Liszt left in the morning, Hans and Cosima in the evening [for Berlin]. Quiet at Starnberg.'

His 'good sense' consisted in his agreement not to force the situation to a violent resolution. Liszt probably hoped privately that Cosima would be reconciled within herself to returning to her husband. There seem still to have been certain reservations on what Hans had been told. On 30 September Wagner wrote to him: 'The state Cosima is in worries me too. Everything about her is uncommon and out of the ordinary: she has a right to freedom in the noblest sense. She is childlike and deep – the laws governing her nature will always lead her only to what is sublime. Nor will anyone ever help her except herself! She belongs to a special order of creation that we must learn to apprehend through her. – In future you will have more favourable opportunity and greater freedom to observe this and to find your own worthy place at her side. And that, too, consoles me!' Whether this veiled confession was followed by an explicit one is a question to which we shall return.

The week with Cosima at Starnberg found its artistic outlet in the melody – called in German the 'Peace melody' – which Wagner used in 1869 in the third act of *Siegfried* at Brünnhilde's words 'Ewig war ich, ewig bin ich' in E major and then in E minor, and again in 1870 in the *Siegfried Idyll*. He promised her a quartet on the melody, which entered his head during the time that they were together at Starnberg, as he later told her. 'Oh, yes, we know very well where it all comes from!' (DMCW, I, pp. 546, 819) In fact a musical sketch survives of the Peace melody, dated 14 November 1864. Newman points out that the theme that directly follows it in the third act, at the words 'O Siegfried, Herrlicher! Hort der Welt!', which is also used in the *Idyll*, must also have been conceived for the 'Starnberg' Quartet: why else would Wagner have constructed the two themes so that they can combine in double counterpoint, when he makes no use of that valuable attribute in *Siegfried*, but only in the *Idyll*, composed fourteen months later? Both melodies meant so much to him for their entirely personal associations that he was prepared to introduce a slight stylistic discrepancy in the final scene of *Siegfried* for their sake, and even to alter the words, not altogether happily, in order to fit them to the second theme.

The sheet with the sketch of the Peace melody also bears a first version of the World Inheritance motive which is heard in the Wanderer–Erda scene, after the lines

> Was in des Zwiespalts wildem Schmerze
> verzweifelnd einst ich beschloß,
> froh und freudig
> führe frei ich nun aus . . .

In a way it symbolizes the re-invigoration of his creative power as a result of King Ludwig's summons. 'My head is in a whirl!' he wrote to Bülow. 'I need every drop of optimism and energy that I possess: for – seriously – I am now getting down to finishing the *Ring*.' That work was the only thing that was now congenial to him: he was far too tense to bother with Beckmesser and Pogner. (23 September 1864) And a week later he wrote to tell him of his move from Starnberg to Munich: his longing to compose had swelled to a passion. 'I am now wonderfully in the mood for the third act of *Siegfried*: and particularly for the first scene with Wotan: it shall be a prelude, short but – significant.'

He drew up a programme at this time, to show the king:

1865
Spring: performance of *Tristan*
Beginning of the winter season: performance of *Die Meistersinger*
1867–8
Performance of the entire *Ring* cycle
1869–70
*Die Sieger*
1871–2
*Parsifal*

Ludwig had asked him for a written account of whether and in what way his views on politics and religion had altered since his writings on art in the early years in Zürich, and Wagner responded with *On the State and Religion*, written in July 1864, in which he developed some of the ideas 'our greatest poet' expressed in *Wilhelm Meisters Wanderjahre* (*Über Staat und Religion*, RWGS, VIII, pp. 3ff.). Never was a king addressed in more worthy or philosophical a fashion, Nietzsche wrote to Gersdorff: 'I was completely exalted and overpowered by the ideality, which seemed to have originated entirely in the spirit of Schopenhauer.' (4 August 1869)

At the same time Wagner was eager to thank his benefactor in words and music. He wrote the *Huldigungsmarsch* (March of Homage) for the king's nineteenth birthday on 25 August, though it was not actually performed until 5 October. Its blend of rapturous idealism and solemn ceremony matches the feelings that he expressed in the poem *An meinen König* ('To my King') in the September.

> es war Dein Ruf, der mich der Nacht entrückte,
> die winterlich erstarrt hielt meine Kraft . . .
> so wandl' ich stolz beglückt nun neue Pfade
> im sommerlichen Königreich der Gnade.

('It was your summons snatched me from the night that numbed my strength in winter's cold . . . Now I tread new paths in pride and joy, in the summer kingdom of grace.' RWGS, VIII, pp. 1f.)

'I have resolved to place all other works on one side for the time being,' he informed the king on 26 September 1864, 'so as to be able to devote myself exclusively and without delay to completing the composition of my major work, the *Ring*.' The following day he began the fair copy of the score of the second act of *Siegfried*, which he had put aside more than seven years before.

A formal ten-clause contract between Wagner and the Court Secretary's office was concluded on 18 October, in which he undertook, for a fee of 30,000 gulden, to compose the music to his drama *Der Ring des Nibelungen* and 'to deliver a complete fair copy into the hands of Hofrat Hofmann within at most three years from today'. For Wagner as for Ludwig this contract was simply a form, to give the work they were doing together plausibility in the eyes of the world.

The king looked forward with impatience to the realization of their hopes. 'I have decided to have a large stone theatre built, so that the performance of *Der Ring des Nibelungen* shall be perfect,' he wrote to Wagner on 26 November. Wagner in turn wrote to Gottfried Semper in Zürich, to find out if he would undertake the project. The famous architect was received by the king on 29 December and commissioned to design the theatre. Shortly afterwards, when the Augsburg *Allgemeine Zeitung* published a report that there was no intention, in the seat of power, of carrying out the plan, Semper's anxiety was stilled by Wagner: 'Have faith – and work for us!' There were in fact two concurrent, alternative plans: a monumental theatre, approached by a new processional way and bridge, to be built on the Gasteig hills on the far bank of the Isar, which it was estimated would cost in the region of 5,000,000 gulden; or a temporary structure in the Glaspalast, the glass exhibition hall, costing about 200,000 gulden.

While the king was all for splendour, Wagner was most concerned to have a functional interior. A letter Semper wrote him on 26 November 1865, after working out the designs in detail, shows what he wanted: an auditorium in the shape of an amphitheatre, its walls articulated by a line of columns, a sunken orchestra pit and, 'in accordance with what we agreed', two prosceniums one behind the other, with the smaller rear one an exact repetition of the front one, only giving a smaller opening. 'This will create a complete dislocation of scale and in consequence everything on the stage will appear enlarged, and we shall achieve the aim of separating the ideal world on the stage from the real world on the far side of the divide represented by the orchestra pit.' In the end this theatre was never built in Munich, but Wagner incorporated these features, which he regarded as his intellectual property, in the Festspielhaus in Bayreuth.

For the moment the building was less important to him than training singers and attracting to Munich the assistants that he would need. 'I have great hopes of Bülow and his help: Peter Cornelius must come soon too. But I still lack a very great deal in spite of those two! In particular a genius of dramatic stagecraft, to look out for people and coach them.' (To Mathilde Maier, 17 December 1864)

Bülow, with his wife and children, had already moved from Berlin to Munich on 20 November. Cornelius and Porges followed after a slight delay. Wagner was less fortunate in his choice of a singing teacher, Friedrich Schmitt, whom he had known as a tenor in Magdeburg. Schmitt, known as 'Blacksmith' for his rough manner, had worked out a method for a kind of German bel canto, which he applied successfully to *Tannhäuser* and *Lohengrin*, but which failed him over *Tristan*. 'Just you wait,' Wagner shouted at him in broad Saxon after one rehearsal, 'when I've finished my *Siegfried*, I'll write another opera specially for you and your pupils in the very best Flotow style!' and threw his velvet cap at him.

Meanwhile Ludwig, in all innocence, had appointed an inveterate enemy of Wagner's as foreign minister and chairman of the council of ministers. Ludwig von der Pfordten, sometime professor of Roman Law in Leipzig, was an old acquaintance of Wagner's from the Dresden days: in 1848 it had been he, as Saxon minister of culture, who had had the last word on Wagner's plan for the organization of a national theatre. Since then he had followed Wagner's career with undisguised disapproval; as late as 1858 he had told the actor Emil Devrient that if the princes stuck together like the democrats none of Wagner's operas would ever get performed anywhere.

From the very first there was an influential circle in Munich, composed of the aristocracy, the civil service and the Catholic clergy, who were suspicious of the parvenu, notorious revolutionary and Lutheran musician whom the king had made his confidant. To begin with they bided their time; indeed it has been claimed that the cabinet would have been quite glad to see the king distracted from the business of government, so that they could pursue their policies with less interference. But when Semper's audience with the king made public the plan to build the new theatre, they made their first attempt, in February 1865, to discredit Wagner with Ludwig. Cabinet Secretary Pfistermeister cannot be absolved of complicity in the scheme. It was a matter of the payment for a portrait of Wagner painted for the king by Friedrich Pecht,[4] and it is obvious that the king was deliberately misled. This was the first occasion on which Wagner experienced Ludwig's capriciousness. Summoned to an audience on 6 February, he was refused admission by the king, who then, a few days later, caused a démenti to be issued, describing the by then widespread rumour that Wagner had fallen into disfavour as 'completely unfounded'. 'Wretched, short-sighted people, who can speak of disfavour,' he assured Wagner, 'who have no notion of Our Love, and can have none.' (14 February)

The enemy faction, who saw the weak point in this denial, launched an attack with an article in the *Allgemeine Zeitung* on 19 February entitled 'Richard Wagner and Public Opinion'. The anonymous author (he turned out to be the poet Oskar von Redwitz, whose *Amaranth* is unlikely to mean much to anybody today) did not scorn to make an issue of such private matters as that Wagner was buying expensive carpets. Wagner replied in sensible, moderate terms on 22 February: he could rightly regard himself not as a royal favourite but as an artist who was being paid a fee commensurate to his work, and he believed he was not obliged to account to anybody for how he spent his salary. (KLRW, IV, pp. 47ff.)

The attack had been fended off. But for all his protestations of love the king still appeared to be avoiding Wagner. The latter therefore put the king's trust to the test in a letter of 11 March, with a direct question: 'Shall I go away? Shall I stay?' '*Stay, stay* here,' Ludwig replied on the same day, 'everything will be *splendid* as it used to be.'

Thus confirmed in his position, Wagner was now able to concentrate on his next major undertakings: the first performance of *Tristan* – for which, at his request, Bülow was appointed kapellmeister – and the composition of a report on the establishment of a national school of music in Munich (*Bericht an Seine Majestät den König Ludwig II. von Bayern über eine in München zu errichtende deutsche Musikschule*, RWGS, VIII, pp. 125ff.). 'It marks a new phase in my life,' he told Mathilde Maier; 'If I find the people who will more or less meet my needs, then I shall have found ... Archimedes' fulcrum, from which I shall lever the musical world out of its dozy nooks.' (17 March) Unlike the Italians and French, he argued, the Germans possessed no tradition in the performance of their great masters. The first need, therefore, was to evolve an intrinsically German style. What he proposed was a method of instruction that would produce a complete, integrated style: it should be based on singing, as the foundation of all music, but would extend as far as gymnastics and mime. He was conscious from the first that such proposals represented a challenge to 'the whole artisanry of art with its pitiful proletariat'.

Bülow took the first orchestral rehearsal of *Tristan* on 10 April. Wagner's daughter Isolde Josepha Ludovica was born on the same day.

Before the dress rehearsal, which took place on 11 May before an audience of about six hundred, Wagner addressed a few words to the orchestra, in a voice trembling with excitement: 'My work has entered into you, out of you it returns to me again: I can enjoy it in serenity. This is unique happiness. We have achieved the best thing of all, the work allows the artist to be forgotten!'

The first performance was fixed for 15 May. On the evening before, news came from Pusinelli in Dresden that Minna was dying, followed the next morning by the assurance that the danger had passed for this once. Relieved, Wagner wrote a short note to the king, dating it '*Tristan*-day'. 'How I am looking forward to the evening!' Ludwig replied. 'If only it would come soon! When will day yield to night?'

Then all of a sudden a court officer appeared at Wagner's house in the Briennerstrasse, armed with a bill of exchange for 2400 gulden and the authority to distrain the furniture on non-payment. The prehistory of the incident went back to the Paris concerts of 1860, when Malwida had introduced Wagner to a wealthy English widow, Julie Salis-Schwabe, who paid him a subvention of 5000 francs to cover his deficit. Unbidden, Wagner made out a promissory note, and when he applied to Malwida to get it extended for him, she replied that he could save himself the trouble, as Mrs Schwabe had never regarded the sum as anything other than a contribution to the success of the concerts. Wagner was therefore all the more amazed to receive a request for payment of the debt from a Munich lawyer, Dr von Schauss, on 20 March 1865: delay might lead to an interruption in the execution of his 'ingenious compositions' and hinder his preparations for the production of his 'magnificent opera *Tristan und Isolde*'. This threat proves that the presentation of the bill by Schauss and those who may be presumed to have been behind him on the very day of the planned première was no coincidence but a deliberate act of malevolence. Wagner barely had time to send to the Cabinet Treasury for help, but this was at once afforded him.[5]

But that was not the end to the day's calamities. At midday Ludwig Schnorr, who was to sing Tristan, arrived to tell Wagner with tears in his eyes that his wife had suddenly turned hoarse and would be unable to sing Isolde that evening. 'My old daemon has been stirring', Wagner wrote to the king, 'and has frustrated the work for whose sake friends have made the most arduous sacrifices in order to get here from great distances.' They had come from all over Europe, from Paris, London, Vienna, Königsberg. Only a few of his friends were absent: Cornelius, who was in Weimar preparing the production of his own *Der Cid*; Liszt, who was kept in Rome by Princess Wittgenstein; and the Willes and Wesendonks from Zürich. It had been the climax of his life, he told Frau Wille in a letter, 'and yet it was made bitter by – absences! – Truly, bitter!' (26 September)[6]

The première finally took place on 10 June, followed by three more performances on 13 and 19 June and 1 July. The house was full, even the standing room. The king entered the royal box on the dot of six, greeted by fanfares and cheers. When Bülow raised his baton, probably no one there realized that he was signalling the completion of an epoch, not in musical history alone but in the history of western culture. A century later the literature on *Tristan* is worldwide, and the work's fascination is as strong as on the first day. Its epoch-making significance was best expressed by Richard Strauss, writing to Joseph Gregor after reading his history of world theatre. Gregor had claimed that in his *Iphigenie* Goethe gave the theatre of the world a final intellectual and spiritual form that had never been equalled since. Strauss objected that 'this "final intellectual and spiritual form" is – thanks to the music – not only equalled but surpassed in *Tristan* . . . *Tristan* is the ultimate conclusion of Schiller and Goethe and the highest fulfilment of a 2000–year–long evolution of the theatre.'

According to Schopenhauer, it is impossible for a genius not to recognize himself and know his worth. This is supported by the pen-portrait of Wagner at this period of his life by Édouard Schuré, a young Alsatian who later became well known for his book *Le drame musical*. In the conversations he had with Wagner at that date he was overwhelmed by the composer's unshakable faith in himself and his great ideas: in his blue eyes, which seemed to Schuré to be fixed immovably on a distant goal, there was a vision that dominated everything else and lent him an air Schuré could only call an eternal chastity. Now his face was that of Faust, now that of Mephistopheles, and then again he looked like a fallen angel thinking about heaven and saying 'it does not exist but I shall find a way to create it'.[7]

The purest realization of Wagner's artistic ideal was achieved, for him, in Ludwig Schnorr's performance of Tristan's great monologue in the third act. Recalling it, he advised anyone who wanted to gain some impression of what it had been like to pick up the score and look first at the orchestral writing alone, the motives restlessly entering, developing, joining, parting, almost consuming each other, possessing an expressive significance that required the most sophisticated harmonization and flexible orchestration, with instrumental combinations of a richness such as no purely symphonic writing could encompass. And yet, as Schnorr sang, this whole immense orchestra 'completely disappeared, or – more accurately – appeared to be subsumed in his delivery'. (*Erinnerungen an Ludwig Schnorr von Carolsfeld*, RWGS, VIII, p. 186) In that one sentence, too, Wagner concisely defined the performance style he had in mind for his works.

But the hopes he now entertained of establishing and disseminating this new style with Schnorr's aid were dashed in a matter of weeks by the news of the tenor's death of typhus on 21 July in Dresden. Wagner and Bülow arrived there to find the city en fête to receive singers pouring in from all over Germany for a festival. 'Yes,' he said to himself, 'but the *one* singer has left us.'

Back in Munich he went for a walk with Schuré in the Englischer Garten, and they sat down beside one of the streams running through the park. 'Everyone has his own daemon,' he began, as his eyes followed the swift flow of the water, 'and mine is a terrible monster. When he rages round me the air is filled with disaster. The only time I crossed the open sea I was shipwrecked; and if I went to America the Atlantic would certainly whip up a hurricane for my benefit. The world has treated me in exactly the same way, and strangely enough, I keep going back to it. But you could say that the fate that cannot do me down lays its hands on my supporters. No sooner has a man dedicated himself to me unreservedly than I can be sure that destiny has marked him for its own. Today we have lost not just *a* singer, but *the* singer, and now we shall have to build with bricks the house that we had hoped to build in granite.' Suddenly he stood up. 'Let's go! If we are to wage war against fate, we must look not backwards, but forwards!'

The teaching staff at the Munich Conservatory had been given notice for 31 July, but there was no date in prospect for the opening of Wagner's school of music. His plan had been considered by a committee, which finally rejected it on the grounds of expense and made alternative proposals of its own to the king. 'Has the human brain ever hatched a greater piece of nonsense than this?' Ludwig stormed. 'No, this will not do, we must follow a different path to salvation.' But in spite of such emotional outbursts, neither the school of music nor the festival theatre moved a step nearer realization.

Wagner saw very plainly that his opponents hoped to wear out his patience. His suspicion that Pfistermeister was playing a key role in this was not without foundation. Without communicating his suspicions to Ludwig in so many words, he felt obliged to advise the king to limit his cabinet secretary's activities 'to the natural sphere of his original appointment'. He wished that Ludwig would appoint a loyal nobleman of his court to see that the royal directives in artistic matters were not thwarted by self-seeking interests. He confessed in a later letter to his embarrassment at seeming to meddle in administrative matters, but before dropping the subject he had to tell the king what the situation looked like from his point of view. Apart from the school of music and the theatre, he was greatly troubled in his conscience by the distress of the chorus and orchestra; it was all the more difficult for him to close his eyes to their grievances because of his own apparently easy position – though, he hinted, he was going to have to ask for greater independence in his own financial arrangements. (30 July)

The request took the form of a report sent to the king at the beginning of August, in which he suggested that he should be allowed the usufruct for life from a capital of 200,000 florins. Of this sum, 40,000 florins should be assigned to him to manage himself, while the remainder should be administered by the Cabinet Treasury to yield 5 per cent interest per annum, to be paid him in quarterly instalments of 2000 florins. This arrangement would cancel all existing payments already being made to him. (KLRW, I, pp. 146ff.)

Wagner was driven to make this request by the uncertainty of his position. Everything he received from the king, liberal though it was, was bounty, and even the contracted fee for the *Ring* depended on the condition that it would be finished within three years, which he already realized was not going to be possible. Though he was sure he could count on Ludwig's generosity, experience was teaching him that he had no way of knowing what decisions the cabinet might not force upon the king, even against his will.

The intransigence with which this request was discussed by the king and his cabinet can be judged by the fact that their decision was delayed until 19 October. The correspondence on the matter was carried on between Cosima on the one hand and Pfistermeister or the Deputy Secretary, Lutz, on the other, until Wagner himself intervened on 17 October with a letter to Lutz in which he stated roundly that the opposition to his request could not possibly stem from the king, as he had been officially informed. Once that had been delivered Cosima was able to write triumphantly, on 23 October: 'Jusqu'ici Lutz n'a pas répondu. La somme est donnée, le roi n'a pas écrit!!!' (KLRW, IV, p. 94)

In the event Wagner's request was granted only in part. The cabinet refused to make available the capital of 160,000 florins, though they agreed to increase the annual ex gratia payment to 8000 florins; this meant that his income would be what it would have been, but without the same independence. On the other hand he was awarded the lump sum of 40,000 florins and invited to collect it from the Cabinet Treasury.

Since Wagner was not well, as Cosima wrote to tell the king later, she offered to go to collect it herself, with her eldest daughter, in the expectation of being given nothing more onerous than a few large notes. Imagine her astonishment on being told that she could have only silver coins. Since there were no members of the public to witness the event she placed her trust in the clerks' discretion where a lady was concerned, and conveyed the bags of money to Wagner in two hansom cabs. 'He was utterly horrified by the affair, thanked me and came close to scolding me; then he praised my courage and said he was burdened by the thought that it was my friendship for him that had placed me in such a position.' (KLRW, I, pp. lxx f.)[8] The transport of the money went unobserved by passers-by, but the treasury officials made sure that it was adequately publicized later.

Wagner's personal doubts and concerns were the cause of greater anguish to him at this time than that kind of hostility. We must go back to the beginning of August 1865. To restore his health, undermined by the death of Schnorr and even more by his struggle to be united with Cosima, the king placed his hunting lodge on the Hochkopf above the Walchensee at Wagner's disposal: 'Get better in the bracing mountain air!' (29 July) 'And now, in spite of wind and weather, off to the mountains!' Wagner replied. 'My faithful servant [Franz] and my good old dog go with me. An old Indian epic, the *Râmâyana*, comes too: Siegfried in manifold forms shall breathe afresh on the mountain heights.' (8 August) (He intended to work on the score of the second act.)

Cosima, who left for Pest with Hans on the same day, to hear Liszt conduct *St Elisabeth,* had given Wagner a diary, known as the Brown Book on account of its binding. He entered in it everything that was on his mind during their separation.[9]

> *Hochkopf, 10 August 1865.* Late yesterday evening, as we toiled up the path, I looked longingly – dead tired – towards the summit, in the hope of seeing our goal at last: my eye was met above the rim of the mountain by the first shining star: without bothering much about whether it was in the right direction or not, I took it for the evening star and greeted it aloud – 'Cosima'. That gave me courage . . .
>
> Marvellous morning, the most beautiful weather. A ramble all round the mountain top. All my expectations exceeded: quite incomparable. My sure refuge for the future has been found. Over there is a daybed, and I can already see you lying on it. – Many thanks for your message! Of course, of course! – I love you with my last loving. – And I hope for better health too. Forgetting and remembering!

The view into the depths below inspired him to write a sequence of verses:

Am Abgrund steh' ich; Grausen hemmt die Schritte,
der mich geführt, verloren ist der Pfad . . .

('I stand at the abyss; horror slows my steps, the path that led me here
is lost.')

But everything that he experienced came to have a symbolic meaning for him:

Was mich dem steilen Gipfel zugetrieben,
hält jetzt gebannt mich an des Abgrunds Rand:
verlassen mußt' ich, die zurück mir blieben,
dem Druck entglitt wohl manche Freundeshand;
wo einst ich mich gesehnt nach letztem Lieben,
der Nebel deckt mir manches Heimatland.
Und darf ich zögernd nicht mehr rückwärts schauen,
wie späht' ich in den Abgrund nun mit Grauen?

('What drove me to the sheer summit now holds me spellbound on
the brink of the abyss: I have had to leave those who remained behind
me, full many a friend's hand has slipped from my grasp; where once
I yearned to find a last love, more than one homeland is hid from me
in mist. And if I may no longer hesitate and look back, how is it that I
now look into the abyss with dread?')

The summer heat gave way to cool, rainy weather.

> *13 August.* Ill and wretched. A very bad cold: high
> temperature. Lonely here . . . I thought I would at least
> write something in the book: complaining to you ought
> to help me. We'll see! I hope it will . . .
> *14 August.* Oh, my dearest woman! The world is
> appalling! I would choose to read Hugo's abominations[10]
> when I've got a temperature: trust me to do something
> clever like that . . . Immense talent! I had to shout that
> aloud several times. But why go on about these horrible
> things all the time, right up to old age, like Hugo? They
> should be left to the police, the chamber of deputies,
> boards and councils and so on. Plain statistical reports
> can say it all better, anyway. Surely a poet is nothing if
> not someone who knows all that without ever having
> made a study of it and, just because it is so obvious and
> easy to understand, doesn't waste any more words on it
> but concentrates on finding and preserving the ways of

redemption from the evil. It's true! there are some
sublime passages even then: e.g. the erstwhile Jean
Valjean's internal struggles before giving himself up are
masterly. Oh, what ghastly stuff! What a beautiful
world! . . .

*15 August.* Was so worn out that I had to leave the two
letters from you that both arrived together today lying
there – opened – but unread for several hours: I saw at
first glance that I wouldn't be able to bear them . . . In
the end, though, I read them. And now – I am
speechless! I stare blankly in front of me and I think I
shall give up speech altogether again. What madness,
what madness!! And that idiot Hans, not to let you go
to Penzing,[11] and to show you the shops of Vienna
instead! Is it to be believed? Is it to be believed? And *he*
is now my only friend! – Oh, cloddish hearts! blind
eyes! Ah, but how beautiful, how beautiful you are, my
dear woman! – Yes, you are mine and only *you* have any
claim on *me*. Nobody else knows anything about me.

God in heaven, how long shall we have to go on
tormenting ourselves in this manner of existence? But –
what am I saying? didn't we find each other in it?

What else can I do but read a book again? –
*Râmâyana!*[12] Adieu!

*16 August.* Good morning, dearest woman! I feel better
again . . . The *Râmâyana* is a great poem and getting
more beautiful as I read! – Truly, just to get into the
right mood for something like this, one has to be able to
withdraw from all the trash of the present day . . . What
a world it is, and how it is constructed and realized! It's
an astounding work of art . . . everything is alive,
resounding and moving round me . . .

Râma is godlike!! Everything seems grander and more
spacious, simply from having to do with such people! –
A magnificent drama, unlike any other, takes shape
before me. But who could write it? . . .

*17 August.* Good morning! Slept very well. – Today at
last I shall get down to the score of *Siegfried* again.
Perhaps I shall have a letter too? . . .

There is a letter! – –

That was a sad letter! a real letter of separation . . .
To make up for it I worked hard at *Siegfried*: the spell
has been lifted! – Good night, dearest woman!

His friendly relations with Mathilde Maier had by no means been
severed after her rejection of his plea to come and keep house for
him and his talk of the possibility of marriage after Minna's death.
(22 June 1864; see above) He did not omit, however, to give her
some hint of the change that had since arisen in his situation: 'Your
coming to me on the only conditions that are possible now . . .
would be a source of nameless, now quite unbearable anguish for
my heart; no silence or concealment on your part, however tender
or loving, could shield me from it.' (19 July 1864)

Cosima evidently made his continuing correspondence with
Mathilde the cause of understandable, though unjustified,
reproaches in the 'letter of separation' mentioned above (cf.
Bergfeld ed., *Das Braune Buch*, pp. 37ff.). The following entry is one
that Eva Chamberlain pasted over:

18 *August*. Good morning, you wicked child! What a
nasty letter that was you wrote me yesterday! Just how
horrid it is, is still sinking in. Really what you say in it
is that you were wrong to love me so much, and on the
other hand to treat your father so badly, when he's the
only person who loves you . . . And now unlucky M.
M. must bear the brunt: my God, the plans I have for
her – no! what haven't I already been up to with her –
what endearments I lavish on her! and so on – That's all
very nicely put, and looks exactly as if you wanted to
make a 'break' with me. Just keep it up! – Well! Well! –

And all this, while you are afloat in joy and happiness,
and I am wasting away up here in the mist and clouds,
sick and sad.

The next three pages in the Brown Book had not been published
before 1975. Wagner writes about his future and his future work.
Bergfeld takes what he says as fantasies brought on by his illness,
but in my opinion it is a conscious flight into illusion:

I can and must live only in a kind of cloud. Since I am
solely an artist, the only kind of life I can lead is an
artificial one . . . Cosima must always be with me –

always: there's no other way . . . Given that, then, I
believe, I shall still achieve the full earnest of my works:
but my work is the only place where there must be any
earnest, everything else must be light-hearted and
joyous.
*19 August.* What useless babble all this is; as if you could
answer me! –

Strange! How shall I feel when I am sitting again,
entire and single-minded, at that miraculous loom. It is
the only thing that is right for me. The world that *I*
cannot shape I must just forget; that is the only possible
relationship I can have with it.

There is one really bad thing! The fact that the
imagination is filled in the end with the essential image
of the world, and that there's no longer much that can
be changed in it, nor anything new that can be added,
engenders a kind of disgust with existence.

No matter what thoughts I have, finally I turn away
from it with a kind of satiety, because I feel that I've
thought it all before. Everywhere I keep coming upon
ideas I've already had: the thrill of discovery has entirely
vanished.

He drew the following conclusion:

There remains nothing absorbing any more except – the
processes of form, the pure artistic joy of perfecting the
portrayal. It is my hope that I shall find great satisfaction
in that again.

But he had an important reservation:

All the same, it will be distracting to be forever casting
an imperceptible[13] sideways glance at the realism of the
portrayal to be expected from most performers.
*20 August.* Good morning, my soul! – Hearing nothing
more from you at all is dreadful. To put an end to
feeling so ill, too, I have decided to return to the
lowlands again tomorrow. – I am really ill. Nothing can
help me except – – God knows? Since what will help
may still not be said aloud. But – for the time being let
us call it – work!

. . . You can still draw my work out of my very soul. But, oh, give me peace as well! Stay with me, do not go away again. Tell poor Hans plainly that I cannot do without you any more. God in Heaven, if only you could simply be my wife in the eyes of the world!

*21 August.* Now a last good morning from the forest lodge! – It's grey. Everything is packed. Except not the book yet. – I'm coming closer to you. Tomorrow I shall already be able to send you a telegram. – There you have ten days from my life . . . Far away from you, I've been coming closer to you all the time! I feel sure of it!

Adieu, mountain-top forest! . . . 5 a.m.

*Munich, 22 August.* When I was crossing the Walchensee in the boat yesterday I saw something beautiful.

The shallows: how clear, how light everything on the bottom was; the water was just glass: lovely white sand bottom, every individual stone, there and there and here a plant, there a stem – everything distinct. Then it was deep: the water dark, dark, all clarity gone, all closed over; but instead suddenly the sky, the sun, the mountains – all bright and clear enough to touch in the mirror – – shallow souls, deep souls! I have seen to the bottom of many shallow souls: how few deep souls there have been who have mirrored the world for me! . . .

I found everything in order at home in the evening.

My clean, polished rooms make me laugh: – that will last, or at least it *can* be made to last! Lovely weather and everything else that gives me such swift and strong delight disappears so swiftly and leaves such long, dull days behind. Curious, how we bring ourselves – or our daemon brings us – to endure it.

The following day, 22 August, Wagner went to visit the children, who had remained behind in the Bülows' house. The baby Isolde had woken up at once and was about to start crying: 'then she laughed up at me instead . . . How much longer will you be away? I suspect a very, very long time.'

He went on to refer to a letter Cosima had sent him from Pest:

I didn't like the sound of those gypsies. Artificially
polished barbarians: not entire nature, not entire art.
Their music, half arranged, mutilated in a
barbaric-cum-dilettante way. Not everything that rouses
our enthusiasm, in our disgust with German
philistinism, is worth it. It's good enough to intoxicate
us, but we ought to be beyond intoxication. Your father
as much as I. Those Eljen, Rakoczy etc. are very nice –
but they lead nowhere, or only backwards, that's a
weakness: it's not that I don't feel the attraction, but I
steer clear of it . . .

Oh, I'm very different from all the rest! – Where can I
expect my joys to spring from?
24 August. I am more reluctant each time I turn to the
Brown Book. I feel as though I ought to be deprived
now even of being close to you. No letter for three
days. – I can understand why!! But I cannot and never
shall be able to understand these pious worldlings! God
alone knows how genuine they are! To me most of it is
alien and incomprehensible! Good morning!

The next day, 25 August, was King Ludwig's twentieth birthday.
After some lines celebrating it:

Kanonen dröhnt! Hallt laut und hell ihr Glocken!
Mich will dem Gram der frohe Tag entlocken! . . .

('Cannons roar! Ye bells ring loud and clear! The joyful day will rescue
me from grief!')

the following lines for Cosima were written sideways across the
page:

Vom fernen Ost, vom Land der Magyaren,
kam morgens mir ein Traumbild bang und wüst:
dem Liebchen ist groß' Freude widerfahren,
mein Weib ward dort viertausendmal gegrüßt.
'Mein Weib?' Du Tor! Frag' erst bei kund'gen Leuten,
was solcher Freudentraum Dir mag bedeuten!

('From the far east, from the land of the Magyars, a wild and fearful
vision came to me this morning: great joy has befallen my darling, four
thousand came to greet my wife. "My wife"? You fool! Just ask those
who know what such a dream of joy can mean to you!')

He wrote to Bülow on the same day. 'The 4000 Magyars would have been the last straw for me. Give Liszt my dearest and warmest regards! What he can do is beyond my power: – from Rome to Pest and then still to be relaxed and in good spirits – I cannot do that. Above all – not *now*! God knows what's wrong with me. I am a bull that has been stunned but hasn't died of it.'

While he was in this mood of recoiling from the world Wagner received a request from the king: 'Tell me something of your plans for "die Sieger" and "Parcival"! I am longing to hear about them!'

> *26 August.* How wonderful! – The king longs
> passionately to hear something about *Parzival*.

The very next day Wagner began to write the first detailed prose scenario, which fills twenty-eight closely written pages in the Brown Book. At the end he wrote '*30 August 1865.* There! That was help in the hour of need!!' It was in the same mood that he was to write the text and music of his 'work of farewell to the world' twelve years later, and this mood – even more than the work's subject – is what conveys the sense of withdrawal from the world.

But already on 31 August he was back with Tristan:

> 'Das Schiff – siehst Du's noch nicht?'
> As long as I was sitting over *Parzival*, my imagination
> was a wonderful help: – whenever the red curtain over
> the door moved, my heart trembled: – she is going to
> come through it! –
> Now the tension of my ideas has dispersed. –
> Reality is back, entire and unvarnished, to be
> mastered. Tomorrow she is going to Szegźard [the
> country house of Liszt's friend Baron Augusz] for four
> days, – then to Venice, wherever they take her. – And
> she doesn't understand me! . . .
> Dearest woman! I know that you are suffering in all
> this! But that you can't even imagine what my suffering
> is like!

The next page is one that Eva Chamberlain pasted over.

> *1 September.* No! It's only tomorrow that she's going to
> Szegzárd. – 'Father says we'll stay in Pest until
> Saturday.' 'Father says "I need a holiday".'[14] – And all

the time she's persuading herself that I meant to hurt her
feelings; I probably don't love her any more! Her father
was right in the end, – he told me a year ago – 'that's
how it will be – he will treat me despicably!' . . . And
there will be more letters from Rome.

Here Wagner was referring to Princess Wittgenstein, who was
using her influence with Liszt against Wagner and Cosima.

All this Catholic rubbish is repugnant to me in the
depths of my soul; whoever takes flight in that must
have a great deal to do penance for.

Wagner returned to *Parsifal*, and sketched two alternative versions of lines about the spear, then asked (2 September), as though
she could answer him, 'Which is the better, Cos?'

Oh, anything, anything is better than to be so
God-forsaken as I was yesterday! . . . Oh, if only a
magic word could be found to explain you completely
to your family!

After entries made on 3, 4 and 5 September, that for 9 September
is another that was pasted over and proves informative:

A shock: Semper is here! Unfortunately Franz told him
that I was not away. I am in such a state that Semper's
visit is very unwelcome. God, what do I care about a
temporary theatre, or a definitive festival theatre, what
do I care about all the architecture in the world! . . .
How I hate this theatre project, indeed – how childish
the king seems to insist so passionately on the plan.

In the next day's entry, Wagner quotes an old proverb, that
everything in life repeats itself. He speculates that in the end it will
turn into a 'life-art-form' [an art-form for the art of living], and goes
on to reflect on the incredible power of music to express this: canon
is a representation of the life of ordinary people, but then there is
fugue: the theme remains always the same, but the free counter-
points which accompany it make it appear in a perpetually new
light.

There is nothing richer or greater in life than the theme
of a beautiful fugue by Bach: unless perhaps a beautiful

countersubject: that then is the greatest triumph, and
when a double fugue displays both themes all the time
with equal clarity and significance, then it achieves the
most beautiful course life can take . . . We two live in a
beautiful Bachian double fugue like that. –

In this same vein of fantasy he essayed an evaluation of Liszt:

Your father's career strikes me as being in 'variation
form'. There is nothing there except the one theme,
repeated afresh over and over again, but slightly changed
each time, ornamented, decorated, refurbished, now the
virtuoso, now the diplomat, now bellicose, now
spiritual, always the artist, always endearing, always
himself . . . I have nothing against variation form, I
think Beethoven used it to the most wonderful creative
ends . . . I myself am simply at a loss with it: I can't
write so much as one variation on any theme!

On 11 September he read a report in the Leipzig *Illustrierte
Zeitung* on the jubilee of the Students' Association of the University
of Jena.

The three Nestors of those founder-members who are
still alive include a Pastor Riemann: his picture made a
deep, deep impression on me. I should like to make that
man's acquaintance . . . You must see Riemann's head.
That is *German* ideality . . .
   You can keep Rome – and Hungary! – that's all
galimatias!

Then he pondered the meaning of 'German'. It was to be the
subject of the 'diary' of 14–27 September 1865 that he wrote for
King Ludwig.[15] The king was so fired with enthusiasm that he had
copies of these impromptu notes distributed among his various
ministers 'for implementation' of the ideas contained in them,
as Wagner wrote to Constantin Frantz. 'I hardly need to describe
to you the almost farcical confusion this caused!' (19 March
1866)

The next part of the entry for 11 September was pasted over. It
refers to a letter of Cosima's that had just arrived, and demonstrates
the whole conflict of her emotions.

1. Wagner and his circle, Munich 1865
From left to right: Friedrich Uhl, Richard Pohl, H. von Rosti, August Roeckel, Auguste de Gasperini, Wagner and his dog Pohl, Hans von Bülow, Adolf Jensen, Carl Grille, Franz Müller, Felix Draeseke, Alexander Ritter, Leopold Damrosch, Heinrich Porges, Michael Moszonyi

2b. Hans Richter

2a. Heinrich Porges

3b. Elisabeth Förster-Nietzsche

3a. Friedrich Nietzsche

4a. *Dionysus among the Muses of Apollo* by Bonaventura Genelli

4b. Wagner's house Tribschen

5b. Liszt with his daughter Cosima in 1867

5a. Mathilde Maier

6. Autograph title-page of the *Siegfried Idyll*, 1870

7. Wagner and Cosima, Vienna 1872

8a. Wagner: sketch in red pencil by Franz von Lenbach, Munich 1880 (based on photographs of 1871)

8b. Judith Gautier

9b. Angelo Neumann

9a. Karl Tausig

10a. The Festspielhaus in Bayreuth: wood-engraving around 1880

10b. The Festspielhaus: a modern photograph

11b. Engelbert Humperdinck

11a. From left to right: Heinrich von Stein, Carl Friedrich Glasenapp and Hans von Wolzogen

12. Family photograph on the steps of Wahnfried, 1881
Front row, from left to right: Isolde and Daniela von Bülow, the dog Marke,
Eva and Siegfried Wagner
Back row, from left to right: Blandine von Bülow, Heinrich von Stein, Cosima,
Wagner, Paul Zhukovsky

13a. Wahnfried seen from the front

13b. Tea at Wahnfried, 1881
From left to right: Wagner, Cosima, Heinrich von Stein, Paul Zhukovsky, Daniela and Blandine von Bülow

14a. Titian's *Assumption of the Virgin* (detail)

14b. The Grail scene in *Parsifal*: Zhukovsky's sketch of 1882

15b. Hermann Levi

15a. Paul Zhukovsky

16b. Zhukovsky's pencil sketch of Wagner, Venice 1883: the inscription in Cosima's handwriting reads 'R. lesend 12. Febr. 1883'

16a. Arthur, Count Gobineau

Your letter, my dear! Pure madness again! Madness and
no end to it! Surrounded by unalloyed bliss, love,
adoration, nature, music, enthusiasm – and full of terrors
and fears, shrieking and swooning! – There is nothing
more that I can say about it. If it must be, then let it be:
I submit to it. Perhaps it is necessary to you.

Then follows the passage already quoted, about her return from the
Karlsruhe festival the year before:

God knows what you'll be like when you return. I
know how you were a year ago, when your father
brought you back here! It was dreadful: you sleepless,
restless, weak, frail, miserable, ravaged! There's nothing
to which I can compare the pain I felt . . . It will be the
same again now . . .
     If you go off adventuring again, I shall take charge of
the child, and you . . .

The entry breaks off here, because the next two pages – four sides –
were cut out by Eva Chamberlain.[16]
     The Bülows returned from Budapest on 13 September. 'She has
survived it bravely,' Wagner wrote to Mathilde Maier, 'and completely astonished me. He was ill when they arrived, and still is.
They are dining with me tomorrow again for the first time.' (22
September) Cosima was now able to resume the running of
Wagner's household, as well as her own. Above all, they now
embarked together on a literary project that was to occupy them for
years to come.
     'You would cause me inexpressible happiness, if you were to give
me a detailed account of your intellectual and spiritual development
and of the external events of your life as well,' the king had written
to him on 28 May. 'May I nurture the hope of seeing this wish of
mine fulfilled one day?' When he asked again on 19 July, Wagner
replied: 'What do you think I was doing when your letter of
yesterday reached me? To save you guessing, I will tell you: – I was
dictating my biography! Friend Cosima does not cease reminding
me of our king's wish. So now the opportune hours of the day are
occupied with my faithfully telling my tale to our friend, while she
diligently writes it down.'
     The growth of the autobiography, virtually under the king's

eyes, can be traced in their correspondence. Thanking Wagner for the first part, Ludwig wrote: 'Ah, continue with it, I beg of you.' Even during the unhappy time of the Prusso-Bavarian war he looked forward longingly to the arrival of each new instalment, and continued to do so through the years until a telegram from Siena, dated 24 August 1880, announced that Wagner had sent off the last part, in the hope that it would reach the king in time for his thirty-fifth birthday.

He amazed Cosima by the fluency with which he dictated, as if he were reading from a book, making it difficult for her to keep up, skilled as she was. He was helped by the notes he had started to make for his 'future biography' at the age of twenty-two in Magdeburg, in the Red Pocket Book: set down while his impressions were fresh, they kept his recollection clear.

Meanwhile Cosima had completed a work of her own: she had copied in her own hand a large number of Wagner's earlier shorter writings and presented this 'Wagner Book' to the king on 25 October. 'I would not wish anyone but Your Majesty to see this book. One must have known Wagner entirely and seen into his inmost depths to be able to mount these steps of his development retrospectively with joyful understanding.' 'How absorbing and profoundly moving every word is , that comes from the pen of our great friend,' the king replied, and he enclosed a ring as a small token of his gratitude. 'May the blue of the sapphire . . . be to you a symbol of firm faith and unshakable confidence.' (KLRW, I, pp. lxxi f.)

Seeing that they were on the point of losing the game, Wagner's opponents thrust the king's grandfather on to the field as a last resort. Returning from a trip to Switzerland, the young Ludwig found a letter from ex-King Ludwig I waiting for him, 'full of coarse reprimands'. His response was to invite Wagner to spend a week with him at Hohenschwangau. (To Julius Fröbel, 28 November; to Mathilde Maier, 30 November) The Indian-summer weather, the freedom from constraint between himself and the king, the beauty of the little castle's setting among lakes, woods and mountains all made the visit an unforgettable experience for him. But already on the second day he wrote presciently in the Brown Book: 'My Cosima! Who takes thought today, that the daemon will have to be paid for this beauty!'

In conversation with the king he raised the subject of his relationship with the cabinet, which had become untenable. He showed him a document which reflected badly on Pfistermeister. An old Viennese friend, Julius Fröbel, whom Wagner had recommended as editor of a journal to publicize the purpose and outlook of the new school of music, had received a letter dated 4 October 1865 from Police Assessor Pfister, a confidant and colleague of Pfistermeister, urging him in the strongest terms not to accept the appointment, since Wagner's stay in Munich, in spite of everything, would be only temporary and his fall would bring down all his 'creatures'. (KLRW, I, p. 212)

'There is only one person, namely your king, to whom you should show this letter,' Fröbel wrote when he forwarded this document to Wagner. (KLRW, IV, p. 102) The king read this unambiguous evidence of an intrigue with anger, but, as usual, drew no conclusions from it and soon appeared to have forgotten about it.

In order to understand the process leading to Wagner's prophesied fall, we must go back to the events of the preceding February. He received an offer of help in that crisis from an unexpected quarter. Prince Maximilian of Thurn und Taxis had conceived an ambitious plan to found a kingdom for his eldest son, consisting of Rhineland–Westphalia and half of Belgium. Feelers had been put out to Berlin and Munich, to ensure the non-intervention of Prussia in the north and Bavaria in the south. The plan was backed by ultramontane circles, as it contributed to their strategy of manoeuvring the Prussians out of western Germany. In order to render the parliaments of the German Federation tractable, a banking enterprise was to be founded, which would gain control of German agriculture and so control elections. This part of the plan was in fact realized, with the foundation of the notorious Langrand–Dumonceau Bank in Antwerp, the liquidation of which is believed to have cost the Taxis family millions.

In Bavaria those party to the plan wanted above all to use Wagner. On 12 February he received a visit from his old acquaintance Councillor Klindworth of Brussels and Baron von Gruben from Regensburg, the Thurn und Taxis estate manager. At table the two hinted to Wagner that the prince had authorized them to cut him in on a banking venture.

'I played the innocent,' Wagner recounts. But the two agents came again, this time accompanied by the lovely Agnes Street-

Klindworth. This time the three put their cards on the table: Wagner was to use his influence with the king to have Pfistermeister replaced by Klindworth; in return he – Wagner – would be given capital to finance his plans in the form of bonus shares in the new bank.

'Once more I failed to understand,' Wagner says. 'The Jesuits wanted to give me two festival theatres, two music schools, and as many villas and securities as I wanted,' he told Mathilde Maier, 'all I had to do was show myself compliant.' And to August Röckel he wrote: 'The Jesuits . . . made my path to everything I could desire so smooth that really I betrayed my artistic ideal by not showing myself at all compliant.' (KLRW, IV, pp. 116f.)[17]

Even if he did not seize the opportunity of benefiting directly from the intrigue, it nevertheless brought him, though only temporarily, a certain relief in his own difficulties, without his seeking it. The king's adjutant Prince Paul of Thurn und Taxis, a younger son of Prince Maximilian, got wind of the plot and warned Pfistermeister he was threatened, as Pfistermeister noted in his diary on 19 February. In the circumstances he thought it prudent to adopt a more moderate attitude to Wagner. He not only now shook the hand of friendship Wagner offered him but also took the initiative in showing him 'favour and flattery', arranging for the purchase of the house in Briennerstrasse from the Civil List, presenting Wagner with the possibility of 'unlimited credit', and above all rendering him every assistance in the preparation of the performance of *Tristan*. 'Pfistermeister is clinging passionately to Wagner, who has kept his footing but has been unfortunately under severe attack,' Bülow wrote to Carl Bechstein on 4 May.[18]

But as Pfistermeister saw his own danger recede, so his good will was replaced by a hostility of which Wagner remained unaware for a time.

Another temptation to busy himself with politics came to Wagner from a strange quarter. We read in the Annals for 22 February: 'Frau Dangl; "the care of Bavaria".' Fröbel's diary contains the explanation: Wagner had told him of a curious incident with a mysterious old woman, with a humble Munich background, who came to his house one evening and said she had to talk to him about the young king and his destiny. The king was destined for great things, she said, it was written in the stars. 'Do you believe in the stars?' she asked, in a loud, solemn voice. 'I want tranquillity for my king and you, Herr Wagner, must protect him.' Even repeating it to Fröbel, Wagner had become extremely excited again. (SRLW, II, p. 217)

Just how greatly he was stirred by this appeal to a belief in the stars that he in fact held is demonstrated by what he wrote the very next day to Mathilde Maier: the fate of this young man was placed in his, *his* hands. To leave him to be the prey of intrigues was a treason for which he had no excuse. An almost miraculous experience had revealed to him his duty to the king. 'Now I ask myself: Why this cup to me? I, who expected to find only rest, rest, obligation to myself alone? I, now holding in my hand the fate of a people, of a glorious, uniquely gifted king?' (23 February) Three days later he wrote to Eliza Wille in almost exactly the same terms: he had to shudder at the idea of thinking only of his own peace and quiet while abandoning the king to the mercy of his entourage. 'I feel dread in the depths of my soul, and I ask my daemon: why this cup to me?' (26 February)

In spite of these feelings he still tried to restrain himself, but when he had to fight the cabinet for the sake of his artistic goals he was drawn unwillingly ever deeper into politics. ' "New age", "new principle" mean – "new men",' he declared to Ludwig. 'They will be found just at soon as the "old men" have been driven out.' (26 November) With alarm his friends watched him assuming the Schillerian role of a Marquis Posa, attempting to influence the policies of Ludwig's Philip II.

More than ever Pfistermeister and his colleagues felt their position threatened. 'Now – in the twelfth hour – Lutz had to ask me in plain language at Hohenschwangau to lend my support to their precisely delineated reactionary plans, "for the love of the king, the enhancement of whose authority is at stake",' Wagner wrote to Röckel. 'How easy it would have been for me to say "yes, yes – of course!" for the sake of peace and my own advantage!' And he went on presciently: 'And I am afraid that if they do not get the upper hand over him . . . they will kill him!' (16 December, KLRW, IV, pp. 116ff.)

Wagner later revealed the cabinet's 'reactionary plans' in a letter to Dr Schanzenbach, the confidant of Prince Chlodwig Hohenlohe. During his stay at Hohenschwangau in November 1865, the deputy Cabinet Secretary, Lutz, had made him privy to the trend of cabinet thinking, with the unconcealed intention of winning his co-operation: namely, that negotiations were afoot to come to an agreement with Bismarck, which would enable them to restore the Bavarian constitution to what it had been before 1848. 'Since this would mean the restoration of full monarchical powers, as the king's particular friend I would surely – so Herr Lutz surmised – go along with the government of the day. All I said to this was that these confidences were completely useless, as I had nothing to do with politics and in particular knew nothing whatever about the interests of the kingdom of Bavaria.' (17 January 1867) Newman is right when he comments that the politicians were only trying to trick Wagner, so as to bring him down later: his downfall had long been decided upon. (NLRW, III, p. 486)

'Now they've finally set the dogs on me,' Wagner wrote to Mathilde Maier, 'I've grown tired of it and have denounced the brutes fairly publicly.' (17 December) On the face of it the cause was remote. A democratic newspaper in Nuremberg had criticized the institution of a Cabinet Secretariat in Bavaria as 'thoroughly uncon-stitutional', to which the Munich *Volksbote* had responded on 26 November with a sharp attack on Wagner: 'Pfistermeister and Hofmann . . . are to be removed, so that certain desires anent the plundering of the royal treasury can obtain easy satisfaction.'[19]

The article, inspired by the Cabinet Secretariat, was quite obvi-ously calculated to draw Wagner out of his covert. He stepped into the trap, with an anonymous open letter that appeared in the *Neueste Nachrichten* on 29 November, and whose authorship was easy enough to guess. It concluded: 'For there is one thing of which you may be sure: it is not a matter of some principle or another, of some partisan policy to which Wagner is opposed, it is simply a matter of the *shabbiest personal interests,* and these can moreover be traced back to an uncommonly small number of individuals; I dare to assure you that the removal of two or three persons, who do not enjoy the least respect among the people of Bavaria, would rid the king and the people of Bavaria at one stroke of these tiresome disturbances.' (KLRW, IV, pp. 107ff).

At last the cabinet had the lever to topple Wagner that they had so long sought. The first to make use of it was the minister of state, Ludwig von der Pfordten, who levelled an imposing charge against Wagner.

'Your Majesty stands at a fateful crossroads and has to choose between the love and respect of your loyal subjects and the friendship of Richard Wagner. This man . . . is despised by every class of the people . . . despised . . . for his ingratitude and betrayal of patrons and friends, for his arrogant and dissolute self-indulgence and squandering, for the shameless way he exploits the undeserved favour he has received from Your Majesty.' (FHKF, p. 143)

How painfully this letter touched the king, and how powerless it was to alter his trust, is demonstrated by his letter to Wagner, quoting Schiller, two days later: 'Oh, my beloved friend, "great was the agony of these last days",' and concluding: 'Take comfort, your friend will never desert you.' (3 December) He returned to Munich and was besieged by visitors on the morning of 6 December: the cabinet threatened to resign if Wagner was not sent away, the Queen Mother and the Bishop of Munich–Freising supported the demand, his great-uncle Prince Karl spoke of the threat of a revolution, which the military would join. The young king was not strong enough to withstand this concerted onslaught. 'His imagination ran away with him,' Wagner told Röckel, 'he saw me as the victim of a popular uprising, wanted to save me and asked me to leave Bavaria for a few months.' (KLRW, IV, pp. 112f.)

It gave the deputy Cabinet Secretary Lutz a peculiar satisfaction to convey this message personally to Wagner in the afternoon of 6 December. The king confirmed it the next day in a brief note: 'It is not for ever, of course. Until death, your faithful Ludwig.'

'I am sure that you, too, do not deceive yourself as to the length of my absence,' replied Wagner, who had made up his mind never to return. 'My child! it was no longer endurable,' he confessed to Mathilde Maier. 'One day, riding four-in-hand with a king, the next, torn to pieces by the priests – and trying to find peace to do some work in between. It was madness!' (17 December)

The most astonishing thing about this whole astonishing episode is that in the midst of all the events that have filled the pages of this chapter, Wagner found the spirits to orchestrate his heroic fairy tale, the second act of *Siegfried*. Unlike his other creative periods he referred only rarely and fleetingly to this occupation at the time, by word of mouth or in letters: for instance, when he and the king used 'Mime' and 'Fafner' as nicknames for Pfistermeister and the treasury minister Hofmann.

In spite of his emotional turmoil and all that weighed on his mind, Cosima told the king on 2 December, he was at that moment in the act of writing the jubilant orchestral passage that ends the act, with the bird first teasing Siegfried and then leading him off:

> So wird mir den Weg gewiesen:
> wohin du flatterst
> folg' ich dem Flug!

And the instruments – flutes, oboes, clarinets, cor anglais, trumpets, violins – play tag with each other, chasing the Woodbird's motive up and down imitatively, with the effect that earned Richard Strauss's praise, the *single* 'ting' of the triangle falling on the strings' pizzicato like a ray of sunshine through the leaves.

The end of the first draft of the score is dated '2 December 1865 (still on board the ship)'. 'The ship' was what they called the house in Briennerstrasse, because it 'was always swaying', as Cosima told her daughter Daniela: 'Uncle Richard can tell you about it, we were on the ship together.'

Wagner asked the king for a few days to put his affairs in order. Porges and Cornelius went down to the station to see him off at five in the morning of 10 December. 'At last the carriage arrived,' Peter recorded in his diary. 'Wagner looked like a ghost; pale, distraught, his long lank hair looking quite grey. We accompanied him to the train . . . Cosima had broken down completely. When his carriage disappeared beyond the pillars, it was like the fading of a vision.'

# 26

*Die Meistersinger*

'Lake Constance again,' Wagner noted in the Annals for 10 December 1865. He went on, via Berne and Vevey, to Geneva, where he found a temporary haven nearby in the Campagne aux Artichauts. It was a large villa, furnished in a 'mesquin' fashion, just for appearances, he told Cosima, 'still – it was a port in the storm: I am undisturbed here, as if I had left the world . . . The view is wonderful, Mont Blanc right in front of me, when I look out from my seat at the piano.' (5 January 1866) By 10 January he was ready to resume the composition sketch of *Die Meistersinger* at the point where it had been interrupted at Penzing two years previously, at Beckmesser's words, as he holds out his slate covered with chalk marks, 'Seid Ihr nun fertig?'

The fact that he did not go on with *Siegfried* at this date shows that the belief that he would see the *Ring* performed, revived by the call to Munich, had once again deserted him. Much as the king and Cosima hoped he would return, he was determined never to go back to Munich. On 1 January he asked a French friend, Monsieur S. (probably Schuré), to commission an agent to find a house in the country for him to rent for five or six years, somewhere in the south of France between Avignon, Arles and Perpignan. His main concern was to settle somewhere away from the world and to sever all the ties that still linked him to his dreadful past. 'C'est le seul moyen pour moi de sauver mes oeuvres conçues, qui seront perdues, si je passe encore une année dans des convulsions du genre de mon ordinaire.' (TWLF, pp. 267f.) His income appeared to be assured, even though Lutz, informing him of this, made the following reservation: 'unless some completely unforeseen circumstance should compel His Majesty the King to act other than His

Allhighness would wish to act when following the dictates of His Allhighness's heart and enthusiasm for art'. (KLRW, IV, pp. 113ff.)

Wagner's most difficult task was breaking the news of his decision to the king. 'I cannot yet bring myself to write to Parzival,' he told Cosima. 'Every day what I have to tell him seems to take on a different form. I am becoming increasingly unsure of myself on this point.' Ludwig poured out his heart to her in a profoundly moving letter: 'Oh, I had hoped, hoped, and that enabled me to suppress my pain; but now the enemy star is in the ascendant, it rends me violently from my friend, hurls me towards a future full of torments, robs me of my hope, my life, my all!' (2 January 1866)

It was a genuinely tragic situation: the young king believing that even in his friend's best interests no other course of action was open to him; and Wagner seeing that the king had been the victim of a conspiracy. At last, on 8 January, he found the courage to write a long and affectionate letter, which could leave Ludwig in no doubt of the irrevocability of his decision: 'Two questions on which our fate depends, my king.' Did Ludwig still believe that his subjects had been stirred by their relationship to an anger that could be appeased only by Wagner's departure? In that case he must keep Wagner at a distance from himself for ever. But if he saw now that he had been shamefully deceived and lied to – what should be the offender's punishment? If Pfistermeister and Pfordten were not dismissed, then, to spare the king and himself further humiliations, Wagner had no alternative but voluntary self-banishment.

He would submit to the decree of fate, Ludwig replied, if he could be sure that this was the only way for Wagner to find happiness and peace of mind. For, as he added in a second letter, the dismissal of those persons was at present out of the question. (15 and 28 January)

The king was the only person to whom the political background to the plot was not becoming daily more obvious. The *Neue Freie Presse* of Vienna declared openly that Wagner had been the victim of a reactionary palace revolution. It was a fact that the liberals had pinned their hopes on his opposition to the unconstitutional Cabinet Secretariat, but their behaviour after his fall aroused his contempt. 'Look at those sheep and foxes washing their hands of anything to do with me, I'm nothing to them but that voluptuous musician!' (To Röckel, 16 December 1865)

For his part he no longer hesitated to give the king political advice. 'I wish you suitable, genuinely valuable guidance in the serious career you must now follow,' he wrote at the end of his letter of 8 January. He implored him to read without delay two books by Constantin Frantz, *Thirty-three Propositions concerning the German Federation* and *The Restoration of Germany*. 'His is the most competent, truly statesmanlike brain that I have yet encountered among Germans. The second and larger book, in particular, expounds what I, too, have felt to be the right, truly German policy; the author has written to me that my harmonies revealed the future of Germany to him.'

Frantz was a political publicist who did not owe his reputation to his pen alone, and whom Bismarck, on coming to office in 1862, had tried in vain to win for his party. He first approached Wagner in November 1865. On his return from Hohenschwangau a letter was waiting for him, in which he made the discovery of a new person, Wagner had told the king. He was going to find out who Constantin Frantz was. A few days later: 'Frau Cosima knew more about him: she describes him as one of the "famous unknown". He is supposed to be significant, profound and completely unflawed.' He was to exercise a formative influence on Wagner's political views similar to Schopenhauer's on his philosophy.

A fire in one of the rooms at Les Artichauts, necessitating redecoration, lent urgency to Wagner's decision to find somewhere to live in southern France. Then a telegram from Cosima arrived on 20 January, asking him to wait just a few days, and when he replied refusing, a second telegram followed: 'Wanted to travel to you tomorrow . . . May I still come?' 'Will my friend please not disturb my resolve,' he replied; 'it must be!' His fears of an attempt to make him change his mind were not unjustified. The same evening he sent her a 'musical letter', direct from the stage he had reached in the *Meistersinger* composition sketch: after the bars from 'Singt dem Herrn Merker zum Verdruß' to 'Ade! Ihr Meister hienied!', with the stage direction 'The masters greatly scandalized: you know!', he scribbled a few lines: 'Nothing more about *Munich*: last hope of deliverance! Do not misunderstand me! You see! merely to write about it is really almost impossible for me!'

He reached Lyons on the evening of 22 January. In a dire mood he had stepped out on to the balcony, he confided to the Brown Book. 'Night, slender crescent moon. On the left Orion's sword with the point to the north-east. Slash, slash, my sword, that a royal heart may feel what true sorrows are!'

The next day he was in Toulon and the following in Hyères. 'Nothing in Hyères,' he telegraphed Cosima. But for the pure chance of not being able to find a suitable haven in the south of France, *Meistersinger* and the *Ring* would have been completed under the halcyon Mediterranean skies that Nietzsche, in his later alienation from Wagner, used to imply would greatly have benefited his outlook!

So he returned to Marseilles. Scarcely had he gone to sleep when he was woken with a telegram from Pusinelli, announcing Minna's sudden death. Since it had been forwarded from Geneva he could not even be sure what was meant by 'last night'. After all the shocks that had assailed him, he confessed to Pusinelli, he had sensed that the next bad news to reach him would either make him break down completely or rouse almost no sensation at all. 'So far, this morning, after a weary night, I can describe my condition in no other way than as one of complete numbness, in which I dully brood – brood – without knowing what, if anything, I have got to think about . . . I am sure that in your friendly solicitude you showed the body of my poor unhappy wife the same honour in my name that I would have shown her, if she had departed from life happily at the side of a husband to whom she gave happiness.'[1]

Minna's letters had become more and more of a torment to him, till in the end he told her on 5 October 1865 that he had not read her most recent one: 'Since the letter I had from you last spring, which depressed me so shamefully, I have decided not to embitter my heart and my memories unnecessarily.' (RWBC, p. 565) An undated draft of a letter, written in a shaking hand, perhaps her last sign of life, begins conciliatingly: 'You *are* good, at the bottom of your heart; I have always known it, it is only in your head, where there is so much that is beautiful and splendid, that sometimes there sprouts much that hurts those closest to you' – and then she goes on to rehearse all the old complaints and accusations. (RWBC, pp. 563ff.)

Just how out of sympathy she had remained with his development as an artist emerges with horrifying clarity from a letter to a friend, dated 14 October 1864: 'It looks as though he won't be writing anything very enjoyable in future, if he's already composed all he had in him and has to force it out now. It's a very poor outlook

– compared with what a Meyerbeer wrote, every one in his own style, he left whole crates whose contents the world still does not know.'[2]

In the will she made in 1865 she left no memento to her husband but bequeathed everything to her 'sister' Natalie. But it was destined that her last act should be one of reconciliation. When the Munich *Volksbote* sank to asserting that Wagner was content to let his wife starve and depend on the charity of strangers, she published a denial on 15 January, ten days before her death, declaring that she received sufficient support from her husband to live a decent life, free from care.[3]

'In great love she endured much sorrow and little joy at my side,' Wagner told a friend later, in Bayreuth, and Glasenapp's unfavourable depiction of her met with his disapproval.[4]

Now, in Marseilles, he took refuge from the recent turmoils in the world of the imagination. A book published by the French railway company had reminded him of the tale of the death of Roland. He drafted a short sketch of it in the Brown Book ending: 'The horn goes unheard – the traitor remains at the king's side – the hero perishes – only love redeems.' He was so filled with the immediacy of experience of the legend, that he wrote to tell the king about it the same day. 'What a sad and dreadful allegory,' Ludwig commented to Cosima.

Wagner got back to Geneva from his wasted journey on the evening of 29 January. 'I am too tired for everything and anything,' he wrote to Cosima. 'Perhaps this condition will be my deliverance. I have two months in front of me that I shall really be able to spend in the same place – here. What I can do for the good of my soul in those two months is the only thing that occupies me at the moment . . . I have rented this place for another two months. Nobody has the right to drive me away for another two months: – methinks life is at my feet, the knowledge is so reassuring.' (KLRW, I, p. 261)

What he could do for the good of his soul was work. And so he settled down to *Die Meistersinger* as if the two remaining months in Les Artichauts were a lifetime. Already in the sketch he worked out the first-act finale on fifteen staves in careful detail. When he received a letter from Cosima on 21 February, bringing him reassuring news that he had been greatly hoping for, he was able to tell her by telegram: 'That did the old shoemaker good. In return the act finale was finished today. Sachs.'

As so often before, his literary imagination was stimulated while he was composing. The thoughts he committed to the Brown Book on 7 February about the holiness of night-time are a fine example. He referred to the performance of the *Oresteia* in the Greek world, when its grim tale of bloodshed and vengeance was begun in broad daylight, only to finish in reconciliation as night fell, whereupon the tragedy was followed by the satyr play. 'The night induces a sense of holiness that sanctions comedy and light-heartedness as well . . . The world sheds its solemn burden in foolery.'[5]

He had been expecting Cosima on 3 March, but she delayed her journey for a few days for an important reason. The king had encouraged her to seek an interview with Pfordten, in order to gain his approval for Wagner's return. His response had been that either the matter was a private concern of the king's – in which case he had nothing to say – or it was an affair of state – in which case it was not proper for him to discuss it. 'Honourable and blinkered' was the impression he made on her: 'truly he thinks our friend is a menace to the state!' (KLRW, I, pp. 262f.)

She arrived at Les Artichauts with Daniela on 8 March, and he resumed dictating his autobiography to her the next day. But above all he devoted himself to orchestrating the first act of *Meistersinger*, which he finished on 23 March.

At this time, too, he wrote a long letter to Constantin Frantz (19 March), which is especially interesting for what he has to say about King Ludwig: he believed his abilities to be exceptional, even though the question of how his capacities as a ruler might develop was still open; a senseless education had succeeded in imbuing him with an insuperable reluctance to concern himself with affairs of state, and this unrealistic attitude made Wagner anxious lest he decline into weakness of character. Representations and reasoning with him would do no good at all, but on the other hand he, Wagner, was in a position to make the king 'lucid and clear-sighted' by means of his art.

All the same he recognized the limits to the influence a king could wield, and the need to seek out supporters among the educated people scattered throughout the nation, who would strive with him to further his artistic undertakings. He thought of writing an occasional series of open letters to Frantz, who he hoped would advise him on the moderate and discreet treatment of any personal topics. His experiences in Bavaria had convinced him that nothing could be accomplished without the concerted action of like minds against the 'so well-organized phalanx of the common sort'. 'My artistic ideal stands and falls with the weal of Germany.'

Cosima went back to Munich on 31 March. Before she left they searched in vain for a new 'Asyl', while making a round trip through Lausanne, Vevey, Berne, Interlaken and the Lake of Lucerne. She reported to the king that she had found their friend changed, restless and unquiet. He had been so pale, so gaunt, so depressed. As they were parting in Romanshorn he had said he supposed he would have to move into a hotel. 'But *Die Meistersinger?*' she had had time to exclaim. He had just smiled sadly as her steamer pulled away from the shore. (KLRW, IV, p. 140)

Without hesitation the king offered to lend him his hunting lodge in the Riss as temporary accommodation, even though it was in Bavaria. 'He must be saved, though it destroy me!' But the very next day, 5 April, Cosima had a telegram from Wagner, telling her he had taken a year's lease on a large villa on the Tribschen peninsula just outside Lucerne, which they had noticed when they were crossing the lake. A fortnight earlier the king's letter would have changed everything, everything, he wrote to her on 7 April, but now it was too late. 'And so: welcome, fate! Let Asyl be Tribschen!' (KLRW, IV, p. 141) Ludwig accepted this turn of events, probably with some relief, and also undertook to defray the expenses of the move and settling in. 'Let us allow him to go his way in peace,' he agreed with Cosima; 'he will surely find what is right for him.'

On 15 April Wagner moved into Tribschen. Two days later he wrote to Cosima:

> Today, Tuesday, glorious morning, market day. Boat after boat from Ury, Schwyz and Unterwalden going to Lucerne market: a delightful sight, quite unspeakably beautiful – especially against this background, on the lovely smooth surface of the lake, where every boat is lapped round by a radiating silver circle. A hard month of winter is not too great a price to pay for a morning like this. Now I can understand the choice I have made and the winter that lies in front of me: Walther has already sung about it, 'am stillen Herd zur Winterzeit, wenn Hof und Haus [sic] mir eingeschneit', and so I shall remember the spring morning, how I shall love the

winter here! Truth, the highest truth be our dogma! See, there is only one other person I can admit to this alliance! Only Parzival [King Ludwig]. And let him be our guardian angel. Once more, let no one disturb us here, let holy peace reign here. These are the last years of a difficult, tormented life, which shall now find their goal, their crown.

Nothing has moved me so greatly for a very long time as renewing my acquaintance with the legend of Melusine. Oh God – Melusine, departing, returning as a ghost in future ages. A fever made me tremble: melancholy and pity threatened to dissolve me into atoms. God! what poetry the human race has produced in its exploration of the fearful riddle of existence – and it's all useless, they play with their immense poems like silly children. What is there for me in this world?

I am sending you *Melusine*, read it, and give it to Parzival to read too.

This mystery of enchantment! By an evil chance Raymond kills his uncle in the forest at night – moonlight – wild flight; a wonderful voice calls to him: Melusine, in sore need of release from enchantment – woos him, brings him boundless happiness, is betrayed by him. On moonlit nights she tends the youngest children – then nothing more is known of her. Night – the elements. Guilt – magic: disbelief – doubt – the breaking of the spell. A long lament through the night – through the air. Moonlight! The birds are undaunted and sing merrily . . .

I have just finished reading *Melusine*, ah! ah God! My heart is breaking!

Have you ever heard starlings rattling and chattering? There are beautiful cows in the meadows all round. Day and night you can hear their bells ringing. That ringing is lovelier than any sound I know. The arbitrary alternation of the sounds, the beauty of the bells, the pride of their owners, possess an indescribable magic. I would give all the bells of Rome for them. (DMCW, I, pp. 279f.; KLRW, V, p. 150)

Cosima wrote to the king on 20 April: 'I take the liberty of sending you *Melusine*, as I was asked to do so.'

The prospect in Wagner's heart was less smiling than the view from his window. His faithful housekeeper Verena Weidmann saw how depressed he was. He was not well, he complained, he was going to settle who was to have his things after his death. '*May*: great distress; provision for my death,' he wrote in the Annals. One evening, Verena recounted, he stayed out unusually late, night fell and to her alarm the dog Russ came home on his own. Accompanied by the groom Jost, she set out towards the town with a lantern. They met Wagner along the road. 'Why, I thought no one cared about me any more; even Russ, who has always been faithful, abandoned me.' (GLRW, IV, p. 174)

What was upsetting him were his hopes and fears concerning Cosima. 'You are invited, with wife, children and servants . . . to come and stay with me in the villa and enjoy my humble hospitality,' he implored Bülow. 'If you fulfil my request you will be making the greatest, the only effective contribution to my well-being, to the well-being of my work – and of my future work.'

Cosima and her daughters arrived at Tribschen on 12 May; Hans was kept in Munich by his duties. In *The Women in Wagner's Life* Julius Kapp writes that, immediately after Cosima's departure, an ardent love letter from Wagner arrived for her, which Bülow opened in the belief that it might contain something urgent that he would have to telegraph after her. 'It revealed the whole bitter truth to him! The great lie of the last two years suddenly stared him implacably in the face.'

When Kapp's book was published in 1912 this story was generally accepted without question, until Ernest Newman poured cold water on it: why, he asked, would Wagner have sent Cosima a letter that would in all probability not arrive until after the time at which he knew she would be leaving home? And, above all, why would Bülow think he might need to telegraph Cosima the contents of a letter from Wagner, when she was already on her way to Tribschen?

Kapp based his story on a letter Peter Cornelius wrote from Munich to his fiancée on 13 May 1866.[6] 'We discussed serious matters at Bülow's yesterday. He had written a very firm letter to Perfall [the intendant of the Munich theatre], complaining bitterly about the bad performance of [Liszt's] *Elisabeth*, demanding four

new violinists for *Lohengrin*, etc. Bülow thought it depended on
these things whether he might not refuse his cooperation at the last
minute. Just after his family had left he had opened a letter, something he normally never does, but he thought he might have to
telegraph his wife immediately. The letter was such that he was
horrified by it. He is very much afraid that nothing will come of the
Conservatory or anything else, and perhaps he will take his leave
and go to Italy.'

No mention there of an ardent love letter, or any other kind of
letter, from *Wagner*, let alone any of Kapp's sensational deductions.
Both Newman and Cosima's biographer Max Millenkovich-
Morold held the view that it would hardly have needed an acciden-
tally opened letter at this late date to open Bülow's eyes. His friend
Cornelius told his fiancée six months earlier that a 'full-blown
affair' was going on between Wagner and Cosima, and wondered
whether Bülow might not have completely surrendered his wife to
Wagner 'in a highly romantic agreement'. 'Was Wagner's embrace
at the station [when leaving Munich] his thanks for it? The actual
marriage between Hans and Cosima has probably been only a
marriage of appearances for some time now. There's no other
explanation for Hans's behaviour.' (10 December 1865)

We know what the reasons were that stood in the way of a
solution to the marital deadlock: regard for public opinion and,
perhaps more important, for the king, who, as events were to
prove, had no comprehension or sympathy for such infringements;
Liszt's disapproval; the fact that the Bülow marriage had been
celebrated in the Catholic church; and finally the opposition of
Bülow himself, who wished to preserve appearances at least – and
who would have lost, as well as his wife, the friend to whom he
clung in spite of everything.

Elucidation of the mysterious letter may lie in quite a different
direction.

On 15 May Wagner had just started the composition sketch of the
second act of *Meistersinger* when a horrifying telegram (well over a
hundred words long!) arrived from the king, disclosing his intention, 'if it is my Dear Friend's wish and will', to renounce the throne
and come and live with him in Switzerland. 'I cannot endure any
longer to remain separate and *alone*.' (KLRW, II, pp. 34f.)

The growing threat of war between Prussia and Austria, in which
Bavaria could not escape involvement, had been worrying Ludwig

for some time. On this particular 15 May, as Pfistermeister told the king's doctor, he had been very agitated, and had spoken of abdicating on grounds of his mental health so as to be able to go and live in Switzerland. (KLRW, II, p. xv)

And suddenly light dawns: the letter to Cosima that Hans opened was *from the king*. He wanted to inform *her* of his intention to abdicate, as he did again two months later, after the Austro-Prussian war had run its unhappy course. Then, on 21 July, he wrote that he had not written directly to Wagner about his decision, once again, to abdicate, 'the shock might have been harmful to him; I ask you to convey to him the content of this letter in your own words.' (KLRW, II, p. 75)

Now we can understand why Bülow was 'horrified' by what he read in the letter he opened on 12 May, and why he feared that it was all up with the school of music and everything else, and that he would have to leave Munich. This letter had crossed with a letter Cosima sent to the king on 10 May, telling him that she would be leaving 'tomorrow morning'[7] with the children to spend some weeks in Lucerne. On receiving that, Ludwig sent her a telegram at Tribschen on 13 May. 'Now you, my friend, will be united with our dear friend, I am with the two dearest ones on earth in spirit. I too dream of future happiness and have every hope that the dream of blissful hours on the shores and waters of the Lake of Lucerne will be fulfilled.' The final sentence, 'I long for news soon', proves that the telegram must have been preceded by another missive to which the king had not yet received an answer: namely the letter opened by Hans. (KLRW, IV, p. 145)

The reference to a 'dream', which only Wagner and Cosima would have understood, even enables us to guess what was in the letter. 'I had a vivid dream about you today,' Ludwig had written to Wagner on 12 November 1865; 'we were talking together on the shore of the Lake of Lucerne, when we heard music on the approaching steamer, we had to part; the ship carried me far away.' Three months later he had a very similar dream, as he wrote to Cosima on 4 February. 'We were sailing on the Lake of Lucerne, our friend was telling me about his plans and talking about his works. It was an elevating dream.' 'The dream . . .' Cosima replied; 'sometimes I feel as though it must come true, but in what worlds?' (KLRW, I, p. 211)

'In what worlds?' On 15 May Ludwig made up his mind that the dream was going to come true here and now. He did not wait for the answer to his telegram of 13 May, but sent off the telegram informing Wagner of his decision to abdicate at 6.40 a.m. Pfistermeister's letter to the king's doctor tells us that he spent an hour and a half with the king that same morning persuading him that in view of the political situation he ought not to go away but stay and open parliament in person. (KLRW, II, pp. 35f.)

In his despair Ludwig sent Wagner a letter like a single, sustained 'cry of pain'. He implores his friend to come to him; he would easily find a suitable house close to Schloss Berg, where he himself was then living. 'You cannot ignore this entreaty; otherwise the strength of my ardent enthusiasm . . . will be shaken to its very foundation and "madness" will overcome me!' (KLRW, II, pp. 35f.)[8]

Wagner's reply was a psychological masterpiece, demonstrating to the full his sympathetic understanding of the king. He appealed to Ludwig's love for himself. '*Six months' patience*!! You must make this sacrifice – for my sake, who stand for ever on the brink of the abyss, tormented by worry, sensing that my future creativity, my very life, depend on these six months, if they allow me the peace to create, undisturbed; – for your own sake, who would fail in your high calling, if you did not steel yourself in these fateful six months for the whole of your life.' (15 May)

But the king's impatience to talk everything over with his friend was no longer to be controlled. On the morning of 22 May, after sending Wagner a birthday telegram, so as to pull the wool over his household's eyes, and listening as usual to the report from Cabinet Secretary Lutz, he rode, accompanied only by a groom, to the railway station at Biessenhofen, caught the express to Lindau, crossed Lake Constance on the steamer to Rorschach in Switzerland, and arrived at Tribschen during the afternoon, to Wagner's complete surprise. His journey did not go unnoticed in Munich for long, however, and in the very tense political climate of the time it aroused general anger. The blame was wrongly placed at Wagner's door, and a flood of abuse burst over him, Bülow and 'Madame Hans the carrier pigeon'.

On Wagner's advice the king opened parliament in person on 27 May, but he was conscious of the deputies' disapprobation. 'Parliament opened today,' he telegraphed to Tribschen, 'reception icecold! Press disgraceful!'

As the stormclouds of war thickened Wagner drew up a 'Political Programme' early in June, though it is not known whether it was actually printed at that time. It reflects Constantin Frantz's conception of a Germany united as a 'triad' or 'trinomium', in which the central states should stand together under the leadership of Bavaria, between the two giants, Prussia and Austria. War between the two latter automatically meant that both would leave the German Federation, and it was incumbent on the remaining member states to form their own independent policy without delay. The King of Bavaria, as head of the oldest state, should summon the other princes to Nuremberg, with the exception of the King of Prussia and the emperor. This reduced Federation, backed by their own armed forces, should then negotiate with Austria and Prussia and prescribe to them the terms for a new federation.

Though the programme rested on a false estimate of the relative military strengths of the different states, it nevertheless shows that what Wagner had in mind was not Bavarian particularism. The idea of a united Germany inspired him so profoundly that he thought of using music to win support for it. Frantz had already asked him in the spring if he would not give a musical expression to the idea of the German cause and compose a morning song to rouse the German nation from its slumbers, and now a Count Enzenberg appealed to him: 'Write the German national anthem that our great banner still lacks, and give it the eloquence of Demosthenes!'

The count's letter was rather formal and old-fashioned, Wagner told the king, but it betrayed a strong, warm heart, such as he rejoiced to find still beat in a manly breast in those sorry times. 'This is the language through which Germany speaks to me.' He wrote back to the count that he, too, dreamed of an earnest German anthem 'that may inspire our will to act with its simple, solemn gravity'. The right idea would come to him, not after days spent pondering on it but in the moment of fervour, of crisis, of inspiration: 'The days of greatest danger are at hand: may the princes apprehend them.' (15 June)

Wagner had started the orchestral sketch of the second act of *Meistersinger* on 8 June, and the exuberant woodwind trills and string figurations are prefaced by the sombre heading 'Still on the brink – as usual'. Things were now so bad that the pressure on Bülow, who was now accused of making one in the 'tricksy race to the treasury', made it impossible for him to stay in Munich any longer. After suing the *Neuer Bayerischer Courier*, and challenging the editor of the *Volksbote* to a duel, he asked the king to accept his resignation and arrived at Tribschen on 10 June. Four days previously Wagner had already drafted a letter, as from the king to Bülow, vindicating Bülow's honour, and sent it to Ludwig with a covering letter urging him to sign the document. 'I fall to my knees before my king,' Cosima added, 'and pray in humility and distress for the letter to my husband, so that we need not leave in shame and disgrace the country where we desired only good.' (DMCW, I, p. 290)

The king yielded to his friends' urging and Bülow hastened to publish the letter – with a foreseeable lack of effect, in view of the fact that the Austro-Prussian war had broken out on 14 June and Bavaria's fate was in the balance.

Wagner had hoped that the new Progressive Party, to which he was close through Röckel, would succeed in blocking Pfordten's policies in the Landtag. In this hope he had implored the king to listen to the voice of the people and follow the majority will of the chamber of deputies, but – 'what does the chamber do? Almost without debating the matter it gives Pfordten a more glowing vote of confidence than scarcely any minister has ever received.' (To Röckel, 23 June) The outcome was that Bavaria abandoned the neutrality Wagner had argued for in his 'Political Programme', and joined the war on Austria's side.

He wrote to the king on 18 June of his regret at seeing that the latter had not found the right man, that 'incompetence, short-sightedness, weakness of character' had led the statesman, who was now at the head of the government, to the ruinous half-measures to which the present sorry state of German affairs was due. Wagner's opinion of Pfordten was shared by Bismarck, who referred to him in his memoirs as 'an honourable and learned German professor of no political acumen'.

The Bavarian army suffered a decisive defeat on 10 July at Kissingen. 'For days I have been wondering how to begin still being something to you now,' Wagner told the king. There must, he thought, be some deep-seated and perhaps painful reason why he should have regained his most carefree creative powers at a moment of national crisis. 'World destiny, unable to realize the glory of the German spirit in the political life worthy of a great nation . . . created the two of us to realize what is too beautiful for life in the eternal mirror of art and – perhaps to preserve it there for posterity, so that one day people will recognize beyond all doubt that the nation that created something like that must have truly lived!' (14 July)

God grant, Ludwig replied, that Bavaria's independence would be preserved; 'if not . . . then away, I will not be a puppet king'. (18 July) This hint of abdicating became passionately explicit in a letter to Cosima three days later: 'Gain for me my dear friend's consent! . . . It is not the difficult political circumstances that drive me to this decision, that would be cowardice – but the thought that my true destiny will never be reached along this road!' (21 July)

Once again Wagner knew what to say to him. He did not stipulate any fixed term for reconsideration, but asked the king whether the world would always appear to him as it did at the present time. When he grew to maturity he would find the world a larger place; and his sense of manhood would also make him aware of his capacities for the exercise of royal power. A king believed in himself, or was no king. What if he should become conscious of his belief in himself only after resigning his rights? If he should ever regret it?

Completely under the spell of the atmosphere of *Meistersinger* himself, he suggested to Ludwig that he should move the seat of government to Nuremberg, 'the heart of Germany': 'Nuremberg, the old, true home of German art, original German inspiration and splendour, the vigorous, ancient imperial city, preserved like a noble diadem.' One can almost hear the words accompanied by the music he had just written to Pogner's lines:

> Nürenberg, die ganze Stadt,
> mit Bürgern und Gemeinen,
> mit Zünften, Volk und hohem Rat . . .

And then he went on to mention Bayreuth. A short while before, in dictating his autobiography, he had described a journey to Nuremberg in 1835 and how he had seen Bayreuth for the first time, bathed in the light of a lovely summer evening. Now, in this same letter, he pictured to the king how Bayreuth could turn out to be his 'best-loved residence'. (24 July)

But while he seemed to lose himself in building such castles in the air, in reality he retained an astonishingly cool head for the changed political situation. 'Send for Prince Hohenlohe-Schillingsfürst at once,' he advised the king on 26 July. He followed up the advice the next day with a long letter justifying it: 'I implore you on my knees: send for Prince Hohenlohe at once . . . new men! new men! You are betrayed if you do not!'

Hohenlohe was known to be opposed to the ultramontane party and to favour an alliance with Prussia, and for that very reason he did not enjoy the king's confidence, as Ludwig informed Wagner through his adjutant, Prince Paul of Taxis. (29 July) However, he bestirred himself to make two ministerial changes: the Treasury Secretary Julius von Hofmann was asked to resign in August and Cabinet Secretary Pfistermeister in October. It was exactly as if the Emperor of Austria had kicked out Metternich, Wagner wrote to Mathilde Maier: all at once the whole pack of baying hounds was silent. He took the opportunity to recommend Prince Hohenlohe to the king again: 'if you could bring yourself to have confidence in Prince Hohenlohe, I think it would be a great advantage.' It was necessary to adopt a dignified and circumspect attitude towards Prussia, and that called for a man possessing rank and the free deportment of a prince. On 31 December the king appointed Prince Chlodwig zu Hohenlohe-Schillingsfürst Minister of Domestic and Foreign Affairs and Chairman of the Council of Ministers, in place of Pfordten.

While Wagner lived in a state of permanent tension and, as he put it, was frightened to death once a fortnight, he nonetheless managed to finish the composition sketch of the second act. Taking refuge from the 'miserable world of experiences' in this occupation was what kept him alive. (To Heinrich Esser; RWBC, p. 806) '6 September 66, 11 p.m. Good night, Cosima!' he wrote on the sketch, after the full moon had risen over the rooftops of Nuremberg and the Night Watchman had called eleven o'clock. It is interesting to see that he originally sketched the Riot scene (which Alfred Lorenz describes as a chorale fantasy in form, with Beckmesser's serenade as a cantus firmus) as an orchestral piece, and then fitted the text to it quite freely, writing each part on a separate stave, with the orchestral part on three staves. He finished the orchestral sketch on 23 September and, without losing the impetus, went straight on to start the composition sketch of the third act on 2 October.

He described his day to Mathilde Maier, that 'dear, loyal soul': up at seven, breakfast between eight and nine, work until one. At three in the afternoon a long walk, returning between five and six, half an hour with the children in the nursery, teaching little Isolde to walk. Work, while Cosima gave the two older girls a French lesson. At eight tea in his room, nine to ten-thirty dictation of his autobiography. 'And that was that! Every day is like this. It's beginning to do Cosima some good, which she needed. Meanwhile the mastersingers are making progress . . . My finest work: everything is turning out well: I weep and laugh over it.'

'Is there anything more you would like?' he concludes. 'I can't think of anything. I cannot write you my music. We live in the air, out of the world – and – have earned it . . .

Den Tag—— seh ich er-schei-nen, der mir wohl ge - fall'n tut.

Wagner was working with a quite unusual application and vigour, Bülow wrote to Jessie Laussot. Overpowering though the effect was of witnessing the work at such close quarters, he did not think he was deluded in forming the opinion that *Die Meistersinger* would be Wagner's 'most classical (please forgive the banality of the word), most German, ripest and most *generally* accessible work of art . . . You cannot begin to imagine its wealth in terms of absolute music, the Cellini-workmanship in every detail. It is unshakable dogma with me: Wagner is the greatest composer, absolutely the equal of a Beethoven, of a Bach – and much more besides. He is the incarnation of the spirit of German art, its most enduring monument even when German, and perhaps music too, may have become a "dead" language.' (14 August)

There was a new shock in store for Wagner, when Ludwig Schnorr's widow Malvina arrived at Tribschen in November. She brought with her her pupil Isidore von Reutter, who was in nightly communication with the spirit of Schnorr. He had told Isidore that she was to marry the king, and Malvina was to marry Wagner – 'all on express ghostly command'. They had led him a fine dance, he told Mathilde Maier, especially as he had realized that the Reutter girl was an impudent fraud, whom he had had to forbid his house. Frau Schnorr had departed in fury and was now stirring up all kinds of trouble. 'Once again it was like an abscess growing in perfectly healthy flesh, when you've no idea what caused it! In short, there's always something pestering my poor mastersingers.' (15 December)

Frau Schnorr was a friend of Cosima's, but she saw to the bottom of her relationship with Wagner, whereupon her feelings changed to raving jealousy, and she denounced the pair to the king. At first Ludwig simply refused to believe the tale, but later grew puzzled. He wrote to Court Secretary Düfflipp, expressing surprise that the latter should think there was something 'not kosher' (in Ludwig's phrase) about the business of Wagner, Frau von Bülow and Frau Schnorr: 'Can the sorry rumour be true after all? I was never able to bring myself to believe it, but can it really be a question of adultery? – Then alas for it!' (KLRW, V, p. xlix)[9]

Coming to the prelude of the third act Wagner referred to the sketch he had made on the morning of his forty-ninth birthday. 'I was the lonely man then,' he told Cosima later. (BBL 1937, p. 2) A second sketch survives showing the reworking of the original 'profoundly melancholy' 'Wahn' motive, so that we can trace how the diatonic descent of the melodic line came to acquire the expressive inflexion it needed.[10]

The Prize Song, too, in the version Walther sings in Sachs's workshop, was conceived before Wagner actually started the composition sketch of the third act. The sheet of paper is dated '28 September [1866], afternoon, because waiting for C[osima]', while the Abgesang is hastily scribbled in 3/4 time on the back of the sheet (it had figured in the prelude in common time). He wrote the text of the song after the music and gave it to Cosima at midnight on Christmas Eve as a birthday present. It had been granted to him, Cosima told the king, at a time when the world outside had nothing but ugliness and evil for them.

In another letter she told him: 'Today Beckmesser was given his musical entrance after the incredibly beautiful scene between Walther and Sachs. When our friend was playing me the words he had just set, and sang "das waren hochbedürft'ge Meister, von Lebensmüh' bedrängte Geister", we both burst into tears. If only I could send you the music our friend has written for these words.' (DMCW, I, pp. 312f.) Beckmesser's musical entrance had a special significance. The ghostly doings with Malvina Schnorr had prevented Wagner from working for a week, and he had picked the sketch up again at the Marker's enraged outburst 'O Schuster voller Ränke'. Cosima had to laugh out loud when he played her the passage.

He often felt his heart was breaking over the sad, dreadfully disturbing times that lay behind him, Wagner wrote to the king on 11 January 1867. 'And – in the midst of all the turmoil – I am near to finishing *Die Meistersinger*! Who will believe it?' Barely recovered, he had been thinking about a curious dream he had had and suddenly laughed aloud, for at that instant the tune for the Tailors' song on the festival meadow had come to him. The strange, really quite unique character of the work itself had helped him once again: Sachs and Walther had been his doctors.

He had a lot of difficulty with the Prize Song. He decided it was impossible to have the same song twice in the one act: it had to be the same and yet different. Moreover it would have been out of character for Walther to repeat the very personal song, in which he had recounted his dream to Sachs and Eva in the privacy of the workshop, in exactly the same form before the masters and the crowd in the festival meadow. So Wagner changed the text in such a way that the second version of the song interprets the dream. His solution to the musical side of the problem is a stroke of genius. In place of the workshop version with its three stanzas (each in Bar-form)[11] the festival-meadow version consists of only one stanza, but its three sections are expanded so skilfully that the listener is under the impression that there are again three complete stanzas. In fact, if we compare just the first Stollen in each version, we find that only seven bars are the same, and no fewer than sixteen are new in the festival-meadow version; nevertheless, as Alfred Lorenz emphasizes, the listener is perfectly satisfied by the similarity. It was the work of a master to shape the two musical periods so that, although not the same, their relationship is evident.

At last, early in 1867, after so many interruptions and grave crises, Wagner came to the composition of Sachs's final monologue, where he was suddenly overcome with doubts. Cosima told the king she had spent a whole day talking about the ending; Wagner felt that Walther's song concluded the drama and Sachs's speech had nothing to add, but was rather a direct address to the audience by the composer: he would do better to leave it out altogether. 'I pulled such a horrible face at that, and said besides that "Will ohne Meister selig sein" was completely in character for Walther – so he thought it over, although he naturally held to his own opinion. It would not let him rest at night, he wrote the new lines, crossed out [his other version] as I had proposed, and sketched the music as well in pencil.'

The passage in question was that beginning 'Habt acht! Uns dräuen üble Streich' '. The sketch Cosima referred to is in the Wagner Archives in Bayreuth, dated '(at night) 28 Jan. 67'. There is no doubt that the lines, like the essay *German Art and German Politics* written shortly afterwards, reflect something of the political feeling of the period 1866–70. But besides its ideological significance, the new stanza performs a dramatic function as well. Wagner recognized that the original ending was static and did nothing to raise the dramatic temperature. Sachs's prophetic warning here adds a new, stirring emotional element that gives the action – which would otherwise float out on a wave of lyricism induced by Walther's song – a last surprising, dramatic upbeat.

One may indeed make a further observation about this ending that touches on the nature of comedy as a whole. Comedy, Schopenhauer remarks, resolves the sorrows and adversities of human life in pure joy. 'But then it must make haste to let the curtain fall at the moment of joy, so that we do not see what comes after.' That is why every happy ending is slightly unsatisfactory for those who see further and deeper than the majority. By changing the focus of attention, in the last moments of *Die Meistersinger*, from the joys and sorrows of the protagonists to something higher than purely personal concerns, the fate and the mission of art, Wagner found an incomparable means of avoiding the dangers of a customary happy ending. The added lines remind us of the realities of life once again, but only in order to raise us to a higher ideality.

With the dismissal of 'Pfi' and 'Pfo' and the appointment of Prince Hohenlohe, all obstacles to the king's artistic plans seemed to have been removed. He was determined to usher in a new Periclean age. 'On the very day that von der Pfordten left the Foreign Ministry in Munich a royal decree created me "kapellmeister in extraordinary to the Bavarian court",' Bülow wrote to Raff. 'That is, hofkapellmeister in partibus infidelium. I solicit your silent commiseration.' Semper was permitted to show the king the long-awaited model of the festival theatre and was appointed architect in charge of the project with the 'royal word and handshake'. The plan for a journal, to be the organ of the new political and artistic movement, also moved nearer realization: in May the Foreign Ministry opened negotiations with the Viennese publicist Julius Fröbel, whom Wagner had recommended as editor.

But it soon became apparent that the obstacles had not only lain in external opposition, but were also rooted in the king's own complex personality. As long as he was talking enthusiastically about his plans in the abstract, he was with Wagner in heart and soul; but when it came to their practical execution he allowed 'all matters of energy and of principle, everything that goes beyond purely personal amiability' to be set at naught by officials. (Wagner to Röckel, 29 January 1867) It has been conjectured whether the king was merely weak or devious, but this schizoid contradictoriness combined with a perfectly clear conscience points rather to a psychopathic element in his character. Wagner did not express any views on it, but he wrote in the Annals on 17 March, after seeing the king: 'Physiognomic change.' (KLRW, II, p. 6)

He was delighted at the news of Ludwig's engagement to his cousin Princess Sophie, of which the king lost no time in informing him by telegram. (22 January) When he made the princess's acquaintance in Munich he was impressed by her unpretentious nature, and by the obvious love and concern she felt for the king. 'If only you could be wholly united with her soon, soon,' he wrote to the king with foreboding. (16 March) Liszt, who was able to observe the young couple during a performance of *Tannhäuser*, remarked: 'Les ardeurs matrimoniales de sa Majesté semblent fort tempérées. Some suspect that the wedding will be postponed for ever.' The termination of the engagement 'by mutual agreement' was announced officially on 11 October. In explaining to Cosima how the engagement had come about and how he had suffered under it, Ludwig showed a clarity in self-analysis that is almost uncanny in so young a man. (DMCW, I. pp. 379ff.)

Wagner discovered that the governmental changes still did not mean an end to his difficulties as early as 6 January, when the king, at Hohenlohe's instigation, asked him to postpone a planned visit to Munich: 'A large faction claims that there is a very close connection between Hohenlohe's appointment and your visit.' Hohenlohe's personal physician of many years' standing, Dr. Schanzenbach, undertook to explain the minister's reasons to Wagner in a letter, to which the latter replied on 17 January with a comprehensive review of the political events before and after his departure from Munich.[12]

At the end of January Schanzenbach went to Tribschen in person, to acquaint Wagner with Hohenlohe's political plans and to recruit Wagner's powerful influence on their behalf. The prince does not mention this mission in his memoirs, and it has been questioned whether it actually took place, but it is confirmed by a letter Wagner wrote to Röckel, swearing him to 'ignorance' of the visit. (KLRW, IV, p. 181) Obviously Hohenlohe would not want the help an opera composer could give him to become common knowledge.

A few weeks later Schanzenbach had to report new scheming against Hohenlohe in circles close to the king. 'Stand by Prince Hohenlohe in preference to anybody, to anybody,' Wagner implored Ludwig. 'If he succumbed to the plotting against him I should regard the misfortune as immeasurable. For once, just this once, stand firm. Whatever may be said against him, for once at last you *must* stand by the man of your choice, or you are lost.' (21 February)

Having finished the orchestral sketch of the last act of *Meistersinger* on 5 March, he would have preferred to get on with the scoring of it 'unmolested and forgotten', but he made the long-postponed journey to Munich at last. While he was there he paid a call on Hohenlohe. The prince set the ball rolling by remarking that they were united by their devotion to the king and by the hatred of the ultramontanes. Wagner spoke of the way the king had been tormented to the point of twice contemplating abdication, then moved on to Bavaria's role in German affairs, to his own art and finally to the Cabinet. He stressed the importance of Hohenlohe's remaining in office. The prince replied that that did not depend on himself; he could not guarantee that the king's confidence in him would not be undermined by someone else; his uncertainty was the greater because, according to custom, the king communicated with him only through the Cabinet. To Wagner's objection that that could not be allowed to continue, Hohenlohe reminded him of the grave danger of issuing a challenge to the Cabinet: he – Wagner – knew that better than anyone![13]

The situation in foreign affairs all too soon gave Wagner occasion to urge Hohenlohe's policies on the king. Louis Napoleon attempted to assuage French disappointment over the outcome of the Austro-Prussian war by annexing Luxemburg at virtually no cost to France. Prussia prevented this, though without exercising her right to occupy Luxemburg herself. While the negotiations were still in the balance Bismarck put out feelers in Munich to discover the likely Bavarian reaction in the event of a Franco–Prussian war (April 1867). An important letter from Wagner to the king dates from this time, urging that it was obvious that every sympathy in

Bavaria was turning towards Prussia, while the Austrian party was still working hard to maintain its influence. If that went on then eventually Austria would simply annex Bavaria, and there would be no more question then of Germany or of Bavaria. 'Therefore, firmly and honourably, an alliance with Prussia.' That would preserve the integrity of Germany and would still permit Austria to join the alliance later. When he had told Prince Hohenlohe of his ideas, Wagner assured the king, the unemotional minister's face had lit up. 'Forwards! Forwards! Now is the time to throw the weight of Bavaria into the scales with Prussia: thus you will make yourself the leader of southern Germany, and Austria – must follow you – must! – There: that was my last will and testament!' (25 April)[14]

Of the king's plans for the arts, his favourite project, the festival theatre, was the first to go by the board. When Röckel told Wagner of the strong opposition in Munich to the clearance that would be necessary along the proposed route of Ludwig's processional way, Wagner answered that the last thing he had on his mind was a Wagner Theatre, let alone a Wagner Avenue. In any case he was used by now to keeping calm when heated resolutions were passed, and waiting until natural developments damped the fire down and poured water over it. Court Secretary Düfflipp had told him recently that the money would be found, by 'economies etc.', at least to start building the theatre and keep it going 'doucement' for five or six years. (29 January) The 'economies', however, failed to be made, as all available monies were swallowed up in the preparations for the king's marriage: the wedding coach alone was said to have cost a million gulden.

Ludwig's second project, the school of music, was almost ruined by Bülow. When his appointment as court kapellmeister and director of the Royal School of Music was at last officially confirmed, the terms of his contract were expressed so vaguely that he felt obliged 'to answer the allhighest proposals with his simple refusal'. He was only able to serve a king who also thought and acted like a king and did not merely have the sensibilities of an artist, he told Raff. In discussing the matter face to face with Düfflipp, he must have referred to himself as a 'Prussian nobleman', an expression Wagner deplored in a letter to the king. The latter had been gracious enough not to pay any attention to Bülow's insane behaviour. 'I could not treat it so lightly and my decision to break with him completely . . . had really already been taken.' (20 February)

On the morning of 17 February Cosima gave birth to Wagner's second daughter, Eva. When her labour started Wagner sat in the next room and softly played Walther's Dream Song.[15] Bülow arrived at Tribschen in the afternoon. According to his second wife, he stood at Cosima's bedside in tears and said 'Je pardonne', to which she replied, 'Il ne faut pas pardonner, il faut comprendre.' Max Morold, her biographer, adds: 'Bülow had long understood, and *because* he understood he also forgave her from the bottom of his heart.' The child was christened Eva Maria three days later in Lucerne. Driving home from the church, Wagner told the king, he had sung to himself Sachs's lines (with some minor alterations obviously to relate the words to himself):

> gar manche Not in Leben,
> manch ehlich Glück daneben –
> Kindtauf', Geschäfte, Zwist und Streit: –
> wem's dann noch will gelingen,
> ein schönes Lied zu singen, –
> seht, Meister nennt man den!

A great misfortune had misfallen the king's faithful servants, he went on in this veiled confession, and if they should recover from it, it would be of no little significance. (20 February)

In order to preserve the appearances of the Bülow marriage in the eyes of the king and the world, Cosima had to leave Tribschen on 16 April and go back to Munich with her husband. En route she telegraphed Wagner:

> Es ist bestimmt in Gottes Rat,
> daß man vom Liebsten, was man hat,
> muß scheiden.

('It is determined in God's counsels that we must part from what we hold most dear'; see above, vol. I, p. 253.)

He wrote in the Brown Book that evening: 'I have probably never been so sad in all my life as at this moment!! – How easy it is to say that, and how inexpressible it is! I went home on foot and sank down exhausted. A short leaden sleep . . . dredged up all the misery of my life as if from the bottommost depths of my soul. I yearn for a severe illness and death. I do not want any more – will not have any more! Would it but have an end, an end!' (KLRW, II, pp. xxi f.)

It was the king's dearest wish that Wagner would spend his birthday with him at Starnberg. Although Wagner's own instinct warned him against it, rightly, and he excused himself on the grounds of needing to work on *Meistersinger*, Cosima, fearing Ludwig's displeasure, persuaded him to change his mind, in a vigorous exchange of telegrams. 'Come here . . . otherwise complete break. Take last wish to heart, will write no more.' (19 May) So Wagner arrived on the morning of his birthday at Starnberg, where the king had rented the Villa Prestele for him, so as to have him nearby. They spent the afternoon together at Schloss Berg. As the villa was not yet ready for him to move in, he went to Munich to stay with the Bülows for a few days. In the evening various events were put on to celebrate his birthday, including a concert in the Westendhalle of excerpts from *Tannhäuser* and *Lohengrin*, and *Das Liebesmahl der Apostel*. Public interest was so great that hundreds had to stand in tight-packed rows.

He moved into Villa Prestele on 30 May – and the king left on 31 May on a sightseeing trip to the Wartburg. Then, late at night on 6 June, there was a knock at Wagner's door. It was Ludwig, who stayed with him for several hours, discussing the model performances of *Lohengrin* and *Tannhäuser* that Bülow was to rehearse under Wagner's supervision. Unfortunately Wagner had recommended his old companion-in-arms from Dresden, Tichatschek, for the role of Lohengrin. It then occurred to him that this might have been a mistake, and he tried to prepare Ludwig for the ageing tenor by telling him that he would be seeing a Holbein rather than a Dürer. He embraced his old friend after the dress rehearsal, greatly moved and delighted that his voice still possessed the same firm, silvery timbre that he remembered. But the king was appalled: this 'knight of the dolorous countenance' was so far from his ideal of the Swan Knight that he dismissed Tichatschek, in spite of Wagner's pleas.

He could not help but feel humiliated by this, Wagner wrote to Ludwig the next day, and in order to get over it he had no choice but to return to Tribschen. 'Farewell, deeply beloved friend!' He heard nothing from the king for a fortnight, then a long letter arrived: 'Lord of my life. . . I kiss the hand that has chastised me!' (21 June)

Ludwig's third project, the newspaper, got under way more auspiciously. After Fröbel had acquainted Hohenlohe with his editorial programme, a state subvention of 20,000 gulden for fifteen months was approved. Wagner and Fröbel were agreed that the paper should be run in a spirit of 'humane patriotism'. Wagner himself was to contribute a series of articles on cultural policy, but otherwise his artistic standpoint was to be represented by Heinrich Porges, 'this diligent, truly industrious, good young man of refined feelings'. That Wagner should have chosen a Jew for this task is an interesting reflection on his alleged anti-Semitism. He hoped that Semper might be persuaded to write something about the spirit of his style of architecture and its application to the crafts, but he advised Fröbel to take his time over finding the right man to deal with literature: on no account should battalions of 'intellectual' collaborators be allowed to draw up in too much of a hurry in this field. (2 September)

The first, trial issue of the *Süddeutsche Presse* appeared on 24 September, and Wagner's articles on German art and German politics began publication in the evening edition. 'By God, anyone who is not delighted, who is not persuaded and won over by the magic of the discourse, the profundity of the spirit that manifests itself therein, does not deserve to live,' the king exclaimed. (21 November) Relations between Wagner and Fröbel were soon clouded. 'Wagner says "beauty serves no end",' Fröbel wrote to Cosima on 10 December, 'but I say, what serves no end is useless, good for nothing, should not exist.' 'What you say about the theory of beauty', she replied, 'surprised me all the more because I thought that since Kant (and Goethe and Schiller after him) the principle of beauty as something that is an end in itself was established beyond question.' This illustrated a division between the artist and the politician that was to prove impossible to bridge in the long run. 'If Fröbel believes the world will be saved by the Americanization of Europe . . . we should appear very strange neighbours in the future,' Wagner commented. He felt inclined to withdraw from the *Süddeutsche Presse* at once, without fuss, simply in the name of common sense, and edit an independent paper, *Der deutsche Stil*, but he would first publish the last two articles in the series on German art and politics.

'Decide for yourself,' Cosima wrote to Fröbel on 19 December, after hearing this from Wagner. 'Do you think it possible to go on together? Wagner *can no other*. That is his strength, but also the danger, in his dealings with the world.'

However, the matter had already been decided in another quarter. That same morning a government official presented himself at the editorial office with an order from the Ministry of the Interior, commanding in the king's name the immediate cessation of the appearance of Wagner's articles. 'His Majesty regards these articles as suicidal.'

'Of course: I write all of it for you alone in reality,' Wagner had admitted in a letter to the king of 30 November, 'I might almost say as a substitute for our conversations at Hohenschwangau . . . I have great hopes of the impression my insights will make on the better sort of those who are themselves active in the theatre; perhaps that ought to be our chief hope.' And he went on percipiently: 'Those honoured gentlemen, the officials of the court and government, will probably be the last . . .' His instinct did not deceive him. The government official, Otto Freiherr von Völderndorff, still boasted in 1900 of the success he had once had in 'executing an express royal command which was the beginning of the end for that tapeworm'.[16] (KLRW, II, p. 209)

Another important event took place in the autumn of that year. Liszt, who had come to Munich to attend the model performances, took the opportunity to see his daughter as well and attend a party in celebration of her nameday at the house of their friend the painter Wilhelm von Kaulbach, where his attitude towards her was affectionate and attentive. This gave the lie to the rumour current in Catholic circles that the Abbé still condemned her behaviour. From Munich he went incognito to Tribschen, where he arrived on 9 October, to have a serious discussion with Wagner.

'Liszt's visit: dreaded but a pleasant relief,' the Annals record. It is not hard to guess the subject of the six hours' private conversation they had together. Wagner sent Cosima a telegram the next morning: 'One word only. Agreeably pacific guest left early today. Completely sleepless but hopeful.'

The two friends had sat up till past midnight, with Liszt's travelling companion Richard Pohl and Wagner's 'apprentice' Hans Richter. Liszt played *Die Meistersinger* from the manuscript, while Wagner sang all the voice parts. Liszt's sight-reading from a score he had never set eyes on before was a unique experience, Pohl recalled. 'I have never heard a finer performance of *Die Meistersinger*. The truth of the expression, the beauty of the phrasing, the clarity in every detail was thrilling . . . The third act delighted him most of all – nobody could have written anything like that except

Wagner, he said when he stopped in delight and admiration to play a passage over again.'

Wagner was greatly changed in appearance, Liszt wrote to Princess Wittgenstein. He had grown thin and his face was deeply furrowed. But his genius was as vigorous as ever. Liszt went back to Munich for another week and while he was there told people he had been to see Wagner. 'That was the best thing I did. I feel as if I had seen Napoleon on St Helena.'

The 'apprentice' mentioned above, Hans Richter, a horn-player in the orchestra of the Vienna opera, had become Wagner's amanuensis a year earlier, when he was barely twenty-four. He had a room on the first floor of Tribschen, and while Wagner was scoring *Meistersinger* downstairs in his study Richter was making a fair copy of the completed pages for Schott's. Once Wagner asked his advice over the point in the finale of the second act where the horn takes up the melody of Beckmesser's serenade: was it possible to play it at that tempo? It was possible, Richter replied, but it would sound very odd and nasal. Excellent, Wagner exclaimed, that was exactly what he wanted. In all other respects, Richter recorded, he always knew exactly how the score was going to sound.

What Richard Strauss admired most about the *Meistersinger* orchestra was its moderation: although it was approximately the same as that of Beethoven's C minor Symphony, with the addition of valve horn, a third trumpet, tuba and harp, yet it produced quite different and original sound-combinations in every bar. He mentions Wagner's writing for the string section, the five parts often reduced to four by the omission of the double basses, which makes full use of the range of registers in the part-writing, so that all the upper partials are heard, for instance, at the words 'Das schönste Weib' in the Prize Song; or producing a fortissimo pizzicato chord to express Beckmesser's nervous start when he thinks he hears mocking laughter; or, finally, making the effect of distant organ-playing with the whole section playing pianissimo. Wagner's treatment of the clarinet throughout its four different registers also wins Strauss's praise: when David is complaining of Lene's not giving him any supper because of Walther's failure in the singing trial, the solo clarinet dives out of its cantabile region and down by two octaves to where it suddenly takes on a cold, menacing timbre. Strauss quotes any number of examples of the valve horn's 'Protean nature', from the Riot scene, where it is the ringleader of the wildest parts of the fighting, to the warm-hearted solo accompanying Sachs's 'Schön Dank, mein Jung . . .'[17]

'This evening on the stroke of eight the last C was written. I solicit your silent concelebration. Sachs,' Wagner telegraphed Bülow on 24 October. The end of the autograph score is in fact inscribed: 'End of the *Meistersinger*. Tribschen, Thursday 24 October 1867, 8 p.m.'

After his recent exertions and emotional disturbances, Wagner felt the need for a brief holiday. Snow had already fallen in the Alps, and getting to Italy would take too much time, so he decided to spend six days in the 'old, strange nest of his fate, Paris'. But this time he found that the interest he could muster in the 'curio' was significantly diminished. The streets he had once known so well had been torn up and he hated the new buildings so much that he could hardly bring himself to look at them. He lived quietly, away from the public eye, in the Grand Hôtel and looked up only one friend, Charles Truinet.

In the Annals he wrote two catchwords: 'schoolchildren; butterflies'. On the final day of the Universal Exhibition he bought a collection of large, brightly coloured Indian butterflies from an impecunious dealer, which later adorned the study in Wahnfried. The other experience made so indelible an impression on him that he was still gripped with emotion when he recalled it in the last year of his life. Trying to leave the exhibition hall he was prevented by the entrance of thousands of schoolchildren. He stood for nearly an hour watching this youthful horde who represented an entire future, and saw prefigured in it every vice and misfortune that could befall the population of a metropolis. His description recalls Balzac's portrayal of the population of a great city in *La fille aux yeux d'or*. Wagner went on: 'All this was under the supervision of teachers, most of them members of religious orders, wearing the grotesquely elegant habits of the newfangled priesthood; themselves without a will of their own, stern and strict, but obeying rather than commanding. All completely soulless' – except for one young sister in a teaching order, who was in charge of a file of girls, and in whose face he read an inexpressibly beautiful concern for others which was the very soul of her life. She symbolized for him the spirit of a 'nation vraiment généreuse', as he described the French in a letter to Catulle and Judith Mendès, governed under the Second Empire by a rigid, soulless educational system.

Wagner travelled to Munich on 23 December, to spend Christmas with the Bülows, loaded with all sorts of 'Parisian toys' for the children. He suffered another unpleasant surprise. Fröbel had told the king that Cosima was involved in political machinations, and Düfflipp was sent to warn them on 27 December. 'I am thunderstruck,' Ludwig told his minister; 'the refined, intelligent Frau von Bülow is devoting herself to gutter journalism, writing these infamous articles! Truly, I would not have thought the cultivated Cosima capable of such a knavish trick!' 'The next day to the king,' Wagner wrote in the Annals. '2½ hours of reconciliations and apologies to C.' 'One thing I implore of you, beloved friend,' Ludwig wrote to Cosima, 'forget the last conversation with Düfflipp . . . I gladly take everything back; it was a passing wisp of fog.' It was a matter of the utmost urgency that Fröbel should leave Munich for good now that the king had seen into his 'black soul'.

All the same, Wagner thought it prudent not to take the initiative in resuming his correspondence with the king, and it was not until 9 March that Ludwig broke the silence: 'I cannot go on like this any longer, with no news of you!' The reserve with which Wagner replied drew a further outburst: 'I will tear, tear with all my strength at my friend's heart, until the wall that keeps us apart collapses.'

In the meantime Wagner had again come to Munich, on 17 March. Two days later a city-court writ was served on him, demanding the payment of a total of 2197 gulden 32 kreuzer to Advocate Simmerl acting on behalf of Widow Klepperbein of Dresden. The document, which is kept in the Wagner Archives as a curiosity, authorizes the court messenger to arrest Wagner, if he does not at once settle the principal and the interest on the debt, and 'to bring him to the New Tower'. Wilhelmine Klepperbein was a motherly friend who had lent him money in Dresden in 1847. God might know, Wagner wrote to Düfflipp, under what pretext the old lady had been persuaded to issue the document. For his part, in the letter covering an advance on Wagner's allowance from the Cabinet Treasury, Düfflipp could express only repugnance at yet another proceeding carried out in the shabbiest fashion. (KLRW, II, p. 9; IV, p. 260; V, p. 76)

Another financial settlement claimed Wagner's attention at the same time. Since the plan to build a festival theatre, which the king had entrusted to Semper three years before, and confirmed with word and handshake only the previous year, now seemed to have been abandoned for good, Semper presented the Treasury, through his lawyer Dr von Schauss, with a bill for 42,305 gulden in payment for his plans and models. At the same time Schauss asked Wagner to ensure that the settlement was made in a way that would not harm Semper. While Wagner was still toying with the idea of acting personally as go-betweeen with his old friend in Zürich, he learned that the king had broken with Semper and would not permit his name to be mentioned in his presence. It was ten months before the architect's account was finally settled, and yet another ambitious scheme ended in discord.

Wagner returned to Tribschen on 22 April 1868, without having seen the king once in the five weeks. He occupied himself with minor literary projects: a preface to the second edition of *Opera and Drama*, which he dedicated to Constantin Frantz, and his *Reminiscences of Ludwig Schnorr von Carolsfeld*, from which I have already quoted. (RWGS, VIII, pp. 195ff.; 177ff.) His prevailing mood was of an enervating melancholy. He noted in the Annals: 'Buddhism: rethought *Sieger*'; and he outlined a mythological and philosophical background for the work in the Brown Book: 'Creation of a new world: the beings from the Dhyana descend to the world again . . . Paradise is lost. The music of the Brahman world recalls it as memory: it leads to truth.' (KLRW, V, p. 159) He also wrote the opening of a Funeral Symphony to *Romeo and Juliet,* with a melancholy A♭ minor melody as principal theme.[18]

Cosima and her children arrived for a short visit in the middle of May. The jottings in the Annals illustrate his feelings: 'Great emotional turbulence: continual new difficulties. Inexpressible pangs of love. Am tempted to flight and disappearance.' Then all at once: 'Continual rapid change: blissful solace. Deliverance essential.' Their need for a decision to be made, once and for all, grew more and more urgent, set aside only for the sake of *Die Meistersinger*, which was soon to be performed.

On 21 May Wagner returned to Munich to stay with the Bülows and supervise the rehearsals. 'A present: my mother's portrait! Great, profound happiness!' he noted on his birthday; 'Lunch with the king on the Roseninsel.' 'What a day! What a life! What a memory!' he wrote to Ludwig in the evening after his return from Schloss Berg. Evidently he talked to him about *Die Sieger* on that occasion, for a few days later he sent him the copy of Burnouf where he had found his source material twelve years previously.

But as with the Volsunga saga he realized how much his imagination had shaped and developed the material in the interim. (31 May)

Meanwhile rehearsals had started. Wagner insisted on a faithful recreation of old Nuremberg: the sketches for the sets had been drawn 'on location' a year before. The street fight, too, was to be arranged by Madame Lucile Grahn 'with the utmost choreographic precision'. 'Singers good,' he recorded, 'but management [Perfall] evasive in everything.' His greatest anguish was caused by an obscure, heavy sense of 'profound hostility and alienation from Hans'. His friends Cornelius and Weissheimer had no idea of what it was, apart from the exhausting rehearsals, that was oppressing him and making him irritable and impatient in those weeks. '*Now* association with him is not exactly enjoyable,' Draeseke wrote, 'but later, perhaps in thirty or forty years' time, we shall be *envied* by the entire world, because he is so gigantic a phenomenon, and his stature will only grow and grow after his death.'[19]

When Schott's published Tausig's superb piano score of the work, Wagner did not forget to send two copies to Editha von Rhaden in St Petersburg, for herself and Grand Duchess Helene: 'If you are kind enough to keep it, then I may hope not to be forgotten by you, just as you, noble lady, are unforgettable to me.' (7 June)

Gradually visitors began to assemble in Munich for the première. In the Annals Wagner mentions, among others, Mathilde Maier – and Jessie Laussot, with whom he wanted to run away to the Far East eighteen years before. 'Nobody can write like I can,' he noted after her name, evidently recording something she had said after seeing a rehearsal. '[*German*] *Art and Politics* written to her from the heart.' He took particular note of a group of French friends: curiously enough it was they, he wrote, who pounced on the popular element in the work and acclaimed it. 'French enthusiasts: German detraction.'

After the last ensemble rehearsal, attended by a considerable audience, he spoke a few cordial words to his artists: the moment of performance, upon them at last after so much hard work, was of decisive importance; for it was their task to show the eminence and dignity to which German art could rise, if people would dedicate themselves to its service in all seriousness. This simple speech profoundly moved all who heard it. There could have been few among them, Newman remarks, who did not realize that with Wagner a new day had dawned for German art. (NLRW, IV, p. 141)

The king attended the dress rehearsal on 19 June, which was in effect a full performance. After he had written to Wagner that same evening saying that it had exceeded his highest expectations, Wagner replied: 'I knew it: He understands me!! Impossible that He should not have sensed and clearly recognized, behind the comic wrappings of popular humour, the profound sadness, the lamentation, the cry of distress of the enchained poetry.' (20 June)

He had sworn in a dark hour not to attend the first performance of *Die Meistersinger*, but in the event, out of consideration for the king and his artists, he was there in the theatre on Sunday 21 June. He was sitting with Cosima at the back of a box and the prelude had already started, when the king sent for him to join him in the Royal Box. 'Had to hear *Meistersinger* at his side, under the public gaze. Very tired and exhausted. Cosima sad that I didn't stay with her.' In vain the audience called for the work's creator at the end of the first act. After the second, at the king's insistence, he advanced to the parapet of the box and acknowledged the applause without speaking, deeply moved, and again after the third act. A murmur ran through the audience: 'Horace at the side of Augustus.' And a newspaper reported that one involuntarily looked up at the ceiling to see if it was not about to collapse.

'Took my leave of Parzival after the performance,' Wagner goes on in the Annals. Presciently he told Ludwig that they would not see each other again for a long time. (KLRW, III, p. 79) It was another eight years, in fact, in Bayreuth. In the ancient republics deserving citizens were accorded royal honours for a day, he wrote to the king: 'The purple mantle was permitted to rest on their shoulders. The next day, humbly, they retired again into the quietness of their private life.' On 24 June he arrived back at Tribschen, whence he wrote to Bülow, to thank him once more for his conducting: Wagner thought it 'incomparable', a view shared by a number of conductors who had come to Munich specially to hear the performance. He also expressed a few wishes with regard to the remaining performances, above all concerning the 'discretion', the 'conscious restraining of the orchestral volume', in the symphonic accompaniment to the musical dialogue on the stage. 'Lucky for us, that we have nothing more to face!' And he signed himself 'Lykurgos, far from Sparta'. (25 June)

Cosima gave the king the autograph score of *Meistersinger* as a Christmas present in 1867 (it is now in the Germanisches

Nationalmuseum in Nuremberg). For his birthday on 25 August 1868, Wagner gave the king a dedicatory copy of the engraved score. (KLRW, V, p. 207) The poem of dedication ends:

> Nun lasse demutsvoll das Glück mich büßen,
> daß ich so herrlich hoch Dir nahe stand:
> hat ferne Dir der Meister weichen müssen,
> drückt' er zum Abschied Dir die Freundeshand;
> nun lieg' sein Werk zu seines Königs Füßen,
> dort wo es Schutz und höchste Gnade fand.
> Und durft' ihm wonnig eine Weise glücken,
> die mög' ans Herz nun hold der Freund sich drücken!

('Now may fortune allow me humbly to repay the honour of having been so close to your glory; when the master had to go far away from you he pressed your hand in friendship and farewell; now let his work lie at his king's feet, where it was accorded protection and highest grace. And if a melody gave him pleasure, may his friend now press it to his heart in happiness!' KLRW, II, pp. 240f.)

Otto Wesendonk attended two of the later performances. Hearing Pogner's address to the masters, he will have remembered Wagner once writing to him that when he read the text to the Grand Duchess of Baden, the particular warmth in his rendering of the part of Pogner gave her the impression that the character had associations with some beneficent experience in his own life. 'I was quite delighted [by her comment]. I really do feel that in the love with which I have created this part – musically, too, now – I have set up a monument to a friend.' (26 July 1862) Though we must deplore the fact that that friend is not treated as he deserved in *Mein Leben* – for which we may blame the coolness of Easter 1864 – Otto Wesendonk's abiding *musical* memorial is in the figure of the art-loving goldsmith:

> Was wert die Kunst und was sie gilt,
> das ward ich der Welt zu zeigen gewillt.

Part VI: *Der Ring des Nibelungen* (II) (1868–1877)

# 27

## From Tribschen to Bayreuth

### I

'Mood: Siegfried's exultant theme . . . recurred, persisted,' Wagner
telegraphed Cosima on his way back to Tribschen. But he soon fell
prey to depression, aggravated by a feverish cold. 'Ensuing great
clarity as to my condition and the state of our affairs,' he wrote in
the Annals. 'Too deeply despondent to make any move: in the fate
of my relationship with Cosima and Hans recognized the reason for
the impotence of all desire. Everything null; Munich experiments
complete failure. Seemed essential never to return there.' He was
determined to force a decisive issue in his relations with Cosima and
with Munich alike, even though it meant new struggles and disturbances on both fronts.

He had realized during the *Meistersinger* rehearsals, when he had
had to fight for every one of his wishes against the opposition of
Perfall, the theatre intendant, that any future collaboration with the
Munich opera, even as guest producer, would be impossible. It was
time now to take the last step on the long road to the realization of
his idea for a festival, and to take it in the direction of his original
idea of a theatre of his own where, even if it was built of wood, he
would be master under his own roof.

Where the requests from other theatres to perform *Die Meistersinger* were concerned, he had to resign himself in advance to the
impossibility of protecting the work from distortions and to the
prospect of its at least surviving as an 'ordinary theatrical success'.
He proposed not to worry any further about it, he told Schott. 'The
work itself . . . will live on; but how?' (To King Ludwig, 14
October 1868)

Nevertheless *Die Meistersinger* made the general public begin to
realize, for the first time, that what was at stake here was not just the

career of one operatic composer but German art itself. Wagner was all the more angry, therefore, when the friend of his youth, his 'discoverer' Heinrich Laube, published a scurrilous article about it in the Vienna *Neue Freie Presse*, Hanslick's paper. Laube had applied for the post of intendant at the Munich opera in 1867 and blamed Wagner for his failure to obtain it. In reality it was the king who turned him down, being reluctant to have a commoner in the post, while Wagner took some pains to find an acceptable alternative for his friend. 'Read Laube's letter,' he wrote to Bülow. 'Believe me, you could do a lot worse than him. If Perfall was appointed, he could hardly ask for a better chief producer or technical director.' (3 October 1867)

Wagner vented his feelings at Laube's attack in three sonnets. (RWGS, XII, pp. 373f.) In the meantime Laube had become director of the theatre in Leipzig. 'Dear Laube,' Wagner wrote on 6 March 1869, 'You would give me cause for sincere gratitude if you were to use your position at the Leipzig Stadttheater to ensure that my operas were absolutely never given there again.'

Cosima had promised Wagner in Munich to follow him a week later. Her departure was delayed, and before she could leave her relationship with Wagner was once again denounced to the king. Röckel's gossiping was to blame, and the incident led to a complete rupture between the two old brothers–in–arms, but it also hastened the decision that had to be taken: Wagner sent for Cosima to come to him at once. 'She comes 22 July. Welcoming the children,' he noted in the Annals. 'Reports difficulties over decision: Plutonic and Neptunian solutions! – Agreed on the main issue.'

Peter Cornelius, who spent five days at Tribschen in August, was impressed by the patriarchal life Wagner led in surroundings that were a standing invitation to dreaming and composition. And when, during his stay, the Parisian impresario Pasdeloup made enquiries about *Lohengrin* and *Meistersinger*, while Signora Giovanna Lucca, the wife of the Milan music publisher, arrived in person with an offer of 50,000 francs for the Italian publishing rights to his works, Peter could not restrain his astonishment over the way 'Wagner's stock is now rising insanely'. Wagner himself was to be amused by Lucca's announcement of the forthcoming score of *Rheingold*. 'Who would have thought it?' he wrote to Schott. 'The barber of Seville sings about the "prodigious, omnipotent metal", but it's intriguing to see it turn into *Oro del Rheno*!' (Autumn 1870)

A passage in the Annals reveals his private mood: 'Melancholy and passionate days.' On 19 and 22 August he drafted a scenario in the Brown Book of a drama on the subject of Luther's marriage, in which the character of a wholly personal confession is more pronounced than in any other of his dramatic conceptions.

The first scene is set in the Wartburg, where Luther took refuge after the Diet of Worms. Dreadfully disturbed at this turning point in his life's work, he has opened the window, and the mildness of the air, the view over green countryside, the song of a bird and a draught of Einbeck beer all help to calm him. Then he is suddenly visited by the memory of the enigmatic look of a woman, containing the peace of ignorance, refreshing gentleness, certainty and moderation. But would it not be a humiliation, if the man in whom a whole world is in ferment submitted to the yoke of a woman? Is it not a trick of the devil? It is something other than the solace of nature. The words that he now has to pronounce to himself are spoken by the hand that gives him the drink, the lips that bless it: 'Brother, forget and remember!'

But if Catharina's blonde plaits fall over the pillow, will they not also fall across his desk? 'Exactly! That would be worth trying . . . It's there, in the priest's pride, that the devil lurks: I must drive him out! I'll take a wife, and it shall be Catharina.'

The sketch contains only a few sentences outlining the final scene, the wedding celebrations, but they indicate the general tenor of the whole. The chorus to the words 'Wine, women and song' harks back to Wagner's reflections on Buddha and Luther in the dark spring of 1864, on the shores of the Lake of Zürich. And if Lucas Cranach figures far more prominently among the guests than Philipp Melanchthon, then it shows Wagner is invoking Protestant *art* as the living testimony to the spirit of Luther.

As in *Die Meistersinger*, the limits of the stage are transcended at the end and attention directed away from the characters of the drama to the life of the nation. 'Genial indication of the goals of the German "rebirth" through philosophy, poetry and music – prefigured in the evolution of Protestantism and given popular expression in Luther's marriage.'

Wagner was to return to the sketch again, notably at a significant point in the writing of *Parsifal*. On 1 September, again in the Brown Book, he sketched a 'comedy in one act' to follow it, which satirizes the theatrical tribulations he had to contend with all his working life; the setting, in a third-rate touring company, is vividly reminiscent of his description of the Bethmann troupe in Lauchstädt. 'Counter to serious depression', he wrote beneath it.

Though Wagner and Cosima were agreed on the 'main issue', the necessity of her divorce, they were now faced with the task of overcoming public and private obstacles and the choice of a 'Plutonic or Neptunian' solution. They thought they would arrive soonest at a clear view if they had a complete change of scene. On 14 September, accompanied by Wagner's servant Jakob Stocker, the faithful Verena's husband, they set off for a holiday in northern Italy.

In Genoa – 'wonderful Genoa, loved from earlier days' – Wagner took Cosima to the street with the palazzos of the nobility where, fifteen years before, alone in the world, he had first felt the spell cast by an Italian city. 'Great joy. Cosima full of life,' he noted in the Annals. In Milan, where they called on the Luccas, heavy rain began to fall and as they started back they heard reports of flooding. 'Bellinzona. Wait or turn back?' After two days they continued their journey. From Biasca onwards the Ticino was swollen to a lake, bridges were down and further progress was possible only on foot. Stepping out from Giornico they were surprised by a dreadful thunderstorm: 'A most terrifying hour.' In the Lavorgo valley with its waterfalls they began a long trek through the mud: 'Lanterns! Broken bridges: through the water.' In this manner they reached Faido, whose woods and orchards had been turned into a watery waste. They found accommodation of a sort in the Hôtel de la Poste: 'Sharing one room with Cosima. Noah's Flood continues: further advance by carriage impossible. Three foul but profound days. 3 October (Saturday): very low spirits. Cosima writing. Close to death.' What Cosima was writing was obviously the letter in which she informed Bülow of the decision she had taken. 'Sunday, 4 October, still pouring . . . indecision: the road increasingly difficult. Post-chaises in caravans. Midday, decide to go on. Off at 1.30. Cosima in oilskins. Pouring with rain. Terrible march: four hours to go the same number of post-hours. Arrival in Airolo. (Coupé!) Spent the night. 5th, morning, posted over the Gotthard (with difficulty) . . . 6th (Tuesday) arrived home. What did our fate mean by it?'

'I've never met a woman with courage like that,' Jakob Stocker declared, 'sharing the most awful hardships without a word of complaint.'

An entry in the Annals betrays that Wagner and Cosima were not yet agreed about everything. 'Understanding and agreement. Melancholy, most important days. Cosima's promise.' On 14 October she set off back to Munich to talk things over with Hans once and for all. Wagner went with her as far as Augsburg. Before leaving he wrote to the king, admitting for the first time what he had hitherto kept from him.

On 14 September he had undertaken a journey to Italy for a holiday, he wrote. A stroke of fate, whose meaning he was still striving in vain to guess, had delayed his return journey, so that he had been caught among the landslides and floods of the Ticino and had had a forewarning of his end. His incredible exertions had been shared by a suffering woman, their mutual friend, to alleviate the grievous state of whose soul he had conceived the idea of this journey. 'On the brink of the abyss, illuminated by long lightning flashes, life revealed itself to us once more with its fearful earnest. Deception could no longer stand its ground! To see death face to face is to turn one's back on all deceit.'

Cosima had now returned to Munich, to set her position to rights and carry out her decisions. 'My blessing went with her: I have reason to honour her as the purest witness for truthfulness and inexhaustible deeps that life has yet shown me: she is the most perfect being I have encountered in my human experience. She belongs to another order of existence.'

Back in Tribschen Wagner endured several days of suspense. Evidently Cosima won Bülow's consent to the divorce without any delay, for on 16 October he was already writing to Carl Bechstein that his wife had been advised to try a change of climate and he would probably have to be separated from her for a considerable length of time – 'in several respects that is very hard for me'. But at the same time he wanted her to promise to go to see her father in Rome first, and move into Tribschen only later, after the divorce had gone through.

'To Rome?' Wagner exclaimed aghast in the Annals; 'bewilderment and passionate concern.' He feared that Liszt would shake her resolve. In desperation he turned to Cosima's half-sister Claire Charnacé, asking her to go and see Cosima in Munich and dissuade her from the idea of going to Rome. He had not foreseen Cosima's anger at this interference in her freedom of decision: 'Cosima beside herself.' She sent him a telegram: 'Wilful interference makes existence intolerable. Bitterly hurt by play with peace of the weary.' And after her sister's arrival in Munich she sent another: 'Claire's arrival has most disagreeable effect, opposition to Rome the saddest thing.'

'Great despondency,' he mourned in the Annals, 'decide to leave' – for Munich, where Cosima had gone to stay with a couple who were former servants of Wagner. After crossing Lake Constance by moonlight Wagner arrived in Munich on 2 November, but went on to Leipzig that same afternoon to seek the relaxation and sense of security that he had found in his sister Ottilie's house in the old days. One disappointment was still in store: he sent a plea to King Ludwig for an audience on his return journey – 'de profundis clamo' – but the answer, sent through the Cabinet Secretariat, was a refusal on a transparent pretext. The king could not get over Wagner's deceiving him as to the true nature of his relations with Cosima.

Wagner returned to Tribschen on 11 November, where he was joined by Cosima, with Isolde and Eva, on 16 November: this time for good. She arrived in Lucerne at night. Bülow wanted to preserve appearances to the last possible moment and she had had to promise him that her presence at Tribschen would be kept a secret for the time being. 'Distress over Hans,' the Annals note significantly.[1]

It was from this time forward that Cosima kept a diary, which she prefaced with a note to her children. 'You shall know about every hour of my life, so that one day you will be able to know me . . . Thus you will help me to fulfil my duty – yes, children, my duty. You will see later what I mean by that . . . 1868 is the most important turning point of my life: it was in this year that it was granted to me to enact what had been my inspiration and hope for five years. This action was not sought, not procured, fate willed it upon me.' (DMCW, I, pp. 422f.)

'She did not share the opinion that many of my friends were content to hold about me, to the relief of their consciences, namely that I was past helping,' Wagner wrote to Madame Muchanoff-Kalergis. 'She knew where and how I could be helped once and for all and did not hesitate for an instant to offer me that help in the possession of herself.' (24 August 1869)

Nevertheless, joy and a sense of guilt were at war in her heart. 'I will bear the world's abhorrence gladly and lightly, but Hans's suffering robs me of all happiness.' It could be thought of Wagner that he demanded and accepted this sacrifice from his friend with the naive egoism of genius, but a comment he made to Cosima after reading the text of *Tristan* to her reveals his inner feelings: he could only depict his relationship to her in Tristan's words in the second act. 'How long I grieved for Hans's sake, until I recognized that in our case, as in *Tristan*, something was at work which nothing else in the world could withstand.' (DMCW, I, p. 542)

Bülow himself was fully aware of the deeper consequence of his sacrifice. 'If Wagner writes but *one* note more,' he admitted to Klindworth, 'then it will be due to Cosima alone.' He and Wagner even began to write to each other again early in December 1868: he signed himself 'in steadfast admiration,' and once used one of his uncomfortable puns, 'With all my head, your sincere Hans von Bülow.'

'Little from without,' the Annals record of Wagner's life in the winter and spring of 1868–9. 'Within: dictation of the biography, score of *Siegfried*.' There were other, minor, literary activities, 'parentheses': his good-natured *Reminiscences of Rossini* and his less good-natured 'censures', his attack on Eduard Devrient and his *Clarifications of Jewry in Music*, an open letter to Marie Muchanoff-Kalergis, which formed the preface to a new edition of *Jewry in music.* (*Aufklärungen über das Judentum in der Musik*, RWGS, VIII, pp. 220ff.) Why he chose to publish something of that sort at that time is rather a mystery. Bülow may have had an inkling of the true reason when he wrote that the 'maestro' was now very isolated and by his action had 'to a certain extent severed the possibility of associating with the world'. (To Jessie Laussot, 13 April 1869)

Having completed the fair copy of the score of the second act of *Siegfried* on 23 February 1869, Wagner at last began to sketch the third act on 1 March. It was a peculiar characteristic of his creative personality that a period of passionate stress and disturbance in his personal life was on each occasion transmuted, sublimated, in renewed, heightened artistic creativity, and in this way was accorded a justification before which all moralizing must fall silent.

Reading Homer and the Edda with Cosima in the evenings revived in him once more the fundamental spirit of his myth, born as it was of the conjunction of ancient Greece and ancient Germany.

Work on the score of the second act restored his familiarity with the mass of motivic material, which he now set about developing further. 'A break of twelve years in a work must be without precedent in the history of art,' he wrote to King Ludwig, 'and if it transpires that this break has in no way impaired the vitality of my conception, then I can probably cite it as proof that these conceptions have an everlasting life, they are not yesterday's and not for tomorrow alone.'

In the same letter he reflected on his compositional technique. The realizing of his initial inspiration demanded long, wearisome labour. One reason why so little was wholly perfected in the world was that true genius manifested itself not only in the speed with which a great plan was conceived, but more specifically in the passionate, even painful perseverance required if the plan was to be realized in full. 'Nothing will come of scribbled jottings in a case like this; from an artistic point of view what transfixes us like a flash of lightning is a miraculously linked, delicately articulated piece of jewellery, in which every stone, every pearl, every link in the chain has to be fixed in its proper place with painstaking diligence, like a work of art in its own right.'

His creative imagination now concentrated on the scene between the Wanderer and Erda. It was already in his thoughts five years before, when he wrote to Bülow: 'It shall be a prelude, short but – significant.'

Now, in his letter to the king, he went on: 'If I wanted to tell you more about *Siegfried* today, I should have to speak of the dark, sublime, aweful dread with which I enter the world of my third act. We come here, like the Hellenes at the steaming cleft in the earth at Delphi, to the heart of the great cosmic tragedy: a world order is on the brink of destruction; the god is concerned for the rebirth of the world, for he himself is the world's will to become. Everything in this scene is instinct with a sublime terror that can be invoked only in riddles.' Since his return to Munich from visiting the king at Hohenschwangau in 1864, when he had put his fearful question to fate, he had been haunted by the theme that greets us as the curtain rises:

'Awe has prevented me until now from writing down what has often flared up in me as brightly as lightning when I have been walking alone in a storm.' (23–4 February 1869)

The music he was now sketching is developed out of motives that are already familiar: but what a change has come over the musical structure compared with the preceding parts of the work! The texture has become denser, the part-writing more polyphonic, and the melos surges irresistibly forward. The technical profit from the composition of *Tristan* and *Meistersinger* is manifest. If he set Wotan's words 'Um der Götter Ende grämt mich die Angst nicht, seit mein Wunsch es will' as recitative it would create an extraordinary theatrical effect, Wagner told Cosima; 'but', he added in a tone of great seriousness, 'then it would cease to be art'.

The consequence is that when the new motive of 'World Inheritance' is introduced at the climax of the scene it is thrown into all the greater relief. It is the motive that he had once conceived in connection with *Die Sieger*:

During the rehearsals at Bayreuth in 1876 Wagner asked for this to be taken 'a little faster' than what immediately preceded it and 'very clearly projected': 'It must sound like the proclamation of a new religion.' The slight increase in tempo has the effect of the illumination that has suddenly burst upon Wotan himself.

On their headland, encircled by the snow-covered mountains, Wagner was living entirely in this world of the gods evoked in his music, and despair seized Cosima when he gave way to doubt about his contemporaries and brooded on the futility of his work: 'This great, passionate work for this mean, petty age of Puritans!'

The king's silence worried her and it began to seem not unlikely that either he would cancel Wagner's allowance, or Wagner would have to renounce it. 'We discuss the possibilities of life in a garret in Paris in the future. A living room and two bedrooms for ourselves and the children. God knows what fate has in store for us.' But on 10 February a letter arrived from the king, couched entirely in the old, warm tone, to which Wagner replied with the long letter about his progress that has been quoted above. It is true that Ludwig had a particular motive in writing, which was to plead for performances of *Tristan* and *Rheingold*. 'I *implore* you, do what you can, beloved friend, to make this possible; ah, I need such pleasures if I am not to be overwhelmed in the whirl of everyday life.'

Although Wagner, believing Heinrich and Therese Vogl not up to the title roles, advised Bülow to throw away his baton rather than have anything to do with the 'botching of a work like *Tristan*', Hans nevertheless did not spare himself or his artists in carrying out the king's wish: 'First and foremost I could not but consider it my duty, and I was satisfied, too, that the reverence your work deserves was consistent with that duty. There was no question of botching or profanation, I do assure you.' (21 June)

It was his own farewell to the Munich theatre. The performance of *Tristan* would see him directing this orchestra for the last time, he told Cosima in a letter written four days earlier. 'Mon séjour à Munich finira par où il a commencé – cela lui donnera une espèce de "Abrundung" ["rounding off"] (cercle plus fatal que vicieux!).' He believed it would make it easier for him eventually to look on the whole sequence of events and suffering – 'la punition de mes fautes envers toi' – contained between the performance of one and the same work at an interval of four years, as a nightmare. 'Truly, without intending any reproach to its mighty creator – *Tristan* gave me the coup de grâce.' (17 June 1869, NBB, pp. 477ff.)

Ludwig's other desire, to see *Das Rheingold*, was to lead to the profoundest disaffection between the king and the composer.

But before that took place, several notable events happened at Tribschen. Friedrich Nietzsche paid his first visit there on 17 May; Wagner and Cosima's third child, Siegfried Helferich Richard, was born on 6 June; and Judith, the daughter of Théophile Gautier, and her husband Catulle Mendès stayed in Lucerne 16–25 July.

Nietzsche, then twenty-four years old, had first made the acquaintance of Wagner, whom he already admired, on 8 November in the previous year in Leipzig, in the house of the composer's sister, Ottilie Brockhaus. 'At the end . . . he pressed my hand very warmly and invited me in a very friendly tone to visit him, to talk music and philosophy.' (Nietzsche to Erwin Rohde, 9 November 1868) Newly appointed professor of Classical Philology at Basel University, he set out on foot from Lucerne to Tribschen on Whit Saturday, 15 May 1869. He stood outside the house for a long time, and heard an anguished chord played over and over again. 'It was, as my brother later discovered,' Elizabeth Förster-

Nietzsche wrote, 'the passage from the third act of *Siegfried*, "Verwundet hat mich, der mich erweckt".' (EFWN, p. 9) Thus at the very start we come across an example of Nietzsche's predilection for embellishing his experiences: it would require an uncommon musical memory to recognize that 'ominous' but motivically not especially individual passage again.

He was invited for the Monday, when he arrived at midday and spent the afternoon with Wagner and Cosima. From the walls of the drawing room, papered in a faded red with gold arabesques, flanked by portraits of Goethe, Schiller and Beethoven, Genelli's *Dionysus among the Muses* presided over this fateful meeting. When Nietzsche wrote at the end of 1871 to announce that *The Birth of Tragedy* was very nearly finished, Wagner referred to the picture in his reply:

> Only the other day, when I was looking at Genelli's *Dionysus among the Muses*, I experienced true amazement, as if suddenly understanding an oracular pronouncement about your latest work . . . In your ideas, as from that picture, I read a remarkable, even wonderful coherence, I venture to say, of each part of my life with every other.

When Nietzsche wrote to Erwin Rohde six months later about the essential, underlying idea of his book (which was proscribed by the academic establishment, though Rohde for one championed it), saying that that world of purity and beauty had not dropped from heaven, but had been preceded by an immense, savage struggle to escape from darkness, crudity and cruelty, he added: he had been thinking of Genelli's watercolour of the Muses gathering around Dionysus, which he had seen in Wagner's house Tribschen.

Obviously the picture, which possessed a deep significance for both, was the point of departure for their discussions at that first visit. A kind of intuition enabled Nietzsche to grasp the symbolic significance of the moment. He did not come unprepared: he had been a Wagnerian since Bülow's vocal score of *Tristan* had come his way while he was still a schoolboy. Now the *Dionysus* was the key that unlocked the problem of the Greeks and the problem of Wagner for him and simultaneously presented new, unfamiliar problems.

Nietzsche's French biographer, Charles Andler, remarks that contemporary classicists would have been less taken aback had not a badly taught generation forgotten the works of their predecessors:

Otfried Müller, Creuzer, Welcker. Nietzsche's attention was drawn to these forgotten works not by his colleagues but by Wagner himself. A comparison between the dates of his visits to Tribschen and the record of his borrowings of these authors from the library in Basel supports the conclusion. He filled his notebooks with extracts from these books, and their basic ideas take shape in his preparatory work for *The Birth of Tragedy*.[2]

But what were intellectual stimuli compared with the direct personal experience of the problem of the Apollonian and the Dionysian in the art and personality of Wagner! It is greatly to the credit of the young classicist that he recognized the question of Greek culture as being one and the same thing as the question of the phenomenon of Wagner. Thus he was able to speak of the Greeks not like those classical scholars who knew them only by hearsay, but as one who had walked among them; and to refer to Wagner not like contemporary writers who looked at him from the narrow angle of the nineteenth century, but as to a contemporary of Aeschylus.

'What I learn and see, hear and understand there, is indescribable,' he confessed to Rohde, 'Aeschylus and Pindar are still alive, believe me.' (3 September 1869) The fruit of his experiences was one of the most remarkable books ever to have come from the pen of a classical scholar: *The Birth of Tragedy from the Spirit of Music*.

Meanwhile Wagner was continuing to work on *Siegfried*. The letter to the king that has already been quoted included an account of his daily round, though omitting any mention of Cosima's presence in the house. His rule, religiously kept, was 'Nulla dies sine linea!' In the morning, after a cold wash, a light breakfast and a quick look at the newspapers; then his letters, of which he sometimes got large numbers, the great majority nonsense or idiotic imputations. At ten he got down to his score, which gave him three beautiful and profitable hours before lunch every day. His principal concern, in furnishing his green study, had been with the library, which was now gradually increasing again after sustaining so many depredations. At one Jakob summoned him to a not too luxuriously or elaborately prepared meal, at the end of which the dogs generally joined him. Then he withdrew to his salon for coffee, after which he took a short nap or played the piano a little. At three he placed upon his head the mighty Wotan hat that struck fear into the hearts of all beholders, and in the company of Russ, the Newfoundland, and

Koss, a rough-haired terrier – 'Falstaff and his page!' – he set off on his constitutional, which in bad weather was usually confined to a walk to Lucerne, where he sometimes browsed among the books in a second-hand shop and had recently found four volumes of Schiller's *Die Horen*. He returned to Tribschen at five, and went back to his score again. The evenings were devoted to reading, in which he constantly returned to the great spirits, Schiller, Goethe, and Shakespeare; sometimes Homer and Calderón, too, less often scholars like Winckelmann. 'And that gives me my blessing for the night; I am in good company and know which of my friends deserve my loyalty.' (24 February 1869)

It was with the celebrated first-violin unison passage that Wagner led Siegfried up on to the 'blessed desert on blissful height' where he recreated in sound the 'sublime impression of the holiness of the empty waste' he had received sixteen years before on his way to the Roseg glacier. There is a daemonic moment when the earth seems to open when Siegfried 'as if dying' presses his lips to the mouth of the sleeping woman, while Freia's motive is heard very softly rising out of the depths. 'The kiss of love is the first intimation of death, the cessation of individuality,' Wagner said to Cosima; 'that is why Siegfried is so frightened.' With Brünnhilde's greeting to the sun, Siegfried's key of C major is asserted with an almost physical brilliance: true religion is when the human being, forgetting self, surrenders everything to the universe, Wagner commented on another occasion. It is again characteristic that this high point of musical expression is simultaneously an outstanding example of musical form: the whole period, as Lorenz has shown, represents a potentiation of Bar-form so that the intensification rests not only on the quality of the sound but above all on a formal, intellectual principle.

The use of the two themes from the 'Starnberg' Quartet in homage to Cosima has already been mentioned in Chapter 25. But the themes of the close of the act, where the pair exclaim their joy aloud, as it were 'to the high Alps, so as to bequeath it to eternity in the undying echo', had also long been in Wagner's mind. Nevertheless, the work on the 'crystallization of the jewel that is intended to be the cornerstone' made such demands on him that he decided against celebrating his birthday in any special way. How wonderful it was, he mused, that Siegfried's exultant theme, 'Sie ist mir ewig, ist mir immer, Erb und Eigen, Ein und All', fitted itself so naturally to the motive of 'Heil dem Tage, der uns umleuchtet' to provide a contrapuntal accompaniment, which continues on its jubilant way in the horns.

'Safely delivered, 14 June 1869', he wrote at the end of the composition sketch, and when he showed the finished pages to Cosima she said: 'Only now has our child been born.'

But their joy in the completion of *Siegfried* was clouded by the prospect of the impending performance of *Rheingold* in Munich. Wagner wrote to Düfflipp that he had no right to oppose his benefactor, if the latter wished to see his works, and as far as he reasonably could he would gladly advise on the production. (18 May) The producer Reinhard Hallwachs and the machinist Karl Brandt had been to see him in April, to receive his instructions. In the middle of August it was the turn of Hans Richter, who was to conduct at Wagner's wish, to arrive at Tribschen with the singers who were to take the parts of Wotan, Loge and Alberich. In the evening Wagner complained that he was like Falstaff, he had lost his voice with singing of anthems, Cosima wrote to Nietzsche: 'he gave the good people a demonstration of everything'. (19 August)

The dress rehearsal took place on 27 August, and an alarming telegram from Richter arrived the next day, urging Wagner to prevent the première at any price, because of the inadequacies of the scenery. Hot on its heels came a letter from the Wotan, Franz Betz, which spoke of a 'crime against the work' and an 'insult to the public'; the root of the trouble, he said, was that the intendant, Perfall, had not given Hallwachs and Brandt the freedom to act as Wagner's plenipotentiaries. Wagner at once sent a telegram to the king, begging him to postpone the performance, following it up with a letter explaining the reasons for the request: in spite of everything he was still confident, he wrote, that if his suggestions were followed they would result in improvements that would salvage the production. It was of course essential that Richter should remain the conductor. (30 August)

For Richter, in order to lend weight to his demand, had refused to conduct a public performance, which Perfall countered by declaring he was seeking a replacement as quickly as possible. In his letter to the king Wagner affirmed his belief that his name commanded enough respect in every musician to deter any conductor from consenting to the act of infamy he was asked to perform. And in fact, with Bülow having already left Munich, Lassen of Weimar, Herbeck of Vienna, Levi of Karlsruhe and Saint-Saëns of Paris all refused.

The king was beside himself: 'The way "Wagner" and the theatrical rabble are behaving is truly criminal and quite shameless,' he raged to Düfflipp. '"Richter" is on no account to conduct again, and is to be dismissed forthwith . . . Pereat the theatre pack! With my usual thoughts and good wishes for yourself, but with curses on the coterie of chicanery and impudence!' (30 August) The next day he sent a telegram after the letter: an end must be put as soon as possible to the disgraceful intrigues of '"Wagner" and accomplices'. 'If W. dares to object again, his allowance is to be stopped for good, and no work of his is ever to be performed in Munich again.' (31 August)

As Wagner had let it be known that he was coming to Munich to supervise the rehearsals himself, the king instructed Düfflipp to try to prevent it. 'But there is no need for him to know that this is my wish, or there will be the devil to pay!' (31 August) Wagner arrived in Munich nonetheless on 1 September, and Ludwig, who had fled to his hunting lodge on the Hochkopf, wrote to, of all people, Pfistermeister: 'The last straw in the insufferable *Rheingold* affair is that completely against my wishes R. Wagner has come to Munich; it will serve him right if there is a hostile demonstration against him, now, when the Bülow scandal is au comble. J'en ai assez!' (KLRW, II, p. 286) Unable to come to any agreement with the intendant, Wagner left the next day with nothing accomplished, but he implored Düfflipp once more to persuade the king to postpone the performance: there was a point, he wrote, 'beyond which no more demands can be made on a man of my sort: or else the reserve of strength I have for creation will be exhausted once and for all'. (3 September)

But the affair ran its course. When finally the Munich kapellmeister Franz Wüllner agreed to conduct, Wagner could not restrain himself from telling him 'in plain German' that he was not up to it:

> Keep your hands off my score! Take my advice, Sir, or the devil take you! Go and beat time for choral societies and glee clubs, or if you must have opera scores at all costs, get hold of the ones your friend Perfall has

written! . . . You gentlemen are going to have to take a lot of lessons from a man like me, before you realize that you have no understanding of anything. (September 1869)[3]

The Augsburg *Allgemeine Zeitung* published an article instigated by Perfall, which represented the whole affair as an intrigue of Wagner's, and drew a reply from him. (*Das Münchener Hoftheater*, RWGS, XII, pp. 304ff.) It seemed, he wrote to Schott, that his name and his fame served only to draw a whole pack of hounds after him. 'I believe that this time I have stood my ground against this sort of agitation for the last time.' (21 September) The first performance of *Rheingold* took place under Wüllner on 22 September. All the published comment agreed in finding the performance splendid but the work itself insupportable, Cosima told Nietzsche: 'But some beautiful, profound words of great congeniality were written à propos of *Rheingold* by Heinrich Porges (a Jew).' (29 September)

Wagner wrote the epilogue to the whole affair in verse:

Spielt nur, ihr Nebelzwerge, mit dem Ringe,
wohl dien' er euch zu eurer Torheit Sold!
Doch habet acht: euch wird der Reif zur Schlinge;
ihr kennt den Fluch: seht, ob er Schächern hold!

('So play with the ring, you foggy dwarves, may it repay you well for your folly! But beware: the ring will trap you; you know the curse: see if it will do rogues any good!' RWGS, VIII, p.338)

Among those who travelled to Munich from far afield to attend the performance was Judith, the beautiful and intelligent daughter of Théophile Gautier and the Italian singer Ernesta Grisi, together with her husband Catulle Mendès and the poet Villiers de L'Isle-Adam. Wagner had thanked her in 1868 for sending him three articles about himself. However, when she invited him in the following year to attend the Paris production of *Rienzi* at the Théâtre Lyrique, he declined in a letter she published in the *Liberté*: people would think, if he came, that he was trying to win back with *Rienzi* what he had lost with *Tannhäuser*. 'Therefore I refrain, so as not to make stonier the stony path my French friends have chosen to tread in attempting to naturalize in France "une individualité essentiellement germanique". If such naturalization is possible, they will clear the road for it without my help.' (RWGS, XVI, pp. 114ff.; LJG, pp. 41ff.)

Thenceforward she had but a single thought: to visit Wagner and hear his works in Munich. When he asked her, on her enquiry, to extend her stay in Lucerne a little, she arrived on 16 July with Catulle and Villiers for a stay of ten days. They spent the days at Tribschen: swimming in the lake, arguing about literature and philosophy, Villiers reading his poems, Wagner organizing excursions and playing to them from the *Ring*. One evening as dusk fell and they sat in the salon looking out over the garden, Villiers broke the silence by asking Wagner without any preamble whether it was by an act of conscious deliberation that he had imbued his works with the sublime, mystical spirit that proceeded from them: in short, whether he was a free-thinker, and a Christian only insofar as the material of his lyric dramas required it. There was one particular circumstance that justified his question, he felt: that is, the fact that the name of God is not once invoked in *Tristan*.

In his own account of the incident Villiers goes on: 'I shall never forget the look Wagner turned on me from the depth of his exceptionally blue eyes: "If I did not feel in my soul the light and the love of the Christian faith you mean, then my works, which all testify to it, would be those of a liar, a jackanapes. My art is my prayer. And believe me: every true artist sings only of what he believes, speaks only of what he loves; for liars betray themselves by the sterility and worthlessness of their work. So far as I am concerned, since you ask, you should know that I am a Christian before all else, and that the accents that impress you in my works are inspired at bottom by that alone." '[4]

By the time the French visitors left for Munich on 25 July they were all firm friends, Judith and Cosima having become particularly intimate. They attended the dress rehearsal, and Judith lost no time in sending a report, 'un tableau très vivant': it was impossible, she wrote, for *Rheingold* to be presented in that form. Ill will and stupidity had formed an alliance. The singers and orchestra were very good, but the sets and machines were impossible: the shabbiest fairground booth would blush to own them. There was nothing to choose between the producer and the intendant: 'je crois que je vais mourir de rage . . . 27 août 2 h du matin.' She had had a good look at the king in his box: 'Féminin et volontaire, candide et dominateur.'

Judith also had a confidential message for Cosima, who was grieving at the thought that it was her father who was influencing Bülow against their divorce. Judith discussed the matter with Liszt during her visit to Munich, and he empowered her to assure his daughter that he, more than anyone, desired the legal resolution of the crisis.

'You have done me a great deal of good,' Cosima replied. She had wept all night long, and then the letter had come and acted like balm. She knew that she and her father were agreed in those areas where the clamour of the world did not penetrate, and she understood that he had to keep silent about her situation. 'If I sleep tonight, then I shall have you to thank for it. I embrace you with my whole heart and the Meister kisses your hand.' (28 August)

But the stresses of the last few weeks had told on him: Judith would find him looking ten years older, 'he is not working so regularly any more, and that worries me now more than anything else'. (7 September) Even so, he had started to 'paint' the score of the third act of *Siegfried* on 25 August, and swore that it was not tiring him in the least. On 2 October he began the composition sketch of *Götterdämmerung* with the first bars of the Norns' scene.

It was nearly twenty years since he had written down the first sketch of this scene, mentioned in Chapter 16. The change in his style since then is plainest to see in the following scene, Siegfried's leavetaking from Brünnhilde. Here, the fact that the words in the two versions are identical and the melodic lines of the vocal parts are also basically similar makes the difference in the outcome all the more prominent. The note values are now doubled, so that the singing is further removed from recitative and elevated to a kind of German bel canto. Syncopations and wider intervals enhance the vigour of the melody; individual notes are changed, an ordinary triad is replaced by the *Tristan* chord; a repeated phrase is raised by a third on repetition, so that it undergoes sequential intensification and gains mediant colouring. Everything is more plastic and more colourful. Above all the inner tension which keeps the flow of the infinite melody in motion has become far stronger:

*Siegfrieds Tod*, composition sketch (1850)

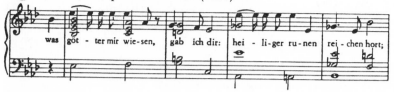

*Götterdämmerung*, full score (1873)

It is interesting to see that Wagner did not begin to sketch the short orchestral prelude to the Norns' scene until three months later, on 9 January 1870. 'My preludes must all be elemental, not dramatic like the *Leonore* overtures,' he once said, 'for then the drama is superfluous.' After the 'elemental' preludes to *Rheingold*, *Walküre* and *Siegfried*, that to *Götterdämmerung* evidently caused him trouble. The choice of the chords that had accompanied Brünnhilde's awakening and greeting of the world shows how instinctive, rather than rational, his own apprehension of his motives was. Certainly the motivic combination is incomparably successful in creating a mood of tense, uneasy expectation, and the return of the chords at Siegfried's death means that the whole of the intervening musical and dramatic action is enclosed within a huge frame.

The 1850 sketch contains no hint of the orchestral passage between the first and second scenes: first light, sunrise, full daylight. This owes its existence not only to the growth of Wagner's compositional technique, but also to the experience of a natural phenomenon: the crescendo of the triplets in the strings depicts mist dispersing as sunlight breaks through, as Wagner could see it looking out from Tribschen towards the Rigi.

While he was 'weaving at the Norns' rope', he also composed his essay *On Conducting,* a truly classic piece in its mixture of earnest and irony. (*Über das Dirigieren*, RWGS, VIII, pp. 261ff.) Cosima wrote to Nietzsche that he wanted to set down on record the whole of his experience in the musical life of the day. In a free adaptation of Goethe he apostrophized his fellow-conductors:

> Fliegenschnauz' und Mückennas'
> Mit euren Anverwandten,
> Frosch im Laub und Grill' im Gras,
> Ihr seid mir Musikanten!

('Buzzing flies and whining gnats and your kinsmen the frog in the undergrowth and the cricket in the grass, you're the musicians for me!')

He used a series of examples, mostly from Beethoven, to expound his own method of interpretation, and also revealed its fons et origo: the inspired singing of Schröder-Devrient, and the performance of the Ninth by the Paris Conservatoire orchestra. The right tempo can be judged only by approaching the music as song, and grasping the thread of the melos. Wagner was the first, Furtwängler wrote, to draw attention to the slight but continuous variation of tempo required by Beethoven's works, which is the only thing that turns a piece of classical music in performance from the notes printed on a page into a living process, something that comes into being and grows as it is heard.[5]

'It's all gold – wonderful,' Bülow exclaimed after reading the essay, of which he at once ordered several more copies. (To E. Spitzweg, 11 May 1870) It was in fact he who schooled a new generation of conductors on the Wagnerian model.

As Christmas approached Cosima began to prepare her surprises. Nietzsche was commissioned to look in Basel for a copy of Dürer's *Melencolia* and a puppet theatre for the children. 'My warmest thanks for undertaking all this, if the king is not as kingly or the devil as black as one might wish, it doesn't matter, children's imaginations are satisfied with an approximation to the real thing.' (9 December) 'Please do not lose patience over the Christ-child at all costs! Yet another request – some tulle with gold stars or spots on it . . . You see, we want to dress a Christ-child and cannot find the proper heavenly clothes anywhere in Lucerne! When I ask you for things like this I cannot help forgetting that you are Professor and Doctor and a classical philologist, and just remember that you are twenty-five and a good friend to us Tribscheners.' (15 December)

When the puppet theatre arrived she sent a telegram: 'Marionettes heavenly. Greetings and thanks.'

Nietzsche was of course invited to spend Christmas at Tribschen. In another letter Cosima told him of Wagner's instructions that he was to arrange things so that he could spend the whole holiday period with them. '*Ifthikar* has already arrived,' she went on mysteriously, 'but I shall only tell you who or what Ifthikar is if you are a good twenty-five-year-old and get here a little earlier to help me gild apples and nuts. But perhaps you will guess what Ifthikar is if I tell you that you will not see it shining where it was intended to, but on the proscenium of our puppet theatre.' (18 December) It was, in fact, the 'Order of Fame', the Nischân el Ifthikar, which the Bey of Tunis had awarded Wagner, and which the latter hung on the theatre in an access of high spirits.

Something doctrinaire about Nietzsche had grated on Cosima, but he made a better impression on Christmas Eve, when she read him the detailed prose scenario of *Parsifal*. 'Dreadfully impressed,' she noted in her diary. Wagner had 'a sublime discussion' with Nietzsche about the philosophy of music, expressing ideas that she hoped he would develop further. (DMCW, I, pp. 472f.) These are two facts that should be remembered, since they contradict certain assertions of the Nietzsche legend: namely that *Parsifal* later took him completely by surprise, and that he played a formative part in Wagner's metaphysics of music.

'J'en ai assez,' the king had written to Pfistermeister on 1 September, but he proved unable to endure silence for long either. 'Is it not so, my beloved friend, you never mistake me!? . . . Oh, God, the desire to hear your divine work was so powerful, so uncontrollable! If I erred, be lenient and forgive me . . . Are you writing *Götterdämmerung*? Will you soon be starting the text of *Parcival*? A thousand greetings to our beloved friend [Cosima]; I shall never lose faith in you, in any respect, you understand me.' (From Linderhof castle, 22 October 1869)[6]

Wagner told Cosima on 1 November that he had decided to write and tell the king that he could not write to him. He read her the restrained letter he had composed, which she would have wished even more reserved. (KLRW, II, pp. 288f.; CT, I, p. 166)

But the matter did not rest there. On 13 November he told her he was going to reproach the king with what they had had to suffer, emphasizing at the same time that, on the other hand, he owed him everything and would not have been able to work at all without him, and asking him finally not to have anything performed for the time being, to have nothing to do with the theatre for a while. She advised him to wait before doing so.

'Still worried about Richard, who looks ill,' she wrote in her diary on 18 November. 'This morning he wrote to the king; I asked him to alter some things that might cause offence and he said he would.' 19 November: 'He will not post his letter to the king because it is Friday.' 20 November: 'Richard read me his letter to the king and posted it.' (CT, I, pp. 169ff.)

'My noble friend and gracious benefactor! . . . The head wars with the heart, emotion with reason, and in the end what is established all over again is what we are and cannot help but be. When I received and read your last, quite unexpected letter, the first thing I said to myself was "we have had all this before", and that depressed me: the last thing I wanted was that it should all be repeated in exactly the same way . . . There is one question I must put to you, and your answer will determine our whole future: Do you want my work as I want it to be – or do you not?' (KLRW, II, pp. 290ff.)

Overjoyed by Wagner's expression of his 'trust' in a letter of New Year greetings, Ludwig wrote: 'Ah, I knew we could not misunderstand each other! I may say I deserve it.' (6 January 1870)

And yet it was from a newspaper that Wagner learned on 12 January that the king had ordered *Die Walküre* to be put into production. 'Greatly alarmed at it; once again his will to work completely halted.' (CT, I, p. 187) His young king was once again causing him the greatest distress, Wagner wrote to Klindworth: 'You will soon learn that the *Rheingold* shambles is going to be repeated with *Die Walküre*. This is the price I have to pay for enough peace and quiet to be able at least to finish composing my works.' (4 February)

He had already written to the king on 12 January, begging 'put my works on, but not without me', and had listed the conditions on which he would be ready to take part in preparing model performances of *Rheingold* and *Walküre*: the king was to give him absolute authority, the performers were to be at his exclusive disposal, the theatre to be closed for six weeks, the intendant to be given leave of absence.

He had read the entire letter to the king, Düfflipp wrote to Tribschen, but had gained nothing by it, except that the king had finally called him 'Richard Wagner's advocate'. Düfflipp also wrote to Bülow appealing for his help, and giving the significant information that 'it is impossible for His Majesty to approve a formal appointment for Wagner in the prevailing regrettable circumstances' – meaning Wagner's relationship with Cosima. When he had asked for other, more acceptable suggestions, Frau von Bülow-Liszt had replied that the Meister was not in a position to make any others. (BB, IV, pp. 364ff.)

Bülow excused himself on the grounds of his health: 'I regard a return to Munich as tantamount to suicide.' Levi, too, again refused an invitation, which earned him Wagner's undying respect.

As 3 May approached, the anniversary of his first summons from Ludwig, he wrote him a poem:

> Noch einmal mögest Du die Stimme hören,
> die einstens aus Dir selber zu mir sprach . . .

('May you hear once more the voice that once spoke to me from you'; KLRW, II, pp. 303f.)

Under the draft in the Brown Book he wrote '(dernier effort!)'. This last effort to dissuade the king from his purpose was as unsuccessful as the rest: the first performance of *Die Walküre* was given on 26 June, conducted by Wüllner.

## II

In the meantime a new avenue had opened for Wagner. 'I really would not know what to balance against the infamy of the present production of *Die Walküre*, if it were not for the Bayreuth hopes,' Cosima wrote to Nietzsche on 24 June 1870. Wagner had never forgotten the pleasing impression the town had made on him on the occasion of his one visit thirty-five years before, but it was only when he looked it up in an encyclopedia on 5 March that he learned of the existence of the old Margraves' Opera House with its unusually large stage, which he at once thought might make it suitable for the *Ring*. As Glasenapp emphasizes, however, it was not what might be called the physical or topographical considerations that constituted the new element in the idea of Bayreuth which was born at that moment, but the fundamental rejection of the modern civilization of the large cities.

Nietzsche was one of the first to be told of the idea, since Wagner was confident of gaining his support for it. Early in 1870 Wagner read Nietzsche's paper *Socrates and Greek Tragedy*, which attributes the decadence of Greek drama from Aeschylus to Euripides to the decline of the lyric and the proliferation of dialectic – an idea he himself had expressed twenty years before in connection with the artwork of the future.[7] He wrote to assure the author of his own conviction as to the correctness of the theory. 'But I am worried about you, and pray with my whole heart that you won't ruin yourself. I would advise you, if I may, not to handle such very implausible views in short papers, with an eye to making an easy effect for considerations that will prove fatal in the long run, but. . . to gird yourself to write a larger, more comprehensive work on the subject.' (4 February 1870) 'Turn your paper into a book,' Cosima agreed; 'certainly it is too good for just a nibble.' Reading the paper had wrought a change in the gloom that had been affecting Trib-schen, she went on. The pilgrimage to the finest age of human history had had such a beneficial effect that the next morning Wagner had got his Siegfried as far as the Rhine, blowing his high-spirited theme accompanied by the boldest and most exuber-ant violin figure; hearing it the Rhinemaidens were filled with joy and hope and let their own song be heard, broad and strong. (8 February)

'I now have no one with whom I can discuss things so seriously as with you – except for the one and only Cosima,' Wagner confessed to Nietzsche. But he was concerned from the first that his young friend should not permit himself to be distracted from his true calling for his sake. 'If you had become a musician, then you would be approximately where I would be if I had stuck to the classics . . . Remain a classicist now, so that, as such, you may let yourself be guided by music . . . Show what classical studies are for, and help me to bring about the great "renaissance", in which Plato embraces Homer and Homer, now imbued with Plato's ideas, at last becomes great Homer indeed.'

'Pater Seraphice,' Nietzsche wrote, to greet Wagner on his birth-day, 'if what you once wrote – to my pride – is true, and music shall guide me, then you at all events are the conductor of this my music.' He signed himself, continuing the allusion to the last scene of *Faust*, 'one of the blessed boys'. (21 May) He brought his friend Erwin Rohde to stay at Tribschen from 11 to 13 May. Rohde, later to be famous as the author of *Psyche*, a two-volume work on the Greek belief in the immortality of the soul, amazed Wagner and Cosima by his apparently inexhaustible knowledge of the Greek world. Cosima thought him more impressive than Nietzsche himself. For his part, Rohde told Nietzsche that the visit to Tribschen had been the climax of the fifteen months he had spent in Italy; he had left the house with a respect and admiration for every aspect of the life lived there that bordered on the religious. Reporting this to Cosima, Nietzsche went on: 'I understand how the Athenians could erect altars to Aeschylus and Sophocles, and give Sophocles the heroic name of "Dexion", because he entertained the gods in his house. This presence of the gods in the house of genius creates that religious atmosphere of which I write . . . In the matter of Bayreuth, I have been thinking that the best thing for me would be to suspend my professional activities for a few years and join your pilgrimage to the Fichtelgebirge.[8] Those are just hopes, to which I gladly surrender.' (19 June)

Cosima replied that they had been finding out all they could about Bayreuth from their bookseller, who came from Wunsiedel, and the auspices sounded very favourable. 'You shall write your book in Bayreuth, and we shall do honour to your book. And if they are castles in the air . . . I shall tend them and make them more productive than any real estates have ever been.' (24 June)

The Bayreuth plan, even if it was only a castle in the air, was what saved Wagner at this time from a paralysis of his creative powers. All the same, as he wrote to Schott, he postponed completing the score of *Siegfried* deliberately, having learned that his Most Serene patron, after 'executing' the *Walküre,* was bending his bow at the next score, so as to lose no time in performing the same experiment on it. He was now quietly working on a counter-plan of his own, to produce the entire *Ring* according to *his* wishes, and it was that that had encouraged him to get on with the composition of *Götterdämmerung.* (Autumn 1870)

Exuberantly, he went on with the composition sketch of the first act: 'Family council', he wrote above the scene in the Gibichungs' Hall, where the plot against Siegfried is hatched. (7 February) By 25 March he was writing to Judith Mendès that on the previous day Siegfried had drunk Gutrune's fateful potion; 'I wager that will bring about some misfortune that I shall have to set to music.' And when he had written the final scene of the act, which Cosima found almost unbearable in its cruelty, he wrote below that 'Fidi', their own small Siegfried, 'thinks it's funny!!' (5 June) But on the back of the sheet of manuscript paper he wrote down his first notes, evoking the names of Schiller and Goethe, for the commemorative essay on Beethoven.

The committee set up in Bonn to celebrate the centenary of Beethoven's birth pointedly made no approach to Wagner. From Vienna, on the other hand, there came an invitation to conduct the Choral Symphony, but as the signatories of the letter included his old adversaries Eduard Schelle and Eduard Hanslick he had regretfully to reply that any document that appeared over those two names belonged necessarily to the category of what was barred to him. (To N. Dumba, 24 June)

The first rumours of war had reached Tribschen, when Wagner, Cosima, the two eldest girls, a student named Schobinger and the servant Jakob set out on 10 July on an expedition that had been planned for a long time, to climb the Pilatus. In spite of her weariness, Cosima was impressed by the sublime quiet and solitude, the more so as Wagner reminded her that experiences like this in the past had inspired his representation of the gods' existence in the *Ring*. 'While we were up there we read the *Parerga* diligently,' she wrote to Nietzsche, 'since recently the Meister has taken up Schopenhauer's aesthetics. You will soon be able to read his – the Meister's – ideas on the philosophy of music in an essay on Beethoven.' (16 July)

Their return to Tribschen on 15 July heralded a rush of events. The marriage of Hans and Cosima was legally dissolved in Berlin on 18 July, France declared war on Prussia on 19 July, and on the same day their French friends, their ranks swollen by Camille Saint-Saëns, Henri Duparc and René Joly, arrived in Lucerne, on their way home from 'model' performances in Weimar and Munich. The declaration of war touched Cosima in a very personal way, for it was her brother-in-law Emile Ollivier, now president of the French Council of Ministers, who issued it, 'le coeur léger'. At Tribschen they agreed not to mention the burning questions on which they would not be able to agree, but to keep to the subject of art, where they all agreed so well. Judith sensed Wagner's passionate excitement at the events. 'I admit', she wrote, 'that I would not have liked him so much if he had not succumbed to patriotic enthusiasm like the rest of us at that moment of decision.'

There was music. Wagner sang passages from *Walküre* and *Siegfried* and, from *Götterdämmerung*, the Norns' scene, of which he had just finished the orchestral sketch. Saint-Saëns, who accompanied him, reading admirably at sight, was so carried away that at the end he cried: 'You owe it to the French to write them a *Charlemagne*!'

The Mendès and Villiers stayed until the end of the month before going on to Paris.

The fact that King Ludwig mobilized the Bavarian army and took the side of Prussia helped to turn away Wagner's wrath from him. For his birthday on 25 August, Wagner sent him a copy of the orchestral sketch of the prelude and first act of *Götterdämmerung*, with a topical poem of dedication:

> Gesprochen ist das Königswort,
> dem Deutschland neu erstanden . . .

('The royal word has been spoken to Germany, newly risen . . .' RWGS, VIII, pp. 339f.)

On the same day Wagner and Cosima were married in the Protestant church in Lucerne. Messages of congratulation and good wishes arrived from far and wide. Mathilde Wesendonk sent a wonderful bouquet of edelweiss, the flower which is to be found only on dangerous mountain slopes.

While following the events of the war with growing interest, Wagner continued to work at the essay on Beethoven which he had started while their guests were with them. Throughout the essay, ideas inspired by the events of the time, on the relationship of the German artist to his people and the national spirit, chime in among the reflections on the metaphysics of music. 'So let us celebrate the great pathfinder in the wilderness to which Paradise degenerated!' the essay ends. 'But let us celebrate him worthily – no less worthily than the victories of German courage: for he who enriches the world with joy has precedence over him who conquers the world!' (RWGS, IX, pp. 61ff.)

'The voice of the prophet in the desert,' Rohde wrote to Nietzsche, when it was published at the end of the year, 'an elevating reminder of the existence of a better life in the midst of this time when one is daily driven ever further from one's true life. The book is a true revelation of the inner meaning and purpose of music, a revelation which no one could make as profoundly or as convincingly as this genius.' (29 December)

A private Beethoven festival also took place at Tribschen during the winter of 1870–1, with a cycle of the quartets, which Wagner rehearsed with three players from Zürich and Hans Richter on the viola. One of them left a memoir of the sessions, remarking that they soon recognized Wagner's calibre. 'His blue eyes flashed, he jumped up, now just beating time gently, to indicate a nuance with a graphic gesture. But then when the pieces were played again in their proper context everything came together as if fashioned in bronze, and the most easily overlooked phrases acquired life and consequence.' (FWSZ, II, pp. 318ff.)

Nietzsche, who had been taken ill while serving as a volunteer medical orderly, was invited to come and hear the quartets when he recovered. In her letter Cosima referred to E. T. A. Hoffmann's fairy tale of the Golden Pot: Wagner was Lindhorst, the archivist with magical powers, Nietzsche the dreaming student Anselmus, and she herself the Orange Lily. 'The Archivist wishes me to invite you to the quartet recital, which I hereby do. If you come you will find the Isle of Spirits in its usual dream state and as always concerned about you and your dreams.' (21 January 1871)

Alluding to Goethe's praise of German courage,[9] Wagner wrote in his *Beethoven*: 'Let the Germans now be courageous in peace as well; let them cherish their true merit and cast false appearances away; let them not aspire to seem something that they are not, and let them on the other hand recognize what is uniquely theirs.' Is he to be blamed if for once he relaxed and shrugged off a troublesome subject that had depressed him for days at a time with a sudden burst of laughter? In the middle of November 1870 he wrote in the Brown Book the outline of 'The Capitulation, Comedy by Aristop Hanes'. The point of the piece is that what it ultimately mocks is not the Parisian capitulation to the German army, but the German surrender to Parisian opera and operetta. So that there should be no doubt as to his intention, when he came to write the play he changed 'The' to 'A' in the title – *A Capitulation: Comedy in the Antique Manner*. 'My subject inspects no other aspect of the French but the one in the reflection of whose light we Germans truly show ourselves more ridiculous than they, who, in all their follies, are always original, while we, in our sickening imitation of them, sink far below the ridiculous.' (RWGS, IX, pp. 3f.)

As German writers seem to take pride in misunderstanding this comedy, a Frenchman should be allowed to speak. In reality it is a play on words, G. Leprince writes, it is about a German capitulation in the world of the theatre. What else does the indefinite article in the title mean, if not that the word 'capitulation' is to be understood as having been transferred? 'Admittedly, one can be mistaken as to that, if one has read only the title. But if one is going to make the comedy the grounds for a destructive condemnation of its author, then one has the duty at least to read it and take all its allusions into account. Otherwise one is open to a charge of bad faith.'[10]

Without revealing his authorship, Wagner asked Hans Richter to write some incidental music for it: 'it ought to parody Offenbach's parodies'. (28 November) After the play had been turned down by the Berlin Vorstadttheater, where it had been sent anonymously, Richter admitted to great relief, as it would have been impossible for him to compose à la Offenbach.

Astonishingly, while Wagner was writing this revue piece, he was simultaneously engaged on the composition of his most personal piece of music. On 4 December he completed the score of the 'Tribschen Idyll with Fidi-Birdsong and Orange Sunrise, a symphonic birthday greeting to his Cosima from her Richard'. 'The first Christmas Eve when I have given Richard nothing and had nothing from him,' she wrote in her diary. But when she woke the next morning a sound fell on her ears that grew richer as she listened: 'I heard music, and what music! When it had died away, Richard came in with the five children and gave me the score of the symphonic birthday composition.' He had rehearsed the *Idyll* in secret with his fifteen players, and they had performed on the stairs. Richter had learnt to play the trumpet for the occasion and played the birdcall so lustily that it was a joy to hear.

This was the only one of his compositions, Wagner said, that he could write a programme for, down to the last 'and'. A sequence of experiences – 'our whole existence', as Cosima put it – is woven together and transformed into absolute music in such a way that no programmatic exposition is needed. At the same time this occasional piece opens completely new paths for symphonic music. Wagner confessed to the king that he felt a little vain about it, and he told Cosima that it was his favourite composition.

The brazen notes of world events still penetrated into the idyll of Tribschen. 'It is right that we should be silent in the face of this awesome greatness, no boasting about victories, no complaining about sufferings,' Wagner said, 'silent, profound recognition that the god disposes.' The same thought is expressed in his poem *To the German Army before Paris*: 'In ernstem Schweigen schlägst du deine Schlachten' ('In solemn silence you fight your battles') (RWGS, IX, pp. 1f.). He wanted to express gratitude for the army's achievements and sacrifice in a Symphony for the Fallen, but when he made discreet enquiries in Berlin he was told that he should not imagine he had a monopoly of the German spirit, and moreover they did not intend to make special arrangements to furnish unpleasant impressions for themselves. His proposal for a festive march, with a chorus to be sung by the people as the troops returned home, also failed to gain approval. So he contented himself with writing a concert piece, the *Kaisermarsch*, a piece of strength and tenderness, its symbolism a happy blend of patriotism and humane sentiment. While he was writing it, he at last, on 5 February 1871, accomplished the long-deferred task of finishing the score of *Siegfried*. The last page of the composition sketch of the march shows clearly enough how the descending fourths of Siegfried's and Brünnhilde's rejoicing were the inspiration of the melody of the closing chorus:

> Feind zum Trutz,
> Freund zum Schutz,
> Allem Volk das deutsche Reich zu Heil und Nutz!

('Defying foes, defending friends, the German Empire is for the good of all people'; RWGS, XII, p. 376)

Nevertheless, the idea of a Funeral Symphony, based on the grave A♭ minor theme he had originally conceived in connection with *Romeo and Juliet*, was to recur constantly in the years to come.

If judgement is to be passed on Wagner's four 'occasional' pieces of 1870–1, then they must all be taken as a whole: the Beethoven essay, as serious and impassioned as the first movement of a symphony, the burlesque scherzo of *A Capitulation*, the Andante con moto of the *Siegfried Idyll*, and the Allegro maestoso of the *Kaisermarsch*. It is only together that they reveal the whole Wagner – and we must also remember that his principal concern throughout the whole period was always the *Ring*.

Wagner's and Cosima's reactions to the events of the war, which ran through the whole gamut of conflicting emotions, from approval of the bombardment of Paris to concern for their French friends, is reflected in their correspondence with the Mendès. On 5 September 1870 Wagner wrote to Catulle: 'Your letter, my dear Catulle, touched me profoundly. Thank you! Yes, happily there is a realm of existence where we are, and shall always be, united . . . For we are in perfect accord on these two great principles: Love and Music. Those are the two lights, shining from the same hearth, that, when placed behind the bad painting of this earthly life, render it transparent and reveal it to us as a mirage!. . . . If only you had stayed with us! I would have made you prisoners. Not of war. Solely in all honour, but in love and in music above all.'

The entry in Cosima's diary for 12 September reads: 'Letter from C. Mendès, very elegiac, he thinks he will die below the walls of Paris.' Catulle had enclosed a 'proclamation from Victor Hugo to the Germans', 'the sort of pure nonsense', Cosima commented, 'that the French find sublime'. (CT, I, p. 284) It stirred Wagner to sit down the same day and write both the Mendès a 'vigorous' letter, running to four pages in print: 'My dears, I do not need to tell you how sad your letter made me. It is truly a tragedy that is taking place between us.' When he had been in a similar situation, it was a 'hydropathic cure by philosophy' that had helped him. But they fortified themselves with 'a kind of false poetry' – referring to Hugo – 'which, for quite a long time, has been upheld as true poetry by a propitious chance which flattered the spirit of a sanguine nation'.

He recommended them, instead, to try 'to find a true statesman . . . capable, above all, of explaining to the French nation what the German nation is, and what its intentions are'.

In his closing paragraphs Wagner rehearsed his theory of the danger of this 'nation vraiment généreuse' becoming too centralized in Paris, in combination with his own disappointments in trying to win the city's favour. 'I see myself – in your place – on the ramparts of Paris, and I say to myself: should this enormous capital city fall in ruins, perhaps!

'But not perhaps! Rather, assuredly! It would be the point of departure for the regeneration of the French people . . . Blessings from your friends! We are with you! Au revoir! Ever yours.'[11]

Communications into and out of Paris were cut directly after this, but as soon as they were re-opened Catulle lost no time in sending a seven-page letter to his 'bien-aimé maître' on 3 July 1871: 'I regret your not having received my letter all the more because in it I said a host of things, in complete disorder, which . . . would be singularly meaningless by now. One of them, however, remains eternally true, it is something that you know: that events do not undo the ties joining people's spirits, the sword does not exist that can cut through that kind of Gordian knot, and our friendship, composed of your kindness and my gratitude, exists without end, and has not even been threatened.'

The prophecy proved false nevertheless. Wagner's inclusion of A

*Capitulation* in Volume IX of his collected writings in 1873 ('he didn't have enough manuscripts', Cosima wrote; CT, I, p. 698) offended Catulle, 'who was especially disgusted by the gratuitous insult to Victor Hugo'. He attended the Bayreuth Festival of 1876, but did not set foot inside the gates of Wahnfried.[12] In all probability, too, he wanted to avoid running into Judith, from whom he was by then divorced.

In May 1869 Wagner had been elected a corresponding member of the musical section of the Royal Academy of Arts in Berlin. In the spring of 1871, as he girded himself for his first visit to the new empire, to inform himself as to the practical and personal preconditions for realizing his idea for a festival, he wrote a paper entitled *On the Destiny of Opera*, which he hoped to deliver to the Academy. The difficulty, he was to write in the preface, lay in treating at length for the second time a subject that he had already discussed in detail years before in *Opera and Drama*. But a glance at the text is enough to see that he gave the subject a quite new turn, in the emphasis on an 'improvisatory' element in drama and in music, which ought to be more successful in blending the two into a whole than the rigid formalism of opera had so far managed to be. It should be like the difference between a 'scene in nature' and a 'work of architecture'. (*Über die Bestimmung der Oper*; RWGS, IX, pp. 127ff.)

Nietzsche arrived in Tribschen on 3 April, on his way from Lugano. He had applied for a chair of philosophy at Basel, and since he still had to demonstrate his qualifications as a philosopher, he had used his holiday to write an essay on the 'origin and aim of tragedy', based on his lectures on Greek music drama, Socrates and tragedy, and the Dionysian world view, and intended to be the first part of his 'major book on the Greeks'. 'I live in a state of derisive alienation from classical philology, and can think of nothing worse,' he wrote to Rohde from Lugano on 29 March. 'So I am gradually getting accustomed to my philosopherhood, and already believe in myself.' His principal reason for breaking his journey back to Basel at Tribschen, his sister tells us, was to read the piece to Wagner. 'But my brother must have suffered a slight disappointment. Being so sensitive, he probably noticed that Wagner had hoped that the new essay would serve in some way to glorify his own art. Great as my brother's enthusiasm for Wagner and his music was, his conscientiousness as a scholar at first refused to associate two very disparate things in the essay, which was at that time entitled "Greek Gaiety".

But regard for his friend won, for as soon as my brother was back in Basel he set to with the greatest enthusiasm to rework it, cutting some chapters and restricting himself now to the subject of Greek tragedy, so as to be able to refer to Wagner's art.' (EFWN, pp. 71f.)

The genesis of the book and the papers that had preceded it had been stimulated by Wagner's ideas and art, under the aegis of the Genelli *Dionysus*, and the six days Nietzsche spent at Tribschen at this stage in its writing will have played a decisive role in its reworking. But his sister's inference that moral pressure was brought to bear on him, by either Wagner or Cosima, and that the reworking was a 'burnt offering on the altar of his friendship', is completely unconfirmed.[13]

'I shall devote tomorrow to packing,' Cosima wrote to Nietzsche on 13 April, 'and I want to get a last letter from Tribschen to you today.' On 15 April she and Wagner started their journey to the 'empire'. In Augsburg they were met by Düfflipp, who conveyed the king's wish to have the first two acts of *Siegfried* performed. Wagner replied that he would sooner burn them and go a-begging than consent. The next day they arrived in Bayreuth. 'A charming edifice,' Cosima commented after they had seen the Margraves' Opera House, 'but the theatre is not in the least suitable for us. Therefore, build, so much the better.' In Leipzig their friends and relatives gathered for a festive reception. His sister Luise Brockhaus found he had become benign and fatherly, and thanked Cosima for having the courage to marry him. In Dresden he had a joyful reunion with the faithful Pusinelli. Then he took Cosima on a tour of the streets and the secluded corners of his boyhood and told her of the impressions the Brühl Terrace, the Frauenkirche and so on had made on him then.

All the preparations for their stay in Berlin, where they arrived at the Tiergarten Hotel on 25 April, had been made by Karl Tausig and Countess von Schleinitz, the wife of the Minister of the Royal House [Internal Affairs]. 'The lecture at the Academy . . . was a curious proceeding,' Cosima reported to Nietzsche. 'The "Scientific" has nothing to do with its sister institution, so the scholars were absent, and our Meister delivered his paper at the conference table to Dorn, Joachim, Taubert and a few, admittedly very well-disposed, painters.' (12 May)

On 5 May Wagner conducted a concert in the Royal Opera House in aid of the King Wilhelm Association. While the emperor had assured him of every facility, Hülsen the intendant told the orchestra to pay no attention to Wagner: the man was there to wave his baton, he said, not to give orders. Only Frau von Schleinitz's last-minute intervention frustrated another high-handed act by the intendant, who had forbidden the decoration of the conductor's desk and the admission of any people carrying flowers: asked by her for an explanation, he excused himself by saying it had been a misunderstanding. Every seat in the house was filled when the emperor and empress entered their box. The concert began with the *Kaisermarsch,* followed by Beethoven's C minor Symphony, the *Lohengrin* prelude, Wotan's Farewell and the Magic Fire music, and the finale of Act I of *Lohengrin*. In response to tumultuous appeals from the audience, after some hesitation, Wagner played an encore of the *Kaisermarsch*.

The emperor declared that he had never heard anything so accomplished as this concert, and his opinion was confirmed by what the leader of the orchestra said to Wagner, apropos of the symphony: 'You have no idea of the casual attitude they take here to things like this.'

In the week before the concert he had had an interview with Bismarck, a historic meeting. At the beginning of the year Cosima had sent Wagner's poem *To the German Army before Paris* to the German headquarters, addressing it to the chancellor's confidant, Lothar Bucher. Bismarck thanked Wagner in a cordial letter written in his own hand, concluding: 'You, too, have overcome the resistance of the Parisians after a long struggle, with your works, in which I have always had the keenest interest, although at times inclining towards the opposition party; it is my belief and my hope that many more victories will be granted them, at home and abroad.' (21 February 1871)

Even before the end of the war Wagner had told Cosima of his wish to pay homage to the great man, the founder of the empire, who continued to be the subject of controversy even in court circles. At the special instigation of Bucher, on arrival in Berlin he left his card at·the chancellor's residence, and received an invitation to call on the evening of 3 May. Bismarck received him in an intimate family circle with as much exquisite courtesy 'as if he were greeting perhaps the minister of an allied state'.

'You know something that none of us know,' Wagner said, meaning the secret of the political strength of the nation. 'The only thing that can be said in my praise', the prince replied with a subtle smile, 'is that now and then I have managed to procure a signature. I have found the hole in the crown' – 'in the spiked helmet' according to another version – 'that lets the smoke through.'

The subject of books arose, but Bismarck was dismissive, saying that nowadays he only ever saw their spines. To Wagner's regret the conversation dwindled into diplomatic and parliamentary gossip.

He had never encountered such self-confidence, Bismarck told Bucher after the meeting. Wagner himself acknowledged the foundations on which his confidence rested, when he said in his *Review of the Festival of 1876* that his faith in the secret artistic strength of the nation had truly required a courage to match it. (RWGS, X, pp. 103ff.)

For his part he was delighted by the prince's genuine amiability. 'No trace of reticence or reserve. Easy of speech, cordially interested in others, inspiring complete confidence and sympathy. But', he added, 'we can only watch each other at work, each can act only in his own sphere. I would not so much as try to win him for me, or ask his support for my cause. The meeting remains something that I value very highly.' (GLRW, IV, pp. 355f., 451; DMCW, I, p. 561)

Cosima wrote to Eliza Wille, mentioning the fact that François Wille and Bismarck had been students at Göttingen together: Wagner would be delighted to see her and her husband again. 'He would have a lot to say to the latter about his princely friend, who made the most significant and agreeable impression on him.' (June 1871, FWSZ, II, pp. 461f.)

There are thus no grounds for the interpretation that has been put on the meeting, to the effect that Wagner sought it in the hope of gaining Bismarck's support and, on being refused, turned against the chancellor. On the contrary: when he wrote the preface to his collected writings shortly afterwards he came out firmly against those self-appointed critics of the founder of the empire, who expected 'a statesman to justify his successes to those who previously had had no idea that such things were even possible, and to subject his measures to the approval of people who first have to have explained to them what is at issue'. (RWGS, I, pp. iii ff.)

His other important activity while in Berlin was to discuss the Bayreuth Festival with Karl Tausig. As the provisional business manager of the undertaking, under the patronage of Countess von Schleinitz, Tausig, 'undeterred by Wagner's fulminations against the Jews', as Newman comments, 'threw himself wholeheartedly into the Bayreuth scheme'.

Leaving Berlin for home, they stopped again in Leipzig, and it was in the town of his birth, on 12 May, that Wagner made the first public announcement of the festival, to take place in 1873. The patrons and benefactors who raised the necessary financial means would receive 'the title and rights of Patrons of the Stage Festival in Bayreuth, while the realization of the undertaking itself will be entrusted to my experience and skills and to my endeavours alone'.

Wagner had written to tell King Ludwig of his plan on 1 March. The king's comment to Düfflipp had been 'I do not like Wagner's plan at all' (19 April), but he now wrote to Wagner himself: 'The gods have inspired your plan for performing the "Nibelungs" in Bayreuth.' (26 May)

One of the last stops on the way back to Tribschen was in Heidelberg, which they reached on 15 May. Absorbed in the view of the castle bathed in the evening sunlight, Wagner's attention was caught suddenly by a puppet show set up on the street, and they watched to the end as the hero, Kaspar, outwitted the foppish count, kept just out of reach of every representative of the law, cocked a snook at devil and priest alike, vanquished death and hell and took his leave of the enthralled audience with a saucy bow: 'Spit out the lights!'

'It was the best moment in the whole trip,' Cosima thought, and, not least, the most instructive in Wagner's view. He could not remember when he had last had so forceful a reminder of the living spirit of the theatre. What a daemonic being that puppeteer was! By creating a world of characters from nothing and animating them with his own breath, he demonstrated in the plainest possible way that mimetic genius consists not in 'affectation', however polished, but in the intrinsic ability to forget one's self and enter into other souls and bodies. At the same time he confirmed what Wagner had said so recently in his paper to the Berlin Academy: that this mimic capability originates in the art of improvisation. And so the unknown puppeteer of Heidelberg was commemorated side by side with Schröder-Devrient in Wagner's essay *On Actors and Singers* (RWGS, IX, pp. 157ff.)

'Unique happiness at being in his own world again,' Cosima

confessed as they at last ended their journey on 16 May. But Wagner did not have the chance to spin himself back into his cocoon. In the twelve months between then and the laying of the foundation stone of the festival theatre, he brought off the incredible double feat of writing the composition sketches of the second and third acts of *Götterdämmerung* at the same time as he was organizing the preparations for the Bayreuth Festival.

When he read Cosima his pamphlet *On the Performance of the Festival Drama 'Der Ring des Nibelungen'*, he remarked: 'As for us, we can do without it. Our pleasure lies in the idea.' He foresaw that the realization of the idea would bring struggles and disappointment in its wake. 'I curse the music that puts me to this torture, that will not let me enjoy my good fortune for a moment,' he exclaimed when one such crisis was upon him. 'It's a madness, or I ought to have been made fierce like Beethoven. It's not true, what you think, that this is my element. To spend my life improving my mind, to enjoy my good luck, that was my spur. It was different once. Oh, I feel as though I was trying to build a house on a catalpa flower. I should have to fill the world with airy vapours first, to separate me and my art from the human race. Idylls, quartets, I should like to write some before I die – and all the while there's this bother about performing the *Ring*!' (DMCW, I, pp. 578f.)

The single response to his appeal had come, in the meantime, from a complete stranger, the Mannheim music publisher Emil Heckel, who wrote to Wagner asking what contribution he could make to the success of the great undertaking. (15 May) Wagner sent him a letter of cordial good wishes and referred him to Karl Tausig, to whom Heckel explained the idea he had had of founding a Wagner Society, with branches in various towns: the purpose of these would be to finance the festival by purchasing patronage vouchers corporately, and so give people of modest means the opportunity to buy a share of a voucher.

'Your Wagner Society is an excellent idea,' Tausig replied, and Wagner pronounced his readiness to conduct a concert in Mannheim, in spite of his commitments: 'Be prepared . . . for me to announce my arrival – perhaps in the autumn – at short notice, and then do you see to it that everything is done decently.' (21 June)

He began the composition sketch of Act II on 24 June 1871: '*Midsummer Day!!!*' he wrote at the head of the introduction to the blackest nocturnal music ever written. There is no sign that the composition had been interrupted for a year: for all its motivic complexity the 'ghostly, dreamlike duologue' between Hagen and Alberich, which he later described as one of the high points of the entire work, was written straight down without any corrections or emendations either while he was writing or inserted later.

Then came the news of Tausig's death of typhus in Leipzig on 17 June. Again, as with Schnorr, he felt with daemonic force that fate, unable to touch him, had laid hands on one of his faithful friends instead. He reflected on the tragedy of Tausig's life, his precocity, a Schopenhauer at sixteen, suffering under his Jewishness, taking no pleasure in his immense virtuosity, since Liszt was greater and he was himself too great to be Liszt's pupil. And now this 'stupidity of fate', that snatched him away at the very moment when a great occupation would have given him inner joy and satisfaction. Wagner wrote him an epitaph:

> Reif sein zum Sterben,
> des Lebens zögernd sprießende Frucht,
> früh reif sie erwerben,
> in Lenzes jäh erblühender Flucht,
> war es Dein Los, war es Dein Wagen –
> Wir müssen Dein Los wie Dein Wagen beklagen.

('To be ripe for death, to harvest early the shyly sprouting fruit of life in the frenziedly blooming flight of spring, was it your fate, was it your daring – we must mourn your fate and your daring together.' *Grabschrift für Karl Tausig*, RWGS, IX, p. 324)

Obtaining the king's approval was another cause for anxiety: if he insisted on his contractual right to have the *Ring* performed in Munich then Bayreuth would be in jeopardy. Rumours were beginning to circulate that Ludwig's new enthusiasm was architecture, that he was going to have his hunting lodges gilded and furbished in the style of Louis XIV. 'My thoughts are heavy,' Wagner complained, 'I shall never be happy or well. This disgrace, being dependent on the king, it's unheard-of and insupportable.' He discarded what he had written of Hagen's summoning of the vassals, because it was 'over-composed' – blaming it on external circumstances. But he greeted Cosima with the new version on their wedding anniversary, 25 August. He started the composition of the vassals' scene with contrapuntal studies on 'Was tost das Horn?' When Cosima looked in on him, he clapped his hand to his head:

'My thoughts are itching'; but the next morning he was able to play her the wild chorus, 'Der Hagedorn sticht nun nicht mehr . . .'

In the end his faith always triumphed: 'I expect a miracle, you will see, it will come, how and where I don't know, but it will come.'

He finished the sketch of the second act on 25 October, in exactly four months. On 1 November he wrote to the banker Friedrich Feustel, the chairman of the town council of Bayreuth, and a friend of Wagner's sister Ottilie Brockhaus, asking for a site for the theatre. 'Let me say at once, too, that as a site for a house for myself I was much taken with a longish piece of meadow land, lying between the left side of the palace garden and also [like the proposed site for the theatre] towards its far end, and the road out to the Eremitage.'

After the council had agreed to the proposal, Wagner went to Bayreuth on 15 December to look at the site for the theatre again, and from there to Mannheim, where Cosima and Nietzsche joined him. 'Herr Jesses, I'm not a prince!' he exclaimed in the purest Saxon, when he was greeted at the station with a resounding three cheers from the members of the Mannheim Wagner Society.

The historic 'Mannheim Concert' took place on 20 December: the *Kaisermarsch*, which he interpreted as a dramatic representation of a military procession; the overture to *Die Zauberflöte*; Beethoven's A major Symphony; the *Lohengrin* and *Meistersinger* preludes; and the prelude and close of *Tristan*. In the morning of the same day he had performed the *Siegfried Idyll* to a small circle of friends.

The concert attracted not only Wagner's supporters but also drew his enemies into the open. He referred to this at the banquet after the concert when he spoke of the people who were assisting his undertaking – 'and then there's Heckel here, who is annoying people', shaking his hand heartily as he spoke. Subsequently a Munich professor, W. H. Riehl, cultural historian, author of novellas and composer of salon music, bestirred himself and gave public lectures in Mannheim, calling for the foundation of Anti-Wagner Societies. Wagner got his own back on Riehl, who, he said, had broken out of his retreat in order to stir up 'all kinds of petty but malicious mischief', by having an article he had written on Riehl's collection of novellas reprinted with a new satirical afterword. (RWGS, VIII, pp. 205ff.)

Nietzsche wrote to Rohde that he felt wonderfully confirmed in his ideas about music by what he had experienced in Mannheim that week. 'If only you could have been there! Other artistic memories and experiences are nothing, compared to this latest one! I was like a person who has had a premonition, at the moment of its fulfilment. For music is precisely that and nothing else. And that, and nothing else, is precisely what I mean by the word "music", when I am writing about the Dionysian!' (21 December)

Nietzsche sent his new book to Tribschen on 2 January 1872. To please Cosima he had had their copy printed on paper in a yellowish shade she particularly liked. 'May my book be to at least some degree worthy of the interest you have taken in its genesis until now, really to my shame,' he wrote to Wagner. 'And if I myself think that I am right in the main argument, it means no more than that *you* with *your art* must be eternally right.' (2 January)

Cosima's letter thanking him took off in a flight of lyrical eloquence: 'How beautiful your book is! How beautiful and how profound, how profound and how audacious! . . . In this book you have conjured spirits that I had believed obeyed the bidding only of our Meister; there are two worlds, one we do not see because it is too remote, and one we do not recognize because it is too close to us, and you have thrown a brilliant light upon them both . . . I have read this book like a poem which reveals to us the essence of the deepest problems, and I can no more tear myself away from it than the Meister can, for it answers all the unconscious questions of my inner being.' (18 January)

On the same day Wagner wrote an important letter to his nephew Clemens Brockhaus, in which he refuted the latter's criticisms of *Socrates and Greek Tragedy*, and at the same time gave his own opinion of *The Birth of Tragedy*: 'It is a truly godlike thought that the profoundly significant rebirth of art under the influence of the German spirit has been seen by this mind as simultaneously the rebirth . . . of the essence of Greek art. If it is my influence that has guided him in this, then certainly none can judge better than I how deeply and inwardly my thought has become the property of this man who is academically so formidably well equipped with everything that I have had to leave uncultivated in myself.' (CWFN, II, pp. 94ff.)

An incident shortly before, of little significance in itself, appears in retrospect as an early symptom of the way the friendship was to develop. In November Nietzsche had completed a composition for piano duet, twenty minutes in duration, entitled *Echo of a New Year's Eve, with processional song, peasant dance and midnight bell.* 'Now I am copying it', he wrote to Gustav Krug, 'in order to make a birthday present of it to my excellent and honoured friend Frau Cosima W.' (13 November 1871) It was a matter of so much importance to him that he also let his friends Karl von Gersdorff and Erwin Rohde into the secret: he was agog to know what Tribschen would think of his music, since he had never yet heard a competent opinion of it. (To Rohde, 21 December 1871)

Just as Wagner had dedicated the *Siegfried Idyll* to Cosima for her birthday in the previous year, so now Nietzsche dedicated his *New Year's Eve* to her. But he sent it to her through the post instead of presenting it in person, refused her cordial invitation on the grounds that he needed time and solitude to think about his lectures, and spent Christmas on his own in Basel.

He left his friends in no doubt that he regarded himself, for all his devotion to Wagner, as his equal as a cultural critic and innovator. 'I have concluded an alliance with Wagner,' he wrote to Rohde on 28 January 1872. 'You can have no conception of how close to each other we now are, and of how our plans coincide.' And his piano duet and its dedication to Cosima was a cautious attempt to put himself on the same footing as Wagner as composer and as Cosima's confidant.

Wagner resumed work on *Götterdämmerung* on 4 January 1872 with the composition sketch of the last act. 'You ought to hear the Rhinemaidens' second song!' Cosima exclaimed in her letter to Nietzsche. (18 January) But only a few days later she was lamenting that their song had been rudely interrupted. Hagen's horn itself would not have intruded so harshly as the 'ruthless summons of the world' to discuss business in Berlin and Weimar. On his return journey Wagner stopped in Bayreuth and on 1 February set up the festival management committee, consisting of the mayor Theodor Muncker and the lawyer Käfferlein, as well as Feustel. Feustel and Muncker had previously visited him at Tribschen, after the negotiations to buy the piece of land on the Stuckberg had fallen through and it had become necessary to find another site. Wagner had been inclined to give up the idea of Bayreuth after all, but Feustel's persistence and Cosima's diplomacy persuaded him at the last moment to approve of the present site.

He was back in Tribschen by 5 February and was at last able to get on with the composition sketch, which he finished on 10 April. 'He has been working less than we had hoped,' Cosima wrote to Judith. 'He has been ill and then there have been many distractions. I don't know when he will find the leisure to devote himself to his work again, for a whole ocean of affairs, conferences, journeys etc. lies before us.' (22 April)

That he was able to complete the composition sketch – thereby fixing the music in all its essentials and most of its details – in this relatively short period, in spite of all the calls on his time and energies, was due once again to the fact that it had long been prepared and waiting in his mind. We know indeed that he had already written down a version of Siegfried's Funeral March. Cosima noted in her diary on 28 September 1871, her nameday, 'Richard refuses to celebrate St. Cosmas's day. My father expressed his good wishes and Richard said: "He's a Catholic, that comes between us," which made us laugh.' But in fact he did have a late surprise for her. The next morning he called to her: 'I have composed a Greek chorus, but one that is, as it were, sung by the orchestra. After Siegfried's death, while the set is being changed, Siegmund's theme will be heard, as though the chorus is saying: that was his father; then the Sword motive, finally his own theme, then the curtain rises and Gutrune comes on thinking she has heard his horn. How could words ever evoke the impression that these serious themes do, newly recreated. Yet the music expresses the immediate present, too.' (CT, I, p. 444)[14]

On the eighteen staves that it occupies on a half-sheet of manuscript paper in the composition sketch of 1872, this powerful passage appears as a delicate tissue of fine pencil lines that can be taken in at a single look. When sketching purely instrumental music Wagner preferred to use this kind of shorthand notation, which enabled him to oversee the musical form with the eye as well as the mind.

He had been uncertain all along as to what Brünnhilde's final words should be, and had drafted more than one set of lines. He had settled on one of these versions, including the lines:

> Nach dem wunsch- und wahnlos
> heiligsten Wahlland,
> der Weltwanderung Ziel,
> von Wiedergeburt erlöst,
> zieht nun die Wissende hin.

('To the holiest chosen land, where striving and delusion are unknown, the goal of world-wandering, thither, absolved from rebirth, she will go who now knows all.')

Now, when he was starting to set her final monologue, Cosima asked him to leave out this conclusion altogether, because it struck her as 'rather artificial'. He must have been alluding to this debate in the cheerful marginal note on the orchestral sketch: 'Enough! Anything to please Cosel!'[15]

The orchestral finale appears in the composition sketch approximately as we now know it. The only major difference is that the sketch lacks the two bars in which the motive of the Gods' Downfall is played fortissimo by the strings and woodwind, so that Siegfried's theme runs directly into that of Redemption through Love.

At the end the sketch is inscribed: 'So enacted and accomplished, seven years from the day on which my Loldchen [Isolde] was born, 10 April 1872. R. W.'

It was Wagner's intention to leave Tribschen for good on 22 April, and go and live in Bayreuth. A curious encounter took place on the eve of his departure. Early in March he had received a letter which began: 'I am a Jew. By telling you that I tell you everything.' The writer went on to describe how he had dragged out his whole life in complete dispiritedness until the day when Wagner's works had first come to his knowledge, whereupon he had immersed himself in this new world and had been able to forget the other, the real world. It had been the happiest period of his life, but it too now lay in the past. Now he found himself once more in a state of the greatest desolation and had already made one attempt to take his own life. 'Perhaps you can help me again. Of course I do not mean help me from sheer pity . . . But could I not be of some use to you in the production of the "Nibelungs"? I believe I understand the work, even if not perfectly yet. I look to you, then, for help, for the help I urgently need. My parents are rich. I would have the means to go to you at once. I look for an answer as soon as possible. My address is as follows . . . Joseph Rubinstein, c/o Isaac Rubinstein, Kharkov . . .'

Before Wagner had made up his mind how to respond to this, Rubinstein arrived at Tribschen in person, in a state of complete demoralization. 'The extraordinary Russian I mentioned before has been here,' Cosima wrote to Nietzsche, 'on the evening before Wagner left, a strange, disturbing incident.' (24 April) Wagner was kindness itself and offered Rubinstein the opportunity to see him often in Bayreuth. In order to avoid seeming to help him 'from sheer pity' he took him into what was called the 'Nibelung Chancellery', where several young musicians were employed in copying parts. (See also Appendix I.)

Cosima's letter to Nietzsche, quoted above, also said she had just had a telegram announcing Wagner's safe arrival in Bayreuth. They would have been very happy to have seen Nietzsche in Tribschen just once more, and had expected him the previous Sunday. A letter would reach her there up to 29 April. 'And so, auf Wiedersehen in Bayreuth.'

Instead of a letter, Nietzsche himself arrived on 25 April for a final visit lasting two days. 'Last Saturday we bade a sad and deeply felt farewell to Tribschen,' he wrote to Gersdorff. 'Tribschen has now ceased to be: we went about as if among actual ruins, the emotion was everywhere, in the air, in the clouds, the dog wouldn't eat, when you spoke to the servants they couldn't stop sobbing. We packed all the manuscripts, letters and books – oh, it was so miserable! These three years which I have spent close to Tribschen, during which I have visited it twenty-three times – what they mean to me! If I had not had them, what would I be! I am glad that I have conserved that Tribschen world for myself in my book.' (1 May)

Cosima too left Tribschen on 29 April – 'le coeur gros, et moi l'esprit inquiet', as she wrote to Judith. Wagner met her and the five children and Russ at Bayreuth and drove with them to the Hotel Fantaisie, which stood in a romantic park seeming to stretch away for ever, in the nearby village of Donndorf. 'The journey was strange and very fatiguing,' she wrote to Nietzsche, 'and here, suddenly, a dream world, a fairyland!'

They had only a few days in which to relax, for on 6 May they were off again to Vienna to rehearse a concert for the Vienna Wagner Society, which took place on 12 May in the concert hall of the Musikverein, whose two thousand seats had been sold out long in advance. The way Wagner was cheered on his appearance, after every item and at the end was without parallel in the annals of concert-giving, an eyewitness wrote. One laurel wreath after another came hurtling down from the gallery to the platform, putting the players in some anxiety for their instruments.

During the performance of Wotan's Farewell, at the words 'Herauf, wabernde Lohe, umlodre mir feurig den Fels!', a thunderstorm broke out. Wagner alluded to it at the end, as he thanked his audience: 'When the Greeks had a great work in mind, they appealed to Zeus to release his lightning as a sign of his approval. Let us, who are all united in the desire to found a home and a hearth-fire for German art, interpret today's lightning as a favourable omen for our national work – as a sign of blessing from on high!'

The foundation stone of the festival theatre was due to be laid at a ceremony on 22 May, Wagner's fifty-ninth birthday, and messages poured in from far and wide from artists and other well-wishers intending to be there. But there was one person who Wagner feared would be absent.

'My great, dear friend,' he wrote to Liszt on 18 May, 'Cosima insists that you would not come, even if I invited you. If so, then we shall have to bear it, as we have had to bear so much! But I cannot *not* invite you. And what do I declare when I say to you: Come? You entered my life as the greatest man whom I have ever been permitted to call my intimate friend; you slowly withdrew yourself from me, perhaps because you could not feel the same intimacy towards me as I towards you. In your place, your reborn, innermost being came to me and fulfilled my longing to enjoy the closest intimacy with you. And so you live within me and in my sight in complete beauty, and we are as if wedded till death and beyond. You were the first person whose love ennobled me; now I am married to her, for a second, higher life, and am able to do what I could never have done alone. Thus you have become everything to me, while I have had to remain so little to you: how immense my advantage is over yours!

'If I now say to you: Come! I am saying: Come to yourself! For you will find yourself here. May you be blessed and beloved, however you decide! Your old friend, Richard.'

But as ever Princess Wittgenstein stood between him and Liszt and sought to prevent a reunion by claiming that Wagner and Cosima had renounced Christ in word and deed.

'Dear, sublime friend!' Liszt replied on 20 May. 'Deeply moved by your letter, I cannot thank you in words. But I hope ardently that all the shadows, the considerations, that keep me far away will disappear and we shall see each other again soon . . . God's blessing be with you both, and all my love. F. L.' He shrank from the idea of putting such a letter in the post, and gave it to Baroness Meyendorff to hand to Wagner in person.

It had looked, in March, as though another crisis was threatening in Wagner's relationship with King Ludwig. The latter had conveyed, through Düfflipp, another request to deliver the score of *Siegfried*, reminding him that, according to the contract of October 1864, it was the king's property. Wagner had no alternative but to deny that he had yet finished scoring the work, though he had in fact done so on 5 February 1871. He wrote back to Düfflipp that a contract had indeed been concluded at the time, but purely as a form, to placate public opinion. 'I sincerely regret that it has occurred to somebody to revert to this contract which has been completely superseded in the meantime by His Majesty's own most unequivocal, gracious assurances.' (27 March 1872)

But on 22 May a telegram arrived for the 'poet–composer Herr Richard Wagner', in which King Ludwig expressed his sincere good wishes for the occasion. 'Felicity and blessings be upon the great undertaking in the next year! Today, more than ever, I am with you in spirit.'

In spite of the rain a dense crowd gathered on the hill. Twenty-one giant flagstaffs marked out the conformation of the future building. The stone was lowered into place to the strains of the *Huldigungsmarsch,* enclosing within it a capsule containing both the king's telegram and a verse by Wagner:

> Hier schließ' ich ein Geheimnis ein,
> da ruh' es viele hundert Jahr':
> so lange es verwahrt der Stein,
> macht es der Welt sich offenbar.

> ('O may the secret buried here
> rest undisturbed for many a year;
> for while it lies beneath this stone,
> the world shall hear its clarion tone.')

Then Wagner took up the hammer: 'Bless you, my stone, long may you stand and firm may you hold!' As he turned round again he was deathly white and there were tears in his eyes.

'On that day in May in the year 1872, when the foundation stone had been laid on the hill in Bayreuth in pouring rain and under darkened skies,' Nietzsche wrote in *Wagner in Bayreuth*, 'Wagner drove back to the town with some of us; he did not speak and communed long with himself with an expression on his face that words cannot describe. He began the sixtieth year of his life on that day: everything that had gone before had been preparation for that moment. We know that at instants of extreme danger or at any decisive turning-point in life people concentrate everything they have ever experienced in an immeasurably accelerated inner vision, and review both the most recent and the most remote things with the rarest clarity of perception. What may Alexander the Great have seen at that moment when he caused Asia and Europe to be drunk from the same cup? But what Wagner inwardly reviewed on that day – what he has been, what he is and what he will be – we, the nearest to him, can also review to a certain degree: and it is only from Wagner's own viewpoint that we shall be able to understand his great deed ourselves – *in order to ensure its fruitfulness through this understanding.*'

The ceremony continued in the Margraves' Opera House, where Wagner made a speech. It had been suggested to him, he said, that he should describe his undertaking as the foundation of a national theatre, but he had no right to use such a term. Where was the 'nation' that erected such a theatre for itself? 'I had only you, the friends of my particular art, of the work and creation that are peculiarly my own, to whom I could turn to find sympathizers for my plans. And it is only in this almost personal relationship that at present I discern the ground on which we will lay the stone that shall support the whole edifice of our noblest German hopes, which as yet hover before us, an audacious vision. Though it is now but a provisional structure, it shall be so only in the same sense that for centuries all outer forms of the essential German nature have been provisional. But the essence of the German spirit is that it builds from within: the eternal god truly lives in it before it builds itself the temple in his honour.' (RWGS, IX, pp. 326ff.)

In the afternoon, again in the rococo Opera House, Wagner conducted Beethoven's Ninth Symphony, the work that had always had so significant a resonance in his life from his earliest youth. A hand-picked orchestra had assembled at his invitation from all over Germany. 'There are no programmes, no announcements, nothing tucked away in corners,' Wagner told them cheerfully at the last rehearsal. 'We're not giving a concert, we're making music for ourselves and only want to show the world how Beethoven should be played, and anyone who criticizes us can go to the devil!'

'Our ceremony is over,' Cosima wrote to Judith, 'and it was, in spite of the atrocious weather, marvellous. What Beethoven sings, "Alle Menschen werden Brüder", became a reality during these four or five days in Bayreuth, whither all our friends, known and unknown, hastened from the ends of the earth, united in one thought, one belief.' (29 May)

She wrote to Nietzsche, too, on the same day. 'The last lamps of our ceremony are now extinguished, it is quiet about us, but not yet quite peaceful within us . . . The bells are ringing – it is Corpus Christi – and the savage screech of the peacocks can be heard from time to time, the children are singing . . . and it is all, all a dream! . . . Farewell, dear, best of friends, may you be proof and steeled for ever!'

# 28

## The First Festival

### I

'I have hopes that the Meister is gradually sinking into the peaceful, twilight mood that he needs for creation,' Cosima wrote to Nietzsche on 14 June 1872; 'yesterday he took up the second act with relish and now I can hear him playing Siegfried and the Rhinemaidens.' After an interruption lasting two months, Wagner was getting himself into the mood to go on with the orchestral sketch of the third act, which he resumed on 15 June at Hagen's line 'Finden wir endlich, wohin du flogest?', and finished on 22 July. 'I lack the power', Cosima confided to her diary, 'to describe the emotion that overcame me when Richard called me to tell me the sketch was finished. He played me the ending, and I do not know whether I am more deeply moved by the sublime music or by the sublime deed.' (DMCW, I, pp. 616f.)

But Wagner's creative quiet was under constant attack and had to be fought for. The act of laying the theatre's foundation stone seemed to unleash a flood of assaults, of which two must be mentioned here, as the retaliation to which they gave rise made them in a sense historic.

The first was an attack on Nietzsche by a former fellow-student, Ulrich von Wilamowitz-Moellendorff, in a pamphlet with the aggressive title: *Philology of the Future! A Rejoinder to Friedrich Nietzsche's 'Birth of Tragedy'* (Berlin, 1872). The Meister had received, read and answered the pamphlet, Cosima told Nietzsche, 'the last in a letter to you, dear Professor, which you will receive any day now'. She would have preferred not to touch the object with a pair of tongs, she added in her impetuous manner. (14 June)

Wagner's answer was his *Open Letter to Friedrich Nietzsche* (RWGS, IX, pp. 295ff.), published on 23 June in the *Norddeutsche*

*Allgemeine Zeitung*. In it he wrote that he had not believed that things were conducted so crudely in the 'service of the Muses' and that their 'favour' could result in such lack of cultivation. 'What can things be like in our German educational institutions?' He put this question to Nietzsche precisely because he had dared, young as he was, to point out with a creative hand the harm that had been done.[1]

The other attack was of a medical nature. A Munich doctor, Theodor Puschmann, published a pamphlet with the title *Richard Wagner: A Psychiatric Study* (Berlin, 1872), purporting to give 'scientific' proof that Wagner suffered from manic delusions, which had already had a malign influence on his mental condition. One can only hope that not too many unfortunates fell into the hands of this 'priceless imbecile', as Newman calls him, who described himself on his title-page as a 'practising physician and psychiatric specialist'. (Cf. NLRW, III, pp. 564f.) But there could be no more striking illustration of the climate of the time than that such a pamphlet could be not only published but also seriously discussed in the press and reprinted three times within a year.

This time it was the disciple who sprang to his master's defence. When the weekly *Im Neuen Reich* published a leader in its issue for New Year 1873, exhorting 'self-examination and the return to the old simplicity', and commending Puschmann for having pointed the finger at the 'guiltiest' in his theoretical demonstration of Wagner's megalomania, Nietzsche's patience snapped and he pilloried the 'scientific-sounding cries of this huckster' in the *Musikalisches Wochenblatt* for 17 January.

Although Liszt, who since 1869 had again been spending part of each year in Weimar, had not attended the foundation-stone ceremony, Wagner was not deterred from extending the hand of friendship again. 'Will our visit be convenient for you and will you be glad to receive us?' he wrote on 29 August, and Liszt replied: 'From what is holiest in my soul I give you thanks and welcome.' Wagner and Cosima stayed in Weimar from 2 to 6 September. They saw Liszt in the Englischer Hof and in his house in the idyllic setting of the palace gardens. Wagner was in an effervescent mood, but Cosima was distressed by her father's 'weariness of soul'. Liszt, who was fully aware of Princess Wittgenstein's hostility towards his daughter, could not refrain from telling her: 'Cosima really is "ma terrible fille", as I once called her, an extraordinary woman and of very great merits, far above every commonplace standard of judgement and certainly worthy of the admiration she arouses in all who know her – beginning with her first husband, Bülow. She has completely and enthusiastically dedicated herself to Wagner, like Senta to the Flying Dutchman.' (DMCW, I, pp. 622f.)

It says much that Liszt even reconciled himself to Cosima's reception into the Evangelical church, which took place on 31 October.[2] She embraced Protestantism with all the fervour of her Catholic heart. 'My entire soul trembled, our dean spoke with a full heart. Richard deeply moved.' 'How beautiful it was after all in that little vestry!' Wagner confessed. 'How powerfully the dean's voice resounded! What could take the place of the feeling aroused when one hears the unspeakably stirring words: "This is my body"?' Still working on *Götterdämmerung*, he had already entered the world of *Parsifal*. He was studying the Grail legend, and was delighted with the idea that in his treatment of it he displayed an affinity to the Greeks, whose mystics were likewise ignorant of a creator.

As well as composition and all the activities involved in organizing the festival, Wagner also found time to continue the series of essays on music and the theatre which had begun with *On Conducting*: no longer fired with the partisan passion of the earlier Zürich essays, they bear witness to the superior achievement of a now unlimited experience.

'The Meister has now settled down to the work he has been planning for a long time, *On Actors and Singers,* which gives a place of honour to our Heidelberg puppeteer,' Cosima told Nietzsche on 22 August. 'It's yet another way of getting to the heart of the matter,' Wagner commented, 'this time directly, through the actors.' Nietzsche replied that after his study of the choreography of Greek tragedy the essay had struck him 'like a revelation', and he longed for someone to take the aesthetic principles that Wagner had established as the basis for a comprehensive demonstration that traditional 'aesthetics' was now a thing of the past.

What was new about Wagner's thesis was that he developed an aesthetic of the drama out of the art of improvisation, the primeval phenomenon of the psychology of the mime. (*Über Schauspieler und Sänger*, RWGS, IX, pp. 157ff.) Similarly, in his subsequent *Letter to an Actor on Dramatic Art* he advised the actor to practise improvising scenes and whole plays: the basis of all mimetic art lay in that. The author who was unable to imagine the full power of his work in performances he improvised in his own mind had been denied the true vocation to drama. (*Brief über das Schauspielerwesen an einen Schauspieler*, RWGS, IX, pp. 258ff.)

Finally, the most illuminating article of all, though only a few pages long, is *On the Term 'Music Drama'*. From criticizing the misleading implications of the expression, Wagner went on to explain the true relationship of 'music' and 'drama' in his works. Revising the view expressed in *Opera and Drama*, he now admitted the primacy of music, 'the constituent that was everything at the beginning'. Music reveals the sense of its sounds to our eyes by means of the 'scenic parable', 'as a mother explains the mysteries of religion to her children by telling them the legends of the saints'. For that reason he was almost inclined to describe his dramas as 'deeds of music made visible' – certainly a high-sounding category of aesthetics for future Poloniuses to add to their lists! While he had once believed that its outcome would be an 'artwork of the future', he no longer thought he had created a genre that all and sundry would be able to adopt. His colleagues should continue to use the term 'opera' for their works: 'It makes their position quite clear, does not make them sail under false colours, raises them above any kind of rivalry with their librettists; and if the ideas they have for an aria, a duet or even a drinking chorus are good ones, then they will please their audiences and produce a respectable piece of work, without unduly exerting themselves to the extent, perhaps, even of spoiling their agreeable little ideas.' (*Über die Benennung 'Musik-drama'*, RWGS, IX, pp. 302ff.)

At the beginning of November 1872 Wagner prepared to set off on a journey of inspection 'hither and thither among the theatrical staging posts', hunting for artists. When his faith in the success of his undertaking faltered, Cosima rallied him: the author of works like his could be allowed to attempt the impossible. And he too decided that in the end it was his vocation to set examples. 'If the light is there it cannot be extinguished, it must go on shining.' But Cosima felt the touch of despair one day, when he said he thought there was something wrong with his heart.

In five weeks, from 10 November to 15 December, they made a round trip that took in Würzburg, Frankfurt, Darmstadt, Mannheim, Stuttgart, Strassburg, Karlsruhe, Wiesbaden, Mainz, Cologne, Düsseldorf, Hanover, Bremen, Magdeburg, Dessau and Leipzig. 'I have already bolted down four theatres and have had to get through a regrettably large number of banquets and dinners,'

Wagner wrote to Feustel from Darmstadt. 'The only certain prize I have captured so far is *one* singer,' and he added with a sigh: 'If there had been anyone who could relieve me of this journey, I would gladly make him a Christmas present of all the honours and festivities!' (20 November)

Cosima excused herself from the banquet in Cologne and used the time to write to Nietzsche. In among her chatter of Lenbach, of the Rhenish school of Old Masters, of the churches of Cologne, she scattered throughout the letter, in parentheses, a commentary on the noises coming up to her from the banqueting room below, which gives a more vivid account of the evening than any formal report: '(They're beginning – a military band – *Tannhäuser* overture; poor, poor Meister, everywhere the same torment, the same wrong tempos)' – '(My God! they won't stop, now they're playing the Soldiers' Chorus from *Faust*. You see, "more appetite than taste", my head is reeling!)' (4 December)

But at the same time the journey took Wagner back into the past and into his own youth. A thousand memories were revived as he roamed through the narrow streets of Würzburg with Cosima. The little house next to the Residenz still stood, where he had lived on his chorus master's pay of ten gulden a month and had written the closing bars of *Die Feen* to the ceremonial accompaniment of all the bells in the city. On the Breiter Weg in Magdeburg he pointed out a fourth-floor window to her: 'Up there we kept our brilliant household, with love, the poodle and the summonses for debt.' The theatre where *Das Liebesverbot* had received its first performance was unchanged, and he told her how he had conducted wearing a sky-blue frock coat with gigantic cuffs and felt himself in heaven.

Wagner cast up the artistic accounts of his journey in his essay *An Insight into Opera in Germany Today*. It is filled with pain and irony: he knew beforehand that he could expect to hear his own works disfigured and he had steeled himself to endure it with the resignation born of long practice. But in every field of opera, from Mozart to Meyerbeer, he had encountered an inability in conductors to do anything right which had far exceeded his worst expectations. It cut him to the quick, as an entry in Cosima's diary shows: the performance of Auber's charming *Le Maçon* in Darmstadt had made him feel sorry for the singers and the composer, to whose memory he had dedicated a warm-hearted reminiscence a year before,[3] and weep for the decline of the theatre.

'In opera,' he appealed to conductors, 'if you are good musicians in other respects, pay attention solely to what is happening on the stage, whether it is a soloist's monologue or a scene of general action; your essential concern should be that that episode, intensified and spiritualized beyond measure by the part taken by the music, is as clear as it possibly can be; if you manage to attain that clarity then you may be sure that you have found the right tempo and the right orchestral delivery as a matter of course.'

He ended by singling out for praise the production of Gluck's *Orpheus* in Dessau: never had he experienced a nobler or more perfect realization of a work as a whole. Everything – grouping, decor, lighting, every movement, every entrance and exit – had been in perfect harmony, and so had achieved that ideal illusionism that envelops us like a 'prohetic dream of something we have never actually known'. 'But this happened, as I say, in little Dessau.' (*Ein Einblick in das heutige deutsche Opernwesen*, RWGS, IX, pp. 264ff.)

On his return to Bayreuth he heard from the festival management committee the sorry news that the Wagner Societies, of which they had had such high hopes, had raised far less than even the most modest estimates had predicted. His own concerts had been the only successful enterprises. Wagner's appalled reaction was that he could not possibly subject himself to the strain of giving a concert for every thousand talers they still needed: it would mean another two hundred or so concerts! But since Feustel and Muncker hesitated to issue new contracts for the building work in these circumstances he had to accept the necessity of doing something of the kind, deciding this time to concentrate his efforts on Berlin and Hamburg.

'It's a bad end to the year,' Cosima wrote to their friend Malwida, 'and a bad beginning to 1873. Richard is tired to death, and I can only follow him, only suffer with him, but I cannot help him!'

As a late gift for Christmas and her birthday, Nietzsche sent *Five Prefaces to Five Unwritten Books*, 'written in a cheerful mood over Christmas 1872 for Frau Cosima Wagner in sincere respect and in answer to oral and epistolary questions'. Worried as they were, Wagner and Cosima were particularly distressed that he did not come himself. Writing to thank him for the *Five Prefaces* on their return from their second tour, on 12 February 1873, she felt obliged to tell him candidly the reason for her delay: Wagner had been hurt by his not coming and by the way he chose to announce the fact. She had been torn between telling and not telling him so, and so she had left it to long-suffering time to erase the minor sense of grievance and allow the purity of their true feelings to flower again. 'Now this has come to pass, and when we talk about you I do not hear the slightest note of offended friendship but only pleasure in what, once more, you have given us.'

'I simply cannot imagine', Nietzsche wrote to Gersdorff, 'how anyone could be more loyal and more deeply devoted to Wagner in every matter of importance than I am; if I could imagine it then I would be it. But in small, less important, subsidiary points, and in the matter of a certain abstention from frequent personal inter-course, which is necessary to me, I might almost say for "sanitary" reasons, I must preserve my freedom, really only in order to be able to sustain that loyalty on a higher plane.' (24 February)

Cosima wrote in her letter of 12 February that they had been particularly struck by the ideas he had aired in the 'Preface to Homer's Contest'. But they will not have read it as we do today with the wisdom of hindsight. The Greek concept of the 'contest', he writes, is inimical to the modern idea of the 'exclusivity' of genius; it presupposes 'that in the natural order of things there are always *several* geniuses, who reciprocally stimulate each other to new achievements and at the same time restrain each other within the bounds of moderation. That belief lies at the heart of the Hellenic idea of the contest: it abhors monocracy and fears its dangers, and as the means of defence against genius it requires – a second genius.' It was typical of Nietzsche's 'paper courage', when he was asserting a new claim, not to do it face to face.

Wagner and Cosima set off on their second tour on 12 January 1873. 'With a heavy heart I ask myself what we think we can accomplish in this iron age of industry,' she confessed as they travelled through the industrial belt, 'the last and highest cry and upward reach of art as it lies stretched in the dust.'

Apart from the concerts in Berlin and Hamburg, the most memorable event was Wagner's reading of the text of *Götter-dämmerung* in the house of Count von Schleinitz on 17 January. In Cosima's view there could seldom have assembled so select a company from all walks of life for a single purpose: princes, ambas-sadors, university professors, the emperor's adjutants, and captains of finance like Strousberg and Bleichröder. 'Then I saw Moltke, too, much older than his pictures, stooping with flashing eyes . . .

The more select and important the people there, and the more interested and sympathetic they showed themselves, the more profoundly one felt the isolation of genius.' (DMCW, I, pp. 647f.; CWFN, II, p. 46)

Wagner used to read his own verse texts as he read Shakespeare, without histrionics but with thrilling effect. Cosima found words inadequate to describe him while he was doing it: his face transfused with light, his eyes visionary, his hands magical, whether gesturing or still, his voice gentle, all soul, but penetrating into the depths and to the furthest horizons. (BBL 1938, p. 11)

He prefaced the reading with a short introduction: whereas in opera, in the usual sense of the term, only those passages of lyrical reflection inserted into the action were considered suitable for musical realization, in his works his dramatic dialogue itself provided the stuff of the musical realization. He believed that the dialogic composition of his text justified him in presenting it to his audience 'naked as it is'. (RWGS, IX, pp. 308ff.)

'We really are back in Bayreuth,' Cosima told Nietzsche in her letter of 12 February, 'though for how long is something we cannot tell.' Wagner used the interval to write another of the short essays for which he drew on the wealth of his artistic experience: *On the Performance of Beethoven's Ninth Symphony*. In it he rehearsed once again all that contributes to clarity in the delivery of the work. (*Zum Vortrag der Neunten Symphonie Beethovens*, RWGS, IX, pp. 231ff.) He also worked on the collected edition of his writings, hoping to have the eighth volume ready before embarking on another concert tour.

One moonlit night he and Cosima went to inspect their new house, which was still in the process of being built, and he showed her the spot he had chosen for their grave. 'Mood serious and light-hearted together', she recorded. The worthy Muncker was very alarmed when Wagner discussed the grave in the garden with him, 'but Richard explained to him the serenity with which we look forward to our eternal rest'.

A telegram from Nietzsche and Rohde announced their intention of arriving for a visit on 6 April. The former confessed to Gersdorff that he himself had not yet grasped quite how it had all suddenly come about. Even on the point of departure he was moved at the thought that the two of them were about to arrive at the railway station of *that* place, where every step would arouse a memory.

They had been the happiest days of his life. 'There was something in the air that I have never sensed anywhere else, something quite outside the scope of verbal expression but full of hope ... I hope my visit will repair what was damaged by my failure to go there for Christmas, and I thank you from my heart for your simple and potent encouragement, which has cleared my vision and shooed away the stupid "midges" that sometimes trouble me.' (5 April)

He brought another manuscript with him, *Philosophy in the Greek Tragic Age*, which he read aloud to them over three evenings. (CT, I, pp. 668f.) However, his sister's claim, in her biography, that Wagner did not disguise his disappointment at Nietzsche's occupying himself with such remote matters, instead of with the Bayreuth undertaking, is yet another of her pet distortions of the truth. Only a short time before, Cosima had referred in her diary to the 'new Nietzsche essay' – probably one of the *Five Prefaces* – saying that for all its profundity it sometimes betrayed a boorishness that made her and Wagner wish he would concentrate on Greek subjects. (DMCW, I, pp. 644f.)

The deep impression Wagner made on his young friend in his ceaseless struggle for Bayreuth is revealed in Nietzsche's letter to him of 18 April: 'It's true, every day I grow more melancholy, feeling so acutely how gladly I would help or benefit you in some way, and how completely incapable I am of doing anything of the kind.' 'Or perhaps I shall have done something', he went on, 'when I have dealt with what I have in hand.'

This was a reference to a book by David Friedrich Strauss, *The Old and the New Belief*, whose intention seemed to be to get rid of 'redemption, prayer and Beethovenian music'. Wagner and Cosima had discovered great enthusiasm for it wherever they went on their recent tour, and it had been the topic of much concerned discussion during Nietzsche's visit. Back in Basel he lost no time in settling to the task of showing the famous historian up as a specimen of the German 'cultural philistine'. 'Emotional tension while working on the first of the *Unseasonal Meditations,*' he recorded, 'anxiety for genius and works of genius, contrasted with the sight of Straussian complacency.' His intention was that it should be the first of a series of essays supporting Wagner in his fight for a German culture, and his original title for them was 'Observations of the Horizon from Bayreuth'. But the expression 'unseasonal' ('unzeitgemäß'), which he now decided to use, was one that he had first thought of in connection with Wagner and what he stood for: in 1869 he had written to Rohde that Wagner stood on his own feet, firmly rooted by his own strength, his eyes fixed far above all ephemerality and not of this age – 'unseasonal in the best sense'.

'I swear to you before God,' Wagner exclaimed after receiving the first of the *Meditations*, 'I believe you are the only person who knows what I want to do!' But he could not suppress the premonition that a time would come when he would have to defend the book against Nietzsche himself. (21 September 1873)

Having received assurances that a concert in Cologne would make a good profit, he agreed to give one in the Gürzenich hall on 24 April. He began a conversation with his agent in Cologne by telling him the story of the Emperor Alexius Comnenus, who, on the eve of battle, asked his commanding general the number of his soldiers. ' "An immense army," the general replied, "a mass of troops reaching as far as the eye can see." The emperor: "I want to know the exact number." – "Ten thousand." – "I am satisfied with that, they will be enough." – Now tell me, my friend,' Wagner went on, 'how much will today's concert make?' – 'Three thousand talers.' – 'Very good, then I am as satisfied as the emperor, and you have done your job well.'

On his way back to Bayreuth Wagner made another trip into his past by breaking his journey at Eisleben, where he had stayed with his step-uncle the goldsmith half a century before and fought the 'autochthonous boy population'.

Now he hoped for three months without disruption in which to orchestrate *Götterdämmerung*. He began the prelude on 3 May, with the chords already heard in Brünnhilde's greeting of the sun from *Siegfried*, not only transformed by being a semitone lower and in 6/4 instead of triple time, but above all darkened by the use of tubas instead of trumpets and trombones, so that they now present not day but night. Here in the Norns' scene he achieves an orchestral sound that in its ebb and flow recalls the swell of an organ. The accompaniment is so symphonic in its treatment that at a concert in Vienna in 1875 he risked performing the whole scene without the vocal parts.

When he came to score the transition leading into Siegfried's Rhine Journey he wished that he could have a second complete orchestra so as to be able to express the state of Brünnhilde's feelings as he would have liked. It was not the desire to make effects for their own sake and play virtuoso games, but the need to enable different instruments to enter and alternate with each other. (BBL 1936, p. 1)

Meanwhile Cosima had begun to prepare in good time for his sixtieth birthday. She enquired of Judith about French translations of the standard works of Indian literature, and gave him the four volumes of the Rig-Veda in Alexandre Langlois's translation.[4] But the most important celebrations took place in the Margraves' Opera House. She arranged for the company temporarily in residence to perform Ludwig Geyer's *Der Bethlehemitische Kindermord*. Peter Cornelius was commissioned to write a play he called *An Artist's Dedication*, in which the painter Genelli introduced the youthful Wagner to the Dramatic Muse. The evening began and ended with two of Wagner's juvenilia, the Concert Overture in C major and a New Year Cantata written in Magdeburg. Wagner listened to the overture very attentively; it was strange, really, he remarked to Cosima, it could not have been written by either Beethoven or Bellini. He left the theatre where these youthful memories had been revived deeply moved.

Wagner had sent a presentation copy of the score of *Rheingold* to King Ludwig, with the dedication:

> Conceived in faith in the German spirit,
> Completed to the glory of his noble benefactor
>     King Ludwig II,
>     by Richard Wagner.

Ludwig thanked him in a birthday telegram: 'Completed the eternal work! I exulted at the news.'

Nietzsche's birthday letter still reflects the distress caused by his visit to Bayreuth the month before: 'What should we be if we could not have you, and what else, for instance, should I be (as I feel at every moment) but stillborn! I tremble every time I think that I might perhaps never have met you: and then life truly would not be worth living and I should not know what to do with myself from one hour to the next.' (20 May)

But the letters and celebrations could do nothing to relieve Wagner of his worries and sometimes he felt like following the advice an old soldier gave Frederick the Great after the battle of Kolin: 'Now, Your Majesty, just let the battle be.' In order to keep his friends informed of how the undertaking stood, he had an essay printed, *The Festival Theatre at Bayreuth*, illustrated with architect's drawings. (*Das Bühnenfestspielhaus zu Bayreuth*, RWGS, IX, pp. 322ff.) He sent a copy to Bismarck, with a covering letter in which he said that some people might think it a regrettable omission if he failed to acquaint the restorer of German hopes with the cultural idea that inspired him. If his enterprise had to be realized without the participation of the only truly beneficial and ennobling authority, then he would have to comfort himself with the thought of the fate that befell the renascence of the German spirit through the agency of the great poets of the second half of the previous century, which Frederick the Great, although the true hero of that renascence, persistently regarded with cold antipathy. (24 June)

He received no reply.

The theatre was topped out on 2 August with due ceremony, attended, to Wagner's joy, by Liszt. They climbed up to the top of the shell of the building on a swaying ladder, accompanied by the children. The world took on the appearance of a dream from up there, Cosima wrote, an artist's dream that had become reality. The foreman carpenter began to recite some verses by the Evangelical dean, asking God to keep the roof on the building, but Wagner cut the final lines, which were addressed to himself, and replaced them by a cheer for the 'German spirit'.

As the funds were increasing only very slowly during this summer, Feustel recommended applying for a loan, for which they would have to find a highly placed guarantor. In the circumstances, Wagner wrote to the king on 11 August, he ventured to ask his only true patron and benefactor to send Secretary Düfflipp to Bayreuth to investigate the financial position for himself. Receiving no answer to that, Wagner addressed himself directly to Düfflipp, telling him that Feustel was coming to see him. Düfflipp replied that the king had not been prepared to give the guarantee Wagner had asked for. He had raised the matter again after Feustel's visit, but in vain. The king was wrapped up in his own plans and he had no interest in anything that might possibly hamper or delay them. (KLRW, IV, pp. 210f.) Those plans centred on the building of Neuschwanstein.

When one thread broke, Wagner commented, he tried to spin another. He discussed with Heckel the idea of launching an appeal representing the festival as a matter of national concern, to capture the interest of those who might not actually want to attend it but could spare ten or twenty talers for a great cause. A conference of Patrons and delegates from the Wagner Societies was called for 31 October in Bayreuth to debate the matter. 'If you take the step of a *manifesto*,' Wagner wrote to Heckel, '. . . then I ask you, if I may, to consult *Nietzsche* in Basel about writing it . . . I have very special confidence in him, specifically, for the task.' (23 September)

But the conference rejected Nietzsche's *Admonition to the Germans* as inopportune, and Cosima, too, felt that if the infant undertaking was capable of survival, then it was too severe an instrument. Instead Professor Adolf Stern of Dresden was entrusted with the composition of an appeal to be sent, with subscription lists, to every book, music and art shop in Germany. 'The whole session was an extraordinary occasion,' Nietzsche told Gersdorff, 'half elevated, half very down to earth; but powerful enough overall to silence all talk of lotteries or anything of that kind . . . The evening ended with a harmless, jolly and very successful banquet at the Sonne, at which Frau Wagner and Fräulein von Meysenbug were the only ladies present. I had the place of honour between them and so was given a nickname from an Italian opera, "Sargino, the pupil of love".'

The four thousand dealers in books and music who received the appeal kept the subscription lists under the counter. Only in Göttingen did a handful of students put their names down for a few talers. An Englishman like Newman cannot restrain himself, in the circumstances, from commenting ironically on Wagner's faith in the 'German spirit'.

Since Düfflipp thought a request coming directly from Wagner might perhaps help, the latter sat down to write to the king on 6 November, reminding him that it had been he who had once adjured him: 'Complete your work: mine be the concern of presenting it worthily to the world!' He also said that he intended to visit Munich with his trusted friend Feustel before the month was out, in the hope of obtaining an audience of the king.

An answer came through Düfflipp. Unfortunately an audience could not be arranged, as 'His Majesty is on the point of moving to Hohenschwangau, and wishes to be undisturbed there'.

Wagner replied that he had almost foreseen the refusal of an audience, but it was essential for him to know very soon whether his request was also to be refused or not. If the *Ring* was to be performed at Bayreuth in 1875, then they must have the security for the credit they needed by the end of the month, so as to be able to give contracts to machinists and scene-painters. (14 November 1873, KLRW, III, p. 25)

On 21 November Wagner saw Düfflipp in Munich, and his hopes were raised that the guarantee might be given. But on 6 January 1874, when more than a month had passed without any confirmation, he asked for a definite decision. It came: His Majesty refused. (SRLW, II, pp. 133f.)

Instead of a guarantee Wagner had received the Order of Maximilian from the king on 12 December, which he was tempted to return when he heard that it had also been awarded to Brahms. 'His Bavarian Majesty sends no word,' Cosima wrote to Countess von Schleinitz, 'but the Order of Maximilian has come instead . . . I besought Wagner to accept the honour in silence, but I thought of Falstaff and his tailor: "I looked a' should have sent me two and twenty yards of satin and he sends me security" – we asked for a guarantee and have been sent an Order.' (DMCW, I, p. 681)

On the morning of her birthday she asked Wagner to drive her to the theatre. The stage was awe-inspiring: 'The whole towers like an Assyrian palace and the pillars are aligned within it like sphinxes, the wings stretch to each side like mysterious passages . . . From the stage we then went into the auditorium. At the moment of entering it, it makes a sublime impression. No amount of instruction can do this for the spectator, but to enter this room prepares him for the mysteries in an instant.'

'Now we must be many things at once,' Wagner warned her, 'cautious, clever, truthful and well bred. You shall hear *Der Ring des Nibelungen* yet.' He had conceived yet another plan in their apparent impasse: the emperor should commission him to produce the *Ring* in the summer of 1876, to celebrate the fifth anniversary of the peace, for the sum of 100,000 talers. He asked Heckel to approach the Grand Duke of Baden to act as intermediary, but the duke, anticipating refusal, advised against the scheme.

In the meantime Wagner had by chance found out why King Ludwig was annoyed with him. Some time earlier the poet Felix Dahn had sent him an ode to King Ludwig with the demand that he set it to music. Finding it impossible, Wagner had simply refused. He could very well understand Dahn's desire to have one of his poems set by himself, who had hitherto set only his own words, he wrote to the king; but he had dismissed Dahn's claim that it was

Ludwig's own wish as just another of the boasts he had heard so often. (9 January 1874)

The king replied that Dahn had indeed expressed the wish that Wagner would set the ode, at an audience he had given him the previous summer; 'I didn't want to put him out, so I agreed rather than disagreed with the idea, voilà tout . . . Thank God that through your genius you are called to higher things than to provide musical illustrations to fulsome odes!' (25 January)[5]

This frank explanation cleared the air. 'No, no, and again *no*! It shall not end thus!' Ludwig exclaimed in the same letter. 'Something must be done. Our plan must not be allowed to come to nothing!' 'Everything is all right with His Majesty,' Wagner reported to Heckel on 9 February; 'the undertaking in which you take so laudably serious an interest is assured.' And referring to his other idea for celebrating the peace of 1871: 'I *knew* that would all lead nowhere; my cause requires a "wise fool".'

And so on 20 February 1874 a contract was drawn up between the festival management committee and the Court Secretary's Office, guaranteeing the committee an advance of 100,000 talers from the Cabinet Treasury. One unwelcome condition was that the entire income from the patronage vouchers was to go to the treasury from thenceforward, and Wagner did everything he could to get round it. But it was not until 27 September 1875 that the king gave his authorization for the Cabinet Treasury to take only 315 gulden out of the 520 brought in by each voucher. Then, as the date of the performances grew closer and rehearsals began, current expenditure began to rise steeply – to 2000 marks a day – and Wagner was forced to ask for a stay in the repayments. 'I received no news! My artists were on the point of coming: I was bold enough to interpret the silence in my own favour . . . So I crossed the Rubicon: I let my players and singers come.' 'Remain favourably inclined towards me,' he begged the king, 'and may you be eternally blessed for it!' (12 June 1876)

On 29 June Düfflipp informed Wagner that the repayments could be suspended until a total of 800 patronage vouchers had been sold, but there was once more a qualification: the Cabinet Treasury would make no further advances over and above the 216,152 marks, 42 pfennigs that had already been indented for of the 300,000 marks guaranteed.

'It is glorious, after all, to have been forsaken by everyone!'

Cosima had declared one evening early in January 1874, after a stormy day of crisis, and Wagner replied: 'It is the only honourable state.'

They had no suspicion then that their most eloquent disciple had also forsaken them. Returning to Basel, Nietzsche found dismaying news from Bayreuth waiting for him. 'Things were in a bad state, without a single ray of comfort, from the New Year onwards,' he wrote to Rohde on 15 February, 'from which I was only able to rescue myself in the end by the strangest method: I began, as coldly as I could, to investigate the reasons why the undertaking had failed; in doing so I learned much, and I believe I now understand Wagner far better than I used to.'

What Nietzsche noted down in the month of January 1874 amounted to the whole of his philosophy of failure. He looked for the causes, not in the uncomprehending obstruction of the world but in Wagner's character: the composer was, Nietzsche decided, an actor and a tyrant; he sought to achieve tyranny through the massed forces of the theatre; he brooked no other individual personality within his own ambit; in respect of musical form he possessed all the crudity for which Germans were notorious; his art was a kind of Counter-Reformation; 'what do we care for a Tannhäuser, a Lohengrin, a Tristan, a Siegfried!' In short, in sixty-nine aphorisms, Nietzsche not merely questioned the worth of Wagner's personality as man and as artist, he roundly denied it.[6]

Nor did he confine himself to private note-taking: Overbeck recalled that Nietzsche spoke to him about Wagner at that time in terms that anticipated *The Wagner Case*.[7]

At all events the condemnation is so complete and so fundamental that even Charles Andler, who was sympathetic to Nietzsche's point of view, had to admit that it was astonishing how Nietzsche managed to continue regarding himself as Wagner's friend, claiming his hospitality and supporting his cause, when he found so many deficiencies in his character, and so many dubious aspects to his cause. 'His silence on the subject of his doubts was an act of great and culpable hypocrisy towards Wagner.'[8]

It is only human, all too human, that an enthusiastic disciple should try to dissociate himself from a cause that he gives up as lost. There is no need to attribute disreputable motives to it. To be forced to watch the downfall of a cause, or a person, to which one has privately and publicly subscribed is painful and humiliating. 'It

is hard to recover from this waiting and fearing,' Nietzsche wrote to
Rohde on 19 March, returning to the same topic; 'there were times
when I gave up hope completely.'

And so he 'rescued' himself by distancing himself 'as coldly as he
could'.

By an irony of fate, immediately after writing that, he received
the long letter in which Cosima thanked him for sending them the
second of the *Unseasonal Meditations*, *Of the Uses and Disadvantages of
History for Life*. 'What has made a particularly deep impression on
me personally in your book is the certainty, which it makes even
clearer, that the suffering endured by genius in this world illumi-
nates the whole order of things for you, and that you see not with
the eyes of the intelligence alone, but with the more penetrating
vision of the heart as well . . . Thus you have been enabled to form
an overall judgement on the cultural world of today by your
compassion for the suffering of genius, and this gives your work its
marvellous warmth.' (20 March)

During the anxious months of the desperate struggle to save
Bayreuth, Wagner finished the score of the first act of *Götterdämmerung* and gave it to Cosima for Christmas. He also had two
encounters with works of contemporary music, each significant in
its own way. He had already gone through Liszt's oratorio *Christus*
at the piano with Cosima in 1872. 'That anyone can so relinquish
the hard-won skills of a great art in order to imitate the droning of
priests is an impoverishment of the spirit,' she wrote in her diary.
'We are saddened by this development of Father's, for which Princess Wittgenstein is undoubtedly the most to blame.' They could
not, however, avoid attending the first complete performance of
the work in the Stadtkirche in Weimar on 29 May 1873, under
Liszt's direction. 'Richard passed through every phase of transport
to downright rage,' she remarked, 'finally achieving a state of
the most profound, loving fair-mindedness.' (DMCW, I, pp. 612,
622)

Anton Bruckner, who visited Wagner in 1873, had first been
introduced to him when he was in Munich to hear the première of
*Tristan* in 1865, and in 1868 he obtained permission to perform the
final chorus of *Die Meistersinger* with the Frohsinn choral society in
Linz, two months before the work's première. He recalled his first
visit to Bayreuth in a letter to Hans von Wolzogen after Wagner's
death:

It was about the beginning of September 1873 . . . when
I asked the Meister if I might show him my No. 2 in C
minor and my No. 3 in D minor. The Thrice-Blessed
refused because of lack of time (theatre-building) and
said he couldn't look at the scores now, since even the
'Nibelungs' had had to be laid on one side. When I
replied: 'Meister, I have no right to rob you of even a
quarter of an hour, and I only thought that with the
Meister's powerful perception, a single glance at the
themes would suffice for the Meister to know the
substance of it.' Thereupon the Meister said, slapping
me on the shoulder, 'Come on, then,' went with me
into the drawing room and looked at the Second
Symphony. 'Very good,' he said, but he seemed to find
it rather tame (for they originally made me very nervous
about it in Vienna), and picked up the Third (D minor),
and exclaiming 'let's see, let's see – well – ah!' he went
through the whole of the first section (the exalted one
singled out the trumpet part) and then said: 'Leave this
work here with me, I will take a closer look at it after
dinner' . . . I thought to myself, shall I make my
request, when Wagner asked me what was on my mind.
Very shyly, my heart pounding , I then said to my
dearly beloved master: 'Meister! I have something in my
heart, that I do not trust myself to say!' The Meister said
'Out with it! You know how much I like you.'
Thereupon I made my request, but only in the event of
the Meister's not disapproving, since I did not want to
profane his thrice-famous name. The Meister said: 'This
evening, at five o'clock, you are invited to Wahnfried, I
shall be there, and after I've had a chance to look at the
D minor symphony properly, we'll talk about this
matter again.' I had been up to the theatre site
immediately before I went Wahnfried at five o'clock.
When I arrived the master of masters hurried to meet
me with open arms, hugged me and said: 'My dear
friend, the dedication is quite all right. The work gives
me uncommonly great pleasure.' For two and a half
hours I had the good fortune to sit beside the Meister,
while he talked about musical affairs in Vienna, offered

> me beer, took me out in the garden and showed me
> his grave!!! Then I had, or rather, was permitted,
> blissfully happy, to accompany the Meister into his
> house.

The sculptor Gustav Adolf Kietz, who was working on a bust of Cosima and had set up his studio in the villa, which was still not completed, was also present during this conversation. According to him, Bruckner kept on trying to talk about Viennese enthusiasm for *Lohengrin*. 'Oh, never mind about that,' Wagner replied, 'I know that, there's a swan comes, bringing a knight, it's something a little different, it makes a change – here, have a drink instead, this is a wonderful beer, Weihenstephan, your health!' – 'For God's sake, Meister, I mustn't, it would be the death of me, I've just come from Karlsbad!' – 'Nonsense, it's good for you, drink it!'

And in spite of his protests, which hilariously punctuated his musical conversation, Bruckner was obliged to drink one glass after another, with the result that the next morning he did not know which symphony Wagner had accepted. Fortunately Kietz, who was staying at the same hotel, remembered that they had talked about a symphony in D minor; at the time he had thought they meant Beethoven's Ninth. To be quite sure, Bruckner wrote to ask Wagner again, if it was to be the symphony 'where the trumpet introduces the theme'. 'Yes! Yes! Cordial greetings!' Wagner scribbled at the bottom of the note, and 'Bruckner the trumpet' became a kind of leitmotiv with him.

Wagner's conscientious study of the score shows that accepting the dedication was no empty act of politeness on his part, as indeed one would hardly expect of him. Cosima's diary tells us that early in 1875 he went through the symphony at the piano with her; the dedicatory copy of it is still in the Wagner Archives. Meeting Bruckner in Vienna in May of the same year, he spoke of performing his symphonies, according to Heckel, and in the letter to Wolzogen Bruckner went on to say: 'Anno 1882, already sick, the Meister took me by the hand and said "Rely upon it, I will myself perform the symphony and all your works." ' In his biography of Bruckner Peter Raabe questions the sincerity of this promise and wonders where and when Wagner thought he would carry it out, but it is obvious that he was thinking not of concert tours, but of the Bayreuth 'school', the project nearest to his heart after the festival, where he intended that the performance style of the widest possible variety of works should be taught and practised.[9]

Wagner also had this to say about Bruckner during the '*Parsifal* summer' of 1882: 'I know of only one who approaches Beethoven, and that is Bruckner.' His behaviour towards the Austrian composer rebuts the legend that he had no time for his contemporaries, but above all it proves that he had completely discarded the theory he had advanced in *The Artwork of the Future* of the 'end of the symphony with Beethoven's Ninth'.

Moreover, while he was scoring *Götterdämmerung* in 1874, he conceived the desire to compose orchestral works himself, 'each having the dimensions and significance of a large-scale overture', 'because truly, while I have been toiling on the large scores of my dramas,' he wrote to Schott, 'a large number of embryo ideas and outline schemes have leapt into my mind for orchestral compositions of the kind that I have now offered you; I have suppressed and ignored them, but when I have finished that last, immense score, I think that it would be a true recreation and pleasure to return to them and realize them'. (23 and 31 January 1874) Although the offer was dictated at that particular time by the hope of obtaining an advance of 10,000 gulden, so as to pay for the final stages in completing the new house and garden, nevertheless the wish kept reviving, showing that he was perfectly serious in seeking a channel for the expression of this side of his nature, too. After he had finished *Götterdämmerung* he talked to Cosima about these new orchestral works, and told her that he would call them 'wavering shapes' ('schwankende Gestalten') from the first two lines of Goethe's *Zueignung*, which he would quote as their motto:

> Ihr naht euch wieder, schwankende Gestalten,
> Die früh sich einst dem trüben Blick gezeigt.

('Once more you approach, you wavering shapes, which appeared to my sad gaze in years gone by.')

These symphonic plans revived in an altered and more definite form while he was working on *Parsifal*.

Work on the house was sufficiently advanced by 28 April for the family to be able to move into it.[10] 'At last – the move into the house. It's not ready yet, but we shall get the better of it,' Cosima wrote in her diary. At four o'clock it was consecrated by a meeting of the festival management committee and Wagner's assistants. 'Richard told me the meeting had a beautiful atmosphere, they had all been filled with a single spirit of dedication to the cause. There could have been no better way of consecrating the house.'

It had been on the very first occasion that Wagner was passing that he had suddenly stopped the carriage, gone for a walk across the site and decided on the position and outlines of the drive, the house and the garden within half an hour.

The drive is an avenue lined with chestnut trees, now replanted, leading up to and encircling a round rosebed with the twice-lifesize bronze bust of King Ludwig by Zumbusch. The plain façade of the house beyond is timeless, its sole ornament the sgraffito by Krausse depicting the 'Artwork of the Future'.

The purely functional character of the lobby and stairwell means that one passes without pause into the hall, a lofty room reaching the full height of the house, with a gallery running round at first-floor level and lit by a skylight. It was intended as a music room. The Pompeian red walls set off the marble statuettes of Wagnerian characters and Kietz's busts of Wagner and Cosima. Cosima's lilac sitting room used to lie to the left, the dining room to the right of the hall. On its far side double doors lead into the great drawing room (destroyed by bombing on 5 April 1945 and restored in 1976), with a huge bay window overlooking the garden. The walls are lined to half their height with the three thousand volumes and more that make up the library of masterpieces of world literature, from the Upanishads of India to Wagner's own contemporaries. In Wagner's day portraits of Goethe, Schiller, Beethoven, Liszt, King Ludwig, Adolf Wagner, Ludwig Geyer, Johanna Wagner, the Comtesse d'Agoult, Wagner and Cosima were hung above the bookcases. Round the edge of the coffered ceiling, and added at a later date, runs a row of the coats of arms of the German towns where Wagner Societies were formed. The taste of the nineteenth century was ennobled and raised wellnigh to timelessness by the genius who lived in this house. This drawing room was where Wagner sat among his family and friends in the evenings, often reading aloud to them, flanked by a grand piano and his desk. It was here, too, that he received visitors, but, except during the first few weeks in the house, the popular idea that he worked in these opulent surroundings is quite without foundation: it was in a simply decorated room on the upper floor, the walls hung with grey satin, its only ornament a portrait of Cosima by Lenbach, that he finished the score of *Götterdämmerung* and wrote *Parsifal*.[11]

When Wagner had resumed his work and was ruminating on a name for his house, he remembered a village in Hessen that he had come across on his travels, called Wanfried, a name which had struck a mystic chord in him for its conjunction of two words, 'Wahn', meaning illusion, delusion or even madness, and 'Fried', meaning peace. Like a poem in Goethe's *Diwan*, recited only to the wise because the mob would at once deride it, 'so only the meditative nature will have any idea of what we mean by it'.

The king gave 25,000 talers towards the house. (His other substantial contributions towards the Bayreuth undertaking were loans and were repaid in full.) But since building a house always costs at least as much again as the original estimate, as Wagner complained, he had to make shift to find the additional sums himself, as we have seen.

'You wish to know the pattern of my daily life?' he wrote to the king. 'Splendid! Because it is the key to the direction of the life that is the sum of my days.' His principle was to wrest as much spiritual tranquillity and cheer as possible from the daemon of earthly existence, so as to be able to perform his duties in the service of genius. His only regret was that he was not ten or fifteen years younger: so much had come to him very late. The fact that destiny had granted him a son had given his life a totally new meaning: property, a home, rights as a citizen, fortune, all now had a significance they had never had for him before. And his wise wife had relieved him of the pressure of daily life and stood guard over his peace.

After his morning bath he took breakfast with Cosima, and then devoted the hours before lunch to work. Unless illness or business worries put him out of the mood for it, 'children's familial lunch' was always a cheering occasion. Then he took coffee in the garden, leafed through the *Bayreuther Tagblatt* – the only newspaper he would now have in the house – and usually discussed some interesting topic with Cosima. After a short rest he looked at his post, considering himself lucky if there was no bad news, but only poems sent for him to set, treatises on the philosophy of art and offers of costumes and suits of armour for the *Ring*, or, the most frequent of all, requests for his autograph from English and American music-lovers. If all was well he did a little more work, perhaps scoring another page of *Götterdämmerung*, then a walk or a drive in the carriage they hired from the landlord of the Sonne to the Eremitage or the Fantaisie, where the children explored the park. At seven in the evening a simple meal with the children. At eight he and Cosima settled in the drawing room for the evening, where they read to each other, or made music with the young men from the Nibelung Chancellery; there were now four of them: a Saxon, Hermann Zumpe; a Hungarian, Anton Seidl; a Russian, Joseph Rubinstein; and finally, of all things, a Macedonian, Demetrius Lalas. These, his journeymen, asserted that they learned more from such evenings than in the conservatories and music schools they had paid such high fees to attend. (To King Ludwig; 1 October)

Like each individual day, all his time was carefully planned. That was the secret of how he accomplished so much work of so many different kinds: scoring, business and private correspondence, supervising the construction of the Festspielhaus, contracting for machines, sets and costumes, engaging players and singers, coaching the principals in their parts, concert tours – and all that in the shadow of not knowing where the next day's money was coming from. He hoped, he wrote to Schott, that fate had good health and great age with unimpaired intelligence in store for him, 'so that for once one person may accomplish and experience all that in Germany takes two lifetimes'. (9 February)

## II

No sooner had Wagner received the king's assurance of a guarantee than he wrote, on 6 March 1874, to his 'foreman', Hans Richter, who in the meantime had been appointed musical director at the Pest opera. He had the following tasks for him: to take charge of the female singers, of whom Wagner had completely lost track, to follow them from place to place, listen to them, report on them, correspond with them and so on; to select the wind players, which would also involve travelling, and also to get the string section in order with the help of the leader, August Wilhelmj; to hear the singers individually with him that summer in Bayreuth. 'How about it? Can you manage it?'

Richter set off on his tour of inspection on 23 May, and from the end of June onwards was assisting Wagner with the preliminary coaching of the singers. These early rehearsals had strengthened his confidence in the success of the whole venture in the most gratifying way, Wagner reported to the king, but the labour and worry involved had made the most extreme demands on his strength and absolutely exhausted him.

Repetiteurs specially trained by him were then to follow the singers to wherever they were working that winter, to continue assisting them to learn their parts. Wagner envisaged rehearsing in the theatre itself in the summer of 1875, with the orchestra and with the major pieces of scenery in place. The months of June and July 1876 were to be devoted to general rehearsals, first of the acts individually, then of the dramas as a whole, and then finally three cycles would be performed in August.

There could naturally be no question, as he had emphasized from the first, of any of those taking part gaining any financial advantage, so he was regretfully obliged to dispense with the services of any prima donnas who performed only for such-and-such a fee. He had fixed the sum of 500 talers a month as the maximum reimbursable to each of the twenty singers he needed, for their travelling and accommodation expenses, in the hope that some of them would manage with less. (To Franz Betz, 8 March 1874) 'And thus you find yourselves called upon, perhaps for the first time in your careers, to dedicate your powers and abilities solely to the one purpose of achieving an ideal artistic end.' (*To the Singers*, 14 January 1875)

The musical demands the *Ring* made on its performers were new and testing. Wagner was able nevertheless to point to a familiar precedent on which he had built to meet his needs. During the 1875 rehearsals he spoke of it to Julius Hey, the singing teacher: 'Didn't Mozart himself bequeath us the basic form of German bel canto in *Die Zauberflöte*? The dialogue between Tamino and the Speaker will stand as the model for all time. What else do you suppose I am trying to achieve in the dialogue between the Wanderer and Mime in the first act of *Siegfried*?'

But the demands made by the staging of this drama drawn from Germanic myth were not only new, but also completely without precedent or model. From the first Wagner knew he could not entrust the task to any run-of-the-mill designers: he would have to have designs by real artists to lay before the very best scene-painters to inspire them to achieve something of a higher order. Cosima would have very much liked to engage the services of Arnold Böcklin, whom she knew from Basel, and she sounded him through Lenbach. But Böcklin declined and, troubled, she wrote to

Lenbach: 'It is sad that the theatre and the fine arts are so separated that when a dramatic artist comes on the scene he finds himself without support.' On the other hand it is not true that Wagner approached Makart. The latter had in fact designed a front curtain with figures from the *Ring*, but Cosima had her doubts as to 'whether a theatre curtain should be painted, whether a picture is the best thing to have in front of another, and whether a beautiful fabric falling in heavy folds does not answer the purpose better'. This idea was the origin of the Bayreuth curtain, which is not raised, but drawn to either side. (MMCW, pp. 298f.)

Through the medallist Anton Scharf, for whom he sat on the occasion of the laying of the foundation stone, Wagner got in touch with Joseph Hoffmann, the landscape and history painter, then forty-one years old. Hoffmann had attended the Vienna academy, travelled extensively, as far afield as Greece and Persia, and studied under Rahl in Vienna, Genelli in Munich, Cornelius, Overbeck and Preller in Rome. He had come to public notice, too, for his beautiful sets for *Die Zauberflöte* and *Der Freischütz*, and his reputation was such that the Uffizi in Florence had bought his self-portrait. His general culture, his sense of the poetic, his gift for landscape in the heroic style with Hellenic and Homeric traits, all these recommended him to Wagner. 'My attention has recently been drawn . . . quite particularly . . . to your exceptional work, the character of which seems already very close to what I need.' (28 July 1872)

Hoffmann submitted his designs, based on studies made in the mountains, by late November 1873. Wagner was surprised and delighted, and had no fault to find with them except for the occasional neglect of the dramatic requirements of a scene in favour of a picturesque effect. The rich decoration Hoffmann gave the Gibichungs' Hall was the subject of lively discussion: it was for that very reason, Wagner declared, that he had got away from the period of the knightly Middle Ages represented in *Tannhäuser* and even *Lohengrin*, in order to do without irrelevant visual splendour and display the characters without conventional clutter.

At first he had thought of letting Hoffmann build the sets too, but then, with his consent, commissioned the Brückner brothers of Coburg. Hoffmann retained the right of supervision, and in the event considerable differences arose between him, the Brückners and the machinist Brandt, who had also worked on the Munich *Rheingold*. A meeting was called in Bayreuth on 5 October 1874, in the hope of persuading Hoffmann to relinquish his supervisory rights; it was a stormy occasion at which Wagner, according to Muncker, displayed admirable restraint. There was something positively sublime about the moment when he averred that if Hoffmann could not win and inspire those who worked under him, as he could his musicians, then he was simply incapable of carrying out the commission assigned to him. It was not his *wish*, Wagner wrote to Hoffmann on 12 October, that the latter should have no further part in it; he had proved as much by his attempts to bring about an understanding between him and his co-workers. 'My only real wish is that you and I, two honourable men, part in peace – for the time being.'

Hoffmann was invited to the festival in 1876, and criticized the sets severely. But Wagner himself was so little satisfied with them that he said he would want to start again from scratch for another production.[12]

How the production was to be costumed presented far more problems than the scenic and architectural aspects. Wagner had objected to the costumes of the Munich *Rheingold* in 1869, which were copied from the series of frescoes based on the *Ring* painted for the king by Michael Echter, because, what with the Greek *peplos* and so on, they suggested almost everything except Germanic gods. The best painters and archaeologists would have to be consulted, and research made into Germanic dress in Roman times, based on Tacitus: 'Just a slight suggestion will give an intelligent and inventive brain all it needs to come up with analogous forms, which then provide the basis for further ideas. Then I wish for *less nudity* and more true clothing, and I don't want the giants replaced by the green men from the Prussian coat of arms . . . No golden ornaments of any kind! That stands to reason in a piece in the course of which gold becomes available for the first time to the gods themselves.' (To Hans Richter, summer 1869)

He commissioned designs in 1874 from Professor Emil Doepler of Berlin, in the hope of his observing these principles: he believed, he wrote, that the commission offered rich opportunities to the imagination. Basically he wanted nothing less than a realization in the form of separate figures of a 'painting' representing personal events from a cultural epoch remote from every known realm of historical experience. The illustrations by Cornelius, Julius Schnorr and others of scenes from the medieval *Nibelungenlied* were to be ignored completely. More recently artists had attempted to represent Nordic mythology by reference to classical antiquity, with suitable modifications. As yet no one had thought of pursuing the clues offered by those Roman writers who had come into contact with the German peoples. 'And so it seems to me that an artist who is willing to adopt my suggestion will find he has the run of a unique field, both for intelligent compilation and for the exercise of his own imagination.' (17 December 1874)

The outcome was discouraging. Wagner did not like Doepler's designs, which were overladen with archaeological minutiae and lacked the grand simplicity of the tragic myth. During the 1876 rehearsals Cosima commented that 'the costumes look like nothing so much as Red Indian chiefs, and apart from the ethnographic nonsense they bear the stamp of petty theatrical tastelessness'.

Immediately before the preliminary sessions with the singers were due to start, on 26 June 1874 Wagner completed the scoring of the second act of *Götterdämmerung*. The instrumentation, spanning the utmost extremes, from Brünnhilde's 'Heilige Götter, himmlische Lenker' to the almost chamber-music-like 'Nicht eine Kunst war mir bekannt', often changing from one bar to the next, represents a peak in his achievement. He began the score of the third act while the rehearsals were in progress, on 10 July. 'I háve had to work on the instrumentation of this concluding work amid incessant interruptions, labouring in torment,' he wrote to King Ludwig on 1 October, 'and I have often cursed myself for having designed it so prodigally; it is the pinnacle which will tower above the whole Nibelung structure, reaching high up into the clouds!' He told Cosima that the fearful work would occupy him for a long time yet, just as the whole undertaking was growing too big for him to cope with. At about midday on 21 November he called to her, asking her to bring the newspaper; assuming that he was too tired to go on working, she did not dare to look at the score on his desk and, thinking it would distract him, she gave him a letter from Liszt that had just arrived. Hurt, he told her that he had just finished the work, but of course a letter from her father banished all interest in him. When he repeated this bitter complaint after lunch, she burst into tears. 'That I have dedicated my life to this work, at the cost of great pain, has not won me the right to celebrate its completion with joy,' she wrote in her diary, 'and so I celebrate in pain.'

That evening, after she had written those lines, Wagner came and put his arms round her, and said he thought they loved each other too much, and that was the reason why they suffered.

For her birthday in 1873 his surprise for her had been a question-and-answer game on the name 'Cosima', set for girls' voices. This year he composed an accompaniment for this 'Children's Catechism' for small orchestra, and concluded it with the last seven bars of *Götterdämmerung*.

'Our Christmas Eve was very jolly,' she wrote to Nietzsche. The tree in the hall had reached as high as the gallery, so that she had had to function as the 'dear Lord' on a real Jacob's ladder, while the Nibelung Chancellery had played the part of angels, flying to and fro, passing her the nuts and apples; the Meister had sat quietly at the foot, not asleep, but deep in Gfrörer's history of early Christianity, which he was reading for the sake of *Parsifal*. (31 December)

On Christmas Eve, to make up for what had happened on 21 November, she found the complete sketches for *Götterdämmerung* on the table with her other presents. On the morning of Christmas Day the *Idyll* was performed and the girls sang their 'catechism', 'Sagt mir, Kinder, was blüht am Maitag?', accompanied by the town orchestra from nearby Hof, which Wagner had secretly engaged. On New Year's Eve, as she walked out on to the terrace to hear the bells ringing, he greeted her with the Indian saying asserting the unity of all life, 'tat tvam asi' – 'that, too, you are'. He had had the snow cleared from the grave, and food scattered for the birds.

A late Christmas present came for him from Lenbach, who sent him his portrait of Schopenhauer. Wagner thanked him for the ' "Idea" of a Schopenhauer' realized in it. 'It expresses the whole of your latest *Unseasonal* [*Schopenhauer as Educator*],' Cosima told Nietzsche, 'a wonderful expression, full of clarity, discernment, concern and melancholy.' (16 January 1875) The picture was hung ceremonially in the library–drawing-room. He did not belong with Goethe, Schiller and Beethoven, Wagner felt: 'the philosopher must stand apart.' So he was given the place high above Wagner's desk.[13]

In retrospect, 1874 was a year that gave Wagner much to reflect on and warned him to make haste. Death had carried away a number of his friends and relatives. His sister Luise Brockhaus had died in February, followed in May by Franz Schott and Madame Muchenoff-Kalergis, and in October by Peter Cornelius, his brother-in-law Heinrich Wolfram and his brother Albert.

Their relationship with Nietzsche was also giving him and Cosima some concern. They knew nothing of his secret disaffection, but they sensed that in some way his friendship had lost its innocence. They had planted three saplings from Tribschen in the garden of Wahnfried, Cosima wrote to him, and the previous day she had got Daniela to read *Der goldene Topf* to them. 'It brought our home at Tribschen back to me all at once, and the curious life that you, too, shared in. Things are different now, and yet not so very different, the bond of trust remains between us, do not let it waste away.' (20 April 1874)

Nietzsche's notes in February 1874 include the observation, again, that the 'tyrant' acknowledged no other individuality beside his own, and that Wagner would be in great danger if he did not acknowledge Brahms etc. He heard Brahms's *Triumphlied* on 9 June and took the vocal score to Bayreuth with him in August, laid it on Wagner's piano and would not leave him in peace until it had been played through. 'Handel, Mendelssohn and Schumann swaddled in leather', Cosima commented in her diary. Wagner had got very bad-tempered and talked about his longing to meet a musical equal, and the superiority of Liszt's *Christus*, which did at least bear witness to a creative urge and sincere emotion.

As usual when there is no other corroboration of Elisabeth Nietzsche's version of an incident, one can take it or leave it. But as Newman craftily points out, when Elisabeth said it had '*since* occurred to her' that the score in its red binding was 'a sort of experimental object', she unwittingly gave her case away. (DMCW, I, p. 705; NLRW, IV, pp. 432ff.)

The year 1875 began with the negotiations for another detested concert tour. The contract with the king contained another disagreeable condition, besides the clause requiring repayment: namely, that the guarantee covered only the cost incurred for sets, machines and gas installations, which would become the property of the Cabinet Treasury in the event of failure to repay; it did not extend to the structural work, which necessarily could not be confiscated. So Wagner had to give concerts in Vienna and Budapest, to pay for the building work. There is no need here to go into the problems that made it necessary for him to change his original programmes. In the end he gave two concerts in Vienna including the first performance of excerpts from *Götterdämmerung* and one concert in Budapest, in which both Liszt and Wagner took part, for the first and only time since a concert at St Gallen in November 1856. Wagner conducted excerpts from *Walküre, Siegfried* and *Götterdämmerung*, and Liszt, 'with his poor ten fingers', played Beethoven's E♭ Concerto. As usual, the concerts were sold out and the audiences wild with enthusiasm. On 3 March Makart gave a fancy-dress party in his studio in Wagner's honour, with the theme of the court of Catharina Cornaro, in fifteenth-century Venice. Amused rather than greatly impressed by the costumes and play-acting, Wagner moved among the guests, chatting in his homely Saxon dialect. When the playwright Adolf Wilbrandt assured him that the German public had warmed to him as to no other great man in his lifetime, Wagner replied, 'Oh, yes, the Sultan and the Khedive of Egypt bought patronage vouchers.' In homage to Wagner, Hellmesberger and his colleagues came to play Beethoven's C♯ minor Quartet, which he was known to value highly, but the noise the guests made, crowding into every room, made serious listening impossible. At the end of the first movement, Wagner shook Hellmesberger by the hand gratefully: 'No more now, all the same, let's not – scatter the pearls any further, but keep them for ourselves, shall we?'

One ray of light came with a reunion with his old friend Gottfried Semper, who had blamed Wagner for the turn taken by the theatre project in Munich. Now he admitted candidly that he had been wrong to trust those who did not deserve it and to withdraw his trust from those who did.[14]

After a short rest, Wagner went to Berlin at the beginning of April to conduct two more concerts. At both of them Siegfried's Funeral March made so enormous an impression that it had to be repeated. After the second concert Wagner and Cosima were invited to the house of Hermann Helmholtz, the physicist, who had listened to 'the godlike music in unceasing tears'. When they visited Adolf Menzel's studio one evening they were greeted by his brother-in-law playing something from *Götterdämmerung*.

Wagner returned to Bayreuth at the end of April, before setting off to give a third concert in Vienna at the beginning of May, and during this brief halt his Newfoundland, Russ, died. The faithful Verena had bought him the dog out of her savings nine years before. 'One has to know from one's own experience how rare unconditional loyalty and affection are among people,' Cosima wrote to her two elder daughters at the Luisenstift boarding school in Dresden, 'to appreciate the friendly wagging tail, the faithful eyes, the unconditional devotion of a dog. Our old friend will be buried tomorrow at the foot of our own grave.' (2 May 1875) A small stone tablet still marks the spot: 'Here Wagner's Russ rests and keeps watch.'

Hagen's Watch was heard for the first time at the third Vienna concert. From the orchestral colouring, you might have thought the strings of the instruments had been spun from ravens' feathers, was Cosima's vivid description of the string syncopations accompanying the eerie tritone in the tubas and double basses. The manner in which Wagner conducted the Allegro introduction (the passage following 'Du, Hagen! Bewache die Halle!') impressed itself on Heinrich Porges's memory: the first two crotchets of the sequence were, so to speak, hurled out, while the downward-swinging triplets dashed onwards exultantly. This drastic rendering, which might be described by the Italian *incalzando*, created an effect that brought the listener to the edge of his seat.

While Cosima was away with Wagner on his concert tours, Elisabeth Nietzsche was at Wahnfried, looking after the children. 'In the last resort it will be a kind of higher education for you,' her brother had written approvingly. And indeed, the future guardian of the Nietzsche archives learned something from observing the mistress of Wahnfried. 'It has often been said to me', she wrote to Cosima on 12 November 1900, 'how remarkable it is that it should be two women who, deputies to a certain extent, stand at the head of both the dominating intellectual trends of the modern world.'

Some light is shed on the inner conflict Nietzsche was experiencing at this time by the letter he wrote Wagner for his birthday in 1875:

> Truly, beloved Meister, writing to you on your birthday is always no more than wishing *ourselves* happiness, wishing *ourselves* good health, so as to interest ourselves in you as we should. For I should think really it is illness, and the egoism that lurks in illness, that force people always to think of themselves: while genius, in its abundant health, always thinks only of others, involuntarily bestowing blessing and health wherever it happens to lay its hand. Every sick person is a

scoundrel, I read recently: and what human condition
isn't sickness! . . . Farewell, honoured Meister, and enjoy
what we do not: good health. (24 May 1875) [15]

His friends seemed to find something thrilling, Wagner
remarked in a letter to the king, in the sight of him busily engaged in
activities that were almost beyond the strength of even a young
man, at an age when everyone thinks only of enjoying the fruits of
toil. And why was he not content with the fruits of his toil, he
wondered; why did he constantly hazard them by devoting all his
endeavours to something for which the world about him had no
desire? But so be it! Schopenhauer had pointed a very fine distinction between talent and genius: while the former hits a target all can
see but cannot themselves reach, the latter hits a target that others
cannot even see. 'That's how it is with me too, and my great work!
At best. . . people substitute for the target perceived by me a target
they all think they can perceive, while mine lies far beyond theirs.'
(30 May)

The preliminary series of rehearsals began on 1 July, using piano
accompaniment until 1 August, and an orchestra from 2 to 12
August. Wagner conducted rehearsals regularly every morning and
afternoon, singing every line and performing every action for the
singers' benefit. Moreover he met the expenses for the 140 people
these rehearsals involved in various capacities – a sum of 12,000
talers, of its nature not covered by the royal guarantee – out of the
profits from his recent concerts.

At the first orchestral rehearsal Hans Richter took the beginning
of the second scene of *Rheingold*. When Wagner arrived he was
greeted by Franz Betz singing Wotan's salute to Valhalla, 'Voll-
endet das ewige Werk'. Deeply moved, he thanked the musicians:
'Opinions about our great enterprise may vary considerably, but I
believe that everyone taking part in it will be convinced that it is a
work of art of great significance, and not a "bag of tricks".' Then he
walked up a gangway on to the stage, near the edge of which stood
his small table, with a box on it supporting an oil lamp and against
which he propped his copy of the score. Richter conducted and
Wagner followed the score, continually waving his arms and legs
about in his excitement.

We owe the description of this scene, recorded by Menzel in a
well-known drawing, to the sculptor Kietz, who had been present

at the first reading of the text of *Siegfrieds Tod* in Dresden in 1848. His memoirs are supplemented by those of two of the people assisting in the production, the singing teacher Julius Hey from Munich and the choreographer Richard Fricke from Dessau.[16] Wagner had asked Hey to come to Bayreuth to administer 'singing therapy' to the tenor who was to take the part of Siegfried. He had discovered Fricke on the occasion when he had seen Gluck's *Orpheus* in Dessau; in his letter inviting him, Wagner told him that he needed not a 'producer' but a 'plastic choreographer', who would clarify his wishes to the performers by visual example.

Hey had ample opportunity to learn to appreciate Wagner's quite unique manner of preparing the realistic stage presentation of his music dramas. 'He spoke, sang and mimed like the most experienced of actors. All his physical movements – even when expressing the most extreme emotions – were governed by the surest instinct for beauty. Always certain of his aims, which he conveyed by suggestion to all the performers . . . his direction was nothing other than the outpouring . . . of his overflowing creative abundance – the emanation of his artistic being as such.'

No less admirable was his skill in coaxing the artists to work together harmoniously, where so much depended on the good will of each one individually. Only Albert Niemann, the Paris Tannhäuser, whom he had cast, not without misgivings, as Siegmund, introduced a discordant note. During a rehearsal of Act I of *Die Walküre* in the hall of Wahnfried, Niemann's intonation became increasingly insecure; growing conscious of it, he walked up to the accompanist, Rubinstein, from behind, seized hold of him by his narrow shoulders and shook him violently, venting his anger on someone who was in no way at fault. As Hey recorded, Wagner was so shocked that for a moment he could find no words with which to resolve this dissonance. He looked at the singer with disgust and finally said, after a general oppressive silence: 'Please, let us go on.' At the informal supper following this rehearsal Niemann assumed the role of the one who had been offended, refusing anything he was offered by the servant, until one of the female singers placated him by giving him food from her own plate. Cosima took her on one side and privately reproved her behaviour, and this so enraged Niemann that he resigned his part and left Bayreuth. At once the press seized on the incident, the artists began to form camps, and it was rumoured that others would follow Niemann's example. None did. 'Niemann was the only one who did not grasp the seriousness of our position.'

At the end of the series of rehearsals Wagner invited everybody to a party in the garden: lights were hung everywhere and the children led a procession along the leafy paths with brightly coloured paper lanterns. Then the trumpeters blew a fanfare to call everyone to the foot of the steps leading from the house, and Wagner addressed them: in performing all the music of his four dramas in a manner rising to virtuoso heights, his singers and orchestral players had accomplished something unbelievable; but they had achieved something far higher still: they had shown the world 'that the only truly vital art now was music'. (KLRW, III, pp. 64f.)

Among those who came to sit in on the rehearsals was the new director of the Vienna court opera, Franz Jauner. As the person with the last word on whether or not Amalie Materna would be free to sing Brünnhilde at Bayreuth, he used this position of strength to angle for Wagner's collaboration in preparing revivals of *Tann-häuser* and *Lohengrin* and, above all, to gain his consent to a produc-tion of *Walküre* in isolation from the rest of the *Ring*. 'No *Walküre* in Vienna, then no Valkyrie Amalie Materna for Bayreuth.' 'The haggling over *Die Walküre*,' Wagner remarked, 'that was a black page, and altogether unworthy of our friendly relations.'

For the present he hoped the plans for *Tannhäuser* and *Lohengrin* would be dropped, as he had stipulated that all the customary cuts must be restored. He wanted to devote his energies now not to new productions of his earlier works, nor even to seeing the *Ring* itself performed: even with that the 'Idea' would have sufficed him personally. 'We have sunk ourselves deep into *Parzival*,' Cosima wrote early in September to Countess Schleinitz. One thing emerged with reasonable certainty: that the Grail was an expression of the longing of the Christian soul to confront the Saviour directly, without the church and its hierarchies intervening – not a protesta-tion but a counter-creation. They had read some of the poetry of Kiot de Provins, the author of a lost *Perceval*, and the first line, 'En ce siècle puant et horrible', had become Wagner's motto.

But to no avail: since Jauner agreed to all his conditions he had to keep his word and on 1 November he moved to Vienna with the whole family for six weeks. He wrote to Feustel complaining of great weariness, and of the exhausting rehearsals, where he had to show them how to do everything.

Whereas in Paris he had had the conclusion of the *Tannhäuser* overture played as well, here in Vienna he went directly from the central section into the Bacchanale, so that, in addition to the Dresden and Paris versions, there is a Vienna version as well. When he appeared on the stage at the end of the performance to acknowledge the enthusiastic applause he promised the audience that he would continue in his efforts to make his works more familiar to them, 'so far as the forces available permit'. Although this qualification quite unmistakably referred to the selection of which works might be performed next, the press represented it as criticism of the artists. On the morning of the day of the second performance, Wagner collected the singers together to thank them and clear up the misunderstanding. It had never entered his head, he assured them, to denigrate the artists who had contributed to the success of the work. If they insisted on public satisfaction, he would ask Jauner to publish the letter of acknowledgement he had sent him. But in that case he would have to abandon his cooperation with them, since he could interpret such a wish on their part in no other way than as mistrust in him. 'I repeat that you are free to publish my letter to the management . . . I myself cannot have any contact with the press.' And he added vehemently: 'For I despise the press' – which was then reported in the newspapers as 'I detest the press'.

The two principals in *Lohengrin* were poorly cast. He wrote to Hey after returning home that his recent survey of tenors in Vienna had profoundly depressed him, 'so that I had to keep on asking myself whatever possessed me to write all the principal parts in my works, where the character's soul is important, for the tenor voice!' (3 January 1876)

The only thing he enjoyed was working with the chorus, which he coached not only to sing as beautifully as possible, as if each member was a soloist, but also to act so intelligently that their personal involvement in the action was credible. Wagner repaid them by returning to Vienna to conduct a performance of *Lohengrin* himself, for the chorus's benefit, on 2 March 1876.

During his stay there in November 1875 he had the opportunity to hear Verdi's Requiem and Bizet's *Carmen*. What he thought of the former is unknown ; Cosima thought it hailed from the regions where Spontini had directed all his compatriots. *Carmen* wrung from her the admission that the French were now the only nation with talent: even this 'unpleasant work' showed talent. Later, of course, in *The Wagner Case*, Nietzsche was to play Bizet off against Wagner. In September 1888 Nietzsche wrote to Gast that Gersdorff had witnessed an angry outburst against Bizet by Wagner: 'On that basis . . . my malice will be even more keenly felt at a certain important passage.' But this is contradicted by the testimony of Joseph Rubinstein, who told Paul Vidal, a professor at the Paris Conservatoire whom he met in Rome in 1884, that Wagner had often asked to hear passages from *Carmen*, especially the first-act duet; the phrase 'Ma mère, je la vois', particularly delighted him; he felt that this naive freshness could be the starting point for a renewal of French dramatic music, drawing new vigour from popular melody.[17]

On the whole Wagner did not enjoy his stay in Vienna. 'Do you suppose those six weeks in the winter of 1875 have lingered in my mind as an agreeable memory?' he asked Jauner as much as three years later. 'No, my dear friend! When I parted from you after your lavish supper on the last evening I was certain that I would never enter Vienna again! There every scoundrelly dog can fall on a man like me and empty his pisspot over me with impunity, but, thank goodness, I need never show my face there again. Never! Never! – Give my respects to Councillor Hanslick and Speidel and all the rest of that crew; I don't blame them for what they do, since it seems to earn them a living in Vienna: consequently the public seems to prefer them to me. Therefore, they have my blessing!' (MWKS, II, p. 184) In fact, the reason for the ferocity of this attack on Vienna lay in an experience of 1877, to which we shall come in due course.

But those Vienna productions of *Tannhäuser* and *Lohengrin* have an enduring importance for posterity because of the chroniclers they found. One of the members of the court opera at the time was a young baritone, Angelo Neumann, who later became world-famous as the director of the touring Wagner Theatre. In his memoirs he wrote that during the rehearsals he gained the indelible impression that Wagner was not only the greatest dramatist, but also the greatest director for the stage and the greatest actor. Fortunately for us Neumann did not content himself with this generalized approbation, but gave a detailed account of Wagner at work with the singers, singing and acting their parts for them to show them how he wanted everything done.[18]

Of even more value are the notes on Wagner's tempos made by a student at the Vienna Conservatory who became a great Wagner conductor, Felix Mottl. While performance styles are tempered more or less by the taste of the time, Wagner's tempos, so far as they can be ascertained, had a sublimity transcending the fashion of any period. At least, they should have had. In Vienna, bad habits had crept in under Richter's predecessor, Esser: 'too fast in the lyrical music', 'too little ardour in dramatic dialogue – too much emphasis on crotchets, instead of a dashing alla breve'. (MWKS II, p. 170) Mottl recorded all Wagner's oral remarks about tempos in his diary, and later used them in the vocal scores of *Tannhäuser* and *Lohengrin* that he made for the Leipzig publishers, Peters, who in turn incorporated them in their editions of the full scores.[19]

Wagner and Cosima got back to Bayreuth on 17 December 1875. 'We are seriously worried,' he wrote to Heckel, 'and when it comes down to it, I have to admit that the idea of holding the festival this year as planned is downright foolhardy. We are up to 490 with the patronage vouchers, but according to the latest calculations we need 1300. So really the original project has totally failed. Now all we can do is hold our breath and see what curiosity will bring in in the end. Even Feustel is inclined to take the risk . . .Otherwise we are putting a good face on things here. Everything will be ready on time (on credit!)' (4 February 1876)

The only really grave fear was that they would not have the ready cash when the singers and players arrived in June and wanted to see the colour of their money. Having heard that the German Emperor was in charge of a fund set up to further enterprises of national interest, Wagner had applied to him directly in October 1875, asking for a loan of 30,000 talers. He was informed that the emperor had approved the request without hesitation, and recommended it to the Imperial Chancellery where, however, it had been refused by Delbrück, the president of the ministry. Bismarck himself had known nothing of the request, Wagner wrote later in the *Review of the Festival*, but Delbrück had acted entirely on his own initiative. (RWGS, X, pp. 106ff.) Instead the Chancellery had advised him to apply to the Reichstag. 'To this suggestion I replied merely that I had thought to apply to the emperor's bounty and the insight of the Imperial Chancellor, but not to the views of the right honourable members of the Reichstag.'

But this version of the story put out for public consumption, namely that Bismarck had known nothing about it, was not true. At the New Year, when they were still waiting to hear the decision,

Wagner said to Cosima that only a man like Bismarck could help, 'otherwise we are lost'. The suggestion that he should apply to the Reichstag arrived a fortnight later. His friends were divided over the likely outcome of such a step. Wagner himself, as he told King Ludwig, felt that a petition to the Reichstag would be 'quite improper'. In the meantime he did not abandon all hope in Bismarck.

All the same he persisted in helping himself by his own endeavours. He started negotiating to give a series of concerts in Brussels. Then he was approached by Theodore Thomas of New York to write something for the centenary of American independence, and replied that he would write something in a broad march form, although it was a long time since he had written a note, and he had got completely out of the habit of composing, as it was called. He expected that the Americans would treat him well, meaning that they would patronize the festival. (See also Appendix II.) He gave the march a motto from Goethe: 'Nur der verdient sich Freiheit wie das Leben, der täglich sie erobern muß' ('the price of liberty, as of life, is daily reconquest'), which gave rise to a comic misunderstanding when the delegates who came to take delivery of the march translated the word 'erobern' ('conquer') as 'rob'. In the gentle passages, Wagner explained, he had been thinking of the 'beautiful and industrious women of North America', who were to be envisaged as taking part in the triumphal procession. As so often when his musical imagination was once roused, it was stimulated in respect of another work altogether. He had shown her his latest album piece, Cosima wrote in her diary on 16 February 1876: it was the song the Flower Maidens sing to entice Parsifal. The sheet of paper was inscribed at the top: '*Parzival*. Act II. *Women*. (Schöner Knabe komm' zu mir)', and at the bottom: '(wanting to be American!)' The remarkable thing about the gentle middle section of the march is a melodic figure which sounds more like Richard Strauss than Richard Wagner:

When a telegram arrived from America, reporting the work's great success, Wagner commented: 'Do you know what the best thing about the march is? The money I got for it.' He had 5000 dollars for the American performing rights, and he asked Schott's for another 9000 marks for the European publishing rights – which they paid.

On 4 March he went to Berlin, in response to an invitation to prepare a performance of *Tristan*, the proceeds of which, by imperial decree, were to go to the festival funds. In his letter to Heckel of a few weeks previously he had said that he wanted to see if he could still do anything about the loan he had requested, but he had no sooner arrived than he learned from Countess Schleinitz that no help was to be expected from the Chancellor.

Tristan was sung by Niemann, with whom Wagner was again reconciled. 'Where else, at the moment, would we find a better Siegmund?' he had asked Hey. 'I know of none. The fact of the matter is that in spite of a certain lack of self-control – or perhaps precisely because of it – he is a fully developed masculine personality. And it is only someone like that who will be capable of entering fully into the role, so that there is not the least vestige left of those all too often pomaded, simpering drawing-room and chamber tenors. Although his acting of a part is always on broad, sweeping lines, he does not display that all-purpose, unintelligent pathos that I so detest and that in the case of the majority of opera singers nowadays turns into a mindless, artistic pose, robbing every performance of the realistic lineaments of dramatic truth.'

Hülsen, who had refused to see Wagner on business thirteen years before, on this occasion gave a glittering dinner party in his honour. Frau von Hülsen, in her memoirs, wrote that she still entertained the most vivid recollection of the festive board, and Wagner at her side, and she still remembered how she involuntarily gave a little start whenever one or other of the singers addressed him as 'Meister'. Hülsen himself behaved like a thorough gentleman towards Wagner. *Der Fliegende Holländer* had proved to be a cast-iron success over the years, and in view of this Hülsen had arranged for Wagner to be paid a retroactive royalty stretching right back to the first Berlin performance in 1844. After deduction of the fee that had been paid at the time, this now amounted to 818 talers and 16 silver groschens. In the case of the new production of *Tristan* it was he who suggested to the emperor that the net proceeds of the first performance should be dedicated to Bayreuth. 'It is a fact that the only operas popular enough to sell out at virtually every performance at the present time are certain of Wagner's.'

The première on 20 March was rapturously received. During one of the intervals Wagner was presented to the emperor, who expressed his admiration and promised to come to Bayreuth for the festival. The net profits amounted to 14,000 marks, which were paid to the festival funds.

But Hülsen made no secret of his opinion that *Tristan* had no future: only *Tannhäuser* and *Lohengrin* would last, *Tristan* and the *Ring* would be forgotten in fifty years' time – according to Julius Kapp, though according to Glasenapp he said fifteen – but either estimate was proved wrong long ago; by 1933, fifty years after Wagner's death, *Tristan* alone had been performed 250 times at the Oper unter den Linden.[20]

King Ludwig replied to Wagner's message on the twelfth anniversary of their first meeting on 3 May with one of his rhapsodic telegrams: 'Wonnemond des Nibelungen-Jahres!'[21] But he did not refer in any way to the request Wagner had by then submitted to suspend the payments on his loan. On 26 May Wagner wrote to Düfflipp that on the very eve of the realization of his undertaking the only remaining means of ensuring it lay in the king's bounty, namely his consent to suspend the repayments as of that moment; otherwise there would not be a pfennig in hand to pay the instrumentalists and singers who would be arriving on 1 June, and he had no alternative but to conceal the whole thing publicly. Nevertheless he crossed the Rubicon, allowed the artists to come and implored the king, once more, to come to his aid. 'The day is nigh when I shall once again behold you, for the first time since I parted from you on the evening of *Meistersinger*, and told you of my profound premonition that we would not see each other again for many a long day. It was fully eight years ago!' (12 June) At last, on 29 June, Düfflipp wrote to tell him that the king had consented to the suspension of the payments, on the conditions already mentioned.

This biography is not the place for a detailed chronicle of the rehearsals and the eventual performances of the *Ring* in 1876. Starting with Glasenapp, the tale has already been told often and adequately. Of greater importance to us are some individual events and personal testimonies which throw light on Wagner's personality, on his work and on the performance of it. In addition to the records by Hey and Fricke, the eyewitness accounts of Felix Mottl and Heinrich Porges are especially valuable.[22]

'Send Mottl immediately!' Wagner telegraphed Richter in Vienna on 20 May. 'I arrive on the Meister's birthday, throw myself into tails and white tie and present myself at Wahnfried for Wagner's great Gaudy! He greets me with a cry of "Enter Count Almaviva!" My forehead was bathed with anxious perspiration, the more so when he said, apparently in all seriousness, that they must be careful in front of me, I came from Vienna and would report everything to Hanslick . . . In the evening, in the Meister's presence, inauguration of the restaurant on the Festival Hill . . . Wagner makes a comic speech about the proprietor, offering to waive his own fame in his favour. Later he appears on the gallery in the restaurant with pike and lantern and sings the Night Watchman's song from *Meistersinger*, producing a hilarious imitation of the F♯ on the steer-horn.'

Mottl was placed in the Nibelung Chancellery to begin with, before being brought into the rehearsals as offstage conductor. His impromptu notes are a first-rate reflection of Wagner's changing moods, his directives on acting – 'Never come down to the front of the stage!' – and singing – 'No "recitatives", there's no such thing in my music! Nothing but "arias"!' – his informal remarks about art and artists in general and his own work in particular: 'When I am composing and need something, it is always to hand.' During a rehearsal of Act II of *Die Walküre* with the orchestra, at the passage 'Gefallner Helden hehre Schar umfängt dich hold mit hochheiligem Gruß' tears came to Mottl's eyes, whereupon Wagner gave him a cheerful nudge and said, to hide his own emotion, 'How about that for sentimentality! Here on the stage we know it's all make-believe! People out there will be duped, but we can stay quite unmoved!'

'I not only respected the Meister deeply, but loved him ardently,' Mottl confessed spontaneously after describing a rehearsal of *Siegfried*. 'If he had wanted it, I would have jumped into the fire for him.'

An article Porges had written about the Bayreuth performance of the Choral Symphony in 1872 gave Wagner the idea at the time of asking him to perform 'an office of the very greatest future importance' to the festivals, 'to follow all my rehearsals very closely . . . and to note down everything I say, even the smallest details, about the interpretation and performance of our work, so that a tradition goes down in writing'. (6 November 1872)

Porges devoted himself to the task conscientiously and with amazing insight and perception. He was not only thoroughly familiar with the score of the *Ring*, but also, thanks to his education and culture, fully able to appreciate its literary and philosophical content. We sense the fresh air of first-hand experience in his descriptions of how Wagner transformed himself into each character, placed himself in each situation, and so inspired all his colleagues, as we might imagine Shakespeare doing, by his playing of the whole drama in his one person. His manner of musico-dramatic delivery impressed as being fundamentally sound, possessing a thoroughly positive vital energy, which was the source of the definitive realism of all his creative directives. For all that, everything he said seemed impromptu, as though what he asked of the performers had only that moment occurred to him.

The distinguishing characteristic of Porges's record is his ability always to locate the endless detail of Wagner's individual instructions to his performers in an overall intellectual context. Thus at the very start, he does not content himself with reporting Wagner's insistence that, as the curtain rises, the violin figurations accompanying Woglinde's 'Weia Waga!' should suddenly be played as softly as possible, but adds that this unexpected reversal after the powerful crescendo of the orchestral introduction, similar in method to Beethoven, is of outstanding stylistic significance: it is a direct expression of the form mastering the material, which Schiller defined as the highest function of art. When, at the end of the second scene, Loge was told to articulate the words 'erstirbt der Götter Stamm', accompanied by pianissimo trombone chords, with temperate but incisive emphasis and quite without personal emotion, it was because at that moment he is the herald of cosmic destiny. 'I shuddered with a feeling as if the spirit of classical tragedy was abroad on the stage.' When Erda appears it should create the impression that as Wotan's lust for power erupts with a daemonic strength it wakens a hidden subterranean force, which normally exercises its sway under the mysterious cover of darkness. The veiled tonal colour for which Wagner asked and the masterly deployment of the verbal accentuation both contributed to this effect: in the passage beginning 'Wie alles war', the next two words, 'weiß ich', marked 'ritenuto', should be sung very slowly and expansively, as if Erda's spirit is sinking back into itself like light fading; on the other hand, the final words, 'meide den Ring', should be sung with an intensity that cuts right through the soul. It is this order of insight that makes Porges's notes on the performance of the *Ring* simultaneously an authoritative commentary on the work per se.

Nietzsche had not come to Bayreuth during the 1875 rehearsals. 'I have just passed through a *very bad* time, and perhaps an even worse one is to come,' he wrote to Gersdorff at the time. 'Will you break it to them in Bayreuth that I am not likely to come in July? Wagner will be thoroughly angry, I am myself.' Nonetheless, with the 'miracle' in which he had ceased to believe on the point of realization after all, he was compelled to make his own contribution in the form of a kind of 'Bayreuth festival sermon'. Having written most of it, in the autumn of 1875 he suddenly claimed that he could write no more. This one of his *Meditations* would not go to the printer, he told Rohde in a letter of 7 October. It was almost finished but he had come nowhere near the standard he set himself.

Elisabeth Nietzsche, on the other hand, claimed to remember his replying to her at the time, asking him if he would continue the essay, 'Oh, Lisbeth, if only I could!' To this Newman adds the ironic comment that there were far too many occasions on which Elisabeth conveniently 'remembered' a little remark of her brother's that came in pat to confirm whatever she happened to be saying at any given moment.

Fortunately we have Peter Gast's account to set against hers. When he urged Nietzsche to go on and complete it, Nietzsche gave no hint of inner reluctance or scruples of conscience, but merely said that it was too personal for publication. It was Gast's enthusiasm after reading the manuscript that finally persuaded him to add the last three of the eleven sections and to publish the book as a 'Festschrift' in July 1876.

The letter he sent Wagner for his birthday a few weeks earlier is enough in itself to refute the later legend that he wrote the fourth of his *Unseasonal Meditations* in despite of his own inner nature: 'It is almost exactly seven years since I first visited you in Tribschen, and I can think of nothing else to say to you on your birthday except that I, too, since then, celebrate my spiritual and intellectual birthday in May each year. For since then you have lived in me and work incessantly as a completely new drop of blood that I certainly did not have before.' (21 May)

The legend, however, not content with representing the book as an offering on the altar of friendship, interprets it as a kind of autobiography. He initiated the process himself in *Ecce Homo*: he would not deny that the fourth *Unseasonal Meditation* is basically about himself alone: '*Wagner in Bayreuth* is a vision of my future.' But, as Newman says, the reading of the composer's nature and character is too penetratingly accurate in most respects not to rank as a painting from life, and the line Nietzsche took twelve years later was 'at once brazen and naive'. And even Andler has to admit that it was 'une construction faite après coup'.

In order to establish his claim that the portrait of the dithyrambic artist in *Wagner in Bayreuth* was in truth that of the 'pre-existent poet of *Zarathustra*' and did not impinge for a moment on the 'reality of Wagner', Nietzsche asserted in *Ecce Homo*, as the acid proof, that Wagner himself had understood it in that light: 'He did not recognize himself in the text.' In reality Wagner wrote to him immediately after reading it: 'Friend! Your book is prodigious! How did you get to know me so well?' How indeed? The answer should have been, from the intimacy of their friendship in the years at Tribschen, and from Nietzsche's acquaintance with Wagner's autobiography.

When Wagner was planning a private edition of his *Life* in 1869 he entrusted it to Nietzsche to deal on his behalf with an Italian printer, Bonfantini, in Basel, and to read the proofs. 'I am committing an act of the most stupendous confidence in you', he wrote to Nietzsche, 'in sending you with these lines quite a tidy quantity of the most valuable manuscript, namely the first part of my autobiography.' Before long, however, he gained the impression that he had perhaps given Nietzsche rather more than he could cope with: 'I . . . now ask you most sincerely to regard yourself as absolutely relieved of this trouble . . . You can be confident that I shall never prevent you from seeing these pages, the more so, I expect, since you know that you are foremost among those I have appointed to continue to watch over these souvenirs of me after my death.' (4 June 1870)

Even if Nietzsche read no more than the history of Wagner's early life on that occasion, it is precisely the knowledge of a person's youth that gives a psychologist the code with which to decipher the adult.

'Come soon, won't you,' Wagner wrote on 12 July 1876, 'and let the rehearsals accustom you to your impressions!' In the first cycle of rehearsals (3 June to 12 July), each act was assigned three working days, but in the second (14 to 26 July) only one. It was a time of hard work and great excitement: the builders were still working on the fabric, the sets were still being painted and repainted, shortcomings in the stage effects had still to be eliminated, and in addition, almost every day there were the usual theatrical tantrums, so that every morning Cosima had personally to seek out whoever happened to have taken offence. And the whole was accompanied by the chorus of the press, which spared no effort to discredit the festival in advance and as far as possible to ruin it. The worst thing of all for Wagner and Cosima was their recognition that the performances would fall as far short of the work as the work itself was remote from the age.

One evening she found him standing at the window. 'He was talking to the stars, especially the Pleiades, his lifelong friends, which were very bright. And he said: "Protect my wife and my children, you good star! With me, do what you like!" He was thinking of his death, he told me.'

Cosima herself had an additional source of distress in Bülow. According to Du Moulin, who presumably learned it from her diary, he had been offered the musical directorship of the festival, and later a tactfully expressed invitation to attend had been sent him. In order to remove himself from the scene entirely he had undertaken an American tour. 'I nurture the warmest wishes – have no doubt on that score – may providence award you the fullest satisfaction in the success of the greatest musical event of the century. Believe me, Madame, that the equal impossibility for me to be there, and not to be there, was the major reason for the irrevocable decision that I took,' he wrote to her from Chicago on 6 February. Now she learned that he had fallen ill and returned to Germany, and was in a sanatorium in Godesberg. 'I have difficulty in overcoming a sense of shame at having come to such decrepitude', he wrote to Richard Pohl, 'and it had to happen of course, in anno Bayreuth, the year I was determined to spend in America because of the, to some extent, two-headed moral impossibility for me . . . not to attend the festival as a Wagnerian de la veille. It is really the bitterest blow in the whole business.'

On 3 August, a rest-day between the first general rehearsals of *Siegfried* and *Götterdämmerung*, after entertaining guests in the evening, Cosima confided to her diary: 'The news is like an overwhelming shadow, engulfing my soul; the very thought of any joy is now impossible, only patience and work.' (DMCW, I, pp. 769f.)

Meanwhile friends wishing to attend the rehearsals were arriving from far and near. When Wagner entertained them at home in the evenings he was friendly and in good spirits, and it troubled him to see Nietzsche, who arrived on 24 July, silent and gloomy. Schuré, who was meeting him for the first time, wrote that 'en présence de Richard Wagner, il était timide, gêné, presque toujours silencieux'.

King Ludwig was expected to arrive for the final dress rehearsals (6 to 9 August). 'To receive . . . the various royal personages, all of whom I detest in some degree or other, and to listen to their idle chatter, to do them the honours there, instead of immersing myself in your sublime, godlike work, is something that I would never ever be able to bring myself to do,' he had written to Wagner back in January. He had decided to stay at the Eremitage palace just outside the town, rather than at the margraves' Neues Schloss in the centre. But the flags and decorations that the townspeople put up to greet him on 5 August were wasted. His special train drew to a halt at one o'clock in the morning on an open stretch of track near the Rollwenzelei inn. The king descended and silently extended his hand to Wagner, who was waiting for him there. The waiting carriage took them both to the Eremitage, where the friends talked until three, when Wagner returned to Wahnfried, charmed and delighted.

The dress rehearsal of *Das Rheingold* was held before an empty auditorium, and was acoustically unsatisfactory, so the guests who had been attending the earlier sessions were allowed in for the remaining three rehearsals. After *Götterdämmerung* the king departed as he had come, in the middle of the night, from the crossing-keeper's house beside the Rollwenzelei, and went back to Hohenschwangau.

'It is impossible for me to describe the impressions with which I came away from the festival at Bayreuth, which afforded me immeasurable ecstasy, and from my happy reunion with you, my revered friend. I came with great expectations and, high as they were, they were all *far, far* surpassed. I was so deeply moved that I may very well have seemed tongue-tied to you! Oh, you understand so well how to shake one's very foundations, to melt with your conquering light the crust of ice which so many sad experiences have caused to form around heart and feelings.' (12 August)

When Wagner went to meet the German Emperor at the railway station on 12 August the building was covered with bunting and the crowd stretched as far as the eye could see. 'I did not believe that you would bring it about,' the emperor replied to his words of welcome, 'and now the sun shines on your work.' Ludwig Schemann recalls that Wagner's face revealed his consciousness that the millennia of human history were speaking through him. The vital clue to understanding Wagner's personality, he adds, was the recognition that as an artist he believed himself a king, and he uses the same comparison as Nietzsche at the beginning of *Wagner in Bayreuth*: no Alexander had ever taken up his daemonic destiny with more profound earnest than Wagner as he assumed the mission that the world spirit had laid upon him. And then, as he climbed into his carriage and drove home through the cheering crowd, shouting hurrah and waving his hat, he was all at once the man of the moment again.[23]

After *Die Walküre*, the emperor sent for him, praised everything he had seen, and expressed his regret at not being able to stay any longer. 'Your graciousness is not to be measured by time and place,' Wagner replied.

Wagner had published a notice asking the audience not to be offended with either the performers or the composer if they did not appear on the stage to acknowledge applause; they had agreed on this act of self-denial, so as not to be seen to step outside the frame of the work. (RWGS, XVI, p. 160) But after *Götterdämmerung* the storm of applause was so prolonged that he felt obliged to appear before the curtain. Gravely, he said: 'It is to your patronage and to the unlimited efforts of my colleagues, the artists, that you owe this achievement. All else that I have to say to you can be summarized in a few words, an axiom. You have now seen what we can do; now it is for you to *want*. And if you want it, then we have an art.' The moment was so impressive that even a dispassionate witness like Dr Strecker, the new director of Schott's, was forced to admit: 'An event of historical importance has taken place, and I can say "I was there".'

The following evening, when seven hundred people gathered for a banquet in the festival restaurant, Wagner, who was sitting with the artists, rose and went to stand on the stairs which joined the upper and lower rooms to make a speech. He wished to refer to what he had said the day before, as he had heard it had been misunderstood. He had not meant that the Germans had had no art until now, but what they had lacked until now was a national art such as the Italians and French possessed. 'Alles Vergängliche ist nur ein Gleichnis' – a work of art, too, is transient, but it is a symbol of what endures, of the eternal. And if what they had presented was still 'inadequate' in some respects, it must nonetheless be recognized as an 'event'. 'My intention is honourable,' he concluded, 'believe me, my intention is really honourable.'

Tumultuous applause and laughter broke out as Signora Giovanna Lucca, his Italian publisher and admirer, produced a 'petit cadeau', a silver laurel wreath which she gracefully pressed upon his brows. But he reverted to a more serious tone, reminding them all of the importance of continuing to have faith in the cause. 'Here is the man who was the first to repose that faith in me, at a time when I was unknown, and without whom you might perhaps today not have heard a note of mine – my dear friend Franz Liszt!' With arms outstretched he walked down the steps and embraced Liszt. Finally, he remarked that so many serious words had been spoken, and an enthusiast had even tried to glorify him in verse: 'So now not one sensible word more!' (GLRW, V, p. 294)

In the midst of all the artistic and social demands on his time Wagner contrived to set the words he had written but not used in Brünnhilde's concluding monologue, beginning 'Verging wie Hauch der Götter Geschlecht', and sent the piece to King Ludwig, who had admired the lines, as a birthday present. It closes in C major with the motive of World Inheritance first heard in the Wanderer/Erda scene in *Siegfried*, where it sounds like 'the proclamation of a new religion'.[24]

At the same time he persuaded the king to come back for the third cycle. 'Nobody will disturb your enjoyment! There will be no "crowned heads" left here for the third performance: perhaps a prince from some little dukedom, but no one with a claim to a seat in the royal box.' (21 August) Before the performance Ludwig spoke a few amiable words to the members of the management committee, but otherwise was accessible to no one except Wagner, since he spent the intervals reading the text. Since it was already apparent that the money they had in hand was not going to be enough, his friends urged Wagner to ask the king personally for more credit, but he vigorously refused to try, saying that he was making every effort to reduce his debts to the king, not to increase them.

At the end of the last *Götterdämmerung* the demonstrations far surpassed everything there had been hitherto. Even Ludwig showed himself at the front of his box and joined in the applause. Wagner appeared before the curtain. His voice shaking, he told them that the festival was now over, and he did not know if it would ever be repeated. He had called this work, which had been so long in the preparing, a 'festival drama', without really knowing what right he had to do so, since there was no festival marked for these days in the calendar of history. Now that it was over and had enjoyed, as the applause indicated, some measure of success, perhaps he could after all claim the right to call it a festival. But credit for the success was due in large part to his colleagues, the artists: 'I wish them to present themselves to me!' The curtains parted; there were the singers and the orchestral players in a broad semicircle with Hans Richter in the middle, waiting to hear the Meister's farewell words: their faith, their dedication had made it possible to keep to the timetable, which nobody had thought beforehand could be done. For the last time he repeated his thanks to them for the long days, and nights too, of work. 'And now that we must part, a heartfelt farewell!' (GLRW, V, pp. 306f.)

But behind the satisfied, confident face Wagner showed the world, he concealed disappointment and despair. Only a few had glimpsed it. The entry in Cosima's diary for 9 September has 'Said goodbye to Mathilde Maier, the last of our friends.[25] Then we discussed the performances and our experiences. Richard does not want the matadors Betz and Niemann again. In his rage at not being allowed to take a bow, Betz's performance was a downright disgrace. Brandt not up to his expectations. Richter not sure of a single tempo [she had remarked at the start of the rehearsals that he had made too much of a meal of beating every crotchet in 4/4 time]. Despondency! Deep distress! Richard very sad, he says he would like to die.' (DMCW, I, pp. 771f.) He may have given some inkling of it to his oldest friend, Anton Pusinelli, with whom he would have liked to retreat to some quiet corner, where they could have enjoyed each other's company. The king was another from whom he did not conceal his mood: the outward success did not serve to hide from him the abyss, from which the last veil had been drawn: 'There is no footing for me and my work in this day and age.' (11

September) He told his Brünnhilde, Amalie Materna, that he was deeply depressed and that he longed only for the moment when he and his family would be able to go to Italy. (9 September) But he revealed himself most unreservedly, to the point of self-forgetfulness, to Judith Gautier, who had come for the second and third cycles and did not leave Bayreuth until 5 September. Her embraces, he confessed a year later, had been a last gift of the gods, who had not wished him to succumb to the 'chagrin de ma fausse gloire des représentations des *Nibelungen*'. (18 November 1877)

The full extent of the financial calamity was one thing he did not yet realize, and he expected to repeat the festival the following year on more favourable terms. What lengthy preparations the Greeks had devoted to their great festivals in honour of Dionysus! Where the ancients had allowed themselves plenty of time, he had to act in all haste. 'Next year we will do everything differently,' he told Richard Fricke. Later, in 1878, when he had recovered from the depression brought on by the immense tension of the preceding years and months, he pronounced a fairer verdict in his *Review of the Festival*: 'A benevolent spell made everything there *good*. And the profound conviction based on that experience is my goodly profit from those weeks.' (*Rückblick auf die Bühnenfestspiele*, RWGS, X, pp 103ff.)

# 29

## Nietzsche in Bayreuth

Wagner had no opportunity to discuss the festival with Nietzsche, for, as he complained, he could not get a single word out of him, even when they spent several hours in each other's company.

By way of explanation the legend offers a sudden insight on Nietzsche's part, the clear recognition of what he had long dimly sensed: that he had deceived himself about Wagner and his work; that Wagner had betrayed his ideal for the sake of quick success; and finally that his music was not really great.

With the thoroughness of the historian and the nose of the detective, Ernest Newman investigated the background and the context of this crisis in three great chapters of his biography: 'Nietzsche in 1876', 'Elisabeth's False Witness' and 'The Realities of the Matter'. (NLRW, IV, pp. 491ff.) No one should forgo the pleasure of reading that masterpiece and model of literary unmasking at first hand. Here I shall do no more than summarize the evidence and supplement it with material from other sources.

As his letters to Gersdorff and Rohde betray, Nietzsche had just gone through a particularly bad year when he went to Bayreuth: violent headaches for days on end, vomiting for hours at a time, general exhaustion, increasing trouble with his eyes. He was so ill at Christmas 1875 that on 18 January 1876 he confided to Gersdorff his fear that he was suffering from a disease of the brain. After a temporary improvement in May, in June he was complaining again that his condition was worsening from day to day.

But he was determined to see Bayreuth through.

After arriving there on 24 July he went to a rehearsal of the first act of *Götterdämmerung*. They were now in the second cycle of rehearsals, with the orchestra but without costumes. Nietzsche had been suffering from a headache for thirty hours without a break and he could not stay in the theatre to the end. The next day he was still so tired, as he told his sister in a letter, that he could hardly write. Nevertheless he went to the rehearsal of the second act that afternoon, and of the third on the following day. On 28 July he reported that he felt better and was now in his element. The third cycle of rehearsals began on 29 July, with the singers in costume; one whole work was taken in a day, but with stops when Wagner had some comment to interpose, and with passages being repeated as necessary. Nietzsche heard *Rheingold*, probably, and, on 31 July, *Walküre*. He was not well, he wrote to Elisabeth the next day: incessant headache and weakness. The day before he had only been able to listen to *Walküre* in the dark: watching had been quite impossible. He wanted to get away, it was absurd for him to stay. The prospect of these long evenings dedicated to art appalled him. This time she would have to see and hear on his behalf. He had had as much as he could stand. He would not even go to the performances, it was such torture for him. He wanted to get away to the Fichtelgebirge or somewhere like that.

Judging by this letter it is improbable that he stayed for *Siegfried* on 2 August. At all events he did not attend a reception at Wahnfried on 3 August, as he had left for Klingenbrunn in the Bavarian Forest because of his continuing headache. He intended to spend about ten days there but not return via Bayreuth – where his sister had arrived in the meantime – as he was running short of money.

It was while he was in Klingenbrunn that he drafted the cutting comments on Wagner and his art that later went into *Human, all too Human*. Cosima had told him, apropos of *Schopenhauer as Educator*, that his writing must 'cut a deep furrow'; it is worth noting that he took up that image and called these notes *The Ploughshare*.

As Newman rightly emphasizes, it would have been impossible even for a person in a normal state of health to judge so vast and novel a work as the *Ring* from such fragmentary acquaintance as Nietzsche had so far had, let alone one in his physical condition, tormented by headaches and eye trouble to the point where he could hardly see.

In fact, he changed his mind and went back to Bayreuth on 12 August. As luck would have it, however, the first cycle of performances took place in a heat wave so enervating, as Schemann recalled, that it was an effort to stand upright. There are no letters by Nietzsche himself to tell us anything about his health during this week, but we have the reliable testimonies of Schuré and Schemann. The former, who also accompanied him on the journey back to Basel, writes that during the performances Nietzsche was gloomy and depressed, and was already suffering from the early stages of the brain disease that later overpowered him. Schemann, who had already known him for some time, visited him on the morning of 18 August, the day after *Götterdämmerung*, and got the impression that he was 'obviously already very ill'.

Back in Basel his condition was so bad that his ophthalmologist reproached himself bitterly for having allowed him to go to Bayreuth. On 27 September Nietzsche wrote to Wagner that he was about to leave for Italy in the hope of putting an end to his suffering. 'It has risen to new heights. . . in these last few years. . . I have put up with incessant pain, as if I had been born for that and no other purpose.'

That these complaints were not just excuses put forward to conceal his disaffection, as has been suggested, is confirmed by the letters written by his physician, Dr Otto Eiser, from Frankfurt am Main to Hans von Wolzogen on 17 October 1877 and to Wagner on 26–7 October 1877.[1] Nietzsche spent a week in Frankfurt in the autumn of that year, to allow Eiser the opportunity to give him a thorough examination, in collaboration with an ophthalmologist. In anamnesis he said that he had been suffering from headaches with paroxysmal intensification for four years. The medical report gave particular emphasis to a 'chronic inflammation of the choroid and the retina (chorio–retinitis centralis)', with morbid alteration of the fundus of the eye, in the right eye reaching as far as the macula lutea; in the absence of any other evidence this optic disorder was taken to be the probable cause of his headaches.

In short, there can be no doubt that Nietzsche was in great pain during the 1876 festival. 'One must really be in good health to receive artistic impressions,' Cosima once wrote to Houston Stewart Chamberlain. 'I almost believe that the whole of this wretched business with Nietzsche arose from the fact that he was tormented by raging headaches in 76.'

Elisabeth Nietzsche did her utmost to conceal this circumstance, which was such as to cast doubt on the objective validity of what Nietzsche later wrote about Bayreuth. In 1895, when she came to the episode in her biography of her brother, she published for the first time extracts from the letters he wrote her from Bayreuth and Klingenbrunn, but suppressing the complaints about his physical suffering which do much to explain his negative response to the *Ring*. Only twelve years later was she able to bring herself to publish the letters in full (ostensibly) in the edition of his collected letters. But even then, as Newman proves, she took the precaution of falsifying the date of every letter, so as to place the greatest possible hindrance in the way of discovery of what her brother really had heard and seen in the crucial days before he left for Klingenbrunn. Newman also demonstrates convincingly that she must have suppressed one letter, if not several, entirely: no doubt they contradicted too blatantly the legend that Nietzsche was in full enjoyment of his receptive and critical faculties during the festival. Newman's suspicions have since been proved absolutely correct by Erich F. Podach and Karl Schlechta.

The very fact that Elisabeth tried to conceal her brother's state of health is the best proof that his condition must have had a decisive influence on his judgement.

There remains the question whether, even had he been in good health, Nietzsche was competent to form a judgement on the music of the *Ring* that would have been in any sense a valuable one. His pronouncements on Beethoven, his adulation of Peter Gast, his high estimation of his own compositions, his later falling away from music to *musiquette*, all make it seem doubtful, to say the least. Newman, at any rate, believed he was swept off his feet for a while by *Tristan*, but 'his natal bias . . . was towards the simple in music'. On the other hand it is probably only fair to the musician in Nietzsche to take his sister's claim that he had expected Wagner to say to him in Bayreuth in 1876: 'Oh, my friend . . . my music will have to change completely, I will return to simplicity and melody!' as yet another of her simplistic fabrications.[2]

There will have been another factor, something human, all too human, of which Nietzsche himself was perhaps quite unconscious. Schuré paints a vivid portrait of Wagner during the rehearsals, commanding the immense assemblage of soloists, chorus, orchestra and stage machinery, and enjoying the well-deserved triumph of bringing the world of his own creation to life. He had to inspire all these beings of flesh and blood with his own spirit. A consummate spellbinder, he pursued his object with a blend of ferocity and friendliness, rage and tenderness, never losing sight of his goal for a moment. In the few hours of relaxation from his superhuman labours he let off steam in a display of high spirits. 'Presented with the spectacle of this artistic miracle that he was performing before our very eyes, every one of us felt . . . Mime's astonishment as he watches Siegfried forging his sword.'

Schuré goes on to speculate whether Nietzsche's self-esteem suffered from a sense of inferiority, and that is undoubtedly a profound psychological insight. It is known that in moods of depression Nietzsche complained of lacking the artist's ability to point to deeds accomplished. And now he sensed the existence of a 'genius that lies in actions', to use Goethe's phrase, that was denied himself.

But even if Nietzsche's later pronouncements on Wagner's music carry little weight today, there is still his charge that Wagner betrayed his ideals and profaned the vision they had shared – in Ernst Bertram's words – 'by its grotesque realization'. 'Utopia had arrived,' Thomas Mann writes, 'and Nietzsche fled.'

He told the story of his flight later in *Ecce Homo*: 'Enough, in the middle of it, on the spur of the moment, I left for a few weeks, in spite of a charming Parisienne's attempts to console me; I made my excuses to Wagner simply by means of a fatalistic telegram. In Klingenbrunn, a little town buried deep in the Bohemian Forest, I carried my melancholia and my contempt for the Germans about with me like an illness – and from time to time I noted down a maxim in my pocketbook, nothing but hard psychological dicta, under the general title *The Ploughshare.*'

But his memory for facts was always poor. He did not leave 'in the middle of it' – 'it', in the context, meaning the festival – but during the rehearsals; it was not 'for a few weeks' but for ten days; he did not make the acquaintance of the 'charming Parisienne' – Madame Louise Ott – until after his return from Klingenbrunn; he makes no reference to the state of his health or to his return to Bayreuth. Both would have contradicted the fiction of his shaking the Wagnerian dust from his feet.

Podach has published an alternative passage from the manuscript of *Ecce Homo* which Nietzsche had pasted over: instead of the story of the 'charming Parisienne' there is one about the old emperor applauding and shouting the while to his adjutant, 'dreadful! dreadful!'[3]

But the heart of the matter is this: has anyone the right to reproach an artist, in his sixty-fourth year, at last realizing the work he has struggled for a generation to create – to reproach him for not having been able to wait? Apart from every other consideration, an idea achieves life and temporal existence only when it risks taking the step from concept to action. For Wagner the meaning of Bayreuth was the giving of an 'active example', and his friends understood as much: as Schemann says, they saw the true significance of the 1876 festival not in the material accomplishment of the performance, but in the symbolic act of performing it at all.

'And Nietzsche fled' – not simply into the Bohemian Forest, but (as we gather from the letter to Mathilde Maier of 15 July 1878 which contains the first version of the legend) to his cherished Greeks. But how, Newman permits himself to ask,

> would this same Nietzsche have behaved if, instead of envisaging his beloved and admired Greeks in the pathos of distance bestowed on them by more than twenty intervening centuries, he had been in Athens some year in the month of Elaphebolion, a studious young Greek from Corinth who had been privileged to visit Euripides [on Salamis] occasionally and discuss the problems of tragedy, myth, ritual and religion with the great artist, and who now, for the first time, was to attend one of the famous festivals?
>
> What would he have found? Assuredly not the ideal spectator dreamt of in *Richard Wagner in Bayreuth*. He would have found the streets of Athens and the Attic equivalent of Angermann's filled with an excited, noisy, garrulous crowd, not all the members of which, perhaps, were strictly sober. In the theatre he would have found, of course, Sophocles and Agathon and Socrates . . . but also the wild Alcibiades, and the crafty demagogic Cleon . . . the Sausage-seller and the Lamp-seller . . .
>
> And if in the evening our suppositious young Corinthian had called on Euripides and found his idol behaving diplomatically to a miscellaneous crowd of admirers and flatterers, would he not, especially if he had been suffering agonies from headache and eyestrain all through the festival, have . . . fled to Delphi or somewhere, and there filled his tablets with bitter

reflections on the poet and his devotees and the Hellenes
in general? And yet, and yet! these strangely composite
audiences . . . bent the knee to an art which they knew
to be higher than themselves . . . and placed Aeschylus
and Sophocles and Euripides on the pedestals from
which all the fluctuations in European taste since then
have failed to dislodge them. (NLRW, IV, pp. 527f.)

# 30

## The Nation's Thanks

'Everybody else left soon after you', Cosima wrote to Judith Gautier, 'and a sudden solitude followed the hubbub you witnessed . . . Everything vanished as if by magic, only the silhouette of our theatre in the distance reminded us of what had been, and we seemed to have awoken from a dream. My husband was too exhausted to do any work, and he was even less capable of dealing with the rather complicated business matters arising from the festival; so I had to promise him to put the house in order within a week, and on 14 September we set off on our travels with bag and baggage, that is, four children and their governess and all their paraphernalia.' (Early October 1876)

Wagner hoped to spend a full three months in Italy, 'resting on the laurels of his American march'. Verona reminded him of the melody for *Romeo and Juliet* he had once written down in a dark hour. In Venice he revisited the Palazzo Giustiniani where he had written the second act of *Tristan* eighteen years before. But the 'silhouette of the theatre' pursued him everywhere, looming larger and larger and darkening the Italian skies; a letter from Feustel caught up with them on the road with the news that it was feared that the deficit would be 120,000 marks, an estimate that climbed to 150,000 marks in the next few weeks.

On 29 September they reached Naples and on 5 October they crossed the bay to Sorrento, where they took rooms in a little annexe of the Hotel Vittoria. 'I expect you know that Sorrento is the native city of Tasso,' Cosima wrote to Daniela, who had stayed behind at the Luisenstift; 'this is where he returned to his sister Cornelia, dressed as a pilgrim, after much suffering,' and she reminded her daughter of the anticipation of that return in Goethe's

506

play about the poet, which is suffused with the resignation of a woman's noble heart like a gentler, purer air.

It was her own mood, too, lulled by the beautiful monodic singing of the peasants at the olive harvest, a moonlit evening on the terrace, an excursion to Capri, riding to Tiberius's villa on donkeys, and returning by the light of the stars and the phosphorescent sea. They were both reading Sismondi's *Histoire des républiques italiennes du moyen âge*: just as Wagner had studied Arabian history in the previous winter, now he was instructing her in Italian history, she told a friend. She begged him to forget the whole 'woe of the Nibelungs'[1] and start a new work. But in the midst of all that sunlight and beauty the only thing that came into his mind was a symphony in memory of the fallen. It would have his *Romeo and Juliet* theme as the basis; he imagined biers being carried into a hall, more and more of them, until the sorrow of the individual was subsumed in the general grief.

It was impossible for him to forget the 'woe of the Nibelungs'. He wrote to Feustel on 7 October, outlining ideas for dealing with it: a general appeal to the Patrons; a specific request to some of the foremost Patrons to organize subscription lists with themselves at the head; a petition to the German Emperor to propose to the Reichstag that the government should take over responsibility for the festival.

A rhapsodic letter from King Ludwig, imploring him to banish his lethal worries and preserve himself for many years to come, 'to the glory and loftiest pride of the German nation', encouraged him to write of his scheme to him too. ' "Arise now," I exhort myself, "Arise, despairing soul! Speak now to *Him*!"' He put very little faith in the patrons, in fact. What had to be done was to bring the matter before the nation as a whole: a proposal could either be moved in the Reichstag by a deputy, or be introduced through the Imperial Chancellery. A third possibility would be for King Ludwig himself to place the matter before the Federal Council, from where it would then go to the Reichstag.

The proposal might be worded something like this: that the Imperial Government should take possession of the Festspielhaus as a national property, against defrayment of the outstanding debts; it should then be assigned to the municipality of Bayreuth with the obligation to promote festivals annually in accordance with the founder's intentions.

It would, of course, be preferable, more seemly and more rational, if Bavaria and her king could execute this plan alone! But there . . .

' "Ah! Fantasia!" that is what the donkeyman kept calling to my wife's mount in encouragement, when we were out for a ride recently. "Fantasia" really was the good beast's name, but she had not the least interest in getting anywhere, so the "Ahs" became more and more exasperated until the donkeyman tried a new ploy: "Corragio, Fantasia! Allegro! Buoni maccheroni, tutto formaggio!" Astonished, we asked him if he would really give his donkey cheese and macaroni; whereupon he answered, oh no, she would be perfectly content with hay; but he liked enticing her with the idea of macaroni. So "Ah, Fantasia!" is what I now say to encourage my weary soul, and perhaps my plan and the motion I drafted have been nothing more than the "buoni maccheroni tutto formaggio" with which that donkeyman spurred on the imagination of his weary animal.' (21 October)

His doubts were confirmed only too soon. He had drawn up and sent off his circular, he told Heckel on 3 November, he had made approaches in Berlin and to the King of Bavaria – and had had no answer. 'So the only thing I can expect now is a truly humiliating issue that will leave me no choice but to demolish everything, quite literally. Without a word or sound I shall assign everything to the creditors, just like a bankrupt . . . In these circumstances my health is not of the best: my inner concern and my anxiety at the uncertainty are too great.'

During October Malwida had arrived in Sorrento, to prepare quarters for the ailing Nietzsche in the Villa Rubinacci, only a few steps from their own lodgings. With characteristic unselfishness, she had undertaken to look after him, together with his friends Brenner and Dr Rée. 'I really do not know how to thank you for what you said and what you offered in your letter,' Nietzsche confessed to her. Later, he found a way, in Aphorism 419 of *Human, all too Human*, where he wrote about the 'dead places' in the head of an old woman who was capable of enthusing in turn over the champions of completely opposing causes.

From a letter Cosima wrote to Daniela on 29 October we learn that the 'quartet', as Malwida described herself and her three charges, had paid their first visit the evening before. Wagner noticed, according to Glasenapp, that Nietzsche, who had already been silent and introspective in Bayreuth, appeared drained and almost entirely wrapped up in his own health. As a consequence, in spite of their proximity, only two or three evenings were spent in each other's company.

On the last of these, according to Elisabeth Nietzsche, the following memorable scene took place. Wagner and Nietzsche went for a marvellous walk along the deserted coast. It was a beautiful autumn evening, mild but with a certain melancholy in the air, hinting at the approach of winter, 'a mood of farewell', as Wagner said. Suddenly he began to talk about *Parsifal* in detail for the first time, in terms not of a projected work of art, but of a religious, Christian experience. While Wagner talked on and on the last ray of sunlight disappeared across the water. 'Have you nothing at all to say, dear friend?' Wagner asked. Her brother explained away his silence with some excuse, but his heart had been full to bursting with his distress at this charade of Wagner's. (EFWN, pp. 262ff.)

This moving story, which Elisabeth paints with such affectionate detail, ought to have been regarded with suspicion from the first. Yet Newman was the first to call it 'highly coloured'. There can be no doubt that the false sentimentality sounds more like Elisabeth Nietzsche than Richard Wagner. It seems very unlikely, too, that the latter would suddenly have made an intimate religious confession to the young friend whose behaviour had been so reserved for so long. In any case the tale can be checked against facts: as we know, Cosima had read Nietzsche the detailed prose scenario of *Parsifal* at Christmas 1869. Schuré, too, tells of their conversation about Wagner's next work when they were travelling together from Bayreuth to Basel after the festival: Nietzsche said that Wagner had told him he was going to read world history before writing the verse text of *Parsifal*. So even if the subject did arise again in conversation in Sorrento it cannot have caused Nietzsche any surprise, and certainly not the disillusion claimed by his sister: that is clearly demonstrated by a letter, first published in 1964, which Nietzsche wrote to Cosima on 10 October 1877, a year after their meeting in Sorrento, where he says: 'The glories *Parcival* promises us can comfort us in all the matters where we need comfort.'[2]

In Elisabeth's glowing painting, it is not only the human figures but the scenery, too, that is imaginary. Instead of the beautiful autumn sunset, with its mood of farewell, which is supposed to have stimulated the fictitious conversation, a cold north wind had been blowing since the beginning of November, the skies were grey, and a blue-black sea hurled foaming waves against the cliffs, so that the Wagners decided on 6 November to leave the very next day.

Should there be any lingering hesitation to accuse Elisabeth Nietzsche of flagrant invention, it will be dispelled in due course when we come to a no less famous scene some six years later which can, by chance, be proved to be an outright lie.[3]

But after the disappointment with Wagner as artist and as champion of an ideal that her brother was supposed to have experienced in Bayreuth, she needed to find a trait that would disappoint him in Wagner the man as well. Since her fictions were only advanced in support of the legend Nietzsche himself propagated in *Ecce Homo*, she can perhaps be excused somewhat, if one is so inclined.

Wagner's troubles continued to follow him through Italy. The honours he was shown there made him all the more painfully aware of his situation in Germany, whence he received no news except the concern of his friends and the denigration of the press.

In Rome, where they spent four weeks, the German ambassador, Herr von Keudell, gave a soirée in his honour in the Palazzo Caffarelli. A deputation from the Regia Accademia di Santa Cecilia informed him of his election as 'socio illustre'. The German artists' colony invited him to a festive gathering in the Palazzo Poli, where he made a stirring reply to a speech of welcome.

At Keudell's reception he met a young Italian composer, Giovanni Sgambati, who was there to take part in one of his piano quintets. Wagner advised him to approach Schott's about publication, and himself wrote to Dr Strecker: he had had Sgambati's two quintets played to him several times, and wanted to recommend them very seriously. For once he had had the pleasure of becoming acquainted with a truly great and original talent, which he would be very happy to present to the wider musical world. 'I advise him to tour Germany, starting with Vienna, as soon as possible, performing his works, which I would expect to have an outstanding success after the tedium of recent *German* chamber music (even Brahms etc.) . . . Please waste no time . . . If he does not suit you, I shall go elsewhere; but I would appreciate a speedy reply, as I am only here for a week.' (23 November) Schott's published not only the two quintets but all Sgambati's later compositions, including a symphony and his fine requiem.

Wagner was able to pass on Schott's affirmative reply to Sgambati before he left Rome, at a reception for Italian artists. Pietro Cossa, whose play *Nerone* Wagner had seen in Venice, was also present and Wagner suggested to them both that they should write an opera on the subject of one of those Italian adventurers he had read about in Sismondi, who might have been an Alexander or a Hannibal on different terrain.

The sights and art treasures of Rome were not neglected. Of the façade of St Peter's Wagner commented that it ought to have been the palace of a Caesar, but in the Sistine Chapel he said: 'This is like being in my theatre, you recognize at once that it was built for a serious purpose.' The tragic lot of genius seemed to him to be epitomized in the life and work of Michelangelo, which he felt were comparable to his own.

He wrote to Feustel that he had to call a halt once and for all and show the world what was involved in entering the financial maze. To stay in it, to be at the mercy of every accident, to be exposed to ever new anxieties – these were things he refused to submit to any longer, since he had never had a financial end in view. If the deficit could not be met in reasonable time, then he would have no alternative but to declare the festival undertaking bankrupt. What belonged to the King of Bavaria would have to revert to him; all other assets would have to go to the highest bidders and the outstanding debts paid with the proceeds. In the suspense of the last few months he had had plenty of time to think about his relationship to the age. 'I have shown what I can do and now feel justified . . . in closing my public career.' (23 November)

This letter brought anxious enquiries from Feustel, to which he replied in clarification that his sole purpose in opting for bankruptcy would be to pay off the debts by selling the material assets. 'The idea of swindling the carpenters and upholsterers of Bayreuth has never entered my head, and if I used the word "bankruptcy" it was intended as a forthright designation of my own position, and I will not hesitate voluntarily to declare myself and my artistic undertaking bankrupt.' He also wanted there to be no doubt that he would, as a matter of course, designate his property in Bayreuth and his income to settling the debts. (29 November)

Having arrived in Florence on 3 December, he went on the very next day to Bologna, which greeted its honorary citizen with a performance of *Rienzi*, at the end of which he was positively buried in flowers, and a banquet, at which he gave thanks for his welcome with a speech on the text of the city's two mottoes: 'Bononia docet' and 'Libertas'.

Back in Florence, he and Cosima made the most of the city's art treasures, and Glasenapp later heard him speak 'with true enthusiasm' of their repeated visits to the Uffizi and the Palazzo Pitti. There were also some inspiriting meetings with the former Jessie Laussot, who now lived in Florence.

His worries continued to hound him in sleepless nights, and he grew bitter and unjust towards those who were loyally looking after his affairs in Germany. He reproached them with being concerned with financial matters to the exclusion of any concern for himself and his well-being. 'I am very sorry to see that even you can find it in your heart to pay me and the position I am in no further attention, and to talk about the business in exactly the same terms as all my other friends,' he wrote to Heckel. If the deficit was not met he was thinking of handing the theatre over to some other agency, perhaps even the court theatre in Munich, and then he would concern himself with it no longer. 'I have reached the end of my strength, my dear friend. Up to this point my undertaking has been a question put to the people of Germany: "Do you want this?" Now I assume that they do not, and so I have come to the end of the road.' (9 December)

Two days later he approached Düfflipp officially with a new suggestion.

Since coping further with the financial side of his undertaking was undermining his health and destroying all further desire to create, he suggested as the most natural and honourable solution that the Hoftheater should take over the enterprise. His works could then be performed in the 'Royal' Festival Theatre in Bayreuth, with the personnel of the Munich court opera. 'For me this solution would also be a release from the pains and torments which make my life a misery, and the continuance of which could easily drive me to surrender all my property and my income in order to pay what must be paid, and to turn my back on Germany.' (11 December)

Arriving in Munich on 18 December, he learned that Düfflipp proposed to visit Bayreuth between Christmas and the New Year, in order to discuss matters with the festival management committee.

For the meantime things remained in the balance. For her birthday Cosima received comforting words from an unexpected quarter: 'Everything on which your life now depends had to happen as it did,' Nietzsche wrote to her from Sorrento, 'and specifically it is impossible to imagine the whole post-Bayreuth present taking any other form than it does, because it corresponds exactly to the whole pre-Bayreuth past: what was wretched and cheerless before is still the same, and what was great remains so, indeed has only now truly become so.' This is another of the three letters first published in 1964, in which he also admits his alienation from Schopenhauer's philosophy, of which, though it must have happened gradually, he had suddenly become aware. (19 December)

Wagner and Cosima, too, took refuge with the Greeks. They read Thucydides' *History of the Peloponnesian War*, and saw a parallel between the fall of the city of Pericles and the defeat of their own work in Bayreuth. Yet at the same time Wagner's mind, which never ceased to dwell on the subject, was at work on a new plan to save it. He wrote to Standhartner that he was rousing himself from the depths of his discouragement to make another experiment. He would shortly be issuing an appeal to the Wagner Societies to form a permanent Society of Patrons, the purpose of which would be to support and maintain the future festivals, to which only the members would be admitted, not the ordinary 'public and the journalistic rabble'. (2 January 1877)

In the appeal, dated 1 January 1877, he said that if there were Germans of discernment to join the ranks of French, English and Americans who had already demonstrated their recognition of the merit of his work, then he would leave it to a Society of Patrons, formed on the lines he envisaged, to lobby the Reichstag for support. To be of any effective use the Reichstag would have to make an annual grant of at least 100,000 marks, and in recognition of this state support free tickets would have to be awarded to deserving applicants. If this plan was put into effect it would be the first time that a theatrical institution received the seal of national importance. (RWGS, X, pp. 11ff.)

Düfflipp arrived at last on 21 January. The next day Wagner made his proposals known to him and the management committee: If the deficit was met by the king or the Reich, then he would be

available to resume the festival on this surer basis; alternatively, let
the king take over the theatre, and let it be run by the Hofoper, until
all the money he had received had been recovered; or, finally, let an
impresario like Pollini take on the festivals, with the same end in
view of repaying the king. (GLRW, V, pp. 331f.)

Düfflipp made himself very pleasant, recalled his visit to Tribschen ten years previously and expressed his thanks for their hospitality as he left, but said neither yes nor no to the proposals.

Wagner wrote to the king that he would have written long before
this, and had only postponed doing so because of Düfflipp's
impending visit and his expectation that the king's wishes would be
made known then. 'Now that I have discovered he was not to
convey any such wishes to me, I shall resort to the course of action I
had previously decided on, undeterred by this incident.' He had
intended to use the leisure hours of his Italian holiday to write the
text of *Parsifal*; but the worries that pursued him there had made his
every step a painful one. 'I admit it was an act of great folly to have
written my great work "in faith in the German spirit", and I must
even fear that I did not serve "the glory of my noble benefactor".'
(23 January)

Shortly afterwards he heard from the Court Secretary's office
that the king rejected the suggestion that the Munich opera should
take over the running of the Bayreuth festivals.

But as Cosima was speaking of the sufferings of genius, Wagner
interrupted her with a smile: 'I'm not going to tell you something.'
– 'Oh, tell me, tell me!' – 'I'm going to start *Parzival*, and I shan't
stop until it is finished.' (DMCW, I, p. 789) Writing a new prose
scenario took him until 23 February, and the verse text until 19
April, and all the time his struggle with the overwhelming deficit
grew greater. He actually had three concurrent and complementary
plans: his 'experimental' proposal for a Society of Patrons, a series
of concerts in London, and negotiations with Dr Förster, the director of the Stadttheater in Leipzig.

Förster had made the first approach in August 1876, with the
request for permission to stage the *Ring* in its composer's birthplace. At the time Wagner was evasive: 'My work is not yet
finished: the actual performances of it have shown me many things
that remain unfinished. Give me time to present my work once
more in a carefully corrected form next year, here in Bayreuth.' (6
September 1876)

Now Wagner himself turned to Leipzig, primarily in the hope of finding his Siegfried, Georg Unger, a suitable place in a theatre where he would not have to 'go back on the haphazard treadmill of the routine repertory'. In return for this favour he would enter negotiations about the *Ring*, if, as he hoped, Leipzig was still interested. (To Kapellmeister Sucher, 31 January 1877)

The offer was taken up with alacrity, but immediately struck an unexpected difficulty when Düfflipp reminded Wagner that according to the 1864 contract the *Ring* belonged to the King of Bavaria and Wagner had no right to sell it to Leipzig or Vienna. Jauner in Vienna had also announced his interest in producing the *Ring* there, and was putting the thumbscrews on Wagner over the matter of Richter's leave of absence for the London concerts.

In response, Wagner argued, as he had done before, that that contract, which he would in any case like to see revised or cancelled, had only been a form in which a gift from the king had been dressed. It would be sad, he wrote, if – someone – wanted to abuse it! Ever since he had been in receipt of a regular allowance and gifts from the king's bounty, he had voluntarily waived all fees and royalties from performances of his works in the Munich court theatre: he had never asked for anything in return for the fact that *Rienzi, Tristan, Meistersinger, Rheingold* and *Walküre* had been 'of profit solely to the box office of the Royal Hoftheater'. (To Düfflipp, 17 April)

Düfflipp replied that it was not primarily a matter of the 1864 contract but of the one of February 1874, in consequence of which the Cabinet Treasury had advanced the sum of 216,152 marks and 42 pfennigs. If the *Ring* were to be given to Munich, Leipzig and Vienna, it would diminish any hope of recovering anything on that advance, since Bayreuth would then lose its particular pull. 'For years I have made no secret of the fact that His Majesty's building plans make such demands on the resources of the Cabinet Treasury as to exclude expenditure of monies for other purposes.' (20 April)

But these objections were overcome, and coordinated terms were agreed for production in the three 'preferred' theatres: Munich in south Germany, Leipzig in the north, and Vienna in Austria. The contract with Förster seemed to be in the bag at last. In the course of the negotiations Wagner came up with an idea that has a quite modern ring to it, to the effect that the three theatres ought to be able 'in time to mount the festivals [in Bayreuth] by combining their artistic forces as appropriate, and similarly to manage the technical administration of the same'. (To Düfflipp, 28 April)

'I reaffirm my acceptance of your proposals of last year,' Wagner telegraphed Förster on 24 April, and received by return the reply: 'Regard your telegram . . . as binding agreement.'

The 'proposals' as Wagner had understood them constituted an honorarium of 10,000 marks for the preferential rights to the *Ring*, and a 10 per cent royalty for each performance. He now discovered in the small print of the contract that by 'honorarium' Förster meant an advance to be repaid within a very short term. In spite of attempts to find a compromise the negotiations foundered on this point. Angelo Neumann, whom we have already encountered as a young singer in Vienna, was now Förster's assistant; he revealed that Förster, under the influence of the anti-Wagner faction in Leipzig, was not unwilling to withdraw from the contract. At a dinner in Förster's house in honour of a prima donna, one of these influential people got carried away and proposed a toast to the happy cancellation of the *Ring* contract; when it was Neumann's turn to clink glasses with this enthusiast he instead threw his glass on the floor and smashed it.

Eventually it was Neumann who revived the project that had failed in Leipzig, in an epoch-making new form.

The last two letters to Förster were written from London, where Wagner had gone at the end of April to give a series of concerts. In January he had been approached by the leader of the Bayreuth orchestra, August Wilhelmj, acting on behalf of the concert agents Hodge & Essex, to give twenty concerts in the 10,000-seat Royal Albert Hall, each of which ought to make £500. In spite of this tempting prospect Wagner hesitated: his London experience of twenty-two years before was still a bad memory, and Bülow, who had lost £1500 there, also warned him against it through his American manager Ullmann. But Wagner gave in to the urgings of his Bayreuth friends, in order to show that it was not lethargy or the thought of his own convenience that held him back. Once the matter was agreed he took it up with his usual energy and first of all made sure of the services of some of his Bayreuth artists, who needed some coaxing, apart from the guarantee of high fees: 'You will sing at twenty concerts, nice cosy English affairs, one or two "pièces", and will get 500 marks an evening.'

Finding Hodge & Essex's proposals obscure, he was delighted

when Alfred Jachmann, the husband of his niece Johanna, offered to go to England to represent him legally. 'Well now, dearest Alfred (a highly auspicious name for England!), let me wish you the best of luck! . . . Act for Bayreuth and Wahnfried in the land of Alfred the Great exactly as your heart inspires you to.' (22 February)

It immediately transpired that the ambitious young agents had overreached themselves, and the number of the concerts had to be cut from twenty to six. The contract was signed on 15 March, and Cosima and Wagner arrived in London on 1 May. She was enthralled – 'If I had to choose a great city it would be London' – while he got the impression, on a steamer trip on the Thames, that Alberich's dream had come true: Nibelheim, world dominion, work, business and everywhere oppressive smoke and fog!

But he could not fail to be struck by the contrast with his 1855 visit. They were welcomed like royalty, and although Wagner did his best to live quietly he was, in Newman's words, 'dined and wined and toasted in public and private', and was received at Windsor on 17 May by Queen Victoria and her youngest son Prince Leopold. He did not forget to look up his old friends Sainton and Lüders. Only Judith, whom he had hoped to see again, did not come. 'Chère âme! douce amie! Et tu n'es pas venue me voir? Agreed, you would have had little joy at the sight of me, drained of my strength by incessant strains and bitterness.'[4]

The concerts, employing an orchestra of 169, led by Wilhelmj and conducted by Wagner and Richter, proved an immense artistic and social success, and two extra ones had to be given at the end of the series. But unfortunately Hodge & Essex had overlooked a factor that had also escaped Jachmann: the fact that *two thousand* of the most expensive seats in the Albert Hall were privately owned and the owners either sat in them themselves for nothing or leased them for their own profit, meaning a loss to the agency of £12,000 over the six concerts. After only three it looked as though the takings would not even cover the expenses. He had been right to have doubts, Wagner wrote to Feustel on 13 May. They must at once find another way of meeting the Bayreuth deficit. He asked the management committee to open a subscription list and to put his own name at the head of it for the sum of 3000 marks.

'Should this expedient fail too, I have decided to make a deal with Ullmann for America, which would also mean putting my house in Bayreuth on the market, crossing the ocean with all my family and never coming back to Germany again.' Cosima's diary shows that he spoke in all seriousness; following a reference to the offer he had had from Ullmann, she wrote: 'In that case no return to Germany!'

To redeem the losses in London, Wagner paid the singers' fees, a total of £1200, out of his own pocket. As for the £700 Hodge & Essex were then able to pay him, he sent it at once to Feustel, asking him to put him down for a subscription of 10,000 marks instead of 3000, and to hold the remainder for him for the time being.

The London Wagner festival had a happier epilogue. His friends in London, knowing that he had not only received no fee but had also dug into his own pocket to the tune of £1200, organized a subscription which raised £561. But when Edward Dannreuther, who had been his host in London, called on him in Bayreuth in the middle of August to present him with this sum on their behalf, Wagner, who would gladly have accepted it as a contribution to the festival funds, had to refuse it as a personal gift, courteously but firmly.

Wagner and Cosima left London on 4 June for Bad Ems, where he was going to drink the waters. His two Mathildes came to see him there – 'good, true' Mathilde Maier and Frau Wesendonk, who had acclaimed Brahms in the meantime but returned to the Wagnerian fold after Bayreuth. Kaiser Wilhelm was in Ems at the same time, and when Siegfried gave him a bunch of cornflowers on the promenade he chatted amiably to the boy. But when Feustel urged Wagner to enjoy some dolce far niente, he could only heave a sigh. 'Yes! Yes! Do nothing! No: *accomplish* nothing! That's my holiday. Well, God's will be done!' To satisfy the most pressing of the Bayreuth creditors he authorized the payment of a considerable sum from his and his wife's private means, which, with the fees paid to the singers in London, amounted to 50,000 marks. 'Let's hope that these inroads on my family's existence will at least purchase us the time and leisure to find out how my affairs really stand.' (14 June)

He had noticed that when they had been rejoined by the children all of them, and especially little Siegfried, had greeted him with looks of such 'tender commiseration' as to make him realize that some really bad blow had been struck him while he was away. It turned out that the *Bayreuther Tagblatt* had published the false reports, circulating elsewhere, that the London concerts had been not only financially but also artistically a flop. Just as after the festival, another flood of hatred and scorn washed over Wagner and his work. One has to read at least a selection of the gems published by contemporary critics to gain a notion of the infamy to which journalism can sink.[5]

Now his enemies in Vienna deemed the time ripe to launch a well-prepared attack from the rear. On 16 and 17 June 1877 the *Neue Freie Presse* published 'Richard Wagner's Letters to a Milliner' (Bertha Goldwag) with an ironic commentary by Daniel Spitzer, a colleague of Hanslick. These letters, concerned with the ordering of silk curtains, bedspreads and dressing gowns, would raise, it was hoped, what Newman calls 'a Philistine horse-laugh' at Wagner's expense. This was the experience that made Wagner assure Jauner that he would never darken Vienna's doors again: 'Never! Never!'[6]

When the king heard from Düfflipp that Wagner was thinking of emigrating to America, he wrote imploring him, by the love and friendship that had bound them for so many years, not to entertain the 'horrifying' idea for one moment: it would be an ineradicable disgrace for all Germans, if they allowed their greatest genius to depart from their midst! (Mid-June)

Still completely beset by the 'chaos of demeaning impressions received daily, even hourly', Wagner sent the king a fair copy in Cosima's hand of the text of *Parsifal*, which he had written as a way of escaping disgust and dread. 'There it is! May it give you some pleasure and perhaps strengthen you in your view that preserving me for my art a few years longer was not completely without value.' (22 June)

Now that the Leipzig plan had fallen through, the only course he could envisage was the earlier one of consigning the Bayreuth festival to the Munich theatre. 'As it will be my last effort, I will gladly talk to anybody I am referred to . . . But my fate, grave and heavy, lies in your royal hand!' At the same time he told Düfflipp he would be coming to Munich in the third week in July to discuss matters.

He got there on 20 July, and Düfflipp called on him in his hotel the next morning. He later reported to the king that Wagner had at once got down to business and asked if the king had made any decision about his request. 'When I was obliged to answer that I knew nothing of any such decision on Your Majesty's part, Wagner looked very surprised and shocked, leant back in his chair, drew his hand over his forehead and said in a tone of the deepest emotion:

"Ah! Now I know where I am. So I have nothing more to hope! – And yet the king's last letters were so cordial and showed such good will that I thought the old days were coming back again." '

Since Düfflipp had been commissioned by the king to persuade Wagner to stay in Bayreuth at all costs, he suggested discussing the new plan with the intendant as well. The fact that Wagner agreed, after a little hesitation, to see Perfall, shows how much in earnest he was when he said that he would talk to anybody at all.

Perfall duly worked out a plan, and Wagner agreed to it. But in the end the king rejected it and commanded the production of the complete *Ring* in Munich.

It seemed that what Wagner had predicted in June was already coming to pass, that it would be Bayreuth that would suffer, rather than the *Ring*. 'My work will be performed everywhere and draw huge audiences – but no one will come to Bayreuth again . . . The only charge I can lay against the town is that *I* chose it. But I did it for the sake of a great idea: I wanted to set up a completely independent, new creation, with the aid of the nation, in a town that would owe its importance solely to that creation – a kind of Washington of art. I had too good an opinion of the upper ranks of our society.' (To Feustel, 14 June)

'A great idea': but the king's decision seemed to drive the last nail into its coffin. As to others, so it seemed to Wagner, who had consented to the decision, compelled by circumstances against his will – and yet not solely against his will. When he entered the Festspielhaus for the first time after his return from England the solemn lofty interior struck him once again with the sense of dedication. But the costumes and production photographs filled him with aversion to the idea of ever repeating the festival. Perhaps Rome or Florence had helped to strengthen his dissatisfaction with the visual realization of his drama. He had spoken so emphatically in London of the impression Michelangelo's frescoes had made on him that some of his friends there now sent him a portfolio of reproductions of them.

The idea seemed dead and buried, but it was to rise again, transfigured. He had gradually come to realize the one thing he still had to do, he wrote to Düfflipp. He was now in his sixty-fifth year and had to husband his strength. 'But in extemporized productions like last year's, I squander my strength . . . I have therefore turned my attention to an idea I have long cherished . . . carrying it out will

set the seal on my effectiveness and influence. What I have in mind is
not a school strictly speaking, but systematic exercises in performance technique under my direction.' (19 September)

Delegates from the Wagner Societies gathered in Bayreuth on 15
September. They met in the Festspielhaus, sitting on the stage in a
wide semicircle round Wagner as he gave them a frank report on the
festival's affairs.

In 1876 he had believed that it would occur to some of the patrons
to ask among themselves: 'Honestly, what are we to do about
Wagner?' They would have agreed: 'Don't trouble with him any
longer, he is physically done up.' And then they might have asked:
'What about paying the bills?' Whereupon it would have transpired
that they could not regard their subscriptions as the end of their
contributions, but would take responsibility for the whole affair. 'It
didn't happen. Everyone went heedlessly home again. It was all just
an entertainment, something out of the ordinary, without any
further consequence or significance. I had been shown the greatest
honours, afforded the happiness of seeing the best singers and
musicians in Germany assemble in a theatre built specially for me to
perform one of my works. Emperors and princes had graced the
festival with their presence. "What more does the man want?" I was
forced to accept that that was the general reaction.'

He went on to tell them about his efforts to cover the deficit. The
circular of the previous November had not produced a single
subscription – only 'the aunt of Herr Plüddemann from Kolberg'
had sent 100 marks. 'Have no fear, gentlemen, that I am losing my
thread among unimportant details: you must be acquainted with all
this, in order to understand my mood.'

After that disappointment he had decided he was too weak to
bear the burden of the theatre. He had turned to the king; he had
been given reason to have hopes of the Reichstag. All in vain!

> We must admit, gentlemen, that we are back at the
> beginning again, though it is true to say that our
> handicap has been greatly reduced, as they say on the
> sports field . . . We have the impression made by last
> year's festival, and we have this theatre. Otherwise,
> though, we are starting again from the beginning . . .
>    You know the goal of all my efforts, of our entire
> undertaking here in Bayreuth: a style and an art of a

kind that cannot be cultivated in our wretched present-day theatres. My intention now would be to build up slowly the means whereby I can make the festivals here truly enduring, self-renewing, a true creation. If you like we can call it a 'school', though our music schools, where the students learn nothing at all, have given me a strong aversion to the expression! It is also appropriate to the modest means that are now at our disposal. We shall achieve much with little in this way. But it will take resolution, and the support of all the friends of our cause. So I ask you now, gentlemen, if you are willing to stand shoulder to shoulder with me in this, if you are willing to devote patience and tenacity to an undertaking that is directed towards a great artistic goal, or whether you would prefer simply to come here again on some future occasion to see something out of the ordinary. If the latter is the case, then this had better be the parting of our ways.

I have had the idea of founding a school here for training singers, instrumentalists and conductors in the correct performance of musico-dramatic works of a truly German style, and I will take the liberty of explaining to you in a few words the form I envisage it taking.[7]

He then outlined his plan for building up the school over the next six years, from the performance of the classics of the instrumental repertory to the higher reaches of operatic style and the performance of his own works. Like his earlier schemes drafted in Riga, Dresden, Zürich and Munich, the plan as expounded here and augmented by further remarks, spoken and in letters to friends, is distinguished by its firm grasp of the ideal and the practical, and like them it came to nothing because of the indifference of his contemporaries. The school could have been started for a miserable 20,000 marks, which was not forthcoming.[8]

The only part of the plan that was realized was the founding of *Bayreuther Blätter*, originally intended as a newssheet about the school for circulation among the members of the Wagner Society who were not actively involved in running it. After the rest of the plan came to nothing it was published as the monthly magazine of the Society. His experiences were repeating themselves, Wagner wrote in his preface to the first issue on 1 January 1878: while his sole interest had always been in concrete artistic achievements, he had been obliged all his life to pick up the pen of the theorist to explain himself.

On the day after the meeting Wagner invited the delegates to Wahnfried, where he read them the text of *Parsifal*, the first time he had done so outside his immediate circle. After reading the subtitle, 'a festival drama of dedication', Schemann recalled, he paused and mimicked the foreseeable reaction of his detractors: 'What's Wagner's caper this time?' After the first act he said to Julius Hey, 'well, well, my dear Hey, how are we going to set *that* to music?' and after the second, 'there's a nice little ballet in it, too'. The sun was just setting as he came to Titurel's obsequies in the last act and his vigorous head was transfigured in the light of its last rays.

No performance of any of Wagner's works made a greater impression on him, Schemann avowed, than that reading. Never again did Amfortas's laments so pierce him through and through as they did on that occasion, when Wagner seemed to be consumed in a passionate ecstasy. He returned home afterwards a new man, in a quite different sense from 1876. 'The line "Hört ihr den Ruf? Nun danket Gott, daß ihr berufen, ihn zu hören" had become the truth for me in a quite miraculous way.'

It all made a very optimistic impression. But Wagner was still not a step closer to paying off the deficit. Cosima had a letter from Feustel on 15 January 1878, in which he summarized his calculations that the outstanding debt was still 98,028 marks and 57 pfennigs, not including a certain amount of interest. He was being pressed for the money and although he could delay legal proceedings for a time yet, he would not be able to do so indefinitely.

'I see only one remaining possibility of averting catastrophe, namely that the Hoftheater in Munich guarantee your husband a royalty for his works of 10,000 marks a year for about ten years.'

Cosima wrote a note covering this letter and sent it on to the king: she lacked the courage to go to her husband with this cry of anguish, now that he was caught up in the anguish of Amfortas. 'I beg Your Majesty most humbly to pay heed to these lines which I venture respectfully to lay before my most gracious sovereign.' (16 January)

'Most honoured lady and friend,' Ludwig replied, 'I shall know no peace until I have told you of the great joy it gave me that you turned to me personally in the matter which is the subject of your so esteemed letter. As soon as I had received it I gave instructions in accordance with your wishes to my Court Secretary, who will get in touch at once with Feustel and Perfall, so that the deficit can be met in the said manner, beyond all doubt.' (27 January)

And so on 31 March 1878 a contract was concluded between the management of the Hoftheater and the Court Secretary's office on the one hand and Richard Wagner and the Bayreuth festival management committee on the other, making provision for the deficit to be defrayed by a loan, at 5 per cent interest, repayable in regular instalments. The repayments were to be raised by the payment of a royalty of 10 per cent of the gross receipts from performances of Wagner's works in all the royal theatres.

Wagner had already written to Feustel on 3 February to thank him for the exceptional patience, wisdom and energy he had exercised in their plight. 'The outcome has been this – to me – very satisfactory turn of events, that it will be due essentially to the success of my own works that we shall be given the means to overcome the evil material consequences of 1876. It is honourable.'

He added: 'The profit from all this is that I can now apply myself to a new work with that beautiful equanimity, the disturbance or overshadowing of which drives the good spirits away from us strange "geniuses"!'

His English biographer cannot refrain from making this comment:

> This, then, was the sharply realistic ending to Wagner's dream in 1850 of 'the German spirit' voluntarily 'co-operating' with him in the achievement of his ideal! In the strictest sense of the words, it was he who paid for conferring Bayreuth on a frigid and largely hostile German world. But at any rate, thanks to the only man who really understood him – the 'mad' King of Bavaria – he could now sleep at night unracked by cares of all kinds, and devote what remained of his health to the completion of his *Parsifal*. (NLRW, IV, p. 579)

Part VII: *Parsifal* (1877–1883)

# 31

'My Farewell to the World'

I

'Oui, il est question de la musique de *Parsifal*. I could not have gone on living without throwing myself into something of the kind,' Wagner wrote to Judith Gautier on 1 October 1877. Cosima had heard the first notes coming from his music room early in August, and he had played her the 'Last Supper' theme on 11 August: he told her that he had written it down all of a sudden when he already had his hat and coat on, ready to go and fetch her. Only the day before he had said a composer should beware of expanding the text for the sake of a melody, and now he had done it after all. In the case of the Prize Song in *Die Meistersinger* he had also written the tune first and shaped the text to fit it, but this new instance was something different again: it was not the beauty of the melody that had tempted him to take this course, but the recognition of the musical fecundity of this central theme coming in the Grail Supper scene, 'the most important scene, the nucleus of the whole'. It contains the anguish of Amfortas,' he told Cosima, and it contains much else besides: specifically the motivic germs of no fewer than five of the principal themes of the work as a whole.[1] It illustrates the principle of motivic development taken to its furthest logical consequences.

He began the composition and orchestral sketches during that September. Each time he sat down to it he felt as though he was writing music for the first time in his life. He was sixty-four years old, harassed by worries and disappointment, and now he was embarking once more on the 'agonizingly difficult work' of creating a completely new world. 'Aidez-moi!' he appealed to Judith, the cry of an ageing man for the youth he has lost, for a renewal of his youth, for the 'recurrent puberty' of genius of which Goethe speaks.

Judith was then thirty-two, in the full flower of her classical beauty. The most celebrated poets and writers of the day praised her dark, deep eyes, the golden tint of her skin, her Grecian profile, comparable to the purest of the reliefs of Aegina. Baudelaire had called her 'petite fille grecque' in her girlhood, Laurent Tailhade wrote of her as 'cette femme au profil de camée, dont le masque faisait penser à la Junon de Velletri'; and in old age Victor Hugo saluted her in his sonnet, 'Ave, dea, moriturus te salutat!'

She and Wagner had been friends since the Tribschen days, but deeper feelings were not aroused until the summer of 1876, when his distress at the 'false fame' that the festival was attracting threatened to overwhelm him. He was disappointed when she did not follow his suggestion that they meet in London: 'Oh, que c'est méchant!' But now commissions for her to buy the surprises he planned for Cosima's birthday created the opportunity for a heady, half-clandestine correspondence, in which Wagner's barber, Bernhard Schnappauf of Ochsengasse in Bayreuth, may be guessed to have played the role of postman as adroitly as his classic colleagues in Seville and Baghdad.

'You behold me in a frivolous mood,' Wagner wrote on 9 November. 'Ah! I am making music, I laugh at life, I laugh at the world. Je me sens aimé, et j'aime. Enfin, je fais la musique du *Parsifal*.' The subject of fabrics and perfumes constantly recurs in the letters: 'There is nothing of the sort here, we live in a desert.' He recalls their stolen embraces: 'C'était un dernier don des dieux.' He asks her to pardon him: he is old enough to be allowed to indulge himself with childish things. And then abruptly he writes about his music, his creation. She wants to translate the text into French, and as she does not know a word of German (though she does know Chinese) Cosima is making a prose translation, which Wagner will annotate for her. He gives the name Parsifal an Arabic derivation after Görres: 'parsi' means 'pure', 'fal', 'fool' in an elevated sense, 'c'est à dire, homme sans érudition mais de génie'. She makes enquiries among noted scholars, who tell her there are no such words in Arabic. Wagner replies that he doesn't know any Arabic, and perhaps Görres didn't either, but he is not worried: he fancies there will not be an excessive number of Orientalists among his future audiences.

And 'les charmeuses de Klingsor'? Those are the flowers that the sorcerer picks in his tropical garden in the spring and which live until the autumn as young girls, 'très gracieusement et naïvement', in order to seduce the knights of the Grail. But he almost despairs of the French language when it comes to translating 'ein furchtbar schönes Weib'. 'Terrible' sounds funny; 'fatal' won't satisfy him; 'terrifiant' is not an approved form, the French have to say 'terrifié'. 'So much for logic! Perhaps there's too much logic, when language is the product of nature and totally irrational, whereas an academy is highly rational, logical and everything else you care to mention – but it is not creative, it merely arranges and lays down conventions. But what is the point of patriotic disputes about languages? It is you, my dear, who make me regret more bitterly than ever that I cannot immerse myself in you entirely through the means of your language!' (4 December)

Judith had obtained a divorce from Catulle Mendès and now lived with her lover Ludwig (né Louis) Benedictus. He was the cause of the only difference between her and Wagner – not jealousy, there was no question of that on either side. But Wagner wrote that Benedictus had fallen greatly in his esteem since he had learned that he composed. Everybody he met was a composer these days and nearly all of them contemptibly weak and idle. 'When I think how much music there is in the world, and how few works have gained my genuine affection, in the sense that these few works comprise everything that I mean by the word "music" – you would be amazed if I told you! But I will not tell you. My heart sinks at your mere mention of "audacious instrumentation": I know all these young people begin with nothing but "audacities", either in the instrumentation or in the harmony – but never in the melody!'

A few days later he explained: 'I did not say that I do not want to see the music of Benedictus, but I am afraid to see it. That's all! I speak from experience. Of late a number of my ardent followers have appealed to me for my opinion of their musical future: against my better judgement I have concealed my despair from them, but they have sensed it and grown cool – or, rather, bitter. That is something that distresses and saddens me.' And to emphasize that his aversion to 'audacities' had not made him an opponent of true innovation in music he added: 'Benedictus qui venit in nomine verae novationis! I embrace him in anticipation!' (23 December)

He imagined her in the room with him as he wrote to her, sitting on the chaise-longue to the right of his desk and looking at him, 'Dieu! avec quels yeux!' To have her there with him and talk to her thus would be an incomparable pleasure. Over and over again, he assured her that she was his only wealth, the 'belle abondance', the 'superflu enivrant' of his life.

Then one day it was all over. 'I have asked Cosima to take those commissions in hand . . . I am so troubled at present by business matters which are not in the least agreeable, that I no longer have the leisure to get on with *Parsifal*. Have pity on me! It will all be over soon, and I shall find again those beautiful moments in which I love to talk to you about myself! . . . Et enfin nous nous reverrons un jour! A vous, R.' (15 February 1878)

What had happened? There is no indication that the relationship had become an issue between Wagner and Cosima. The extracts from her diary for the period available to date (May 1977) report on his work on *Parsifal*, and conversations about Haydn and Mozart symphonies, with which he was much preoccupied at the time. There is nothing to suggest marital discord. Nor, indeed, did the former warm friendship between Wahnfried and Judith fall off at all. She had provided Wagner with a creative impulse, but now that she had played her part passion was converted back into friendship and a grateful memory.

The publication in 1964 of Cosima's letters to Judith also threw a new light on those which Wagner wrote to her. Cosima must have known of the affair at the time, and we can now see it through her eyes. 'She had the wisdom', the editor writes, 'to regard it as passing and unimportant, and the skill to betray nothing to either her husband or her friend and to allow the crisis to run its course.'[2] That is not to say that the experience left no scar on his heart. Two years later, when he was talking to Cosima about Goethe and Ulrike von Levetzow, he said: 'He felt it very deeply – it was a farewell to life.' And perhaps this thought was already in his mind when he asked Judith, in one of his last letters to her, 'shall I forget it?' then goes on: 'No! – But everything is tragic – everything inclines – at best – to elegy' ('tout penche – au melieur [sic] cas – à l'élégie!'). It could well be an allusion to Goethe's *Marienbad Elegies*, the outcome of his passion for Ulrike von Levetzow:

> Wenn Liebe je den Liebenden begeistet,
> Ward es an mir auf's lieblichste geleistet . . .

('If ever love inspirited the lover, it happened to me in the loveliest way.')

Meanwhile the progress of *Parsifal* can be followed in Cosima's diary, almost from day to day. When Wagner played her the prelude from the orchestral sketch he spoke about the attraction of the Grail mystery:'That the blood becomes wine strengthens us and we are therefore able to turn to the earth, while the transformation of the wine into blood draws us away from the earth.' The modulation of the Faith theme to D major in the prelude he compared to the spread of revelation through the whole world. He had been on the verge of giving it all up, he told her one day after he had started the first act. He had picked up his Darwin and then suddenly thrown it down again, 'for while I was reading everything came to me and that put me in such good fettle that I positively had to force myself to stop, so as not to keep lunch waiting. It's an insane state of affairs.' And another evening he played her a marvellous theme for a symphony: he had so many ideas of that kind, new ones occurred to him all the time, but he couldn't use the happy tunes for *Parsifal*.

'When you get the next page,' he said a few days later, 'you'll see that I've had a lot of trouble with it.' He wanted a weighty 3/2 for Amfortas's approach in the first scene, and had had difficulty fitting in Gurnemanz's words: 'Er naht, sie bringen ihn getragen . . .' 'Ingenuity is not what is wanted here, it must sound as though it had to be as it is. But now I've got it!'

One afternoon when he was working, he formed the impression that something that had seemed a good idea that morning now sounded harsh. So he closed the lid of his grand piano, and played it with the soft pedal down, and found it was satisfactory after all. To signal his pleasure to Cosima, who was helping the children with their lessons, he played the lovely theme from the coda of the first movement of Mozart's C major Symphony.

Another day he told her he had had an inspiration that would please her: at the very moment when the esquires were repeating the prophecy, Parsifal would fire his arrow interrupting them at the words 'der reine Tor'.

Sometimes the modulation into another key was what caused him difficulty, sometimes a 'rhythmic battle' he had to win. We learn of his satisfaction with a chromatically descending major third in the transformation music, out of which he then developed the counterpoint in the theme of the lament to the Saviour. When he played her what he had composed of Amfortas's complaint he admitted that the phrase 'nach Ihm, nach Seinem Weihegruße' had occupied him for the whole morning. He had never done anything as 'fantastic' as this before, it was getting greater all the time!

But he had only now come to the most difficult part of all, he told her, and the next day he improvised the Grail Scene from his sketches. In order to represent the spirituality of the words of the Saviour, the complete divorce from all materiality, he wanted to use a blend of voices, 'a baritone solo would make everything material, it must be neither male nor female, neuter in the highest sense of the word'. And so he set the first statement of the Last Supper theme ('Nehmet hin meinen Leib . . .') in the major mode, for altos and tenors, and the second, more urgent statement in the minor, for sopranos and altos. 'The drums will accompany the voices like a soft earth tremor!' He took a look at the scores of Berlioz's Requiem and Te Deum and laughed at all the directions for the timpani: it was like nothing so much as a director in the theatre straightening the actors' wigs.

The work absorbed him completely. He decided not to have Titurel speak again after the Mystery. One afternoon he had a tussle with a modulation and that night, when Cosima was already in bed and on the point of falling asleep, she heard him shout: 'A flat, G flat, F, it must be!' On 22 January 1878 he played and sang her the Grail scene. The words 'Wein und Brot des letzten Mahles' sounded like an age-old story, told by angels. 'But I won't have the old man coming back.' The next evening he told her, 'this will make you laugh', and showed her where he had allowed Titurel to sing again after all.

He was already thinking about the second act before he began to sketch it at the beginning of March. Klingsor was going to be very savage: 'Did you expect him to be brooding?' He was quite clear about how the prelude would be, and Kundry's scream, too. While this was all in his mind he sketched a canon for a 'domestic symphony', lost his temper with one of his adherents who disparaged Mozart's G minor Symphony, and praised Haydn's 'Military' Symphony: 'All our music goes back to these works.' He kept returning to Haydn and Mozart for several days in succession after that. There were things in *Zauberflöte*, he said, that made a chapter in the history of art in themselves: Sarastro introduced an innate, intelligent dignity instead of the conventional operatic kind – and we, the readers, at once recognize the creator of Gurnemanz – and there were things in Mozart, Wagner added, that would never be surpassed. Another evening, Cosima writes, he picked up Haydn's 'Bear' Symphony, and then drew Anton Seidl's attention to the Andante of his G major Symphony [presumably the 'Surprise'], which was one of the most beautiful things ever written – and what a marvellous sound!

While working on Klingsor's scene with Kundry he compared Klingsor to Alberich: at one time, he said, he had felt complete sympathy with Alberich, who represented ugliness yearning for beauty. Alberich possessed the naivety of the pre-Christian world, Klingsor that specific kind of evil that Christianity had brought into the world: 'He does not believe in goodness, like the Jesuits, that is his strength – but also his downfall; there is always *one* individual at any time throughout the ages.' Wagner was glad when he had finished the scene, and had 'thrown Klingsor off the battlements'.

'Ah! Music!' he exclaimed of Parsifal's appearance in the magic garden. 'What could take its place? In spoken dialogue this pause would be impossible. The *speaking pause* is the property of music.' But he was soon dejected again. 'I was so looking forward to my Flower Maidens, and now that's difficult too!' First of all he worked out the contrapuntal vocal writing on four or five staves, and then wrote the words for it: it reminded him of how he had written the words after the music when he was working on the finale of the first act of *Lohengrin* and the street fight in the second act of *Meistersinger*. 'My girls shall rush in with a wail, like children whose toys have been taken away – without anger.' And of the graceful motion of the Ab major passage 'Komm! Komm! Holder Knabe!': 'In the first act I was very sparing with the more sensuous intervals but now I'm using my old paint pot again.'

It was the beginning of April, but the skies were still grey. While he was giving his Flower Maidens something to sing he was thinking about the birds outside: 'Why do the birds sing so? They don't worry about what the sky looks like, they sing as children laugh – for no reason.'

It was in the midst of this happy absorption in writing music, at the beginning of May, that Nietzsche sent them *Human, all too Human*. By a miracle of significance and chance, according to *Ecce Homo*, a copy of the text of *Parsifal* reached Nietzsche at exactly the same time, inscribed 'To his dear friend, Friedrich Nietzsche, from

Richard Wagner, Councillor of the Church'. 'The crossing of these two books – I seemed to hear an ominous note. Was it not the sound of *swords* crossing?'

The truth was less melodramatic: the copy of *Parsifal* had reached him on 3 January 1878. (And the dedication actually ran: 'Cordial greetings and best wishes to his dear friend Friedrich Nietzsche, Richard Wagner (Supreme Councillor of the Church – for the information of Professor Overbeck).' The allusion to Overbeck's book on 'the Christlike-ness of present-day theology' was intended to stress the unecclesiastical nature of the text, as Nietzsche understood very well, but twisted out of malice.)

It reached him, as his sister admits, 'in the middle' of the compilation of *Human, all too Human*, which did not appear until the May of that year. There is no need to go into Nietzsche's allegation of astonishment at the work again, but the publication of *Human, all too Human* had a prehistory that cannot be passed over here. Nietzsche originally wanted to issue it under a pseudonym, but this idea was quashed by the publisher, who did not want to let slip the chance of causing a sensation. Thereupon Nietzsche replaced Wagner's name throughout by 'the artist'. Writers on Nietzsche have claimed that that was all that was necessary to remove any possible cause of offence to Wagner, but this is not borne out by the facts.

Quite the reverse: tempering the text was the last thing he intended. As his confidant Peter Gast told Joseph Hofmiller, he actually added a particularly savage dig after completion. Gast had written three quite long essays, purely atheistic in character – we may assume that they were written in the spirit of Nietzsche's newly adopted positivism, as they met with his approval – and sent them to Hans von Wolzogen for inclusion in the first number of *Bayreuther Blätter*, presumably to serve as a kind of 'programme' for the periodical. Wolzogen rejected the articles in a seven-page letter which, according to Gast, enraged Nietzsche more than Wagner's later reception of *Human, all too Human*, and was the decisive factor in his alienation. It was then that he added to Aphorism 109 the tailpiece probably aimed not only at Wolzogen's letter but also, and primarily, at Wagner's *Parsifal*, which he had since received:

> But certainly frivolity or melancholy of whatever degree is better than romantic retreat and desertion of the flag,

an approach to Christianity in any form; for in the
present state of knowledge, no one can have anything at
all to do with that without irredeemably besmirching his
intellectual conscience.

Above all, avoiding Wagner's name concealed absolutely
nothing. Everyone knew at once who was meant, not least Wagner
and Cosima themselves. It would have been one thing if the criticism had been confined only to his ideas and his works, but the
ruthless assault on Wagner's whole personality as man and as artist
– notably in the chapter 'Out of the Soul of Artists and Writers' –
was quite another matter. The climax comes in Aphorism
164:

> It is at all events a dangerous sign when a person is
> overcome with the sense of awe at himself, whether it is
> that famous awe of the Caesars, or the awe inspired by
> genius that is under consideration here; when the scent
> of the sacrifice . . . penetrates into the brain of the
> genius, so that he begins to waver and to believe himself
> more than human. Slowly the consequences follow: the
> sense of not being answerable, of possessing exceptional
> rights, the belief that his very society bestows a blessing,
> insane rage when the attempt is made to compare him
> with others, or even to assess his worth at a lower rate,
> to draw attention to weaknesses in his work . . .
> In rare individual cases this insane trait may also have
> been the means of holding a nature of this kind together,
> in spite of its tendency to overreach in all directions at
> once: in the life, too, of individuals delusions often have
> the value of those medicines which are in fact poisons;
> but [and now the dagger is thrust home] in the end, in
> the case of every 'genius' who believes in his own
> divinity, the poison reveals itself in exact proportion to
> the ageing of the 'genius'.

(When one reflects on the horrifying way in which Nietzsche
himself was later to succumb to the awe inspired by his own genius,
it is tempting to believe in the working of Nemesis.)
'I could make a comment on every sentence that I have read,'

Cosima wrote to Countess von Schleinitz, 'and I know that it represents the victory of evil.'

She had not been spared. 'One always loses by too close an intimacy with women and friends; one of the losses is the pearl of one's own life.' (428) But she was most deeply wounded, on her own personal account, by the aphorism on 'the voluntary sacrificial animal' (430):

> There is no way in which remarkable women can so effectively ease the lives of their menfolk, if the latter are great and famous, as by becoming, so to speak, the receptacle of the general disapprobation and occasional resentment of other people. Contemporaries will customarily tolerate a large number of blunders and follies, even acts of crude injustice, on the part of their great men, if only there is someone else to play the part of sacrificial animal, whom they may mistreat and slaughter, and so relieve their feelings.
>
> It is by no means uncommon for a woman to conceive the ambition to offer herself for this sacrifice, and the man can then feel well contented – assuming, that is, that he is enough of an egoist to consent to the presence of such a voluntary deflector of lightning, storm and rain in his vicinity.

Elisabeth Förster-Nietzsche confirmed what is easy enough to guess, that her brother was consciously alluding to Cosima in the aphorism.

Cosima was forced to ask herself what had given Nietzsche the right to parade before the public gaze the most intimate aspects of what she had experienced and suffered for Wagner's sake. She wrote a long letter to Elisabeth in which she expressed herself, as the latter observed, 'with remarkable agitation'. And an extraordinary lack of sensitivity is displayed by the occasion, nine years later, when Nietzsche is supposed to have asked his sister, 'By the bye, why did Frau Wagner take such exception to *this* aphorism in particular that time? On Wagner's behalf? On her own? It's always been a puzzle to me.'

This was the book, then, that Nietzsche despatched to Wahnfried in May 1878. He sent two copies, according to *Ecce Homo*, with a cheerful verse of dedication:

Dem Meister und der Meisterin
entbietet Gruß mit frohem Sinn,
beglückt ob einem neuen Kind
von Basel Friedrich Freigesinnt . . .

('Friedrich the liberal-minded of Basel, rejoicing in his new infant, offers glad greetings to the master and the master's wife.')

The affair of *Human, all too Human* poses more than one psychological riddle. What caused Nietzsche suddenly to lash out at Cosima, almost directly after his last letter of 10 October, in which he had assured her of his sincere devotion 'in good times and in bad'? Charles Andler is probably right in seeing it as the sudden bursting of the dam behind which jealousy had been mounting for a long time: some dark instinct in him had been spoiling for a fight. 'And the decision to attack, long taken in secret and suppressed by his conscience, peremptorily and irresistibly overpowered him on one of his days of crisis, when it was imperative for him to make a clean sweep of things within himself.' Andler considers that Cosima herself may well have been one, and not the least, of the causes of his jealousy of Wagner, and the theory certainly finds confirmation in the aphorism on the voluntary sacrificial animal: reading it we can sense the pleasure Nietzsche is taking at the thought of inflicting pain, sharpening his arrow-point at each word, finally aiming at her heart, at the heart of her heart, her sacrifice of herself for Wagner.

With the aid of references to utterances of Nietzsche from the Tribschen period and to the interpretation of the 'Empedocles' fragments, Erich F. Podach has shown that there is a substantial body of evidence that even at the height of his friendship with Wagner Nietzsche was already planning to 'dethrone' him. He believed Wagner incapable of carrying out their common aim of bringing about the rebirth of Greek culture out of the German spirit and the spirit of music. That role was reserved for himself. Wagner's 'dethronement' was to take place with Cosima's aid, and she was to fall to Nietzsche as the victor's prize.[3]

This plan to reverse the master–disciple relationship shows through in one of Elisabeth Förster-Nietzsche's anecdotes, according to which she once said to her brother at a later date: 'Oh, I wish Wagner had been twenty years younger when you first met him; I think you might have converted him to your ideas.' Nietzsche replied: 'I too used to believe and hope the same; but then *Parsifal* came and destroyed every hope, every possibility.' (EFWN, pp. 266f.)

The role assigned to Cosima is revealed in Nietzsche's 'Ariadne' fantasy: 'The divine bride Ariadne–Cosima was supposed to turn away from the inadequate demigod Theseus–Wagner and turn to the god Dionysus–Nietzsche who alone was worthy of her . . . Many years later madness presented Nietzsche with the illusion of fulfilment.'[4] In the first week of January 1889, at the onset of his madness, Nietzsche sent a number of letters to his friends. To Jacob Burckhardt he wrote that together with Ariadne he was the golden equilibrium of all things, and to Cosima, 'Princess Ariadne, my beloved', he wrote: 'Of late I was . . . perhaps Richard Wagner, too . . . But this time I come as conquering Dionysus, who will make of the earth a festival . . .' (3 January 1889)[5]

That was the final act in the tragedy of Dionysus, which had begun twenty years earlier under Bonaventura Genelli's picture, and in which the publication of *Human, all too Human* marked the peripeteia.

The other psychological riddle the book poses is what on earth was in Nietzsche's mind when he sent Wagner a book with such contents, with every appearance of innocence and harmlessness. Did he really think that Wagner would take this blow, dealt him in full public view, with a smile and in silence? At all events Nietzsche had no difficulty in laying the blame for the inevitable rupture on Wagner – at least to the satisfaction of his adherents, who treated as sacrilege the latter's daring to comment ironically, in the August 1878 number of *Bayreuther Blätter*, without naming names any more than Nietzsche had, on 'the quite illimitable advance in the field of criticism of everything human and inhuman'. (*Publikum und Popularität*, RWGS, X, pp. 79ff.)

'It does me no great honour to have been praised by that man,' he remarked to Cosima, then added, unable to disguise his hurt, 'one can't forget it.'

May of 1878 was an eventful month. On 12 May Hödel made his unsuccessful attempt on the life of the aged Kaiser. Bismarck's response was to lay the 'Sozialistengesetz' – an emergency bill containing a number of repressive measures against socialists – before the Reichstag, where it was defeated by the National Liberal party under their leader Bennigsen. Amid the public stir, Wagner confessed that he could hear only the voice of indignation, and no note of horror: nobody seemed to be shocked at being a member of a society in which such actions were possible. He condemned the attempt to pass emergency measures, instead of rooting out the causes of the emergency. Bennigsen, normally a weakling, had acted sensibly but had not touched the core of the matter, though he had been close to it when he had spoken of 'our guilt'. To Feustel's admission that, as a deputy, he had voted against the bill with a heavy heart, Wagner replied that reaction was always bad. The leaders of the socialist movement might be muddle-headed and were perhaps a bunch of intriguers, but the future belonged to socialism.

At the beginning of June, as he and his family returned from an enjoyable outing, he was shocked by the news of another assassination attempt: a Dr Nobiling had fired at the emperor on Unter den Linden, and the old man had fainted, covered in blood. If he had anything to do with it, Wagner said, a Day of Repentance would be decreed, so that the whole nation could examine its conscience! In the following days, as details of the event became known, he expressed his admiration for the emperor's unpretentious greatness: his first question had been about his coachman, and his second concern had been with who was to represent him for the time being; not one complaint about what had befallen himself. When Feustel asked him why he did not write to congratulate the old monarch on his recovery, he replied, in a resigned tone: 'What would be the point? The emperor would ask himself: what does he want? Ah, he's got that deficit, he wants money!'

There followed the depressing news of mass internments for lèse-majesté, terms of imprisonment of the order of five and ten years, which Wagner predicted would mean the release of an appalling generation in ten years' time! And then the emperor's birthday was celebrated with illuminations, under siege conditions! Wagner turned to Goethe and read the scene in *Egmont* where the hero discusses the same topic with the repressive Spanish general, the Duke of Alba, in purely human terms, far removed from any political commonplaces:

> Doesn't the world, and posterity too, praise kings who
> proved able to forgive offences against their dignity, to

forgive them, regret them and treat them with disdain?
Isn't that the reason why they are regarded as being like
God, who is far too great for any offence to touch him?

Everything about the event struck him as crude and stupid: the
socialists, who wanted to gain control of the state in order to
organize something impossible, and the government, who couldn't
come up with anything but prohibition and repressive police
regulations. He disapproved of the socialists making a party matter
out of something that concerned all Germans. He hoped that no one
believed that the forces at work in the socialist movement were
capable of being directed by theories and organizations: if that were
so there would be nothing in it. But ethics could be influenced, and
human feelings could be prepared to accept the violent changes that
would inevitably come with revolution. He had hopes of a new
religion issuing from industrialists' love of their workers. He was
pleased to hear that Sulzer, his old friend from the days in Zürich,
was now at the head of the socialist party there. 'We could do with
someone like him in Germany: I'm sure his efforts are directed, not
*against* property, but towards property for all.' He re-read the letters
he had written to Uhlig a quarter of a century before, and said that
then as now he looked forward to the advent of socialism, only now
he no longer expected it to happen in the near future. Wagner's
political views were in fact far more consistent throughout his life
than is commonly realized.

The impression that Bismarck, in his concern with military
might, was neglecting cultural and social advances encouraged
Wagner in an increasingly urgent private opposition to all forms of
militarism in his last years.[6] He admitted now that he had keenly
supported the constitution of the army in the past, but the way
things were now – the people exhausted, incessant new levies,
incessant increase of military strength – it was barbaric. 'Conquering new provinces and never even asking oneself how to win them
over; not giving a thought to how to make a friend of Holland,
Switzerland etc. – nothing at all – and only the army!'

Schemann tells of an occasion in December 1877 when Wagner
had launched a passionate complaint about the distress the German
people were in. 'And it's all happening right under the nose of
Bismarck, the German of the old school!' Schemann had never seen
him flare up in such holy wrath before. After those last words he

had rushed out into the wintry night and worked off his agitation in a boisterous game with his Newfoundland dog.

In the same year 1878, which we can regard as marking the climax of the crisis in Wagner's relationship to the empire, he published in the *Bayreuther Blätter*, under the title 'What is German?', the notes he had written for King Ludwig in 1865, the springtime of his German hopes, bringing the article to an abrupt conclusion by asking earnestly whether Constantin Frantz might be able to help answer the question in his title. (*Was ist deutsch?*, RWGS, X, pp. 36ff.)

Frantz answered in an 'Open Letter to Richard Wagner', which was published in the June issue of *Bayreuther Blätter*. To be German, politics needed to have an aim beyond its own immediate ends; it must raise itself to 'metapolitics', which bore the same relationship to ordinary politics as metaphysics to physics. This open letter with its severe criticism of Bismarck, appearing so close in time to the two assassination attempts of the summer of 1878, caused such a shock – 'like a purgative', as Wagner put it – that the members of the Berlin Wagner Society resigned in droves.

Wagner found all his feelings about the Reich expressed in a new book Frantz published the following year, on federalism. 'It's a book I would like to commend in clarion tones to the serious consideration of the entire population,' Wagner wrote to King Ludwig; 'it contains the complete solution to the problems of this world expounded in the clearest and most thorough way, and it is precisely the solution that I myself sense is the only right one.' (7 July 1879)

Constantin Frantz has remained a relevant and controversial figure.[7] He numbers among his champions men like the Austrian historian Srbik, who praised him as a 'national cosmopolitan' in the second volume of his work on German unity, and, in his own time, Jacob Burckhardt, who wrote to Friedrich von Preen in 1872, after reading Frantz's *Das neue Deutschland*, 'That one's got a clear head on his shoulders.'

Once, when Wagner was reading a book by Frantz, a fascinating enough occupation in itself, he remarked that it nonetheless required something of a struggle to occupy himself so much with the 'phenomenal world' when his thoughts were really always with the 'thing in itself'. Even then neither *Human, all too Human* nor political events were able to draw him away from the inner world of

*Parsifal*. On 29 May, after a boil on his leg had forced him to stop composing for a while, he declared that he felt so well that it was his duty to work. He played Cosima the conclusion of Kundry's narration, which was the most recent passage he had set, up to '. . . und Herzeleide – starb'. 'Herzeleide dies very simply, like the branch of a tree, she gradually fades.' He wanted to orchestrate some bars straight away, he thought it would help, as when he had written the prelude to *Rheingold* straight out in full score. 'The sound of horns' was something he absolutely had to have in certain passages.

'I'm well away now!' he exclaimed to Cosima on 3 June: Kundry's kiss, 'an instant of daemonic oblivion', and Parsifal's cry: 'Amfortas! Die Wunde! Die Wunde! Sie brennt in meinem Herzen!' 'What I've got myself into! It goes beyond *Tristan*.' Of Kundry's attempt at consolation, 'Die Liebe lerne kennen', he remarked that he had put nothing *Tristan*-like into it: it was not, for instance, like anything Isolde says about love, 'it is something different'. But he had to stop work again at that point, to go to a spa for a cure. 'We are listening to the blackbirds,' Cosima recorded; 'I say that I will miss their song.' 'I shall start then,' Wagner replied, 'now it is the summer that is the composer. I'm thinking about the third act, I prefer not to think about the second.' And a few days later: 'I have written some more of the canon [for the Domestic Symphony], and made up a very pretty figure. This will be the only sort of thing I shall write one day, it needn't be in four movements. I shall ask Lachner for his recipe for suites, I have a great mass of suitable ideas stored away unused.'

Then he suddenly came back to his old idea for a comedy: 'I shall write another piece, *Luthers Hochzeit*, in prose.' (5 July 1878; BBL 1937, p. 7) In other words, he wanted to confront the image of Parsifal, repulsing Kundry because of the danger of forgetting his mission in her embrace, with the contrary image of Luther taking Catharina as his wife, because her gaze brings peace and security to 'the boundless imagination of the striving, desiring male heart'. They represent two variations on the theme of male and female, which measure the full extent of the topic only when placed side by side. Nietzsche's doctrinaire attitude, his inability to understand the composer's multitudinous soul, is never more tellingly revealed than by his playing off the plan of *Luthers Hochzeit*, which Wagner had mentioned to him, against *Parsifal*, as proof of backsliding, of an espousal of 'ascetic ideals'.[8]

Nothing could have been further from the tenor of Wagner's life. In the middle of composing the Good Friday scene he wrote to the king about the happiness the work was giving him, and could not restrain himself from writing, too, about the happiness his wife and children gave him. He expressed his gratitude for the new meaning and new dimension his life had gained with the birth of his son. There is paternal pride in his description of how the boy was developing, and affectionate concern in his outline of the plans he and Cosima had made to bring him up as a free human being. Added to this was the artist's satisfaction with the way *Parsifal* was turning out: 'I feel happier than I have ever been: my work is for me the fountainhead of a life that surrounds me with ever new images arising out of the soul, giving calm and contentment. And there – there, laughing with the joy of being alive, is my son, bonny as a Wälsung; and over and above all my thoughts, presentiments, wishes, a world rises before me, a world not of hope, but of confidence.' (9 February 1879)

Only six weeks after beginning his cure, on 26 July 1878, he took up the composition sketch again, with the great scene between Parsifal and Kundry: the 'duet' in *Die Walküre* was pure joy by comparison, he moaned to Cosima, and in *Tristan* there had at least been the bliss of longing, 'but here there is only the wild suffering of love'. Other remarks he made to her about individual passages illustrate the artistic conscientiousness with which he went about his work. He had thought of a melody for Kundry's words 'Nun such' ich ihn von Welt zu Welt' that had greatly appealed to him but had been too long for the text. He had even begun to think of writing some extra lines when all of a sudden a counter-theme had occurred to him, which had given him everything he needed: the violins got the leaping melody expressing the state of her soul, while she had the theme for her urgent words. But he was still not satisfied. When he came to look at the composition and orchestral sketches again a year later, when he was starting the full score, something in the sequential writing did not please him and he did not rest until it was exactly what he wanted, as we now hear it: 'Nun such' ich ihn von Welt zu Welt, ihm wieder zu begegnen.'

'Oh, my heart sinks at the thought of everything to do with costumes and make-up, when I think that characters like Kundry are going to be impersonated on a stage, it immediately puts me in mind of those dreadful artists' balls, and now I've created the invisible orchestra, I'd like to invent invisible acting too!' (23 September)

When he began the third act on 24 October he talked about the mournful sounds he now had to compose: there must not be a single ray of light, for it would be very misleading. A few days later he asked Cosima to listen to something he had written and give him her advice. He played the prelude, depicting Parsifal's wanderings on 'der Irrnis und der Leiden Pfade', and showed her the pile of manuscript paper he had covered with sketches. 'Improvising like this, having ideas, that's not difficult, my difficulty always is knowing how to cut it down to size.' And when he saw how moved she was he commented: 'So it's good, I'm glad!' He was still not satisfied himself, but the next morning at the moment of waking an idea came to him for an insertion in the middle of the prelude: it only amounted to two bars but made a great difference.

All the time that he was working on *Parsifal*, the evenings were devoted to music: Beethoven, Weber and a lot of Mozart. Then there was Bach: he and Rubinstein went through all the preludes and fugues of the *Well-Tempered Clavier* together, and Cosima's diary contains a wealth of the comments he made.

'This is music *eo ipso*,' he said, 'it's like the root of the word. This is in the same relationship to other music that Sanskrit is to other languages.' Bach's music contained the germ of everything that subsequently ripened in the rich soil of Beethoven's imagination. But then he added: 'That distinction isn't just; he – Bach – is already perfect in himself, incomparable.' Compared with Beethoven and Mozart, Bach was the purest musician, while they had something in common with poets. He played some Italian airs by Bellini: 'This is *pour le monde*'; and then the first part of the C♯ minor Prelude: 'But this here, this *is* the world.'

He started to score the prelude of the first act while he was still sketching the third. More and more, he said, he wanted to avoid anything that sounded strange or jarring; he supposed that what he was attempting was the equivalent of Titian's use of colour. He did not dare give the Last Supper theme to a single instrument, an oboe or a clarinet for instance, so he devised that mysterious, impersonal blend of strings and woodwind, with the addition of the characteristically dry sound of a pianissimo trumpet when the theme is repeated in the higher register. In the orchestral sketch he had anticipated this repeat being accompanied by harps, but in the score the arpeggios are given to the violins and violas, creating a gentle glow (which he liked to compare to the gold background of the mosaics in St Mark's in Venice) by the conjunction of their demisemiquavers with the triplet chords of the flutes and clarinets. He had already said on an earlier occasion that the instrumentation would be completely different from the *Ring*: 'like layers of cloud, separating and re-forming'.

'I pretended that I was doing nothing but reading (Lecky's *History of European Morals* . . . highly recommended!),' he wrote to the king, 'but secretly I was scoring the prelude to *Parsifal* and I decided to surprise Cosima on the morning of her birthday with a performance of it.' The Duke of Meiningen lent him his orchestra for two days, the parts were copied, rehearsals were held in Meiningen and the players arrived in Bayreuth on 23 December in the greatest secrecy. The next day the first rehearsal under Wagner took place in the banqueting room of the Sonne, where it transpired that whenever the Meiningen kapellmeister had been at a loss as to the rhythm of a passage he had doubled the tempo.[9] The rehearsal was chaotic to begin with, according to Anton Seidl; the musicians were thrown into utter confusion by the unaccustomed movements of Wagner's long baton until they grasped that the pre-eminent consideration was the phrase, the melody, not the beat. Later, Bülow was to take over the Meiningen orchestra, but this rehearsal under Wagner raised them to a level they had never reached before. At seven in the morning of 25 December they assembled in the drawing room in Wahnfried, the Christmas tree was moved to one side, the music stands were arranged in the large bay window overlooking the garden. The players hung on Wagner's gaze, while the emotional expression was reflected in his face. Cosima had no chance to give way to her feelings, for he at once told her to prepare the room for a concert that very evening. He had invited about sixty people and played some movements from Beethoven's symphonies, in addition to the *Siegfried Idyll* and the *Parsifal* prelude. Afterwards he himself spoke with satisfaction of the musicians' delight, even ecstasy, when he had shown them how to play the Minuet of the Eighth Symphony, which was normally gabbled. And how beautifully in the end, how exactly as he had wanted, the clarinets had played the Trio, that most charming of all idylls!

Judith had invited them to visit her at her seaside villa in Saint-Enogat near Dinard during the following year, but Cosima wrote on 6 January that they would prefer not to accept: 'All of us, including *Parsifal*, feel so well after our year of complete seclusion that we have promised ourselves to spend 1879 like its predecssor.'

After the 'diversion' of the concert on Christmas Day, which had been like a tonic, on New Year's Day, with Cosima's permission, as Wagner told the king, he returned to *Parsifal* in the best of spirits. By 14 January he was able to sing Gurnemanz's Act III narration to her, up to 'er starb – ein Mensch wie alle'. When she tried to express to him how deeply this simple intensity of feeling moved her, he said: 'Yes, that's something you might call the most German of characteristics, the combination of simplicity with an unshakable faith, and the need to affirm this faith through good deeds.'

'When Parsifal faints – that's where it begins,' he said cheerfully, 'it will be the most beautiful thing – I already have a lot sketched.' And as the melos unfolded, depicting the spring meadow and all its flowers on the 'day of innocence' when nature is 'absolved from sin', with the richest of polyphonic writing, he confessed that he thought it very important that the inner and subordinate parts should sound well, which was why he liked to have a piano handy when he was writing. There were quite often 'squeezed' passages in Beethoven which made him think that if the composer had been able to hear them he would not have written them like that!

'People will ask how it is that Parsifal recognizes Kundry in her altered appearance – but does he recognize her? It is all an unspoken ecstasy, how he comes home and turns to look at this unhappy woman.' He called the end of the Good Friday scene – 'Du weinest – sieh, es lacht die Aue' – an elegy: an awesome transformation takes place in Parsifal's soul, he is wholly man once more before he becomes king.

He finished the composition sketch on 16 April and the orchestral sketch on 26 April. The following day he played through the last scene, from the transformation interlude. He remarked that just as it was the naivety of nature that kept *Siegfried* from sentimentality, so *Parsifal* was saved from it by the naivety of holiness, which was innocent of any of the dross of sentimentality. He illustrated certain intervals on the piano and said: 'That is simply impossible in *Parsifal*.' He turned to Hans von Wolzogen: 'To show you what sort of a fool I am, I will play you something I'm going to alter in the first act.' He failed to find the chord: 'Of course, it's in the prelude; as I heard it I said to myself: that's all very fine, but that chord will have to go.' It was too sentimental. He was talking about bars 99–100; at the performances on Christmas Day 1878 there was only one bar there, in which the Pity motive ended in a colourless imperfect cadence. It was not until he looked through the entire sketch again in August 1879 that he at last decided how to alter it.

On this occasion, too, he gave the ending of the whole work its final form: he said he had gone through the whole thing in his head thirty or forty times before settling on this particular version. Alfred Lorenz has analysed the closing scene as being in three periods: two arch forms (a–b–a) and a Bar (a–a–b), which put together make a larger Bar (A–A–B); to that we may add that, in its final form at least, the structure, building up according to an inner dynamic, was consciously determined by the artist's mind working at its highest level.

'Complete seclusion' – Cosima's words make a motto for the period from August 1879 to January 1882, during which Wagner wrote the score of *Parsifal*. 'What does the man of genius need?' he once asked, when thinking about the lives of Beethoven and Liszt; 'independence shielded by love.' That was what Cosima did her best to give him: an inner world to which he could retire, a world filled with the magical sounds of his own composition, the secret interpretation of the characters of his dramas, daily communion with the masters of music and poetry. It was a state such as he had once described to the king, long before he attained it:

> Only when Jupiter has set his sign on a man's forehead do the storms cease that have dissipated his vital strength until then . . . Now at last he knows blue skies, peace, mild, gentle air, the shady grove; now the man enters into the enjoyment of his divine powers. (30 November 1867)

## II

Inevitably some things from the world outside penetrated into Wagner's seclusion, to be met by him with circumspection.

First and foremost was the question of productions of the *Ring* outside Bayreuth, which there was now no way of preventing. In November 1877 Angelo Neumann had made a new approach to obtain the work for the Leipzig opera, of which he was now director. In his reply Wagner consented in principle: since Hamburg had acquired the performance rights in the meantime, Leipzig would no longer be asked to pay a fee for the exclusive right. Neumann came to visit him in Wahnfried in January 1878. 'I am glad you are seeking to renew the arrangements for which the ground was broken last year,' Wagner said; 'I was very sorry at the failure of the plan.' The contract was signed there and then. Leipzig staged *Rheingold* and *Walküre* in April 1878, *Siegfried* and *Götterdämmerung* in the following September, and three complete cycles in January, February and April 1879.

Wagner did not stint his praise and appreciation of Neumann's 'courage, zeal and great skill', but excused himself from going to Leipzig in person on the grounds of his reluctance to become embroiled again in the excitements of musical and scenic direction, which he would certainly be unable to resist if he were there. He meant this to be understood as a reflection of his own 'peculiarity' rather than lack of faith in the capabilities of the Leipzig production team. 'May it prove to be a happy return for me to my home town, from which strange musical circumstances have so long kept me absent!' (23 September 1878)

Munich was eager not to be left behind Leipzig. 'I permit myself to hope', Düfflipp's successor as the king's secretary, Ludwig von Bürkel, wrote to Cosima, 'that Leipzig will not succeed . . . in stealing the honour of the first complete performance from the capital of our gracious sovereign.' (27 June 1878) On the matter of Wagner's participation in the Munich production, Bürkel wrote that His Majesty was most emphatic 'that the Meister was not to be disturbed in his work on *Parsifal*, which he awaits with feverish impatience'. In one of his letters Bürkel enclosed a sketch of the proposed design for Valhalla, on which Wagner commented simply: 'Fasolt and Fafner were not acquainted with this architectural style.' He refused Perfall's invitation to attend the final rehearsals of *Götterdämmerung*. The first performance of the complete tetralogy took place in November 1878, a month and a half before Leipzig. The king did not attend it, but in the following April had a complete cycle performed for himself in private, which aroused his enthusiasm as much as the performances he had seen in Bayreuth. Wagner was embarrassed and vexed by the praise lavished on Therese Vogl, as Brünnhilde, for her 'magnificent equestrian daring' as she jumped on to Grane's bare back in order to leap into (or rather, over) the blazing funeral pyre, making the moment the 'culmination' for many people in the audience: it is perfectly true that this action is in his stage directions and forms part of the whole, but if the audience was distracted by it to that extent, he said, then he would really prefer to cut it.

Schwerin, Vienna, Brunswick, Cologne, Mannheim and Hamburg, too, had all started to build up their own *Rings*, beginning with productions of the separate parts. Wagner steadfastly refused all invitations to attend these performances so that the audiences could honour the work's author in person. As he wrote to Jauner, he realized that the conditions in normal theatres made cuts necessary, but for him that was a reason both for not attending such performances and for preferring not to learn about the changes in too much detail. 'It is a weakness for which I must be pardoned . . . Oh! how well I appreciate that the Viennese – especially if he is sitting in the stalls – wants his supper and a glass of wine by eleven o'clock at the latest! No, no! I understand that perfectly; and, let's face it, it is absurd to expect a theatre audience to exert itself in any way, even in the interests of its enjoyment; after all, it was in order to obviate such exertions that I invented the Bayreuth festival.' (GLRW, VI, pp. 157f.)

But though Wagner kept aloof from performances of the *Ring* he could not ignore the prospect of staging *Parsifal*. 'I told you once before, my sublime friend,' he wrote to the king, 'that in making the last stroke of the pen on a score like this I consign it to the hell that can turn every bar of it into an instrument of torture for me. I often hear the devilish voice mocking me: "Why did you do it all with such love and joy? Do you want to enjoy it *eternally*?" I believe that anyone who loves me will not grudge my right to keep this one last work of mine from the rough paws of my comrades-in-art and the cawing of that polymorphic monster, our audiences and the public at large, for as long as I can – even, indeed, for ever.' (27 March 1879)

But there were two clauses in the contract of March 1878 that prevented him from doing entirely as he wished with *Parsifal*. One stated that the first performance of his most recent work was to be given at Bayreuth in 1880 and the other that thereafter 'the unconditional right of performance was to be made over to the management of the Hoftheater'. He was determined to free himself from these shackles. He argued that the purpose of the contract had been only to arrange the repayment of his debts, and the schedule about the performance of *Parsifal* constituted 'in no way an integral part of the contract'. His management committee, however, considered it would be more suitable to add a supplementary clause which would leave the date of the first performance to his discretion alone. (7 July 1879) Only three days later Bürkel replied that: 'His Majesty the King. . . had no objection to the postponement of the performance of this work to such later date as seemed fit to the Meister, Richard Wagner.'

With that Wagner was relieved of the pressure of a deadline, and he could now contemplate escaping for a while from the harsh climate of Bayreuth, which he was unable to stand for too long at a time. He took a six months' lease from 1 January 1880 on the Villa Angri at Posilipo above Naples, for a very low rent, as he told the king, which was nevertheless almost beyond the means of a German opera composer. On their way there they celebrated the New Year in Munich with Lenbach, Levi and Bürkel, and Cosima persuaded Bürkel to suggest to the king the establishment of a protectorate over Bayreuth. The suggestion interested Ludwig and he also enquired what he could do to help Wagner fulfil his wish to prolong his stay in the south.

However, the over-enthusiasm of Wolzogen, who on his own initiative proposed a protectorate formed by all the German princes, with the Kaiser at their head, very nearly caused a serious upset. Ludwig was furious at the idea that he should take third or fourth place behind other crowned heads who would have done virtually nothing for the cause. It took all Muncker's diplomacy to make the king understand, through Bürkel, that this was not a new version of the plan proposed by Cosima, but merely the antics of 'our over-eager Wagnerians'.

Wagner and his family arrived in Naples on 4 January. 'The most beautiful scenery in Europe, nothing like it anywhere else . . . then there is our piece of land, the most glorious site in Naples. A Prince Doria once had colossal terraces constructed here and we can now climb from the sea to the level of Posilipo in a garden that is green and full of flowers even at this time of the year . . . All this, which I expect to be able to enjoy until the end of May, already fills me with kindly hope.' (KLRW, III, pp. 167ff.) But then two attacks of erysipelas, recurring for the first time in twenty-four years, confined him to his room until the end of January. In this 'lethargic state' he had obscure dreams that recalled the 'most terrible time in his life, the *Tannhäuser* year in Paris'. A conversation about German current affairs with his doctor, Professor Schrön, brought flooding back the complete hopelessness of his Bayreuth undertaking and made him think seriously once again, as in London in 1877, of emigrating to America. In his imagination he pictured himself turning his back on Europe and building his theatre, his school and his house in Minnesota – after raising a million dollars by subscription. America was the only place on the globe that it gave him any pleasure to think about, he declared: what the Hellenes were among the peoples of Europe, that country was among the nations of the earth. 'Yes, they will outstrip us! We are a hotch-potch destined for ruin.' And he remembered something his uncle, Adolf Wagner, had said: 'Our continent is an overripe fruit that a storm will shake from the branch; the tide of history is moving towards America.' (GLRW, VI, pp. 303f.)

It was in this frame of mind that Wagner wrote on 8 February 1880 to Dr Newell S. Jenkins, an American dentist in practice in Dresden, with whom he had become friendly, and asked him for advice.

> Dear, honoured Sir and Friend!
> I feel as though my patience will soon run out where my hopes of Germany and its future are concerned, and that I may well come to regret not having transplanted the seeds of my artistic ideas to a more fertile and hopeful soil long ago.
> I do not think it impossible that I may yet decide to emigrate for ever to America with my whole family and my last works. As I am no longer young I should require a very substantial accommodation from across the ocean to make it possible. For my moving expenses and to defray all my trouble, an association would have to be formed there which would place at my disposal in a lump sum a capital of a million dollars, half to be paid directly on my settling in a climatically advantageous state of the union, and the other half to be deposited at 5 per cent in a state bank. With that America would have bought me for all time. The association would also have to raise the funds for the annual festivals, in which I would gradually present all my works in model

productions: these would start at once with the *first* performance of my latest work *Parsifal*, which I shall not permit to be performed anywhere else until then. All future work on my part, whether as producer or as creative artist, would, in consideration of the capital sum paid to me, belong unconditionally for all time to the American nation.

I recall that at your last visit you kindly and eagerly offered to make the arrangements for me if I wished to make a so-called artistic tour of America. I hope you will understand why I now turn to you and no one else with these far more drastic ideas. A mere tour, to earn a limited sum of money by giving concerts, and then to return to Germany, would never suit my book. Nothing but a complete move to America would be worth my while!

Would you be so kind as to ponder the matter a little, and, if you think it a good idea, let me know your views! In the greatest friendship and with sincere regards,

Richard Wagner

8 Febr. 1880.        Naples – Villa Angri. Posilipo.[10]

Jenkins, not trusting his own competence in the matter, consulted John Sullivan Dwight, the 'musical sage of Boston', the American Ambassador in Berlin, and other American friends in Germany. 'The consensus was that the plan was not feasible, for both artistic and financial reasons.'

Wagner made no secret of his plan to King Ludwig. 'The news about the performances of my work causes me nothing but concern; I wish I could withdraw permission to give them everywhere, and have already seriously thought about emigrating for good to America, because there I would receive the means to buy back all the performance rights that have been granted. For many other reasons, including my total loss of hope in Germany, I must still look on the project as not yet abandoned; I am waiting for a clear statement of their views, and if I find their account satisfactory then the only thing that could prevent me from the execution of the plan is the consideration of my already advanced years.

'In truth, there is no more ironic fate than mine!' (31 March 1880)

The following day, 1 April, Dr and Mrs Jenkins came to talk to him at the Villa Angri. 'We went to Constantinople by way of Naples expressly to talk with him and Frau Cosima and found they were so full of illusions as to the conditions in America that arguments against this plan had no force.' It took Jenkins another year, with the help of other American friends, to convince the Meister that the place for his future triumphs was in his homeland, and not abroad. 'I rejoiced that that end was attained without a cloud resting upon our friendship.'[11]

But privately Wagner had already begun to think in terms of making his trip to America a concert tour only, starting in September 1880 and going as far as California. He visualized the moment of his arrival in San Francisco. 'It will be the fulfilment of my boyhood wish, for I always had the thought: what? shall I die without having seen this little planet and everything on it? That at least, since we can't go to the stars!' (GLRW, VI, pp. 385f., note)

In the event, as we shall see, another attack of erysipelas forced him to postpone the tour until the next year. But he did not relinquish his determination to have set aside the other clause in the 1878 contract, according to which *Parsifal* was to be placed at the disposal of the Munich theatre after its Bayreuth première.

He had had to surrender all his works, however ideal their conception, to the exigencies of ordinary theatrical practice, he wrote to the king on 28 September 1880, and he wondered whether he ought not to preserve at least this last and most sacred of them from that fate. His allusion to the representation in the work of the Christian mysteries is more likely to have been calculated to influence the king than to be an exhaustive reflection of his own view. 'Was heilig mir' – his criterion of sacredness was the same as Walther von Stolzing's: that in artistic matters it is not the material but the spirit that is decisive.

'Only there [in Bayreuth] let *Parsifal* be performed, only there, in all futurity; never must *Parsifal* be offered to the public as entertainment in any other theatre; that this should be so is the only thought in my head, as I review the ways and means of ensuring my work this destiny . . . I have therefore decided to spend about six months in the United States of North America in the autumn of next year, in order to earn a capital sum which will rid me and my heirs for all time of the necessity of losing control over the performing rights of my works.'

'Although I do not in the least approve of your intention of going to America for six months,' Ludwig replied, 'since the exertions awaiting you there might well undermine your health, on the other hand I am completely in agreement with you that *Parsifal*, your sacred festival drama of dedication, should be given only in Bayreuth and is not to be desecrated on another, profane stage.' (24 October 1880) He had in fact issued the following instructions on 15 October: 'In the furtherance of the great aims of the Meister, Richard Wagner, it is my wish that the orchestra and chorus of my court theatre be placed at the disposal of the Bayreuth festival for two months in the year annually from 1882 onwards;' and, further, 'that all previous agreements about the performances of the festival drama of dedication, *Parsifal*, are herewith annulled.'

The story of how *Parsifal* was accorded this special dispensation, which was so hotly disputed when the copyright expired, has taken our narrative ahead of events. While Wagner was trying to school himself to contemplate the state of affairs in the public sphere of art with 'ironic serenity', other concerns, at first blush completely unrelated, were tormenting him and robbing his nights of sleep.

When Malwida, visiting Wahnfried in 1878, had defended the experiments carried out on living dogs by a certain Professor Goltz, Wagner had turned a thunderous look on her: never, ever, would such bloody methods bring anyone closer to the essence of things. In 1879 he was asked by animal protection societies to raise his voice with theirs against the torture of animals in the name of science.

If he were a young man, he told Cosima, he would not rest until he had raised a general outcry against this barbarism. A religion could be founded on compassion for animals; compassion between humans was more difficult, they were so malicious, they recoiled from each other and it was hard to apply the sublime doctrine of Christianity. But one could make a start with patient, dumb animals, and anyone who was kind to animals would certainly also not be hard on men. (BBL 1937, p. 109)

'Your important pamphlet had already reached me,' he wrote on 14 August 1879 to Ernst von Weber, the author of *The Torture Chambers of Science*, 'and I confess to you my weakness, that I have not had the courage yet to read it properly, since the first glance at it moved me excessively. My son shall be and learn whatever he wants, but I shall urge him to learn enough surgery to be able to dress simple wounds on humans and animals and – doing better than his father – to steel himself to the sight of physical suffering.'

Weber visited him a short time later, and they had some serious conversations about vivisection. Wagner had hesitated as to how he could best contribute to the debate, but now decided to write an 'Open Letter to Herr Ernst von Weber', which he published in the October 1879 issue of *Bayreuther Blätter*, and also as a pamphlet, in an edition of 3000 copies, printed at his own expense. (*Offenes Schreiben an Herrn Ernst von Weber*, RWGS, X, pp. 194ff.)

That the anti-vivisectionists wanted to enlist Wagner's support illustrates, as Newman points out, how great his influence now was in Germany. It was also his opportunity to prove that his heart was in the right place. (NLRW, IV, pp. 601f.) The new and distinctive feature of the 'Open Letter' is its complete rejection of utility as a criterion and its appeal solely to the ethic of compassion. 'For where human dignity is concerned, let us agree that the first evidence of it appears at the point where the human being distinguishes himself from the animal by showing compassion even for the animal.' In this unmasking of the cold sophism that pity is only a sublimated form of egoism, he must have been thinking of Aphorism 46 of *Human, all too Human*: 'Compassion Stronger than Suffering'. Wagner in fact underwent an experience similar to that of his Parsifal: as the latter's compassion for an animal is the first stage in his progress towards recognition of a metaphysical guilt in all existence, so Wagner himself advanced from preoccupation with the special case of vivisection to a more general problem of modern civilization which has only increased in earnest since his day: whether it is right to purchase scientific progress at the cost of compromising traditional ethics. It is perhaps an insoluble dilemma, but one that has to be examined frankly.

Early in April 1880 a petition was delivered to the Reichstag, requesting the abolition or at least restriction of vivisection; the 6000 signatories included 25 generals and 88 staff officers out of a total of 257 officers – a sign, as Glasenapp remarks, that manliness and compassion are by no means mutually exclusive. Bismarck himself later affirmed in a letter to Ernst von Weber: 'Ever since I learned of the excesses of vivisection, I have shared your sense of outrage;' although he lacked any legal powers, he would have tried to use his influence to introduce restraints on experiments with animals, were it not that the strength that remained to him barely sufficed for carrying out the duties of his office.[12]

The petition was not even presented on the floor of the Reichstag, but was dealt with by a committee, who consulted the expert opinion of only one man, the pathologist Rudolf Virchow. When Wagner was sitting down to lunch with his family on Ascension Day in the Villa Angri, he was unable to prevent himself from blurting out what he had intended to keep from them: the news that the decision in Berlin on the vivisection question had gone against them. 'Things look gloomy in my German heart,' he wrote to Wolzogen, 'and I am thinking more and more of removing myself and my children – by opting for America – from the German empire. But it shall have *Parsifal* first.' He dated the letter: '7 May 1880 (Ascension, whoopee!)'

The household had been joined in the middle of January by the young poet and philosopher Heinrich von Stein, whom Malwida had recommended as a tutor for Siegfried. Fate had brought them a third person, Wagner wrote to the king, who would now share their life for some years as a welcome member of the family. He went on to describe Stein as a man of a kind that he had hitherto encountered only in novels. He came from an old noble family with a wide network of kindred, possessing substantial estates in Thuringia. He was a graduate in philosophy, but would not regard his studies as completed until he had devoted some time to the education of a gifted boy. 'He is slender and blond, like a German youth out of Schiller . . . a very remarkable person, who has come to me like a miraculous gift!' (Naples, 25 January 1880) Nietzsche also had great hopes of Stein, greeting his announcement that he was coming to see him in Sils-Maria in 1884 with '*very* welcome! *Much* wished for – I will not say more today'. And after the visit he dedicated a poem to him, *Einsiedlers Sehnsucht* ('The Recluse's Longing'):

> Der Freunde harr' ich, Tag und Nacht bereit:
> Wo bleibt ihr, Freunde? Kommt! 's ist Zeit! 's ist Zeit!

('I look for my friends, waiting day and night: where are you tarrying, friends? Come! 'tis time!, 'tis time!')

As late as 1888 Nietzsche could still not forgive the dead Wagner for coming between Stein and him even then: 'Oh, that old robber! He robs us of our young men, he even robs us of our women still and carries them off into his cave.' (*The Wagner Case*, postscript) He was referring to Stein – and to Cosima.[13] It is indeed pertinent to wonder whether jealousy of Wagner was not more potent in this than love of Stein. Only a year after the Sils-Maria episode he had written to his sister: 'Do you really believe that Stein's works, which I would not have perpetrated even at the height of my worst Wagnerism and Schopenhauery, are as important as the immense task that is mine?' (Early March 1885)

Soon after Stein's arrival in Naples a young Russian painter, Paul Zhukovsky [Joukowsky], called at the Villa Angri. He had a studio only twenty minutes away, had known Frau Wagner in Munich, and thought it his duty to pay a neighbourly call on her and Wagner. This courtesy visit flowered into an enduring friendship. By an interesting coincidence his father, Vasily Alexandreyevich Zhukovsky, an eminent Russian poet and tutor to the future Tsar Alexander II, had once paid his respects to Goethe more than half a century earlier.[14]

Zhukovsky had hitherto spent most of his life in Italy, but he now decided to make Bayreuth his permanent home. For this reason, Wagner wrote to the king, he had asked him to execute drawings and designs not only for *Parsifal* but for all his works: 'Since it will be done exactly according to my specifications we can expect something to come of it which will be of use to posterity.' They had been to Amalfi together, and visited the Palazzo Rufolo at Ravello high above the bay of Salerno. 'There we discovered splendid motives for Klingsor's magic garden, which were sketched at once with a view to their being adapted for the second act of *Parsifal*.' (31 May 1880)[15]

A third visitor had presented himself at the Villa Angri at the beginning of March: Engelbert Humperdinck, then twenty-six years old. He had received a bursary from the Mendelssohn Foundation 'to pursue his musical studies', but in reality, as he confessed, he used it to traverse 'Italiens holde Auen' with his eyes un-Tannhäuserly wide open. After presenting his visiting card, which bore the resounding title 'Member of the Order of the Grail' – the name adopted by a bunch of young musicians in Munich – Humperdinck was received by Wagner in a large room with half the blinds down. After a searching look, Wagner asked, 'Well, what are you doing here in Naples, you knight of the Grail?' Humperdinck explained about his bursary. 'How extraordinary!' Wagner exclaimed. 'Can a young musician's art still profit today in Italy? Tempi passati!' Then he enquired about his further plans, and when Humperdinck told him he was about to leave for Sicily, he said: 'Now, that's sensible of you. See all the sights, and don't forget Palermo. I shall probably get there again. And when you get back come up and see me again; perhaps you will learn something quite new up here if you do. So, auf Wiedersehen in May!'[16]

The contemporary musical scene in Italy had not made a very good impression on Wagner. His lifelong fondness for Halévy's *La Juive*, which had impressed him by a 'certain spine-chilling sublimity, shot through by an elegiac breath' in 1837 in Dresden,[17] tempted him to see a performance of it in the Teatro San Carlo. '*La Juive* in the evening,' Cosima wrote in her diary, 'delighted by San Carlo – everything an opera house should be, delighted by all the beauties of the work, delighted by the orchestra, especially the playing of the two cors anglais, but horrified by the singing and acting and the production: constant incongruity between the music and the theatrical action. Richard emphasized how this work, from the school of Méhul and Cherubini, is full of life and emotional sensitivity, and not the least Jewish in its emphasis, just rightly delineated.' *La Juive* belonged to the same period as Hugo's *Notre Dame*, he said; Halévy was the first musical genre painter and was more sensitive than Cherubini: 'I liked him very much; his was a yearning, sensual nature.' (BBL 1937, p.154)

But when a Roman prince, a syndic of Rome, sent Wagner a deputation inviting him in the name of the Senate and the Roman people to be the guest of honour at a performance of *Lohengrin* in the Teatro Apollo, he was cautious enough to decline politely. Not even the tempestuous eloquence of Signora Lucca, who came all the way to Naples to persuade him to go, could change his mind. Undeterred, she sent off telegrams to him in both intervals, to report on the tumultuous applause. 'Ah! quel bonheur! j'ai réussi,' he sighed ironically, 'my God, how ungrateful we are!' To King Ludwig he wrote: 'Nobody could understand why I refused the invitation, and I had to hold forth so vehemently and so long that it made me ill . . . Really, my position vis-à-vis this world is so senseless and ridiculous that reminders of it are often our only source of laughter.' (31 March 1880)

On the other hand he had no cause to regret accepting an invitation from the Duke of Bagnara, the president of the Conservatorio di Musica of Naples, to hear a performance of the *Miserere* of Leonardo Leo, a contemporary of Bach. 'The awesome, sublime effect of that music! This is the one, true music, beside which all else is trivial. The composition builds up like a mighty cathedral, meticulously constructed, sublime and necessary, every modulation immensely effective because it follows logically from the part-writing.' According to Cosima, he went on talking long after they got home about this style of church music, 'this most sublime, completely impersonal art'.

On a second, official visit to the conservatory, the 250 pupils saluted him with three 'Evvivas', and then performed for him *La Bataille de Marignan* by the Flemish master Jannequin, as well as an operetta by one of their own number, which earned its composer a hearty 'Bravo!' from the distinguished guest. Wagner also met the aged music teacher, Francesco Florimo, the friend of Bellini, on this occasion. He embraced him, deeply moved, crying 'Bellini! Bellini!' And as he took his leave, with an 'Evviva' for Naples and Italian music, he turned once more to Florimo, who was trembling with emotion, and said, 'Long live the great Bellini!'[18]

Although he had not stinted his applause for the young performers, he could not help but observe the general decline in Italian operatic practice. He felt that the best way he could thank the Duke of Bagnara for his courtesy was candidly to draw his attention to the depredations. 'How are we . . . to get away from trying to achieve results with means that are totally alien to great dramatic art? How are we to impress the feeling for beauty indelibly upon richly talented young natures such as these?' He suggested that the answer lay in deep and sustained study of Mozart's *Figaro*, both versions of Gluck's *Iphigenia*, Spontini's *La Vestale* and the old Italian masters. 'There is in art, just as in life, such a thing as good society.' (RWGS, XVI, pp. 125ff.)

'Perhaps you will learn something quite new up here,' he had told Humperdinck as he was leaving. On the latter's returning now from Sicily, with another of the 'knights of the Grail', Martin Plüddemann, later a well-known composer of ballads, both were at once co-opted to take part in a performance of the Grail scene to celebrate Wagner's birthday. Humperdinck described the occasion. Rubinstein and Plüddemann undertook the task of teaching the four girls the by no means easy choral music sung from the height of the dome. As the sun was shedding its last light over the hills and the coastline, Rubinstein began to play the opening bars of the transformation music. The girls, in their best dresses, stood to the right of the grand piano, their childish faces shining with excitement; Plüddemann and Humperdinck himself stood on the other side, each with a Grail Knight's part in his hand. The audience, across the room, consisted of Cosima, Siegfried, Malwida and Zhukovsky. 'In the middle of the circle sat Wagner, before him on a stand the sketch of *Parsifal*, from which he sang and conducted, soloist, composer and producer in one person. He knew just how to use his voice, which was not large but sonorous and ranged over a wide compass to reach every register, so as to render each passage impressively.' Dusk had fallen as the last notes died away and their rapt attention dissolved in tumults of admiration.

'Well, my children,' Wagner smiled, 'you ought to be pleased with me. I knew what I was doing, all right, when I wrote that. But now, outside, we all need some fresh air!' When Humperdinck took his leave Wagner paused in thought for a moment. 'Young friend, wouldn't you care to come to Bayreuth? There would be all kinds of things for you to do there, which you might enjoy.' While Rubinstein made the vocal score Humperdinck could make a duplicate copy of the autograph full score for everyday use. 'Oh, yes, my dear fellow, the old, great masters of painting had to grind colours, too, before they were allowed to start working on their own.'

As Humperdinck, Rubinstein and Plüddemann were walking away from the house in the mild night, lit by a full moon, they heard a familiar voice singing softly behind and above them:

> Drei Knäblein, jung, schön, hold und weise,
> begleiten euch auf eurer Reise . . .

It was Wagner, on the balcony, sending them on their way with the Three Ladies' song from *Zauberflöte*. The young men burst into Tamino and Papageno's reply, 'So lebet wohl! Auf Wiedersehn!'

Wagner and Cosima kept up their regular practice of reading aloud in the evenings. On 23 June he decided it had to be Aeschylus's *Agamemnon*. 'So he's reading it,' Cosima wrote, 'and I feel as though I've never seen Richard like this, transfigured, inspired, completely at one with what he's reading, the performance could not have been more sublime. Cassandra's first cries were heartbreaking.' A quarter of a century later Zhukovsky confirmed: 'I can still hear her cry of "Apollo! Apollo!" ' Two days later, when he completed the reading with the glorious close of the *Eumenides*, Cosima exclaimed: 'Do you know what work I think has a similar combination of the ideal world and the real, and reminds me of the founding of the Areopagus? In *Meistersinger*, Sachs's address at the end.' – 'That's exactly what I was about to say,' Wagner replied.

He praised Droysen's translation and recalled the impression it had made on him all those years ago in Dresden, when he had immersed himself in the Greek world. And now that, like a sculptor, he had 'worked' his own artistic ideal from the Greek in the intervening years, he experienced that impression anew in the setting of the heroic landscape of the Bay of Naples, where something of the Greek spirit still lives.

Such reliving of earlier experiences – above all of the Ninth Symphony and the *Oresteia* – is characteristic of Wagner's personality, lending it something of the formal integrity, coupled with inner richness, of a Beethovenian symphonic movement.

The time that they had planned to spend in the south really ran out at the end of May, but on 16 June the king ordered: 'To enable the Meister Richard Wagner to prolong his stay in Italy to the benefit of his health, I grant him as a contribution to his costs during the five months June to October inclusive of the current year, the sum of 5200 lire.' Conveying the news of this grant to Cosima, Bürkel was also told to explain that 'the mention of October as the expiry date in no way exercises any kind of pressure to return to frosty Germany'.[19]

'My health gives cause for optimism in this unbelievably wonderful air,' Wagner wrote to Wolzogen early in May, 'but I am idle beyond all measure!' He was referring to a sizeable contribution he had promised for *Bayreuther Blätter*. He wrote regularly for it, not only articles on topics of current interest such as 'Public and Popularity', 'The Public in Time and Place' (1878), 'Shall we Hope?' and 'Open Letter to Ernst von Weber' (1879), but also the essays 'On Writing Poetry and Music' and 'On Writing Poetry and Music for Operas in Particular' (both 1879), which continue the series of writings based on his own unique, personal artistic experience. The 'affinities' that were now looming in his head 'to biblical proportions' related to one of the more important of these works, one of those that encircle the conception and creation of his dramatic works like a philosophical aura; what *The Artwork of the Future* and *Opera and Drama* are to the *Ring*, *Beethoven* (conceived in Venice though not written until later) to *Tristan,* and *German Art and German Politics* to *Meistersinger, Religion and Art,* first published in the October 1880 issue of *Bayreuther Blätter,* is to *Parsifal. (Religion und Kunst,* RWGS, X, pp. 211ff.)

He prefaced it with an epigraph from one of Schiller's letters to Goethe: 'I find in the Christian religion *virtualiter* the lineaments of what is highest and noblest, and the various manifestations of the same in real life seem so repugnant and vacuous to me simply because they are failed representations of those ideals.' (17 August 1795) The words are unmistakably Wagner's answer to Nietzsche's assertion that one cannot have anything to do with Christianity 'without soiling one's intellectual conscience beyond redemption'.

A return of his erysipelas at the beginning of July forced him to leave Naples earlier than planned, to seek a change of air in the hills further north, in Siena. He found spacious lodgings in the Villa Torre Fiorentina, outside the city gates; the furnishings included a state bed that Pope Pius VI had slept in and which was big enough, Wagner opined, for a whole schism. When the shadows deepened in the gentle evening light he could trace the graceful outlines of chain after chain of the Umbrian hills, reaching to the horizon. He excused the expense of this brief six-week rental by saying: 'For people like us all extravagances have only one meaning, the achievement of peace and ease, so that the spirit can be free.'

His spirits benefited further from a visit from Liszt, which went off harmoniously, and the completion of the next stage in the composition of *Parsifal.* He had begun what he called 'drawing the bar lines' on 7 August 1879 and now finished it on 24 September 1880; we have Humperdinck's description and explanation of the process. The orchestral sketch, a kind of short score, comprises a complete 'skeleton' of the composition, written down on two or three, occasionally more, staves, while the margins are filled with mysterious symbols and series of numbers, comprehensible only to initiates, pertaining not only to details of the orchestration but also to the planning of the score. By working out the spacing in advance, Wagner was able to paginate the entire full score, already finished in his head, before putting pen to paper. When he finally started to write the work out in full score back in Bayreuth, he worked so fluently that Humperdinck, as copyist, had difficulty in keeping up with him. He writes that it was the spirit of order, creative self-discipline, the logic of his systematic working methods, that led

Wagner to measure with his own hand the depth and width of the trenches and the foundations on which was to arise the miraculous edifice of the Grail Castle. 'That is the reason for the noble architectural line, for the serene sense of proportion in the deployment of the means, not a note too many and not one too few; the reason, too, for the clarity and transparency of the part-writing and the eurhythmic movement that we admire in Richard Wagner's last work.'[20]

In the meantime, while they were still in Naples, Wagner had finished another work that had occupied him on and off since 1865: his autobiography, *Mein Leben*. He was in time to have the fourth part, covering the years 1861–4, printed in Bayreuth, and to send it to the king for his birthday. He sent him a telegram from Siena, saying he hoped the book would arrive in time. (24 August 1880)

'With all my heart,' Ludwig replied, 'I render you, my faithfully loved friend, my deep innermost thanks . . . for the very welcome, much valued gift with which you surprised me.'

'The chief satisfaction, as far as I'm concerned, is the good weather and the beautiful clear skies!' Wagner had recently written to Hans von Wolzogen, not entirely seriously. But he was to owe his most powerful experience in Siena to a work of art. He went to see the cathedral, and after viewing the exterior, at once sumptuous and high-spirited in its decorative use of Gothic style, the lofty, earnest interior, vaulted over by the massive dome, moved him to tears: it was the most powerful impression any building had ever made on him. He lost his temper with Jacob Burckhardt's strictures, in his *Cicerone*, on some irregularity in the lines: 'Where does he find the rules by which to criticize the builders of such a unique work?' Zhukovsky had to make a drawing of the interior, which later served as the basis for the design of the Grail Temple at Bayreuth. It was the solution, for him, to this difficult scenic problem, and all subsequent designs have been variations on it, with greater or lesser degrees of success. Anyone who still remembers seeing Zhukovsky's Grail Temple at Bayreuth will agree that it was distinguished by two features above all else: its obliviousness to conventional theatrical ideas of flats and backcloths and, arising from that but intensified by perspective illusion, the impression that one was not watching from the far side of a proscenium arch but, like Parsifal, attending the ceremony from within the lines of pillars. This effect was helped by the great depth of the stage at

Bayreuth, which enabled the files of knights and esquires to enter down the two aisles on either side of the brightly lit central apse, approaching gradually in the dimmer, bluish light as if from some immeasurable distance.

Making another stop, from 4 to 30 October, in Venice, where they stayed in the Palazzo Contarini dalle Figure on the Grand Canal, Wagner and Cosima renewed their acquaintance with Comte Arthur de Gobineau. 'Diplomate, grand seigneur, courtisan de salon, chroniqueur politique, orientaliste, sculpteur, philologue, feuilletoniste', as a modern biographer, R. Gérard-Doscot, describes him, Gobineau had represented France in three continents, visited Persia, Greece, Brazil, Scandinavia and Russia on ethnological expeditions, and carried out his duties as *maire* of his country community with diplomacy and vigour during the occupation of 1870–1. His writings ranged from political commentary and the history of remote peoples and cultures to authorship of *Nouvelles Asiatiques*, *La Renaissance* and the tragedy *Alexandre*, to name only three of his best-known works. He took up the chisel in order to conjure to life from stone figures of his imagination – a Valkyrie, a Sonata appassionata. In his versatility he seemed a scion of Renaissance man, such as he had depicted in his *Leonardo da Vinci*. At the same time he loved to preserve an intellectual incognito and once at a party successfully denied his authorship of the later famous *Scènes historiques*.

'Je suis passé par Venise et j'ai vu Wagner, qui voulait m'emmener à Bayreuth où il va donner *Perceval*,' he wrote to Arrigo Boito, one person who admired both Wagner and Verdi. But Gobineau's first visit to Bayreuth did not take place until May 1881.

On the last stage of the journey home, Wagner halted in Munich for two and a half weeks, to give himself and his family the opportunity to see some of his works. He was much moved by *Tristan*, at which he was warmly received by the audience: he told Cosima how he felt for and with each character in turn, with Marke, with Kurwenal – it was as though he was each of them.

On the afternoon of 12 November he conducted for the king a private performance of the prelude to *Parsifal*. He wrote a programme note for the occasion, heading it 'Love – Faith: – Hope?' (RWGS, XII, p. 349) Only a few close friends attended, keeping well in the background. Deeply impressed, the king asked for it to be played again, but when he asked to hear the *Lohengrin* prelude, for purposes of comparison, Wagner handed the baton to Levi. The action was later construed as a sign that Wagner had taken umbrage, and was associated with an outburst in a conversation about politics with Lenbach and some others later the same day, when he referred to 'the great and powerful of the earth': 'whether king, Kaiser or Bismarck, they're all the same!' But this story comes at second hand, and both Glasenapp and Newman doubted its authenticity. The performance had been preceded by a rehearsal and Wagner was tired; his surrender of the baton to Levi for the *Lohengrin* prelude was a matter of no special moment.[21]

After more than ten months away they arrived back in Bayreuth on 17 November. 'We are back among our domestic penates,' Cosima wrote to Judith, 'and it is as though we had never left them. Like all beautiful things Italy has turned into a dream for us, and even if we have left her, she has not left us, and we live on the memories.' Then, referring to Munich, 'in order to forget the sky, the sun and the beauty, we immersed ourselves in the sublime. It proved a good idea, and thanks to it we feel happy to be here, and we are both working in our own way, he for eternity and I for this mortal span. We could go on living like this for hundreds of years!' (28 December 1880)

Wagner resumed work on his score on 23 December. He complained that really he needed more instruments than he had, not to make more noise but to express what he wanted. But by blending the instruments he had, he created completely new timbres, quite distinct from those of the *Ring* or *Tristan*. About to score the passage in the first scene where Amfortas is lifted and carried off to the lake, he told Cosima that he intended to use trombones and trumpets; strange though it might be, it would work well. So it is that we now hear the forest voices of the separate instruments above a soft, warm background of a pianissimo second-inversion B♭ major chord sustained by the trombones and trumpets, as well as woodwind.

In the evenings they read Gobineau's *Nouvelles Asiatiques* and *La Renaissance* together, which gave them great pleasure. Her husband thought it admirable in the latter, Cosima wrote to the count, that he showed the epoch ending with the last evening in the life of its greatest artist, who, while incapable of preventing the decline of the age, was yet seen in the light of his own immortality. 'And how well you have succeeded in representing his temperament!' she added; 'I think one has to have lived with a genius to be able to appreciate the truth of the scene in which you introduce Michelangelo!'

Wagner was even more enraptured with the *Nouvelles Asiatiques*, which Cosima gave him for Christmas. 'That I had to make the acquaintance of this unique, original writer so late! I am consuming the *Nouvelles* slowly, so as to savour them.' In his view that he was discovering completely new delights in the French language, he was far ahead of the writer's compatriots. It was half a century before Jean Prévost called Stendhal and Gobineau 'the two greatest prose writers of the nineteenth century' and Roger Nimier declared: 'Should we put Gobineau and Stendhal on the same footing? Undoubtedly! Indeed, I regard the former as superior, because he is inimitable.'[22]

Otherwise they had the usual miscellany of worries and nuisances to cope with. One source of trouble was Wagner's relationship with his agents, Voltz & Batz of Mainz. When a new copyright law came into force in 1871 this pair recognized it as a sign of the times and offered Wagner their services in negotiating with theatres and collecting his fees – for a consideration of 25 per cent. They relieved him of an immense burden of business correspondence, but on the other hand they involved him in embarrassing difficulties by overstepping their responsibilities. Franz Schott had seen through them at once and refused to countenance their high-handed behaviour. By now Wagner too was ready to dissolve his arrangement with them but since they demanded 100,000 marks by way of settlement, he had no alternative but to contest each one of their officious actions on his behalf as it came up, a constant source of irritation. 'For one last time I want to try to bring home to you the explanation that you apparently need concerning me and my relationship to yourselves. I will keep it short and say no more than this: after a lifetime of experience, I have reached my sixty-ninth year and wish to be treated accordingly. There is no question of "business obligations" or anything of that sort between us; your only obligation is to account, and render an account, for your services, and otherwise to wait until I ask you for them again.' (23 September 1881)[23]

Meanwhile it seemed as though Angelo Neumann's efforts to get the *Ring* produced in Berlin were to be crowned with success after years of haggling. On 28 November 1880 Wagner granted him 'the exclusive performance rights . . . at one of the Berlin theatres in the summer or spring of the coming year, 1881,' which gave him a free hand to negotiate with the Viktoria-Theater and the Royal Opera. After considerable hesitation, Hülsen agreed to have the production in his theatre, under the direction of Neumann and Seidl, 'if', as he telegraphed to Wagner, 'rights for *Walküre* are made available to me afterwards'. Neumann forecast that the message would not even raise a reply, and on Hülsen's commenting that it would be rather rude, Neumann asked him if he thought Wagner would feel flattered by the implication that *Rheingold, Siegfried* and *Götterdämmerung* were worthless. Neumann was right; on 7 December the intendant told him: 'The old rascal really has not answered.' The upshot was that Neumann came to an arrangement with the Viktoria-Theater, which had been his original intention.

At the same time he was negotiating with London. 'Rather tempestuous! But I am not disinclined . . .' Wagner replied to his request for approval. That was enough to encourage the impresario to hatch even more ambitious plans. 'To be the herald, abroad and beyond the oceans, of that new musical world your genius has revealed to us all – that sublime mission stirs me to such a degree that I have abandoned all other plans for the future.' (8 January 1881) 'I have no objections to make to all your plans and suggestions,' Wagner answered, 'as I see very well that you are the right man for the business.' (10 January) So was born the idea of a 'travelling Wagnerian theatre'.

In view of the anti-Semitism that was particularly rife in Berlin in those days, George Davidsohn of the *Berliner Börsencourier*, one of the few pro-Wagner journalists, wrote to Neumann to point out the serious threat it would be to the success of the Berlin *Ring* if the idea got about that Wagner had any part in the controversy. Neumann relayed this warning to Cosima and a few days later had the following reply from Wagner: 'Dear friend and patron! I have no connection with the present "anti-Semitic" movement: an essay by me in the forthcoming issue of *Bayreuther Blätter* will testify to this in a way that ought to make it impossible, even, for *people of intelligence* to connect me with that movement.' (23 February)[24] 'We will try to spread the assurance you ask for,' Cosima added, 'but it is all the more difficult because my husband has taken no part in the controversy.' Wagner's desire to dissociate himself from the matter was not, in any event, influenced by fears for his success in Berlin, as emerges from his advice to Neumann, in the same letter, to abandon Berlin altogether: 'It would be the last straw if your – our – enterprise got off on completely the wrong foot as a result of idiocies of the kind that are flourishing in Berlin at the moment.' But Neumann was neither willing nor able to follow that advice.

A year before, indeed, Wagner had refused to sign the mass petition 'against the growing influence of the Jews' which Bernhard Förster, later the husband of Elisabeth Nietzsche, organized for presentation to Bismarck.

After finishing the score of the first act of *Parsifal* on 25 April, Wagner set off with Cosima on 29 April for Berlin, to attend the rehearsals and the first cycle. 'We are here, my heart, when can you come?' Cosima wrote the following morning to Daniela, who had been staying with Countess Schleinitz in the Home Office for some time. 'Frau Wesendonk has just sent this basket of flowers – but they suit you and Mimi better than me, so I am sending them to you.' But she was shocked when she saw her daughter the next day: 'I suffered for you yesterday, for I saw how you trembled, how your speech, your movements, everything had changed.' It so happened that there had been a Liszt festival in Berlin only a few days before, including a concert conducted by Bülow, at which Liszt had presented Daniela to her father, who had not seen her for twelve years. 'Once more, madame,' Bülow wrote to Cosima, 'I thank you on my knees. What an adorable child! What a soul you have formed! I can only weep when I think of it, and I think of it incessantly. This 27 April brought me a revelation. Je remercie la Providence de m'avoir gardé cette indicible joie.' (28 April) But the meeting had aroused a fearful conflict in the heart of his daughter, who was accustomed to regard Wagner's house as her home; Liszt, who had witnessed it, evaded the embarrassment, in the circumstances, of seeing Cosima and Wagner, by leaving Berlin before they got there, but this was enough in itself to draw public attention to a purely family event.

Although the production was not all that Wagner might have desired, and although the Siegfried had not fully recovered from a recent illness, the first cycle was a brilliant success. 'Richard and I, we are – in spite of all the failings in the performance – very moved by it,' Cosima wrote in her diary. 'At Brünnhilde's closing words we were propped up against each other, my head on his arm, and

Richard exclaimed "the things we go through together". He went on to the stage and made a speech.'

Waiting for them in Wahnfried, they found Count Gobineau, who had been made thoroughly at home under the 'petit gouvernement' of Blandine. Animated conversations on every topic under the sun during the next fortnight revealed that happy mixture of agreement and dissent which is the foundation of a creative friendship. Wagner, who had just got to know Gobineau's *Essai sur l'inégalité des races humaines*, read him a section from his chapter on the Germanic races and then played the prelude to *Parsifal*. It was a symbolic act, an attempt to express his desire to override the severity of Gobineau's ideas on race by the spirit of Christianity. This idea was the basis of his last essay, *Heroism and Christianity*: that a true equality needed to be based on what could be gained from a general moral consensus, such as true Christianity was ideally suited to develop. (*Heldentum und Christentum*, RWGS, X, pp. 275ff.)

On 25 May Wagner, Cosima, Gobineau, Zhukovsky and the children set off together for Berlin again, to attend the fourth cycle. 'C'est sublime!' Gobineau wrote to Comtesse La Tour. 'C'est un chef d'oeuvre extraordinaire! C'est le comble de la gloire et du triomphe pour Wagner!'

At the end of *Götterdämmerung*, which was attended by the emperor and his entourage, Neumann had decided to surprise Wagner with a special tribute. When the composer, looking unusually pale, arrived on the stage to thank the artists, Neumann had the curtain raised and began a well-prepared speech, expressing his thanks 'to the gracious members of the imperial family, the art-loving audience and those who represent their views in public'. At these words Wagner turned and left the stage, so that Neumann had to direct his thanks to him into the wings. It was not only the press that interpreted this as an affront to the imperial family: Neumann too would not believe Wagner when he said he had been on the verge of a heart attack. 'It was not until two years later,' he wrote in his memoirs, 'when the news reached us from Venice that the Meister had died of heart failure, that I realized the tragic truth of his words.'[25]

'My husband began scoring the second act today,' Cosima wrote to Judith on 6 June, 'and we're already at work on the sets and costumes.' But the peace that allowed them to work was soon disturbed again. Levi arrived at Wahnfried on 26 June to discuss *Parsifal* with Wagner. As he returned from a walk on the morning of 28 June Wagner received him with a joke about his unpunctuality. 'Well – now let's go and eat,' he went on in a friendly tone, 'but, no, first of all, go and read the letter I've left on your table.' Levi went to his room and found there an anonymous letter from Munich, casting the vilest aspersions on his character and his relations with Wahnfried, and imploring Wagner to keep his work pure and not allow it to be conducted by a Jew. (GLRW, VI, pp. 500ff.)

At table Levi asked Wagner why he had not simply thrown the letter on the fire, to which Wagner replied: 'I'll tell you why: if I hadn't shown the letter to anyone, had just destroyed it, then perhaps something of its contents would have stayed with me, but as it is I can assure you that now I shall not retain the slightest recollection of it.' After the meal Levi packed his bags and went off to Bamberg without saying goodbye, and then sent Wagner a long letter asking to be relieved of the duty of conducting *Parsifal*.

'Friend, you are requested most earnestly to come back to us quickly,' Wagner telegraphed; 'that is the main thing if we are to get the matter straight.' Levi only reiterated his request to be released, so Wagner wrote him the following letter, which succeeded in bringing him back.

> Dear, best friend! I have the greatest respect for your feelings, but you do not make anything easy for yourself or for us. It is precisely your proneness to gloomy introspection that might make our relationship with you a little oppressive! We are quite agreed on telling the whole world this sh—, and your part will be not to run away, leaving people to draw completely nonsensical conclusions. For God's sake, turn round at once and get to know us properly at long last. Do not lose any of your faith, but gain the courage to go on with it!
>
> Perhaps – it will be a turning point in your life – but in any event – you are my conductor for *Parsifal*! (1 July)

So far I have followed Glasenapp's account of the events leading up to this letter, but it lacks one important factor, which we learn from a letter that Julius Kniese, who was later influential in developing the Bayreuth style, wrote his wife on 17 July 1883: the anonymous letter also contained the assertion 'that Frau Wagner was more than kind to Herr Levi, and her relationship with him was perhaps an intimate one'.[26] This is confirmed by Cosima herself, who wrote to Daniela that the day of 28 June had brought 'all manner of unpleasantness . . . namely an anonymous letter to Papa, making such scandalous accusations against poor Levi (and in association with me!) that he completely lost his head and left without warning'. (1 July) It is this element that fully explains both Wagner's attitude and Levi's sensitivity to the charges.[27]

Wagner had never been shy of talking to Levi about his Jewishness. The spirit of their conversations can be deduced from this entry in Cosima's diary: 'When our friend Levi told us his father was a rabbi, the talk came round to the Israelites again, and we discussed the idea that they had impinged on our culture at too early a stage, and that the element of general humanity that should have developed out of the German character, to the benefit of the Jewish character as well, was hindered in its evolution by their premature encroachment on our culture.' (13 January 1879) A short time before that conversation Wagner had said to her that if he ever wrote about the Jews again he would say there was no objection to be made against them, only they had come to the Germans too early, when they (the Germans) were not firmly rooted enough to absorb that element. (BBL 1937, pp. 106, 59)

Levi was far from resenting this frankness, though Newman supposed he must have done. The publication of a letter to his father, who was chief rabbi in Giessen, shows as much:

> You write: 'If only I could really like Wagner' – But of course you can, and you should! He is the best and noblest of men. Of course the rest of the world misunderstands him and slanders him . . . Goethe fared no better. But one day posterity will recognize that Wagner was as great a man as he was artist, which those close to him know already. Even his fight against what he calls 'Jewry' in music and modern literature springs from the noblest motives, and that he's not just narrow-mindedly anti-Semitic . . . is shown by his attitude to me and Joseph Rubinstein and by the cʟ friendship he used to have with Tausig, whom he loved dearly. The most wonderful thing I have experienced in

my life is the privilege of being close to such a man, and I thank God for it every day. (13 April 1882)[28]

An unpleasant task fell to Cosima immediately after the episode of Levi's departure and return. She and Wagner wished to adopt her daughters by Bülow, who were growing up with them. Apart from the fact that Bülow's itinerant life would have made it impossible for him to devote the proper attention to his daughters, he did not possess the temperament for fatherhood. But although he had now had an opportunity to see for himself how Daniela had prospered in her mother's care, he refused point-blank to consent to the adoption, so that Cosima decided she must see him and discuss the matter face to face.

They arranged to meet in Nuremberg in July; but before we come to that, there is another episode to mention which affected Bülow's relations with Bayreuth and has often been misrepresented. In view of the loss made by the 1876 festival and the financial disaster of the London concerts, Bülow made up his mind to do something for Bayreuth and at the same time to shame his fellow-countrymen. He had another, purely personal motive, as Newman points out: not having attended the festival in 1876 had deeply grieved him, and he wanted to purchase, as it were, by a generous act, the right to be present, with head held high, at the first performance of *Parsifal*. 'The day after tomorrow I am playing for Bayreuth again in Berlin,' he wrote to Klindworth on 20 January 1879; '. . . my real concern is not nearly so much with the 10,000 marks as such – which, incidentally, are taking me far more time and trouble in "shabby Germany" [in English] than I expected – as with the *moral significance* of my strumming . . . and (egoistically) with making it possible for me to be present at *Parsifal*!' (NBB, p. 60)

By 10 September 1880 he was able to tell Wolzogen that he had sent Feustel the 40,000 marks he had set himself as a target, though since his concerts had brought him only 28,000 marks he had had to make up the remaining 12,000 marks from his savings, a not inconsiderable sacrifice. If the Bayreuth school for training musicians in Wagnerian style failed to materialize, 'then it would be my wish, as you well know, that the 40,000-mark obolus should be used to erect a statue of Wagner in B.[ayreuth] – the Bismarck monument in Cologne cost exactly that'. (BB, VI, pp. 28–31)

There was only one thing Wagner could do, which was to find a tactful form whereby the money could be, in effect, given back to Bülow. According to Glasenapp he wanted it to be diverted to Bülow's daughters instead, though the festival management committee were reluctant to lose it. (GLRW, VI, pp. 439ff.) This version of the story is confirmed by Cosima's letter to Daniela of 16 March 1881: 'Your Papa [Wagner] is sending the fund of 40,000 marks back to him [Bülow] with the request to invest it for you [the girls], as I have given my inheritance from my mother to the [festival] theatre. Papa further wishes to adopt you all.'

Newman is probably right when he comments that this 'palpable snub' must have played a part in strengthening Bülow's determination not to agree to the adoption.[29]

Cosima's diary contains an account of the meeting in Nuremberg:

> Hans with me from 4 to 6.30, try to subdue his violent surges of emotion and overcome his injustice towards Daniela. Impossible task! He asks me to stay until tomorrow morning, as he has not put the proposal he wanted to in the manner he wished. I agree. [The next day:] Second interview. Hans tells me he doesn't know whether white is black or black white. He no longer has a guiding star, he starts to twitch nervously. We take our leave! . . . After this meeting I return home as if a new life were beginning for me, I am without comfort and yet at peace, made happy only by his [Wagner's] happiness and deep in my heart the consciousness of an inexpiable guilt. God help me to enjoy the one and never to forget the other! (DMCW, I, pp. 944f.)

The next event in their lives was of a more agreeable kind. Wagner was working hard every morning and afternoon, and told Cosima on 28 September that he had reached Parsifal's words in the second act: 'Ja! Diese Stimme! So rief sie ihm . . .', with an accompaniment featuring alternating figures for solo violin and clarinet. The next day Judith Gautier and Benedictus, who had been opera-going in Munich, arrived in Bayreuth. Judith's heart beat fast as she mounted the steps of Wahnfried: it was to be her first meeting for five years with the 'terrible, gentle master', as she had addressed him in a sonnet she had written for his sixty-sixth birthday:

> Maître terrible et doux! laisse, de l'humble apôtre,
> l'amour fervent monter vers toi comme un encens.

She found him unchanged or, rather, rejuvenated. 'He received us with the moving sincerity that comes over him in the presence of those of his faithful friends by whom he knows himself truly loved.'

He took her into Zhukovsky's studio to see the designs for *Parsifal*. 'The magical garden created by the sorcerer Klingsor had not been easy to realize. Wagner wanted it to be completely unrealistic, a dream, a vision, a fantastic flowering brought into being by a stroke of a wand, not by earthly increase. Nothing that they tried satisfied him . . . The costumes were no less difficult, because the Meister was not content with approximations: the enchantresses, who are flowers to the extent that sirens are fishes, caused the most trouble. Wagner wanted not seductive young women but flowers with souls – des fleurs animées.'

'He told us about his stay in Naples and Venice, of the joy Italy had given him, and we sensed his homesickness for the sun, his longing for other horizons.'[30]

She left him with the promise to return the next year for *Parsifal*.

His longing for other horizons was not merely the desire for sunshine and health, it was a new stage in his idea of emigrating: 'To go away like Lykurgos and see what they make of my affairs!' But then he would stand by the tall French windows in the drawing room of Wahnfried, look out at the trees tossing in the autumn wind and wonder if he had the right to uproot the children so entirely from their native soil. He had expressed something of his doubt and uncertainty in a birthday poem to King Ludwig that year:

> Wie birgt in Nebeldunst und Dämmergrauen
> vor mir doch immer dichter sich die Welt?

('How obscure the world grows, concealing itself from me in mist and eerie twilight.')

In this dilemma the idea increasingly took the shape of a consoling vision of the future: 'In the expectation of the bad times which will inevitably come, we ought to raise a thousand million by subscription, with which to pay off everything and found a new society over there, but until that time comes we should work to establish the religious basis of this society.' There is something in his visions of the 'wild lyricism' that always appealed so strongly to him in *Wilhelm Meisters Wanderjahre*:

> Bleibe nicht am Boden heften,
> Frisch gewagt und frisch hinaus . . .

('Don't remain rooted to the spot, up and out!')

While his imagination was working, Cosima had to look for the land of his fantasies on the great schoolroom globe. Zhukovsky captured the significance of the scene in a symbolic drawing: the globe becomes the planet earth, carried by an elephant and a tortoise, the symbols of wisdom and patience. To the left there are a ruined castle, a broken pillar and an antique torso – emblems of the Old World; to the right a ship with sails set, ready to cast off from the quay and sail for the New World. At the top of the drawing there is the motto 'One wingbeat, and aeons lie behind us.'

His own doctor had sent to Erlangen for a specialist in internal ailments, who told Wagner that his organs were perfectly healthy and that he needed only a strict diet and fresh air. That year he set off for the south as early as 1 November. 'Sun! Sun!' he exclaimed in a letter to King Ludwig. 'On the one day that we spent in Naples our eyes could hardly endure the sea of light that flooded over everything! We made a night crossing, staying on deck in glorious moonlight, and in the morning reached Palermo: sun and warmth; everywhere we looked, gardens and groves of orange trees laden with fruit! . . . Oh! My king! And where are *we* living? We've settled ourselves so comfortably – between two gardens of palm trees! [in the Hôtel des Palmes] – that I look forward with complete confidence to full recovery.' (22 November)

He started to score the third act of *Parsifal* immediately after their arrival, and since Rubinstein was staying in the same place he was able to pass each page virtually into his hands for him to prepare the vocal score. He enjoyed pointing out the finer points of the orchestration, for instance the way the first violins cease playing and are replaced imperceptibly by the second. 'For Parsifal's entry I have horns *and* trumpets; horns alone seemed to me too soft, not ceremonial enough; trumpets alone too tinny, too clattery – in such a case one must *invent* something; and on top of that I want it played well.' He thought everyone would marvel at *Parsifal*: especially at the praying to the spear. That was the crux: it would be impossible to express what was happening at that moment with words; it was beyond the scope of concepts or of any other means, nor was any proper impression of it to be gained at the piano: 'At the piano, ah, that's nothing, the instrumentation is all-important there!' (GLRW, VI, pp. 537f.)

(In this instance the strings play an expansive, wide-arching melody that swells and falls away three times; one note in the second phrase is held diminuendo through seven bars plus one beat while the horns announce Parsifal's motive.)

What news they had from the world outside Sicily, such as the thwarting of Neumann's plans to produce *Lohengrin* in Paris by the hostility of the chauvinistic French press, oppressed his spirits and his health. He was already looking forward to the journey up the Nile that they planned to take in twelve months' time: for once he would be free of all such news for three whole months! But in the last analysis he agreed that his work was the principal cause of the recurrence of cramps in his chest, since the excessive concentration of his mind and spirit completely arrested his physical functions. He used to raise his hands to heaven and pray for 'easy pages'.

The thought of the instrumentation of the close of the work worried him: he felt he would need many more instruments than the orchestra actually possessed at the time. Just as he had had an alto oboe built as a substitute for the cor anglais, he would similarly have to augment all the wind sections, to provide him with the 'groups' he needed. Cosima could have no idea, he told her, of *how* the thought tormented him. (20 December)

He looked back over the events of the last few years: the building of the theatre, the rehearsals, the performances and the cares of the months following the festival; how he had written the text of *Parsifal* in order to save himself from despair: and now finishing the work was as difficult as anything he had ever done, because the task demanded concentration such as came only in trance.

All the same he could not help but find it remarkable that he had saved up this work, the subject of which had occupied him from a very early stage of his career and which he called his most 'reconciliatory work', to the highest maturity of his old age: 'I know what I know, and what is in it.'

He had vowed to have finished it entirely by Cosima's birthday:

'Then – predictably, my abdomen started its usual devilish games, rendering me incapable of working for several days: – Adieu, vow! The score will have to wait until the New Year.'[31] It had to wait longer still, in fact: the page including the harps, on which he consulted Rubinstein, took a very great deal out of him and he did not finish the work until 13 January 1882.[32]

The day before, a French visitor to Sicily had left a letter at the Hôtel des Palmes, asking for permission to call on the Meister, so as to give himself the pleasure of taking news of him back to Paris for, among others, M. Lascoux – one of Wagner's devoted French admirers – and Madame Judith Gautier. It was Auguste Renoir, who was touring Italy and had been begged by various mutual friends in Paris to do all he could to get a sketch, at least, of Wagner. When he called at the hotel again the next day, as Wagner was not well, he was received by Zhukovsky, who asked him whether he would not care to stay a little longer in Palermo, as the Meister was just writing the last notes of *Parsifal*, was in a state of nervous debility and no longer able to eat, and so on. Amiably, the young Russian suggested that he return the following afternoon. Renoir wrote a friend a long letter about his attempts to see Wagner, which were at last crowned with success.

> I hear muffled steps approaching across the thick carpets. It is the master in his velvet gown with wide sleeves faced with black satin. He is very handsome and kind and shakes my hand, invites me to sit down again and then we launch into the craziest conversation, interspersed with 'hi' and 'oh', half in French, half in German . . . What a lot of rubbish I must have talked! Towards the end I was burning with embarrassment, I felt quite giddy and red as a turkey cock . . .

Wagner consented to sit for Renoir the next day.

> He was very cheerful, I very nervous and sorry that I was not Ingres. In short, I believe I made good use of my time: thirty-five minutes is not long, but if I had stopped sooner it would have been very good, as my sitter lost some of his cheerfulness towards the end and became stiff. I responded to these changes too faithfully . . .

At the end Wagner wanted to see it. He said: 'Ah! Ah! I look like a Protestant minister.' Which is perfectly true. In short, I was very glad I didn't make too much of a fiasco of it. At least it's some sort of souvenir of that wonderful head.[33]

Wagner's art and personality were probably too alien to Renoir's for any more satisfactory result. One of the other Impressionist masters might have done better – or Van Gogh, who himself once compared his palette with Wagner's orchestra, saying it is only when all the colours are used intensively that the artist recovers repose and harmony. 'The process is comparable to the music of Wagner, the intimacy of which is not impaired in spite of its being performed by a large orchestra.'[34]

Life in a hotel was not without its inconveniences, and early in February Wagner gratefully accepted the offer, from a Prince Gangi, of the use of a house on the Piazza dei Porazzi. One of the last melodies he ever wrote is a souvenir of the time he spent there: it was one he had originally sketched at the time when he was writing the second act of *Tristan*, on which he now improvised until he found the shape he wanted for it. Eva Chamberlain gave the autograph fair copy of it to Arturo Toscanini in 1931, after he had conducted his first *Parsifal* in Bayreuth, and it then came to be referred to as the 'Porazzi theme'.[35]

Like Goethe before him, Wagner discovered that the image of Italy impressed upon his soul became complete only when he came to know Sicily. But while Goethe grumbled at his 'incompetent' guide for spoiling his enjoyment of the scenery by his parade of historical learning – the imagination ought not to be startled out of its peaceful dreaming by such nocturnal alarums – it was precisely the great historical figures and reminiscences that stirred Wagner, from the Greeks to the Normans and Hohenstaufens, right up to the dying Garibaldi, whose passage through Acireale he witnessed.

Stopping in Venice on their way home in the middle of April, Wagner learned by chance the address of his former friend Karl Ritter, whom he had not seen since the year of *Tristan*. A woman with a baby in her arms opened the door to him: Herr Ritter was not at home. When Wagner objected strenuously that he was sure Ritter *was* at home, she ventured in some embarrassment that he must be Herr Wagner. 'Yes, yes!' he replied and asked for a piece of paper, on which he wrote, 'What sort of a person are you?' It was yet another experience of friendship to add to his store.

He got back to Bayreuth on 1 May. Gobineau arrived shortly afterwards for quite a long stay. They had a number of lively conversations about religion, in which the only thing they could not agree on was the relative merits of Catholicism and Protestantism: in spite of his Germanophilia the count remained a faithful son of Rome. All the same, when Wagner offered him a glass of beer, referring to the invigorating effect that 'Einbecker', from the famous breweries in Lower Saxony, had on Luther, Gobineau was happy to accept. But he was visibly very tired, as Cosima recalled in her memoir of him,[36] and it was with great concern that she saw him leave for Gastein, whither he had been sent by his doctors. Wagner gave him as leaving present an expensive first edition of *Faust*.

He finished one of his most important articles on the day Gobineau left, the *Open Letter to Herr Friedrich Schön of Worms*, in which he called for the setting-up of a grant-awarding foundation. Forced by experience to open his festival theatre to audiences that would pay generously for it, he foresaw that in future, 'though no camel will go through a needle's eye and no rich man will enter the kingdom of heaven, we shall have to admit only the rich as a rule to our theatre'. There was an urgent need for a new foundation 'to create the means to allow completely free access, and even providing travel and accommodation costs where necessary, to those who, in their want, share the lot of the greater number and often the most deserving of Germany's sons'. (RWGS, X, pp. 291ff.)

Just how seriously Wagner persisted in regarding his artistic mission, in spite of all the disappointments he had suffered, emerged in a conversation he had about that time with Schemann and Wolzogen. The sound of a military band, carrying over to Wahnfried from the nearby barracks of a light cavalry regiment, elicited from him a complaint about the 'whores' dances' the military marched to nowadays. Music was dragged in the mud in order to amuse the crowd, and some charity concerts and conservatory galas were not much better. 'I renounce everything that is purveyed as music nowadays: I am no musician; I renounce music for music's good!' As he went on talking, the words 'I am no musician' recurred like a refrain; the art, as he understood it, could be saved only if it were guarded like the most precious of treasures, locked up in a shrine. And there and then he vowed with a passionate intensity to do what he could to that end.[37]

When Wagner spoke, at moments such as this, of 'the art, as he understood it', he was never referring primarily to his own works; he was exhilarated, he said, by the thought that one's forebears always remained one's criterion of what was highest: it was always the works of others that came into his mind, never his own. (GLRW, VI, pp. 604f.)

In the meantime, thanks to Levi[38] and his assistant Franz Fischer and the chorus master and 'flower-father' Heinrich Porges, the preliminary rehearsals had made good progress: though after a rehearsal of the great scene between Parsifal (Hermann Winkelmann) and Kundry (Amalie Materna), Wagner said privately that it would probably never be performed as he had heard it in his imagination. The performers had simply no conception of all that was inherent in the scene and their roles. And *how* Schröder-Devrient would have delivered the line 'So war es mein Kuß, der welthellsichtig dich machte'!

He had suffered a heavy loss, at the end of 1881, with the sudden death of the resourceful machinist, Karl Brandt. 'To think that this deeply devoted man – for he was that to me – had to die!' His place was taken by his son Fritz, who now had to answer for the fact that the transformation in the first act now took too long. Placidly he asked for so many minutes' more music, as the machine could not run any faster. Wagner's patience was near breaking-point, and Humperdinck volunteered to save the situation. 'I ran home, quickly sketched some transitional bars [to lead into a repeat], orchestrated them and dovetailed them into the score. Then I showed the Meister the manuscript, torn between hope and fear. He looked through the pages, then nodded amiably and said: 'Well, why not? That will do all right.'

Adolphe Appia was to describe the transformations in *Parsifal*, carried out in full view of the audience, as an attempt by Wagner to overcome the limitations of realism by realistic means. But whether the designer works with perspective and movable sets or with what Appia himself called 'active light', the essential factor is that what is seen must correspond to what is heard: the harmonic progressions of the transformation music in the first act clearly prescribe movement in a specific direction, for which fade-out, however visionary, can never be a substitute.

On the rest-day following the dress rehearsal on 24 July a banquet took place in the theatre restaurant. The guests sat at a long, festively decked table. Richard Wagner sat in the middle of one side, talking vivaciously to a young woman who answered him in melodious French, punctuated with peals of laughter. In contrast to the evening dress of the other women she wore a linen blouse *à la matelote*, with a brilliant red cravat round her neck. Word passed that it was the daughter of a French poet called Théophile Gautier. Franz Liszt and Cosima sat across the table from them. After Bürgermeister Muncker had made a speech Wagner leapt to his feet, commanded silence by striking his glass twice and began to speak. He reminded them of the misunderstanding that had arisen from the speech he had made at the end of the previous festival and of the general and inexpungible uncomprehension of his purpose that had resulted from it. 'Now': as he spoke the word his voice broke and he stopped; then he said 'now' again, this time in a whisper, and then again very quietly, unable to control his voice: 'Now I have learned to be silent.'[39]

The murmur of excitement that ran round the room slowly died away, then someone proposed a toast to Liszt. Hardly had his name been spoken than Liszt jumped up and moved quickly along the back of the line of seats, stooping as though he wanted to remain unobserved, until he reached the back of his great friend's chair, where he stopped. Knowing Liszt's reluctance to speak in public, Wagner stood up and thanked the company in his name. Then in simple, sincere words that touched the heart he recalled all that Liszt had done for him. 'To be blunt with you I was a bloke without a hope, and then Liszt came and showed a deep understanding of me and my work that sprang from within himself. He helped my work to become known, he gave me his support, he did more to help me rise than anyone else. He has been the link between the world that lived in me and the other world outside.'[40]

As tongues began gradually to wag more and more noisily, Wagner asked a third time for silence. His brief final words, bubbling over with exuberance, reminded Chamberlain irresistibly of Beethoven: it was like the last movement, or rather the coda of the last movement, of some of his string quartets. 'Children!' Wagner cried emphatically, 'Children, tomorrow is the day we've all been waiting for! Tomorrow the devil's abroad! So make sure, all of you who are taking part, that the devil gets into you, and all of you who are here to listen, that you receive him aright!'[41]

The first two performances, on 26 and 28 July, were reserved for Patrons, and the general public were admitted to the other fourteen. At the first performance the applause that broke out at the end of the first act, and even more at the end of the second, seemed unending. Wagner stepped forward to the front of his box and asked the audience not to insist further on the singers' taking a bow. This was interpreted by some members of the audience as meaning that he did not want to hear any applause, and when it broke out at the end of the third act they attempted to shush it. Once again Wagner stood up and assured them that he had not meant to stop them applauding, only that they should not expect the singers to come out before the curtain to take their customary bows, and with that he gave the signal to renew clapping himself. This was the origin of a tradition that is still observed: silence in the auditorium after the first act, applause after the second and third, while the curtains part to show the final tableau again.

The second performance, the last ever given for the patrons alone, closed a chapter in the history of the festival. At the end the curtains parted and the audience saw Wagner on the stage surrounded by the entire company: the members of that day's cast in their costumes and the two other casts in their everyday clothes, as well as the musical staff, the technicians and stage hands and the machinists in their blue overalls. Wagner stood in the middle with his back to the audience, wearing a black frock coat and a light-coloured overcoat and with his top hat in his hand. Those in the auditorium caught only a few words of his speech of thanks to everyone on the stage, according to Chamberlain. But then he turned round and walked to the edge of the stage and peered down into the orchestra pit: 'You too, my dear minstrels', at which his voice sounded particularly affectionate, even tender. Then he stepped back a few paces, drew himself up and, with a brief flourish of his hat, said in a somewhat harsh tone of voice: 'And with this, meine Herren Patrone, I take leave of you.' The way he pronounced the word 'leave' [Abschied] forcibly reminded some hearers of Gurnemanz's dismissal of Parsifal. According to another eye-witness a trace of proud contempt played on his lips.[42]

It would be impossible to list the names of all the friends who flocked from near and far. But three were absent.

Nietzsche had written to his sister on 30 January that he was very glad to hear she was going to Bayreuth. 'But I – forgive me! – am certainly not going, unless Wagner himself personally invites me and treats me as the most honoured of his guests.' As Newman says, Wagner could have seen no reason why he should humble himself to that extent. He had indeed rid himself of all sentimental feelings towards Nietzsche by then. Lou von Salomé recalls an attempt that was made during the festival to mention Nietzsche's name in Wahnfried, in the hope of bringing about a reconciliation: Wagner left the room in great agitation and forbade the name to be spoken in his hearing ever again.

In contrast to that, we have Elisabeth Nietzsche's tale of how, when she was at Bayreuth for *Parsifal* in 1882, Wagner asked to see her privately. 'We talked about *Parsifal* at first, but as I was leaving Wagner said softly: "Tell your brother, since *he* went from me, I have been quite alone." ' It is a touching story that both Newman and the present author nevertheless ventured to doubt, and the truth emerged as even worse than we suspected. Professor Podach drew my attention to a publication of his, dated 1937, which Newman and I both overlooked, and which establishes that Elisabeth Nietzsche did not exchange a single word with Wagner in the summer of 1882. After his death on 13 February 1883 she wrote to Frau Overbeck on 15 April, from Rome, where she was staying with Malwida:

'How it still grieves me that last summer I did not have the courage to meet Wagner. Malwida reiterates that Wagner positively lamented last summer that he did not see me at all . . . And now I have deprived myself of that last pleasure by my own timidity.'[43]

There could be no more illuminating example of what we are up against when we consider the Nietzsche–Wagner legend.

Bülow, too, who had been one of the first generation of Wagner's disciples, was absent. It is not hard for us to imagine the emotional struggle it cost him. But Adelheid von Schorn, the friend of both Stein and Zhukovsky, received a printed communication from him in Bayreuth during the festival:

Marie Schanzer, member of the Ducal Theatre Company, and
Hans von Bülow, intendant of the Ducal Orchestra,
have the honour to notify you herewith of their marriage,
Meiningen, 29 July 1882.

Bülow also added a handwritten note on the card: 'With a request for your silent commiseration for the sacrifice.'[44]

To Wagner's great distress King Ludwig, too, stayed away: he wrote that he had not felt well for some time and the pure air of the mountains was doing him good. 'And now, to conclude, the *heartfelt request*: let me remain dear to you.' (17 July)

Wagner replied in verse:

> Verschmähtest Du des Grales Labe,
> sie war mein alles dir zur Gabe,
> sei nun der Arme nicht verachtet,
> der dir nur gönnen, nicht geben mehr kann.

('Though you have refused the Grail's consolation, it was all I had to give you; do not now despise the poor man who can only wish you well, having nothing more to give you.' 25 August.)

During the last performance on 29 August Wagner took the baton from Levi's hand during the transformation in the last act and conducted the work to the end. 'I stayed at his side because I was afraid that he might make a mistake,' Levi wrote to his father, 'but my fears were groundless – he conducted with as much assurance as if he had been nothing but a kapellmeister all his life.' He conducted the solemn passages with an impressive breadth, and Amfortas's scene surpassed in power anything that had yet been heard. When the cheering and applauding showed no sign of abating after the reappearance of the final tableau, Levi shouted for silence, whereupon Wagner, still at the conductor's desk, spoke some warm words of farewell to the orchestra and the people on the stage: 'You have done everything perfectly, the greatest perfection of dramatic art above, a continual symphony below.' He concluded with the invitation to return the following year, which met with a thunderous 'Yes!'

# 32

La lugubre gondola

'Dramatic perfection above, a continual symphony below' – it has the ring of an affirmation of the artistic ideal that had been Wagner's guiding star since his teens, when he saw Schröder-Devrient as Leonora and first read the score of the Choral Symphony. At the end of Chapter 4 I wrote that the whole story of Wagner's artistic endeavours, as theorist and practitioner, was his struggle to synthesize dramatic and symphonic music in symphonic drama; we can now add that the synthesis, the union, is most completely perfected in *Parsifal*. There is even the temptation to say 'most effortlessly', except that we know how hard he found it at the last: but there is no trace of the effort in the finished work.

The 'festival drama of dedication' is a work of old age: not only in the sense of artistic perfection, not only in its inclusion of individual musical and poetic traits that run through his work from *Die Feen* onwards, but above and beyond that in the mysterious way in which it sums up the world's great currents of feeling (philosophies would be already too rationalistic a term) that had moved his heart: echoes of Indian and Greek, Christian and non-Christian ideas are all to be found in it, without any one of them singly dominating the others.

But if the expression 'a work of old age' is taken to imply one in which the creator's powers manifestly slacken their spiritual tension, then *Parsifal* is nothing of the kind. On the contrary, Thomas Mann is absolutely right when he calls it 'the most extreme of his works . . . with a capacity for accommodating the psychological to the stylistic and vice versa that surpasses at the close even Wagner's own usual standards'.[1]

Some perception that this work represents the artistic fulfilment

585

of all that he had struggled for throughout a long life, the sublimation of his completely personal style, struck his contemporaries; even criticism was more moderate and restrained in its expression. People recognized first and foremost that this 'work of farewell to the world' owed its conception to Wagner's recoil, in his own words, from 'this world of murder and robbery, organized and legalized by lies, deceit and hypocrisy'. 'That, in truth, is the meaning and the magic of this last work of the old artist who had seen so much, suffered so much, in his pilgrimage through life . . . We feel in the presence of it as we do in that of the only other music that inhabits the same sphere – the last quartets of Beethoven: the men who can dream such music must have made up their account with time and are ripe for eternity.' (NLRW, IV, p. 705)

It was not a day too soon when Wagner set off for Venice on 14 September. His heart attacks had worsened to an alarming degree as a consequence of the exertions of the last few months, sustained under incessantly grey skies. But on this occasion Italy received him, as it did the first time he and Cosima went there together, with cloudbursts and floods. They set up house on the mezzanine floor of a wing of the Palazzo Vendramin, 'like a puppy in a lion's cage', Cosima joked. One of the double windows of the drawing room gave on to the Grand Canal, the others overlooked a small formal garden in the French style, and Wagner was greatly soothed by looking across the foliage, still a summery green, to the gondolas flitting past 'like elves' on the canal beyond.

'It ought to be possible to close every door behind us and hear nothing more,' he said to Cosima once when they were riding in a gondola. 'In order to endure life, we should be dead in it.' But she had to admit to herself resignedly, 'I cannot hold life at bay, and it always brings disturbances.' There was the correspondence with Bürkel about the private performances of *Parsifal* that King Ludwig wanted to have staged in the Hoftheater in Munich, which upset Wagner profoundly. (1 October) There was the equally tiresome dispute with Signora Lucca, who laid claim to *Parsifal* on the grounds of the expression 'oeuvres inédites' in the 1868 contract. It was an interpretation that the courts might well have endorsed, had things gone so far, and it was only due to the generosity of Dr Strecker that a compromise was reached that did not involve the annulment of the contract giving Schott's the sole right to *Parsifal*. The worst and most persistent disagreement was with the agents

16

Voltz & Batz, who withheld the fees for performances of *Tristan* on the grounds of their interpretation of a clause in their contract. 'Whoever thought I had earned a fortune?' Wagner exclaimed. 'Once I was no better than a beggar, glad when somebody gave me something. Now they all cling to me and suck me dry.' In no event did he intend to let himself be treated as a fool. 'This pack gives me a strong desire to sharpen my teeth.' (To Feustel, 27 November) In the end Adolf von Gross, Feustel's son-in-law, won the case against Voltz & Batz, and freed Wahnfried from the toils of their contract, but not until after Wagner's death.[2]

One of the last unwelcome provocations came with the publication of the first four books of Nietzsche's *Gay Science*. Did Wagner perhaps read the famous Aphorism 279 on 'friendship that is the will of the stars'? It has been read variously as referring to his friendship with Paul Rée, Jacob Burckhardt, Franz Overbeck or Wagner. Nietzsche himself told Lou von Salomé that it was Rée but he later associated it with Wagner: we can take it as yet another of those fine-sounding dedications that he so loved to make, capable of address to any number of different people. His sister finally gave out that Aphorism 279 was his answer to the message Wagner had allegedly given her for him in the summer of 1882, which, as Podach says, is not only one of the most brazen of her fabrications but one of the stupidest: 'It would not be to Nietzsche's credit if he had continued to pursue Wagner with hatred after receiving a cri de coeur like that.'[3]

There was a comet to be seen in the skies above Venice that autumn, as there had been in 1858, the year of *Tristan*. One clear night when there was a full moon Wagner and Cosima looked out of the window and saw it travelling across the sky between the Plough and Orion, with a fiery tail of shooting stars.

They were deeply shocked by the news of Gobineau's death, on his way through Turin, alone, on 13 October. 'Barely has one met such a man, when everything runs away like water through one's fingers,' Wagner mourned. At his suggestion Cosima wrote a memoir of Gobineau for *Bayreuther Blätter*, the *Erinnerungsbild aus Wahnfried* which, as Wagner said, only a woman could have written. Reading it the king would recognize, he wrote to Ludwig, the lot that had fallen to one of the most excellent of men. Then, alluding to himself: 'So much lies in ruins about me, all-powerful death has snatched away almost everything that once had value in my life: there is just a something in me that remains as young and vital as on the day when a prophetic vision of my life first dawned on me. "Noch losch das Licht nicht aus!" ' (18 November)

Shortly afterwards Liszt arrived to stay in the Palazzo Vendramin. Welcome though he was, he brought with him the particular unrest that was his natural element. 'As a result of his uncommonly rich and restless life, wherever he goes he is surrounded by a tide of acquaintances, who ferret him out, draw him into an incessant life of matinées, dinners and soirées, and thereby completely conceal him from our sight, since we give all that a wide berth and keep ourselves exclusively to ourselves.' (To King Ludwig, 10 January 1883)

Wagner was reading Hermann Oldenberg's recently published *Buddha* at this time. He found it fascinating and talked about it a lot, but in the end it led him to decide once and for all to abandon any idea of writing *Die Sieger*. Oldenberg tore aside the veil of legend and revealed the true face of the Buddha, cool, thoughtful and remote from all our ideas and emotions.

But Wagner's mind was accustomed to be engaged with some great project, and even now it did not rest. On 1 November he finished writing a review of the performances of *Parsifal* that summer, 'a didactic treatise, to further the development of the style I wish to promote'. (*Das Bühnenweihfestspiel in Bayreuth 1882*, RWGS, X, pp. 297ff.) Once more he rehearsed his case for avoidance of trivial operatic effects in words and music, for economy in the control of breath and use of gesture, for movement in stage action never coming completely to a standstill, for noble simplicity of sets and costumes – in short, for the opposite of all that has since been practised in performances of his works under the title of Wagnerian style. He concluded by writing about the 'beauty and intelligence' of the orchestral playing, which all who heard it must have sorely missed when they returned to the usual rough treatment of orchestral music in the world's grandest opera houses.

Heinrich von Stein left them on 15 October, in order to go to Halle and complete his formal qualifications for a university teaching career, at his father's wish. He dedicated his collection of 'dramatic pictures', bearing the title *Helden und Welt* ('Heroes and World'), to Wagner 'in love and respect'.

'There is certainly no happier advance that you could have made than this from musing philosopher to clear-sighted dramatist,'

Wagner replied in a letter, written on 31 January 1883, that was intended to serve as the book's preface, and also turned out to be his last literary utterance. 'Seeing, seeing, truly seeing: that is what is universally lacking. "Have you no eyes?" – again and again one would like to put that question to this world that only ever chatters and hearkens.' The words of Stein's Solon, which he wanted to see emphasized typographically in some way, could serve as his own testament.

> Whatever may be the true nature of the immense,
> obscure background of things, the only way by which
> we approach it is here in this poor life of ours, and even
> our transitory actions have this same earnest, profound
> and inescapable significance.[4]

For the celebration of Cosima's birthday as a 'family jubilee' he dedicated to her the C major Symphony he had written fifty years before (see vol. I, Chapter 5). He rehearsed it with the students and professors of the Liceo Benedetto Marcello and it was performed before a small audience on the evening of 24 December. He was delighted by his 'old-fashioned' early work, especially by its exclusive concern with the sublime and its lack of sentimentality. 'Young Hercules, taming the serpents', Liszt wrote to Princess Wittgenstein, while Cosima thought 'it was written by someone who has not learned to fear'.

When Wagner walked into the brilliantly lit auditorium in the Teatro La Fenice, briskly climbed the steps to the conductor's rostrum and raised his baton, it was for the last time. After the concert they went back to the Palazzo Vendramin by gondola, gliding along the Grand Canal in the quiet of Christmas Night, bathed in moonlight such as is perhaps seen only in Venice. He was silent, happy, his heart full of memories.

This re-encounter with his early symphony was not an accident. Let us recall that he felt an urge to write orchestral pieces while he was composing Götterdämmerung and Parsifal: the most high-spirited symphonic themes kept coming into his head, he complained, which he could not possibly use then. What increasingly interested him was the form in which to cast his symphonies. He thought of calling them 'symphonic dialogues'. There was no question of his tackling traditional four-movement form, but there had to be two subjects which should be allowed to converse.

'I would go back to the old [preclassical] form of the one-movement symphony with an andante middle section; people cannot write four-movement symphonies any more after Beethoven, they all seem imitative, for instance when they try to write big scherzos like his.' (1 December 1878, BBL 1937, pp. 59f.) 'Last movements are the stumbling block,' he had said more recently, referring to the Pastoral Symphony – only Beethoven could have got away with what was ventured there. 'I shall take care, I shall only write one-movement symphonies.' (17 November 1881)

His idea of symphonic dialogues was still not his last word. Now in Venice, when some beautiful melodies for a symphony came to him he said to Liszt: 'When we write symphonies, Franz, the one thing we must avoid is thematic contrast, Beethoven exhausted the possibilities of that! Instead we must take a melodic thread and spin it out to its furthest extent. *But at all costs no drama!*' (GLRW, VI, p. 752)

He was often to be heard, in these last days, playing the piano softly to himself in his room, a rhapsodic melody in the style of an English folk song that was often in his head. And when he sat down of an evening to improvise on the beautiful grand piano, an Ibach with a particularly soft tone, it was like new blossoms springing up under his fingers from the stems of one lovely melody after another. One recalls something he once said of Beethoven: 'Sometimes it was a Scottish folk tune, sometimes a Russian, or again an old French tune, in which he recognized the kind of nobility of innocence that one dreams of, and at whose feet he laid all his art in homage.'

The first few days in Venice left Wagner feeling refreshed. But there was no let-up in the attacks of cramp, though he surprised everyone by the speed with which he recovered each time and indeed by how well he looked. He had to be especially careful in the mornings: he would say that he had kept his balance well today. Only Cosima suffered from his irritability, which was exacerbated by his old jealousy of her father. 'You must be careful with me, but also considerate,' he pleaded, putting the blame on his 'bad character'.

Humperdinck, who had hastened from Paris to help rehearse the symphony, said goodbye on 3 January. 'It seemed', he wrote, 'as though the setting sun of his life cast a shimmer of transfiguration over the Meister's face, uniquely transforming everything that was astringent and stern into gentleness and kindness. "Auf Wiedersehen, dear Meister," I cried, deeply moved. He looked at me gravely and said softly: "I wish you a good journey, my dear friend." '

Liszt went too, on 13 January, his itinerant life calling him to Budapest. Only the faithful Zhukovsky remained, though he was looked for in Russia to attend his father's hundredth birthday celebrations: an inexplicable anxiety kept him in Venice. Levi arrived on 4 February for a week. He brought news of Nietzsche, who had recommended a 'young Mozart' [Peter Gast] to him, who was an absolute dud as a musician. They discussed all manner of preparations that would be needed for the festival in the coming summer. Wagner said he was thinking of producing *Tannhäuser* next in Bayreuth: a definitive production of that would be more worth while even than doing *Tristan*.

On Shrove Tuesday, 6 February, he and the children went out in the evening to mingle with the carnival crowds streaming from the Riva and the Merceria towards the bright lights of the Piazza San Marco. 'His step was elastic, youthful even, his head was high,' a friend who met them recalled; he was visibly enjoying himself among the jubilant throng. At the stroke of midnight all the countless lights went out, plunging the square into deep darkness. When he got back to the Palazzo Vendramin towards one o'clock, he slapped the old porter who was waiting up for them on the shoulder: 'Amico mio, il carnevale è andato.'

Levi, who was unwell during the last days of his stay, left on 12 February. 'The Meister went with me to the stairs, kissed me again and again – I was very moved.' (To his father, 15 February 1883)

That evening Wagner picked up Fouqué's *Undine* again, which he had started to read the day before. Cosima passed her notebook to Zhukovsky, who made a quick sketch of his face: 'R. reading. 12 Febr. 1883'. Then Wagner played the Porazzi theme and a few bars for a scherzo that he had thought of. 'Children, stay a little while yet,' he pleaded repeatedly. Around eleven o'clock, when everyone else had gone to bed, he struck up the Rhinemaidens' lament on the piano:

> Traulich und treu
> ist's nur in der Tiefe:
> falsch und feig
> ist, was dort oben sich freut!

'To think that I already knew that in those days,' he said to Cosima and then talked about the Undines of legend, water sprites longing for a human soul. 'They are dear to me, these beings of the deep, with their longings. Are you, too, one of them?' He stayed up very late, and she could hear him talking to himself, as if he was writing poetry.

'I must go carefully today,' he said when he got up the next morning, 13 February. He stayed in his study and went on with the essay on the feminine in human nature which he had started two days before. 'In the contrasting opinions held of polygamy and monogamy we encounter the point of contact of the purely human with the eternally natural . . .' (*Über das Weibliche im Menschlichen*, RWGS, XII, pp. 343ff.)

When Zhukovsky arrived as usual for lunch at about two, for the first and only time he found Cosima at the piano, playing Schubert's *Lob der Tränen* to Siegfried, her own tears falling as she did so. Wagner sent word that he did not feel altogether well, there was no need to worry but they were to start the meal without him. Cosima ventured into his study once more and came back with the news: 'My husband has his cramps and rather strongly in fact; but it was better for me to leave him alone.' The maid she left in the room next to his study heard him groan: he sat at his desk, with his cap in front of him and appeared to be waiting for the pain to pass. Suddenly he tugged at the bell: 'My wife and the doctor!' As Cosima ran to him she found him struggling violently. He collapsed in her arms exhausted. She thought he had fallen asleep, but when the doctor came there was nothing he could do but pronounce him already dead.

The sheet of paper he had been writing on lay on the desk. The last two words were 'love – tragedy', then the pen had traced a scrawl across to the edge of the paper.

During his stay at the Palazzo Vendramin, though apparently completely absorbed in the social whirl, Liszt had been strangely impressed by a funeral procession he had seen on the Grand Canal, and it is almost as though a premonition moved him to write, unknown to anyone, the two versions of *La lugubre gondola* for piano, which pushed back the frontiers of harmony. A few weeks later, on 16 February 1883, a procession of gondolas accompanied the boat bearing Richard Wagner's coffin as he set out on his last journey.[5]

The body was embalmed, taken to Bayreuth and interred in the vault in the garden of Wahnfried.

The world was stunned by the news of Wagner's death. He had ended his last letter to King Ludwig, 10 January, with the words: 'So may the circle of my existence close for today . . .' When Bürkel broke the news to him, Ludwig cried out: 'Horrible, dreadful!' Then: 'Now leave me alone.' 'May the Almighty give you the strength to bear this terrible test,' he wrote to Cosima. When Bürkel returned from the funeral in Bayreuth and reported on the attendance and the messages that had poured in from all over Germany and from abroad, he said proudly: 'I was the first to recognize the artist whom the whole world now mourns; I saved him for the world.' (SRLW, II, p. 208)

The news reached Meiningen at a moment when Bülow was just on the verge of recovery from a serious illness. It was not until the evening of the following day that his wife plucked up the courage to tell him, and then in the presence of his doctor. She had had no idea, she wrote to her mother, of the passionate love he still felt for Wagner, in spite of everything, in the very depths of his heart. 'Bülow's life has been so closely interwoven with that name that he now feels, in his own words, spoken with the greatest difficulty, as if his own spirit has died with that spirit of fire, and that only a fragment of his body still remains to wander the earth.'[6]

When he heard that Cosima was refusing all food, to the point that her own life was in danger, he sent her a telegram: 'Soeur, il faut vivre.'

Nietzsche wrote to Cosima and contrived to blend his expression of condolence with that of his admiration for her: 'You have not refused in the past to listen to my voice, too, in grave moments; and now, when the news has just reached me that you have suffered the gravest experience of all, I know of no other way to pour out my feelings but by directing them wholly to you and solely to you . . . I look upon you today, as I have always looked upon you, even from afar, as the woman my heart best honours.'

He had been very ill for several days, he wrote to Peter Gast on 19 February. 'I'm all right again now, and I even believe that Wagner's death was the most necessary relief that could have been granted me at this time.'

'Triste, triste, triste! Wagner è morto!' Verdi wrote to Giulio

Ricordi on 14 February. 'When I read the news yesterday, I may truly say I was crushed. Not a word more! – A great individual has gone from us, a name that will leave a powerful impress in the history of art.' Then, as he read his letter through, he crossed out the word 'potente' and wrote 'potentissima' in its place: 'a *most* powerful impress'.

The most universal, enduring expression of grief for Wagner's passing came from the pen of Anton Bruckner. He was working on the Adagio of his Seventh Symphony at the time, and had just come to the powerful outburst in C major when the news reached him. 'I wept, oh, how I wept!' He went on to write the coda, which he himself called 'Music in mourning for the thrice-blessed master', and in which the C♯ minor of the tubas resolves into the C♯ major of the last bars: 'Non confundar in aeternum.'

Bruckner's biographer Erich Schwebsch wrote: 'This movement was born not of Wagner's *death* but of the awe-inspiring recognition of the *immortal* in a doomed, mortal body.'[7]

# APPENDIX I

(cf. p. 444)

Joseph Rubinstein's morbid sensitivity meant that Wagner soon discovered that he had taken on a heavier responsibility than he had expected. In such circumstances, where it was often necessary to restrain the young man's suicidal tendency, he had had to exercise uncommon patience, he confessed to King Ludwig, 'and on the subject of treating the Jews humanely, I think I may claim my share of praise'.

His patience held out for more than ten years, until his own death. He may well have foreseen that Rubinstein would not have survived a separation. He did not disguise his fears from Joseph's father, who wished his son to pursue a career as a concert pianist. After yet another reiteration of this wish, Wagner sent the following letter to Kharkov on 22 January 1882.

> Honoured Sir,
> Pray permit me to write to you briefly once more about your son Joseph, in the hope of persuading you to adopt an attitude towards the young man that I believe would be beneficial.
>
> Easily though I can grasp your misgivings, as a father, at the way of life your son has adopted, which is certainly open to misinterpretation, yet in my opinion it would take only a determined effort of will to dispel once and for all not only those fears but also the anxiety they cause your son.
>
> Joseph's honourable efforts to comply with your wishes concerning the exercise of his talent to establish a position in life have been as honourable in intent as they have been rendered useless in effect by his own temperament. Without doubt one reason for this lies in certain morbid dispositions,

which, however, I believe I am right in saying, might lead to the most regrettable excess if he was obliged obstinately to persist in those efforts. In him the recognition of the essence and the value of true art has grown to a truly religious belief, rooted in his soul where it has engendered a sensitivity that amounts to a passion. If you will assure him, without opposition, of the modest means he needs for his exceptionally sober and temperate mode of life, you will support him contentedly in the service of a noble cause to which all too few are able to devote themselves freely and unconditionally. By comparison, I venture to ask again, to what nobler use could a substantial fortune, even one acquired only by hard work, be put than, at a time like this, in a case where there are special gifts to be developed and nurtured in tranquillity, to put another human being, one's own son, on a footing of true freedom. Had the King of Bavaria, for instance, not once given *me* the basis for that freedom, I should long ago have subsided in silence, for the necessity of employing my art to earn my living had made it a thing of disgust to me. I am raising my own son in such a way that – should he decide upon any kind of artistic career – he will be able, with the modest means I expect to leave him, to be of use to the world, as a free man, dependent on no one.

If particular temperamental dispositions perhaps prevent your son from attaining to the highest goals, he will nevertheless assist them in the most beneficial possible way as a free man. Not all are able to do everything!

One thing is certain, however, that forcing him to adopt a course alien to his nature will inevitably make him thoroughly unhappy.

Forgive me these utterances, honoured sir, which I have felt compelled to make for no other reason than awareness of the silent conflicts of your son, whom I have grown to value; and permit me to assure you at the same time of my greatest regard. Yours sincerely . . .

Events soon proved the accuracy of Wagner's forebodings. When, after his death, Rubinstein took up a career as a pianist again, he was unable to adapt himself to a world where what he held most sacred was degraded to a commercial undertaking. He was often much in Frau Cosima's thoughts, Du Moulin writes. (DMCW, II, pp. 42ff.) No one gave this lonely man so much encouragement as she. But how was she to offer comfort to anyone after Wagner's death, when she herself was completely without comfort? In spite of that Rubinstein continued to receive a certain life-giving elixir from Wahnfried. He wrote in reply to a letter from Daniela: 'Your letter was once again something for me to cherish and value. Believe me, I could write to you almost every day (I am such a fool), to pour out everything that whirls about in me so violently.' 'The people are so hard,' he wrote to Cosima from London. 'A creature like that. . . thinks that his conscience is clear and truly believes in the maxim "life is business" . . . I believe that maxim is false.'

So he returned to Lucerne, where he had first met Wagner, and took his own life on 22 September 1884.

His father wrote to Wahnfried,

> I see very clearly that my misfortune was incalculable; for where, as with my Joseph, there is a major imbalance of intellect and will, sooner or later – according to Schopenhauer – catastrophe will inevitably ensue. His successes, especially in Rome, while fostering his self-confidence, simultaneously increased his nervousness – a case of monstrum per excessum. The immediate cause is of no importance. 'No one can run away from his fate,' he wrote to me a few years ago. He did not run away from his. According to what they wrote from Lucerne, he went to his death with the lightest of hearts. On his way to an old mill he distributed, it is said, a considerable sum among the poor (which gave rise to the rumour that it was a count who had shot himself) and it was all over in a minute. You see . . . with what premeditation he did it . . . Proof that it was inevitable. I know, too, that it would be in vain for me to seek him on another planet; it is only here that I shall be able to find the traces of his being, which was so dear to me. It is only in memory that I can live on with him. But the heart has no ears and is inaccessible to the promptings of reason. Besides, I am already too old and weak, so I shall not have to wait very much longer for my release. Good old Plutarch, in that famous letter to Appolonius, thought that we should not give way to grief, but honour the memory of the beloved dead instead; well, I mean to do so.

Rubinstein's body was taken to Bayreuth, where he had found his spiritual home under the aegis of Wagner's music. A simple marble obelisk in the Jewish cemetery bears his name.

# APPENDIX II

(cf. p. 486)

Draft of a letter to someone in the USA (perhaps Gustav Schirmer, the New York music publisher).

The original manuscript of this draft is in the Wagner Archives; the text is published here by kind permission of Frau Winifred Wagner.

Dear Sir!
I have been racking my brains as to what more I can say of particular interest to my friends in America about an undertaking that I believe I can say I have discussed and explained perfectly adequately already in a number of writings and announcements. I prefer, therefore, to send you today my three principal essays along with other documents relevant to my plans, although most of the material is also to be found in the ninth volume of my collected writings, so that you can adapt it as you see fit for communication in detail to your fellow-countrymen. Perhaps they will then grasp my ideas faster than the princes and governments of the German Empire, whose concept of German culture remains a complete mystery to me to this day.

But the main, and perhaps the only necessary piece of advice I have to give Americans is that they should abandon from henceforth Fra Diavolo's maxim, 'Long live art, and above all lady artistes!' for if they cling to it their money is extremely unlikely to attract any but the avaricious, while it cannot possibly furnish them with any notion of what the noblest minds of Europe – and especially of Germany – are struggling, in the teeth of an utterly degenerate culture, to give life to.

The presence of Americans at next year's festival is greatly to be desired, and you will see that I have taken that into consideration in the choice of dates in the second half of August, having taken to heart your request that the performances should be so late.

I must ask you then to be content with these brief remarks for today; permit me to hope that what I am sending will be of use to you in carrying out your good intentions!

Respectfully,

yours most sincerely,

Richard Wagner

Bayreuth, 8 September 1875

# APPENDIX III

(cf. p. 538)

Three letters in the Wagner Archives in Bayreuth, addressed to Cosima Wagner by Friedrich Nietzsche when deranged. (First published by kind permission of Frau Winifred Wagner in Westernhagen, *Wagner* (1956), with facsimiles.)

The dots ( . . . ) do not signify omissions, but are as found in the originals.

(1)

*Address:* Madame Cosima feu Wagner / Bayreuth / Allemagne
*Postmark:* Torino / Ferrovia / 3.1.89

They tell me that a certain divine Hanswurst has of late completed the dithyrambs of Dionysus . . .

(2)

*Address:* Frau Cosima Wagner / Bayreuth / Germania
*Postmark:* Torino / Ferrovia /3.1.89

To the Princess Ariadne, my beloved.

The belief that I am a man is prejudice. But I have often lived among men and I know everything that men can experience, from the lowest to the highest. I was Buddha among the Indians, Dionysus among the Greeks; Alexander and Caesar are my incarnations, likewise Lord Bakon who wrote Shakespeare. Of late I was Voltaire and Napoleon, and perhaps Richard Wagner too . . . But this time I come as the conquering Dionysus, who will make of the earth a festival . . . Not that I have much time . . . The heavens rejoice at my existence . . . I also hung on the cross . . .

600

(3)

*Address:* Frau Cosima Wagner / in / Bayreuth / Germania
*Postmark:* Torino / Ferrovia / 3.1.89
*You* shall publish this breve to mankind [misspelt] from
Bayreuth, with the title:

*The joyful tidings.*

# APPENDIX IV

(cf. pp. 551–3)

From Dr Newell Sill Jenkins, *Reminiscences*, by courtesy of Professor Klaus Liepmann.

He [Wagner] was unwilling to speak English, of which he had only a literary knowledge, and was accustomed to say: 'I speak English, but only in the dialect of North Wales.' One day he asked me the origin of my name, saying that it should have a meaning, as German names generally did. Then I told him there was once a great king in Wales, of whom the English 'King Cole' was but a degenerate copy. This king, whose name was Jen, was a model of all a monarch should be, pious, learned, just, generous and, above all, jovial. In his court were assembled all the great artists of his time and they were more honoured than princes. His happy subjects basked in the light of his jolly countenance and lived so happily under his gentle and prosperous reign, that, when at last he died childless, they decided that no successor should bear that beloved name. Only when later a man appeared who in his person and character reminded them of their lamented monarch, they called him 'of the kin of Jen', and so originated the name Jen-kins.

The next morning he gave me a copy of the 'Ring' [in Alfred Forman's translation], which the author had sent to the *Meister* and with which we had all amused ourselves the previous evening. It bore . . . written in Wagner's hand [and in his own English], the following inscription: 'Translated in the dialect of North Wales, in the time of King Jen, forefather of my noble friend, Jenkins.'

Among other 'mementoes of the great *Meister*' Jenkins also had

> Joseph Rubinstein's arrangement for the piano of the great
> Festive March composed by Wagner for the opening of the
> celebration in America of the hundredth anniversary of the
> United States' Declaration of Independence. The flyleaf of the
> book bears these words [in German]:

> My dear Mr Jenkins! In recognition of our mutual hopes, I
> proclaim this dedication to you in friendship: 'Long live
> America!' Yours, Richard Wagner.

> This refers partly to a hope we both entertained that he
> might sometime visit America and partly his sympathy with
> my belief that Europe would eventually become republican
> and not Cossack.

The Wagner Archives possesses the sheet of paper, dated 25 January
1879, on which Wagner drafted the inscription he wrote in Jenkins's copy
of the *Ring*. Forman's version was not a singing translation but intended
for the study; Wagner described it as a 'monument'.

# CHRONOLOGY

## Summary of Wagner's Life and Work

Specific dates (day and month) are based on the revised version of Otto Strobel's *Zeittafel*.

### Part 1 (1813–1849)

1813 Richard Wagner is born in Leipzig on 22 May. His father, Friedrich Wagner, the registrar of police, dies on 23 November.

1814 Wagner's mother, Johanna Rosine née Pätz, marries the painter, actor and playwright Ludwig Heinrich Christian Geyer on 28 August, and the family then moves to Dresden.

1821 Wagner's stepfather dies on 30 September.

1822 Richard enters the Kreuzschule in Dresden.

1826 He displays a particular liking for Greek, and translates the first three books of the *Odyssey* as 'extra homework'.

1828 After moving back to Leipzig he enters the Nicolaischule. He plays truant, writes *Leubald*, 'a great tragedy', and secretly takes lessons in harmony.

1829 He sees Schröder-Devrient in *Fidelio*.

1830 Wagner makes a piano reduction of the Choral Symphony. First essays in composition, including a 'Pastoral', for which he writes words and music 'simultaneously'. Transfers to the Thomasschule.

1831 Wagner enrols as a music student at Leipzig University. Lessons in counterpoint and composition from Theodor Weinlig. Compositions for voice, piano and orchestra.

1832 He begins his first opera, *Die Hochzeit*. He abandons the composition sketch after the first numbers and destroys the text.

1833 A Symphony in C major is performed in the Gewandhaus. Wagner writes his second opera, *Die Feen* (based on Gozzi's *La donna serpente*). He goes to Würzburg as chorus master.

1834 He becomes musical director of the Bethmann theatre company in Lauchstädt, where he meets the actress, Minna Planer. He writes the text for his next opera, *Das Liebesverbot* (based on Shakespeare's *Measure for Measure*). He goes to Rudolstadt and Magdeburg with the company.

1835 On a journey undertaken to audition singers, he sees Bayreuth for the first time; in Nuremberg he witnesses a street fight provoked by a caterwauling carpenter; in Frankfurt am Main he begins making notes for his future biography.

1836 First performance of *Das Liebesverbot* in Magdeburg. Wagner follows Minna to Königsberg, where she has been engaged at the theatre. They are married in the church at Tragheim near Königsberg on 24 November.

1837 Wagner is appointed musical director at the theatre in Riga. He takes back Minna, who deserted him in Königsberg.

1838 He begins the composition of *Rienzi*.

1839 The Wagners do a 'moonlight flit' from Riga, and board the *Thetis* at Pillau for a stormy voyage to London, stopping en route at Sandviken on Boröya. The legend of the Flying Dutchman takes shape. They reach Paris on 17 September. Wagner hears a rehearsal of the Ninth Symphony by the Conservatoire orchestra. Under its impact he composes a *Faust* Overture.

1840 Wagner writes settings of French poems and completes the score of *Rienzi*. Writes arrangements of numbers from French and Italian operas to earn a living. Spends some time in a debtors' prison in October or November. *Eine Pilgerfahrt zu Beethoven* is published in the *Gazette musicale*.

1841 *Ein Ende in Paris* published in the *Gazette musicale*. Conception of Senta's Ballad. Wagner and Minna move to Meudon, where he writes the text and music of *Der Fliegende Holländer*. *Rienzi* is accepted by the Dresden court theatre.

1842 Return to Dresden. On a holiday, Wagner begins the prose sketch of *Tannhäuser* at Schreckenstein near Aussig. First performance of *Rienzi* in Dresden.

1843 First performance of *Der Fliegende Holländer* in Dresden. Wagner is appointed kapellmeister to the King of Saxony. His oratorio *Das Liebesmahl der Apostel* receives its first performance in the Frauenkirche. Holidaying in Teplitz, Wagner reads Jacob Grimm's *Deutsche Mythologie*.

1844 The remains of Carl Maria von Weber are brought from London to Dresden. Wagner composes a funeral march for the occasion.

1845 The score of *Tannhäuser* is finished. Wagner writes the first prose sketch of *Die Meistersinger* and the prose sketch of *Lohengrin* in Marienbad. First performance of *Tannhäuser* in Dresden.

1846 Palm Sunday: Wagner conducts the epoch-making performance of the Choral Symphony. During the summer the Wagners spend three months in Gross-Graupa, where he finishes the composition sketch of *Lohengrin*. Prose sketch for a play about Frederick Barbarossa. Edition of Gluck's *Iphigenia in Aulis*.

1847  While scoring *Lohengrin*, Wagner studies Greek literature and culture; decisive impact of the *Oresteia* of Aeschylus.

1848  The completion of the score of *Lohengrin* is followed by a gap of five and a half years before Wagner writes music again. He addresses the Vaterlandsverein in Dresden on 'Republicanism and the Monarchy'. He tackles the material of the *Ring* for the first time in *Der Nibelungen-Mythus als Entwurf zu einem Drama*, and writes the verse text of *Siegfrieds Tod*.

1849  Prose draft of a play, *Jesus von Nazareth*. The May rising in Dresden, in which Wagner takes part, and during which he has an idea for a play about Achilles.

### Part 2 (1849–1883)

1849  Wagner flees Dresden on 9 May, escaping arrest by pure chance. Liszt helps his flight on from Weimar. The Dresden police issue a warrant for his arrest. He reaches Zürich on 28 May. He writes *Das Kunstwerk der Zukunft*.

1850  Wagner goes to Paris and drafts a text for submission to the Opéra, *Wieland der Schmied*. He meets with no success. His plan of going to Greece and Asia Minor with Jessie Laussot is thwarted. He returns to Zürich and to Minna, and begins and abandons a composition sketch for *Siegfrieds Tod*. Liszt gives the first performance of *Lohengrin* in Weimar.

1851  Wagner completes his major theoretical work, *Oper und Drama*, the verse text of *Der Junge Siegfried*, and his autobiographical *Mitteilung an meine Freunde*. The ideas of casting the Nibelung material as a four-part work and of holding a festival to perform it evolve simultaneously.

1852  First visit to northern Italy. Completion of the text of the *Ring*.

1853  Private edition of the text of the *Ring* appears, and Wagner reads it to an invited audience in the Hotel Baur au Lac in Zürich. The scenery of the Julier Pass and Roseg Glacier makes an indelible impression on him, on his way to St Moritz, and is later to leave its mark on the music of the *Ring*. On a second visit to Italy, at La Spezia, the music of the *Rheingold* prelude comes to him in a kind of vision. He returns to Zürich and begins to compose *Das Rheingold*.

1854  Wagner completes the score of *Das Rheingold* and begins *Die Walküre*. He reads Schopenhauer's *Die Welt als Wille und Vorstellung*. First conception of *Tristan*.

1855  Wagner conducts eight concerts in London, but fails to realize any financial profit. Returns to Zürich. *Tristan* takes more definite shape, and Wagner considers introducing Parsifal on his Grail quest.

1856  Completion of the score of *Die Walküre*. Prose scenario of *Die Sieger*. After a cure in Mornex, Wagner resumes the composition of the *Ring* with *Siegfried*. He makes the first musical sketches for *Tristan*.

1857  Good Friday: the first prose sketch of *Parsifal* (then spelt *Parzival*).

The Wagners move into the house Asyl, lent them by the Wesendonks, on the outskirts of Zürich. Wagner finishes the orchestral sketch of Act II of *Siegfried*, then lays the *Ring* aside for twelve years. Begins *Tristan*. Composes the *Wesendonk Lieder*.

1858 Hans and Cosima von Bülow visit Asyl. Crisis in the relationship with the Wesendonks. Wagner leaves Asyl for ever on 17 August and goes to Venice. In the Palazzo Giustiniani he resumes the composition of the second act of *Tristan*. He sketches a song, *Es ist bestimmt in Gottes Rat*. Draft of a letter to Schopenhauer on the metaphysics of sexual love.

1859 Wagner leaves Venice on 24 March (after pressure is exerted by the Saxon government) and goes to Lucerne, where he begins the third act of *Tristan*. In conversation with the composer Felix Draeseke he expounds Beethoven's compositional technique, taking the 'Eroica' as his example. He finishes *Tristan*. In September he moves to Paris, where Minna follows him.

1860 Three concerts of excerpts from his works in the Théâtre Italien. A circle of French admirers forms round Wagner. 22 July: a partial amnesty, permitting him to return to Germany with the exception of Saxony.

1861 He scores the Paris version of the Bacchanal and Venus's scene in *Tannhäuser*. It receives three performances at the Opéra, and is then withdrawn at the composer's request. The possibility arises of producing *Tristan*, first in Karlsruhe and then in Vienna. On 14 August Wagner leaves for Vienna, to supervise early rehearsals, but the whole project falls through. On a train returning to Vienna after a short trip to Venice he conceives the major part of the *Meistersinger* prelude, and thereupon writes a second prose sketch. He moves to Paris, where he writes the verse text and conceives the melody of the 'Wach auf' chorus.

1862 Wagner moves to Biebrich, near Mainz, in order to start the music of *Die Meistersinger*. A last brief visit from Minna, who lives apart from him in Dresden. Wagner's friendship with Mathilde Maier. He conducts the first performance of the *Meistersinger* prelude in an almost empty Gewandhaus in Leipzig. He gives a private reading of the text in Vienna; Eduard Hanslick, believing himself caricatured in the figure of Beckmesser, becomes Wagner's implacable enemy.

1863 January to April: concerts in Vienna, Prague, St Petersburg, Moscow. Wagner furnishes an apartment in Penzing, a Viennese suburb, at great expense. Concerts in Budapest, Prague, Karlsruhe, Löwenberg, Breslau, Vienna.

1864 In flight from his creditors, Wagner leaves Vienna in haste. After staying with Frau Wille at Mariafeld near Zürich, he goes on to Stuttgart, where a messenger from the King of Bavaria finds him. Ludwig II receives him in the Residenz in Munich on 4 May. Wagner dedicates the *Huldigungsmarsch* to the king, who commissions the *Ring*. Hans and Cosima von Bülow come to live in Munich.

1865 First performance of *Tristan und Isolde* in Munich. Wagner begins to
     dictate his autobiography, *Mein Leben*, to Cosima. He writes the
     prose sketch of *Parsifal* and a 'diary' for King Ludwig on the subject
     'What is German?' A press campaign of mounting hostility and
     Wagner's vigorous defence lead to catastrophe: on 6 December the
     king asks him to leave Bavaria for the time being. Wagner goes to
     Switzerland and rents a villa near Geneva.

1866 Determined never to return to Munich, Wagner searches for a house
     in southern France, without success. In Marseilles he receives the
     news of Minna's death. He rents the villa Tribschen outside Lucerne,
     and resumes the composition of *Meistersinger* with Act II. 22–4 May:
     surprise visit from King Ludwig.

1867 Wagner finishes *Die Meistersinger* and takes a brief holiday in Paris.

1868 First performance of *Die Meistersinger* in Munich, with Wagner in the
     royal box. He returns to Tribschen, where Cosima follows him after
     the denunciation of their relationship to the king. Wagner drafts
     scenarios for *Luthers Hochzeit* and a 'Comedy in one act' ('to counter
     grave depression'). Cosima and Wagner go to northern Italy and she
     decides to stay with him permanently.

1869 Wagner resumes the *Ring* after twelve years, scores Act II of *Siegfried*
     and begins the composition sketch of Act III. Nietzsche comes over
     from Basel to pay his first call on 17 May. Wagner's son (and third
     child) Siegfried is born on 6 June. Serious differences between
     Wagner and King Ludwig over the Munich première of *Das
     Rheingold*. He begins *Götterdämmerung*, composes *Wahlspruch für die
     deutsche Feuerwehr* ('Motto for the German Fire Service'), and writes
     *Über das Dirigieren*.

1870 Recalling his visit to Bayreuth in 1835, Wagner looks it up in an
     encyclopedia and learns of the large stage in its opera house, which
     gives him the idea of performing the *Ring* there. *Die Walküre* receives
     its first performance in Munich, against Wagner's wishes. Judith
     Mendès-Gautier and other French friends visit Tribschen. Wagner
     and Cosima are married. He writes the centenary essay *Beethoven*,
     and the 'comedy in the antique manner' *Eine Kapitulation*, and
     composes the *Siegfried Idyll*.

1871 Wagner composes the *Kaisermarsch* and makes his first visit to the
     new German Empire. After seeing the Bayreuth opera house he
     decides to build his own theatre. He reads his paper *Über die
     Bestimmung der Oper* to the Royal Academy of Arts in Berlin, calls on
     Bismarck, and conducts a charity concert in the royal opera house, in
     the presence of the emperor. He returns to Tribschen. The town
     council in Bayreuth decides to let him have a site for the
     Festspielhaus. The Wagner Society is founded. Wagner conducts in
     Mannheim.

1872 Nietzsche publishes *Die Geburt der Tragödie aus dem Geist der Musik*.
     The Society of Patrons of the Bayreuth Festival is founded. Wagner
     moves to Bayreuth. 22 May: he lays the foundation stone of the

Festspielhaus, and in the evening conducts the Choral Symphony in the Margraves' Opera House. He writes the essay *Über Schauspieler und Sänger*. Cosima is baptized a Protestant. Wagner begins the search for performers with a tour of Germany.

1873 Concerts in Hamburg, Berlin, Cologne. Wagner reads the text of *Götterdämmerung* in Berlin, in the house of Count von Schleinitz, before an audience including Field-Marshal Moltke and Adolf Menzel. Anton Bruckner visits Wagner in Bayreuth and dedicates his Third Symphony to him.

1874 Financial crisis of the festival undertaking. King Ludwig guarantees a credit of 100,000 talers. The Wagner family moves into Wahnfried. 21 November: Wagner completes the score of *Götterdämmerung* (having started *Das Rheingold* on 1 November 1853). Composes *Kinderkatechismus* for four girls' voices and small orchestra.

1875 Concerts in Vienna, Budapest (jointly with Liszt), Berlin. The preliminary rehearsals for the *Ring* are held in Bayreuth.

1876 Composition of the Festival March in celebration of the centenary of the American Declaration of Independence: while working on it Wagner gets the idea for the Flower Maidens' 'Komm', komm' holder Knabe'. The first Bayreuth festival, with three complete cycles of the *Ring*. The emperors Wilhelm I of Germany and Pedro II of Brazil are present at the opening performances (while King Ludwig attends the dress rehearsals and the third cycle). September–December: the Wagners are in Italy, spending a month in Sorrento, where Wagner and Nietzsche meet for the last time. News of the festival's deficit of 147,851·82 marks reaches Wagner. They return to Bayreuth just before Christmas.

1877 Wagner writes the second prose sketch and the verse text of *Parsifal*. He gives eight concerts in the Royal Albert Hall in London, in aid of the Bayreuth deficit, and is received at Windsor Castle by Queen Victoria. He discloses his plan for a school of music in Bayreuth (never realized) to delegates of the Wagner Societies. He begins the composition of *Parsifal*.

1878 *Bayreuther Blätter* begins publication, edited by Hans von Wolzogen. The prelude to *Parsifal* is performed in Wahnfried for the first time.

1879 While continuing to work on *Parsifal*, Wagner writes a number of articles for *Bayreuther Blätter*. Heinrich von Stein joins the household as Siegfried's tutor.

1880 January–October: residence in Italy (Naples, Siena, Venice). Wagner writes *Religion und Kunst*. On the way home, Wagner stops in Munich and conducts the *Parsifal* prelude at a private concert for King Ludwig.

1881 Angelo Neumann produces the *Ring* at the Viktoria-Theater in Berlin. Wagner, his family and Count Gobineau, a guest in Wahnfried, attend the fourth cycle. From November: residence in Italy (Palermo, Acireale).

1882 Wagner finishes the score of *Parsifal* on 13 January in Palermo. May:
return to Bayreuth, where Count Gobineau again visits.
Establishment of the Bayreuth Stipendiary Fund. Sixteen
performances of *Parsifal* in Bayreuth. Wagner and his family leave for
Venice on 14 September and take up residence on the mezzanine
floor of the Palazzo Vendramin. On Christmas Eve Wagner conducts
his C major Symphony (first performed in the Gewandhaus in 1833)
in the Teatro La Fenice.

1883 12 February: before going to bed, Wagner plays the Rhinemaidens'
lament: 'Traulich und treu ist's nur in der Tiefe: falsch und feig ist,
was dort oben sich freut!' 13 February: while working on the essay
*Über das Weibliche im Menschlichen*, Wagner is struck by another heart
attack and dies in Cosima's arms. The last words he writes are 'Love
– tragedy'. 18 February: Wagner's burial in the garden of Wahnfried.

# THE WORKS

The author's article on Wagner in *Die Musik in Geschichte und Gegenwart*, XIV, incorporates a list of the works, compiled by Gertrud Strobel, with notes on their first performances and first publication.

### 1. The Operas and Music Dramas

*Die Hochzeit* (Fragment, 1832)

*Die Feen* (1833–4)

*Das Liebesverbot, oder Die Novize von Palermo* (1834–5)

*Rienzi, der Letzte der Tribunen* (1838–40)

*Der Fliegende Holländer* (1841)

*Tannhäuser und der Sängerkrieg auf Wartburg* (1843–5) (Act III finale rewritten 1847; Bacchanal and Venus's scene in Act I rewritten 1860–1)

*Lohengrin* (1845–8)

*Tristan und Isolde* (1857–9)

*Die Meistersinger von Nürnberg* (1861–7) (First sketch 1845)

*Der Ring des Nibelungen. Ein Bühnenfestspiel für drei Tage und einen Vorabend* (First prose sketch, *Die Nibelungensage (Mythus)*, 4 October 1848; complete score finished 21 November 1874)

   – *Das Rheingold* (Text 1852; music 1853–4)

   – *Die Walküre* (Text 1852; music 1854–6)

   – *Siegfried* (Original title *Der Junge Siegfried*; text 1851; music: Acts I and II 1856–7 (Act II orchestrated 1869), Act III 1869–71)

   – *Götterdämmerung* (Original title *Siegfrieds Tod*; text 1848, revised 1852; music 1869–74)

   – Composition sketch for *Siegfrieds Tod*, scenes 1 and 2 (1850; abandoned)

*Parsifal. Ein Bühnenweihfestspiel* (First prose sketch 10 April 1857; first prose draft 1865; verse text and music 1877–82)

### 2. Plays, Fragments, Sketches: including operatic texts written but not composed by Wagner

*Leubald. Ein Trauerspiel* (1825)

*Die Hohe Braut* (1836 and 1842; libretto, set by Johann Kittl as *Bianca und Giuseppe, oder Die Franzosen vor Nizza*)

*Die Glückliche Bärenfamilie (Männerlist größer als Frauenlist)* (1837; libretto; some music written)

*Die Sarazenin* (Prose draft 1841–2, verse text 1843)

*Die Bergwerke zu Falun* (Prose draft for an unwritten libretto, 1841-2)

*Friedrich I.* (Sketch for a play, 1846 and 1848)

*Alexander der Große* (Sketch for a play, 184?; does not survive)

*Jesus von Nazareth* (Draft of a play; 1849)

*Achilleus* (Sketch for a play, 1849)

*Wieland der Schmied* (Prose draft of a libretto, 1850)

*Die Sieger* (Sketch for a music drama, 1850)

*Luther / Luthers Hochzeit* (Sketch for a play in prose, 1868)

*Lustspiel in 1 Akt* (Draft, 1868)

*Eine Kapitulation. Lustspiel in antiker Manier* (1870)

*Lessing und Friedrich der Große* (Idea for a comedy, 187?; mentioned GLRW, V, p. 381, Correspondence 16, p. 47)

*Hans Sachs / Hans Sachs' zweite Ehe* (Idea for a play, 187?; mentioned Correspondence 16, p. 47)

*Herzog Bernhard von Weimar* (Idea for a play, 187?; mentioned KLRW, II, p. 7; Correspondence 16, p. 47)

### 3. Orchestral Works

Overture in B♭ major ('Drumbeat') (1830)

Overture to Schiller's *Die Braut von Messina* (1830)

Overture in C major (1830)

Concert overture in D minor (1831)

Overture to Raupach's *König Enzio* (1832)

Concert Overture in C major (1832)

Symphony in C major (1832)

Symphony in E major, first movement (1834)

*Beim Antritt des neuen Jahres* (cantata, five numbers; 1835)

Overture to T. Apel's *Columbus* (1835)

*Polonia* Overture (1836)

'*Rule Britannia*' Overture (1837)

Overture to Goethe's *Faust* (Originally intended as the first movement of a *Faust* Symphony; first version 1840; revised as a *Faust* Overture 1855)

*Trauermusik nach Motiven aus 'Euryanthe'* (1844)

*Träume* for small orchestra and solo violin (Arrangement of one of the *Wesendonk Lieder*; 1857)

*Huldigungsmarsch* (1864)

*Romeo und Julia* (Sketch for a symphony in A♭ minor; 1868)

*Siegfried Idyll* (1870)

*Kaisermarsch* (1871)

*Großer Festmarsch* (Celebrating the centenary of the American Declaration of Independence; 1876)

### 4. Vocal Compositions

Seven Compositions for Goethe's *Faust*: *Lied der Soldaten, Bauern unter der Linde, Branders Lied, 'Es war einmal ein König', 'Was machst du mir vor Liebchens Tür', 'Meine Ruh' ist hin', 'Ach neige, du Schmerzensreiche'* (melodrama) (1831)

*'Dein ist das Reich'* (Four-part vocal fugue, exercise; 1832)

*Abendglocken* (Text by T. Apel; 1832)

Scene and Aria for soprano (1832)

Tenor aria for insertion in Marschner's *Der Vampyr* (1833)

Bass aria for insertion in Karl Blum's *Maria, Max und Michel* (1837)

Bass aria for insertion in Joseph Weigl's *Die Schweizerfamilie* (1837)

*Nicolay-Volkshymne* for chorus (Text by H. von Brackel; 1837)

*Der Tannenbaum* (Ballad by G. Scheurlin; 1838)

*La Descente de la Courtille* for chorus (Text by Dumanoir; 1840)

Bass aria for insertion in Bellini's *Norma* (1840)

*'Tout n'est qu'images fugitives'* (Text by J. Reboul; 1840)

*Les Adieux de Maria Stuart* (Text by Béranger; 1840)

*'Dors entre mes bras, enfant plein de charmes'* (Poet unknown; 1840)

*Mignonne* (Text by Ronsard; 1840)

*L'attente* (Text by Victor Hugo; 1840)

*Les deux grenadiers* (Setting of Heine's poem in a French translation made at Wagner's request by Professor Loeve-Veimars; 1840)

*Gesang zur Enthüllung des Denkmals Sr. Majestät des hochseligen Königs Friedrich August der Gerechte*, for chorus (1843)

*Das Liebesmahl der Apostel.* A biblical scene for men's voices and large orchestra (Text by Wagner; 1843)

*Gruß seiner Treuen an Friedrich August den Geliebten*, for chorus (Text by Wagner; 1844)

*'Hebt an den Sang'* for chorus (Text by Wagner; 1844)

*Fünf Gedichte für eine Frauenstimme: Der Engel, Stehe still, Im Treibhaus, Schmerzen, Träume* (Texts by Mathilde Wesendonk; 1857–8)

*Wahlspruch für die deutsche Feuerwehr* (Text by F. Gilardone; 1869)

*Kinder-Katechismus zu Kosels Geburtstag*, for girls' voices (Text by Wagner; first version with piano, 1873; second version, with the accompaniment arranged for small orchestra, 1874)

### 5. Works for the Piano

Sonata in D minor (1829)

Sonata in F minor (1829)

Sonata in B♭ major for piano duet (1831)

Sonata in B♭ major, opus 1 (1831)

Polonaise in D major for piano duet, opus 2 (1831)

Fantasia in F♯ minor, opus 3 (1831)

*Große Sonate* in A major, opus 4 (1832)

*Albumblatt* in E major, for E. B. Kietz (1840)

Polka in G major, for Mathilde Wesendonk (1853)

'*Eine Sonate für das Album von Frau M. W.*', in A♭ major (1853)
'*Züricher Vielliebchen / Walzer, Polka oder sonst 'was*', in E♭ major (1854)
'*Notenbriefchen für Mathilde Wesendonk*', in G major (1857)
*Albumblatt* in C major, for Princess Pauline Metternich (1861)
*Albumblatt*, '*Ankunft bei den schwarzen Schwänen*', in A♭ major, for Countess
      Pourtalès (1861)
*Albumblatt* in E♭ major, for Betty Schott (1875)
'Porazzi' Theme, in A♭ major (1858 and 1882)

## 6. Performing Arrangements

Rossini, *I Marinari*, duet, orchestrated by Wagner (1838)
Gluck, *Iphigenia in Aulis* (1846–7)
Palestrina, *Stabat mater* (1848)
Mozart, *Don Giovanni* (1850)


A complete edition of the works of Wagner is in process of publication at the
      present time, under the auspices of the Munich Academy of Fine Arts
      *Gesamtausgabe der Werke Richard Wagners*, Mainz, (1970– ).

# THE CORRESPONDENCE OF RICHARD
# AND COSIMA WAGNER

Letters are quoted from the following editions:

Wagner, Richard, *Briefe in Originalausgaben.* Leipzig, 1912:

    vol. 1/2 An Minna Wagner

    vol. 3 Familienbriefe

    vol. 4 An Theodor Uhlig, Wilhelm Fischer, Ferdinand Heine

    vol. 5 An Mathilde Wesendonk

    vol. 6 An Otto Wesendonk

    vol. 7 Briefwechsel mit Breitkopf & Härtel

    vol. 8 Briefwechsel mit B. Schott's Söhne

    vol. 9 Briefwechsel Wagner–Liszt

    vol. 10 An Theodor Apel

    vol. 11 An August Röckel

    vol. 12 An Ferdinand Praeger

    vol. 13 An Eliza Wille

    vol. 14 An seine Künstler

    vol. 15 Bayreuther Briefe

    vol. 16 An Emil Heckel

    vol. 17 An Freunde und Zeitgenossen

  – *Gesammelte Briefe (1830–50)*, see RWGB, p. xxvi

  – *Briefe nach Zeitfolge und Inhalt*, ed. by Wilhelm Altmann. Leipzig, 1905

  – *Briefe*, selected and ed. by Wilhelm Altmann, 2 vols. Leipzig, 1925

  – *Briefe. Die Sammlung Burrell*, see RWBC, p. xxvi

  – *Lettres françaises*, see TWLF, p. xxvi

  – *An Hans von Bülow.* Jena, 1916

  – *An Judith Gautier*, ed. by Willi Schuh. Zürich, 1936

  – and Cosima Wagner, *Lettres à Judith Gautier*, see LJG, p. xxv

  – 'Richard Wagner und Judith Gautier. Neue Dokumente', ed. by
    Willi Schuh, in *Schweizerische Musikzeitung* 1963 / 3

  – *Zwei unveröffentlichte Briefe an Robert von Hornstein*, ed. by Ferdinand
    von Hornstein. Munich, 1911

  – 'Briefe an Dr Theodor Kafka', ed. by Wilhelm Kienzl, in *Die Musik*,
    1906–7 / 19

- and King Ludwig II, *Briefwechsel*, see KLRW, p. xxv
- *An Mathilde Maier (1862—78)*, ed. by Hans Scholz. Leipzig, 1930
- 'Fünf neu aufgefundene Briefe . . .' [to Princess Pauline Metternich], ed. by Maria Ullrichowa, in *Beiträge zur Musikwissenschaft*, 1964 / 4
- 'Fünf ungedruckte Briefe . . . an Meyerbeer', ed. by Georg Kinsky, in *Schweizerische Musikzeitung*, 15 November 1934
- *The letters to Anton Pusinelli*, see RWAP, p. xxvi
- *Briefe an eine Putzmacherin*, ed. by Daniel Spitzer. Vienna, 1906
- *und die Putzmacherin, oder Die Macht der Verleumdung*, ed. by Ludwig Kusche. Wilhelmshaven, 1967
- 'Briefe . . . an Editha von Rhaden', ed. by Wilhelm Altmann, in *Die Musik* 1924 / 10
- *An Hans Richter*, ed. by Ludwig Karpath. Berlin, Vienna, Leipzig, 1924
- *An Frau Julie Ritter*, ed. by Siegmund von Hausegger. Munich, 1920
- *Die Briefsammlungen des Richard-Wagner-Museums in Tribschen bei Luzern*, ed. by Adolf Zinsstag. Basel, 1961

Other letters are published in:

Fehr, Max, *Richard Wagners Schweizer Zeit*, see FWSZ, p. xxv
Förster-Nietzsche, E., *Wagner und Nietzsche*, see EFWN, p. xxv
Fricke, Richard, *Bayreuth vor dreißig Jahren*
Hey, Julius, *Richard Wagner als Vortragsmeister 1864–76*
Kapp, Julius, *Wagner und die Frauen*, see JKWF, p. xxv
Kapp, Julius, and Hans Jachmann, *Richard Wagner und seine erste Elisabeth*. Berlin, 1927
Lippert, Woldemar, *Richard Wagners Verbannung und Rückkehr*, see LWVR, p. xxv
Neumann, Angelo, *Erinnerungen an Richard Wagner*
Niemann, Gottfried, and Wilhelm Altmann, *Richard Wagner und Albert Niemann*. Berlin, 1924
Röckl, Sebastian, *Ludwig II. und Richard Wagner*, see SRLW, p. xxvi
Schemann, Ludwig, *Lebensfahrten eines Deutschen*
Weissheimer, Wendelin, *Erlebnisse mit Richard Wagner, Franz Liszt und vielen anderen Zeitgenossen*
Westernhagen, Curt von, *Richard Wagner* (1956)
Wille, Eliza, *Fünfzehn Briefe von Richard Wagner*

Wagner, Cosima *und Houston Stewart Chamberlain im Briefwechsel 1888–1901*, ed. by Paul Pretzsch. Leipzig, 1934
- *Briefe an ihre Tochter Daniela von Bülow 1866–85. Nebst 5 Briefen Richard Wagners*, ed. by Max von Waldberg. Stuttgart and Berlin, 1933
- 'Lettres à Gobineau', ed. by C. Serpeille de Gobineau, in *La Revue Hebdomadaire* 1938, pp. 263ff., 400ff.
- *Briefwechsel zwischen C. W. und Fürst Ernst zu Hohenlohe-Langenburg*. Stuttgart, 1937
- *Briefe an Friedrich Nietzsche*, see CWFN, p. xxv
- *Briefe an Ludwig Schemann*. Regensburg, 1937

Other letters by Cosima Wagner are published in:
Du Moulin Eckart, Richard, *Cosima Wagner*, see DMCW, p. xxv

A complete edition of Wagner's letters in fifteen volumes is in process of publication at the present time, commissioned by the Richard-Wagner-Familien-Archiv Bayreuth and edited by Gertrud Strobel and Werner Wolf. The first volume appeared just before the first edition of the present work and is cited herein as RWSB (Richard Wagner, *Sämtliche Briefe*, Leipzig, 1967– ).

### Chapter 25. Munich

1 Pfistermeister transmitted this message by word of mouth and not, as Wagner says in *Mein Leben*, in a letter from the king. (KLRW, I, pp. xxxiv f.)

2 Ludwig's diary was published in 1925. Newman calls the editing and commentary of Edir Grein 'a deplorable exhibition of pseudo-psychiatry'. (NLRW, iii, p. 244)

3 On the Brown Book see note 9 of this chapter.

4 The painting (oil on canvas) disappeared until it was identified in the Metropolitan Museum, New York, by Martin Geck, who published it in colour in his book *Die Bildnisse Richard Wagners*. See Vol. I, pl. 16b.

5 The Annals twice refer to 'Schwabe–Schwind'. At the time Wagner suspected that the painter Moritz von Schwind, who was hostile to him, was behind the presentation of the bill, but this appears not to have been the case. Cf. KLRW, V, pp. 229f.

6 Otto Wesendonk remained a generous friend to Wagner, in spite of everything. At Wagner's request he even surrendered the autograph score of *Das Rheingold* to King Ludwig, who wrote him a cordial letter of thanks in his own hand (28 August 1865).

7 Schuré, *Souvenirs sur Richard Wagner*.

8 Wagner's account of the incident in a letter to the king of 9 June 1866 is slightly different. 'Curtly and brusquely they asked her if she wanted to carry the sacks of silver coin herself. When she asked them in amazement to give her notes they explained that they did not have enough in paper, and she would have to take at least half in silver. In the face of this discourtesy she drew some consolation at least from having spared me similar humiliation.' (KLRW, II, p. 57)

9 The Brown Book is kept in the Wagner Museum in Bayreuth. Extracts from it had been published, principally in BBL and KLRW, but it was first published in full in 1975, edited and with a commentary by Joachim Bergfeld (*Das Braune Buch*, Zürich). At some time Eva Chamberlain, the daughter of Richard and Cosima Wagner, unfortunately took it upon herself to interfere with the

manuscript, removing and destroying seven pages and pasting blank paper over five more sides. These last have now been uncovered and rendered legible, and their content reveals that Eva's filial piety was excessive; the conclusion is that the seven pages she destroyed probably did not contain any 'sensations' either. The text of the Brown Book, as now made available, sheds new light on the events of the following weeks in Wagner's life (10 August to 11 September 1865), so this section of the present biography has been revised and expanded for this edition.

10  *Les Misérables*. Hugo's treatment of social, economic and communal questions extends even to the drainage system, a considerable problem in Paris. Reading the book made such an impression on Wagner that he made it the starting point of his 'comedy in the antique manner', *Eine Kapitulation*, in 1870.

11  The suburb of Vienna where Wagner had lived from May 1863 to March 1864.

12  The Hindu epic by Valmiki. On that occasion, at least, Wagner was reading it in the French translation by Fauche, which was later in his library at Wahnfried.

13  'unvermerklich': this should perhaps be read as 'unvermeidlich' ('unavoidable').

14  'The visit to Venice that we had planned had unfortunately to be abandoned for various reasons.' (BB, IV, p. 59)

15  Part of this was published in the second issue of BBL in 1878 and so made its way into the complete *Schriften* (RWGS, X, pp. 36ff.). Published in full in KLRW, IV, pp. 5ff.

16  Wagner was later to look back on his own situation during Cosima's journey to Pest: 'He . . . spoke about the despicable position for a lover of knowing that his beloved is in the power of another, who governs her life. It is endurable in the first raptures of love, but in time the situation becomes thoroughly dishonourable.' (5 April 1873; CT, I, p. 667)

17  Cosima wrote to Auguste de Gaspérini on 14 December: 'Ils auraient bâti des palais et six théâtres pour un à W., s'il avait voulu se faire leur agent auprès du roi; je le sais par les tentatives qu'ils ont faites.'

18  Cf. KLRW, I, pp. lxvi f., and IV, pp. 116f.; SRLW, II, pp. 1f.; GLRW, IV, pp.51ff.; NLRW, III, pp. 396ff.

19  Remarkably, in 1937 Otto Strobel found it impossible to track down the complete text of this article, since *the relevant pages were missing* from the Bavarian State Library's copy of the *Volksbote*! (KLRW, IV, pp. 106f.)

### Chapter 26. Die Meistersinger

1  The text as given in *Richard Wagner an Freunde und Zeitgenossen* is incomplete; it is supplemented here from KLRW, I, pp. 257f.

2  In Friedrich Herzfeld, *Minna Planer*, pp. 330f.

3 The text is published in KLRW, IV, p. 124; a draft of it in RWBC, p. 565. Light is shed on the methods adopted by Wagner's enemies by further reference to the *Volksbote*: on 6 February the paper claimed to have learned from a person of some rank in Dresden that Minna Wagner had been receiving poor relief; it could therefore be assumed that her denial had been extorted from her. On 21 February the paper had to publish an official statement from the Dresden Commission for the Welfare of the Poor that Frau Wagner had by no means lived in straitened circumstances and had neither claimed nor received any relief. (KLRW, IV, pp. 128f.)

4 Herzfeld, *Minna Planer*, p. 354.

5 Published in Westernhagen, *Vom Holländer zum Parsifal*, pp. 132f.

6 Peter Cornelius, *Ausgewählte Briefe*, II (Leipzig, 1905), pp. 370ff. The editor of his correspondence, his son Carl Maria Cornelius, dated this letter '(12 May)', which Otto Strobel later showed to be incorrect; it must be '13 May'. (KLRW, V, p. 194, note 3)

7 The departure took place on 12 May, not on 11 May as planned. (KLRW, V, p. 194)

8 Editing his father's correspondence in 1904, Carl Maria Cornelius evidently decided he ought to make certain omissions so as to prevent identification of the author of the letter to Cosima that Bülow opened, out of consideration for the house of Wittelsbach. At all events, his editing of the letter of 13 May allowed Kapp to invent the legend of 'the great lie of the last two years', and it has taken the combined efforts of Strobel, Newman and myself to refute it.

9 This improbable story is to be found in KLRW, II and IV. A relative of Malvina Schnorr, C. H. N. Garrigues, took up her cause in his book *Ludwig und Malvina Schnorr* (Copenhagen, 1937), in which he put Wagner's version of the events in a bad light. Otto Strobel annihilated the charges in 1939 in KLRW, V.

10 Westernhagen, *Vom Holländer zum Parsifal*, p. 136.

11 Each stanza in Bar-form has three sections: the first two (the Stollen) are musically identical or nearly so; the third (the Abgesang) is different but shows some resemblance to the Stollen.

12 According to KLRW, II, p. 134, note, the text of the letter as given in *Richard Wagner an Freunde und Zeitgenossen* is incomplete. The full text was published in the *Münchner Neueste Nachrichten* of 19/20 May 1929.

13 *Denkwürdigkeiten des Fürsten Chlodwig zu Hohenlohe-Schillingsfürst*, I (Stuttgart and Leipzig, 1906), p. 211.

14 Newman's refusal to see anything more in this than the 'tirade' of a political amateur concerned only with his own interests illustrates the limits of his treatment of his subject. He did not appreciate that this letter related to a quite specific occasion and that Wagner was quite obviously inspired by Hohenlohe to champion his pro-Prussian policies. (Cf. NLRW, IV, pp. 71ff.)

15 On Eva's first birthday, 17 February 1868, Cosima was in Munich, and Wagner sent her a telegram to mark the day:

Was die Weise mir gebar,
mehr als Morgentraum nur war;
vom Parnaß zum Paradies
sie den Weg dem Leben wies.

('What the song bore me was more than a morning dream; it showed me the path of my life, from Parnassus to Paradise.')

He also recorded in the Brown Book: 'Eva sat on the piano and listened to the birth-song and then the Apprentices' Dance: very attentive and pleased.'

16 Otto Strobel gives a further illustration of the noble Freiherr's mentality by quoting a poem Völderndorff wrote and recited at a social gathering in Munich a few days after Wagner's death. (KLRW, II, p. 209, note)

So bist du hin, du Schwindler sondergleichen,
Hat dich der Teufel endlich doch ergriffen,
Du hast dein letztes Leitmotiv gepfiffen,
Dem Himmel Dank, jetzt mußt du einmal schweigen . . .
Fahr hin, du schlechter Mensch und schlechter Dichter,
Und sei der Teufel dir ein strenger Richter!

('So you've gone, you incomparable swindler, Old Nick's collared you at last, you've warbled your last leitmotiv, heaven be thanked, you must be quiet now . . . Good riddance, bad man and bad poet, and may the devil judge you severely.')

17 Strauss (ed.), *Instrumentationslehre von Hector Berlioz*.
18 First version 21 April, second draft 7 May 1868. Published in facsimile and transcription in Westernhagen, *Wagner* (1956), p. 57. A transcription is also to be found in *Das Braune Buch*, p. 175.
19 W. Weissheimer, *Erlebnisse*, p. 391.

### Chapter 27. From Tribschen to Bayreuth

1 O. Strobel, 'Flucht nach Tribschen', *Bayreuther Festspielführer* 1937, pp. 77ff.
2 Andler, *Nietzsche, sa vie et sa pensée*, II (Paris, 1921), pp. 219ff.: 'Les sources du livre sur la naissance de la Tragédie'.
3 The various documents relating to the *Rheingold* affair are to be found, according to date, in KLRW II, IV and V.
4 From the *Revue Wagnérienne* (Paris), February 1887 (abbreviated).
5 Furtwängler, *Ton und Wort*, p. 11.
6 This letter is printed in two parts in KLRW, II, the *latter* half on pp. 287f., correctly dated 22 October, and the *first* part on p. 290, speculatively dated mid-November, as though it were a separate letter. I am indebted to Herr Erich Neumann of East Berlin for drawing my attention to Strobel's correction in KLRW, IV, p. 261.
7 Westernhagen, *Wagner* (1956), p. 154.

8 The 'Pine Forest Mountains' to the east of Bayreuth. Wunsiedel (mentioned in the next paragraph) is one of many small spas in the district.

9 'There is no braver nation in the world, if they have the right leaders.' (*Wilhelm Meisters Lehrjahre*, Book 4, chapter 16.)

10 Leprince, *Présence de Wagner*, pp. 45, 72.

11 In TWLF this letter of Wagner's is wrongly dated 12 August, instead of September, 1870, which reverses the order of the two letters and makes nonsense of the sequence.

12 Zuckerman, *The first hundred years of Wagner's 'Tristan'*, pp. 100f.

13 Cf. Podach, *Ein Blick in Notizbücher Nietzsches*, pp. 72f. CT. I, pp. 375f., confirms the doubts as to Elisabeth's version of events. Wednesday, 5 April 1871: 'Professor Nietzsche reads to me from his work (origin and goal of Greek tragedy), which he wishes to dedicate to Richard; greatly delighted by it; it reveals a very gifted man who has absorbed Richard's ideas and made them his own.' 6 April : 'Further reading.' 7 April: 'The last reading from the essay.'

14 DMCW, I, pp. 583f. has two differences here: 'a great chorus' instead of 'a Greek chorus' and 'those themes' instead of 'these serious themes'. In answer to my enquiries, Dr Dietrich Mack, the co-editor of the diaries, has assured me that in this instance there can be no doubt as to the correctness of the reading in CT. The obvious conclusion to be drawn is that on 29 September 1871 Wagner was talking about a preliminary sketch which has not survived and in which the funeral music was not yet conceived as a march, but as a passage of reminiscence, comparable to a Greek *stasimon*, and concluding with the statement of Siegfried's theme, instead of going on to the Hero theme. Further evidence that this sketch was not identical with the composition sketch of the third act is offered by the fact that in the latter the Funeral March follows straight on, on the same page, from the setting of Siegfried's dying words (cf. my *Forging of the 'Ring'*, p. 226). Du Moulin could not have known this, and evidently thought Cosima was in error.

15 Later, in an edition of the text of *Götterdämmerung*, he could speak of other, less personal reasons for the decision. (Cf. vol. I, p. 219)

### Chapter 28. The First Festival

1 Erwin Rohde, too, his 'beloved philologist of the future', wasted no time in coming to Nietzsche's defence, in *A philologist's letter to Richard Wagner: Pseudo-philology*. The title itself ('*Afterphilologie*': 'hideous word', in Wagner's view) was coined by Nietzsche's friend Professor Overbeck of Basel, who therewith aligned himself in their camp. (Cf. Erwin Rohde, *Kleine Schriften*, Tübingen, 1901.) Wilamowitz followed up with a *Second part: a rejoinder to the attempts to salvage Friedrich Nietzsche's 'Birth of tragedy'* (Berlin, 1873).

2 The anniversary of Luther's nailing of the Ninety-five Theses to the church door in Wittenberg, celebrated as Reformation Day.

3 *Erinnerungen an Auber*, RWGS, IX, pp. 42ff.

4 Of the other works that she and Judith discussed, Wagner asked the Mendès, in a letter of 12 December 1873, to get him the following: Anquetil Duperon's *Oupnekhat* (the Persian version of the Upanishads, in a Latin translation favoured by Schopenhauer), E. L. Burnouf's translation of the Bhagavad-Gita and H. Fauche's translation of the Maha-Bharata. All are in the library at Wahnfried.

5 An entry in Cosima's diary indicates that though the king now denied it by implication, he had indeed been angry. 'Thursday, 29 January 1874. After dinner, Richard went to see Herr Feustel, who was very puzzled by what the king said about Dahn's poem, since when he was at Hofrat Düfflipp's he had seen telegrams from Secretary Eisenhart saying that the king was extremely displeased with Richard!' (CT, I, p. 787)

6 Nietzsche, *Die Unschuld des Werdens. Der Nachlaß*, selected and ed. by Alfred Baeumler, I (Leipzig, 1931), pp. 97ff.

7 C. A. Bernouilli, *Franz Overbeck und Friedrich Nietzsche*, I (Jena, 1908), p. 137.

8 Andler, *Nietzsche*, II, p. 400.

9 Anton Bruckner, *Gesammelte Briefe*, Neue Folge (Regensburg, 1924), p. 166; *Richard Wagner an Emil Heckel* (Leipzig, 1899), p. 99; *Bayreuther Festspielführer*, 1938, pp. 35f.; G. A. Kietz, *Richard Wagner . . . Erinnerungen*, pp. 182ff.; H. v. Wolzogen, *Erinnerungen an Richard Wagner*, pp. 28f.; Peter Raabe, *Bruckner* (Regensburg, 1944).

10 Wagner lived in Bayreuth, at no. 7 Dammallee, from the end of September 1872 to 28 April 1874.

11 Cf. Franz Stassen, 'Wahnfried', in *Bayreuth* (Munich, 1943). During the Second World War the books and pictures were placed in safe keeping. Some of the pictures are now in the Siegfried-Wagner-Haus, but the books were returned to the drawing room, to their original places on the shelves, in 1976.

12 GLRW, V, pp. 151f., 390ff.; MWKS, II, pp. 130ff.; *Richard Wagner an seine Künstler (Briefe in Originalausgaben*, vol. 14), p. 349, note 1: 'The very detailed discussions and clarifications of the Meister's intentions necessitated various alterations in the execution of the Hoffmann designs; there was not time enough in the end to meet the Meister's wishes in everything.' (Max Brückner to the editor)

13 The original painting is now in the Siegfried-Wagner-Haus.

14 MWKS, II, pp. 141ff.; DMCW, I, pp. 722ff.; GLRW, V, pp. 164ff.

15 KLRW, IV, pp. 214f.; also published in full in Nietzsche, *Werke*, ed. by Karl Schlechta, III, pp. 1105ff.

16 Kietz, *Richard Wagner . . . Erinnerungen*; Hey, *Richard Wagner als Vortragsmeister*; Fricke, *Bayreuth vor dreißig Jahren*.

17 Leprince, *Présence de Wagner*, pp. 90f. There can be no doubt as to the reliability of Vidal's statements.

18 Neumann, *Erinnerungen an Richard Wagner*.

19 Material from Mottl's diary was published by Willy Krienitz in *Neue Wagner-Forschungen* [I].
20 Kapp, *Wagner und die Berliner Oper* (Berlin, 1933), pp. 56ff.
21 The translator is inclined to adapt Andrew Porter's version of the Spring Song: 'Winter storms have vanished at your command.' The telegram went on to quote Brünnhilde's apostrophe to Siegfried: 'O Heil der Mutter, die Dich gebar!' etc.
22 Mottl kept a record in his diary (cf. note 19 of this chapter); Porges's *Die Bühnenproben zu den Bayreuther Festspielen 1876* was first published in instalments in BBL, from 1880 onwards, and appeared later in four booklets, published variously by Schmeitzner in Chemnitz and Siegismund und Volkening in Leipzig, 1881–96.
23 Schemann, *Meine Erinnerungen an Richard Wagner*.
24 Published in facsimile in KLRW, III, facing p. 88.
25 'Abschied von Mathilde Maier, der letzten Freundin'; 'der letzten Fremden' ('the last stranger') in CT, I, p. 1001 is obviously an erroneous reading of the manuscript: Cosima would never have referred to Mathilde Maier as a stranger. Cf. also GLRW, V, p. 308: 'Their close friends, such as . . . Mathilde Maier . . . remained until the first week in September.'

### Chapter 29. Nietzsche in Bayreuth

1 Published in Westernhagen, *Wagner* (1956), pp. 524ff.
2 Cf. Martin Vogel's reference to Nietzsche as a 'music-lover who persisted in his dilettantism' in his essay 'Nietzsches Wettkampf mit Wagner'.
3 Podach, *Friedrich Nietzsches Werke des Zusammenbruchs*, pp. 274ff.

### Chapter 30. The Nation's Thanks

1 A mild pun: apart from its obvious meaning, 'die Nibelungen-Not' is the alternative title of the medieval *Nibelungenlied*. [Tr.]
2 Joachim Bergfeld, 'Drei Briefe Nietzsches an Cosima Wagner', in *Maske und Kothurn*, 10 (1964), 3/4, pp. 597ff.
3 CT, I, pp. 1011ff. now proves beyond doubt that the 'walk' and the 'confession' *cannot* have taken place.
4 This undated letter must have been written in London in May 1877. It reveals that Wagner still hoped she would come over for the two additional concerts.
5 See Max Chop, 'Richard Wagner im Spiegel der Kritik seiner Zeit'.
6 The letters ended up in the possession of Brahms, who bequeathed them to the Gesellschaft der Musikfreunde, but since he only initialled his will instead of signing it, his relatives contested it. The letters later turned up in the catalogue of a dealer in Boston, Mass., and were bought by the Library of Congress. The prehistory of their publication in the *Neue Freie Presse*, including the role Brahms is alleged to have played, will be found in an appendix, 'The Putzmacherin Letters', in NLRW, III, pp. 567ff. In 1967 Ludwig

Kusche published more letters he had found in the Wagner Museum in Eisenach, in *Richard Wagner und die Putzmacherin, oder die Macht der Verleumdung* ('Richard Wagner and the Milliner, or The Power of Calumny'). Kusche appears not to be acquainted with Newman's account. (The siglum KBMG, which Newman uses on p. 569, is omitted from his own key: it refers to Ludwig Karpath's *Begegnung mit dem Genius*, Vienna, 1934.)

7 The speech was taken down in shorthand by Franz Muncker and is to be found in RWGS, XII, pp. 326ff. The editor, Richard Sternfeld, remarks that the rare pleasure of reading an authentic transcript of one of the Meister's longer oral pronouncements surely justified its publication there.

8 The plan is published in full, with the statutes of the Society of Patrons, in RWGS, X, pp. 16ff.

**Chapter 31. 'My Farewell to the World'**

1 Alfred Lorenz, *Das Geheimnis der Form bei Richard Wagner, IV: Der musikalische Aufbau von Richard Wagners 'Parsifal'*, pp. 13ff.

2 Cf. the present author's review in *Die Musikforschung*, 1966 / 2.

3 Podach, *Friedrich Nietzsche und Lou Salomé*, pp. 96ff.

4 Ibid.

5 The text of the three letters to Cosima is given in Appendix III. They were first published in Westernhagen, *Wagner* (1956), pp. 470ff., where they were given both in transcription and in facsimile, reproduced from the originals in the Wagner Archives. Karl Schlechta's edition of Nietzsche's works has a version based on an erroneous oral tradition: 'Ariadne, I love you, Dionysus.' (5th, rev. edn, 1966, III, p. 1350) Cf. also Podach, 'Nietzsches Ariadne', in *Ein Blick in Notizbücher Nietzsches*, pp. 115ff., and Westernhagen, 'Nietzsches Dionysos-Mythos, im Lichte neuer Dokumente', in *Neue Zeitschrift für Musik*, 1958, pp. 419ff.

6 Wagner no doubt took note of the 'Imperial Message' of 17 November 1881 announcing new social measures, but he did not live to see its implementation.

7 Cf. Eugen Stamm, *Ein berühmter Unberühmter. Neue Studien über Constantin Frantz* (Konstanz, 1948).

8 *The genealogy of morals, 3: What is the meaning of ascetic ideals?*

9 The prelude to *Parsifal* is the only composition of Wagner's for which there is a record of the playing-time under his direction. He conducted it twice at one sitting in a private concert for King Ludwig in Munich on 12 November 1880, and Dr Strecker, who was also present, timed both performances at exactly 14½ minutes. (Strecker, *Richard Wagner als Verlagsgefährte*, p. 299)

10 From the text published in facsimile in *High Fidelity*, December 1975: Klaus Liepmann, 'Wagner's proposal to America' (by kind permission of Professor Liepmann).

11 Jenkins had the satisfaction of witnessing such a triumph when he

attended the first performance of *Parsifal* in Bayreuth in 1882. 'I can recall nothing of the close. I do not remember if we applauded or not, for even like those who had the ability to understand the music, I was overwhelmed with the sublime effect of this magnificent drama.' (Dr Newell Sill Jenkins, *Reminiscences*, privately published; communicated to me by Professor Klaus Liepmann and quoted here by kind permission of Dr Jenkins's grandson, the musicologist Newell Jenkins jr.) See also Appendix IV.

12 Bismarck's letter is published in *Bisher ungedruckte Briefe von Richard Wagner an Ernst von Weber* (Dresden, 1883).

13 Cf. H. von Stein, *Gesammelte Dichtungen*, 3 vols. (Leipzig, n.d.), and *Goethe und Schiller* (Leipzig, n.d.); Günter Ralfs, *H. von Stein, Idee und Welt* (Stuttgart, 1940). When I mentioned Stein in my first book, *Wagner* (1956), somebody objected that his name was by now completely unknown in Germany. So far as I know, nobody had anything to comment on what I said. But in 1965 Iwao Takahashi, lecturer in aesthetics at Keio University, Tokyo, wrote to me: 'The "Wagnerian" H. von Stein, who died young and about whom I once published an article in a Japanese periodical, remains my ideal of an aesthetician.'

14 *Goethes Unterhaltungen mit dem Kanzler von Müller*, 5–7 September 1827.

15 Wagner wrote in the visitors' book in the Palazzo Rufolo: 'Klingsor's magic garden has been found! 26 May 1880. RW.'

16 Humperdinck, *Parsifal–Skizzen*.

17 *Halévy and French opera* (1842), RWGS, XII, pp. 131ff., 423.

18 Florimo, *Riccardo Wagner ed i wagneristi* (Ancona, 1883).

19 King Ludwig's gifts, in cash and other forms, to Richard Wagner over the period – little short of nineteen years – from 1 May 1864 to 13 February 1883 amounted to a total of 521,063 marks. Anyone who feels driven to tot up the other side of the account should bear in mind the valuable manuscripts Wagner gave the king, including, for instance, the autograph scores of *Die Feen, Das Liebesverbot, Rienzi, Meistersinger, Rheingold* and *Walküre*. Cf. Otto Strobel, 'Richard Wagner und die Königlich Bayerische Kabinettskasse', *Neue Wagner-Forschungen*, [I] pp. 101ff.

20 Humperdinck, *Parsifal–Skizzen*, pp. 7f.

21 The other version purports to be that told by Lenbach to Heinrich von Poschinger, who published it (only in 1903) in his book *Bausteine zur Bismarckpyramide*.

22 'Cosima Wagner: Lettres à Gobineau', in *La Revue Hebdomadaire* 1938, pp. 263ff., 400ff.; Arthur Gobineau, *Nouvelles Asiatiques*, ed. R. Gérard-Doscot (Paris, 1963).

23 Some of Wagner's letters to Voltz & Batz (though not this one) were listed and selectively quoted for the first time in RWBC, pp. 737ff. Cf. also Strecker, *Richard Wagner als Verlagsgefährte*, pp. 234ff., and GLRW, V and VI, passim.

24 The essay in question was *Know Thyself*. (*Erkenne dich selbst*, RWGS, X, pp. 263ff.)
25 Neumann, *Erinnerungen*, pp. 188f.
26 *Der Kampf zweier Welten um das Bayreuther Erbe. J. Knieses Tagebuchblätter aus dem Jahre 1883* (Leipzig, 1931), pp. 95f.
27 The grounds for this calumny were presumably the numerous letters exchanged between Cosima and Levi while the Wagners were in Naples: cf. DMCW, I, pp. 886–918. In Du Moulin's opinion her letters to Levi were among the most beautiful and expressive she ever wrote, and he adds: 'That may well be because it was there that Levi had bade farewell, for ever in this life, to the woman he had hoped to make his wife.'
28 Bayreuth Festival programme, *Parsifal*, 1959, p. 9.
29 Cf. NLRW, IV, pp. 641ff. Newman's account of the episode is illuminating as a whole.
30 From Judith Gautier, *Richard Wagner et son oeuvre poétique*. Liszt was visiting at the same time and told Princess Wittgenstein that Judith remained in an incessant state of 'heavenly rapture'; Cosima's diary betrays her own jealousy (CT, II, pp. 798f.), but it did not prevent her from writing to Schott's on Wagner's behalf to recommend Judith's translation of *Parsifal* as 'excellent in every respect'. (14 October 1881)
31 To Albert Niemann, 16 December 1881. Wagner wrote the last page of the score in time for 25 December, which he was able to do in consequence of his working out the pagination in advance. (KLRW, III, p. 232, note.)
32 Schott's paid Wagner 100,000 marks for *Parsifal*, the highest fee ever paid by a German music publisher at that date. There is a detailed account of the negotiations in Strecker, *Richard Wagner als Verlagsgefährte*, pp. 308ff.
33 Willi Schuh, *Renoir und Wagner*.
34 Van Gogh, *Briefe an die jüngere Schwester und an die Mutter* (Munich, 1961), pp. 52f.
35 *Bayreuther Festspielführer* 1934, pp. 183ff., with a facsimile.
36 *Graf Arthur Gobineau. Ein Erinnerungsbild aus Wahnfried* (2nd edn, Stuttgart, 1916).
37 Schemann, *Meine Erinnerungen an Richard Wagner*, pp. 14, 22; *Lebensfahrten eines Deutschen*, pp. 110f.
38 'To me he [Wagner] remarked that if he was in the orchestra he wouldn't like to be conducted by a Jew.' (CT, II, p. 983) On the other hand he had earlier told Levi that he had had the idea of getting him baptized, and taking Holy Communion with him.' (CT, II, p. 755) And there is his emphatic statement in the letter to Levi of 1 July 1881: 'In any event – you are my conductor for *Parsifal*!'
39 Taken from the eyewitness account by Houston Chamberlain in *Lebenswege meines Denkens*, pp. 237ff.
40 Ibid., and GLRW, VI, p. 632.

41 Chamberlain, op. cit., and Friedrich Eckstein, *Alte unnennbare Tage* (Vienna, 1936), quoted in MWKS, II, p. 208.

42 Ehrenfels, *Richard Wagner und seine Apostaten*, p. 55.

43 Podach, *Friedrich Nietzsche und Lou Salomé*.

44 A. von Schorn, *Zwei Menschenalter* (Stuttgart, 1920), pp. 342f.

### Chapter 32. La lugubre gondola

1 *An einen Opern-Spielleiter* (1927).

2 Cf. GLRW, VI, p. 716; DMCW, II, pp. 67f.

3 Podach, *Ein Blick in Notizbücher Nietzsches*, p. 159 (apropos of a draft of *Nietzsche contra Wagner*); p. 212. The germ of the aphorism lies in a letter to Overbeck of 14 November 1882.

4 Stein, *Gesammelte Dichtungen*, II: *Solon und Krösos*. Wagner, *Brief an H. von Stein*, RWGS, X, pp. 316ff.

5 Cf. Westernhagen, 'Wagners Beziehungen zu . . . Liszt'. 'With Béla Bartók, we hold the view that Liszt hit upon new possibilities without exploiting them.' (English summary, p. 332.)

6 Marie von Bülow, *Hans von Bülows Leben*, 2nd edn (Leipzig, 1921), pp. 389f.

7 Schwebsch, *Anton Bruckner* (Stuttgart, 1923), pp. 299f.

# BIBLIOGRAPHY

(See also the Summary Bibliography on pp. xxv–xxvi, which has a key to the abbreviations used in the text, and the bibliography of published correspondence on pp. 615–7. Readers are also referred to *The New Grove Dictionary of Music and Musicians* (London, 1980), which includes a fuller bibliography than is appropriate in a book of this compass.)

Periodicals are listed separately at the end.

Abraham, Gerald, *A hundred years of music*, 4th edn. London, 1974

Adler, Guido, *Richard Wagner. Vorlesungen gehalten an der Universität Wien.* Leipzig, 1904

Adorno, T. W. *Versuch über Wagner*. Frankfurt am Main, 1952

Appia, Adolf, *Die Musik und die Inszenierung*. Munich, 1899

Arnswaldt, W. K. von, *Ahnentafel des Komponisten Richard Wagner*. Leipzig, 1930

Bailey, Robert, 'The genesis of *Tristan* . . . a study of Wagner's sketches and drafts for Act I'. Unpublished dissertation, Princeton University

Barth, Herbert, *Internationale Wagner-Bibliographie*. 2 vols: 1945–55 and 1956–60. Bayreuth, 1956, 1961

Barth, Herbert, Dietrich Mack and Egon Voss, compiled and ed. *Wagner. Sein Leben und seine Welt in zeitgenössischen Bildern und Texten*. Vienna, 1975
 – *Wagner; a documentary study* [translation of the foregoing]. London, 1975

Baudelaire, Charles, 'Richard Wagner et *Tannhaeuser* à Paris', *Revue Européenne*, 1 April 1861. Reprinted in *Oeuvres Complètes*, vol. 2, *L'Art Romantique*, ed. by Jacques Crépet. Paris, 1925

Beeson, Roger, 'The *Tristan* chord and others: harmonic analysis and harmonic explanation', *Soundings*, 5 (1975), p. 55

Bekker, Paul, *Wagner. Das Leben im Werk*. Stuttgart, 1924
 – *Richard Wagner: his life in his work* [translation of the foregoing]. London and Toronto, 1931

Bergfeld, Joachim, *Wagners Werk und unsere Zeit*. Berlin and Wunsiedel, 1963

Blunt, Wilfrid, *The Dream King: Ludwig II of Bavaria*. London, 1970

Bory, R. *Richard Wagner. Sein Leben und sein Werk in Bildern*. Frauenfeld and Leipzig, 1938
- *La vie et l'oeuvre de Richard Wagner par l'image* [French edn of the foregoing]. Lausanne, 1938

Boulez, Pierre, 'Time re-explored' (German–English–French). *Rheingold* programme, Bayreuth Festival, 1976

Bournot, Otto, *Ludwig Heinrich Christian Geyer, der Stiefvater Richard Wagners*. Leipzig, 1913

Braschowanoff, Georg, *Richard Wagner und die Antike*. Leipzig, 1910

Burrell, Mary, *Richard Wagner: his life and works 1813–34*. London, 1898

Chamberlain, Houston Stewart, *Das Drama Richard Wagners*. Leipzig, 1892
- *Lebenswege meines Denkens*. Munich, 1919
- *Richard Wagner*. Munich, 1896 [and later edns]
- *Richard Wagner* [English translation of the foregoing]. London and Philadelphia, 1897 [and later edns]

Chop, Max, 'Richard Wagner im Spiegel der Kritik seiner Zeit', *Richard-Wagner-Jahrbuch*. Leipzig, 1906

Dahlhaus, Carl, ed. *Das Drama Richard Wagners als musikalisches Kunstwerk*. Studien zur Musikgeschichte des 19. Jahrhunderts, vol. 23. Regensburg, 1970

Dahlhaus, Carl, 'Wagner, Richard: musical works', in *The New Grove Dictionary of Music and Musicians*. London, 1979

Daube, Otto, '*Ich schreibe keine Symphonien mehr*'. *Richard Wagners Lehrjahre*. Cologne, 1960

Deathridge, John, *Wagner's 'Rienzi': a reappraisal based on a study of the sketches and drafts*. Oxford, 1977

Donington, Robert, *Wagner's 'Ring' and its symbols*. 3rd edn. London, 1974

Drews, Arthur, *Der Ideengehalt von Richard Wagners dramatische Dichtungen, nebst einem Anhang Nietzsche und Wagner*. Leipzig, 1931

Du Moulin Eckart, Richard, *Cosima Wagner*, see DMCW, p. xxv
- *Cosima Wagner* [English translation of the foregoing]. 2 vols. New York, 1931

Ehrenfels, Christian von, *Richard Wagner und seine Apostaten*. Vienna and Leipzig, 1913

Einstein, Alfred, *Music in the Romantic era*. New York, 1947
- *Die Romantik in der Musik* [German edn of the foregoing]. Liechtenstein and Munich, 1950
- *Von Schütz bis Hindemith*. Zürich and Stuttgart, 1957

Ellis, William Ashton, *Life of Richard Wagner*. 6 vols. London, 1900–8. (The first three volumes are mainly a translation of Glasenapp's biography.)

Engelsmann, Walter, *Erlösung dem Erlöser. Richard Wagners religiöse Weltgestalt*. Leipzig, 1936
- *Wagners klingendes Universum*. Potsdam, 1933

Faerber, Uwe, *Der Jubiläums-Ring in Bayreuth 1976*. Berlin, 1976 [English edn: Berlin, 1977]

*Der Fall Bayreuth*, with contributions by S. Skraup, E. Stradler, H. Altmann, W. Abendroth, P. O. Schneider. Munich, 1962

Fehr, Max, *Richard Wagners Schweizer Zeit*, see FWSZ, p. xxv

Fricke, Richard, *Bayreuth vor dreißig Jahren. Erinnerungen* . . . Dresden, 1906

Fries, Othmar, *Wagner und die deutsche Romantik*. Zürich, 1952

Fuchs, Eduard and Ernst Kreowski, *Richard Wagner in der Karikatur*. Berlin, 1907

Furtwängler, Wilhelm, *Briefe*, ed. by Frank Thiess. Wiesbaden, 1965
 – *Gespräche über Musik*. Zürich, 1949
 – *Ton und Wort. Aufsätze und Vorträge, 1918–54*. Wiesbaden, 1954
 – *Vermächtnis. Nachgelassene Schriften*. Wiesbaden, 1956

Gautier, Judith, *Richard Wagner et son oeuvre poétique*. Paris, 1882
 – *Richard Wagner and his poetical works* [translation of the foregoing]. Boston, 1883

Gautier, Judith, *Le troisième rang du collier*. Paris, 1909

Geck, Martin, *Die Bildnisse Richard Wagners*. Studien zur Kunst des 19. Jahrhunderts, vol. 9. Munich, 1970

Glasenapp, Carl Friedrich, *Das Leben Richard Wagners*, see GLRW, p. xxv
 – *Wagner-Encyklopädie*, 2 vols., Leipzig, 1891. (Reprint: Hildesheim, New York, 1977)

Glasenapp, C. F. and Heinrich von Stein, *Wagner-Lexikon*. Stuttgart, 1883

Gollancz, Victor, *The 'Ring' at Bayreuth* . . . with an afterword by Wieland Wagner. London and New York, 1960

Golther, Wolfgang, *Richard Wagner als Dichter*. Die Literatur. Berlin, 1904
 – *Die sagengeschichtlichen Grundlagen der 'Ring'-Dichtung*. Charlottenburg, 1902

Grand-Carteret, John, *Wagner en caricatures*. Paris, 1891

Gregor-Dellin, Martin, *Wagner-Chronik. Daten zu Leben und Werk*. Munich, 1972

Grimm, Jacob, *Deutsche Mythologie*. 2 vols. Göttingen, 1844. (Reprint, 3 vols. Darmstadt, 1965)
 – *Teutonic mythology* [translation of the foregoing by J. S. Stallybrass]. London, 1882

Guichard, Léon, *La musique et les lettres en France au temps du wagnérisme*. Paris, 1963

Gutman, Robert W. *Richard Wagner: the man, his mind and his music*. London, 1968

Halm, August, *Von Grenzen und Ländern der Musik*. Munich, 1916
 – *Von zwei Kulturen der Musik*. 3rd edn. Munich, 1947

Hanslick, Eduard, *Musikalische Stationen*. Berlin, 1880
 – *Vom Musikalisch-Schönen*. Vienna, 1854
 – *The beautiful in music* [translation of the foregoing by G. Cohen]. New York, 1957

Herzfeld, Friedrich, *Königsfreundschaft*, see FHKF, p. xxv
 – *Minna Planer und ihre Ehe mit Richard Wagner*. Leipzig, 1938

Hey, Julius, *Richard Wagner als Vortragsmeister 1864–76*, ed. by Hans Hey.
    Leipzig, 1911
Holloway, Robin, 'The problems of music drama', *Music and Musicians*
    (April–July 1973)
Hopkinson, Cecil, *'Tannhäuser': an examination of 36 editions*.
    Musikbibliographische Arbeiten, vol. 1. Tutzing, 1973
Humperdinck, Engelbert, *Parsifal-Skizzen*. *Persönliche Erinnerungen an Richard
    Wagner*. Siegburg, n.d. (Reproduced from ms.)
Indy, Vincent d', *Richard Wagner et son influence sur l'art musical français*. Paris,
    1930
Jacobs, Robert L. *Wagner*. The Master Musicians. London, 1947
Jäckel, Kurt, *Richard Wagner in der französischen Literatur*, vol. 1, *Die Lyrik*; vol.
    2, *Die Prosa*. Breslau, 1931–2. (A projected vol. 3, *Das Drama*, was
    not published.)
Jung, Carl Gustav, *Symbole der Wandlung*. Zürich, 1962, etc.
    – *Symbols of transformation* [translation of the foregoing by R. F. C.
    Hull]. Coll. Edn, vol. 5. London 1956
Jung, Ute, *Die Rezeption der Kunst Richard Wagners in Italien*. Studien zur
    Musikgeschichte des 19. Jahrhunderts, vol. 35. Regensburg,
    1974
Kapp, Julius, *Richard Wagner. Eine Biographie*. Rev. edn. Berlin, 1929
    – *Richard Wagner und die Frauen*, see JKWF, p. xxv
    – *The women in Wagner's life* [translation of the foregoing]. London,
    1932
Katz, Adele T. *Challenge to musical tradition*, chapter 6: 'Richard Wagner'. New
    York, 1972
Kietz, Gustav Adolf, *Richard Wagner in den Jahren 1842–9 und 1873–5*.
    *Erinnerungen, aufgezeichnet von Marie Kietz*. Dresden, 1905
Koch, Max, *Richard Wagner*. 3 vols. Berlin, 1907–19
Kurth, Ernst, *Romantische Harmonik und ihre Krise in Wagners 'Tristan'*. Bern and
    Leipzig, 1920
Lange, Walter, *Richard Wagner und seine Vaterstadt Leipzig*. Leipzig, 1933
    – *Richard Wagners Sippe*. Leipzig, 1938
Leprince, G. *Présence de Wagner*. Paris, 1963
Leroy, Maxime, *Les premiers amis français de Wagner*. Paris, 1925
Liess, Andreas, *Beethoven und Wagner im Pariser Musikleben*. Hamburg, 1939
Lindau, Paul, *Nüchterne Briefe aus Bayreuth*. Breslau, 1876
Lippert, Woldemar, *Richard Wagners Verbannung und Rückkehr*, see LWVR,
    p. xxv
Liszt, Franz, *Richard Wagner (Tannhäuser, Lohengrin, Holländer, Rheingold)*.
    *Gesammelte Schriften*, vol. 3, pt 2. 2nd edn. Leipzig, 1899
Loos, Paul Arthur, *Richard Wagner. Vollendung und Tragik der deutschen
    Romantik*. Munich, 1952
Lorenz, Alfred, *Das Geheimnis der Form bei Richard Wagner*. Vol. 1: *Der
    musikalische Aufbau des Bühnenfestspiels 'Der Ring des Nibelungen'*; vol.
    2: *Der musikalische Aufbau von Richard Wagners 'Tristan und Isolde'*; vol.
    3: *Der musikalische Aufbau von . . . 'Die Meistersinger von Nürnberg'*;

vol. 4: *Der musikalische Aufbau von . . . 'Parsifal'*. Berlin, 1924–33. 2nd edn. Tutzing, 1966

Ludwig, Emil, *Wagner oder die Entzauberten*. Berlin, 1913

Machlin, Paul S. 'Genesis, publication history and revisions of Wagner's *Flying Dutchman*'. Unpublished dissertation, University of California, Berkeley
  - 'A sketch for the *Dutchman*', *Musical Times*, 117 (1976), p. 727

Magee, Bryan, *Aspects of Wagner*. London, 1968

Mann, Thomas, *Leiden und Größe Richard Wagners*. Various edns
  - *Wagner und unsere Zeit. Aufsätze, Betrachtungen, Briefe*, ed. by Willi Schuh. Frankfurt am Main, 1963

Mayer, Hans, *Richard Wagner in Bayreuth, 1876–1976*. Zürich, Stuttgart and London, 1976. [English and German edns]

Meyerbeer, Giacomo, *Briefwechsel und Tagebücher*, ed. by Heinz Becker. Berlin, 1960–

Meysenbug, Malwida von, *Memoiren einer Idealistin*. 2 vols. 3rd edn. Berlin, 1881. [English translation: New York, 1936]

Millenkovich-Morold, Max, *Cosima Wagner. Ein Lebensbild*, see MMCW, p. xxv

Mitchell, William J. 'The *Tristan* prelude: techniques and structure'. *Music Forum*, vol. 1. New York, 1967

Morold, Max, *Wagner Kampf und Sieg*, see MWKS, p. xxv

Moser, Max, *Richard Wagner in der englischen Literatur des 19. Jahrhunderts*. Bern, 1938

Neumann, Angelo, *Erinnerungen an Richard Wagner*. 3rd edn. Leipzig, 1907

Newman, Ernest, *The life of Richard Wagner*, see NLRW, p. xxvi
  - *Wagner nights*. London, 1949. [Reprint, London, 1977; American edn: *The Wagner operas*, New York, 1949]

Nietzsche, Friedrich, *Richard Wagner in Bayreuth* (*Unzeitgemäße Betrachtungen*, 4), 1876. *Der Fall Wagner*, 1880. *Nietzsche contra Wagner*, 1901. Various edns
  - *Werke*, ed. by Karl Schlechta. 3 vols. 5th, rev. edn. Munich, 1966
  - *The Complete Works*, ed. Oscar Levy. New York, 1924

Österlein, Nicolaus, *Katalog einer Wagner-Bibliothek*. 4 vols. Leipzig, 1882–95 [Modern reprint, Wiesbaden and Liechtenstein]

Pfitzner, Hans, *Die Ästhetik der musikalischen Impotenz*. Munich, 1920
  - *Werk und Wiedergabe*. In *Gesammelte Schriften*, vol. 3. Augsburg, 1929

Podach, Erich F. *Ein Blick in Notizbücher Nietzsches*. Heidelberg, 1963. (Includes accounts of the writing of *Die Geburt der Tragödie* and the origins of the 'Ariadne' myth.)
  - *Friedrich Nietzsche und Lou Salomé. Ihre Begegnung 1882*. Zürich and Leipzig n.d. [1937] (Contains Elisabeth Nietzsche's account of the 1882 Bayreuth Festival.)
  - *Friedrich Nietzsches Werke des Zusammenbruchs*. Heidelberg, 1961. (Contains authentic texts of *Nietzsche contra Wagner* and *Ecce homo*.)
  - *The madness of Nietzsche*. London, 1931

Porges, Heinrich, *Die Bühnenproben zu den Bayreuther Festspielen des Jahres 1876*. Leipzig, 1896

Pourtalès, Guy de, *Wagner*. *Histoire d'un artiste*. Paris, 1932

Preetorius, Emil, *Wagner*. *Bild und Vision*. 3rd edn. Godesberg, 1949

Redlich, H. F. 'Wagnerian elements in pre-Wagnerian operas', in *Essays presented to Egon Wellesz*. Oxford, 1966

Röckl, Sebastian, *Ludwig II. und Richard Wagner*, see SRLW, p. xxvi

Roeder, Erich, *Felix Draeseke*. *Der Lebens- und Leidensweg eines deutschen Meisters*. Vol. 1: *Richard Wagner in der Schweiz*. Dresden, n.d. [1931]

Rolland, Romain, *Musicians of today*. New York, 1915

Schemann, Ludwig, *Meine Erinnerungen an Richard Wagner*. Leipzig and Hartenstein, 1924

– *Lebensfahrten eines Deutschen*. Leipzig and Hartenstein, 1925

Schrenck, Erich von, *Richard Wagner als Dichter*. Munich, 1913

Schuh, Willi, *Renoir und Wagner*. Erlenbach–Zürich and Stuttgart, 1959

– 'Renoir und Wagner (neue Folge)', in *Umgang mit Musik*. Zürich, 1970

– *Richard Strauss, Lebenschronik 1864–98*. Zürich, 1976

Schuré, Edouard, *Le drame musical*. 2: *Richard Wagner*. *Son oeuvre et son idée*. Paris, 1875

– *Souvenirs sur Richard Wagner*. Paris, 1900

Schweitzer, Albert, *J. S. Bach*, chapter 20: 'Dichterische und malerische Musik'. Various edns. [English translation: New York, 1911]

Shaw, George Bernard, *The Perfect Wagnerite*. Various edns

Silège, H. *Bibliographie wagnérienne française*. Paris, 1902

Sitwell, Sacheverell, *Liszt*. London, 1934

Skelton, Geoffrey, *Wagner at Bayreuth*. London, 1965

Spengler, Oswald, *Der Untergang des Abendlandes*. Vol. 1: *Pergamon und Bayreuth*. Munich, 1923

Staehelin, Martin, 'Wagners Persönlichkeit im Urteil eines Zürcher Freundes, Jakob Sulzer', *Neue Zürcher Zeitung*, 20/21 March 1976

Stein, Herbert, *Dichtung und Musik im Werke Richard Wagners*. Berlin, 1962

Stein, Jack, *Richard Wagner and the synthesis of the arts*. Detroit, 1960

Strauss, Richard, *Betrachtungen und Erinnerungen*. Zürich, 1949

– *Briefe an die Eltern*. Zürich, 1954

– *Briefwechsel mit Joseph Gregor*. Salzburg, 1955

– *Briefwechsel mit Hugo von Hofmannsthal*. 4th edn. Zürich, 1975

– *Briefwechsel mit Willi Schuh*. Zürich, 1969

– ed. *Instrumentationslehre von Hector Berlioz*. Leipzig, 1904

Strecker, Ludwig, *Richard Wagner als Verlagsgefährte*. Mainz, 1951

Strobel, Otto, 'Eingebung und bewußte Arbeit im musikalischen Schaffen Richard Wagners', *Bayreuther Festspielbuch*, 1951

– ' "Geschenke des Himmels": Über die ältesten überlieferten Tristan-Themen', *Bayreuther Festspielführer*, 1938

– *Richard Wagner. Leben und Schaffen. Eine Zeittafel*. Bayreuth, 1952

– *Richard Wagner über sein Schaffen*. Munich, 1924

– ed. *Skizzen und Entwürfe zur 'Ring'-Dichtung*, see SERD, p. xxvi

- 'Über einen unbekannten Brief Richard Wagners an Mathilde
  Wesendonk', *Bayreuther Festspielführer*, 1937
- 'Unbekannte Dokumente Richard Wagners', *Die Sonne*, February
  1933
- 'Die Urgestalt des *Lohengrin*', *Bayreuther Festspielführer*, 1936
- 'Wagners Prosaentwurf zum *Fliegenden Holländer*', *Bayreuther Blätter*,
  1933
- 'Zur Entstehungsgeschichte der *Götterdämmerung*', *Die Musik*,
  February 1933

Stuckenschmidt, H. H. *Schönberg*. Zürich, 1974

Tappert, Wilhelm, *Richard Wagner im Spiegel der Kritik. Wörterbuch der
  Unhöflichkeit*. 2nd edn. Leipzig, 1903 [Reprint, Munich, 1967]

Turing, Penelope, *New Bayreuth*. St Martin, Jersey, 1969

Vanselow, A. *Richard Wagners photographische Bildnisse*. Munich, 1908

Vogel, Martin, *Apollinisch und Dionysisch*. Studien zur Musikgeschichte des 19.
  Jahrhunderts, vol. 6. Regensburg, 1966
- 'Nietzsches Wettkampf mit Wagner', in Salmen, Walter, ed. *Beiträge
  zur Geschichte der Musikanschauung im 19. Jahrhundert*. Studien zur
  Musikgeschichte des 19. Jahrhunderts, vol. 1. Regensburg, 1965

Voss, Egon, *Studien zur Instrumentation Richard Wagners*. Studien zur
  Musikgeschichte des 19. Jahrhunderts, vol. 24. Regensburg, 1970

Wagner, Cosima, *Die Tagebücher*, see CT, p. xxv
- *Cosima Wagner's Diaries* [translation of the foregoing by Geoffrey
  Skelton], 2 vols. London, 1978–80

Wagner, Richard, *Das Braune Buch. Tagebuchaufzeichnungen 1865–82*, ed. by
  Joachim Bergfeld. Zürich and Freiburg im Breisgau, 1975
- *Mein Leben*, see ML, p. xxv
- *My life* [translation of the first edition of the foregoing]. London and
  New York, 1911
- 'The work and mission of my life', *The North American Review*, 1879
- *Lebensbericht* [back translation of the foregoing]. Hanover, n.d.
- *The Ring of the Nibelung*. A new translation by Andrew Porter.
  [Parallel German and English texts.] London, 1977

Wagner, Siegfried, *Erinnerungen*. Stuttgart, 1923

Wagner, Wieland, ed. *Richard Wagner und das neue Bayreuth*. Munich, 1962

Wagner, Wolf-Siegfried, *Die Geschichte unserer Familie in Bildern*. Munich, 1976
- *The Wagner Family Albums* [translation of the foregoing]. London,
  1976

Wagner-Archiv, Bayreuth, *Katalog der Bibliothek von Richard Wagner in
  Wahnfried*. [Ms., compiled 1888]

*The Wagner companion*, ed. by P. Burbidge and R. Sutton. London and
  Boston, 1979.

*The Wagner companion*, ed. by R. Mander and J. Mitchenson. London, 1977

*Wagner 1976: a celebration of the Bayreuth Festival*, ed. by Stewart Spencer. The
  Wagner Society. London, 1976

Warrack, John, *Carl Maria von Weber*. 2nd edn. Cambridge, 1976

Weissheimer, Wendelin, *Erlebnisse mit Richard Wagner, Franz Liszt und vielen anderen Zeitgenossen nebst deren Briefen.* 2nd edn. Stuttgart and Leipzig, 1898

Westernhagen, Curt von, *Die Entstehung des 'Ring'.* Zürich, 1973
- *The forging of the 'Ring'* [translation of the foregoing]. Cambridge, 1976
- *Gespräch um Wagner. Discussion on Wagner. Entretiens sur Wagner.* Bayreuth, 1961
- *Richard Wagner. Sein Werk, sein Wesen, seine Welt.* Zürich, 1956
- 'Richard Wagner und das Ausland' [German–French–English], *Rheingold* programme, Bayreuth Festival, 1972
- *Richard Wagners Dresdener Bibliothek 1842–1849.* Wiesbaden, 1966
- *Vom Holländer zum Parsifal. Neue Wagner-Studien.* Zürich, 1962
- *Wagner.* Zürich, 1968. [First edn of the present work. Italian translation, Milan, 1973; Japanese translation, Tokyo, 1973. Second German edn, Zürich, 1979.]
- 'Wagner, Wilhem Richard', in *Dictionnaire de la Musique*, ed. by Marc Honegger, vol. II, Paris, 1970
- 'Wagner, Richard: biography; literary works', in *The New Grove Dictionary of Music and Musicians.* London, 1980
- 'Wagner, Wilhelm Richard', in *Die Musik in Geschichte und Gegenwart*, vol. 14. Kassel, 1968. [Includes a list of the works, compiled by Gertrud Strobel.]
- 'Wagner, Wilhelm Richard', in *Sohlman's Musiklexikon.* Stockholm, 1977
- 'Wagners Auswanderungsutopie' [German–French–English]. *Götterdämmerung* programme, Bayreuth Festival, 1976
- 'Wagners Beziehungen zu dem Komponisten Liszt' (with English summary 'Wagner's connection with . . . Liszt'), in Bonis, Ferenc, *Magyar Zenetörténeti Tanulmányok.* Budapest, 1973
- 'Wagners Dresdener Studien über unbekannte Quellen von *Tristan und Isolde*' [German–French–English], *Tristan* programme, Bayreuth Festival, 1970
- 'Wagner's last day', *Musical Times*, 120 (1979), pp. 395–7

White, Chappell, *An introduction to the life and works of Richard Wagner.* Englewood Cliffs, N.J., 1967

Wille, Eliza, *Fünfzehn Briefe von Richard Wagner mit Erinnerungen und Erläuterungen.* 3rd enl. edn. Munich, Berlin and Leipzig, 1935

Wolzogen, Hans von, *Bayreuth. Die Musik*, ed. by R. Strauss. Berlin, n.d.
- *Erinnerungen an Richard Wagner.* Leipzig, n.d.
- *Musikalisch–dramatische Parallelen.* Leipzig, 1910

Zuckerman, Elliott, *The first hundred years of Wagner's 'Tristan'.* New York and London, 1964

### Defunct Periodicals

*Bayreuther Blätter*, see BBL, p. xxv
*La Revue Wagnérienne*, ed. by Edouard Dujardin. Paris, 1885–8
*Richard-Wagner-Jahrbuch*, ed. by J. Kürschner. 1 vol. Stuttgart, 1886

*The Meister.* The quarterly journal of the British Wagner Society, ed. by
W. A. Ellis. London, 1888–95

*Bayreuth. Handbuch für Festspielbesucher,* ed. by F. Wild. Bayreuth, 1894–1930

*Bayreuther Festspielführer* (various titles). Bayreuth, 1901–39

*Richard-Wagner-Jahrbuch,* ed. by Ludwig Frankenstein. 5 vols. (Various
publishers) 1906, 1907, 1908, 1912, 1913

*Neue Wagner-Forschungen. Veröffentlichungen der Richard-Wagner-
Forschungsstätte Bayreuth,* ed. by Otto Strobel. 1 vol.
Karlsruhe, 1943

*Das Bayreuther Festspielbuch,* published by the administration of the
Bayreuth festivals. Bayreuth, 1950–1

**Current Periodicals**

*'Bayreuth'-Jahreshefte,* published by the administration of the Bayreuth
festivals. Bayreuth, 1954–

*Programmhefte der Bayreuther Festspiele* [Bayreuth Festival programmes].
Bayreuth, 1953–

Newsletter (untitled) of the Österreichische Richard-Wagner-
Gesellschaft. Graz

*Tribschener Blätter,* Zeitschrift der Schweizerischen Richard-Wagner-
Gesellschaft. Lucerne, 1956–

*Bulletin de Cercle National Richard Wagner.* Paris

*Bulletin de L'Association Européenne pour la Musique Wagnérienne.* Paris

*Feuilles Wagnériennes,* Bulletin d'Information de l'Association
Wagnérienne de Belgique. Brussels, 1960–

*Wagner,* The Wagner Society. London, 1971–

Periodical (untitled) of the Wagner Genootschap, Amsterdam, 1961–

*Monsalvat. Revista Wagneriana.* Barcelona, 1973–

# INDEX

## Compiled by G. M. Tucker

Note:
pp. ix–xxi = preliminary pages of Vol. I; pp. 1–327 = Vol. I; pp. 329–628 = Vol. II.
Wagner's literary and musical works are indexed under their respective titles.

Abt, Franz, 170, 174
Achilleus (Wagner), 127, 139
Aeschylus, 98–9, 110, 274, 412, 423, 505, 560
Agoult, Comtesse Marie d' (Cosima Wagner's mother), 248, 334, 469
Alexander II, Tsar of Russia, 312, 557
Alexander der Große (Wagner), 127
Alexander the Great, 447
America, 164, 212, 256, 344, 470, 486–7, 493, 517–18, 519, 551–3, 556, 598–9, 603
Ander, Alois, 295, 296, 298, 310, 311
Anders, Gottfried Engelbert, 52, 54, 70
Anderson, G. F., 200
Andler, Charles, xiii, 411, 464, 492, 537
Apel, Theodor, 32, 35, 37, 39, 42, 51, 61, 62
Appia, Adolphe, 580
Ariosto, Ludovico, 20
Aristophanes, 100
Art and Revolution (Wagner), 143, 145
Artwork of the Future, The (Wagner), 143, 144–6, 332, 468, 469, 561
Assing, Ludmilla, 214
Auber, Daniel François, 47, 273, 453
Augusta, Princess, of Prussia, 280, 282
Avenarius, Cäcilie, see Geyer, Cäcilie

Bach, Johann Sebastian, 4, 29, 38, 317, 319, 355–6, 381, 559; influence on W, 31, 262; works, 31, 237, 262, 544
Bagnara, Duke of, 558–9
Bailey, Robert W., xi, 322
Bakunin, Mikhail, 133, 137

Balzac, Honoré de, 393
Banck, Carl, 83, 155
Barthou, Louis, 322
Baudelaire, Charles Pierre, 111, 273, 275, 290–1, 528
Baumgartner, Wilhelm, 172, 175
Bayreuth, 10, 425, 557, 560, 562, 565; Margraves' Opera House, 423, 433, 447, 459; W's early visits to, 379, 423; W's move to, 443–4, 623; see also Wahnfried
– festival, 78, 116, 232, 432, 435–7, 451, 474, 485, 488–98, 503–4, 515–16, 549, 563, 572, 576, 579, 582–4, 591; finance of, 454, 460–4, 480, 485–6, 487–8, 506, 507–8, 511–14, 517–18, 519–24; management committee, 441, 454, 463, 469, 513, 517, 524, 550, 573; theatre, 340, 437, 439, 441, 445, 446–7, 449, 460, 462, 466, 471–3, 506–7, 512, 520–1, 563–4, 576; Wagner Societies and Society of Patrons, 82, 141, 245, 436, 437, 439, 444, 454, 461, 463, 469, 507, 513, 514, 521, 522, 541, 582
Bayreuther Blätter, xii, 160, 522–3, 534, 538, 541, 555, 561–2, 567, 587
Bechstein, Carl, 360, 405
Becker (Justice), 304
Becker, Dr Heinz, 321
Beethoven, Ludwig van, 32, 62, 112, 207, 296, 331, 356, 381, 411, 420, 437, 457, 459, 468, 469, 476, 490, 502, 544, 546, 547, 581, 590; conducted by W, 48, 86–90, 133, 170, 172–3, 203, 204, 241–2, 434, 439, 447, 545;

Beethoven, Ludwig van—*cont.*
  influence on W, 22–6, 28, 31–3, 38, 81, 173, 174, 180, 189, 262, 265; W's planned biography of, 54
  – works, 22, 25, 48, 148, 172, 184, 186, 204, 262, 419, 427, 478, 486; *Fidelio*, 22–3, 132, 144, 170, 274, 585; symphonies, 25, 32, 33, 48, 62, 172–3, 194, 203, 204, 242, 265, 392, 434, 439, 545, 590, Ninth Symphony, xiii, 22, 24–6, 53–4, 62, 86–90, 105, 107, 133, 145, 184, 197, 242, 276, 420, 426, 447–8, 456, 467, 468, 489, 561, 585
*Beethoven* (Wagner), 425–6, 427–8, 430, 561
Bekker, Paul, 32
Bellini, Vincenzo, 47, 459, 544, 559; influence on W, 39; works, 38–9, 170
Benedictus, Ludwig, 529, 573
Bennigsen, Rudolf von, 539
Bergfeld, Joachim, x, xiv, 350, 618
Berlin, 116, 129, 191, 429, 430; Court Opera, 68, 70, 73, 141, 204, 282; Königstadt theatre, 41, 44; Royal Academy of Arts, 432, 433, 436; W's visits to, 44, 49, 70, 119–20, 335, 433–6, 441, 455, 478, 487–8, 568, 569; W's works performed in, 70, 117, 118, 119–20, 121, 128, 152, 180, 204–5, 256, 487–8, 566–9
Berlioz, Hector, 63, 87, 110, 114, 153, 207, 272, 273, 278, 327; meeting with W, 208; on W's works, 274; W on, 62; works, 62, 274, 288, 532
Berthold (schoolteacher), 139
Bertram, Ernst, 503
Bethmann, Frau Heinrich, 40
Bethmann, Heinrich, 40, 404
Betz, Franz, 414, 472, 480, 497
Beust, Friedrich Ferdinand von, 282
Biebrich, 303–6, 308
Bischoff, Professor, 146
Bismarck, Otto von, 362, 367, 378, 386, 434–5, 460, 485–6, 538, 540–1, 555, 565, 568, 572
Bissing, Harriet von, 314–15
Bizet, Georges, 483–4
Blasewitz, 45–6
Bleichröder, Gerson von, 455
Böcklin, Arnold, 472
Boieldieu, François, 47, 170
Boito, Arrigo, 181, 564
Bonfanti, G. A., 492
Bote & Bock (publishers), 191
Bourget, Paul, 96

Bournot, Otto, 8
Brahms, Johannes, 39, 86, 193, 200, 308, 310, 327, 462, 477, 510, 518, 624
Brandt, Fritz, 580
Brandt, Karl, 414, 473, 497, 580
Breitkopf & Härtel (publishers), 31, 81, 94, 114–15, 122, 159, 173, 190–1, 209, 220, 227, 254, 256–7
Brendel, Franz, 146, 264
Brenner, Albert, 508
Brockhaus, Clemens, 440
Brockhaus, Friedrich, 12, 27, 94
Brockhaus, Heinrich, x, 94, 102, 117
Brockhaus, Hermann, 45–6, 94
Brockhaus, Luise, *see* Wagner, Luise
Brockhaus, Ottilie, *see* Wagner, Ottilie
Bruckner, Anton, xiii, 465–8, 594
Brückner, Gotthold, 473
Brückner, Max, 473, 623
Brussels, 277, 486
Bruyck, Karl Debrois von, 77
Buch, Marie von, *see* Schleinitz, Marie von
Bucher, Lothar, 434–5
Bülow, Blandine von, 333, 373, 381, 426, 569, 572
Bülow, Cosima von, *see* Wagner, Cosima
Bülow, Daniela von, 215, 333, 364, 370, 373, 381, 426, 477, 506, 508, 568, 571, 572
Bülow, Franziska von, 15, 169–70
Bülow, Hans von, xii, 14–15, 83, 106, 135–6, 141, 149, 171, 173, 194, 198, 201, 256, 259, 264, 268, 280, 287, 290, 307, 340, 354, 360, 411, 415, 451, 516, 583, 593; and Bayreuth, 493, 572–3, 583–4; and his children, 568, 572–3; and Ludwig II, 331, 335, 375, 377, 387, 422–3; as conductor, 169–70, 342, 343, 389, 397, 410, 420, 545; as husband to Cosima, 233, 247, 249, 334, 340, 347, 349, 352; kapellmeister in Munich, 341, 373, 377–8, 384, 387, 410; on the Cosima/W affair, 373–4, 388, 396, 405–7, 493; on W's works, 48, 77, 262, 381; on the Wesendonk affair, 252
Bulwer Lytton, Edward George, 46
Buol-Schauenstein, Karl Graf von, 257–8
Burckhardt, Jacob, 127, 538, 541, 563, 587
Burk, John N. (editor of the Burrell Collection), 41, 48, 183, 277
Bürkel, Ludwig von, 548, 550, 586, 593
Burnouf, Eugène, 212, 395, 623
Burrell Collection, ix, 41, 47, 61, 72, 75, 148, 149, 183, 214, 243, 277, 289

Burrell, Mary, 10, 28, 41, 48, 243
Büsching, Johann Gustav Gottlieb, 35

Calderón de la Barca, Pedro, 239, 413
Capitulation, A (Wagner), 428, 429, 430, 432, 619
Carl Alexander, Grand Duke of Saxe–Weimar–Eisenach, 176–7, 217–18, 250, 257, 263
Carlyle, Thomas, xi, 319
Chabrol de (pseudonym Lorbac), 271
Challemel-Lacour, Paul, 271, 283
Chamberlain, Eva, see Wagner, Eva
Chamberlain, Houston Stewart, xvii, 9, 208–9, 270, 293, 501, 581, 582
Champfleury, Jules, 270, 273–4, 297
Charnacé, Claire (half-sister of Cosima Wagner), 405–6
Cherubini, Luigi, xix, 47, 148, 170, 558
Chopin, Frédéric François, 277
Chorley, Henry, 206
Communication to my Friends, A (Wagner), 43, 104–5, 112, 132, 143, 159, 160
Constantin, Prince Friedrich Ferdinand, of Weimar, 9–10
Cornelius, Carl Maria, 620
Cornelius, Peter (composer), 296, 298, 300, 302, 303, 308, 314, 316, 340, 343, 364, 373–4, 396, 402, 459, 476
Cornelius, Peter (painter), 94, 133, 473, 474
Cossa, Pietro, 511
Crespi, Angelo, 258
Creuzer, Professor Friedrich, 20, 412
Curtis, Mary, 243

Dahlmann, F. C., 95
Dahn, Felix, 462–3
Dangl, Frau, 360–1
Dannreuther, Edward, 29, 319, 518
Dante Alighieri, 20, 207, 242
Daru, Count Pierre Antoine Bruno, 254
Darwin, Charles, 531
Daube, Otto, xi, 24, 28, 30, 31
Davidsohn, George, 567
Davison, J. W., 206
Delacroix, Eugène, 304
Delbrück, Rudolf von, 485
Devrient, Eduard, 135, 140, 231, 232, 257, 272, 321, 325, 326, 407
Devrient, Emil, 340
Dietrich (lover of Minna Wagner), 45, 47, 320

Dietsch, Pierre Louis, 64, 289
Doepler, Karl Emil, 474–5
Dolci, Carlo, 71
Dolgoruki, Prince, 251
Donizetti, Gaetano, 60
Doré, Gustave, 270
Dorn, Heinrich, 28, 49, 50, 433
Draeseke, Felix, 264–5, 325, 396
Dresden, 171, 178; court theatre, 11, 12, 22, 62, 67, 91, 135; Kreuzschule, 19, 21; Liedertafel choral society, 84, 115; revolution in, 15, 130, 137–40, 175, 213, 257; Vaterlandsverein, 122, 130–2; W kapellmeister in, 75, 80–92, 113, 119, 121–2, 150; W's flight from, 94, 118, 123, 139–49; W's friends in, 115; W's library in, xi, 94–5, 103, 117, 133, 136, 145, 219, 233, 235, 320, 326; W's residence in, 11, 18–20, 23–4, 71–4, 94, 97–8, 106, 340, 522, 561; W's visits to, 45, 308, 344, 433; W's works performed in, 14, 67, 70, 73, 78, 116, 178
Drews, Arthur, 136
Droysen, Johann Gustav, 98, 127, 143, 561
Düfflipp, Lorenz von, 382, 387, 394, 414–15, 422, 433, 436, 446, 460, 461–2, 463, 488, 512–14, 515, 516, 519–20, 548, 623
Dumba, N., 426
Du Moulin Eckart, Richard, xii, 493, 596, 622, 627
Duncker, Lina, 213, 223
Duparc, Henri, 426
Duperon, Anquetil, 623
Dürer, Albrecht, 420
Dustmann, Luise, see Meyer-Dustmann, Luise
Dwight, John Sullivan, 552
Dysart, Lord, 208

Echter, Michael, 474
Eckermann, Johann Peter, xv, xix
Eckert, Karl, 329–30
Eckstein, Friedrich, xviii
Eger, Manfred, 327
Eichel, Gottlob Friedrich, 4
Eichelin, Johanna Sophie, see Wagner, Johanna Sophie
Einsiedel, Ernst Rudolf von, 41
Einstein, Alfred, 49
Eisenhart (Secretary), 623
Eiser, Otto, x, 501
Elisabeth, Empress of Austria, 296, 309
Ellis, William Ashton, 324

Engels, Friedrich, 133
Enzenberg, Karl Graf, 377
Erard, Mme, 241
Erlanger, Emile, 294, 326
Esser, Heinrich, 276, 295, 298, 380, 485
Ettmüller, Ludwig, 95, 219
Eugénie, Empress of France, 280
Euripides, 107, 423, 504, 505

Fauche, H., 619, 623
Feen, Die (Wagner), 36–8, 42, 43, 76, 453, 585
Fehr, Max, ix, 202, 205
Ferreira-França, Ernesto, 232
Ferry, Jules, 271
Fétis, F. J., 267
Feuerbach, Ludwig, 145
Feustel, Friedrich, 439, 441, 453, 454, 460, 461, 482, 485, 506, 511, 517, 518, 523–4, 539, 572, 587, 623
Fischer, Franz, 580
Fischer, Wilhelm, 67, 71, 75, 135
Flaubert, Gustave, 60
Flaxland (publisher), 326
Fliegende Holländer, Der (Wagner), 132, 271; composition of, 63–5; conception of, 51, 59–60; musical language of, 49, 65, 66, 109, 174, 189; performances (projected and actual), 67–8, 70, 73–4, 114, 117, 174, 177, 204, 273, 487; publication of, 114–16, 118, 122–3, 159; revisions of, 65–6; sources, 60
Florence, 148, 511–12, 520
Florimo, Francesco, 559
Forman, Alfred, 602–3
Förster, August, 514, 515–16
Förster, Bernhard, 568
Förster-Nietzsche, Elisabeth, see Nietzsche, Elisabeth
Fould, Achille, 280, 286
Fouqué, Friedrich Heinrich Carl, 591
Franck, Dr Hermann, 104, 106, 120
Franco-Prussian War, 426–8, 429–31, 434
Frantz, Constantin, 356, 367, 370, 377, 395, 541
Frauenstädt, Julius, 199, 200
Frederick the Great, 4, 317, 459, 460
Freiligrath, Ferdinand, 214
Fricke, Richard, 481, 489, 498
Friedrich I, Grand Duke of Baden, 232, 257, 295, 304, 325, 326, 462
Friedrich I. (Wagner), 127–8

Friedrich August I, King of Saxony, 84
Friedrich August II, King of Saxony, 72, 75, 84, 86, 91, 121, 129, 132, 137, 176, 204, 258
Friedrich Wilhelm III, King of Prussia, 40
Friedrich Wilhelm IV, King of Prussia, 120–1, 152
Fritzsch, Ernst Wilhelm, 32
Fröbel, Julius, 359, 360–1, 384, 389–90, 394
Frommann, Alwine, 55
Fürstner, Adolf, 78, 123
Furtwängler, Wilhelm, xv, 77, 187, 420

Gade, Niels, 88
Gaillard, Karl, 76, 101, 105, 113
Gangi, Prince, 578
Garibaldi, Giuseppe, 578
Garrigues, C. H. N., 620
Gaspérini, Auguste de, 268–9, 270, 272, 273, 276, 287, 297, 619·
Gast, Peter, 484, 491, 502, 534, 591, 593
Gautier (Mendès), Judith, ix, xiii, xvii, xviii, 17, 56, 270, 393, 410, 416–18, 425, 426–7, 442, 444, 448, 498, 506, 517, 527, 528–30, 545, 565, 569, 573–4, 577, 581, 623, 627
Gautier, Théophile, 277, 410, 416, 581
Geck, Martin, xi, xx, 618
Genelli, Bonaventura, 144–5, 411, 433, 459, 473, 538
Georg, Mitalis, 175
Gérard-Doscot, R., 564
Gersdorff, Karl Freiherr von, 338, 441, 444, 455, 456, 461, 484, 491, 499
Gevaert, François Auguste, 273
Geyer, Benjamin, 9
Geyer (Avenarius), Cäcilie (W's half-sister), 7, 11, 13, 18, 71, 270
Geyer, Christian Gottlieb (Ludwig Geyer's father), 6
Geyer, Ludwig Heinrich Christian (W's stepfather), 6–9, 11, 12, 17–18, 19, 67, 459, 469
Gfrörer, August Friedrich, 476
Glasenapp, Carl Friedrich, xi, xii, 121, 278, 369, 423, 488, 508, 512, 555, 565, 570, 573
Gluck, Christoph Willibald, 38, 296; works, 80, 106–7, 121, 204, 454, 481, 559, conducted by W, 80, 106, 204
Gobineau, Comte Joseph Arthur de, ix, xvii, 564, 565–6, 569, 579, 587
Goethe, Johann Wolfgang von, xv, xix, 4, 7, 9, 10, 20, 69, 95, 98, 138, 199, 224, 254, 279, 304, 323–4, 390, 411, 413, 420, 425,

428, 469, 476, 486, 503, 528, 530, 557, 562, 571, 578; influence on W, 23, 284; works, 5, 106, 140, 320, 343, 468, 470, 539, *Faust*, xv, 90, 243–4, 284, 304, 424, 579, *Tasso*, 237, 255, 260, 271, 324, 506–7, *Wilhelm Meister*, 19, 296, 338, 575, 622

Golther, Wolfgang, 236

Goltz, Professor, 554

Görres, Joseph, 103, 528

*Götterdämmerung* (Wagner), 19, 421, 427; compared with *Siegfrieds Tod*, 151–2, 162–3, 418; completion of, 468, 470, 475; composition of, 231, 418–19, 424, 425, 426, 437–9, 441–3, 449, 451, 465, 468, 470, 475, 589; motives in, 202, 419, 438, 442; new ending for, xiv, 219, 442–3, 622; orchestration, 458–9, 475, 479; performances, 426, 477–8, 479; readings of, 455–6; sketches for, 442–3, 476, 622

Gottfried von Strassburg, 232

Gounod, Charles, 270, 273, 292

Gozzi, Carlo, 36

Grahn, Lucile, 396

Grässe, J. G. T., 94

Gregor, Joseph, 343

Grein, Edir, 618

Grimm, Jacob, 93–6, 103, 152, 158, 161, 185, 284, 320

Grimm, Wilhelm, 94, 96, 103, 158, 193

Grisi, Ernesta, 416

Gross, Adolf von, 294, 587

Gruben, Baron von, 359

Gutzkow, Karl, 91–2

Habeneck, François Antoine, 51, 53, 87

Hagen, F. H. von der, 94, 233

Hagenbuch, Franz, 142

Haimberger (violinist), 175

Halévy, Jacques Fromental, 60, 71, 558

Hallwachs, Reinhard, 414

Halm, August, 186

Handel, George Frideric, 477

Hanslick, Eduard, 28, 107, 295–6, 301, 308, 402, 426, 484, 489, 519

Härtel, Dr Hermann, 220–1, 227, 240–1, 263

Härtel, Raymund, 114, 220–1, 227, 263

Hartenfels (impresario), 256

Hatzfeld-Wildenburg, Paul Graf von, 280

Hauser, Franz, 38

Haussmann, Georges Eugène, 285

Haydn, Joseph, 530, 532–3

Hebbel, Friedrich, 310

Heckel, Emil, 437, 439, 460–2, 463, 467, 485, 487, 508, 512

Hegel, Georg Wilhelm Friedrich, 145

Heine, Ferdinand, 62, 67, 71, 72, 92, 103, 114, 135–6, 177

Heine, Heinrich, 51, 53, 60, 61, 64, 65

Heinse, Wilhelm, 39

Helene Pavlovna, Grand Duchess, 312, 314, 315, 396

Hellmesberger, Joseph, 478

Helmholtz, Hermann, 478

Herbeck, Johann, 415

Herder, Johann Gottfried von, 99

Hermann, Gustav, 322

Hermann, Paul, 94

Herwegh, Emma, 241, 245, 248, 334

Herwegh, Georg, 163, 165, 179, 180, 197, 198, 334

Herwegh, Marcel, 214

Herzen, Alexander von, 292

Herzen, Olga von, 292

Hettner, Hermann, 214

Heusler, Andreas, 95

Hey, Julius, 472, 481, 483, 487, 489, 523

Hiebendahl (oboist), 115–16

Hillebrand, Karl, 148

Hiller, Ferdinand, 103, 117, 119

Hindemith, Paul, 238

*Hochzeit, Die* (Wagner), 35–6

Hödel, Max, 538

Hodge & Essex (concert agents), 516–18

Hoffmann, E. T. A., 5, 61, 72, 281; influence on W, 19, 24; works, 10, 19, 29, 70, 215, 477

Hoffmann, Joseph, 473–4, 623

Hofmann, Julius von, 339, 362, 363, 380

Hofmannsthal, Hugo von, 108

Hofmiller, Joseph, 534

*Hohe Braut, Die* (Wagner), 49, 73, 128

Hohenlohe, Prince Konstantin von, 183

Hohenlohe-Schillingsfürst, Prince Chlodwig, 361–2, 379–80, 384, 385–7, 389–90, 620

Hohenzollern-Hechingen, Prince of, 313

Holtei, Karl von, 46, 50

Holtzmann, Adolf, 207

Homer, 20, 211, 407, 413, 424, 473

Hornstein, Robert von, 198, 199

Hugo, Victor, 96, 348, 431–2, 528, 558, 619

Hülsen, Botho von, 141, 204–5, 256, 434, 487–8, 567

Hülsen, Helene von, 487

Humboldt, Wilhelm von, 98, 254
Hummel, Johann Nepomuk, 25, 27
Humperdinck, Engelbert, 82, 289, 557–8, 559–60, 562, 580, 590
Hürlimann, Dr Martin, 319
Hurn, Philip Dutton, 243

Jachmann, Alfred, 517
Jahn, Otto, 81, 191, 221
Janin, Jules, 271, 291
Jannequin, Clément, 559
Jauner, Franz, 482–3, 484, 515, 519, 549
Jenkins, Dr Newell Sill, x, 551–3, 602–3, 625–6
*Jesus von Nazareth* (Wagner), 136–7, 145
*Jewry in Music* (Wagner), 153, 407
Joachim, Joseph, 308, 433
Johann, King of Saxony, 217–18, 264, 282
Joly, Anténor, 52
Joly, René, 426
Joukowsky, see Zhukovsky
*Junge Siegfried, Der* (Wagner), 46, 158, 161, 163

Käfferlein (Bayreuth lawyer), 441
Kalergis (Muchanoff), Marie, 277–8, 406, 407, 476
Kant, Immanuel, 390
*Kapitulation, Eine* (Wagner), see *Capitulation, A*
Kapp, Julius, 90, 243, 271, 277, 291, 325, 373–4, 488, 620
Karl, Prince of Bavaria, 363
Karl August, Grand Duke of Saxony, 9–10
Kaulbach, Wilhelm von, 391
Keller, Gottfried, 172, 175, 213–15, 223, 241, 280
Kempen von Fichtenstamm, Johann, 257–8
Keudell, Robert von, 510
Kietz, Ernst Benedikt, 52, 70, 71, 73, 74, 105, 113, 116, 150, 156, 163, 176, 178, 294
Kietz, Gustav Adolf, 105–6, 133, 135–6, 467, 469, 480
Kittl, Johann, 128, 322
Kleist, Heinrich von, 199
Klemm, Gustav, 79
Klepperbein, Wilhelmine, 394
Klindworth, Georg Heinrich, 277, 281, 359–60
Klindworth, Karl, 149, 189, 208, 209, 222, 227, 247–8, 256, 271, 278, 326, 407, 572
Knebel, Karl von, 9

Kniese, Julius, 570–1
Köhler, Louis, 189
Königsberg, 13, 44, 47
Köppen, C. F., 255
Kossak, Ernst, 128, 199
Kranz, Walter, 98
Krausse, Robert, 469
Kriele, Hans,. 115–16
Krug, Gustav, 441
Kummer, Friedrich August, 87
Kurth, Ernst, 186–7, 237
Kurtz, Hermann, 233
Kusche, Ludwig, 624–5
Küstner, Theodor, 67, 70, 120

Lachmann, Karl, 103
Lachner, Ignaz, 542
Lalas, Demetrius, 471
Lamprecht, Pfaffe, 128
Lanckoronski, Count, 296
Langlois, Alexandre, 459
Lascoux, M., 577
Lassen, Eduard, 415
Laube, Heinrich, 36, 39, 52–3, 54, 296, 402
Laussot, Eugène, 147–8, 149
Laussot, Jessie (Taylor), 147–50, 222, 381, 396, 512
Lecky, William Edward Hartpole, 545
Lehrs, Samuel, 52, 70, 71, 75, 80, 93, 97, 99, 153
Leipzig, 117; Battle of, 6; Euterpe Society, 33; Gewandhaus, 6, 33, 53, 77, 307; Nikolaischule, 27, 144; theatre, 22, 28, 33, 37, 402, 514; Thomaskirche, 4, 6, 29; Thomasschule, 4, 27; University of, 4, 7, 27–8, 29; W born in, 5–6; W's residence in, 20, 27, 35; W's visits to, 102, 307–8, 406, 410, 433, 436, 452; W's works performed in, 515, 519, 547–8
Lenbach, Franz von, 453, 472–3, 476, 550, 565, 626
Leo, Leonardo, 559
Leonardo da Vinci, 259
Leopold, Prince (son of Queen Victoria), 517
Leprince, G., xi, 428
Leroy, Adolphe, 270
Leroy, Léon, 268, 270
Leroy, Maxime, 268, 283
Lessing, Gotthold Ephraim, 5
*Leubald* (Wagner), 21, 28
Levetzow, Ulrike von, 304, 530

Levi, Hermann, 415, 423, 550, 565, 570–2, 580, 584, 591, 627
Lewald, August, 50
*Liebesverbot, Das* (Wagner), 40, 42–3, 50, 52, 76, 102; performances, 12–13, 42, 43–4, 272, 453
Lindau, Paul, 326
Lindau, Rudolf, 281, 326
Lipinski, Karl, 81
Lippert, Woldemar, 258
Liszt (Ollivier), Blandine, 240, 271, 278, 298
Liszt, Eduard, 315, 327
Liszt, Franz, 73, 109, 122, 141, 142, 146, 147, 148, 152, 153, 156, 158, 160, 164, 175, 176, 185, 189, 191, 194, 200, 217, 227, 250, 257, 264, 267, 277, 343, 354, 356, 385, 438, 469, 547, 627; and his daughter Cosima, 334, 335–6, 350, 354–5, 405–6, 450–1, 475, 590; as conductor of W's works, 151, 154–5, 204; friendship with W, 178, 198, 216, 220, 231, 241, 248, 259, 278–9, 297, 442, 445–6, 496, 581; meetings with W, 140, 178–9, 183–4, 221, 222–4, 336, 391–2, 450–1, 460, 477–8, 496, 562, 581, 588–91; on the Cosima/W affair, 336, 355, 374, 391, 418, 568; on W's works, 104–5, 111, 267, 589; W on the music of, 225, 465, 477; works, 148, 207, 222, 225, 261, 322, 347, 373, 465, 477, 592
Lobe, J. C., 155
Logier, Johann Bernhard, 28
*Lohengrin* (Wagner), 66, 267, 340, 464, 467, 473, 488; alternative endings for, 104–5; as romantic opera, 111–12; composition of, 98, 102, 105–6, 107, 113, 127, 129, 533; influences on, 86, 107; Ludwig II and, 109, 329, 331–2, 333, 565; motives in, 108–9; musical language of, 55, 108–11; orchestration in, 110–11; performances (projected and actual), 103, 120, 135, 151, 154–6, 159, 177, 191, 256, 271, 272, 273, 277, 295, 311, 332, 374, 389, 402, 434, 439, 482–3, 484, 558, 576; publications of, 122, 190, 485; sources, 93, 101–3; text, 107–8, 119, 271; W's first hearing of, 177, 295
London, 140, 149, 514, 567; W in, 87, 114, 206–10, 516–18, 520, 528, 551, 572
Lorenz, Alfred, 109, 186, 201, 259, 380, 383, 547
Louis Napoleon, Prince, *see* Napoleon III
Louis Philippe, King, 129
Lucas, C. T. L., 70, 103

Lucca, Giovanna, 402, 404, 496, 558, 586
Lucerne, 154, 260–6, 413; *see also* Tribschen
Lüders, Karl, 208, 517
Ludwig I, King of Bavaria, 358
Ludwig II, King of Bavaria, xi, 63, 139, 227, 316, 353, 370–1, 469; and Bayreuth, 436, 438, 446, 460, 461–3, 470, 488, 494–5, 496–7, 507–8, 511, 513–14, 519–20, 523–4, 553–4, 584; and the Bülow/W scandal, 374, 377–8, 382, 388, 402, 405–6, 422–3; and his ministers, 340–1, 345–6, 358–9, 380; and W's banishment from Munich, 363–4, 366, 370, 385–6; artistic plans, 339, 345, 384–5, 387, 389–91, 394–5, 438, 460; as W's patron, 332, 339, 346, 365–6, 371, 463, 470, 471, 477, 488, 524, 550, 561, 596, 626; engagement to Princess Sophie, 330, 385; first meeting with W, 119, 330, 332; intrigues concerning, 341, 359–63, 366, 385–6; performances ordered by, 409–10, 414–17, 422–3, 425, 433, 520, 548, 565, 586, 625; plans to abdicate, 374–6, 379, 386; relationship with W, 330–2, 341, 358, 363, 366, 389, 394, 397, 421–2, 427, 519, 593; W's works dedicated to, 43, 397–8, 459; W's works owned by, 438, 446, 515, 549–50, 618, 626; W's works written for, 338, 354, 356, 357–8, 496, 519, 541
Luther, Martin, 9, 317, 340, 579, 622
*Luthers Hochzeit* (Wagner), 403, 542
Lüttichau, Ida von, 104, 140
Lüttichau, Wolf Adolf August von, 67, 73, 74, 85, 87, 91–2, 118, 120–2, 131, 135, 258
Lutz, Johann von, 346, 361–2, 363, 365, 376

Mack, Dietrich, 622
Magdeburg, 12–13, 40, 43, 51, 67, 113, 452–3, 459
Magnan, Bernard Pierre, Marshal of France, 273
Maier, Mathilde, xviii, 304, 305, 308, 310, 311–13, 315, 333, 350, 361, 380, 396, 497, 504, 518, 624
Mainz, 294, 301, 302, 304, 315, 452, 566
Makart, Hans, 473, 478
Mallarmé, Stéphane, 283
Mann, Thomas, 111, 112, 164, 193, 214, 236, 324, 503, 585
Mannheim, 82, 437, 439, 452, 549
Marbach, Dr Oswald, 13
Maria Pavlovna, Grand Duchess of Saxony, 140

Marienbad, 102, 295, 299–300
Marschner, Heinrich August, 39, 66
Martini, Giovanni Battista, 29
Marx, Karl, 133
Massmann, H. F., 233
Materna, Amalie, 482, 498, 580
Maurin-Chevillard Quartet, 184
Mauro, Seraphine, 298, 302
Maximilian, Archduke, 258
Maximilian II, King of Bavaria, 316, 332
Maximilian, Prince of Thurn und Taxis, 359–60
Méhul, Etienne, 47, 170, 558
*Mein Leben* (Wagner), xv, 8, 9, 41, 47, 51, 85, 93, 94, 121, 137, 147, 153, 327, 335, 492; dictation of, 137–8, 232, 242, 357–8, 370, 379, 381, 407; written for Ludwig II, 138, 242, 357–8, 563
*Meistersinger von Nürnberg, Die* (Wagner), 409, 489, 515, 562; completion of, 66, 393; composition of, 299–302, 304–6, 313, 318, 329, 365, 367–8, 369–70, 374, 377, 379, 380–3, 386, 389, 392, 527, 533; conception of, 102, 294, 299; ending of, 383–4; influences on, 30, 255, 561; musical language of, 110, 231, 297; orchestration in, 308, 392–3; performances (projected and actual), 307, 309, 338, 391, 395, 396–8, 401, 402, 439, 465, 488; readings of, 301, 302–3, 304, 308, 312; rehearsals, 395–7, 401; sketches for, 305, 380, 382, 384
Mendelssohn-Bartholdy, Felix, 77, 120, 206, 477, 557
Mendès, Catulle, xii, 270, 393, 416–17, 427, 430–2, 529, 623
Mendès, Judith, *see* Gautier, Judith
Menzel, Adolf, 478, 480
Meser, C. F., 115–17, 123
Metternich-Sándor, Princess Pauline, 280–1, 286, 291, 296, 300–1
Meyendorff, Baroness, 446
Meyer, Friederike, 308
Meyerbeer, Giacomo, 36, 47, 52, 63–4, 67–8, 117–18, 121, 273, 280, 291, 321, 322, 330, 369, 453; influence on W, 48, 55; meetings with W, 51, 119–20, 208; W on, 50, 152–4, 281; works, 73, 147, 153, 154
Meyer-Dustmann, Luise, 82, 296, 301, 308
Meysenbug, Malwida von, 61, 208, 270, 271, 286, 290, 291–2, 301, 342, 454, 461, 508, 554, 556, 560, 583
Michaelson (agent), 191

Michelangelo Buonarotti, 511, 520, 566
Milan, 259, 404
Millenkovich-Morold, Max, 374, 388
Mitterwurzer, Anton, 89
Moltke, Helmut Graf von, 455
Mottl, Felix, 484, 489, 624
Mozart, Wolfgang Amadeus, 30, 38, 62, 107, 191, 199, 296, 453, 544; conducted by W, 47, 80, 82, 171, 203–4, 439; influence on W, 31, 81–3; works, 82, 203–4, 213, 237, 530, 531, 532, *Don Giovanni*, 40, 41, 80, 82–3, 171, 213, 329, *Le Nozze di Figaro*, 82–3, 559, *Die Zauberflöte*, 82, 171, 439, 472, 473, 532, 560
Muchanoff, Marie, *see* Kalergis, Marie
Müller, Alexander, 142
Müller, Christian Gottlieb, 29
Müller, Franz, 155, 219
Müller, Karl Otfried, 143, 412
Muncker, Theodor, 441, 454, 456, 474, 550, 581, 625
Munich, 177, 557, 573; court opera, 67, 116, 256, 300, 401–2, 512, 513–14, 515, 519–20, 523–4, 549, 553, 586; W's residence in, 263, 329–64 *passim*, 522; W's visits to, 144, 316, 386, 389, 393, 395, 406, 415, 462, 512, 519, 550, 564–5; W's works performed in, xiii, 38, 66, 341–3, 391, 396–8, 414–17, 422–3, 426, 465, 473, 474, 515, 548, 564
*Music of the Future* (Wagner), 283, 332

Naples, 550–62, 563, 574, 575, 626
Napoleon Bonaparte, 4, 6
Napoleon III, Emperor, 162, 272, 280–1, 286, 386
Nerval, Gérard de, 155
*Neue Zeitschrift für Musik*, 107, 146, 153, 155, 173, 225
Neumann, Angelo, 484, 516, 547–8, 566–8, 569, 576
Neumann, Erich, 621
Newman, Ernest, ix, x, 7, 9–10, 20, 31, 47, 50, 52, 77, 91, 107, 113, 115, 123, 133, 155, 179, 191, 236, 238, 245, 276, 308, 324, 331, 336, 362, 373–4, 396, 450, 461, 477, 491, 492, 499, 500–5, 509, 555, 565, 571, 572, 583, 618, 620, 625
Niemann, Albert, 55, 247, 286, 287, 289, 292, 298, 481–2, 487, 497, 627
Nietzsche, Elisabeth (sister of Friedrich), x, 410–11, 432–3, 457, 477, 479, 491, 500,

501–2, 509–10, 534, 536, 537–8, 568, 583, 587, 622
Nietzsche, Friedrich, ix, x, xvii, 28, 99, 427, 562, 591, 593; alienation from W, 368, 464–5, 477, 494, 508–9, 534–5, 537–8, 556–7, 583; and the Bayreuth festival, 425, 461, 491, 499–505, 513; friendship with W, 423–4, 433, 440–1, 449–50, 454–5, 456–7, 459, 479–80, 491–2; illness, 428, 499–502, 508; influenced by W, 412, 433, 440, 622; on W's works, 96, 259, 338, 421, 439–40, 451, 538, 542; visits to W, xiii, 410–11, 421, 424, 432, 444, 456–7; works, 423–4, 432–3, 440, 446–7, 454, 457–8, 461, 465, 476, 491–2, 500, 503, 510, 587, *The Birth of Tragedy*, 411–12, 440, *Human all too Human*, 500, 533–8, 541, 555, *The Wagner Case*, 8, 464, 484, 508, 557
Nimier, Roger, 566
Nobiling, Karl, 539
Nordmann, Johannes, 100
Nottebohm, Gustav, xiii
Novalis (pseudonym of Friedrich von Hardenberg), 235

Oehme (brassfounder), 138
Offenbach, Jacques, 429
Oldenberg, Hermann, 588
Ollivier, Blandine, *see* Liszt, Blandine
Ollivier, Emile, 240, 271, 281–2, 298, 426
*Opera and Drama* (Wagner), 143, 153–4, 156–7, 173, 332, 395, 432, 452, 561
Ott, Louise, 503
Ott-Imhof, Konrad, 178
Overbeck, Franz, 464, 534, 587, 622
Overbeck, Frau Ida, x, 583
Overbeck, Johann Friedrich, 473

Pachta, Jenny, 32–3
Palermo, 575–8
Paris, 49, 140, 577, 590; Conservatoire orchestra, 53, 87, 172, 184, 420; Grand Opéra, 51, 52, 62, 64, 272, 276, 281; Jockey Club, 283, 290–1; Opéra Comique, 50; revolution in, 128–9, 132, 163; Théâtre de la Renaissance, 52, 272; Théâtre Italien, 272–3, 275; W's friends in, 52–3, 59–60, 62, 70, 282, 292–3; W's residence in, 51–4, 60–70 *passim*, 121, 129; W's visits to, 143, 147, 149, 184, 238, 240–1, 267–94 *passim*, 296–7, 301–2, 393, 551; W's works performed in, 290–2, 416, 576

*Parsifal* (Wagner), xviii, 16, 18, 324, 338, 421, 468, 509, 538, 556, 562, 627; as W's last work, 354, 563, 585–6; composition of, xii, 403, 468, 470, 484, 486, 514, 524, 527–30, 531–3, 541–7, 548, 562–3, 568, 569–70, 573, 575–7, 589; designs for the staging of, 557, 563–4, 574, 580; earliest conceptions of, 216, 226–7, 254–5, 262, 279, 355, 451; musical language of, 84–5, 288, 527, 542, 546–7, 585; orchestration in, 16, 544–5, 565, 575–6; performances (projected and actual), x, xvii, 545, 549–50, 552, 559–60, 564, 570, 572, 578, 582–4, 586, 625, 626; prose scenario, xiv, 139, 354, 421, 509; readings of, 523; rehearsals, xvii, 580; restricted to Bayreuth, 553–4; sources, 102, 476, 482; text, 519, 528–9, 533, 576, 627
Pasdeloup, Jules Etienne, 402
Patersi, Madame, 184
Pätz, Johanna, *see* Wagner, Johanna
Paul, Prince, of Thurn und Taxis, 360, 380
Pecht, Friedrich, xi, 52–3, 59, 304, 341
Pedro II, Dom, Emperor of Brazil, 232
Perfall, Karl von, 373, 396, 401–2, 414, 415–16, 520, 524, 548
Perrin, Emile, 271
Pestalozzi, Salomon, 203
Petipa, 285
Petrarch, 20
Pfister (Police Assessor), 359
Pfistermeister, Franz Seraph von, 329, 341, 345–6, 359–62, 363, 366, 375, 376, 380, 384, 415, 421, 618
Pfitzner, Hans, 77, 108, 259
Pfordten, Ludwig von der, 340, 362, 366, 370, 378, 384
*Pilgrimage to Beethoven, A* (Wagner), 26, 54
Pillet, Léon, 64
Planer, Amalie, 46–7, 49
Planer, Minna, *see* Wagner, Minna
Planer, Natalie, 41, 61, 144, 243, 303, 369
Plato, 100, 331, 424
Pleyel, Ignaz Joseph, 31
Plüddemann, Martin, 521, 559–60
Plutarch, 279, 594
Podach, Erich F., x, 502, 503, 537, 583, 587
Pohl, Richard, 84, 238, 391, 493
Pollini, Bernhard, 514
Porges, Heinrich, 109–10, 111, 246, 296, 308, 315, 323, 340, 364, 390, 416, 479, 489–91, 580, 624

Porter, Andrew, 624
Poschinger, Heinrich von, 626
Pourtalès, Albert, Count, 280
Pourtalès, Countess, 297
Pourtalès, Guy de, 274
Praeger, Ferdinand, 208–9
Prague, 19, 33, 128, 137, 311, 313
Preen, Friedrich von, 541
Preller, Friedrich, 473
Prévost, Jean, 565
Proudhon, Pierre Joseph, 143, 163
Puschmann, Theodor, 450
Pusinelli, Anton, 115–16, 117, 118, 122–3,
   217, 252, 269–70, 307, 342, 368, 433, 497

Raabe, Peter, 467
Rackowitz, Baron Joachim, 312
Raff, Joachim, 384
Rahl, Carl, 473
Raumer, Friedrich, 69
Redern, Wilhelm von, 68, 70, 119
Redwitz, Oskar von, 341
Rée, Paul, 508, 587
Reissiger, Gottlieb, 67, 73, 86, 121, 128, 129,
   198, 321
Renoir, Auguste, 577–8
Reutter, Isidore von, 381
Reyer, Ernest, 271, 273
Rhaden, Editha von, 312, 314, 315, 396
Rheingold, Das (Wagner), 193, 202, 239, 419,
   515, 618; composition of, 181–2, 184–90,
   266, 542; conception of, 180, 183; form in,
   186, 188, 225; musical language of, 55,
   109, 187–8, 265; musico-poetic synthesis
   in, 185–6, 188–9; performances, xiii, 232,
   248, 271, 309, 409–10, 414–17, 422, 473,
   474; publications of, 276, 402; scoring of,
   189–90, 221; sketches for, 159, 161, 163,
   184–7
Richter, Hans, 277, 391–2, 427, 429, 471,
   474, 485, 489, 515, 517; as a conductor of
   W's works, 414–15, 480, 497
Richter, Jean Paul Friedrich, 10, 317
Ricordi, Giulio, 593–4
Riehl, W. H., 439
Riemann, Pastor, 356
Rienzi (Wagner), 71, 115, 132, 294, 515;
   composition of, 46, 48–9, 51, 54, 60, 67;
   influence of grand opera on, 48–9, 55; in
   relation to later works, 55; performances
   (projected and actual), 14, 55–6, 67, 70, 73,
   113, 114, 119–20, 121, 128, 152, 177, 204,

256, 416, 512; publication of, 116, 122–3;
   rehearsals, 72–3; sources, 46
Rietz, Julius, 191
Riga, 13, 45, 60, 178, 522; theatre in, 46; W's
   flight from, 51
Ring des Nibelungen, Der (Wagner), 149–50,
   157, 223, 417, 426, 430, 488, 561, 565; and
   Schopenhauer, 197, 199–200; composition of, 66, 172, 218, 227, 263, 339, 346,
   368; conception of, 98–9, 123, 128, 134,
   150; designs for the staging of, 470, 472–5;
   leitmotiv in, 169, 174; musical realization
   of, 74, 136, 169, 176–7, 179; performances
   (projected and actual), 177, 179, 338, 339,
   423, 425, 437, 438, 462–4, 495–8, 514–15,
   516, 520, 547–9, 566–9; publication of,
   220–1, 257, 263–4; readings of, 165, 176,
   179, 214, 312; rehearsals, 190, 195, 471–2,
   475, 480–2, 489–91, 492–4, 499–500, 502,
   503; sources, 93–7; text, 94, 160–5, 199,
   214, 235, 310–11, 332, 602–3; see also Götterdämmerung, Junge Siegfried, Rheingold,
   Siegfried, Siegfrieds Tod, Walküre
Ritter, Alexander, 287, 290
Ritter, Julie, 147–8, 150, 160, 164, 169, 176,
   190, 194, 205, 211, 222, 223–4, 226
Ritter, Karl, 135–6, 147, 149–50, 155,
   169–71, 198, 199, 200, 217, 223, 247,
   248–9, 251, 578–9
Roche, Edmond, 269, 281, 292
Röckel, August, 129, 132–2, 137, 138, 145,
   188, 198, 378, 386, 387, 402
Röckel, Eduard, 208
Rohde, Erwin, 410, 411, 412, 424–5, 427,
   432, 439, 441, 456, 458, 464, 491, 499, 622
Rollett, Hermann, 194
Rome, 510–11, 520, 558, 583, 597
Root, Waverly Lewis, 243
Rossini, Gioacchino, 42, 47, 181, 199, 275
Royer, Alphons, 281, 286, 289
Rubinstein, Joseph, 443–4, 471, 481, 484,
   544, 560, 571, 575, 577, 595–7, 603

Saburoff, General (director of St Petersburg
   theatre), 285
Sainton, Prosper, 208, 517
Saint-Saëns, Camille, 415, 426
St Petersburg, 285, 294, 311, 314, 396
Salis-Schwabe, Julie, 342
Salomé, Lou von, 583, 587
Samuel, Lehmann, 175
Sanctis, Francesco de, 242, 243

San Marte (pseudonym of A. Schulz), 103
Sarazenin, Die (Wagner), 69–70
Sardou, Victorien, 281
Sayn-Wittgenstein, Caroline, Princess, see Wittgenstein, Caroline
Sayn-Wittgenstein, Princess Marie, see Wittgenstein, Princess Marie
Schack, Adolf Friedrich von, 144
Schanzenbach, Dr Oscar, 361, 385–6
Schanzer (von Bülow), Marie, 583, 593
Scharf, Anton, 473
Schauss, Friedrich von, 342–3, 395
Schade, John H., 189
Schelle, Eduard, 426
Schelling, Friedrich Wilhelm, 145
Schemann, Ludwig, xix, xxi, 495, 500–1, 504, 523, 540, 579
Scheuerlin, Georg, 49
Schiller, Johann Christoph Friedrich von, 69, 224, 254, 323, 332, 343, 361, 363, 390, 411, 425, 469, 476, 490, 556, 562; influence on W, 23, 279; works, 5, 7, 33, 160, 279, 413
Schirmer, Gustav, 598
Schladebuch, Julius, 155
Schlechta, Karl, 502, 625
Schleinitz, Alexander, Count, 455
Schleinitz, Marie (von Buch), Countess, 335, 433, 434, 436, 462, 482, 487, 536, 568
Schlesinger, Maurice, 60–1, 71
Schletter, Heinrich, 117
Schmitt, Friedrich, 340
Schnappauf, Bernhard, 528
Schnorr von Carolsfeld, Julius, 474
Schnorr von Carolsfeld, Ludwig, 343, 344–5, 347, 381, 438
Schnorr von Carolsfeld, Malvina, 343, 381–2, 620
Schobinger (student), 426
Schoenberg, Arnold, 325
Schön, Friedrich, 579
Schönaich, Gustav, 296, 315, 316
Schopenhauer, Arthur, xv, 304, 343, 384, 438, 476, 480, 513, 557, 597, 623; influence on W, 105, 162, 197–201, 211–12, 231, 236, 254, 269, 279–80, 367; views on W, 198–9; works, 148, 162, 196, 197, 200, 426
Schorn, Adelheid von, 583
Schott, Betty, 26, 301, 304
Schott, Franz, 24–6, 27, 276, 298, 300, 301, 304, 306–7, 401, 416, 422, 425, 468, 471, 476, 566

Schott's Söhne (publishers), 276, 392, 396, 487, 510, 586, 627
Schrenk, Erich von, 234
Schröder-Devrient, Wilhelmine, 22–3, 38, 67, 69, 72–4, 100, 113, 115, 118, 144, 155, 321, 420, 436, 580, 585
Schrön, Otto von, 551
Schubert, Franz, 592
Schuh, Willi, xi
Schumann, Clara (Wieck), 28, 33, 34
Schumann, Robert, 33, 51, 77, 120, 199, 477
Schuré, Edouard, 344, 365, 494, 501, 502–3, 509
Schwebsch, Erich, 594
Schwind, Moritz von, 618
Scott, Walter, 220
Scribe, Eugène, 49–50, 73
Seebach, Albin Leo von, 282
Seelisberg, 211
Seidl, Anton, 471, 533, 545, 567
Semper, Gottfried, 135, 213–14, 242, 339, 340–1, 355, 384, 390, 394–5, 478
Sgambati, Giovanni, 510–11
Shakespeare, William, 413, 456, 490; influence on W, 21, 22, 23, 28; works, 21, 40, 48
Shaw, George Bernard, 133
Sieger, Die (Wagner), xiv, 218–19, 224, 255, 338, 354, 395–6, 409, 588
Siegfried (Wagner), 15–16, 17, 139, 219, 220, 340, 411, 419, 446, 464; completion of, 414, 425, 430; composition of, xiv, 221–2, 224, 225, 227–8, 232, 266, 337, 347, 349–50, 363–4, 365, 407–9, 412–13, 418; form in, 413; motives in, 237, 407, 409, 413–14; musical language of, 225, 409, 413–14, 474; performances, 426, 433, 477; resumption of, 263, 269, 272, 339, 407; sketches for, 337; see also Junge Siegfried
Siegfried Idyll (Wagner), 336, 429, 430, 439, 441, 476, 545
Siegfrieds Tod (Wagner), 150, 151, 156, 158, 219, 220; readings of, 135, 136, 143, 148, 184, 481; sketches for, xi, 151–2, 157, 169, 188, 322; text, 135, 161–3
Siena, 82, 562–3
Sillig, Julius, 20, 97
Simmerl (advocate), 394
Simrock, Karl, 103
Singer, Otto, 24
Sismondi, Simonde de, 507, 511
Smart, Henry, 206

Sophie Charlotte, Duchess in Bavaria, 330, 385

Sophocles, 20, 504, 505

Sorrento, 506–10, 513

Speidel, 484

Spengler, Oswald, 96, 321

Spitzer, Daniel, 519

Spohr, Louis, 39

Spontini, Gasparo, 483; influence on W, 48–9, 55, 86; works, 49, 85–6, 172, 559

Srbik, Heinrich Ritter von, 541

Stahr, Adolf, 104, 155

Standhartner, Josef, 296, 298, 299, 305, 308, 313, 315, 513

Stein, Heinrich von, xix, 181, 556–7, 583 588, 589, 626

Stendhal (pseudonym of Marie Henri Beyle), 566

Stern, Professor Adolf, 461

Sternfeld, Richard, 50, 90, 154, 271, 325, 615

Stocker, Jakob, 404, 412, 426

Stocker, Verena, see Weidmann, Verena

Strauss, David Friedrich, 457

Strauss, Richard, 28, 108, 110, 207, 261, 265, 288, 343, 364, 392, 486

Strecker, Ludwig, 495, 510, 586, 625

Strecker, Ludwig (son of the above), 300

Street, Agnes, 277, 326, 360

Strobel, Gertrud, 321

Strobel, Otto, 219, 331, 619, 620, 621

Strousberg, Bethel Henry, 455

Stuttgart, 294, 318, 329, 452

Suarès, André, 283

Sucher, Josef, 515

Sulzer, Jakob, 142, 143–4, 173, 175, 192, 209, 213–14, 215, 217, 260, 323, 540

Tacitus, 474

Tailhade, Laurent, 528

*Tannhäuser* (Wagner), 66, 84, 89, 93, 102, 103, 118, 241, 295, 340, 464, 473, 488; and Catholicism, 76; ballet in, 283, 285; completion of, 101; composition of, 75, 78–9, 93, 127; conception of, 69–72; for Paris, 70, 78, 280–93 *passim*, 416, 551; musical language of, 43, 77; performances (projected and actual), 15, 77, 78, 148, 155, 172, 177, 180, 190–1, 204–6, 207, 267, 272, 273, 276, 277, 285, 290–2, 385, 389, 482–3, 484, 591; publication of, 116, 122–3, 159, 485; rehearsals, 281, 286–90; revisions/alterations, 76, 78, 283–5, 286–9, 297, 483; sket-

ches for, 72; text, 76–7, 102, 235; translation of, 269, 271, 281–2

Tasso, Torquato, 20, 506

Taubert, Karl Gottfried Wilhelm, 433

Tauler, Johannes, 318

Tausig, Karl, 245, 247, 262, 264, 296, 308, 310, 315, 396, 433, 435–6, 437–8, 571

Taylor, Jessie, see Laussot, Jessie

Teplitz, 7, 15, 39, 71, 75, 93, 96

Tessarin (piano teacher), 251

Thomas, Theodore, 486

Thucydides, 513

Thum, Professor, 139

Tichatschek, Joseph, 67, 72–3, 78, 155, 247, 298, 389

Tieck, Ludwig, 70

Titian, 299, 544

Toscanini, Arturo, xii, 578

Tribschen, 17, 94, 208, 263, 371–444 *passim*, 477, 491, 492, 514, 528

*Tristan und Isolde* (Wagner), xi, 36, 55, 66, 98, 269, 274, 340, 354, 409, 411, 417, 464, 488, 502, 515, 562, 587; and Schopenhauer, 236, 254; completion of, 266, 274; composition of, xiv, 224, 233, 237, 239, 241, 244–6, 247, 253–6, 258–66, 506, 542, 543, 578; earliest conceptions of, 200, 216; intention to write, 232; musical language of, 31, 110, 231, 237–8, 258, 261–2, 265–6, 279, 288, 344, 565; performances (projected and actual), 257, 271, 272, 273, 276, 278, 280, 295, 296, 326, 337, 341–3, 360, 409–10, 439, 465, 487–8, 564, 587; publication of, 241, 257, 270; readings of, 236, 407; rehearsals, 298, 300, 310, 340, 342; scoring of, 265; sketches for, 242, 246, 263, 325; sources, 233; text, xiv, 233–6, 260, 271

Truinet, Charles (pseudonym Nuitter), 271, 281, 292, 297, 302, 393

Tunis, Bey of, 421

Uhlig, Theodor, 66, 109, 130, 142, 146, 151, 153, 155, 157, 158, 160, 163, 165, 171, 173–4, 176, 540

Ulibishev, Alexander, 81

Ullmann, Bernard (impresario), 516, 517–18

Unger, Georg, 515

United States, see America

Vaez, Gustav, 147

Vaillant (W's doctor), 219–20

Van Gogh, Vincent, 578

Venice, 545, 619; W in, 250–9, 299, 506, 511, 561, 564, 574, 578, 586–91; W's death in, 6, 569, 583, 587, 591–8

Verdi, Giuseppe, 42, 483, 564, 593–4

Verona, 506

Viardot-Garcia, Pauline, 278

Victoria, Queen of England, 207, 517

Vidal, Paul, 484, 623

Viel Castel, Horace de, 281

Vienna, 171, 183, 191, 519; court opera, 296, 392, 482, 484; revolution in, 129, 132; W in, 132, 294, 295–6, 298–301, 308, 312–16, 444, 458, 467, 477–9, 482–4, 619; W's works performed in, 295, 482–3, 515–16, 549

Villiers de l'Isle-Adam, Philippe Auguste, 416–17, 427

Villot, Frédéric, 270, 283

Virchow, Rudolf, 556

Vogel, Martin, xi, 624

Vogl, Heinrich, 410

Vogl, Therese, 410, 548

Völderndorff, Otto Freiherr von, 391, 621

Voltaire, François Marie Arouet de, 317

Voltz & Batz (W's agents), 566, 587, 626

Voss, Johann Heinrich, 20


Wagenseil, Christoph, 300

Wagner, Adolf (W's uncle), 20, 82, 97, 469, 551

Wagner, Albert (W's brother), 12, 37, 74, 102, 118, 204, 476

Wagner, Cosima (Liszt, von Bülow), 189, 200, 215, 241, 289, 294, 461, 469, 560; and Hans von Bülow, xviii, 233, 247, 249, 336, 340, 347, 349, 352, 388, 404–7, 451, 493, 572–3; and Judith Gautier, ix, xiii, xviii, 417–18, 506, 530, 546, 565, 569, 627; and Ludwig II, 346, 358, 370, 371, 375, 385, 389, 394, 397, 409, 523–4, 550; and Friedrich Nietzsche, ix, 414, 416, 419–20, 420–1, 425, 428, 440–1, 443–4, 448, 453, 454, 461, 465, 509, 513, 536–8, 600–1; diaries of, xi–xiv, xvii–xxi, 323, 406, 531, 622; divorce from Hans von Bülow, 404, 405, 418, 426; first meetings with W, 184, 236, 334–5; marriage to W, 427, 433; on W's music, 42, 383, 425, 449, 479, 546, 589; on the Wesendonk affair, 248; permanent residence with W, 406; visits W, 333–5, 337, 370–1, 373–88 passim, 395,

402; W's love for, 331, 347–57, 373–4, 388, 395, 476, 619; writings of, 358, 587

Wagner, Emanuel (schoolmaster and organist), 3

Wagner (Chamberlain), Eva (W's daughter), xii, xiv, 350, 354, 357, 388, 406, 578, 618–19, 621

Wagner, Friederike (W's aunt), 4

Wagner, Gottlob Friedrich (W's grandfather), 4–5

Wagner, Isolde (W's daughter), 342, 352, 381, 406

Wagner, Johanna (W's niece), 78, 118, 204, 517

Wagner, Johanna (Pätz) (W's mother), 5–10, 11–16, 17, 18, 27, 29, 30, 42, 70, 395, 469

Wagner, Johanna Sophie (Eichel) (W's grandmother), 4–5

Wagner, Karl Friedrich (W's father), 5–7, 10

Wagner (Wolfram), Klara (W's sister), 12, 243, 307, 308

Wagner (Brockhaus), Luise (W's sister), 12, 14, 117, 307, 433, 476

Wagner, Martin (schoolmaster), 3

Wagner, Minna (Christiane Wilhelmine Planer) (W's first wife), xviii, 15, 142, 147, 176, 192, 204, 236, 267; alienation from W, 141, 143–4, 158; death of, 368–9; deserts W, 13–14, 45–6; early life, 41; first meeting with W, 40–1, 42; illness of, 244, 342; last meeting with W, 308; marriage, 44; on the Laussot affair, 148–9, 150; on the Wesendonk affair, 242–3, 245, 247, 251, 260, 303–4; reconciliations with W, 46–7, 151; separation from W, 251, 297, 304; W in love with, 41–2; W's relationship with, 140, 154, 158, 183, 251–2, 269–70, 271, 297, 306–7, 310, 312, 333, 368–9

Wagner, Moritz (silver-miner), 3

Wagner (Brockhaus), Ottilie (W's sister), 21, 45–6, 406, 410, 439

Wagner, Richard:
– ancestry and paternity, 3–10
– and the Gesamtkunstwerk, 26, 54, 79, 146–7, 585
– and the press, 81, 114, 117, 155, 174, 206, 213, 267, 272–3, 291, 310, 341, 402, 481, 483, 493, 510, 518–19, 569, 576, 620
– as conductor, 13, 41, 48, 80–4, 87–90, 170–3, 174–5, 177, 203–4, 206–7, 273, 307–11, 313–14, 419–20, 433–4, 437, 439,

Wagner, Richard—*cont.*
444–5, 447, 454, 458, 477–9, 484–5, 517,
545, 584, 589
– as exile, 15, 118, 130, 152, 155, 175–6,
177–8, 191, 199, 204–5, 217–18, 250,
257–8, 264, 267, 282
– as orchestrator, 49, 85, 110–11, 120, 187,
189–90, 202, 207, 265, 309, 364, 392–3,
458–9, 475, 479, 544–5, 565, 575–6, 578
– as poet, 21, 36, 65, 77, 95, 108, 199, 214,
233–6, 260
– as revolutionary, 91, 128–33, 137–41, 143,
150, 157, 159–60, 162–4, 340
–birth and childhood, 4, 5–6, 11, 15, 17–21,
23, 144
– creative technique of, 37, 51, 65, 75, 78–9,
184–6, 189, 221, 254, 302, 442, 527, 533,
562–3
– earliest compositions, 21, 28, 30–4, 35–6
– education, xi, 19–20, 27-31, 82, 97, 198,
319
– financial problems, 13, 28, 45, 50, 60–1,
66, 71, 73, 94, 97, 113–23, 145, 179, 190–2,
204–5, 217, 256, 275–8, 285–6, 294, 310,
315–16, 327, 342–3
– harmony, use of, 75, 109–10, 186, 201–2,
237, 288, 546–7
– illness, 17, 157, 176, 211, 215, 219–20, 287,
346, 347, 350–1, 357, 550, 553, 561–2, 569,
575–7, 586, 590, 592
– influenced by:
German opera, 63
German and Nordic mythology, 93–7,
99–100, 134, 219, 407
grand opera, 48–9, 55
Greek history, mythology and tragedy,
19–20, 93, 97–100, 101, 107, 110, 127,
134, 143, 284, 370, 407, 451, 513,
560–1, 585
Indian literature and philosophy, 105,
207, 211, 218, 236, 255, 269, 347, 349,
395, 459, 585
Italian opera, 39, 42
mediaeval literature and history, 35,
69–70, 94, 101, 103, 112, 127, 233
other composers, *see* Bach, Beethoven, Bellini, Berlioz, Meyerbeer,
Mozart, Spontini, Weber
philosophers, *see* Feuerbach, Hegel,
Nietzsche, Schelling, Schopenhauer
– isolation of, 15, 105, 136, 183, 209, 231,
270, 313, 333, 407

– leitmotiv, use of, 36, 38, 43, 65, 108–9,
152, 169, 174, 179–80, 187–9, 193, 202,
261–2, 419, 527
– marriages, 13, 44, 427, *and see* Wagner,
Cosima; Wagner, Minna
– plans for a music school, 341–2, 345, 359,
467–8, 520–2, 551
– plans for a new theatre, 156, 177, 339–41,
345, 355, 387, 401, 439, 551
– plans to emigrate, x, 517–18, 519, 551–3,
556, 574–5
– plans to write a symphony, 54, 395,
429–30, 468, 507, 531, 532, 542, 589–90
– residences in: Biebrich, 303–6, 308;
Blasewitz, 45–6; Königsberg, 13, 44, 45,
47; Lucerne, 154, 211, 260–6; Magdeburg,
12–13, 40–1, 43–4, 51, 453; Riga, 13, 45,
46–51, 60, 522; Würzburg, 37, 142, 453; *see
also* Bayreuth, Dresden, Munich, Paris,
Tribschen, Venice, Vienna, Wahnfried,
Zürich
– sweethearts and mistresses, *see* Gautier,
Judith; Laussot, Jessie; Maier, Mathilde;
Wagner, Cosima; Wagner, Minna;
Wesendonk, Mathilde
– views on:
Christianity and Catholicism, 136, 355,
417, 442, 484, 533, 562, 569, 579
concert performances and orchestral
reform, 47–8, 74, 90–1, 178, 309
drama, 99, 101, 157, 432, 436, 451–2
France and the French, 62, 393, 428, 431,
484
German art, 39, 342, 390, 396, 445
496
himself as artist, 76, 114, 210, 220, 254,
317, 344, 350–1, 408, 480, 495, 511
Italian opera, 39, 559
Jews, 153, 245, 390, 407, 436, 438, 558,
567–8, 570–1, 595, 627
politics, 130–3, 163–4, 361–2, 367, 377,
378–80, 386–7, 390, 427, 430–1,
539–41
Protestantism, 403, 451, 579
theatrical reform, 47, 129–30, 132,
171–2
vivisection, 554–6
WORKS:
arrangements, 24–5, 49, 60, 71, 106–7,
276
journals: Annals, 162, 200, 216, 226,
253, 254, 335, 336, 360, 365, 385, 391,

393, 394, 395, 396, 401, 402, 403, 404, 405, 406, 407, 619; Brown Book, xiv, 336, 347–57, 367–8, 369–70, 388, 395, 403, 423, 428, 618–19, 621; Red Book, 59, 320, 358; Venetian Diary, 236, 240, 251, 252, 253, 254, 256
operas, *see individual titles*
orchestral works, 28, 31–3, 36, 49, 51, 54, 55, 85, 203, 310, 338, 395, 396, 430, 434, 439, 446, 459, 486–7, 506, 589, 603; see also *Siegfried Idyll*
piano works, 26, 31–2, 297
prose works, 23, 28, 39, 50, 61–2, 96, 123, 129–30, 133, 134, 161, 172, 206–7, 275, 319, 338, 384, 395, 407, 419–20, 429, 432, 434, 436, 437, 449–50, 451–2, 453–4, 456, 460, 498, 541, 561–2, 579, 592; see under their titles *Art and Revolution, Artwork of the Future, Beethoven, Communication to my Friends, Jewry in Music, Mein Leben, Music of the Future, Pilgrimage to Beethoven*
songs and choral music, 36, 49–50, 51, 84–5, 115, 238–40, 253, 260, 389, 459
texts, scenarios and sketches, *see individual titles*
Wagner (Marbach), Rosalie (W's sister), 12, 13–14, 22, 36, 37, 38, 40, 46
Wagner, Samuel (I) (schoolmaster), 3
Wagner, Samuel (II) (W's great-grandfather), 3–4
Wagner, Siegfried (W's son), xix, 410, 425, 470, 518, 543, 554, 556, 560, 592
Wagner Societies, *see under* Bayreuth
Wahnfried, 23, 82, 208, 232, 294, 393, 432, 456, 466–7, 468–71, 477, 479, 481–2, 489, 494, 500, 523, 530, 545, 548, 554, 569, 570, 573–4, 579, 583, 587, 593, 597, 623; library in, xi, 20, 81, 94, 213, 235, 469, 619, 623
Walewski, Count, 292
*Walküre, Die* (Wagner), 419, 515; completion of, xiv, 216–17, 218, 266; composition of, 192–6, 200–2, 207, 211, 215–16, 543; musical language of, 31, 49, 82, 193, 225; performances, xiii, 222, 248, 271, 309, 422–3, 425, 426, 434, 445, 478, 482; scoring of, 202, 221; sketches for, 159, 161, 163, 193–5, 201–2, 323
Warnkönig, Leopold August, 321
Weber, Carl Maria von, 33, 66, 544; con-

ducted by W, 47, 81, 170, 172, 204; influence on W, 18, 22, 33, 38; reburial, 85; works, *Euryanthe*, 39, 73, 81, 85, 172: *Der Freischütz*, 18, 22, 24, 62–3, 170, 204, 473
Weber, Caroline von, 75, 81
Weber, Dionys, 33, 83
Weber, Ernst von, 554–5, 561
Weidmann (Stocker), Verena, 263, 373, 404, 478
Weimar, 160; theatre, 10, 158, 159; W in, 140, 297, 441, 450–1, 465; W's works performed in, 103, 151, 154–6, 177, 426
Weinlig, Theodor, xi, 28, 29–31, 33, 36, 84, 198, 319
Weissheimer, Wendelin, 248, 303, 308, 309, 310, 329–30, 396
Welcker, Friedrich Gottlieb, 412
Wesendonk, Guido, 215, 253
Wesendonk, Mathilde, xviii, 66, 105, 177, 203, 205, 221, 225, 226, 233, 238, 241, 269, 279, 315, 318, 327, 343, 427, 518, 568; W's affair with, 194, 201, 215, 236–7, 238–44, 246–9, 251–3, 260, 299, 303, 314
Wesendonk, Otto, 160, 179, 180, 192, 205, 215, 217, 221, 225–6, 233, 239–40, 241, 246, 249, 253, 260, 263–4, 276, 299, 343, 398, 618
Widmann, Professor, 140
Wieck, Clara (Schumann), 28, 33, 34
Wieck, Friedrich, 28
*Wieland der Schmied* (Wagner), 147, 148
Wigand, Otto, 143
Wilamowitz-Moellendorff, Ulrich von, 449, 622
Wilbrandt, Adolf, 478
Wilhelm I, German Emperor, 433–4, 464, 485, 487–8, 495, 507, 518, 538–9, 569
Wilhelmj, August, 297, 471, 516, 517
Wille, Eliza, 75, 165, 198, 231, 241, 247, 252, 253, 255, 314, 315–18, 343, 435
Wille, François, 165, 179, 198, 253, 316, 318, 343, 435
Winckelmann, Johann Joachim, 145, 413
Winkelmann, Hermann, 580
Winkler, C. T., 67
Winterberger (pupil of Liszt), 251
Wittgenstein, Caroline, Princess, 178, 183, 198, 222–3, 336, 343, 355, 445, 450, 465, 589, 627
Wittgenstein, Princess Marie, 183, 222, 224, 266, 274

Wolfram, Heinrich, 139, 476
Wolfram, Klara, *see* Wagner, Klara
Wolfram von Eschenbach, 101
Wolzogen, Hans von, xii, xix, 22, 65, 82, 465, 467, 534, 546, 550, 556, 561, 563, 572, 579
Wüllner, Franz, 415, 416, 423
Würzburg, 37, 142, 452–3

Zhukovsky, Paul, xx, 557, 560, 563, 569, 574, 575, 577, 583, 591, 592
Zhukovsky, Vasily Alexandreyevich, 557, 591

*Zukunftsmusik* (Wagner), see *Music of the Future*
Zumbusch, Caspar, 469
Zumpe, Hermann, 471
Zürich, 37; municipal theatre, 169; Music Society, 172, 177, 190, 202–3, 212; W conducts in, 169–73, 174–5, 177, 202–4; W's friends in, 143–4, 149, 175–6, 213, 264; W's residence in, 75, 142–5, 147, 151, 159, 178–9, 184, 221–2, 225–6, 522; W's visits to, 294, 316; W's works performed in 205–6

OEMCO